TEIKYO WESTMAR UNIV

O9-ABG-834

THE
GIFTED
AND
TALENTED

*Developmental
Perspectives*

THE GIFTED AND TALENTED

Developmental Perspectives

Edited by

Frances Degen Horowitz
Marion O'Brien

91 - 1933

American Psychological Association
Washington, DC 20036

The Gifted and Talented: Developmental Perspectives was developed and produced with partial support from The Esther Katz Rosen Fund.

Copyright © 1985 by the American Psychological Association. All rights reserved. No part of this book may be copied or reproduced in any form or by any means without written permission of the American Psychological Association.

Copies may be ordered from:
American Psychological Association
Order Department
P.O. Box 2710
Hyattsville, MD 20784

Library of Congress Cataloging-in-Publication Data
Main entry under title:
The Gifted and talented.
  Bibliography: p.
  Includes indexes.
    1. Genius   2.Gifted children.   3. Intelligence levels.
4. Creative ability.   5. Social interactional.   6. Gifted children—
Education.   I. Horowitz, Frances Degen.   II. O'Brien, Marion.
BF412.G56 1985   153.9'8   85-7559
ISBN 1-55798-043-8
Third printing, January 1990

Text and cover design by Jack Gordon, Arlington, Virginia
Composition by Harper Graphics, Waldorf, Maryland
Printing by BookCrafters, Inc., Chelsea, Michigan

Printed in the United States of America

Dedication

*This volume is dedicated
to Lewis Terman, Pauline Snedden Sears, and Robert L. Sears
for pioneering and continuing the study of the gifted*

*and to Esther Katz Rosen—
to her memory, to her contributions, and
to her deep concern for children.*

Contents

Part II. Aspects of Giftedness

Part III. Reflections on the Study of Giftedness

Preface

The publication of this volume is an historic event—one that helps crystallize what we know about those who are identified as being gifted and talented. The project began in 1981 when the Board of Trustees of the American Psychological Foundation began to plan support, through the Esther Katz Rosen Fund, for the publication of a monograph about gifted and talented children. Designed to assist the Trustees in making informed decisions about various policy proposals, the monograph was also designed to inform others about issues related to current knowledge about the gifted and talented and the application of that knowledge to concerns about their welfare and fulfillment. In 1982 a small, one-time grant to pursue the project was provided through the Rosen Fund to the American Psychological Association.

In fact, however, this worthy project has a much longer history. It really began with the work of Esther Katz Rosen, a prominent clinical psychologist who specialized in working with children during her 35-year career. Dr. Rosen was deeply interested in helping gifted children achieve their potential and intensely concerned about issues relevant to the gifted and talented. She was a Fellow of the American Psychological Association and active in many other civic, charitable, and professional organizations. Upon her death, Dr. Rosen bequeathed a substantial gift to the American Psychological Foundation "for the advancement and application of knowledge about gifted children" to be used at the discretion of the Trustees for this or "other significant purposes in the field of clinical psychology."

Through the years, the Esther Katz Rosen Fund has been carefully shepherded by the APF Trustees so that it has grown and, at the same time, has been used to support a series of projects related to the broad array of issues germane to gifted children. In addition to supporting the production of *The Gifted and Talented: Developmental Perspectives*, the Rosen Fund has provided support to Congressional Science Fellows in the area of child policy (Daniel M. Koretz, 1978–1979; Lyn Aubrecht, 1981–1982). Over the last three years, the Fund also has provided support for some 30 Esther Katz Rosen Fellows (primarily ethnic minority children) to attend summer session programs designed for gifted and talented children at the Duke University Talent Identification Program. With the help of the Rosen Fund, Thomas M. Achenbach, C. Keith Conners, and Herbert C. Quay are developing a Descriptive Classification of Children's Behavior as a tool for early diagnosis and intervention (and as a nonmedically-focused alternative to DSM-III) for children's problems.

In the mid-1970s, the Rosen Fund supported the Social Science Research Council's Committee on Gifted Children, and in 1977 a donation was made by the Rosen Fund to Clark University to update archival records of G. Stanley Hall's work because of Hall's relationship to child psychology. Another donation was made by the Rosen Fund (in October 1978) to support a Science Writer's Seminar that emphasized writing related to children. In 1979 the Archives of the History of American Psychology in Akron, Ohio, received a donation from the Rosen Fund to support the child and developmental aspects of the archives. In 1981 the Fund provided support for the 1982 Conference on Child Clinical Psychology. In 1983, through a special effort supported by the Fund, the book *Facilitating Infant and Early Childhood Development* was distributed to 300 institutions (250 libraries in the Third World and 50 institutions in the United States primarily serving minority children). These and other activities have continued the work of Dr. Rosen.

The APF Trustees proposed that *The Gifted and Talented* present the state of the art in research and practice and policy regarding our nation's gifted and talented children as it now stands. Edited and written by experts in each of the areas, it has been written specifically for psychologists and researchers. As they have provided information, the authors have gone beyond the various common stereotypes and provided insight and perspective.

Numerous individuals were involved in developing *The Gifted and Talented*. Members of the APF Board of Trustees throughout the project from 1981 to the present were psychologists Albert Bandura, William Bevan, Theodore H. Blau, Donald T. Campbell, John J. Conger, Nicholas A. Cummings, Florence L. Denmark, Dorothy H. Eichorn, Wilbert S. McKeachie, Michael S. Pallak, Max Siegel, and M. Brewster Smith (and Treasurers for the Board, Charles L. McKay and James D. Causey).

The conceptualization of this monograph has had many contributors. The ultimate tribute, of course, goes to Francis Degen Horowitz and Marion O'Brien, who refined the final organization and coverage and did the substantive editing of the manuscripts, and to the individuals who contributed the excellent chapters that are included in this volume. In addition, appreciation is extended to Edward Zigler, Yale University; Jim Gallagher, University of North Carolina; Julian Stanley, Johns Hopkins University; Donald Treffinger, State University of Buffalo; John Feldhusen, Purdue University; Carolyn Callahan, University of Virginia; Joseph Renzulli, University of Connecticut; Sandford Reichart, Case Western Reserve University; and Dorothy Sisk and Harold Lyn (both formerly of the Department of Education's Office of the Gifted and Talented) for their contribution to the initial planning. Special thanks are extended to Lyn Aubrecht, of Meredith College, for his advice and counsel on issues related to the gifted and talented during his year as the APA/APF Congressional Science Fellow.

Finally, both Ruby Takanishi, Administrative Officer for Scientific Affairs, and Gary R. VandenBos, Deputy Executive Officer for Communications, deserve special thanks for managing and contributing to each stage of the development and completion of this splendid volume. Likewise, the assistance of Adele L. Schaefer, Jack Donahue, Virginia O'Leary, and Joann Horai is greatly appreciated.

But most importantly, each of us involved in creating *The Gifted and Talented* honor Dr. Rosen's professionalism and her dedication to improving our understanding of gifted and talented children, and we acknowledge the continued support of her family for the efforts of the American Psychological Foundation to fulfill her wishes. It is for this reason that this volume is also dedicated to Esther Katz Rosen.

For the Trustees,

Michael S. Pallak
Secretary, American Psychological Foundation, 1979–1985
Executive Officer, American Psychological Association, 1979–1985

Acknowledgments

The editors wish to thank the editorial advisors who contributed substantially to the quality of the writing in the book. These include John Hagen, Aletha Huston, Reva Jenkins-Friedman, Daniel Keating, Sarah Lightfoot, David Perry, Robert Sears, Margaret Spencer, Charles Super, and Ed Zigler. We also express a special thanks to Daniel Keating. He was to have served as co-editor of this volume, and he helped in the initial planning of the contents of the book. Other commitments, however, made it necessary for him to withdraw from the project.

The authors who contributed to the volume are owed our appreciation for making the editorial work a pleasure rather than a chore. Their timely response at all of the steps in the preparation of this book is in no small measure responsible for the currency of its contents.

We also acknowledge with thanks the help and patience of our office staff, especially Connie Emerson, Laura Fine, and Paula Seikel. The University of Kansas contributed time and facilities toward the preparation of the book. And, of course, we want to express our thanks to the Esther Katz Rosen Fund of the American Psychological Foundation.

Finally, we would like to thank the production staff at APA, especially Brenda Bryant, who supervised the project; Deanna Cook, who did a marvelous job of copy editing; and Donna Stewart, who helped us keep track of everything. Their efficient and highly competent work made the difficult final stages of production run smoothly.

Frances Degen Horowitz
Marion O'Brien
Lawrence, Kansas
July, 1985

Part 1. The Nature of Giftedness

The Nature of Giftedness

Conventional wisdom has pinpointed some individuals in all cultures and historical periods as being gifted because they exhibit talents that are not evident in the majority of people. Despite this widespread recognition of the gifted, psychologists and educators have had difficulty reaching a consensus on the precise definition and measurement of giftedness. Some view the gifted as the top end of a continuum of intelligence, which, in turn, is seen as a unitary characteristic perhaps based in genetics. Others see gifted individuals as expressing specific talents that have been nurtured environmentally. The way particular investigators view giftedness influences the types of research questions they ask, the methodology they use to answer those questions, and even the nature of the sample selected for study. Thus, the definition of giftedness is itself a prime area for investigation. The chapters in this section reflect the lack of agreement in past research over the nature of giftedness, but the authors raise similar questions for future investigation.

In his historical review of Western concepts of giftedness, Robert Grinder of Arizona State University directly confronts the problems inherent in defining giftedness and intelligence. Through most of history, giftedness was viewed retrospectively—people were considered gifted by virtue of their accomplishments. The invention of intelligence tests suggested the possibility of identifying potentially gifted people and thus nurturing their unusual talents. Grinder characterizes two major threads in the modern study of giftedness: one, the neurophysiological, information-processing approach, which arises from the pioneering work of Galton, and the other, in the Binet tradition, focuses on the analytical and insight aspects of intelligence. These two lines of work, in Grinder's view, are converging, and, in essence, both are searching for a general intelligence factor similar to what he calls "Spearman's venerable g."

Robert Sternberg and Janet Davidson of Yale University also address the issue of definition as a necessary first step to the study of cognitive processes in gifted individuals. In reviewing four general theoretical approaches to cognition—stimulus–response, Piagetian, psychometric, and information processing—and their application to the gifted and talented, as well as four theories specific to understanding giftedness—figural to formal transition, domain-specific talents, multiple intelligences, and evolving systems—Sternberg and Davidson conclude, with Grinder, that theoretical approaches are highly convergent. Giftedness, they say, may be best understood from a societal perspective in which characteristics of the individual, particularly high general and specific intelligence, and characteristics of the environment both contribute to the expression of talent. The authors see a pressing need for theory-based empirical data that are developmental in nature in order to advance our understanding of giftedness.

The focus of chapter 3 is on the specific characteristics of skilled performance on intellectual tasks. Mitchell Rabinowitz and Robert Glaser, working at the Learning Research and Development Center of the University of Pittsburgh, describe how a well-organized knowledge base permits rapid retrieval of information for use in problem solving and therefore contributes to an individual's ability to perform at a highly competent level. Knowledge is typically domain-specific, but the acquisition, organization, and mechanisms for retrieval of knowledge may be general abilities that apply across diverse fields. Rabinowitz and Glaser echo Sternberg and Davidson in their call for developmental research on knowledge acquisition and application.

The domain-specific aspects of intelligence are also emphasized in chapter 4. Michael Wallach of Duke University decribes the history of creativity testing along with its uses and misuses. According to Wallach, although creativity is an intuitively appealing construct, its application as a general ability has yet to be approved. If creativity is instead viewed as excellence within a particular field, with the concomitant implication of originality in both problem definition and solution in that field, then the most useful approach to identifying and fostering high creativity will be field-specific.

In chapter 5, Jayanthi Mistry and Barbara Rogoff of the University of Utah differentiate between domain-specific abilities, which they term "talents," and general intellectual potential or "giftedness." In these authors' views, the use of a general construct of intelligence is untenable from a cross-cultural point of view. Because so much of human behavior is shaped by its cultural context, tests purporting to measure underlying intelligence are not interpretable across different cultures. By contrast, specific cognitive talents, developed in individuals through experience with culturally central domains of activity, can be defined and assessed within particular cultures. To gain a better understanding of gifted performance, these authors argue, future research should focus on the development of individual talents within particular domains and the transfer of skills from one domain to another.

These five chapters set forth major issues facing investigators in the field of giftedness. From the diverse points of view emerges one commonality: the call for prospective developmental research, guided by theory, to aid our understanding of the complex of factors that contribute to gifted performance.

1. The Gifted in Our Midst: By Their Divine Deeds, Neuroses, and Mental Test Scores We Have Known Them

Robert E. Grinder
Arizona State University

We humans have always been inspired by the gifted and talented because of their ability to solve problems and perform feats that are beyond the capability of ordinary people. Those with extraordinary abilities have been expected to contribute to social survival and cultural advance since perhaps the very origins of communal life. Primitive *Homo sapiens* abetted survival by heeding the advice of peers astute in hunting and fishing, skilled in physical prowess, and adept at anticipating climatic changes. When Plato saw that debilitating wars were corrupting Athenian society, he proposed in his *Republic* to rejuvenate it by assigning citizens to tasks on the basis of individual differences in capabilities (Jowett, 1942, p. 267). People were classified into one of three types: Artisans would produce and market material goods; warriors would master defense and war; and philosophers, by virtue of their superior intellect, would govern society. Plato's rhetorical call has reverberated through the centuries into our own times. No one has ever devised a satisfactory system, however, for the first step in the process; that is, differentiating people on the basis of capabilities. The knotty problem, in respect to giftedness at least, has always been divisible into two mutually related questions: How have people with extraordinary capabilities been identified? How has their giftedness been explained?

Societies have, in fact, only two general approaches for identifying giftedness and talent. First, there is the venerable practice of simply observing who stands out in our midst. We have taken note of novel behavior, unusual accomplishment, and uncommon perspicacity in others. We thus have possessed an oversupply of impressionistic, anecdotal data and subjective interpretations that we have used as bases for elevating certain people to eminence. Second, in more recent times, giftedness has been identified on the basis of a person's potential prominence. Our shift from a retrospective to a prospective practice stems from the invention of mental tests, which, in turn, inspired interest in prediction. Sir Francis Galton, in the 1880s, was first to develop instruments for the purpose of identifying individual differences in intellectual capability. Shortly thereafter, Alfred Binet in France and Lewis M. Terman in America developed tests of general intelligence. Those who scored in the upper ranges on Terman's measures were labeled superior, near-genius, and genius, and collectively they represent the group psychometrists usually identify as *gifted* (Miles, 1954). Unfortunately, however, as is shown in the following discussion, neither the retrospective nor the prospective approach has produced methods that effectively differentiate expressions of giftedness.

Society's interest in identifying exceptional talent has differed as a function of changing configurations of imagery, ideology, and scholarly activity. These changes may be divided, in conjunction with the two methods of identification, into three cultural epochs relative to the ways in which giftedness has been understood. Each epoch produces a distinct "face" by which we have known gifted persons. The first emerged during a cultural epoch when extraordinary intellectual power was believed to transcend the mental processes of ordinary minds. The second extends from early Renaissance to the twentieth century, a time during which people of wisdom were regarded as neuropathic aberrations in the natural scheme of things. Tremendous advances in philosophy and science occurred during these centuries. At first, as a consequence of beliefs about species immutability, giftedness was interpreted as a mental alienation, an incurable, torturous disease to be avoided at all costs. Later, as theories of heritability evolved, neuroses and giftedness were seen as closely linked

I wish to express my gratitude to Sanford J. Cohn, Arthur R. Jensen, James B. Kashner, Ellen G. Kelman, Fred N. Kerlinger, Edward A. Nelsen, and Julian C. Stanley for their suggestions as I developed the manuscript.

components in the genetic structure. The third face of giftedness surfaced when late-nineteenth century naturalists Charles Darwin, Thomas Huxley, Herbert Spencer, and dozens of others opened eyes to new perspectives on human nature and paved the way for empirical investigations of individual differences. At that point, psychometrists, psychologists, educators, and most others interested in giftedness generally assumed that giftedness originated via the workings of natural selection and Mendelian laws of genetics.

The following discussion covers three major topics: giftedness and divinity, giftedness and neurosis, and giftedness and mental test scores. Each section corresponds to one of the three faces of giftedness already noted. Although cultural changes have been enormous, as the commentary reveals implicitly, the practice of identifying giftedness retrospectively, by eminence or prominence, remained fast until the advent of mental testing. No one until then had improved methods of selection. The issues emphasized in the first two sections, consequently, deal less with identification per se than with explaining how giftedness was understood. Mental testing, in contrast, generated a mania for investigating individual differences and inspired the development of new techniques for identifying intellect and talent. The new breed of psychometrists enthusiastically endorsed naturalistic theories of heritability and raised few questions about either biological or mental processes that might underlie expressions of extraordinary capability. Consequently, the third section of the paper differs from the first two in its emphasis on the long-forsaken question of identifying giftedness.

Giftedness and Divinity

When nomadic, quasi-agrarian communities were first formed, humans invented a repertoire of images to explain and deal with the mysteries of reality. As civilizations emerged, individuals who performed outstanding deeds were thought to possess extraordinary power. Their accomplishments appeared to transcend the mental powers of ordinary minds. They were thought to be divinely inspired. When ecclesiastical dogma arose from the shambles of the Roman Empire to rule reason well into the fifteenth and sixteenth centuries, people whose thoughts, pronouncements, and deeds exceeded the narrow bounds of orthodoxy were branded as heretical. They were said to be inspired by devils and demons. Many of these heretofore gifted sages were persecuted unmercifully as witches. A description of why gifted people were first identified in the context of divinity provides a first face of giftedness. The presentation is divided into two parts—transcendental benevolence and transcendental devilry—each of which corresponds to an extended period of social change.

Transcendental Benevolence

Primitive people solved the imperatives of providing for food and safety as best they could. Fanciful analogies about the natural world were accepted as valid causal relations. All matter was assumed to be animate, and human motives were attributed to every event; experiences were limited, so myths were contradicted infrequently. Whenever the wind blew, for instance, some superhuman was assumed to be puffing its cheeks; clearly the wind was alive—did it not shriek, whisper, and move things about? Primitive people also viewed natural events as isolated occurrences caused by different imaginary beings, and in the flow of daily activities different spirits were attributed to every conceivable ideological and practical need. As these imaginary, formless spirits accrued significance, adventures were attributed to them, and they began to acquire a history and identity as good or bad, weak or powerful, kind or cruel. The Greeks described each of these attendant spirits or tutelary gods as a presiding "genius" (Oxford Universal Dictionary, 1955).

Next, or perhaps concurrently, the geniuses or gods were viewed as residing in human beings. Early humans lived in constant awe of mighty wild beasts. Although the night-roaming habits and frightful cries of mammals, birds, and reptiles terrified primitive people, the animals' swiftness, cunning, and strength were an inspiration. Animals were adopted as guardian spirits and were worshiped as holy entities. Totemism (revering powerful animals as gods) soon led people to disguise themselves as animals, perhaps to identify with divinity, to frighten away evil spirits, or to gain some of the powerful attributes of the beasts. The more skilled and cunning of these individuals were venerated by others in the tribe or community as priests, medicine chiefs, or divine kings. This stage in cultural development marks perhaps the first basis for distinguishing gifted people from others.

Primitive people transformed ordinary mortals into deities and geniuses in order to honor them for their beneficent acts (Murray, 1955). Those who appeared to be most successful in controlling rainfall, thunder, and floods; in ensuring crops and bountiful harvests; and in determining what was lawful in community relationships were chosen regularly to wear animal heads or skins because they were the ones who seemed to have powers similar to those of the divine beasts. Although the visible parts of their bodies were still merely human, the holy mantle consecrated them as divine. When these avatars made pronouncements that turned out to be erroneous, others came to realize that they were only imperfect incarnations of the all-powerful gods.

The real, infallible gods were somewhere far away, perhaps hidden in the clouds or on the summit of some inaccessible mountain. When the mountain was climbed, the gods moved off into the upper sky. Meanwhile, the avatars stayed on earth, all the while wielding enormous influence. Their connections with the great gods were more intimate than were those of anyone else, and they knew the rules for approaching the gods and reaching them with prayers. How, then, could primitive people avoid the belief that they were living under divine tutelage? Individual differences between average people and these seers were so vast that surely the seers' special intellectual powers emanated from the supernatural. How, indeed, could excellence so transcendent be due merely to human powers (Lecky, 1905; Murray, 1955; Ribot, 1906)?

About 1100 B.C., the early Greeks sailed into the Aegean Sea to find new homes on the western coast of Asia Minor. They brought with them the epic poems, psalms, songs, and stories that had been passed down from Greek antiquity. The migrant Greeks believed themselves to be the descendants of legendary heroes, and the tales they sang and recounted constituted inspiring myths about their divinity. The Greeks felt the presence of their gods everywhere, especially in times of battles and festivals. From the gods came everything, and it was the task of mortals to make proper use of what they provided. The Greeks took the conventional steps necessary to stay in contact with their gods: They offered them prayers and sacrifices, they consulted oracles, and they built countless shrines to house icons.

Many of the Greek philosophers believed their own wisdom to be the product of the divine work of muses, geniuses, or demons. (These terms were used synonymously in Greek mythology; the term "demon" was denoted as an evil spirit only in Medieval times.) For example, Pythagoras, who is known primarily as a mathematician because of his geometric theorems, was also a religious prophet and mystic; his followers worshiped him as if he were divinely inspired. Empedocles, renowned for his theory of the immutability of the natural elements of earth, air, fire, and water, often boasted about his supernatural powers. He claimed he could bring forth rain and sunshine, change the direction of the wind, heal the sick, cure the infirmity of old age, and raise the dead. Like Pythagoras, Empedocles believed in the migration of the soul and forbade his disciples to kill and eat animals (Nordenskiold, 1935).

Socrates, whom we revere as one of the wisest men who ever lived, was deeply conscious of his demon, whose voice he heard, according to Plato in his *Crito*, "murmuring in my ears, like the sound of the flute in the ears of the mystics" (Jowett, 1942, p. 79). A segment of the Athenian population thought Socrates so dangerous that they executed him when he refused to concede that he had introduced strange gods and had thereby corrupted the young. Socrates's student, Plato, and in turn, his student, Aristotle, developed rational philosophies that tended to upgrade the intellectual powers of humankind and to downplay divine inspiration. Plato thought the physical world was to be explained by developing rational interpretations of the spiritual intentions of the gods. Aristotle, in contrast, chose to investigate qualities of the physical world and to draw inferences about spiritual reality from the conclusions about nature he believed to be warranted.

Although Aristotle did not call Plato a god, he built an altar to him, which suggests that he regarded his teacher as divine (Murray, 1955). On the whole, the Greek prophets who followed Plato and Aristotle were relatively modest. They healed the sick and cast out devils, not in their own names, but in the names of the gods who sent them. Ptolemy, however, who gave us the infamous geocentric interpretation of the universe, claimed divinity upon the death of his wife in 271 B.C., not only for her, but also for himself (Murray, 1955).

Transcendental Devilry

The Romans first came into contact with Greek culture during the third and fourth centuries B.C. Greek thought then began to dominate Roman thinking; Roman priests consulted the Greek oracles, Greek superstitions and philosophy supplanted Roman paganism, and Greek became the language of much of the empire. Augustus established Rome as the center of the empire and created an unprecedented century or two of peace for the societies of the western world. But political, economic, and moral distress ensued as increasingly poor government in the provinces caused the empire to fall prey to hordes of migratory invaders. The material prosperity, governmental structure, and intellectual culture of the Roman empire were destroyed. Christianity, which had superseded pantheism during the prolonged period of peace, thus became the surviving force by which to civilize the predatory barbarians.

The Church promised that a supreme power would save faithful followers from sorrow and suffering. It infused a fresh vitality in the prevailing decadence, and Rome once again became the capital of the world. Cultural life in the Dark Ages (500–1200) and in the Middle Ages (1200–1500) was prescribed by dogmas and doctrines that had been drawn up by ecclesiastics in the first centuries of the Christian era. The priests and monks of the time accepted church writings as infallible truths. Church leaders presumed that truth would be revealed to them in accordance with the divine will, and they demanded absolute obedience from their followers.

People wavered, however, in their allegiance to the Church. Various forms of totemism, animal worship, and magical arts had also survived the onslaught of cultural destruction during the Dark Ages. Thus, a cohort of individuals operating outside of church sanction believed that they, too, were following a divine call. Many afflicted people, especially the physically handicapped, sought the blessing of such self-proclaimed magicians, hoping to be cured. These sorcerers, wizards, astrologers, and fortune-tellers had had counterparts in ancient Greece and Rome; ordinary people revered them for practicing the healing arts, unearthing treasure-troves, and discovering the secrets of the future. But they often ran afoul of the clergy. The Church was equally engrossed in controlling and manipulating natural processes—every saint worked miracles—but such divine deeds always occurred within the context of canon law.

Beginning around the twelfth century, the Church took steps to punish those believed to be subversively collaborating with the devil. For several centuries thereafter, trials and convictions were commonplace throughout Europe and thousands of people were executed. In many instances, the crime of witchcraft was merely a pretext through which the Church persecuted those who would not embrace its dogma. Suspicion fell on everyone—men and women of all ages and social classes, and even children. Many of the sufferers were too poor, ignorant, or feeble to defend themselves; however, any person who showed either unusual intellectual capability or interest in scientific activity—in fact, interest in anything outside the purview of Church dogma—was likely to be persecuted. It was a dangerous time in which to be astute and curious, especially if it led one to embrace heretical ideas or engage in nonconforming behavior, for, ipso facto, it meant being possessed by demons, and hence, condemned to death by burning at the stake (Hyslop, 1925; Robbins, 1959).

Giftedness and Neurosis

Whereas the culture of the Middle Ages wasted human reason, Renaissance culture developed a reverence for it. Medieval political and economic life revolved around the protective walls of the medieval castle, but after Roger Bacon invented gunpowder in the thirteenth century, the development of massive cannons rendered these great citadels obsolete. The political center of gravity thus shifted from country to city, and small-scale agrarian economies soon were overshadowed by the fluid profits of trade and commerce. A middle class thus wedged itself between the feudal lords and serfs. This new merchant class undertook risks for profit, and their enterprise and industry led them to an appreciation of worldly comforts and away from preparations for eternal life.

The new secularism produced an "Age of Reason," that is, an overwhelming confidence in what reason could accomplish. Heretofore, knowledge had been bounded by the authority of Aristotle, the doctrines of Thomas Aquinas, and the proclamations of ecclesiastical revelation. Now, new developments in science revealed that much of this knowledge needed revision. For example, Copernicus (1477–1543) showed that the direct evidence of our senses had deceived us into thinking that the sun revolved around the earth; Galileo (1564–1642) experimented with the pendulum to discover precise, lawful ratios between weight, time, and motion; and Isaac Newton (1642–1726) proved that Galileo's laws, which governed the movement of bodies at the earth's surface, also governed relationships among the stars and planets.

The Age of Reason produced a succession of physicians, naturalists, and social observers who made giftedness an integral component of neurosis. A summary of the thought of some of these distinguished personages constitutes the second face of giftedness. The discussion extends chronologically in roughly two parts from early Renaissance to the turn of the twentieth century. During this period, religious, social, and scientific ideology were dominated, initially, by the doctrine of special creation, and later, by theories of evolution and heredity. These two viewpoints provide different explanations of why giftedness was regarded as having an underlying, organic connection with neurosis.

Special Creation and Mental Alienation

As scientific research revealed that the physical world was governed by natural law, a zeal for systematizing knowledge arose. Aristotle had classified organic life into 500 different species, and it was believed that every one of them had been created at the same instant. But by the time of the Renaissance many new species had been discovered. Church dogma had held for centuries, however, that it was an affront to the majesty and purpose of the Creator to assume that any living creature could be transformed or become extinct. Ecclesiastical affirmation of special creation and immutability thus provoked enthusiasm for cataloging all the members of the plant and animal worlds—in order to demonstrate the wondrous imagination of the Creator. The tempo of the mania, for example, led Carl Linnaeus (1707–1778), perhaps the premier taxonomist of all time, to publish *Systema Naturae*, in which he classified all known botanical, zoological, and mineralogical specimens into genera and species.

Renaissance physicians conceived the mind to be a function of the brain and nervous system, and they surmised that extraordinary ways of reasoning and behaving had less to do with the intentions of demons and other supernatural forces than with changes in nervous energy. As zeal for codifying all manner of phenomena intensified, physicians also meticulously reported and classified their observations of mental activity. William Cullen (1712–1790) was first to use the term "neurosis" to describe such mental symptoms as hysteria, hypochondriasis, and nervous exhaustion or "neurasthenia" (Alexander & Selesnick, 1966). As a byproduct of their enthusiasm for classification, physicians developed strong interest in individual differences in mental behavior. But what were they to make of these differences? The doctrines of special creation and immutability implied that there should be an ideal archetype for mental functions; discussion centered, therefore, on the significance of deviations from what they imagined that the Creator had originally intended. Because the physicians concentrated on unusual, out-of-the-ordinary features of mental activity, these forerunners of modern psychiatry became known as mental alienists.

The mental alienists were phobic about neurasthenia, which was then thought to lead usually to incurable insanity. They believed that the Creator had given everyone an exhaustible quantity of nervous energy. Given demands on the limited supply, wise individuals learned to husband their activities, that is, to be temperate, compliant, obedient, and adaptive (Sicherman, 1981). Lack of emotional control, absent-mindedness, preoccupation in thought, delusions or hallucinations, grandiose ideas, and novel insights represented debilitating deviations. Accordingly, any deviation from general expectations, whether in the direction of lunacy, madness, or insanity on the one hand, or genius and giftedness on the other, indicated mental instability. "Originality of thought and quickness or preponderance of the intellectual faculties were organically much the same thing as madness and idiocy" (Nisbet, 1891, p. vi).

Consequently, for a long period of time, including the eighteenth and nineteenth centuries, expressions of outstanding intellect were assumed to be accompanied by morbid, abnormal, nervous afflictions (Lombroso, 1891; Nisbet, 1891; Nordau, 1895). Importantly, the mental alienists, by drawing ingenuous assumptions about deviation and instability from the doctrine of special creation, came to the conclusion that precocious children were destined to be strange, physically weak, neurotic, and burned-out prodigies. And for generation after generation thereafter, many parents have shielded their children from intellectual activity, sharing the same fears as the early alienists (Freeman, 1983; Hildreth, 1966; Hollingworth, 1926; Terman, 1905).

Evolution and the Hereditary Transmission of Eminence and Neurosis

Early in the nineteenth century, questions began to be raised about the effects of social conditions upon mental alienation. To many alienists, degraded living circumstances, alcoholism, and venereal diseases were drawing individuals into deviancy and thereby into corrupting the progress of civilization. The alienists saw that unhealthy social conditions persisted from generation to generation, but they believed that responsibility for the neuropathology had to be reintroduced in each generation. In a world convinced of species immutability, concepts of heritability were unthinkable. At midcentury, however, heredity was introduced into the equation. Moreau de Tours, a French sociologist and distinguished "expert in mental pathology," offered the world in 1857 its first comprehensive theoretical and empirical discussion of the "traits of degeneration."

In keeping with the conventional wisdom of mental alienists, he said, "The clearest notion we can form of degeneracy is to regard it as a *morbid deviation from an original type*" (Nordau, 1895, p. 16). And "genius," he said, "is but one of the many branches of the neuropathic tree" (James, 1902, p. 16). Importantly, Moreau also proclaimed that "a race which is regularly addicted . . . begets degenerate descendants, who, if they remain exposed to the same influences, rapidly descend to the lowest degrees of degeneracy" (Nordau, 1895, p. 34). To Moreau and a cohort of zealous followers, then, the threat of societal degeneration at the hands of either lunatics or geniuses seemed all the more imminent because heritability indicated acceleration in the degradation of those exposed to social evils.

Hereditary Transmissions

Moreau's reasoning was influenced enormously by the work of Jean Lamarck (1744–1829) who, in the opening decade of the nineteenth century, became the first naturalist to offer a plausible alternative to the doctrine of special creation. Lamarck argued that new habits and behaviors, acquired in the process of adapting to new modes of life and environmental conditions, led to changes in body organs and mental attitudes; these acquired characteristics, he maintained, could be inherited by succeeding generations. From the point of view of modern genetics, of course, only changes in the genetic makeup are heritable. Skills and attitudes acquired in one generation cannot be passed on via the gene structure. Charles Darwin and many other naturalists of the day, however, thought otherwise.

Darwin presented *The Origin of Species* to the world in 1859 after personally collecting observations of plants and animals distributed throughout the world and exhaustively analyzing the patterns of variation that he saw. The infinite variety he found in forms of leaves, flowers, fruits, and animals convinced him that such diversity could not possibly have been brought about, as Lamarck had predicted, by the direct action of external causes. However, Darwin lacked an alternative explanation of the cause of the variation; he simply accepted the obvious fact that variation occurred within all species. Darwin did have an explanation, nonetheless, for the observations that he had made of species mutability. Given random variation within species, some individuals will be better suited than others to a particular environment; these varieties will propagate more successfully and secure a place for themselves. Darwin thereby determined that a uniform principle of evolution accounted for species mutability. In any given population of plants and animals, he said, the environment "naturally selects" which of the random variants will be hereditarily favored.

Perhaps more clearly than anyone else, Darwin recognized that the premise of evolution must rest ultimately on an adequate explanation of hereditary transmission (Grinder, 1967). After publication of *The Origin of Species*, therefore, Darwin turned resolutely toward developing a theoretical basis for explaining variations within species. He could have saved himself the trouble had he availed himself of the research of an inconspicuous Austrian monk, Johann Gregor Mendel, whose work in the seclusion of the cloister at the monastery in Brunn was destined to establish him as the forerunner of modern geneticists. Mendel crossed contrasting characteristics of twenty-two varieties of garden peas and discovered that some characteristics prevailed phenotypically or visibly to the exclusion of the others. By letting the cross-bred plants fertilize themselves, Mendel found in each generation a predictably constant numerical proportion of dominant to recessive characters. Mendel thus recognized that the characters affected hereditary variation in a discrete or particulate fashion. He worked out the numerical ratios between dominant and recessive traits as they were likely to appear in given generations, and in 1865 he published his results in the relatively obscure *Proceedings of the Natural History Society of Brunn*.

Mendel's findings nicely complemented the theory of natural selection, and when, in 1900, two biologists, Carl Correns and Hugo De Vries, recognized their implications, Mendelism became the dominant explanation of hereditary variation. If Mendel's data were made available to Darwin, he ignored them in favor of a fanciful hypothesis that, surprisingly, closely parallels that of Lamarck's theory of acquired characters. Darwin hypothesized that in every body cell a host of atom-like "gemmules" arose, each of which possessed qualities for reproducing that specific cell in progeny. He named his theory "the provisional hypothesis of pangenesis," and published it in 1868, replete with testimonials from domestic breeders, in a massive two-volume series (Darwin, 1868). Darwin proposed that gemmules migrated via the bloodstream to the myriad parts of the body and eventually accumulated in the reproductive cells. "An organic being is a microcosm—a little universe, formed of a host of self-propagating organisms, inconceivably minute and numerous as the stars in heaven" (Darwin, 1868, vol. 2, p. 399). The theory also held that given characteristics in progeny would approximate, first, those of the mother or father, depending on whose gemmules were "prepotent," and second, those of kin—near relatives contributing more gemmules than distant ones.

Intelligence and Heredity

Although Darwin never demonstrated specific interest in intellect as a heritable trait, one of his cousins, Francis Galton, found the issue compelling. When Galton published his epochal *Hereditary Genius*, he aimed to show "whether and to what degree natural ability was hereditarily transmitted" (Galton, 1869/1892, p. x). He depended entirely upon Darwin's theory of pangenesis to explain the mechanisms of heredity; indeed, he used the theory as a blueprint for designing a program, on the one hand, to strengthen the intellectual capabilities of humankind, and on the other, to arrest mental degeneration and foster cultural growth. Galton also relied upon early psychometric techniques to demonstrate empirically the applicability of the theory of pangenesis to questions of both human development and social progress. He established himself, thereby, as Mendel had done in genetics, as the forerunner of contemporary psychometrists.

We hold Galton in inestimable esteem; he developed an explanation of heredity based on quantitative data, introduced statistics to the social sciences, and established psychometrics as the leading method by which to assess individual differences in intellect. But Galton was misguided by the theory of pangenesis. The theory opened the way for outlandish assumptions about how environmental factors might influence heritability. Galton thus was misled into drawing a series of ill-advised conclusions, and in the process, into giving credence, by his considerable prestige, to the belief that giftedness and neurosis were synonymous.

Galton (1869/1892) worried that the quality of life achieved by British society was in serious decline. "Our race is over-weighted," he stated. It was being "drudged into degeneracy" because the mercantile and technological demands of society "call for more brains and mental stamina than the average of our race possess"; philosophers, artisans, and laborers were not up to the complexities (p. 345). Galton, however, did not despair. He was certain that the theory of pangenesis would guide him to the clues that were necessary for both arresting decline and improving society. He assumed that a close parallel existed between societal development and species evolution; indeed, he saw the parallel as "one of the most striking facts in the evolution of mankind" (p. xxiii). He declared, therefore, that

> this theory, propounded by Mr. Darwin as 'provisional' . . . is—whether it be true or not—of enormous service to those who inquire into heredity. It gives a key that unlocks every one of the hitherto unopened barriers to our comprehension of its nature; it binds, within the compass of a singularly simple law, the multifarious forms of reproduction. (p. 364)

The theory of pangenesis persuaded Galton that "each generation has enormous power over the natural gifts of those that follow" (1869/1892, p. 1), whether in matters of species heritability or characteristics of communal life. But the credibility of his theoretical analyses depended on whether he could confirm empirically the predictions of the theory of pangenesis. Could he demonstrate, for example, the likelihood that individuals are affected more by the gemmules of recent ancestors than by those of remote ancestors? Galton knew that confirmation of the pangenesis hypothesis would provide a defensible basis for analyzing the characteristics of given populations, assessing their prospects for social degeneration or prosperity, and even, perhaps, engineering matings in which parents who possessed desirable gemmules could pass them immediately to progeny.

Galton chose to investigate mental abilities because he wanted to show that they are affected by heredity in the same way "as are the form and physical features of the whole organic world" (1869/1892, p. 1). He reckoned that reputation or eminence of men over fifty years of age would constitute an accurate index of high ability, so he decided to study the hereditary transmission of eminence by comparing kinsmen across several generations. Galton anticipated that variations in intellectual ability would follow the pattern of a normal probability curve. He was familiar with the efforts of Lambert Quetelet, a Belgian statistician, who, earlier in the century, had shown that the distribution in a large population of physical characteristics could be described in terms of statistical probabilities. He thus divided the probability distribution patterns into fourteen intervals or grades, seven on each side of the mean, and labeled the groups on the upper side A through G.

People in the A group were near the mean. They constituted a very large group—about one in four persons. The proportion of people in the F group, designated "eminent," however, was much smaller—about one in 4,000 or 233 per million. The G group, designated as "genius," included only one person in 79,000, or 14 per million. Galton derived these figures from census data pertaining to men older than fifty years of age living in the British Isles. Next, he analyzed a current biographical handbook, *Men of the Time*, for clues to eminent men. He selected High Court judges who had lived since the Reformation as the basis of his investigation.

Galton analyzed the kinship relationships of these distinguished individuals by tabulating the percentages by which their eminent relatives fell within the grades of his interval scale. According to Hull (1928), Galton arranged his data on a square chart, stretched a silk thread from the center of the chart through clusters of data, and then measured the angle by which the thread deviated from the vertical. Since the tangent of a zero angle (no correlation) is zero, and since the tangent of the angle showing a perfect correlation (45°) is 1.00, Galton thus obtained indices of the magnitude of correlation between kinship and eminence.

In brief, Galton found through his statistical analyses that the distribution of ability followed kinship patterns. He declared, therefore, that there was no doubt as "to the existence of a law of distribution of ability in families" (Galton, 1869/1892, p. 318). Galton was exhilarated. What marvelous changes would occur in society, he speculated, "if we could raise the average standard of our race only one grade!" The number of eminent men would increase more than tenfold; there would be 2,423 per million at that grade instead of only 233 (p. 343). And far more important to the progress of civilization would be the increases in numbers that would occur in every grade of intellect. Hence, he said, "it seems to me most essential to the well-being of future generations, that the average standard of ability of the present time should be raised" (p. 344).

When Galton classified eminent men and their descendants on the basis of their reputations, he also recorded his impressions of their physical stature and traits of personality; he believed that someday these factors might prove useful in his formulas. Galton was fully aware that "there is a prevalent belief . . . that men of genius are unhealthy, puny beings—all brain and no muscle—weak-sighted, and generally of poor constitutions" (p. 331). Galton said he thought that his readers, however, would be surprised at the stature of "the heroes of history who fill my pages" (p. 331). Thus, he concluded, "I do not deny that many men of extraordinary mental gifts have had wretched constitutions, but deny them to be an essential or even usual accompaniment." (p. 332).

Intelligence and Neurosis

Twenty years later, Cesare Lombroso, an Italian criminologist, a professor of forensic medicine and psychiatry at Turin, and a dedicated disciple of Moreau, argued in *The Man of Genius*, that "genius is a true degenerative psychosis" (Lombroso, 1891, p. 333). It was, he said, "a symptom of hereditary degeneration of the epileptoid variety, and is allied to moral insanity." Lombroso scrutinized encyclopedias, biographical dictionaries, autobiographies, letters, and compositions in prose and verse to distill information about the medical and psychological characteristics of eminent people. He used terms like abnormal, morbid, insane, gifted, and genius interchangeably. In an early chapter of his book, he described Wolfgang Amadeus Mozart, Robert Burns, and John Stuart Mill as mentally ill, but at the end of it he described them as "normal men of genius."

Although his scholarship was shoddy, Lombroso had collated a colossal mass of anecdotal data, and it was superficially persuasive. His data revealed that people of high ability were generally small, pallid, and emaciated. Many were also sexually sterile, left-handed, or restless vagabonds. Some were tortured by religious doubt and abused alcohol and narcotics. Lombroso insisted, therefore, that melancholy, depression, and neurosis must be the price of genius or giftedness. He was positive that he had provided incontrovertible evidence for Moreau's interpretation of degeneracy.

Galton was impressed by Lombroso's reasoning, but he was only partially convinced. Galton indicated in the preface to the first reprinting of *Hereditary Genius* in 1892 that he could accept less than half of Lombroso's data supporting "the connection between ability of a very high order and insanity." Nonetheless, he said, "there is a large residuum of evidence which points to a painfully close relation between the two, and I must add that my own later observations have tended in the same direction, for I have been surprised at finding how often insanity or idiocy has appeared among the near relatives of exceptionally able men" (Galton, 1869/1892, p. vii).

William James, who held consecutive professorships in physiology, philosophy, and psychology at Harvard within a brief span of 17 years and who was America's foremost psychologist at the time (Boring, 1950), shared Galton's initial skepticism toward the neurosis theory. James, too, however, eventually became convinced of its authenticity. James expressed his endorsement of it in his major treatise on human nature, *The Varieties of Religious Experience*. A painstaking review of the literature led him to the following conclusion:

> The nature of genius has been illuminated by the attempts . . . to class it with psychopathical phenomena. Borderland insanity, crankiness, insane temperament, loss of mental balance, psychopathic degeneration . . . has [sic] certain peculiarities and liabilities which, when combined with a superior quality of intellect in an individual, make it more probable that he will make his mark and affect his age, than if his temperament were less neurotic. (James, 1902, pp. 22–23)

Giftedness and Mental Test Scores

The invention of psychological measurement late in the nineteenth century marks a significant turning point in progress toward identifying giftedness. Mental testing revealed convincingly that variability in human abilities was an empirical reality; it showed that individual differences could be operationally defined on the basis of test scores. The social climate of the times virtually cried out for mental testing. A new ideology of individual differences had arisen. It was based in part on laissez faire economics and upward social class mobility. It conveyed a distinct egalitarian flavor in that it asserted that all people, whatever their intellectual capacities, should have a fair chance to develop whatever talents they may have. The theory of evolution had focused attention on the future, and interest grew apace in assessment in order to ensure that every person's potential for accomplishment and contribution to society could be realized.

Social pressures mounted in the United States, England, France, and other Western countries, especially in the context of education. Compulsory education laws had been passed recently, and schools were bulging with children who differed in abilities. The problem of diversity was exacerbated by an influx of immigrants to America whose children must be educated for productive citizenship. But how were young people to be assigned to different kinds of programs? How could schooling be made more efficient and cost-effective? Mental testing would provide the solution. Galton had inspired interest in the functional uses of the mind, and his work stimulated enormous interest in investigating individual differences in human abilities.

The third face of giftedness to be described is thus derived from the way mental test scores have been employed in the twentieth century to identify gifted people. The discussion is divided topically into five parts, which are presented in approximate chronological order. The topics include the invention of mental tests, the relation of intelligence test scores to neurosis, problems of identifying giftedness via test scores, past and present strategies in identifying giftedness, and finally, a few brief comments about how the legacy of the psychometric era apparently is influencing contemporary searches for ways to identify and understand giftedness.

The Invention of Mental Tests

When Galton wrote the preface for the 1892 reprinting of *Hereditary Genius*, he stated that he wished that he could have changed the title of the book to *Hereditary Ability*. He had used "genius" simply to indicate his interest in the hereditary transmission of exceptionally high ability, which he believed to be integral to ordinary behavior. Galton defined intellectual fitness as a product of willpower, aesthetic appreciation, moral sentiments, and capacity for abstract reasoning. He believed that higher mental attributes aggregated as a general ability and were "innate" in that they were transmissible in accordance with Darwin's hypothesis of pangenesis. But he also believed that degeneration in social conditions might destabilize intellect over the course of an individual's lifetime. How, then, were those of highest ability to be identified and protected?

Galton's goal to improve humanity through the selective mating of intellectually capable people propelled him into developing the first mental tests of individual differences. In 1884 he opened a demonstrational anthropometric laboratory in London, as part of an International Health Exhibition, where visitors could be examined. His "mental tests" included measures of physical strength, pitch and sight sensitivity, color and perceptual discrimination, and reaction time. In Galton's judgment, different levels of intellect could be inferred from sensory discriminations. Consequently, his mental tests were measures of sensory capacity because "the more perceptive the senses the larger the field upon which judgment and intellect can act" (Galton, 1883, p. 27). These measures yielded the mental test scores that Galton assigned to his enthusiastic, impressionable subjects. The test scores conveyed to them his view of their personal worth to society. Questions of construct and empirical validity were never raised. Haphazard testing procedures were seen as sources less of contamination than of annoyance: "The magic involved in measurement gave the measures worth" (Travers, 1983, p. 168).

In 1887, James McKeen Cattell, an American student enroute to the University of Pennsylvania from work in Wilhelm Wundt's psychological laboratory, stopped by to assist Galton. Wundt had founded his laboratory in 1879 in Leipzig, and he was using sensory measures similar to those of Galton, but for the purpose of investigating general or normative laws of behavior. Cattell, who later described Galton as the greatest man he had ever known (Travers, 1983), found Galton's approach to the study of human variability irresistible. At Pennsylvania, and later at Columbia University, Cattell built replicas of Galton's laboratory. He and his students investigated individual differences in sensory capacity under controlled conditions, hoping thereby to find among the correlations an explanation for interdependence among mental processes.

The results, however, were disappointing, for the correlations hovered around zero (Wissler, 1901). The studies demonstrated that mental abilities as measured by these tests were unrelated both to one another and to university grades, which the researchers used as corroborative evidence of the capacity to engage in complex intellectual activity (Freeman, 1926). Nonetheless, this turn-of-the-century research marks a transition point in the history of efforts to identify giftedness. For the first time, after thousands of years of subjective, anecdotal, and retrospective speculation about the meaning of accomplishments and deeds, Galton, Cattell, and their students paved the way for the advent of psychometric testing. They provided a rationale, if not respectable empirical support, for identifying giftedness on the basis of mental test scores. Galton and Cattell also set the stage for a resurgence, nearly a century later, in both theory and research regarding the biological bases of intellectual capability (Eysenck, 1982), although no one was sufficiently prescient at the time to recognize it.

Galton's efforts had a strong, immediate impact in the 1890s on Alfred Binet, who was poised to develop mental tests directly from forms of complex reasoning. Binet had set up a psychological laboratory at the Sorbonne in 1890. His initial tests of individual differences paralleled those of Galton and Cattell, and his results were equally unproductive. Binet soon recognized, however, that test items calling for judgment and reasoning differentiated individuals better than did those tapping sensory capacities. Binet thus declared: "If anyone wishes to study the differences between two individuals, it is necessary to begin with the most intellectual and complex processes" (Binet & Henri, 1895, p. 417).

An opportunity to explore his hypothesis empirically arose when he and Theodore Simon were commissioned in 1904 by the Minister of Public Instruction in Paris to develop tests to ensure that "mentally defective" and normal children were not placed inadvertently in the same class-rooms. France had recently passed a compulsory school attendance law, and the Ministry sought to optimize instructional costs. Binet and Simon arranged the items in their 1905 and 1908 scales from easy to hard, and scores children made on the component tests were combined to yield overall scale scores. The tests were classified by age level in the 1908 revision, which meant that children of the same age could be differen-tiated in ability by the proportion of tests that they passed.

Binet and Simon described the average score that children at given chronological ages had attained as their "mental age." Children who passed tests a year or two below their chronological age were designated as inferior or retarded; those who passed tests a year or two in advance of their chronological age were designated as superior or advanced. The implication that scoring well above chronological age signified high abil-ity acquired tremendous significance in the twentieth century in the quest to identify gifted people. The Binet and Simon model, however, did not provide for using mental test scores for comparing children at different ages. Two children, an eight- and a twelve-year-old, for example, might attain the same mental age, but before a conclusion could be drawn about their relative capabilities, one would have to consider whether their chro-nological ages differed. Binet died at age 54 in 1911, at the very height of his promising career; otherwise he surely would have resolved such awkwardness in his procedures for classifying levels of intellect.

When Lewis M. Terman (1916), a professor of psychology at Stanford, revised Binet's scales, he adopted a simple method, which was first pro-posed by Stern (1914), for comparing levels in intellectual ability among persons of different ages. Terman obtained quotient scores by dividing each participant's mental age by his or her chronological age to obtain a measure that brought the two dimensions into relative perspective. That is, a child with a mental and chronological age of 8 years would have the same IQ (100—decimal points ignored) as a child with a mental and chronological age of 12. Terman's rationale for the IQ ratio stemmed from beliefs about intelligence and giftedness that are echoed in contemporary dialogue. He followed conventional wisdom in viewing intellect as a un-itary, global ability.

By this time, however, the Lamarckian and pangenesis assumption that variations in intellect could be induced by outside influences upon genetic makeup had been superseded by Mendelism. Terman thus took the tack that the IQ score reflected a biological, genetically determined level of intelligence that was stable or wholly independent of cultural factors throughout the lifespan. Intelligence obviously developed and ma-tured in childhood, but the IQ ratio took that into account; therefore, from Terman's perspective, children's and adolescents' IQ scores provided reliable, comparative indicators of potential for educational and social accomplishment. He then published probability tables, as Galton had done, which showed the proportion of people who were likely to obtain given IQ scores. For example, Terman determined that about 2 percent of the population would score 130 IQ and above. His calculations provided a precise, easily applied method for deciding what proportion of the population should be identified as gifted. The Stanford-Binet thus became the standardized reference point for determining who should be regarded as ordinary and who as gifted.

Once it was recognized that growth in mental age unevenly parallels growth in chronological age, psychometrists reverted to Binet's strategy of computing deviation scores within age groups. The venerable IQ acronym, however, given its enormous popular acceptance and traditional significance, has been retained to reference differences in deviation scores.

IQ Frees Giftedness From the Taint of Neurosis

Terman launched his life-long interest in giftedness when he was a senior in psychology at Indiana University. He was asked in 1902 to prepare for a seminar separate reports on mental deficiency and on genius (Terman, 1925, 1954). At the time, he had never heard of a mental test. Reading for those two reports, however, acquainted him with the work of Galton, Cattell, and Binet. His master's thesis at Indiana was based in part on tests used by Binet, and when he entered Clark University in 1904, he spent his first year of graduate study reading about both mental tests and child prodigies. Terman was familiar with the work of Moreau and Lombroso, and he assumed, as did everyone else during that era, that precocious young people were highly susceptible to nervous instabilities (Terman, 1905). However, as had Galton earlier, he raised questions about the connection and chose as his doctoral dissertation a comparative study of seven high-ability and seven low-ability boys from a large urban high school (Terman, 1906). He indicated years later that the experiment contributed little or nothing to science, but that it had sold him on the significance of mental testing (Terman, 1954).

After he attained a professorial appointment at Stanford University in 1910, and as he embarked upon the development of the Stanford-Binet, Terman's interest in gifted young people so intensified that he vowed someday to make them the subject of comprehensive study. His dream came true when the Commonwealth Fund of New York City awarded him a grant in 1920 that provided resources for locating and studying the physical, emotional, and personality traits of 1,000 children, 140 IQ or higher, and for following their development into adulthood. The massive investigation was reported over a period of years in *Genetic Studies of Genius*, a five-volume series. Terman found his high-IQ sample to be appreciably superior to ordinary children in physique, health, social adjustment, and mastery of school subjects. Terman's findings exerted enormous impact in bringing about changes in attitudes toward the gifted. "The data show that the physical and mental traits which characterize typical gifted children appear to warrant the belief that . . . the 'eccentricity of genius' is largely a myth" (Terman & DeVoss, 1924, p. 184).

Terman believed that he had disproved the organic or biological basis of the myth, and he and his colleagues affirmed the conclusion in subsequent investigations and publications (Miles, 1954; Miles & Wolfe, 1936). Over the years, as it has filtered into textbooks and other widely read sources, it has become one of the findings associated prominently with Terman's life-long research. Miles (1954, p. 1037) suggests that the contradiction between earlier investigators and Terman and his colleagues was due largely to differences in matters of definition; however, the reasons stem also in part from sharp cleavages in theoretical formulations about the characteristics of personality as they are derived from notions of either special creation or evolution.

Psychometric g Muddles the Identification of Giftedness

Terman regarded ability in abstract, logical, and judgmental reasoning to be the essence of intelligence and giftedness. These skills would mediate success in every endeavor or accomplishment, whatever its nature. Since the mental tasks he devised revealed individual differences empirically, he never questioned their validity as instruments for identifying giftedness. Terman's abiding faith in the Binet scales was strengthened by their conceptual congruence with Charles Spearman's two-factor theory of intelligence. Spearman (1904), a University of London professor of psychometrics, had demonstrated statistically that scores on mental tests could be divided into a general, g factor, which emerged from the degree of intercorrelations among tests, and into specific, s factors, which represented components unique to each test. Spearman envisaged comprehensiveness and application ("eduction of correlates") to be the main power of g. He thought of this power as energy stimulated by cortical activity that could be transferred from one mental operation to another. Terman was cognizant of Spearman's work when he revised the Binet scales; his revision complemented Galton's analysis of intelligence as a general, global composite of abilities. The g factor was thus viewed as the psychometric basis for differentiating levels of giftedness. Terman was so convinced of the reality of g that he said: "We are coming to recognize that from their ranks [children whose IQ is 140 and above] and from no where else our geniuses in every line are recruited" (Witty & Lehman, 1930, p. 486).

Spearman's concept of *g* provided an underlying principle for the arbitrary use of IQ cutoff scores as a way of classifying people as gifted. This application, in both practice and theory, however, drew sharp, scathing criticism. First, on practical grounds, as a measure of general intelligence, the IQ appeared somewhat insensitive to factors that probably influence success and achievement, such as originality, inventiveness, devotion and concentration, creative and productive thinking, and patterns of highly specific abilities. Investigators revealed, for example, that scores on the Stanford-Binet were uncorrelated with those obtained on tests of musical giftedness, poetic ability, and visual art skills (Manuel, 1919; Scheidemann, 1931; Seashore, 1919). And it seemed intuitively obvious that few people would score uniformly on all the Stanford-Binet subscales, even if they did tap every aspect of giftedness. One person might be gifted in mathematics, another in language arts, and another in general reasoning, but given variations in their abilities, all might earn the same IQ. Second, on theoretical grounds, Edward L. Thorndike, America's foremost educational psychologist during the first half of this century, insisted that it was an error to suppose "that some one function is shared by all intellectual traits, and that whatever resemblances or positive correlations the traits show are due to the presence in each of them of this function as a common factor" (quoted in Freeman, 1926, p. 480; originally cited in Thorndike, 1914).

Thorndike, in rejecting Spearman's psychometric *g*, held that intellect was composed of a "multitude of functions." He opened the door thereby for speculation about specific abilities, but in spite of his disavowal, he did not close it on *g*. Whereas Spearman presumed intelligence to be a unique alchemy of mental energy, Thorndike defined intelligence in terms of neurophysiological connections or associations, saying that intellect differs on the basis of the quantity of connections that people are capable of making. "The person whose intellect is greater or higher or better than that of another person," he said, "differs . . . in the last analysis in having, not a new sort of physiological process, but simply a larger number of connections [*c's*] of the ordinary sort" (Pintner, 1931, p. 69).

What, then, was the source of psychometric *g*? Perhaps because scores on so many tests of complex mental abilities are correlated, certain *c's* are common to these measures. Furthermore, people who are gifted in different ways might apply *c's* in different aggregates to create specific abilities. Thorndike's theory of intellect was conceptualized to complement powerful new perspectives then emerging about learning, and its scope is vast indeed. Let me note here that his views shifted interest in giftedness in two new directions. First, Thorndike refocused attention on

the ways that both heredity or original nature and environmental learning might interact to affect the course of intellectual development. Second,
he emphasized that the task of identifying giftedness required a comprehensive range of measures (Thorndike, Bregman, Cobb, & Woodyard, 1927).

The next major attack on Spearman's g occurred when L. L. Thurstone (1938), of the University of Chicago, reported, after analyzing a
large matrix of intercorrelations, that he found more evidence for several
specific abilities than for a general ability. Verbal comprehension, arithmetic computation, perceptual speed, and general reasoning were among
the abilities that stood out among the various "primary factors" that
Thurstone and his followers defended as being independent of one another. However, when subsequent analyses eventually showed that degree of independence among the factors could be interpreted as a statistical
artifact, Thurstone conceded that Spearman probably was right in pos-
tulating g as a latent attribute of intelligence (Eysenck, 1967, 1979;
Sternberg & Powell, 1983).

J. P. Guilford (1967) of the University of Southern California is
the latest of the psychometrists to attempt to annul g. Guilford hypothesized a structure-of-intellect model comprising three classifications of 15 intellectual dimensions. The dimensions, in turn, produce
120 (5 × 4 × 6) different types of abilities via permutations. The three
classifications involve different forms of processing and analyzing information, of organizing information, and of conceptualizing and expressing information. After arriving at the three-classification model
conceptually, Guilford and Hoepfner (1971) proceeded empirically to
demonstrate partially the extent to which the abilities are independent
of one another. The model has attracted a cohort of devotees, especially
among educators and psychologists who long for distinct psychometric
measures of all potential patterns and expressions of giftedness. They
have been aware for a long time that the IQ was too inclusive for their
purposes, but until Guilford stepped forward, neither an alternative
model nor a satisfactory rationale for developing a comprehensive set
of tests had been available to them for escaping the confusion stirred
up by the ubiquitous, psychometric g.

Eysenck (1979), for example, has suggested that one answer to the
dilemma may reside in developing hierarchical models of intellect whereby
g is induced statistically, as a superordinate connotation of general intelligence, from intercorrelations among more basic or specific abilities
(such as verbal, numerical, and reasoning). These basic abilities, in turn,
may be induced from abilities of even greater subordination (such as
addition, subtraction, and multiplication). Hierarchical models that appear congruent with the realities of intellectual functioning have been
described (Burt, 1941; Vernon, 1950; Vernon, Adamson, & Vernon, 1977),
and, as Eysenck (1979) observes, perhaps "we can have our cake and eat
it, too." The cake, however, possesses a soft center, for the entire super-

structure of a hierarchical model is filled with correlations, all of which point ultimately to psychometric *g*.

Another solution is to ignore the psychometric relations produced by *g*. For example, Stanley (1979) has defined giftedness for his purposes as exceptional mathematical reasoning ability. He and his colleagues conduct talent searches, using a difficult test of mathematical reasoning, to identify young people whose potential for success in mathematics and related areas is high. Next, they arrange instructional environments to help these youngsters learn mathematical and scientific skills as swiftly as their talents and interests allow. Such a prescription might also be useful for identifying and using talent potential in literature and writing, music, dance, visual and decorative arts, and so forth.

Vernon, Adamson, and Vernon (1977) describe several tests that have appeared since the abortive struggle earlier in the century to develop tests of special abilities; however, none of them has come into widespread use. A special ability test, even when selection standards are stringent, may confound aspects of a talent with interest level and, indeed, with other talents. The result is that people who will never realize their potential in the particular ability may be selected for special consideration, and that others whose untapped attributes will promote their success in spite of lack of recognition, and special opportunity may be rejected.

Perhaps for these reasons Guilford's model has been touted as the solution to the problem of identifying giftedness. More than any other reputable authority in the field of psychometrics, Guilford inspired hope that the multiple components of individual differences in giftedness can be defined empirically (Gowan, 1977; Khatena, 1982; Michael, 1977). But to the dismay of those who thought a way out of the wilderness was at hand, Guilford's model has been shown to possess little more than heuristic value. Its integrity has been seriously impugned. Critics have reanalyzed his data and, as with Thurstone's data, have argued that Guilford's findings may be used to support rather than to negate Spearman's *g* (Eysenck, 1979; Harris & Harris, 1971; Horn & Knapp, 1973, 1974).

Practical Limitations in Identifying Giftedness

The roots of the dilemma in which Guilford tangled himself were nurtured by the pioneers of mental testing. They toiled under pressure from school administrators to invent ways of identifying children for cost-efficient instructional programs and of providing opportunity for gifted children to reach their potential. The psychology of individual differences in intellect, to the extent that its methodology has been dominated by mental tests, never was elevated to the status of a science. Competing hypotheses regarding the processes of intellect were seldom considered or investigated. Instead, the urgency of meeting a social need led psychometrists into a morass of technological and methodological problems.

The prestigious National Society for the Study of Education commissioned a yearbook for each of the years 1920, 1924, 1958, and 1979 to foster the development of "the extraordinary capacities and interests of the gifted segments of school populations" (Henry, 1958, p. vii). These four yearbooks chronicle the progress practitioners have made in identifying giftedness in the context of the unremitting presence of psychometric g. The promise of mental tests, of course, enlivened contributors to the 1920 yearbook. "Gifted" was declared to have become "the standard designation of children of supernormal ability" (Henry, 1920, p. 9). Gifted children were determined arbitrarily to constitute about 10 percent of the school population, and a cutoff score of 115 on the Stanford-Binet was advocated as the primary basis for distinguishing the gifted from other pupils.

By the time of the 1924 yearbook vexing questions had arisen about whether special abilities, personality attributes, attitudes, aesthetic appreciation, and leadership skills affected the behavior of "superior," "gifted," or "talented" young people. Baldwin, for example, recognized the "strong wave of enthusiasm" sweeping the country to promote superior children "on I.Q.'s alone." But, he said, "intelligence tests are relatively gross. . . . They take into consideration few distinctions of the relative values of the special traits" (Baldwin, 1924, p. 30). On the whole, doubts raised by contributors to the 1920 yearbook were so widespread that its editor declared that, since agreement could not be reached on "fundamental principles," even after extended correspondence and two lengthy face-to-face sessions, readers should regard it as a "preliminary report." He hoped that someday a comprehensive means of identifying giftedness would be achieved; at that time, he said, the Society ought to issue another yearbook (Whipple, 1924).

The contributors to the 1958 yearbook indeed brought forth a comprehensive description for identifying giftedness, but it could not be defined operationally because of its circularity and inclusiveness. According to the yearbook description, a "talented or gifted child is one who shows consistently remarkable performance in any worth-while line of endeavor" (Havighurst, 1958, p. 19). Since giftedness was viewed as a "process of becoming," selection procedures were to be based on multiple measures: mental test cutoff scores and subjective interpretations of characteristics such as persistence, drive, purpose, and quality of interpersonal relationships (Strang, 1958). So many issues appeared to affect the development of gifted children that the 1958 yearbook was devoted "not to the two or five percent with the highest intelligence quotients, but to the twenty percent with promise of exceptionally good performance in a variety of areas of constructive activity" (Havighurst, 1958, p. 19). Each contributor to the yearbook interpreted promise of exceptional performance to fit his or her programmatic needs, and, thereby, the contributors in 1958 revealed themselves to be as divided on "fundamental principles" as were the contributors in 1920. They either ignored the differences, however, or were oblivious to them.

The 1979 yearbook reinforces trends established in the 1958 yearbook, but it does not resolve them. The skimpy 1958 description of giftedness is given more detail. The content of the new prescription for identifying giftedness is borrowed from a 1972 report to Congress by the United States Office of Education:

> Gifted and talented children are those . . . who by virtue of outstanding abilities are capable of high performance. . . . [Included are] those with demonstrated achievement and/or potential ability in any of the following areas: (a) general intellectual ability, (b) a specific academic aptitude, (c) creative or productive thinking, (d) leadership ability, (e) visual and performing arts, and (f) psychomotor ability. (Gallagher, 1979, p. 30; Marland, 1972, p. 10)

Unfortunately, the 1979 description presents a set of categories that are so confounded conceptually that psychometric investigation of their relationships yields nothing but g. Indeed, they are so vague that Gallagher (1979) suggests that both better rhetoric and more sustained research are needed if a more coherent statement is to be passed to the next generation. Zettel's (1979) review of methods and procedures used by different states to identify gifted young people, for example, reveals that today there are virtually as many different strategies, as well as different standards, as there are local school districts.

Fruits of the Legacy

The twenty-first century is upon us, but researchers are hardly any more efficient in identifying giftedness than they were when Terman first developed the intelligence test. Measures of special abilities, aptitudes, and skills tend either to be unrelated to criterion measures or to correlate inescapably with one another via the ever-present psychometric g. As a consequence, they fail to differentiate people satisfactorily on the basis of potential for specific achievements. Practitioners still rely heavily, therefore, on teacher nominations, novel behaviors that appear especially creative, peer nominations, examples of unusual accomplishment, and other data that form the core of impressionistic, anecdotal judgment.

We may take heart, nevertheless, in acknowledging that society has progressed far in its quest to identify giftedness. We now discount the possibility that high intelligence is a product of divine power; rather, we are inclined to view its mysterious ways as measurably continuous with ordinary behavior. And seldom do we assert that giftedness and neurosis are linked inevitably as an outcome of either metaphysical or evolutionary design. The invention of mental tests has sharpened our perspective and centered attention during this century upon the difficult tasks, first, of identifying people who possess the potential for extraordinary attainment, and second, of providing opportunities for them to realize their talents. The fruits of the legacy are significant. Psychometric technology made its mark in defining intelligence empirically as a general ability. But it has failed to explain adequately the processes that account for this ability. Galton, Binet, and other pioneers of mental test development applied their talents to solving practical problems; they and their successors were distracted from exploring hypotheses about why individuals differ in intellect and giftedness. Both Galton and Binet, however, developed sharply divergent theoretical viewpoints about the source of intellectual competence. Although they were unable to investigate them, their ideas form the bedrock for two distinct approaches among contemporary researchers who are seeking to explain individual differences in intellectual fitness.

One group of researchers is exploring the biological or neurological basis of intelligence. Galton hypothesized that individual differences in intellect could be tapped with measures of reaction time, sensory discrimination, and perceptual speed. Eysenck (1982) had made exactly the same assertion, but his measures are more sophisticated. He says that higher mental functions depend on a properly operating central nervous system and that differences in its operation account for individual differences in general intelligence. Eysenck believes that Galton's theoretical approach was fundamentally correct and that it fell into disrepute because it lacked both adequate rationale and sufficiently sensitive instruments for continuing empirical exploration. Information-processing theory and advanced electronic technology have resolved these problems. They enable Eysenck (1982), Jensen (1985), and their colleagues to investigate hypotheses pertaining to individual differences in information processing at neurophysiological levels of analysis.

These researchers have ascertained that choice reaction time is positively correlated with intelligence. Reaction time experiments revealed that high- and low-ability subjects differed negligibly in simple reaction situations but differed markedly in circumstances where choice times required relatively greater amounts of information. The findings led Eysenck and his colleagues to formulate a neurophysiological theory to account for these differences and to seek a direct physiological measure of them. As they continue to explore the speed with which people process information, and as they develop more precise measures of the electrical activity of the cerebral cortex, these researchers are beginning to identify links between intelligence and brain physiology. Eysenck (1982) believes that successful intellectual functioning or competence is dependent on the direct transmission of correct information. He has formulated an "error-in-transmission" hypothesis, which suggests that highly capable people have faster reaction times than do others because they make fewer errors in transmitting neurological information through the cortex.

A second group of researchers is involved in renewing interest in the judgmental and analytic aspects of intelligence. Its activity may be traced directly to Binet's original ideas. Binet applied his hunches to test development rather than to basic research, but he inspired others to formulate theories of intellectual functioning based on them. Frank N. Freeman (1926), for example, integrated definitions of intelligence offered by Binet, Spearman, Terman, Thorndike, and many others in a remarkably thorough review of test theory and development. Freeman's synthesis provided a cogent reformulation of Binet's viewpoint, and given the scholarship upon which it was based, others at the time cited it as if it were the definitive word. As Freeman put it:

> Psychologically, degrees of intelligence seem to depend on the facility with which the subject-matter experience can be organized into new patterns. This rearrangement of thought material is what characterizes particularly the higher mental processes. It is not identified with any one of them, but it underlies them all. (1926, p. 489)

Robert Sternberg and his colleagues (Sternberg & Davidson, 1983; Sternberg & Gardner, 1982; Sternberg & Powell, 1983) presented a theory of intelligence and a corollary theory of giftedness that closely parallel the views of Binet and Freeman. Sternberg and his coauthors explicitly assume, on both theoretical and empirical grounds, that intelligence is represented by a general ability, and they propose that it can best be understood by analyzing the ways in which people "mentally represent and process information."

Sternberg and his colleagues investigate information processing by focusing on the "component" tasks inherent in complex reasoning problems. They reason that, once the information-processing origins of g are isolated, knowledge of individual differences in intellect, as is indicated by step-by-step performances on discrete tasks, may eventually explain individual differences in higher level, complex reasoning. They suggest that intellectual competence is indicated by "metacomponential" or "executive-processing" skills, which include a broad array of problem-solving attributes. They see these skills as representative of general ability, or g, because, as Freeman anticipated, they are presumed to function independently of content domains and specific talents.

According to Sternberg and Davidson (1983), individual differences in general ability are attributable to individual differences in executing metacomponential skills. The psychological basis of giftedness is thus said to be "insight skills." Gifted individuals, they say, are characterized by an unusual ability to acquire, and to think in terms of, novel concepts and conceptual systems. These exceptional insight skills set apart the gifted from the ordinary. The truly gifted are likely to enjoy an abundance of major intellectual insights during their lifetimes, whereas average people may have no insights of significance in their lifetimes. Sternberg and Davidson come uncomfortably close to a definition of giftedness based on a presumption of divine inspiration. Although, of course, this is not their intent, their view of giftedness as being qualitatively distinct from ordinary intellectual activity was certainly common in ancient times.

No one today knows how to integrate the divergent trends in scholarship that Eysenck and Sternberg exemplify. Both conceptualize individual differences in intellectual functioning as cognitive in nature, but each offers different theoretical and methodological ways of investigating Spearman's venerable *g*. Eysenck regards the problem as being as difficult to resolve as that "between the wave and corpuscular theories of light" (1982, p. 7). He says that physicists think in wave terms on even days of the week and in corpuscular terms on odd days. They keep Sunday open for thinking about both theories! When all of the week is available, so to speak, for considering both neurophysiological and metacomponential theories of intellect simultaneously, perhaps the centuries-old struggle to identify and understand giftedness may be elevated to the point where judgments will be made less on the basis of data provided by test technology and more on the premises of theory that is substantiated by verifiable hypotheses.

References

Alexander, F. G., & Selesnick, S. T. (1966). *The history of psychiatry: An evaluation of psychiatric thought and practice from prehistoric times to the present.* New York: Harper & Row.

Baldwin, B. T. (1924). Methods of selecting superior or gifted children. In G. M. Whipple (Ed.), *Twenty-third yearbook of the National Society for the Study of Education* (pp. 25–47). Chicago: University of Chicago Press.

Binet, A., & Henri, V. (1895). La psychologie individuelle. *L'Annee Psychologique, 2,* 411–465.

Boring, E. G. (1950). *A history of experimental psychology* (rev. ed.). New York: Appleton-Century-Crofts.

Burt, C. L. (1941). *The factors of the mind.* New York: Macmillan.

Darwin, C. (1868). *The variations of animals and plants under domestication* (Vols. 1–2). New York: Appleton.

Eysenck, H. J. (1967). Intelligence assessment: A theoretical and experimental approach. *British Journal of Educational Psychology, 37,* 81–98.

Eysenck, H. J. (1979). *The structure and measurement of intelligence.* Berlin, West Germany: Springer-Verlag.

Eysenck, H. J. (1982). Introduction. In H. J. Eysenck (Ed.), *A model for intelligence* (pp. 1–10). Berlin, West Germany: Springer-Verlag.

Freeman, F. N. (1926). *Mental tests: Their history, principles, and applications.* New York: Houghton Mifflin.

Freeman, J. (1983). Emotional problems of the gifted child. *Journal of Child Psychology and Psychiatry. 24,* 481–485.

Gallagher, J. J. (1979). Issues in education for the gifted. In A. H. Passow (Ed.), *Seventy-eighth yearbook of the National Society for the Study of Education* (pp. 28–44). Chicago: University of Chicago Press.

Galton, F. (1883). *Inquiries into human faculty and its development.* London: Macmillan.

Galton, F. (1892). *Hereditary genius.* London: Julian Friedman. (original work published 1869)

Gowan, J. C. (1977). Background and history of the gifted-child movement. In J. C. Stanley, W. C. George, & C. H. Solano (Eds.), *The gifted and the creative: A fifty-year perspective* (pp. 5–27). Baltimore: Johns Hopkins University Press.

Grinder, R. E. (1967). *A history of genetic psychology: The first science of human development.* New York: Wiley.

Guilford, J. P. (1967). *The nature of human intelligence.* New York: McGraw-Hill.

Guilford, J. P., & Hoepfner, R. (1971). *The analysis of intelligence.* New York: McGraw-Hill.

Harris, M. L., & Harris, C. W. (1971). A factor analytic interpretation strategy. *Educational and Psychological Measurement, 31,* 589–606.

Havighurst, R. J. (1958). The importance of education for the gifted. In N. B. Henry (Ed.), *Fifty-seventh yearbook of the National Society for the Study of Education* (pp. 3–20). Chicago: University of Chicago Press.

Henry, N. B. (1958). Editor's preface. In N. B. Henry (Ed.), *Fifty-seventh yearbook of the National Society for the Study of Education* (pp. vii–viii). Chicago: University of Chicago Press.

Henry, T. S. (1920). Classroom problems in the education of gifted children. In T. S. Henry (Ed.), *Nineteenth yearbook of the National Society for the Study of Education* (pp. 7–20). Chicago: University of Chicago Press.

Hildreth, G. H. (1966). *Introduction to the gifted.* New York: McGraw-Hill.

Hollingworth, L. S. (1926). *Gifted children: Their nature and nurture.* New York: Macmillan.

Horn, J. L., & Knapp, J. R. (1973). On the subjective character of the empirical base of Guilford's structure-of-intellect model. *Psychological Bulletin, 80,* 33–43.

Horn, J. L., & Knapp, J. R. (1974). Thirty wrongs do not make a right: Reply to Guilford. *Psychological Bulletin, 81,* 502–504.

Hull, C. L. (1928). *Aptitude testing.* New York: World Book Company.

Hyslop, T. B. (1925). *The great abnormals.* London: Philip Allan & Co.

James, W. (1902). *The varieties of religious experience: A study in human nature.* New York: Longmans, Green.

Jensen, A. R. (1985). The theory of intelligence. In S. Modgil & C. Modgil (Eds.), *Hans Eysenck: Searching for a scientific basis for human behavior.* London: Falmer Press.

Jowett, T. (1942). *Plato: Five great dialogues.* New York: Walter J. Black.

Khatena, J. (1982). *Educational psychology of the gifted.* New York: Wiley.

Lecky, W. E. (1905). *History of European morals* (Vol. 1). London: Longmans, Green.

Lombroso, C. (1891). *The man of genius.* London: Walter Scott.

Manuel, H. T. (1919). *A study of talent in drawing.* Bloomington, IN: Public School Publishing.

Marland, S. P., Jr. (1972). *Education of the gifted and talented.* Washington, DC: U.S. Government Printing Office.

Michael, W. B. (1977). Cognitive and affective components of creativity in mathematics and the physical sciences. In J. C. Stanley, W. C. George, & C. H.

Solano (Eds.), *The gifted and the creative: A fifty-year perspective* (pp. 141–172). Baltimore: Johns Hopkins University Press.

Miles, C. C. (1954). Gifted children. In L. Carmichael (Ed.), *Manual of Child Psychology* (2nd ed., pp. 984–1063). New York: Wiley.

Miles, C. C., & Wolfe, L. S. (1936). Childhood physical and mental health records of historical geniuses. *Psychological Monographs, 47,* 390–400.

Murray, G. (1955). *Five stages of Greek religion.* New York: Doubleday.

Nisbet, J. (1891). *The insanity of genius.* London: Ward & Downey.

Nordau, M. (1895). *Degeneration.* New York: Appleton.

Nordenskiold, E. (1935). *The history of biology.* New York: Tudor.

Pintner, R. (1931). *Intelligence testing: Methods and results* (rev. ed.). New York: Holt.

Ribot, T. (1906). *Essay on the creative imagination.* Chicago: Open Court.

Robbins, R. H. (Ed.). (1959). *The encyclopedia of witchcraft and demonology.* New York: Crown.

Scheidemann, N. V. (1931). *The psychology of exceptional children.* Boston: Houghton Mifflin.

Seashore, C. E. (1919). *The psychology of musical talent.* New York: Silver Burdette.

Sicherman, B. (1981). The paradox of prudence: Mental health in the gilded age. In A. Scull (Ed.), *Madhouses, mad-doctors, and madmen: The social history of psychiatry in the Victorian era* (pp. 218–240). Philadelphia: University of Pennsylvania Press.

Spearman, C. H. (1904). "General intelligence" objectively determined and measured. *American Journal of Psychology, 15,* 201–293.

Stanley, J. C. (1979). The study and facilitation of talent for mathematics. In A. H. Passow (Ed.), *Seventy-eighth yearbook of the National Society for the Study of Education* (pp. 169–185). Chicago: University of Chicago Press.

Stern, W. (1914). *The psychological methods of testing intelligence.* Baltimore: Warwick & York.

Sternberg, R. J., & Davidson, J. E. (1983). Insight in the gifted. *Educational Psychologist, 18,* 51–57.

Sternberg, R. J., & Gardner, M. K.(1982). A componential interpretation of the general factor in human intelligence. In H. J. Eysenck (Ed.), *A model for intelligence* (pp. 231–254). Berlin, West Germany: Springer-Verlag.

Sternberg, R. J., & Powell, J. S. (1983). The development of intelligence. In J. H. Flavell & E. M. Markman (Eds.), *Handbook of child psychology: Vol. 3. Cognitive development* (4th ed., pp. 341–419). New York: Wiley.

Strang, R. (1958). The nature of giftedness. In N. B. Henry (Ed.), *Fifty-seventh yearbook of the National Society for the Study of Education* (pp. 64–86). Chicago: University of Chicago Press.

Terman, L. M. (1905). A study in precocity and prematuration. *American Journal of Psychology, 16,* 145–183.

Terman, L. M. (1906). Genius and stupidity: A study of some of the intellectual processes of seven "bright" and seven "dull" boys. *Pedagogical Seminary, 13,* 307–373.

Terman, L. M. (1916). *The measurement of intelligence.* Boston: Houghton Mifflin.

Terman, L. M. (1925). *Genetic studies of genius: Vol. 1. Mental and physical traits of a thousand gifted children.* Stanford, CA: Stanford University Press.

Terman, L. M. (1954). The discovery and encouragement of exceptional talent. *American Psychologist, 9,* 221–230.

Terman, L. M., & DeVoss, J. C. (1924). The educational achievements of gifted children. In G. M. Whipple (Ed.), *Twenty-third yearbook of the National Society for the Study of Education* (pp. 169–184). Chicago: University of Chicago Press.

Thorndike, E. L. (1914). *Educational psychology* (Vol. 3). New York: Columbia University.

Thorndike, E. L., Bregman, E. O., Cobb, M. V., & Woodyard, E. (1927). *The measurement of intelligence*. New York: Bureau of Publications, Teachers College, Columbia University.

Thurstone, L. L. (1938). *Primary mental abilities*. Chicago: University of Chicago Press.

Travers, R. M. W. (1983). *How research has changed American schools. A history from 1840 to the present*. Kalamazoo, MI: Mythos.

Vernon, P. E. (1950). *The structure of human abilities*. London: Methuen.

Vernon, P. E., Adamson, G., & Vernon, D. F. (1977). *The psychology and education of gifted children*. London: Methuen.

Whipple, G. M. (1924). Editor's preface. In G. M. Whipple (Ed.), *Twenty-third yearbook of the National Society for the Study of Education* (p. vi). Chicago: University of Chicago Press.

Wissler, C. (1901). The correlation of mental and physical tests. *Psychological Review Monograph, 3* (6, Whole No. 16).

Witty, P. A., & Lehman, H. C. (1930). Nervous instability and genius: Some conflicting opinions. *Journal of Abnormal and Social Psychology, 24*, 486–497.

Zettel, J. (1979). State provisions for educating the gifted and talented. In A. H. Passow (Ed.), *Seventy-eighth yearbook of the National Society for the Study of Education* (pp. 63–74). Chicago: University of Chicago Press.

2. Cognitive Development in the Gifted and Talented

Robert J. Sternberg
Janet E. Davidson
Yale University

Everyone admires that handful of individuals who, in a given generation, change the course of civilization by virtue of their gifts and talents—individuals such as Aristotle, Leonardo da Vinci, Napoleon Bonaparte, John Locke, and Albert Einstein. In admiring such extraordinarily talented individuals, it is difficult not to wonder how they came to be so talented: Was it factors in their heredities or environments, or perhaps an unusual interplay of circumstances that turned excellent talents into superlative ones? If ever we are to understand the extraordinary gifts of the highly talented, we will certainly need to consider the origins of these gifts, and how they developed.

The purpose of this chapter is to consider the cognitive development of the gifted and talented. Because of the rich interconnectedness of all of the factors that contribute to the mind's development, we, the authors of this chapter, consider "cognition" in a broad rather than in a narrow sense. Indeed, in order to give any meaning at all to this review and discussion of the literature, we need first to define what we mean both by "gifted and talented" and by "cognitive development." We open our chapter with some definitions, and then review the relevant literature that falls within the purview of the domain carved out by our definitions. Our review consists of two parts: a review of cognitive-developmental theories and how they might help the public understand the gifted and talented, and a review of the empirical literature on the cognitive development of the gifted and talented. The empirical literature, unfortunately, has only minimal interface with the theoretical literature. Finally, we summarize and discuss those aspects of cognitive development that seem central to the development of high levels of talent.

What Does it Mean To Be Gifted or Talented?

Any schoolteacher or administrator knows that an astonishingly high percentage of parents believe their children to be gifted or talented. This large percentage could be written off partially to subjectivity, but it could also be understood in part as due to the willingness of parents to perceive in their own children the full range of skills and behaviors in which talents can manifest themselves. In considering the meaning of "gifted and talented," one must deal with two issues: the range of skills and behaviors that one accepts as representing genuine gifts and talents, and the level at or form in which these skills and behaviors must be manifested in order to set them off from ordinary manifestations.

A Range of Skills and Behaviors

Tannenbaum (1983) has presented a useful taxonomy of kinds of talents, which is helpful in delimiting the range of skills and behaviors with respect to which society seems willing to recognize extraordinary gifts. According to Tannenbaum, there are four basic kinds of talents.

1. Scarcity Talents. These talents are in short supply in the world, and the outcomes of them are products that make the world an easier, safer, healthier, or more intelligible place in which to live. The contributions of individuals such as Jonas Salk (inventor of a polio vaccine), Martin Luther King (a principal bearer of a new age of better race relations), and Sigmund Freud (inventor of the first systematic and widely accepted form of psychotherapy) fall into this domain.

2. Surplus Talents. These talents are also in short supply, but, according to Tannenbaum, they enrich the world in a way that might be characterized as "divine luxury." For example, the contributions of Wolfgang Amadeus Mozart, Pablo Picasso, or Ernest Hemingway have made the world a much better place in which to live, but they have not saved

Preparation of this chapter was supported by a grant from the Spencer Foundation.

lives or changed the commonweal, as have the contributions of those with scarcity talents, such as Jonas Salk or Sir Alexander Fleming (discoverer of penicillin). The surplus talents thus tend to be focused in the areas perceived by the public as entertainment, whereas the scarcity talents tend to be focused in the areas of technology, medicine, politics, and so forth.

3. Quota Talents. These talents include skills and behaviors for which there is only a limited demand. Thus, whereas the world would seem to have unlimited room for the potential Flemings and Picassos, it needs only so many teachers (because of limitations in the number of teaching positions), lawyers (because of limitations in the number of law suits and other legal business), and engineers (because of limitations in the development of technology). These talents, therefore, are very susceptible to the rule of supply and demand as it applies to human talents.

4. Anomalous Talents. These talents reflect powers of humankind that are valued only by virtue of their statistical anomaly, or by virtue of their impressiveness despite social disapproval. Don Juan, with his record conquests, or the idiot savant who can state the day of the week on which any date in the indefinite future falls, are examples of people with anomalous talents. The unusually successful Machiavellian, or the wily demagogue, might also be viewed as having anomalous talents.

Although Tannenbaum's taxonomy is useful, we authors are less comfortable with the four-way distinction than is Tannenbaum. For example, we believe that whether surplus talents are clearly distinguishable from scarcity talents is debatable: The effects of culture upon society may sometimes be more subtle and less immediate than are the effects of politics or medicine, but we suspect that they are equally woven into the fabric of society. The cultural contributions of a given age are not only shaped by, but also help shape, the psyche and mores of that age. Similarly, we doubt that quota talents are readily separable from scarcity and surplus talents; there seems always to be room for the really great lawyers, teachers, and engineers. There seems to be less room for the average ones, but the same could be said of political leaders and medical scientists. Quota talents may really represent lesser degrees of scarcity and surplus talents. Finally, it is often extremely difficult to draw a clear line at just what it is that society disapproves of, but recognizes as talented. Some of the greatest demagogues have received massive approval, either in their own times or posthumously. Similarly, some of the greatest Machiavellians (perhaps Bismarck or Robespierre) have come to be recognized as extraordinary in large part because of their Machiavellian talents. In contrast, Don Juan seems less to represent a genuinely gifted individual than do the various authors and composers (such as Mozart) who have made him the subject of their artistic forays.

The Social Context

If there is any one thing that seems to define the range of behaviors that are gifted or talented, it is society's labeling of them as such. This has been noted before. Becker (1978), a leading proponent of a "labeling" theory of social deviance, has extended this theory to giftedness as well, arguing that giftedness (or, to be exact, "genius") is the result of being labeled as such and has no independent existence in its own right. Individuals may be intrinsically extraordinary in any of a variety of skills, but once one moves to the designation of "giftedness," or at the extreme, "genius," that designation is a product of whatever a given societal milieu is willing to label as such. If this view is correct, then it suggests that the number of unappreciated gifted, at least for posterity if not for their own time, must be less than one might intuitively believe; after all, it is the society that defines the gifts.

Indeed, Lenneberg (1980) has argued that we have almost all fallen victims to the "myth of the unappreciated genius," by which large numbers of great individuals have gone unrecognized in their times. According to Lenneberg, careful historical analysis reveals that in many instances great individuals have been viewed as unappreciated only because of their lack of commercial success, despite the fact that they were widely recognized as gifted and talented within their own fields of endeavor. One would not want to argue, of course, that the gifted are always appreciated in their own time. Many great talents probably go unrecognized, and it seems likely that there is something to the notion that an individual can be "ahead of his or her time." But it may be that the number of the unappreciated is not so great as the conventional wisdom would have us believe.

If gifts and talents are in the eyes of the societal beholder, just what are the gifts and talents to which our society, and others like it, are willing to accord recognition? Various taxonomies have been proposed to answer this question. If a "societally sanctioned" answer to the question exists, it is that of Marland (1972), who, as U.S. Commissioner of Education, proposed six areas in which gifted and talented children were to be identified and nurtured: (a) general intellectual ability, (b) specific academic aptitude, (c) creative or productive thinking, (d) leadership ability, (e) visual and performing arts, and (f) psychomotor ability (see also DeHahn & Havighurst, 1957). Cohn (1981) has proposed a hierarchical model, similar in some respects to hierarchical models of intelligence such as that of Vernon (1971), which lists as major domains of giftedness the (a) intellectual, (b) artistic, (c) social, and (d) other, with subdomains falling under these major domains. Piechowski (1979) has also advanced a hierarchical model, including as major domains the (a) psychomotor, (b) sensual, (c) intellectual, (d) imaginal, and (e) emotional. In contrast, Renzulli (1978) has simply classed various kinds of abilities together, and

offered as his definition of giftedness (a) above-average (but not necessarily exceptional) ability, (b) creativity, and (c) task commitment.

Measuring Giftedness

The taxonomies described clearly aim for breadth in the range of gifts and
talents they acknowledge. Not all theorists of giftedness have sought such
breadth. Terman believed IQ to be a reasonable and sufficient basis for
identifying gifted children. The first major investigation of giftedness in the
United States, the Terman "genetic studies of genius" (e.g., Terman & Oden,
1947, 1959), used Stanford-Binet Intelligence Test scores as the primary
basis for identification. Almost all of the participants in the study had IQs
of at least 140, and some had IQs of 180 and above. Hollingworth (1938), a
contemporary of Terman's, also used IQ as the primary basis for identifying
the gifted, using 130 as a minimum score for identifying gifted individuals
and 180 as a minimum score for identifying intellectual geniuses.

The attempts of both Terman and Hollingworth to identify the gifted
in terms of a single index of intellect find their historical roots in the
thinking of Galton (1869), who represented in terms of the normal curve
the range of ability from idiocy, at the lowest point on the curve, to genius,
at the highest. Although a single IQ score would seem by any standard
to be a narrow basis for defining giftedness, at the same time it appears
likely that those who are gifted by virtue of their exceptional achievements do have IQs considerably above the societal average. Cox (1926),
for example, estimated the average IQ of some of the most distinguished
gifted individuals in history to be 155, although such historical estimates
are imprecise, at best.

Certain more recent theorists of intelligence have followed in the
path of Terman and Hollingworth in their use of intelligence as a basis
for defining giftedness (or at least, intellectual giftedness), but they have
sought to expand considerably the notions of Terman and Hollingworth
in terms of what constitutes human intelligence. Gardner (1983) has
expanded conventional notions of intelligence by harking back to faculty
psychology and suggesting that the mind can be understood in terms of
a set of distinct "multiple intelligences." His list of multiple intelligences
looks very much like the lists of talents provided earlier in this chapter,
which served as bases for defining the range of skills and behaviors in
which giftedness should be recognized. Indeed, Gardner's book is largely
devoted to a consideration of extraordinary levels of talent.

Sternberg (1985) has proposed a "triarchic" theory of human intelligence that he has sought to extend to understanding intellectual giftedness, broadly defined. According to this theory, intellectual giftedness
can be defined only with reference to three domains: (a) the internal,
mental mechanisms responsible for intelligent behavior; (b) the external,
contextual setting, which defines what will be labeled as intelligent within

a given societal milieu; and (c) the level of experience an individual has with a given task or situation intended to measure intelligence. According to Sternberg, individuals may be gifted with respect to (a) cognitive functioning of the kinds measured by conventional intellectual tasks and tests, (b) contextual fitting that requires adaptation to, selection of, or shaping of environments, and (c) the ability to deal with novelty or to automatize information processing effectively. Individuals may show giftedness in any one or more of these aspects of intelligence.

A Working Definition of Giftedness

The sampling of taxonomies of giftedness in this chapter should make clear that although a perfect consensus does not exist regarding the specific skills and behaviors to which the term "giftedness" should be applied, there does exist moderate agreement regarding the kinds of things that should not fall within this purview. Given our view that giftedness is societally defined, it makes sense to seek to find and then use a consensus taxonomy as a basis for defining giftedness, because this taxonomy probably gives a prototypical representation of the societal view. Without claiming uniqueness in our consensus taxonomy, we include within the range of relevant skills and behaviors (a) *intellectual skills* of all kinds (including verbal, quantitative, spatial, memorial, and so on); (b) *artistic skills* of all kinds (including painting, musicianship, drama, dance, and so on); (c) *niche-fitting skills* of all kinds, including adaptation to, selection of, and shaping of those physical and interpersonal environments in which one happens to find oneself (lawyers, business executives, doctors, or whoever must find or make an environment that is well suited to their talents before they can be successful; and (d) *physical skills* of all kinds, including those involved in various sports and in physical survival in less than hospitable terrains.

In sum, we propose a consensus taxonomy to define the range of skills and behaviors that we consider to be bases for unusual gifts and talents. This classification scheme meshes, in one way or another, with many of those previously listed. We claim only heuristic usefulness, not uniqueness or one-to-one mappings to the psychology of the individual for our taxonomy of domains. We agree with Renzulli (1978) that high ability, creativity, and task commitment are probably prerequisite to outstanding performance in any of these domains. At the same time, we doubt that the meaning of any of these three terms is quite the same from one domain to another.

Distinguishing Characteristics of Skills and Behaviors

Although there is some variation among theorists' beliefs regarding the range of skills and behaviors to which the labels "gifted" and "talented" can reasonably be applied, there seems to be relatively little variation among their notions regarding distinguishing characteristics, at least if one defines these distinguishing characteristics at a sufficient level of generality. Individuals who are recognized as gifted or talented tend to be acknowledged as such by virtue of either (a) the precocity of their development (slope of the developmental function) or (b) the ultimate level of their development (asymptote of the developmental function). In some instances, the child prodigies who show exceptionally rapid advancement also end up at exceptionally high levels of accomplishment as adults, although this is by no means always true, for reasons to be discussed later. Thus, in our purview, we consider performance that is exceptional by virtue either of its precocity (slope) or its ultimate level (asymptote). Precocious behavior can readily be identified as exceptional simply by virtue of its timing: A child attains at an early age performance that is not normally demonstrated until much later, if at all. In the case of exceptional ultimate behavior, identification procedures are by no means as direct. Societal consensus, as noted earlier, seems to define such behavior as exceptional (see also Amabile, 1983).

Cognitive Development: A Literature Review

We shall be as brief in our consideration of what we mean by "cognitive development" as we were lengthy in our consideration of what we mean by "gifted" and "talented." Following Flavell (1977), we shall define as cognitive that "complex *system* of interacting processes which generate, code, transform, and otherwise manipulate information of diverse sorts" (p. 12). Like Flavell, we shall attempt a broad construal of both cognition and development, so as not to exclude from our purview any skills or behaviors that might further one's understanding of how exceptional talent develops. In other words, we view cognitive development as referring to the capabilities of the human mind that change as an individual grows older. General intelligence is one of the mind's capabilities; creativity, musical ability, and artistic ability are other examples. Our review of literature covers two areas: theory and empirical research. This separation reflects the state of literature, in which theory and data have developed almost independently.

General Theories

In this section, we consider theories that fall into two basic classes: cognitive-developmental theories that can naturally be extended to the understanding of the development of gifts and talents, although this was not their original aim, and cognitive-developmental theories that have been proposed especially to understand the development of the gifted and talented. Somewhat predictably, there are more theories of the first kind than of the second, and so we shall have to be particularly selective in considering the more general theories. General theories of cognitive development can naturally be divided into four classes (see Sternberg & Powell, 1983), and we shall use a four-class schematization here as a useful heuristic for comparing theoretical approaches.

Stimulus–Response Theory

Stimulus–response theory tends to emphasize the role of learning in cognitive development. Learning, in turn, is seen as the result of the formation of associations. A pure version of the stimulus–response point of view was presented by Thorndike, Bregman, Cobb, and Woodyard (1926), who suggested that

> in their deeper nature the higher forms of intellectual operation are identical with mere association or connection forming, depending upon the same sort of physiological connections but requiring *many more of them.* By the same argument the person whose intellect is greater or higher or better than that of another person differs from him in the last analysis in having, not a new sort of physiological process, but simply a large number of connections of the ordinary sort. (p. 415)

In this view, then, all skills and behavior are seen as emanating from stimulus–response connections, and differences in levels of performance can be traced to differences in the number and range of such connections (see also Hull, 1943).

More sophisticated and differentiated stimulus–response views have been presented in more recent times, for example, by Gagne (1968), by Kendler and Kendler (1975), by White (1965), and by others. Although greater differentiation in the theoretical system is allowed in these newer views, cognitive development is seen as the accumulation of past associative learning. Thus, even in Gagne's hierarchy of types of learning (including signal learning, stimulus–response learning, chaining, verbal association, multiple discrimination, concept learning, principle learning, and problem solving, in order of increasing complexity), the formation of stimulus–response connections is the basis for cognitive development.

The implications of such a view for understanding unusual gifts and talents are straightforward. Precocious children (steep slope in the learning-developmental function) form connections at a much more rapid rate than do ordinary children, and exceptional adults (high asymptote in the learning-developmental function) have formed exceptionally large numbers of variegated stimulus–response connections. Certain current views of expertise, which stress the role of knowledge in expert performance (e.g., Chi, 1978; Larkin, McDermott, Simon, & Simon, 1980), can be viewed as compatible with, although much more complex than, the stimulus–response point of view. Their similarity is in their stress upon the products of knowledge acquisition. Their greater complexity, however, is in allowing for the importance of the role of cognitive structures and contents, rather than simple associations, as the bases for superior cognitive performance.

As a basis for understanding cognitive development in the gifted and talented, stimulus–response theory suffers from many of the same problems that led to its general weakening in psychology. First, it says virtually nothing about the mental processes and structures that intervene between stimulus and response. Even "mediational" stimulus–response accounts, although they acknowledge the existence of mental states between external stimulus and response, say surprisingly little about the forms this mediation can take. Second, stimulus–response accounts seem virtually to equate cognitive development with learning. Although there can be no doubt that learning plays an important role in cognitive development, the work of Piaget (1972, 1977) and others suggests that it is extremely unlikely that learning is all there is to cognitive development. Finally, the account seems in some respects theoretically barren. Viewing the gifted and talented as having more, or more complex, stimulus–response connections, or as having faster-evolving connections, seems to do little more than to restate the fact of their exceptionality. Exceptional individuals may indeed learn quickly and eventually know more, but stimulus–response accounts give only a lean explanation for why these individuals developed as they did. A fuller account is needed.

Piagetian Theory

Piaget's (1972) theory of intelligence and intellectual development is probably the most comprehensive theory of its kind, and so it would seem natural to look to this theory for understanding of exceptional gifts and talents. Indeed, almost everyone seriously interested in the gifted has given at least some study, no matter how cursory, to Piaget's theory.

Piaget viewed intelligence, broadly defined, as a biological process of morphogenesis and adaptation to the environment. Intelligence develops in a series of periods, which are invariant in their order of unfolding: a sensorimotor period, lasting from birth to approximately two years of age; a period of preparation for concrete operations (preoperational period), lasting from approximately two to six years of age; a period of concrete operations, lasting from approximately six to twelve years of age; and a period of formal operations, lasting from approximately twelve years of age through adulthood. A description of children's levels of cognitive accomplishments during each of these periods is outside the range of this chapter and is lengthy. Suggested sources for such a description are Flavell (1963) or Ginsburg and Opper (1979).

Piaget was not particularly interested either in individual differences in intelligence or in exceptionally high levels of talent. Nevertheless, this theory does lend itself to extensions to these areas. Because Piaget's area of inquiry was that of intelligence, any inferences or extrapolations drawn would have to be for the intellectual domain of giftedness only. Piaget's theory suggests a view of intellectual precocity in terms of rapid passage through the Piagetian periods of cognitive development. Indeed, there is at least some indication that intellectually precocious youngsters do move through the periods of development more rapidly than do intellectually typical ones (Keating, 1975). Nevertheless, available evidence suggests that precocity is more likely to show up through rapid movement within rather than between periods (Lovell, 1968; Webb, 1974). Although moderate correlations (at about the .6 level) have been found between scores on Piagetian tasks and standard psychometric intelligence tests (Kaufman, 1971; Zigler & Trickett, 1978), we agree with Tuddenham (1971) that replacing mental age (itself a flawed construct) with Piagetian period level would not lead to an improvement either in the understanding or prediction of intellectual behavior.

Taking Piaget's theory at face value, it would not seem to have much to say about exceptional performance among adults. After all, if everyone reaches the period of formal operations eventually, then it is difficult to say just where the sources of adult individual differences will lie. However, the theory may actually have considerable potential for explaining individual differences at the adult level. First, it now appears that not all adults do, in fact, reach a fully formal-operational level of functioning (Flavell, 1977; Martorano, 1977; Neimark, 1975). Second, neo-Piagetian theorists have attempted in various ways to extend Piaget's theory of intellectual development, arguing that there may be a fifth period that provides a clear and consistent basis for differentiation among levels of performance in adults.

Several proposals have been made regarding the form of adult cognitive development beyond the formal operations period. Arlin (1975), for example, proposed that whereas the primary development during the formal-operational period is in problem-solving ability, the primary development taking place in a post-formal-operational period might be one of problem-finding ability. Gifted adults, therefore, might be those who progress from merely being able to solve significant problems to a level of being able to find and formulate significant problems. This suggestion is consistent with theory and data developed by Getzels and Csikszentmihalyi (1976), who, in studies of gifted artists, demonstrated that perhaps no talent distinguished more from less gifted artists as well as did the talent of finding appropriate artistic problems on which to work. A measure of problem-finding ability showed significant and moderate correlations with rated aesthetic ability (.40) and originality (.54), although the correlation with craftsmanship (.28) was not statistically significant.

Certainly, the importance of problem-finding ability extends beyond the arts; perhaps no skill is as important in scientific research. Zuckerman (1979), for example, has pointed out that among elite scientists, the prime criterion of scientific taste resides in a sense of what constitutes an important problem. For such scientists, deep problems and elegant solutions to these problems are the primary bases for distinguishing excellent from commonplace science.

Another view of post-formal-operational thinking, proposed by Case (1978), is based upon the fact that a primary criterion for designating an individual as formal-operational is the individual's ability to perceive second-order relations, or relations between relations. For example, in the analogy, bench : judge :: pulpit : minister, recognition of the analogy hinges upon recognition of the second-order relation between the first-order relation, bench : judge, on the one hand, and the first-order relation, pulpit : minister, on the other. Case suggested that "the search for 'development beyond formal operations' should. . .concentrate on clarifying the nature of second-order intellectual operations and on searching for third-order operations" (p. 63).

Sternberg and Downing (1982) extended and operationalized Case's notion by constructing a test of the ability to recognize third-order relations, as in analogies between analogies. Subjects in their experiment received third-order analogies such as (bench : judge :: pulpit : minister) :: (head : hair :: lawn : grass), and they had to rate the goodness of such analogies. They found that development in the ability to recognize third-order relations continued through adolescence, even among very bright subjects, and that the acquisition of the ability to solve third-order relations seemed to resemble the acquisition of the ability to solve second-order relations, but during a later time period of life. Scores on the third-order analogies test were moderately correlated (.52) with scores on difficult second-order analogies.

Perhaps the most ambitious extension of Piaget's (1972) theory has been undertaken by Commons, Richards, and Kuhn (1982), who proposed to look at fourth- as well as third-order operations. They proposed a fifth period involving the ability to handle third-order relations that they referred to as requiring "systematic operations," or exhaustive operations on classes of relations-forming systems. The sixth period, according to these investigators, involves the ability to handle fourth-order relations requiring "metasystematic operations" for comparing and contrasting systems with one another. They tested their theory by presenting undergraduate and graduate students with complex stories involving complicated relations, such as preference for different objects or heaviness of various objects. To demonstrate systematic thinking, the subjects had to recognize the complex interrelations among objects. To demonstrate metasystematic thinking, the subjects had to recognize complex interrelations among stories. The investigators found that few undergraduates demonstrated either systematic or metasystematic thinking, but that some graduate students did. Moreover, formal-operational attainments seemed to be a prerequisite for the demonstration of these very advanced kinds of skills. Thus, the data seemed to support the notion that systematic and metasystematic thinking require cognitive attainments beyond those of formal operations.

The research of Arlin (1975), Sternberg and Downing (1982), and Commons et al. (1982) extends Piagetian theory and provides a basis for understanding how Piagetian theory might be applied to understanding cognitive development in the gifted beyond the levels reached by typical adults. The periods beyond the fourth are not yet as well specified as are the four periods proposed by Piaget. At the same time, though, they seem to offer more in the way of understanding advanced intellectual development than does the straightforwardly quantitative concept of mental age, which, beyond the age level of 16 or so, seems not to be a well-articulated concept (Cronbach, 1970).

Another aspect of Piaget's (1972) theory of cognitive development that seems relevant to a discussion of the gifted is the notion of "equilibration." Equilibration consists of two processes: assimilation, which occurs when a newly acquired concept is integrated into an existing mental schema, and accommodation, which occurs when a new mental schema is created in order to understand a new concept, or when an existing mental schema undergoes substantial modification. From a developmental point of view, the gifted individual would be seen as one who is not only better able to assimilate and accommodate new information, but also as one who will have a knack for knowing when to use each of these two processes. Thus, the gifted individual is less likely to attempt to assimilate information that needs to be accommodated and is less likely to see accommodation as necessary when new information can be assimilated, perhaps in a nonobvious way, to an existing schematic structure.

Psychometric Theory

Psychometric theory has given rise to several distinct traditions, each of which has slightly different implications for the understanding of cognitive development in the gifted and talented. The oldest tradition dates back to Sir Francis Galton, a cousin of Charles Darwin. Galton (1883) proposed two general qualities that distinguished the more from the less gifted: energy, or the capacity for labor, and sensitivity to physical stimuli. His views were brought to the United States by James McKean Cattell (1890), who proposed a series of 50 psychophysical tests that could be used to measure people's intellectual ability. These tests included, among others, dynamometer pressure (greatest possible squeeze of one's hand), rate of arm movement over a distance of 50 cm, the distance on the skin by which two points needed to be separated for them to be felt separately, and letter span in memory (a measure of short-term memory capacity). According to this view, the intellectually gifted individual is one who shows unusually high levels of psychophysical talent. The tradition of Galton was short-lived in the United States, however. A study by Clark Wissler (1901), a student of Cattell, on presumably highly intelligent Columbia University undergraduates, found no correlation between scores on Cattell's tests and academic performance at Columbia. This study, although flawed, had considerable impact on the field. But the death-knell for the Galtonian approach was probably sounded not so much by Wissler as by a French competitor with a better idea, Alfred Binet.

Binet represents a second psychometric tradition. Whereas Galton and Cattell emphasized psychophysical responses in their measurement of intelligence, Binet emphasized judgment. To Binet and his collaborator, Theophile Simon, the core of intelligence is "judgment, otherwise called good sense, practical sense, initiative, the faculty of adapting one's self to circumstances. To judge well, to comprehend well, to reason well, these are the essential activities of intelligence" (Binet & Simon, 1916, p. 42). Binet and Simon cited Helen Keller as an example of someone who would have performed very poorly indeed on psychophysical tasks, and yet was clearly near the top of the range in terms of what almost anyone would mean by demonstrated intelligence.

Binet and Simon constructed early versions of an intelligence test to measure the judgmental skills that they thought to be central to intelligence. Lewis Terman brought the ideas of Binet and Simon to the United States and, together with Maud Merrill, formulated the Stanford-Binet Intelligence Scales. The character of the scales differs somewhat from one age to another, but typical tasks measure skills such as vocabulary, inductive reasoning, social judgment, spatial visualization, and arithmetic problem solving.

The key to understanding intellectual giftedness, according to followers of the Binet tradition, is the intelligence quotient, or IQ. This index can be computed in either of two ways. In ratio IQs, a person's mental age, or MA (that chronological age for which the person's performance on the test would be average), is divided by the person's chronological age, and then multiplied by 100. In deviation IQs, scores are computed by converting percentiles to standard scores within a given age level with a mean of 100 and a standard deviation of 15 or 16. The deviation scores are generally preferred today because of conceptual and computational problems involving mental ages (see Sternberg & Powell, 1983). Intellectual giftedness is usually associated with the attainment of a high IQ, such as 130 (98th percentile) or 140 (99+ percentile). Although a high IQ would seem to form only a narrow basis for the identification of giftedness, in general IQ is without question the most frequently used criterion for the assessment of giftedness, and often it is the only criterion in current identification programs.

A third psychometric tradition and, theoretically, probably the richest, is one that dates back to Charles Spearman (1904, 1927). Spearman invented a method of statistical analysis, called factor analysis, by which one can identify the latent structures of intellect responsible for observed individual differences in intelligence test performance. Intelligence tests are "factor analyzed," and the outcome is a set of hypothetical factors representing the structure of intellect. Several theories of the factorial model of intelligence have been proposed. For example, Spearman (1927) argued that a single general factor, or g, best represents the structure of intellect. Thurstone (1938) argued for the existence of eight factors of intellect—verbal comprehension, verbal fluency, memory, inductive reasoning, spatial visualization, perceptual speed, facility with numbers, and possibly deductive reasoning. Guilford (1982) has argued for the existence of as many as 150 factors of the mind.

Developmental theorists have suggested several ways in which a factorial model might account for cognitive development. The number of factors might increase with age, leading to greater differentiation of the intellect (Garrett, 1946); the relevance or weights of various factors may change with age (Hofstaetter, 1954); the contents of particular factors may change with age (McCall, Hogarty, & Hurlburt, 1972); or scores (levels or performance) on a given set of factors may increase with age (Bayley, 1933, 1970). Thus, development might be qualitative or quantitative. These loci of change might also be seen as serving as bases for distinguishing the gifted from others. Gifted individuals might be perceived as having greater cognitive differentiation (more factors of the mind), as having different weights for factors in the overall composition of intellect, or as simply having higher scores on a particular set of factors.

Because IQ (a composite of factor scores) is usually used as a primary indication of giftedness, it is no surprise that children identified as being gifted show higher IQs than do children not found to be gifted. However, there is at least some evidence of differences in patterns of abilities between the gifted and nongifted. For example, Lucito and Gallagher (1960) examined patterns of scores on the Wechsler Intelligence Scale for Children (WISC), a test similar to the Stanford-Binet, but with separate verbal and performance scales. High-IQ children tended to show relatively higher scores in similarities, vocabulary, and general information (relative to their own mean scores). Low-IQ children tended to show higher scores on performance tests involving use of concrete, manipulable objects (again relative to their own mean scores). Bliesmer (1954) also found that high-IQ children showed particular strength in the verbal areas. Thus, on the average, the superiority of children with higher IQs tends to be in the verbal rather than in the performance areas.

Cognitive Theory

Cognitive, or information-processing theory, seeks to account for cognitive development in terms of the kinds and levels of information processing that take place at different points in a child's development. Whereas the emphasis in psychometric theorizing is structural and hence static, the emphasis in cognitive theorizing is process oriented and hence dynamic. Cognitive theorists disagree as to exactly what unit of analysis serves as the most suitable basis for understanding cognitive development. Most of the units that have been proposed, however, are related to what Newell and Simon (1972) have referred to as an elementary information process (eip). Such a process may be used to translate a sensory input into a conceptual representation, transform one conceptual representation into another, or translate a conceptual representation into a motor output.

Sternberg (1981) has proposed a componential theory of giftedness that isolates a fairly well-defined set of loci of cognitive development (see also Brown, 1975). According to this theory, there are three basic kinds of elementary information processes: (a) metacomponents, which are higher order control processes that are used in executive planning and decision making in problem solving; (b) performance components, which are lower order processes used in executing a problem-solving strategy; and (c) knowledge-acquisition components, which are lower order processes used in acquiring, retaining, and transferring new information. Some examples of metacomponents are defining the nature of a problem, selecting a set of lower order processes to solve a problem, and combining the selected processes into a working strategy for solving the problem. Some examples of performance components are inferring a set of relations between two stimuli, mapping a second-order relation between relations, and applying a previously inferred relation to a new domain. Some examples of knowledge-acquisition components include selective encoding, by which relevant information in a stimulus field is separated from irrelevant information; selective combination, by which the relevant information is combined in a usable way; and selective comparison, by which new information is related to old information previously stored in long-term memory.

Sternberg (1982) has suggested several ways in which cognitive development can occur. First, knowledge-acquisition components provide the bases for a steadily developing knowledge base. Second, the solution-monitoring metacomponent monitors the effectiveness of the other components and gives them feedback. This system allows an individual to use the components to learn from their own mistakes and to incorporate the newly learned information into future performance. And third, feedback from performance components and knowledge-acquisition components to metacomponents allows an individual to take corrective action that improves the quality of performance.

According to this view, intellectually gifted individuals are ones who are particularly effective in their componential functioning and in their ability to use the intercommunication among components to correct and improve their task performance. Thus, the gifted would be particularly well able to recognize the nature of problems, to select strategies that are appropriate for solving problems, to map higher order relations, and to distinguish relevant from irrelevant information. Developmentally, they are better able to employ the system of communication among components (described in Sternberg, 1982) to learn how better to solve the various kinds of tasks with which they are confronted in life.

In more recent work, Sternberg and Davidson (1982) have stressed, in particular, the role of insight in intellectual giftedness. They view insights as resulting from applying knowledge-acquisition components in novel ways. Thus, although the gifted may be superior in all kinds of componential functions, truly outstanding individuals in history seem to be those who are particularly well able to attain insights by using selective encoding, selective combination, and selective comparison in original ways. By comparing gifted and nongifted children in the upper elementary grades, Davidson and Sternberg (1984) found that the gifted children (identified through conventional tests) were superior to the nongifted ones in their insight abilities. For example, when solving mathematical problems, the gifted children spontaneously applied the appropriate insight processes of selective encoding, selective combination, and selective comparison, but the children of average intelligence needed cues to use these processes.

A second cognitive view of giftedness and its development can be derived from the theorizing of Pascual-Leone (1970) and of Case (1974, 1978), who have attempted to place some of Piaget's ideas into an information-processing framework. Like Piaget, they have drawn heavily upon the "scheme" as a basic unit of analysis. According to Case (1974), there are three basic kinds of schemes: figurative, operative, and executive. Figurative schemes are "internal representations of items of information with which a subject is familiar, or of perceptual configurations which he can recognize" (p. 545). Operative schemes are "internal representations of functions (rules), which can be applied to one set of figurative schemes, in order to generate a new set" (p. 545). And executive schemes are "internal representations of procedures, which can be applied in the face of particular problem situations, in an attempt to reach particular objectives" (p. 546).

Consider, for example, what happens when an individual recognizes a picture of a house. If an individual described a photograph as depicting a picture of his or her house, one could say that the individual had assimilated the sensory input to a figurative house scheme. If the individual looked at two different photographs of a house and judged them to be depicting the same house, one would describe the individual as having applied an operative scheme representing a sameness function to the figurative schemes representing the features of each of the two photographs. The figurative and operative schemes would only be activated, in the first place, if they were a part of some larger executive scheme that required the particular comparison. Case (1974, 1978) proposed that intellectual development occurs partly as a function of the evolution of the three kinds of schemes. A more variegated and differentiated set of schemes evolves as a child experiences more and more of the surrounding world. A gifted child might be viewed as one who is particularly well able to form new schemes, whose schemes are accurate representations of the world, and who is better able to integrate and differentiate the total set of developing schemes.

A third framework for understanding cognitive development in the gifted and talented derives from the work of Siegler (1978, 1981), Gelman and Gallistel (1978), and others who have emphasized the role of rules, or principles, in cognitive development. The basic assumption underlying this work is that "cognitive development can be characterized in large part as the acquisition of increasingly powerful rules for solving problems (Siegler, 1981, p. 3). Rules can be considered to be ministrategies for solving problems of various kinds. As a child grows older, the complexity of his or her rules increases, generally because earlier-developing rules fail to take into account all of the relevant information in a given problem.

Siegler has used rules most often to translate Piaget's stages of performance on various tasks into information-processing terms (e.g., Siegler, 1976). For example, he has taken Piaget's (1952) description of the developmental sequence in the conservation of liquid quantity, and formulated a series of rules that seem to capture the psychological levels of a child's development in solving the conservation task. Thus, when following Rule 1, a child asks him- or herself only whether the values of the dominant dimension (usually the height of a column of water in each of two jars) are equal. If the heights (or values on some other dominant dimension) are judged to be equal, the child responds that the alternatives are equal; if the heights (or whatever) are judged to be unequal, the child responds that the jar with the water at the greater height has more water in it. When following Rule 2, the child asks him- or herself whether the values of the dominant dimension are equal and, if they are, whether the values on the subordinate dimension are equal. If so, the child responds that the jars contain equal amounts of water; if not, the child responds that the jar with the greater value on the subordinate dimension has more water in it. Siegler posits two successively more advanced rules than these. In each case, the developing rules take into account successively more information about the nature of the problem. In related work, Gelman and Gallistel (1978) sought to describe the principles that children acquire in their developing understanding of number concepts.

If development is seen as the acquisition of successively more complex rules through the application of successively more complete encoding and understanding of problems, then gifted individuals might be seen as those who either acquire more complex rules earlier, or who more effectively apply the rules they have to given problem situations. Because the work of both Siegler and Gelman has tended to involve tasks more suitable for children than for adults, the implications of their work for giftedness in adults is less readily apparent than it is for giftedness in children. Nevertheless, it seems plausible to believe that many problem-solving tasks that adults attempt to deal with involve alternative rules or strategies at differentiated levels of complexity, and that the more gifted adults are able to see more into the problems and hence to apply more complex rules in order to achieve solutions to these problems. Although not all problems have rule-based solutions, a rule-based notion seems to apply at least to that class of problems whose structures are well defined and that can be solved by an algorithmic strategy that is specifiable in advance.

Specific Theories

Although there are any number of theories of cognitive development that could, with augmentation, be applied to an understanding of cognitive development of the gifted and talented, the number of theories directed specifically toward understanding cognitive development in the gifted and talented is limited. Four are described here.

The Figural to Formal Transition

Jeanne Bamberger (1982) has proposed a theory of cognitive development that, although intended primarily to account for development in musical prodigies, might also be extended to other levels of talent, including in areas other than music. Bamberger claimed that there are two basic periods in the development of exceptionally talented individuals, which she refers to as figural and formal periods. The two periods are characterized by qualitatively different modes of mental representation for information in the field of talent.

In the figural mode, information is represented in terms of groupings of events. The primary source of interrelation of structures is related to other structures at the same level of abstraction. For example, "if figural subjects are asked to attend to a singular pitch event, they assign meaning to such an event in relation to its unique situation and function within the figure of which it is a member" (Bamberger, 1982, p. 64). Figural representations are highly dependent upon immediate sensory experience of bodily actions and their juxtaposition in space and time. Child prodigies, at least in music, seem to rely almost exclusively on figural representations. They understand events in relation to one another, and seem to have an uncanny "feel" for what they are doing that is unmatched by any formal cognitive or other structures.

In the formal period, information is represented in terms of relations between discrete elements and higher order, more abstract categories of such elements. Entities are interrelated not so much with each other as with the more abstract units to which they seem to belong. This representation is thus more hierarchical and categorical than is a figural one. For example, "purely formal subjects tend to focus on separate, discrete events—that is, on each note individually. Further, they make use of . . . *fixed reference structures,* such as the ordered set of pitches in a scale or the hierarchy of metric units generated by specific time and pitch relations" (Bamberger, 1982, p. 64). They are thus more likely to ignore the unique figural function or situation of an event and more likely to attend to the event in its total, hierarchical context.

Prodigies almost invariably represent information in a figural mode. The mode is outside the normal range of representations for children of their age, and seems to distinguish them qualitatively from others. At some point in their careers, they must switch from a figural to a formal mode in order to become mature (musical or other) artists. This transition represents a mid-life (although it usually occurs in adolescence) crisis for many prodigies; some are not able to make the transition, or at least to make it well. Those who cannot make the transition never pass to a mature level of functioning and tend to be remembered primarily in their former roles as child prodigies. They never quite reach maturity in their craft. Those who do make the transition become the highly talented adult artists who continue to have successful, or potentially successful, careers.

Bamberger has proposed one of the few theories (if not the only theory) that gives an intuitively plausible account of just what it is that distinguishes talent at the earlier levels of development (slope of the developmental function) from talent at the more mature levels of development (asymptote of the developmental function). Although the nature of the figural and formal modes is in need of further specification, Bamberger's theory represents an important first step to understanding the bases for and distinctions between exceptional levels of childhood and adult talents.

Domain-Specific Development

David Feldman (1980, 1982) has sought to extend Piaget's theory of development in order to account for cognitive development in the gifted and talented—development that he believes is not well accounted for by the universals that tend to be the distinguishing marks of Piagetian theory. He proposes that in addition to an individual's talents and personal qualities, at least four forces must be recognized in the development of exceptional talent.

First, the individual must display exceptional drive and dedication in a domain or field of endeavor that has been recognized by society as a legitimate field for the display of exceptional talent. The greatest drive will be for nought if it is in a domain that society is not prepared to recognize as one in which exceptional talent is to be fostered and valued. Second, the individual must have the good fortune to grow up in an environment that will nurture this particular talent. Even if the individual has an exceptional level of talent, this talent will not develop if the individual's environmental circumstances do not foster and stimulate the growth of talent in the particular domain of the individual's gifts. For example, Gardner (1981) has cited as an instance of the lack of such environmental circumstances the development of the Indian mathematician, Ramanujan, whose exposure to formal mathematics apparently came too late for him to make the outstanding contributions to mathematical theory that he might otherwise have made.

Third, there must not only be recognition in the domain of talent and exposure to instruction in this domain, there must also be outstanding instruction and mentorship in this field. Prodigies have typically been exposed to the very best mentors in the field at a given time, and placed on a regimen that enabled them to exploit their gifts maximally. Finally, the development of exceptional talent hinges, to some extent, not only upon the recognition of the domain as one in which talent is to be recognized and exploited, but also upon the relative prestige and value placed on the field at a given time. At any point in history, some domains are simply more valued than others. The individual whose potential expertise is in a more highly valued domain of endeavor is likely to be better recognized and trained than is the individual whose potential expertise is in a field that, even if recognized, is accorded less value.

Feldman's basic point, therefore, is that giftedness is highly dependent upon a confluence of circumstances, most of which are outside the control of the individual. It is very much a theory of "the right person at the right time in the right place." Because of the great domain-specificity of exceptional talent, many highly talented people will never fully realize their potential simply because the societal means did not exist for them to do so. Born at another time or in another place, they might have been exceptional; born when and where they were, they often do not turn out to be. Tannenbaum (1983) also emphasizes the role of the environment in giftedness. His view involves five kinds of factors: (a) general ability, (b) special ability, (c) nonintellective factors, (d) environmental factors, and (e) chance factors.

Development of Multiple Intelligences

Howard Gardner (1982, 1983) has taken a view similar to that of Feldman, saying less about the factors that lead to development and nurturance of talent, but perhaps more about what Gardner, at least, perceives as the relatively isolable domains in which talent, or intelligence, develops. These domains can foster "multiple intelligences," such as linguistic, musical, and logical-mathematical intelligences. Feldman and Gardner are in basic agreement, though, regarding both the domain specificity of giftedness and the importance of societal reward systems in determining what will constitute extraordinary gifts and talents at a given point in time.

Evolving Systems

Howard Gruber (1980, 1981, 1982) is yet another theorist whose ideas about the cognitive development of the gifted and talented mesh well with Feldman's and Gardner's. In his "evolving systems" approach, Gruber views the highly creative individual as "someone constituted of three loosely coupled systems, each evolving over long periods of time throughout the life history: an organization of knowledge, an organization of affect, and an organization of purposes" (Gruber, 1982, p. 21). Gruber used a case-study method of analysis to understand how these systems develop in outstandingly creative individuals such as Darwin and Piaget. Although he concentrated upon the development of specific individuals, he believes he has found commonalities in the development of these creatively gifted individuals. For example, he noted their use of metaphors and figures of thought in their conceptualizations. Gruber also believes that traditional accounts of giftedness place too much emphasis on spontaneous insights and playful spontaneity and not enough emphasis on the highly creative individual's "organized network of purposes." He said, "Darwin's thought is characterized neither as one great moment of insight nor as an uneventful process of monotonic, gradual change. Rather, his many insights—literally thousands—are the expression of the functioning of a system, moments of qualitative change in a continuous process of structural growth" (Gruber, 1982, p. 23). According to Gruber, the highly gifted seem to work out a global, highly organized plan for their work, and their life consists in part of the realization of this plan.

   In summary, then, those developmental theorists who have emphasized the gifted, in particular, seem to agree upon the importance of both individual talent and the context in which it develops. They believe in the domain-specificity of talent and hence do not see giftedness as having much to do with exceptionally high levels of IQ or any other single personal characteristic. Moreover, they tend to emphasize the systematic nature of the development of giftedness, with only part of the system emanating from the individual. To these theorists, giftedness cannot be understood solely as a cognitive trait, but rather must be understood as a complex interaction between the individual and a peculiarly supportive environment that the individual helps create, but over which the individual has only limited power.

Empirical Studies

The amount of literature on the cognitive development of the gifted and talented and how it compares to the cognitive development of more typical individuals is small. A complete review of developmental and nondevelopmental literature on gifted and talented children can be found in Tannenbaum (1983), upon which the present review is based in part. This section focuses only on those studies that have at least some developmental implications.

Intelligence

How, in general, do children identified as highly intelligent differ from other children? In a review of the literature, Miles (1954) found that high-IQ children tend to be more highly represented among the ethnic and racial majority and among the higher socioeconomic classes; are more likely to be male than female; are generally of better health; walk, talk, and reach puberty earlier; do better in school, especially in verbally oriented subjects; have more hobbies; prefer playmates who are older than they are; and tend to be more popular. With regard to this last finding, there is at least some evidence that the relation between IQ and popularity is curvilinear, with popularity dropping off for very high levels of IQ.

Freehill (1961) compared high-IQ to average-IQ children on a large number of dimensions—including aspects of intellectual performance, academic performance, origin, development, health, character, social life, and play, and found the gifted to excel on almost all of the numerous status and performance variables studied. For example, on the intellectual dimension, the high-IQ children were superior in problem solving, organizing ability, general information, curiosity, originality, memory, rapidity of learning, verbal ability, attention span, qualitative thought, common sense, quantitative thinking, memory for designs, school success, parlor games, hand skills, and mechanical ability. As was the case for popularity, there is at least some evidence that after a certain point, the linear relation between IQ and success may break down. For example, Hollingworth (1942), in a study of children with IQs over 180, found that children with extremely high IQs often find it difficult to relate socially to their age peers and to make close friends (see also Terman & Oden, 1947, for similar findings).

Without doubt, the most comprehensive study of the intellectually gifted is that conducted by Terman and his successors (e.g., Terman, 1925;

Terman & Oden, 1947, 1959). Terman included in his sample Californian children under age 11 with IQs over 140, as well as children in the 11- to 14-year age bracket, some of whom had slightly lower IQs (to take into account the lower ceiling of the Stanford-Binet intelligence test in this higher age bracket). The mean IQ of the 643 subjects selected was 151, and only 22 had IQs under 140. Their accomplishments in later life were quite extraordinary. By 1959, 70 of the subjects were listed in *American Men of Science*, 3 were members of the National Academy of Science, 31 were listed in *Who's Who in America*, and 10 were listed in the *Directory of American Scholars*. The large majority of men were in professional or managerial occupations. Far more of the men had gone to college than would have been true in a normal sample. This has been found by other investigators as well in other studies of the gifted (e.g., Barbe, 1957; MacDonald, Gammie, & Nisbet, 1964; Nichols & Astin, 1966). Among the women, 45 percent were housewives; the social mores of the times when these individuals chose careers make it simply impossible to compare the achievements of the women with those of the men.

An interesting feature of the Terman study was a comparison of more and less successful participants (as of 1940), at least by conventional standards of success (see Oden, 1968). These individuals were labeled as belonging to "A" and "C" groups, respectively, with those in between falling into a "B" group. Whatever differences may have arisen in performance, the differences would not be well understood solely in terms of IQ: The mean IQ for A's was about 157, compared to 150 for C's. Nor can the difference easily be detected early in terms of conventional indices. The two groups did not differ in terms of age of learning to read, amount of reading, or parental indications of special ability in fields such as mathematics, science, art, music, or drama. Compared to the C's, the A's were much more likely to enter college (97% versus 68%), more likely to graduate from college (90% versus 37%), and more likely to give themselves high ratings on ambition for excellence in work, recognition for accomplishments, and vocational advancement.

A's also came from different family backgrounds: They were twice as likely to be Jewish, their parents were better schooled and their fathers had higher occupational attainments, and their parents were less likely to be divorced. The parents of the C's punished their children more often and also were more likely to point out faults in describing the children. Perhaps the most interesting difference between A's and C's was in their responses to a question on a 1950 biographical inventory: "From your point of view, what constitutes success in life?" A's tended to emphasize vocational satisfaction, achievement, realization of potentials, and fulfillment of social responsibilities. Although neither group rated income as highly important, C's tended to emphasize it more than did A's.

The achievements of the gifted group studied by Terman can be perceived in two ways. On the one hand, the members of this group were far more successful, by conventional standards, than would be children with more typical IQs. On the other hand, it has been noted that no Nobel Prize winners have yet come out of the group, nor have there been any individuals who have been generally recognized as being superlatively successful. It is difficult to interpret these data. Although IQ failed to pick out any superlative successes in the California group, it is not clear that any other measure would have, either, or even that one could expect any superlative successes within a highly limited geographical and temporal frame of reference.

Given the certainly notable successes of the group as a whole, one might wonder just how early identification of such intellectually gifted individuals can be made. Can one, for example, identify such individuals in infancy rather than in early to middle childhood? Typical longitudinal studies (e.g., Bayley, 1955) have shown that conventional infant intelligence tests predict later IQ only poorly, if at all. One reason for this is that infant tests seem to measure skills quite different from those measured by the tests given to children and adults. Thus, Hofstaetter (1954), in a factor analysis of Bayley's data, found that in children of up to 20 months of age, the main skill measured by the tests was sensory-motor alertness. From 20 to 40 months, the primary source of variance in scores is persistence. It is only from 48 months on that the conventional verbal and symbolic skills become the primary sources of variance.

In a study of high-IQ children, Willerman and Fiedler (1974, 1977) found the same lack of prediction (in this case, between scores at 8 months and scores at 4 and 7 years of age) as has been found for more typical children. Thus, it would appear that conventional intelligence tests for infants do not predict later IQ in either typical or gifted samples. At the same time, recent research on infants' preference for novelty in habituation paradigms (e.g., Fagan & McGrath, 1981; Lewis & Brooks-Gunn, 1981) suggests that intelligence test scores in infancy may be predictive of later IQ, if only the right kinds of tests are used for the infants.

To summarize, high-IQ children appear to be more successful than typical-IQ children on an extremely wide variety of cognitive and social indices of success, both during childhood and in later life. Because high IQ is confounded with so many other variables, most notably socioeconomic background, it would be improper to draw any strong causal inferences from the association between IQ and life success (see Jencks, 1972). IQ may be one variable leading to greater life success, but its importance is probably overestimated by studies that do not control for correlates of IQ; unfortunately, this includes virtually all of the studies in the literature on gifted children. Although IQ is positively related to a variety of successes, there is at least some evidence that at the upper extremes of IQ, the linear relation breaks down. Empirical studies have shown that children with extremely high IQs tend to have social adjustment problems, but again, such problems may be a result of social and cognitive demands upon these children, rather than of their IQs per se. An interesting set of anecdotal accounts of the demands upon such children can be found in R. Feldman's *Whatever Happened to the Quiz Kids?* (1982). If the IQs or social adjustments of these children are not typical, neither are the demands that are often placed upon them.

Special Talents

Studies of special talents have most often been of two kinds—studies of child prodigies and studies of eminent adults in particular fields of endeavor. The studies of prodigies will not be reviewed here, because it is difficult to draw generalizations from these studies, which are almost without exception case studies of one individual (or a small number of individuals). For reviews of studies of child prodigies, see Barlow (1952) and Feldman (1980). Most studies of special talents focus on one or more occupational domains. A few studies, however, have examined individuals of great eminence, without regard to particular occupation. We consider first these more general studies of eminent individuals, and then studies limited to two particular occupational domains, scientists and artists. For studies of other occupational groups, see Albert (1983).

General Studies. Without doubt, the most famous and influential study of exceptionally eminent individuals is that conducted by Cox (1926). Cox was interested in discovering the early mental traits of 300 geniuses. Cox's method was quite different from Terman's. Whereas Terman identified his sample upon the basis of childhood test scores and then looked forward to their adulthoods, Cox identified her sample on the basis of adult eminence and then looked backward to their childhoods. Cox was far more selective than was Terman in her choice of individuals, basing her choice upon extremely high later achievement rather than upon quite high childhood IQ. Her sample included individuals such as Mozart, Voltaire, Goethe, Coleridge, Penn, and Addison. She found the members of her sample to be above average in 67 "good" traits, but not in "absence of an occasional liability to extreme depression" or in "absence of the liability to anger." The childhood traits she defined as diagnostic of future success were persistence, intellectual energy, originality, and ambition. Her three main conclusions were that the eminent individuals had (a) above-average hereditary and environmental advantages; (b) well above-average IQs, as indicated by precocious intellectual accomplishments; and (c) unusual motivation, confidence in their abilities, and strength of character.

Walberg (1969, 1971; Walberg, Rasher, & Hase, 1978) studied childhood characteristics of the highly eminent, focusing upon childhood IQ. Walberg et al. (1978) noted that converging sources indicate a mean IQ of 159 for the individuals studied by Cox. Breakdowns by occupational groups showed philosophers to have the highest mean IQ (173), followed by scientists (164), writers (162), and artists (150), and soldiers (133). Even within the sample of eminent individuals, IQ proved to be correlated with eminence, as measured by indices such as word count for biographical articles in encyclopedias.

Finally, McCurdy (1957) has also studied childhood correlates of exceptional eminence. McCurdy's study was based upon a somewhat intensive analysis of 20 individuals from Cox's list, including individuals such as J. S. Mill, Leibniz, Grotius, Tasso, Coleridge, and Voltaire. McCurdy reached three major conclusions regarding typical developmental patterns. First, as children, the eminent tend to have received a high degree of attention from parents and other adults, including intensive educational interventions and abundant love. Second, they tend to have been isolated from other children, especially outside the nuclear family. Third, they tend to have had rich fantasy lives, in part because of their intensive education and their isolation.

The studies just described are similar in their emphases upon personal traits in the development of eminent individuals. Not all studies, however, have equally emphasized the role of strictly internal factors. For example, Simonton (1978) has stressed the sociocultural context of eminence and its development. Simonton has concluded that (a) potential geniuses must have access to numerous role models very early in life; (b) exposure to cultural diversity is also important; (c) certain political events, such as political instability, can inhibit the development of geniuses, whereas other political events, such as civil disturbances, can enhance later creativity; and (d) the young genius adapts to the political environment by generating a set of philosophical beliefs.

Studies of Scientists. The most well-known study of the "early background of eminent scientists" is certainly that of Roe (1953). Roe intensively studied the life histories and available test data of 67 scientists, including roughly equal numbers of physical, biological, and social scientists. All were between 31 and 60 years of age and had been judged by their peers to be distinguished in their contributions to their respective fields. Some of Roe's findings closely resemble Terman's. The eminent scientists had a median IQ of 166, which was even higher than that of Terman's group. The groups showed different patterns of aptitudes at the time they were studied. Physical scientists had the highest mathematical scores, followed by biologists and then social scientists. On spatial tests, physical scientists again had the highest scores, followed by social scientists and then biological scientists. And on a verbal test, social scientists had the highest scores, followed by the physical scientists and then the biological scientists. The groups also reported different characteristic modes of thinking. Experimental physicists and biologists reported considerable reliance upon visual imagery in their thinking; theoretical physicists and social scientists relied more on verbal or symbolic modes of thinking. The groups of scientists differed in interests as well as in abilities. Whereas physical scientists showed an early interest in gadgets and inventions, social scientists were more likely to show an early interest in literature and classics.

The differences between the scientists and other individuals extended beyond the cognitive domain. Like Terman's subjects, the scientists were disproportionately likely to be born to professional parents, to be first-borns, to excel in school, and to have enjoyed their education. The three groups of scientists differed somewhat in their childhood development. Although all three groups of scientists showed some tendency toward childhood isolation, only the social scientists attached a notion of superiority to this isolation. As adults, however, the social scientists showed themselves to be less independent of parental ties than did either the physical or biological scientists. In general, the social scientists exhibited from an early age more concern with quality of interpersonal relations than did members of the other two groups.

The Terman data also have revealed a few insights regarding the development of scientists. At age 11, those who later became scientists were already more likely to show interest in the sciences, and this interest pattern continued into adulthood. The science group showed less interest in business occupations than did their nonscientific counterparts and also had poorer social relations than did the others (see Tannenbaum, 1983).

A particularly interesting retrospective study of scientists was conducted by Zuckerman (1979), who was particularly interested in patterns shown during youth by Nobel laureates in sciences. "The most striking fact in the process of self-selection is that future members of the ultra-elite were clearly tuned in to the scientific network early in their careers" (reprinted in Albert, 1983, p. 241). Before becoming laureates, these individuals went to great lengths to apprentice themselves to outstanding senior scientists. Many of these masters themselves later became laureates. But of particular interest is that the apprenticeships tended to occur before rather than after the masters received their Nobel Prize. Thus, the future Nobelists were not merely looking for masters who had won Nobel Prizes, but rather were tuned in to the talented scientists who eventually would win the Prize. Another interesting facet of the development of the Prize winners is that they reported that their education was truly an apprenticeship in form. The most important things they learned were via modeling of the masters, rather than via direct instruction. Their training was truly a process of socialization rather than merely a form of direct learning from classroom or even laboratory instruction.

Studies of Artists. Perhaps the most well-known study of artists is that conducted by Getzels and Csikszentmihalyi (1976). Their sample consisted of 321 students in various areas of art. Their results showed that artistically talented students did not differ significantly from typical college students in conventional cognitive abilities, although they would be at least in the upper third of their overall age group on such measures.

This result is consistent with research on children, which shows that accuracy in representing real objects artistically is not correlated with general intelligence (Hollingworth, 1926). The Getzels and Csikszentmihalyi study, mentioned earlier in this chapter, found that a particularly good index of success in art was artistic problem finding. The better artists were able to choose better problems for artistic study. Since problemfinding ability is not measured on standard psychometric tests, it is not surprising that the standard tests did not pick up differences in this ability. The artists were distinguished from nonartists on tests of values and personality through their higher concern with esthetic values and lower concern with economic and social values than was typical for students of their age level. The art students were also more introspective, alienated, imaginative, radical, and self-sufficient than was typical for students of their age level.

Another approach to investigating artistic talent has been a more exclusively psychometric one. The results of these studies have been fairly uniform: Psychometrically measured artistic talent is either independent of, or only very weakly correlated with, general intelligence (Holland, 1961; Lewerenz, 1928; Wallach & Wing, 1969; Welsh, 1975). Thus, artistic talent appears to be as relatively independent of general intelligence as scientific ability appears to be dependent upon it, at least up to a certain level of IQ. It should be noted, however, that the researchers who conducted these studies did not examine eminent artists, but rather looked at a broad and normal range of talent.

Conclusions and Future Directions

There is no dearth of possible theories of cognitive development that can be applied to understanding development in the gifted and talented. There is, however, a paucity of empirical research testing these theories. Empirical studies of the development of the gifted and talented have been illuminating with respect to childhood correlates of adult giftedness, but they have revealed relatively little about development. Even studies that have included multiple age groups—whether longitudinal or cross-sectional—have been focused upon states of performance rather than its development. It is difficult to find studies that could be seriously viewed as strongly testing a theory of cognitive development in the gifted, with the exception of Bamberger's (1982) and possibly D. H. Feldman's (1982) work. We believe that the most pressing need in the field of cognitive development of the gifted and talented is for research that is clearly linked to theoretical underpinnings.

Paradigms for Studying Cognitive Development in the Gifted and Talented

The question arises as to which theories of cognitive development provide promising leads for such research. We believe that most of the extant ones are, in fact, promising, because they are highly convergent in the directions they suggest. Consider the nature of these convergences.

Stimulus–response theories have traditionally been concerned with the input–output relations that underlie task performance. The other three kinds of theorizing considered in this chapter—Piagetian, psychometric, and cognitive—concentrate upon what happens mentally between the external stimulus and the response. These latter kinds of theories can therefore be viewed as providing the information about mental structures and processes that is missing in conventional stimulus–response theorizing and that is specified in only vague detail in mediational stimulus–response accounts.

Psychometric and Piagetian theories are quite different in form, but their messages are not so different. Consider again the loci of cognitive development that can emerge from psychometric theorizing. One is an increase with age in the number of factors composing intelligence. Because Piaget believed that periods build upon each other, the new skills acquired in later periods are likely to be represented, psychometrically, as additional factors. Indeed, Piaget viewed new periods as increasing the number of cognitive structures available in children's repertoires, and factors of intelligence are, in theory, unitary sources of structural variation. Thus, one might interpret the differentiation hypothesis as being consistent with the notion of later Piagetian structures building upon earlier ones.

A second locus of cognitive development in psychometric theorizing might be, essentially, in the renaming of existing factors. For example, the nature of the general factor of intelligence is likely to change from infancy to adulthood. Such a finding is also consistent with Piagetian theory: Certainly, the most central abilities (and thus the general factor) in the sensory-motor period are quite different from the most central abilities in the formal-operational period. Thus, in addition to increased differentiation of factors, one might expect some change in the composition of existing factors.

Finally, a psychometric viewpoint can predict increases in factor scores with increasing age. The same prediction follows from Piagetian theory: As children grow older, their scores on factors that might be obtained from Piagetian tasks should increase. Within a period, such increases would be attributed to "horizontal decalage," which is a consolidation of skills acquired during that period. Between periods, such increases would be attributed to consolidation of skills of an earlier period. Both psychometric and Piagetian models are primarily structural, and we believe that it takes very little extension of either kind of theorizing to view them as intermappable and complementary.

Similarly, Piagetian theory can be viewed as being compatible, at least in spirit, with cognitive theories. Indeed, researchers such as Pascual-Leone, Case, and Siegler, who are within the cognitive tradition, are sometimes viewed as "neo-Piagetian" because of their attempts to place Piagetian concepts and tasks within an information-processing framework. Indeed, Siegler's rules might be viewed as a description of the information-processing strategies by which children solve Piagetian (or other) tasks at successive periods of cognitive development. Because Piaget's theory is primarily structural, it needs complementation by processing theories.

Finally, psychometric and cognitive theorizing are highly compatible. Indeed, alternative factor theories of intelligence can be intermapped with alternative cognitive theories (Sternberg, 1980). Again, the cognitive theories provide an information-processing basis for understanding the constellations of individual differences that give rise to particular factors. Also, psychometric factors can be seen as providing a foundation for understanding bases for individual differences in processing. Even Spearman (1923), the psychometric theorist par excellence, proposed a preliminary processing model that sought to understand the general factor of intelligence in terms of three operations, which he called apprehension of experience (encoding the stimuli), eduction of relations (inferring relations between various aspects of the stimuli), and eduction of correlates (applying relations from one set of stimuli to another). These processes are essentially the same as three of the processes in Sternberg's (1977) and others' information-processing theories of analogical reasoning. Thus, psychometric and cognitive theories provide complementary ways of looking at the same phenomena.

The same kind of complementarity that exists among theoretical frameworks also seems to exist *within* those frameworks. For example, within the psychometric framework, it can be shown that alternative factorial theories are generally rotational variants of each other and hence mathematically equivalent (Sternberg, 1977). In other words, different rotations of the same factor space will often support different theories. Within the Piagetian framework, the ideas of investigators proposing possible fifth periods beyond formal operations are also surprisingly similar. For example, Case (1978), Sternberg and Downing (1982), and Commons et al. (1982) all view fifth periods in terms of the development of higher order relational thinking. Although Arlin's (1975) proposal regarding problem finding is different, it seems likely that sophisticated problem finding will depend upon the ability to perceive higher order relations. Indeed, those scientists who deal with "big" problems seem to be those who do what Commons et al. refer to as systematic and meta-systematic thinking, rather than limiting themselves to thinking in terms of lower order concepts and relations. Within the cognitive framework, the units of analysis are also largely intermappable: Siegler's (1981) rules seem to correspond closely to what Sternberg (1980) refers to as strategies, and both are close in meaning to Case's (1978) schemas.

Our point, then, is that we believe that one's choice of a theoretical framework is largely one of heuristic convenience. The important issue seems to be that of how well a given theoretical framework is used, rather than that of which framework is chosen. Informative research about the nature of human gifts and talents could probably be done within any of the frameworks we have considered in this chapter. Although we, like everyone else, have our own theoretical preferences, such preferences seem to be more a matter of personal taste and the current paradigms of psychology than they are matters of right and wrong. Indeed, paradigms are not disconfirmable; only the specific empirical claims made by specific theories within these paradigms may be subjected to tests.

Promising Areas for Future Research on the Gifted

There are certain problems in the field that appear to us to be particularly ripe for investigation at this point. Hence, we encourage research on these particular problems, regardless of the paradigm selected. We mention here four problems that seem to emerge from a variety of theories and empirical studies in a variety of paradigms and that we believe to be of central concern to the field. (For a developmental approach to these problems, see Sternberg, 1982.)

The Nature of Problem Finding in the Gifted. The importance of problem finding to exceptional performance has emerged in the theoretical and empirical work of a number of investigators (e.g., in the work of Arlin and in that of Getzels & Csikszentmihalyi) and seems to cross-cut particular domains of giftedness. Problem-finding ability often distinguishes gifted artists, scientists, mathematicians, philosophers, and others. We psychologists need to know more about the cognitive capacities that render some people better problem finders than others. As of now, we have done little more than name the phenomenon.

Representation of Information. Gifted individuals in a variety of fields seem to represent information differently than do more typical individuals. Bamberger (1982) understands these differences in terms of figural and formal modes of representation. Chi (1978), Chase and Simon (1973), and others understand these differences in terms of availability and accessibility of a knowledge base in a domain of expertise. The gifted seem not only to know more about a given field, but to know how to use their knowledge to better advantage. Investigators need to know how their ways of representing information enables them to function at very high levels of performance.

The Role of the Environment. Gifted individuals, without regard to their domain of talent, seem to be particularly well able to shape the domain in which they work (see e.g., Austin, 1978; Sternberg, 1985). Often, they end up either creating a field or substantially changing an existing one. Moreover, the empirical literature makes clear that the environment in which gifted individuals grow up has a major effect in shaping their lives (see, e.g., Lynn, 1979; Simonton, 1978). Psychologists need to understand better how these mutual shaping forces act and interact in the development of gifted individuals.

Combinations of Talents That Lead to Giftedness. If this review has made anything clear, it is that there is no one formula that leads to gifted performance. Although many gifted individuals are highly intelligent in the traditional sense, they also seem to have a diversity of other talents that lead to their highly successful performance. Psychologists need to know what kinds of combinations of talents are synergistic in producing giftedness and what kinds of environmental circumstances foster the development of these talents.

This list of problems is, of course, incomplete, and others might argue whether these are indeed the central problems that the field faces at the present time. Nevertheless, we believe that the list provides a start toward specifying useful directions for the field. And if this chapter has specified some potential directions in which the field might move, then it has accomplished what is perhaps its major purpose.

We also have some ideas about directions in which we, at least, believe research on the cognitive development of the gifted and talented should not proceed. The first is one of atheoretical empirical studies in which the performance of gifted children at various age levels is contrasted. Such studies are not likely to reveal much about the development of gifts and talents, simply because the most common result—improvement with age—is uninformative with regard to both cognitive structures and cognitive processes. We do not believe that the accumulation of facts without any theoretical basis is useful in the development of a science of the gifted, or in that of any other science. The second direction is one of the study of gifted and talented individuals in the absence of control groups containing typical individuals. Such studies allow no way of distinguishing which features of cognitive development are distinctive to the gifted and talented. To the extent that theories of just what is distinctive about cognitive development in the gifted and talented are needed, research that also involves typical individuals is needed as well.

Generalizations About the Gifted and Talented

The last issue to which we address ourselves is whether there are any generalizations about the gifted and talented that seem to apply across domains. Given the domain-specificity of exceptional talents (D. H. Feldman, 1982; Gardner, 1982), such generalizations are difficult to find. Nevertheless, we believe that there are at least five generalizations that hold without regard to domain.

1. High General Intelligence and Exceptional Specific Ability. Gifted individuals tend to have relatively high levels of general intelligence and extremely high levels of specific ability in the fields of their expertise. Although the levels of general intelligence vary as a function of field, studies of highly gifted individuals in a variety of fields repeatedly have suggested distinctly above-average levels of measured intelligence. It seems likely that the requisite level will vary with field. For example, exceptional theoretical physicists will probably require a higher level of general intelligence than will, say, exceptional artists. Nevertheless, the exceptional artists are likely to be distinctly above average in general intellect.

2. Exceptional Capitalization Upon Patterns of Abilities. The gifted not only have high levels of general and specific abilities, but seem to have a knack for making the most of what abilities they have. Everyone is better in some things than in others. The gifted seem particularly well able to bring their strengths to bear upon their domain of expertise, and to find ways of compensating for their relative deficiencies in other areas.

3. Exceptional Environmental Shaping Abilities. Everyone is shaped by his or her environment, and perhaps the gifted and talented are shaped more than most. But exceptional individuals also seem to be able to capitalize upon their environments with much the same flair with which they capitalize upon their abilities. When the environment does not suit them, they mold rather than succumb to it and often end up shaping it for others as well as for themselves. Indeed, those who create paradigms, whether in science, literature, art, or any other field, might be viewed as environmental shapers par excellence.

4. Exceptional Problem-Finding Ability. Although it is not quite known what problem-finding ability consists of, it is clear that the gifted in a great variety of areas are individuals who are able to find problems that are large in scope, important in the context of the field, and tractable in terms of being operationally studied or acted upon. A given quality of product, conditionalized upon the problem it addresses or solves, becomes all the better when it is not conditionalized upon the problem, and when one considers as well the particular problem it addresses.

5. Exceptional Ability to Conceive Higher Order Relations. The gifted seem to have an extraordinary talent for conceptualizing in terms of relations of the third-order and above, that is, to do what Commons et al. (1982) have referred to as systematic and metasystematic thinking. They view their work not only as a series of isolated or loosely related projects, but as pieces of part of an evolving master plan or system that they create over time. Their life's work often reveals a kind of unity and systematization that is lacking in the work of the less gifted.

To summarize, the gifted seem to have high levels of ability, both general and specific; to know how to capitalize both upon their internal abilities and the external environment; and to find important problems that fit into a large-scale system of ideas in which they are working. Perhaps noncoincidentally, problem finding and the ability to see relations of the third order and beyond constitute two of the major proposals for periods beyond formal operations in Piagetian-style thinking. Indeed, the two skills may be interrelated: Finding important problems may be, in part, a function of one's ability to think in terms of large-scale systems and metasystems.

In conclusion, we believe that there now exists a substantial theoretical base upon which empirical studies of development, or further theories of development, can draw. If there is a a pressing need in the field, it is for a union of theory and research. This union seems to be forthcoming.

References

Albert, R. S. (Ed.). (1983). *Genius and eminence: The social psychology of creativity and exceptional achievement.* Elmsford, NY: Pergamon Press.

Amabile, T. (1983). *The social psychology of creativity.* New York: Springer-Verlag.

Arlin, P. (1975). Cognitive development in adulthood: A fifth stage? *Developmental Psychology, 11,* 602–606.

Austin, J. H. (1978). *Chase, chance, and creativity.* New York: Columbia University Press.

Bamberger, J. (1982). Growing up prodigies: The midlife crisis. In D. H. Feldman (Ed.), *Developmental approaches to giftedness and creativity* (pp. 61–77). San Francisco: Jossey-Bass.

Barbe, W. B. (1957). What happens to graduates of special classes for the gifted? *Ohio State University Educational Research Bulletin, 36,* 13–16.

Barlow, F. (1952). *Mental prodigies.* New York: Greenwood Press.

Bayley, N. (1933). Mental growth during the first three years: A developmental study of 61 children by repeated tests. *Genetic Psychology Monographs, 14,* 1–92.

Bayley, N. (1955). On the growth of intelligence. *American Psychologist, 10,* 805–818.

Bayley, N. (1970). Development of mental abilities. In P. H. Mussen (Ed.), *Carmichael's manual of child psychology* (3rd. ed., Vol. 1, pp. 1163–1209). New York: Wiley.

Becker, G. (1978). *The mad genius controversy.* Beverly Hills, CA: Sage.

Binet, A., & Simon, T. (1916). *The development of intelligence in children.* (E. S. Kite, Trans.). Baltimore: Williams & Wilkins.

Bliesmer, E. P. (1954). Reading ability of bright and dull children of comparable mental ages. *Journal of Educational Psychology, 45,* 321–331.

Brown, A. L. (1975). The development of memory: Knowing about knowing, and knowing how to know. In H. W. Reese (Ed.), *Advances in child development and behavior* (Vol. 10, pp. 103–152). New York: Academic Press.

Case, R. (1974). Structures and strictures: Some functional limitations on the course of cognitive growth. *Cognitive Psychology, 6,* 544–573.

Case, R. (1978). Intellectual development from birth to adulthood: A neo-Piagetian interpretation. In R. S. Siegler (Ed.), *Children's thinking: What develops?* (pp. 37–71). Hillsdale, NJ: Erlbaum.

Cattell, J. M. (1890). Mental tests and measurements. *Mind, 15,* p. 373.

Chase, W. G., & Simon, H. A. (1973). The mind's eye in chess. In W. G. Chase (Ed.), *Visual information processing* (pp. 215–281). New York: Academic Press.

Chi, M. T. H. (1978). Knowledge structures and memory development. In R. S. Siegler (Ed.), *Children's thinking: What develops?* (pp. 73–96). Hillsdale, NJ: Erlbaum.

Cohn, S. J. (1981). What is giftedness? A multidimensional approach. In A. H. Kramer (Ed.), *Gifted children* (pp. 33–45). New York: Trillium Press.

Commons, M. L., Richards, F. A., & Kuhn, D. (1982). Systematic and metasystematic reasoning: A case for levels of reasoning beyond Piaget's stage of formal operations. *Child Development, 53,* 1058–1069.

Cox, C. M. (Ed.). (1926). *Genetic studies of genius: Vol. 2. The early mental traits of three hundred geniuses.* Stanford, CA: Stanford University Press.

Cronbach, L. J. (1970). *Essentials of psychological testing* (3rd ed.). New York: Harper & Row.

Davidson, J. E., & Sternberg, R. J. (1984). The role of insight in intellectual giftedness. *Gifted Child Quarterly, 28*(2), 58–64.

DeHahn, R. G., & Havighurst, R. J. (1957). *Educating the gifted.* Chicago: University of Chicago Press.

Fagan, J. F., III, & McGrath, S. K. (1981). Infant recognition memory and later intelligence. *Intelligence, 5,* 121–130.

Feldman, D. H. (1980). *Beyond universals in cognitive development.* Norwood, NJ: Ablex.

Feldman, D. H. (1982). A developmental framework for research with gifted children. In D. H. Feldman (Ed.), *Developmental approaches to giftedness and creativity* (pp. 31–45). San Francisco: Jossey-Bass.

Feldman, R. D. (1982). *Whatever happened to the quiz kids?* Chicago: Chicago Review Press.

Flavell, J. H. (1963). *The developmental psychology of Jean Piaget.* Princeton, NJ: Van Nostrand.

Flavell, J. H. (1977). *Cognitive development.* Englewood Cliffs, NJ: Prentice-Hall.

Freehill, M. (1961). *Gifted children: Their psychology and education.* New York: Macmillan.

Gagne, R. (1968). Contributions of learning to human development. *Psychological Review,* 177–191.

Galton, F. (1869). *Hereditary genius.* London: Macmillan.

Galton, F. (1883). *Inquiries into human faculty and its development.* London: Macmillan.

Gardner, H. (1981, May). Prodigies' progress. *Psychology Today,* pp. 75–79.

Gardner, H. (1982). Giftedness: Speculations from a biological perspective. In D. H. Feldman (Ed.), *Developmental approaches to giftedness and creativity* (pp. 47–60). San Francisco: Jossey-Bass.

Gardner, H. (1983). *Frames of mind: The theory of multiple intelligences.* New York: Basic Books.

Garret, H. E. (1946). A developmental theory of intelligence. *American Psychologist, 1,* 372–378.

Gelman, R., & Gallistel, C. R. (1978). *The child's understanding of number.* Cambridge, MA: Harvard University Press.

Getzels, J. W., & Csikszentmihalyi, M. (1976). *The creative vision: A longitudinal study of problem finding in art.* New York: Wiley.

Ginsburg, H., & Opper, S. (1979). *Piaget's theory of intellectual development: An introduction* (2nd ed.). Englewood Cliffs, NJ: Prentice-Hall.

Gruber, H. E. (1980). The evolving systems approach to creativity. In S. Modgil & C. Modgil (Eds.), *Toward a theory of psychological development* (pp. 269–299). Windsor, England: National Foundation for Educational Research.

Gruber, H. E. (1981). *Darwin on man: A psychological study of scientific creativity* (2nd ed.). Chicago: University of Chicago Press.

Gruber, H. E. (1982). On the hypothesized relation between giftedness and creativity. In D. H. Feldman (Ed.), *Developmental approaches to giftedness and creativity* (pp. 7–29). San Francisco: Jossey-Bass.

Guilford, J. P. (1982). Cognitive psychology's ambiguities: Some suggested remedies. *Psychological Review, 89,* 48–59.

Hofstaetter, P. R. (1954). The changing composition of intelligence: A study of the t-technique. *Journal of Genetic Psychology, 85,* 159–164.

Holland, J. L. (1961). Creative and academic performance among talented adolescents. *Journal of Educational Psychology, 52,* 136–147.

Hollingworth, L. S. (1926). *Gifted children: Their nature and nurture.* New York: Macmillan.

Hollingworth, L. S. (1938). An enrichment curriculum for rapid learners at Public School 500: Speyer School. *Teachers College Record, 39,* 296–306.

Hollingworth, L. S. (1942). *Children above 180 IQ. Stanford-Binet: Origin and development.* Yonkers, NY: The World Book Company.

Hull, C. L. (1943). *Principles of behavior.* New York: Appleton-Century-Crofts.

Jencks, C. (1972). *Inequality.* New York: Basic Books.

Kaufman, A. S. (1971). Piaget and Gesell: A psychometric analysis of tests built from their tasks. *Child Development, 42,* 1341–1360.

Keating, D. P. (1975). Precocious cognitive development at the level of formal operations. *Child Development, 46,* 276–280.

Kendler, H. H., & Kendler, T. S. (1975). From discrimination learning to cognitive development. A neo-behavioristic odyssey. In W. K. Estes (Ed.), *Handbook of learning and cognitive processes: Vol. 1. Introduction to concepts and issues* (pp. 91–247). Hillsdale, NJ: Erlbaum.

Larkin, J. H., McDermott, J., Simon, D. P., & Simon, H. A. (1980). Models of competence in solving physics problems. *Cognitive Science, 4,* 317–345.

Lenneberg, H. (1980). The myth of the unappreciated (musical) genius. *The Musical Quarterly, 54,* 219–231.

Lewerenz, A. S. (1928). I.Q. and ability in art. *School and Society, 27,* 489–490.

Lewis, M., & Brooks-Gunn, J. (1981). Visual attention at three months as a predictor of cognitive functioning at two years of age. *Intelligence, 5,* 131–140.

Lovell, L. (1968). Some recent studies in cognitive and language development. *Merrill-Palmer Quarterly, 14,* 123–138.

Lucito, L. J., & Gallagher, J. J. (1960). Intellectual patterns of highly gifted children on the WISC. *Peabody Journal of Education, 38,* 131–136.

Lynn, R. (1979). The social ecology of intelligence and achievement. *British Journal of Social and Clinical Psychology, 18,* 1–12.

MacDonald, B., Gammie, A., & Nisbet, J. (1964). The careers of a gifted group. *Educational Research, 6,* 216–219.

Marland, S. P., Jr. (1972). *Education of the gifted and talented: Report to the Congress of the United States by the U.S. Commissioner of Education.* Washington, DC: U.S. Government Printing Office.

Martorano, S. C. (1977). A developmental analysis of performance on Piaget's formal operations tasks. *Developmental Psychology, 13,* 666–672.

McCall, R. B., Hogarty, P. S., & Hurlburt, N. (1972). Transitions in infant sensorimotor development and the prediction of childhood IQ. *American Psychologist, 27,* 728–748.

McCurdy, H. G. (1957). The childhood pattern of genius. *Journal of Elisha Mitchell Science Society, 73,* 448–462.

Miles, C. C. (1954). Gifted children. In L. Carmichael (Ed.), *Manual of child psychology* (pp. 984–1063). New York: Wiley.

Neimark, E. D. (1975). Intellectual development during adolescence. In F. D. Horowitz (Ed.), *Review of child development research* (Vol. 4). Chicago: University of Chicago Press.

Newell, A., & Simon, H. A. (1972). *Human problem solving.* Englewood Cliffs, NJ: Prentice-Hall.

Nichols, R. C., & Astin, A. W. (1966). Progress of the merit scholars: An eight-year follow-up. *Personnel and Guidance Journal, 44,* 673–686.

Oden, M. H. (1968). The fulfillment of promise: 40-year follow-up of the Terman gifted group. *Genetic Psychology Monographs, 77,* 3–93.

Pascual-Leone, J. (1970). A mathematical model for the transition rule in Piaget's developmental stages. *Acta Psychologica, 32,* 301–345.

Piaget, J. (1952). *The origins of intelligence in children.* New York: International Universities Press.

Piaget, J. (1972). Intellectual evolution from adolescence to adulthood. *Human Development, 15,* 1–12.

Piaget, J. (1977). *The development of thought: Equilibration of cognitive structures* (A. Rosin, Trans.). New York: Viking.

Piechowski, M. M. (1979). Developmental potential. In N. Colangelo & R. T. Zaffrann (Eds.), *New voices in counselling the gifted* (pp. 25–57). Dubuque, IA: Kendall/Hunt.

Renzulli, J. S. (1978). What makes giftedness? Reexamining a definition. *Phi Delta Kappan, 60,* 180–184, 261.

Roe, A. (1953). *The making of a scientist.* New York: Dodd Mead.

Siegler, R. S. (1976). Three aspects of cognitive development. *Cognitive Psychology, 4,* 481–520.

Siegler, R. S. (1978). The origins of scientific reasoning. In R. S. Siegler (Ed.), *Children's thinking: What develops?* (pp. 109–149). Hillsdale, NJ: Erlbaum.

Siegler, R. S. (1981). Developmental sequences within and between concepts. *Monographs of the Society for Research in Child Development, 46,* (2, Whole No. 189).

Simonton, D. K. (1978). History and the eminent person. *Gifted Child Quarterly, 22,* 187–195.

Spearman, C. (1904). "General intelligence," objectively determined and measured. *American Journal of Psychology, 15,* 201–293.

Spearman, C. (1923). *The nature of "intelligence" and the principles of cognition.* London: Macmillan.

Spearman, C. (1927). *The abilities of man.* New York: Macmillan.

Sternberg, R. J. (1977). *Intelligence, information processing, and analogical reasoning: The componential analysis of human abilities.* Hillsdale, NJ: Erlbaum.

Sternberg, R. J. (1980). Sketch of a componential subtheory of human intelligence. *Behavioral and Brain Sciences, 3,* 573–584.

Sternberg, R. J. (1981). Intelligence and nonentrenchment. *Journal of Educational Psychology, 73,* 1–16.

Sternberg, R. J. (1982). A componential approach to intellectual development. In R. J. Sternberg (Ed.), *Advances in the psychology of human intelligence* (Vol. 1, pp. 413–463). Hillsdale, NJ: Erlbaum.

Sternberg, R. J. (1985). *Beyond IQ: A triarchic theory of human intelligence.* New York: Cambridge University Press.

Sternberg, R. J., & Davidson, J. E. (1982, June). The mind of the puzzler. *Psychology Today,* pp. 37–44.

Sternberg, R. J., & Downing, C. (1982). The development of higher-order reasoning in adolescence. *Child Development, 53,* 209–221.

Sternberg, R. J., & Powell, J. S. (1983). The development of intelligence. In J. H. Flavell & E. M. Markman (Eds.), *Handbook of child psychology: Vol. 3. Cognitive development* (4th ed., pp. 341–419). New York: Wiley.

Tannenbaum, A. J. (1983). *Gifted children: Psychological and educational perspectives.* New York: Macmillan.

Terman, L. M. (1925). *Genetic studies of genius: Vol. 1. Mental and physical traits of a thousand gifted children.* Stanford, CA: Stanford University Press.

Terman, L. M., & Oden, M. H. (1947). *Genetic studies of genius: Vol. 4. The gifted child grows up: Twenty-five years' follow-up of a superior group.* Stanford, CA: Stanford University Press.

Terman, L. M., & Oden, M. H. (1959). *Genetic studies of genius: Vol. 5. The gifted group at mid-life: Thirty-five years' follow-up of the superior child.* Stanford, CA: Stanford University Press.

Thorndike, E. L., Bregman, E. O., Cobb, M. V., & Woodyard, E. I. (1926). *The measurement of intelligence.* New York: Columbia University Teachers College.

Thurstone, L. L. (1938). *Primary mental abilities.* Chicago: University of Chicago Press.

Tuddenham, R. (1971). Theoretical regularities and individual idiosyncrasies. In D. Green, M. Ford, & G. Flamer (Eds.), *Measurement and Piaget* (pp. 64–80). New York: McGraw-Hill.

Vernon, P. E. (1971). *The structure of human abilities.* London: Methuen.

Walberg, H. J. (1969). A portrait of the artist and scientist as young men. *Exceptional Children, 36,* 5–12.

Walberg, H. J. (1971). Varieties of adolescent creativity and the high school environment. *Exceptional Children, 38,* 111–116.

Walberg, H. J., Rasher, S. P., & Hase, K. (1978). IQ correlates with high eminence. *Gifted Child Quarterly, 22,* 196–200.

Wallach, M.A., & Wing, C.W., Jr. (1969). *The talented student: A validation of the creativity-intelligence distinction.* New York: Holt, Rinehart & Winston.

Webb, R. A. (1974). Concrete and formal operations in very bright 6 to 11 year olds. *Human Development, 17,* 292–300.

Welsh, G. S. (1975). *Creativity and intelligence: A personality approach.* Chapel Hill: University of North Carolina at Chapel Hill, Institute for Research in Social Science.

White, S. H. (1965). Evidence for a hierarchical arrangement of learning processes. In L. P. Lipsitt & C. C. Spiker (Eds.), *Advances in child development and behavior* (Vol. 2). New York: Academic Press.

Willerman, L., & Fiedler, M. F. (1974). Infant performance and intellectual precocity. *Child Development, 45,* 483–486.

Willerman, L., & Fiedler, M. F. (1977). Intellectually precocious preschool children: Early development and later intellectual accomplishments. *Journal of Genetic Psychology, 131,* 13–20.

Wissler, C. L. (1901). The correlation of mental and physical tests. *Psychology Review Monograph Supplement, 3*(6).

Zigler, E., & Trickett, P. K. (1978). I.Q., social competence, and evaluation of early childhood intervention programs. *American Psychologist, 33,* 789–796.

Zuckerman, H. (1979). *The scientific elite: Nobel laureates' mutual influences.* New York: Free Press.

3. Cognitive Structure and Process in Highly Competent Performance

Mitchell Rabinowitz
University of Illinois at Chicago
Robert Glaser
University of Pittsburgh

The study of the gifted is a relatively uncharted area of cognitive psychology. Although there is a fairly long history of research investigating the nature of intelligence and superior intellect, there have been few attempts by cognitive psychologists to understand the processing characteristics of people at the upper end of the intelligence/performance continuum. In general educational practice, certain people are considered gifted because they exhibit extremely skilled or competent performance. This is illustrated by the several definitions of giftedness in the first two chapters of this volume, including that of former U.S. Commissioner of Education Sidney P. Marland, who described gifted and talented children as exhibiting "high performance" and "demonstrated achievement" (Marland, 1972).

In this chapter, consistent with this orientation, we ask the question: What allows people to perform in highly competent ways and to exhibit the very skilled performance that is apparent in highly gifted people? From a psychometric point of view, this ability is often attributed to a high level of general intelligence (g) as indexed by high scores on tests of mental abilities or by assessments of various factors of intelligence. Recent attempts to understand the cognitive mechanisms involved utilize an information-processing approach that characterizes factors of intelligence and aptitude in terms of component processes. Variations in intelligence and aptitude test performance have been related to variations in speed of processing (Hunt, 1976, 1978; Keating & Bobbitt, 1978; Vernon, 1983), to variations in problem representation and "insight" skills (Sternberg & Davidson, 1983), to differences in accessible knowledge (Pellegrino & Glaser, 1982), and to variations in the flexible use of strategies (Campione, Brown, & Ferrara, 1982). There has also been considerable discussion of variations in metacognitive skills such as planning, questioning, and solution monitoring (Brown, 1978; Sternberg, 1981). In general, research indicates that people who exhibit highly competent performance have easy and fast access to relevant information, are able to view problem situations in qualitatively distinct ways, can use strategies effectively and flexibly, and have better metacognitive skills.

To help us better understand the performance of the gifted and delimit the importance factors that characterize competent performance, in this chapter we review research in cognitive and developmental psychology in which skilled performance has been compared to less skilled performance. In much of the research comparing children with learning problems to more typical children, young children to older children or adults, and novices to experts, researchers have taken this approach. These comparative studies have shown that an important determinant of skilled performance, related to the components of competence just listed, is the knowledge that people bring to a task. That available organized knowledge exerts a considerable influence on performance characteristics is no longer debated within cognitive and developmental psychology. For example, recent research on developmental differences in memory performance emphasizes the role of knowledge (Chi, in press). Developmental differences in memory performance are dramatically reduced when the familiarity of the materials to be learned is taken into account (Bjorklund & Zeman, 1982; Richman, Nida, & Pittman, 1976). These differences can even be reversed when the younger group is more familiar with the stimulus materials than is the older population (Chi, 1978; Lindberg, 1980).

The work reported in this paper was supported in part by the Learning Research and Development Center, with funds from the National Institute of Education (NIE), United States Department of Education; and was also supported by the Personnel and Training Research Programs, Psychological Sciences Division, Office of Naval Research, under Contract No. N00014-79-C-0215.

In a similar vein, research in which experts and novices are compared in domains such as baseball (Chiesi, Spilich, & Voss, 1979), bridge (Charness, 1979), chess (de Groot, 1965; Chase & Simon, 1973), physics (Chi, Feltovich, & Glaser, 1981; Simon & Simon, 1978), and medical diagnosis (Lesgold, 1984), to name just a few, clearly shows that domain-specific knowledge has significant influence on cognitive skills. In addition, there has been a growing shift in emphasis within various computer simulations of cognitive performance from specifying general procedures or strategies to describing the underlying knowledge structure in a given domain (Anderson, 1983a; Chi, Glaser, & Rees, 1982; Minsky & Papert, 1974).

In this review, our intention is not to present this discussion so that future theorists will list knowledge as yet another separate factor that needs to be considered in the discussion of the gifted. Rather, we review theories and experimental findings from cognitive and developmental psychology that suggest that the operation of a well-organized knowledge base provides a framework in which to discuss and understand the various components of highly competent behavior and the interrelationships among them.

Knowledge as an Associative Network

Prior to discussing the consequences of possessing a well-organized knowledge base for performance, we need to expand upon what we mean by knowledge and some aspects of its architecture. One way in which knowledge has been theoretically described is in terms of an associative network (Anderson & Bower, 1973; Collins & Quillian, 1969; Norman & Rumelhart, 1975). Within an associative network, concepts are represented as the nodes of the net, whereas relations between concepts serve as associative links. Three of the properties of associative links are as follows. They specify the relation among concepts, such as "belongs to the category of," or "has a certain property." Associative links can vary in strength— some concepts are strongly associated with each other, whereas others are only weakly associated. Associative links can be either excitatory or inhibitory.

This associative network is conceptualized to operate on the basis of the "automatic" spread of activation along associative links (Anderson,1983b; Collins & Loftus, 1975). Spread of activation operates such that when a word is encountered, the concept in memory corresponding to it is excited. When a node receives excitation, its level of activation rises, eventually reaching a threshold point, at which time activation spreads to related concepts. This spread of activation to related concepts is termed *secondary activation*. The amount of secondary activation generated depends upon the level of activation of the originally activated node and the strength of the associative links between concepts. A node spreads activation in proportion to its level of activation, and stronger associations lead to stronger secondary activations. Excitatory links increase the level of activation of a related node, whereas inhibitory links decrease the level of activation of associated nodes.

A consideration of how such an associative network might vary among individuals must include at least three aspects. First, there are issues of quantity, that is, the number of specific concepts available to a person. An expert in a given domain is thought to have a greater amount of declarative knowledge (knowledge of concepts and facts) about that domain than does a novice. Similarly, an adult might be considered to have more conceptual knowledge than a young child. Similar comparisons can be made about metaknowledge—knowledge of one's own processing capabilities and regulation of processing. In this architecture, then, knowledge might be indexed theoretically by estimating the number of nodes within memory.

Second, at a different level, are issues of organization, that is, how one piece of information relates to another. Developmental issues of organization have emphasized a shift from a thematic organization, in which things go together because they occur together in space or time, to a taxonomic organization, in which things go together because they belong to the same conceptual categories (see Mandler, 1983, for a review of this literature). Similarly, experts in a field might organize information according to different conceptual categories than do novices (Chi et al., 1981). This knowledge might be indexed within a semantic net through variations in the associative links that connect pieces of information.

The postulated differences within node-link structures for individuals at different levels of competence are illustrated in Figures 1 and 2 (Chi, Glaser, & Rees, 1982). Two kinds of subjects, experts and novices in physics, were asked to tell all they could about a physics problem involving an inclined plane. The subjects categorized the problem according to how they would solve it. The experimenters translated the subjects' protocols into node-link networks and compared the structures of experts and novices.

Inspection of these two figures reveals interesting differences in both the content and organization of these representations. For the novice (Figure 1), the representation consists primarily of surface features, such as the presence of a plane, the angle at which the plane is inclined with respect to the horizontal, the height and mass of the block, and whether or not it has friction. For the expert (Figure 2), the structure is related to and organized around basic laws of physics, such as principles of mechanics, conservation of energy, and Newton's laws of force. At the lowest level of the representation are the structural, or surface features of the problem. The novice represented at least as many surface features of the

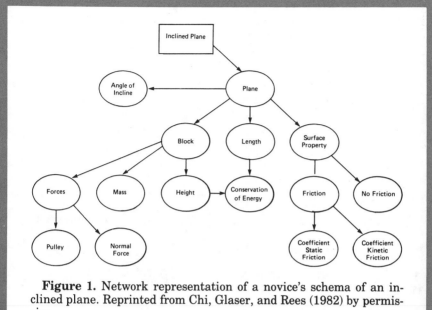

Figure 1. Network representation of a novice's schema of an inclined plane. Reprinted from Chi, Glaser, and Rees (1982) by permission.

problem as did the expert. For the novice, however, these features are not subordinate to basic physics principles but, in fact, appear to be more salient than the principles that are so important to the expert. In addition, the expert's knowledge includes not only principles but also an understanding of the conditions of their use (see dotted-line enclosures). The novice's knowledge fails to include these conditions.

Associative networks can also differ according to the accessibility of information, that is, how easy it is to retrieve a concept or a relation. Thus, a concept might be available, in that there is a node representing that concept in memory, but be relatively inaccessible, in that it receives very little activation from related concepts. Theoretically, one can say whether knowledge of a given concept is available or not: Is there a node representing this concept in the knowledge base? Is there an associative link connecting these two concepts? However, available knowledge might be differentially accessible. Whereas it might require quite a bit of effort to access one piece of available knowledge, other information might become accessible with little or no effort being made. In this chapter, we will conceive of differences in accessibility as being related to variations in the strength of the associative links.

These three ways of describing variations in knowledge—amount, organization, and accessibility—are obviously interrelated. In fact, it is probably impossible to consider one without also taking account of the

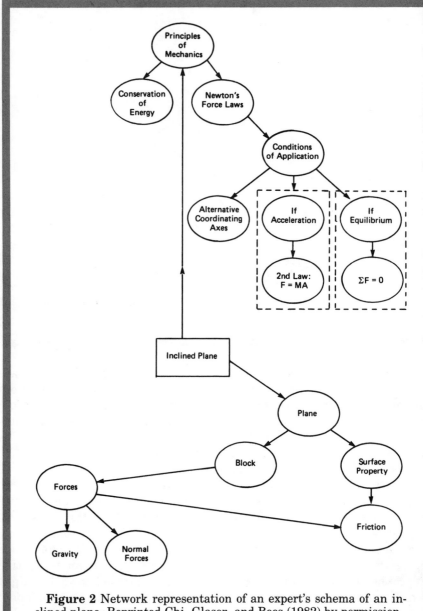

Figure 2 Network representation of an expert's schema of an inclined plane. Reprinted Chi, Glaser, and Rees (1982) by permission.

others. With this interrelationship in mind, we will discuss the consequences of having a well-organized knowledge base. Our particular emphasis is on the consequences of variations in accessibility of knowledge as a significant feature of cognitive skill and gifted performance.

The Retrievability of Knowledge

In some situations people seem to have ready access to information, and in other situations people need to work in a controlled way at deriving such information. There are also large individual and developmental differences in people's ability to access information, and competent performance is often indexed by the ability to retrieve information easily. People who exhibit expertise within a domain of knowledge are able to access information rapidly. Furthermore, Keating and Bobbitt (1978) found that children of above-average ability search memory more rapidly than do those of average ability. An important question is how the ability to quickly access information develops. What are the factors that determine when information is rapidly retrieved and when it must be derived more slowly?

For most tasks there is more than one way to obtain information. There are a variety of problems for which we all seem to have the ability to arrive at an answer in an automatic manner. To take two very simple examples, when asked their name or current address, most people have answers available almost immediately. There is little sense of doing anything special to obtain the answer; the information is automatically accessible. As a matter of fact, there is probably no way one can prevent answers to such questions from coming briefly into awareness.

On other problems, there seems to be a need to run through some procedure in order to derive the answer. Take the question, "How many windows are there in the place where you are currently living?" Most people probably do not have this information encoded in such a way that it can be readily retrieved. A person can derive this information, however, by picturing him- or herself walking through the house counting the number of windows. This procedure requires a person's attention in order to be carried out and can be started or stopped at any point prior to obtaining the answer.

One important aspect of the development of competent performance is a shift from the reliance on conscious controlled processing to derive an answer to the automatic and fast access of an answer. Controlled processing is generally characterized as a slow, primarily serial, effortful, capacity-limited, subject-controlled process. Alternatively, automatic processing is a fast, parallel, fairly effortless process that is not limited by processing capacity constraints and is not under direct conscious control (Neely, 1976; 1977; Schneider & Shiffrin, 1977).

One perception of competence is derived from observing the procedures people use. For example, given the problem $7 + 2$, you might access a store of facts and retrieve the answer 9. Alternately, you can generate the answer by first counting to 7, then counting two more and observing the end result. Adults and older children are able simply to retrieve the answer 9 in an automatic fashion, with no awareness as to how the answer is generated; they simply know that $7 + 2$ equals 9. Children beginning elementary school, however, have to generate most answers by using one of a variety of procedures. From this point of view, most people would judge the adult or older child to be more proficient in arithmetic computation than is the younger child, even though the younger child may be proficient in generating a procedure to produce the answer.

Simple addition is a good task with which to investigate the development of competence. The methods by which people perform addition show a clear developmental progression from using procedures (such as counting) for generating answers (Ashcraft, 1982; Groen & Parkman, 1972; Resnick, 1982; Siegler & Robinson, 1982) to having the ability to access the information easily. Recent research on young children's addition performance has emphasized the derivative nature of children's processing. Groen and Parkman (1972) found that the smallest number within an addition problem was the best predictor of solution times for the children. On this basis, they set forth a *min* model, proposing that children add by selecting the larger of two addends and counting up from it the number of times indicated by the smaller addend. Similarly, Ginsburg (1977) found that children often alluded to counting-on from the larger number when verbalizing about the solution process. Resnick (1982) illustrated other procedures that children use to generate answers to addition problems. For example, given the problem $3 + 4$, a child might change the problem to $3 + 3$, access the answer, and then add 1 to it. Each of these examples shows that children must derive answers to addition problems in a controlled way.

Adults, however, appear to perform simple addition by simply retrieving the answers (Ashcraft, 1982; Ashcraft & Battaglia, 1978; Groen & Parkman, 1972.). For example, in order for Groen and Parkman's data on adults to fit the min model, the incrementing process used by adults would need to be faster than any other known elementary process. On the basis of their results, they postulated that adults retrieve the answer 95 percent of the time and use the min process only 5 percent of the time. Thus, on this task there is a developmental progression of competence from having to derive the answer to simply retrieving the information.

Within this developmental trend away from the use of strategies to derive answers, Siegler and Robinson (1982) observed, in viewing videotapes of four- and five-year-old children working on addition problems,

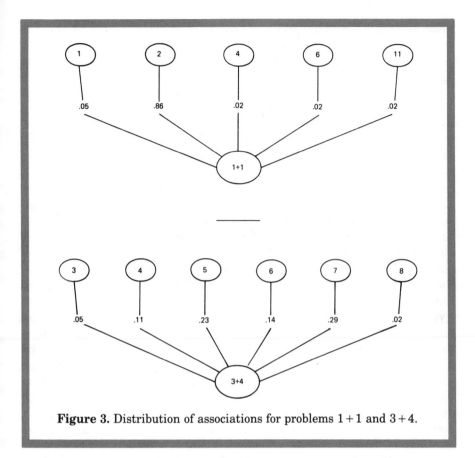

Figure 3. Distribution of associations for problems $1+1$ and $3+4$.

that competence varied from problem to problem. Children overtly used strategies to solve many of the problems, but sometimes they were able simply to retrieve the answer. On retrieval trials, there was no visible or audible intervening behavior and their solution times were faster. To account for this difference, Siegler and Robinson assumed that the representation of addition knowledge consists of associations of varying strengths between each problem and possible answers. From normative data, they were able to estimate the associative weights. Figure 3 shows the resulting distribution for two problems, $1+1$ and $3+4$. The distribution of responses from the problem $1+1$ to possible answers is peaked toward the answer 2. Peaked distributions are those in which the strength of the associative links from the problem to possible answers is much greater for one answer than for other answers. On problem $3+4$, the distribution of the associative weights from problem to possible answers was more even.

Children tended to access the answer (rather than deriving the answer) on problems for which there was a peaked distribution of associations. Furthermore, as the peakedness of the distribution increased, solution times on retrieval trials decreased. On problems for which the strength of the associative links between the problem and answers was more evenly distributed over a variety of answers, children tended to use a procedure to derive the answer. Using such data, Siegler and Shrager (1984) proposed a learning model by which gradually increasing the peakedness of the distributions from addition problems to answers predicted behavior much more similar to that of adults. Within this model, then, learning is assumed to be the strengthening and weakening of associative weights between pieces of information.

The ability to access information easily also affects competence on more complex forms of problem solving. We have suggested that an important component of competent and skilled behavior is the ability to have easy and rapid access to information. One way to think about the issue of accessibility is in relation to the automatic spread of activation along associative pathways in a knowledge structure. If the associative links are weak and few, then the rise in the level of activation of related knowledge will be negligible, and the information should still be relatively inaccessible. In such cases, a person would need to use a procedure to derive information. The greater the amount of excitation a node is receiving, either through stronger or a greater number of inputs, the higher the level of activation will be and thus the more accessible the information becomes. Accessibility, then, can be viewed along a continuum. Weak associative links provide little input to allow information to become automatically accessible. As the spread of activation increases, due to stronger associative links, related information becomes more accessible. To the extent, then, that giftedness is indexed by rapid access to relevant knowledge, gifted people might be characterized as having knowledge with strong associative links connecting related pieces of information. Future research needs to focus on how such knowledge is acquired. This issue is raised again in the last section of this chapter.

Accessibility, Representation, and Problem Solving

Variability in access to relevant information also influences competence in complex forms of problem solving. Consider the following example:

> A block of mass M1 is put on top of mass M2. In order to cause the top block to slip on the bottom one, a horizontal force F1 must be applied to the top block. Assume a frictionless table. Find the maximum force F2 which can be applied to the lower block so that both blocks will move together.

Experts and novices show substantial qualitative differences in the cognitive structures and processes that compose their ability to solve such problems. With problems of this kind, a person must first understand what the problem entails—what the important concepts presented in the problem are and how they are related. In this initial encoding, a person builds a cognitive representation or mental model of the problem. Some of the information used to construct this representation is explicitly stated in the problem statement; other information is inferred. Understanding and insight into the problem comes from the interaction between the information explicitly stated in the problem and a person's prior experiences and knowledge. Variations in the accessibility of relevant information affect the structure and content of the person's initial understanding or mental representation of the problem. The quality of this representation, in turn, has a large impact on determining the efficiency, elegance, and precision of subsequent processing needed for solving the problem (Gentner & Gentner, 1983; Greeno & Simon, in press; Johnson-Laird, 1982, 1983; Larkin, in press).

Finding the Problem

Problem representations are created very rapidly upon presentation of a problem. For example, Hinsley, Hayes, and Simon (1978) found that when college students were asked to categorize algebra word problems into types, they did so very quickly—sometimes after reading just the first phrase of the problem statement. Similarly, Chi et al. (1981) found that experts and novices in physics both were able to categorize physics problems very quickly, although the specific content of the categories differed markedly.

There is much evidence to suggest that variations in the problem representations that are constructed occur because of differences in the ability to perceive the relationships among materials rather than through variations in the strategies with which people approach or solve the task. The now classic studies of de Groot (1965) and Chase and Simon (1973) showed that players at different levels of chess skill were essentially alike in the number of moves they considered, in the depth of their search for move sequences, and in similar measures obtained from spoken protocols, but that substantial differences occurred in their perception of the problem configurations. The chess master is thus seen as a superior problem recognizer rather than a deep thinker, and this theoretical position accounts for some of the extremely competent performance of expert chess players. "It explains how a chess master is able to defeat dozens of weaker players in simultaneous play: because for the most part he simply relies on his pattern recognition abilities—his so called "chess intuition"—to generate potentially good moves" (Chase & Chi, 1981, p. 115).

Thus, as a person gains increased knowledge and familiarity within a domain, his or her representation or understanding of problems changes. As already indicated, in the study of physics problem solving, Chi et al. (1981) found that experts and novices began their problem representations with specifiably different problem categories. When asked to classify problems on the basis of how they would solve them, novices tended to sort physics problems on the basis of surface characteristics of the problem: similar objects (such as a spring or an inclined plane), key words (such as mass or friction), or the interaction of several object components (such as a block on an inclined plane) as depicted in Figure 1. In addition, the novices' verbal explanations of their categories emphasized these structural characteristics. By contrast, experts tended to classify the problems according to major physics principles (or fundamental laws) governing the solution of each problem, as illustrated in Figure 2. The verbal protocols of experts also confirm the basis of these groupings. In a similar vein, Egan and Schwartz (1979) found differences between experts and novices in electronics in the way they reconstructed symbolic drawings of circuit diagrams. Skilled technicians utilized the functional nature of the elements in the circuit, such as amplifiers, rectifiers, and filters, whereas novice technicians produced chunks based more upon the spatial proximity of the elements.

A major difference between experts and novices in these studies is that the representations of the novice are based primarily on information that is explicitly presented in the problem statement—objects, key words, visual proximity. Experts, however, are able to base their representations on higher-level principles—information that is not explicitly stated within the problem. They can quickly retrieve from memory functional or principled relations among the concepts. This ability of the expert can be attributed to the existence and accessibility of structures of prototypical knowledge or problem schemata that unify superficially disparate problems. In line with general schemata theory (Rumelhart, 1981), these schemata provide information structures that can be rapidly accessed to make apparent the inferences needed concerning the relations in the information presented in the problem.

Choosing a Strategy

On the basis of different mental representations of problems and differential accessibility to information, people can use markedly different strategies to work on a problem. Again, clear examples are offered within the context of expert–novice differences in physics problem solving (Larkin, McDermott, Simon, & Simon, 1980; Simon & Simon, 1978). Some of these differences are evidenced in quantitative measures of problem solving. Simon and Simon (1978) noticed a 4 to 1 difference between their experts and novices in the speed with which problems were solved. Also,

Larkin (1979) has claimed that experts were able to retrieve a number of physics equations in successive chunks with very small interresponse intervals followed by a longer pause. The novices did not exhibit this pattern of pause times in equation retrieval.

The most substantial differences between experts and novices are evidenced in the qualitative ways in which they appear to solve problems. While working on physics problems, the expert appears to use a "working forward" strategy, whereas the novice uses a "working backward" strategy. The expert works from the variables given in the problem using the fundamental principles relevant to the problem to suggest which equations should be used. The expert can then successively generate and solve equations from the given information. The novice, on the other hand, starts with an equation containing the unknown of the problem. If it contains a variable that is not among the givens, then the novice selects another equation to solve for it, and so on, using essentially a general means-ends strategy (Newell & Simon, 1972) by which each equation is compared with the desired final state of the problem. The novice then reduces deviations from this desired final state by generating equations to solve for new unknowns. The initial mental representation strongly influences the choice of strategy that is used. When the problem becomes difficult, experts switch from the forward working strategy to a sophisticated means-end analysis, and this occurs, it appears, when they cannot construct an elaborate representation for such problems (Larkin, 1977).

The nature of one's mental representation of a problem has also been shown to affect the ability to use such problem-solving skills as questioning, predicting outcomes, and deriving the main points. Such skills are applicable to a variety of domains, and skilled thinkers have been shown to use them in solving problems, whereas less skilled thinkers do not (Brown, 1978; Sternberg, 1981, 1984). Miyake and Norman (1979) have shown that the ability to spontaneously ask questions about a body of knowledge depends upon one's existing knowledge of the material. They asked people who had different amounts of expertise in computer text editing to work on two editing tasks. People who exhibited high competence and had considerable experience with computer test editing asked more questions about the task when the editing task was difficult. Novices, however, asked many more questions with the easy task. There were no differences between the two groups in the number of questions asked about a baseline task where there were no knowledge differences. Thus, the tendency to spontaneously ask questions regarding the editing task was dependent upon the level of knowledge they possessed when they came to the task. The novice exposed to expert level material does not have a problem representation that is detailed enough to suggest what sorts of questions should be asked and therefore cannot obtain needed information. Asking a question implies a proper structure of knowledge with which to formulate the question. It is on difficult tasks that competent people seem to ask the most questions, suggesting that they have more elaborate, better defined representations of situations.

The ability to predict outcomes or to supply additional information has also been shown to vary with knowledge. Larkin (in press) presented an expert and a novice with problems in reduced forms, in which only the key terms of the problems, such as objects (e.g., blocks, planes, ropes), attributes (e.g., velocity, height), and values were presented. The task was to predict what the original problem statement was. The expert was much better at this task than the novice and was able to construct the problems so that solving the constructed problem was equivalent to solving the original problem. In most cases the novice was unable to derive these problems.

Similarly, Chiesi et al. (1979) tested people for knowledge of the game of baseball. They identified a group of subjects (high-knowledge) who knew quite a bit about the strategies of the game, and a second group (low-knowledge) who knew the basic rules of the game and a bit about which professional teams were currently doing well, but little about the game's finer points. Subjects were asked to write down all the possible outcomes they could think of for specific baseball situations. High-knowledge individuals knew more possible outcomes and could better specify which ones were likely to occur. More important, however, than the number of outcomes people were able to predict was that high-knowledge individuals were more likely to produce basic action sequences involving strategic, goal-oriented plays. Thus, in both of these examples, the ability to predict appeared to be dependent upon the ability to access an elaborated representation of the domain.

Even skills that lead to extraordinary memory performance have been shown to be knowledge dependent. Recent research conducted by Chase and his associates has supported this view (Chase & Ericsson, 1981; Ericsson, Chase, & Faloon, 1980). A student, SF, who had average memory abilities and average intelligence for a college student, spent a year and a half engaged in long-term practice on a memory-span task. Over this time, SF was able to increase his memory span from 7 to 79 digits. (Memory span for most people is approximately 7.) The protocols obtained by the experimenters indicated that during this extensive practice, SF, a good long-distance runner, devised the strategy of recoding digits into running times. For example, SF recoded 3492 as "3:49.2—near world-record time for the mile," which for him was a single chunk. Since SF had many running times stored in memory, he could easily chunk most cases of four digits. In those cases in which he could not, SF recoded the four digits into a familiar date or age. In addition, SF had numerous categories of running times, ranging from half-mile times to marathon times, and many subcategories within each category, for example, near world-record time, very poor mile time, average mile time for the marathon, and average work-out mile time. By organizing the running times hierarchically, SF was able to exhibit large memory spans for digits. However, SF's ability to memorize was limited to digits; when he was switched from digits to letters, his memory span returned to 7. In this situation, SF was not able to use his knowledge to chunk and recode the items. His knowledge of running times was thus an enabling condition for an amazing feat of memory.

In summary, competent behavior is associated with elaborate representations in which many relations not explicitly stated in a problem are rapidly accessed. The initial representation that one constructs during a task is an important determinant of performance characteristics. These initial representations are formed very quickly upon presentation of the problem, and initial variations in these representations arise because of differences in the ability to perceive automatically the relations implicit within the problem. Variations in the initial representation allow people to work on problems in qualitatively different ways and enable them to use various types of strategies. Presumably, individuals with outstanding abilities develop representational competence that leads to high-quality performance and to abilities that enable them to predict, derive questions, and quickly get to main points.

The Interactive Development of Automaticity and Controlled Processing

We have emphasized that highly competent performance seems to involve a good deal of fast and unconscious processing and the ability to perform complex operations with little apparent attention to fundamental details. It appears that rapid accessibility of information, as a function of spread of activation, allows for this ability. In addition, highly organized knowledge structures allow for a richer, more elaborate mental representation of the problem context and for the use of conscious controlled processing when required for complex cognitive effort. Many investigators have recognized the importance of the shift from controlled to automatic processing in enabling skilled performance (Lesgold, 1984; Perfetti & Lesgold, 1978; Schneider & Shiffrin, 1977; Sternberg & Wagner, 1982). This shift in processing is considered important for two primary reasons. First, it frees attentional resources that can then be used for other processing. Second, it allows for a more complex representation of a problem.

Because people have limited attentional resources for processing information, competition for these attentional resources can cause a bottleneck that limits performance capabilities. The implications of this shift in mode of processing were discussed by Schneider and Fisk (1982):

> If every processing task reduces attentional resources by a fixed, task-specific amount, then maximal performance should be a function of subject resources available and resource costs of the component tasks . . . If task resource costs are reduced with practice, then the upper bound on the number of tasks that can be combined increases with task practice. If, with practice, component tasks can be developed to the point that they require no attentional resources, then human processing capacity may have an effectively unlimited upper bound. (p. 261)

The necessity of relying on controlled processing for a substantial portion of cognitive effort imposes a limit on the amount of information with which people can work. This limiting factor might be one way to account for poor performance or, alternately, a way to consider one aspect of highly competent performance. For example, Sternberg and Wagner (1982), in reference to specific learning disabilities, suggested:

> Learning disabilities in general may result from the absence of essential basic skills, but the present authors believe that many specific learning disabilities derive from slow or limited automatization of skills. In particular, the learning disabled individual continues to have to perform in a controlled way (i.e., with conscious attention) tasks that a normally functioning individual will long ago have automatized . . . Processing resources that in others have been freed and used to master new tasks are in the disabled person devoted to tasks that others have already mastered. (p. 2)

In a discussion on reading, Perfetti and Lesgold (1978) suggested that capacity during reading comprehension is limited by momentary data-handling requirements. They proposed three components in reading that, when not fully developed, could increase the working-memory bottleneck: (a) access to long-term memory, (b) automation of decoding, and (c) efficiency of reading strategies. Having to work consciously on any one of these components diverts attentional resources that could be applied to other processing. By automatizing each of these component processes as much as possible, the reader has more resources to apply to the other components or to higher level skills, such as using context, prior knowledge, and inference to aid comprehension.

The need to rely on controlled processing, then, might inhibit competent performance. Some of the processing differences found between experts and novices can be interpreted with the constraint of limited attentional resources in mind. To return to the physics problem, for example, novices use most of their attentional resources on a working backwards strategy; their attention is invested in generating equations and solving for unknowns. Experts, however, use a working forward strategy and put less effort into generating and solving equations, thereby allowing other types of processing to occur. In fact, Simon and Simon (1978) found that experts made many more metacognitive statements than did novices and that they commented more often on observations of errors, the physical meaning of an equation, statements of plans and intentions, and self-evaluations. It appears that automatic accessibility to relevant information helps to ease the bottleneck in attentional resources, freeing them for other processing components that increase performance competence.

Increases in automaticity also allow for a more elaborate mental representation of a situation, and the construction of such a representation enables certain processing to occur. For example, in order to improve a novice's performance, one might suggest that the novice merely needs to be taught to use the working forward strategy. Unfortunately, this approach is unlikely to succeed because the working forward strategy requires a sufficient representation of the problem so that straightforward inferences can lead to solution. A working backwards strategy, however, requires a less sophisticated representation. For a novice, at each step, there is a list of things which, if known, would result in the ability to solve the problem. Less elaborated knowledge is required to use such a strategy. Thus, an expert's representation of the problem appears to be a necessary condition for the use of the working forward strategy. This is not a problem of limited capacity; given less limited attentional resources, it is still unlikely that a novice would be able to construct the expert's problem representation. Rather, it is a matter of having easy access to the relevant knowledge needed to support the use of a given strategy.

The automatic accessibility to relevant information also enables the use of more general strategies, such as questioning and predicting. In the Chiesi et al. (1979) study, novices in baseball were less able to predict goal-oriented or strategic outcomes for a specific baseball situation. This is not necessarily a reflection of the novice's general prediction skills. Rather, in this context they were not able to construct a sufficient mental representation that would enable them to use such skills. A similar explanation could account also for Larkin's (in press) finding that novices were not able to reconstruct problems from the key words of the problem.

In this section we have emphasized the role that the development of automaticity plays in enabling skilled performance. The effects of increased automaticity are twofold. First, it provides for easy accessibility to relevant knowledge, which allows an elaborate mental representation of a problem context to be constructed. These initial mental representations have been shown to influence subsequent processing during problem solving. Second, increasing automaticity frees up attentional resources that can then be directed toward other aspects of the task. Both of these aspects, automatic accessibility to information and the reduction of the bottleneck to attentional resources, are components that depend on well-organized and highly structured knowledge. This increase in automaticity, in turn, allows for increases in skilled performance.

The Structure of Knowledge and Competent Performance

In this chapter we have suggested that certain component processes of highly competent performance can be viewed within a framework of the development of organized and cohesive knowledge structures. The ability to retrieve information rapidly, the manner in which a mental representation of a problem situation is formed, and the ability to use cognitive strategies vary with differences in knowledge. More specifically, each of these skills has been shown to vary with the relative accessibility of information. Thus, knowledge structure in specific domains appears to be an important determinant of competence. Support for these claims comes from developmental research and from comparative research on the cognitive abilities of experts and novices in various domains.

Although we have illustrated that knowledge is an important constraint on allowing competent performance, we have not addressed the issue of how that knowledge is acquired and utilized. Many researchers have shown that there are wide individual differences among people in their tendency to use general cognitive strategies or metacognitive skills for promoting skilled performance (Bransford et al., 1982; Brown, 1978; Sternberg, 1981, 1984). Even with sufficient knowledge, not all people use the skills that may be available to them. Thus, knowledge might enable, but not necessitate, the use of such skills. In fact, training in the use of such skills often noticeably improves performance (Brown, Bransford, Ferrara, & Campione, 1983; Palincsar & Brown, 1984). This approach leads to conceptions of intelligence that emphasize general skills, rather than domain-specific knowledge, and it may be that gifted people are gifted because they are more likely to use such skills to build up and use their knowledge (Sternberg, 1981, 1984; Sternberg & Davidson, 1983).

Knowledge plays a role in accounting for variability in the use of general strategies, for example, as a result of mental representations of a task. Knowledge not only enables the use of such skills, but might also affect how much effort one must apply to use them. Imagine a hypothetical situation in which question-asking behavior is observed for four people who vary in their degree of knowledge of a domain, from expert to novice, and who are presented with a problem. These four people will generate mental representations of the materials that vary in detail. Person A, an expert, studies the problem and generates a very detailed mental representation of it so that there are few gaps or inconsistencies to be filled. In this context, person A does not ask many questions. Person B has less knowledge than does person A, but is able to construct a fairly elaborate mental representation of the problem. However, in this representation, there are gaps that need to be filled. These gaps are relatively obvious from the problem representation so that with the exercise of controlled monitoring skills, the questions that need to be asked are derived. Person C has less knowledge of the domain than does person B. Person C is able to construct a representation of the problem, but the specific information needed to suggest what questions should be asked is not immediately accessible. In such a situation, person C needs first to build up the mental representation, through controlled processing, before asking useful questions. Person D has very little knowledge of that domain and thus cannot build a meaningful representation at all. Consequently, the representation cannot suggest what types of questions should be asked, and the person does not have enough knowledge to consciously build the representation to the point where it will.

The most interesting contrast in this example is that between person B and person C. They have the knowledge necessary to enable them to ask relevant questions of the materials and thus to improve their understanding of the problem. Person B can do this rather effortlessly by generating questions from the problem representation. Person C, however, must consciously and skillfully elaborate the problem representation before asking questions. To exhibit the same performance, person C has to apply more effort than does person B. Competent performance in this case is a joint function of accessible knowledge and available general cognitive skills.

Rabinowitz and Chi (in press) have made a distinction between *general-context* and *specific-context* strategies that is relevant here. A general-context strategy is one that is exhibited in situations in which a person chooses to use a strategy primarily on the basis of the general constraints of the task. In this situation, the person makes the decision to use the strategy at the start of the task, that is, before the actual materials are viewed. An example of such a strategy, in the case of studying behavior, might be the use of an outlining strategy, such as to glance quickly over the material to get an outline of what might be discussed. The decision to use such a strategy is made prior to looking at the specific nature of the materials. The specific information presented in the passage, or how that information is related to prior knowledge, cannot influence the decision to use the strategy. It seems that the important prerequisite for the use of such a strategy is metacognitive knowledge—knowledge of the general aims of the task and knowledge of which strategies might be applicable.

Alternately, the decision to initiate a specific-context strategy is made in response to a specific, rather than the general, situation. This usually entails noticing similarities, differences, or gaps in knowledge. The decision to use a specific-context strategy is not made at the start of the task. For example, the question-asking strategy studied by Miyake and Norman (1979) can be considered to be a specific-context strategy. Subjects used this strategy only in response to certain specific situations, and the ability to notice these specific situations was based on prior knowledge. Similarly, the working forward and working backward strategies used by experts and novices during physics problem solving were generated in response to accessing specific information form the materials. The ability to access such information was determined by the knowledge that the subject had of the domain. Notice that experts switched to a different strategy when less knowledge of the problem was accessible. Thus, although the exhibition of general-context strategies depends primarily on metacognitive skills, the exhibition of specific-context strategies seems to depend to a large extent on domain-specific knowledge.

Although the decision to use a general-context strategy may be made independently of domain-specific knowledge, the effects of using such a strategy might be to help increase knowledge. For example, the use of the outlining strategy discussed earlier might lead to better acquisition and thus greater knowledge. The ability to use such strategies may be a significant component of giftedness (Campione et al., 1982; Sternberg & Davidson, 1983).

How can such strategies be acquired? One way is for them to be explicitly taught at some time (Palincsar & Brown, 1984). By explicitly teaching such strategies, people's metacognitive knowledge would improve and such strategies would then be applied in a variety of situations. However, general-context strategies can also evolve from specific-context strategies. Through experience with a specific task, a person might come to expect some regularities in the stimulus situation. Thus, strategies that were initially a response to some specific context might come to be employed at the beginning of the task with the expectation that it will, in fact, be a useful strategy. It is also possible that strategies used in several specific contexts become decontextualized so that they might be employed in a variety of tasks. Thus, specific-context strategies could become general-context strategies and subsequently be used to build up knowledge in a variety of domains. In this case the ability to use the strategy initially, the specific-context strategy, was strongly dependent upon knowledge. Thus, the acquisition of general strategies, based on this view, is derivative of domain-specific knowledge.

We have emphasized that knowledge can be a framework for understanding highly competent performance. But how the interactive development and use of general cognitive strategies and knowledge-based processes account for gifted performance is an open question (Glaser, 1984; Glaser, in press; Sternberg, in press). To what extent is outstanding competence dependent upon knowledge structures that rapidly provide relevant information and generate representations? In addition, how is such performance dependent upon skills that enable people to build up and use such knowledge bases? What are the task conditions that differentially call upon these abilities? Clearly, research needs to be conducted on the differences between gifted and average people in the acquisition of knowledge and related cognitive skills, in the accessibility of information, in the representations of problem situations, and on how such differences determine the properties of outstanding performance. Such research could contribute a great deal, not only to our understanding of gifted people and to methods of nurturing their talents, but also to educational practices for raising the general level of cognitive competence and intellectual skill.

References

Anderson, J. R. (1983a). *The architecture of cognition.* Cambridge, MA: Harvard University Press.

Anderson, J. R. (1983b). A spreading activation theory of memory. *Journal of Verbal Learning and Verbal Behavior, 22,* 261–295.

Anderson, J. R., & Bower, G. H. (1973). *Human associative memory.* Washington, DC: Hemisphere.

Ashcraft, M. H. (1982). The development of mental arithmetic: A chronometric approach. *Developmental Review, 2,* 213–236.

Ashcraft, M. H., & Battaglia, J. (1978). Cognitive arithmetic: Evidence for retrieval and decision processes in mental addition. *Journal of Experimental Psychology: Human Learning and Memory, 4,* 527–538.

Bjorklund, D. F., & Zeman, B. R. (1982). Children's organization and metamemory awareness in their recall of familiar information. *Child Development, 53,* 799–810.

Bransford, J. D., Stein, B. S., Vye, N. J., Franks, J. J., Auble, P. M., Mezynski, K. J., & Perfetto, G. A. (1982). Differences in approaches to learning: An overview. *Journal of Experimental Psychology: General, 111,* 390–398.

Brown, A. L. (1978). Knowing when, where, and how to remember: A problem of metacognition. In R. Glaser (Ed.), *Advances in instructional psychology* (Vol. 1, pp. 77–165). Hillsdale, NJ: Erlbaum.

Brown, A. L., Bransford, J. D., Ferrara, R. A., & Campione, J. C. (1983). Learning, remembering, and understanding. In J. H. Flavell & E. M. Markman (Eds.), *Handbook of child psychology: Vol. 3. Cognitive development* (4th ed., pp. 77–176). New York: Wiley.

Campione, J. C., Brown, A. L., & Ferrara, R. A. (1982). Mental retardation and intelligence. In R. J. Sternberg (Ed.), *Handbook of human intelligence* (pp. 392–490). New York: Cambridge University Press.

Charness, N. (1979). Components of skill in bridge. *Canadian Journal of Psychology, 33,* 1–50.

Chase, W. G., & Chi, M. T. H. (1981). Cognitive skill: Implications for spatial skill in large-scale environments. In J. Harvey (Ed.), *Cognition, social behavior, and the environment* (pp. 111–136). Hillsdale, NJ: Erlbaum.

Chase, W. G., & Ericsson, K. A. (1981). Skilled memory. In J. R. Anderson (Ed.), *Cognitive skills and their application* (pp. 141–189). Hillsdale, NJ: Erlbaum.

Chase, W. G., & Simon, H. A. (1973). The mind's eye in chess. In W. G. Chase (Ed.), *Visual information processing* (pp. 215–281). New York: Academic Press.

Chi, M. T. H. (1978). Knowledge structures and memory development. In R. S. Siegler (Ed.), *Children's thinking: What develops?* (pp. 73–96). Hillsdale, NJ: Erlbaum.

Chi, M. T. H. (1985). Changing conceptions of sources of memory development. *Human Development, 28,* 50–56.

Chi, M. T. H., Feltovich, P., & Glaser, R. (1981). Categorization and representation of physics problems by experts and novices. *Cognitive Science, 5,* 121–152.

Chi, M. T. H., Glaser, R., & Rees, E. (1982). Expertise in problem solving. In R. J. Sternberg (Ed.), *Advances in the psychology of human intelligence* (Vol. 1, pp. 7–76). Hillsdale, NJ: Erlbaum.

Chiesi, H., Spilich, G. J., & Voss, J. F. (1979). Acquisition of domain-related information in relation to high and low domain knowledge. *Journal of Verbal Learning and Verbal Behavior, 18,* 257–283.

Collins, A. M., & Loftus, E. F. (1975). A spreading activation theory of semantic processing. *Psychological Review, 82,* 407–428.

Collins, A. M., & Quillian, M. R. (1969). Retrieval time from semantic memory. *Journal of Verbal Learning and Verbal Behavior, 8,* 240–247.

de Groot, A. (1965). *Thought and choice in chess.* The Hague: Mouton.

Egan, D., & Schwartz, B. (1979). Chunking in recall of symbolic drawings. *Memory and Cognition, 7,* 149–158.

Ericsson, K. A., Chase, W. G., & Faloon, S. (1980). Acquisition of a memory skill. *Science, 208,* 1181–1182.

Gentner, D., & Gentner, D. R. (1983). Flowing waters or teeming crowds: Mental models of electricity. In D. Gentner & A. Stevens (Eds.), *Mental models* (pp. 99–129). Hillsdale, NJ: Erlbaum.

Ginsburg, H. (1977). *Children's arithmetic: The learning process.* New York: Van Nostrand Reinhold.

Glaser, R. (1984). Education and thinking: The role of knowledge. *American Psychologist, 39,* 93–104.

Glaser, R. (1985). All's well that begins and ends with both knowledge and process: A reply to Sternberg. *American Psychologist, 40,* 573–575.

Greeno, J. G., & Simon, H. A. (in press). Problem solving and reasoning. In R. C. Atkinson, R. Hernstein, G. Lindzey, & R. D. Luce (Eds.), *Stevens' handbook of experimental psychology* (rev. ed.). New York: Wiley

Groen, G. J., & Parkman, J. M. (1972). A chronometric analysis of simple addition. *Psychological Review, 79,* 329–343.

Hinsley, D. A., Hayes, J. R., & Simon, H. A. (1978). From words to equations: Meaning and representation in algebra word problems. In P. A. Carpenter & M. A. Just (Eds.), *Cognitive processes in comprehension.* Hillsdale, NJ: Erlbaum.

Hunt, E. (1976). Varieties of cognitive power. In L. Resnick (Ed.), *The nature of intelligence* (pp. 237–259). Hillsdale, NJ: Erlbaum.

Hunt, E. (1978). Mechanics of verbal ability. *Psychological Review, 85,* 109–130.

Johnson-Laird, P. N. (1982). Ninth Bartlett memorial lecture. Thinking as a skill. *Quarterly Journal of Experimental Psychology, 34A,* 1–29.

Johnson-Laird, P. N. (1983). *Mental models: Towards a cognitive science of language, inference, and consciousness.* Cambridge, MA: Harvard University Press.

Keating, D. P., & Bobbitt, B. L. (1978). Individual and developmental differences in cognitive-processing components of mental ability. *Child Development, 49,* 155–167.

Larkin, J. H. (1977). *Skilled problem solving in physics: A hierarchical planning model.* Unpublished manuscript, University of California at Berkeley.

Larkin, J. H. (1979). Processing information for effective problem solving. *Engineering Education, 70,* 285–288.

Larkin, J. H. (in press). Understanding, problem representations, and skill in physics. In S. F. Chipman, J. W. Siegal, & R. Glaser (Eds.), *Thinking and learning skills: Vol. 2. Research and open questions.* Hillsdale, NJ: Erlbaum.

Larkin, J. H., McDermott, J., Simon, D. P., & Simon, H. A. (1980). Models of competence in solving physics problems. *Cognitive Science, 4,* 317–345.

Lesgold, A. M. (1984). Acquiring expertise. In J. R. Anderson & S. M. Kosslyn (Eds.), *Tutorials in learning and memory: Essays in honor of Gordon Bower* (pp. 31–60). San Francisco: Freeman.

Lindberg, M. (1980). The role of knowledge structures in the ontogeny of learning. *Journal of Experimental Child Psychology, 30,* 401–410.

Mandler, J. M. (1983). Representation. In J. H. Flavell & E. M. Markman (Eds.), *Handbook of child psychology: Vol. 3. Cognitive development* (4th ed., pp. 420–494). New York: Wiley.

Marland, S. P., Jr. (1972). *Education of the gifted and talented* (Vols. 1–2). Washington, DC: U.S. Government Printing Office.

Minsky, M., & Papert, S. (1974). *Artificial intelligence.* Eugene, OR: Oregon State System of Higher Education.

Miyake, N., & Norman, D. A. (1979). To ask a question, one must know enough to know what is not known. *Journal of Verbal Learning and Verbal Behavior, 18,* 357–384.

Neely, J. H. (1976). Semantic priming and retrieval from lexical memory: Evidence for facilitory and inhibition processes. *Memory and Cognition, 4,* 648–654.

Neely, J. H. (1977). Semantic priming and retrieval from lexical memory: Roles of inhibitionless spreading activation and limited-capacity attention. *Journal of Experimental Psychology: General, 106,* 226–254.

Newell, A. & Simon, H. A. (1972). *Human problem solving.* Englewood Cliffs, NJ: Prentice-Hall.

Norman, D. A., & Rumelhart, D. E. (1975). *Explorations in cognition.* San Francisco: Freeman.

Palincsar, A. S., & Brown, A. L. (1984). Reciprocal teaching of comprehension-fostering and comprehension-monitoring activities. *Cognition and Instruction, 1,* 117–175.

Pellegrino, J. W., & Glaser, R. (1982). Analyzing aptitudes for learning inductive reasoning. In R. Glaser (Ed.), *Advances in instructional psychology* (Vol. 2, pp. 269–345). Hillsdale, NJ: Erlbaum.

Perfetti, C. A., & Lesgold, A. M. (1978). Discourse comprehension and sources of individual differences. In M. Just & P. Carpenter (Eds.), *Cognitive processes in comprehension* (pp. 141–183). Hillsdale, NJ: Erlbaum.

Rabinowitz, M., & Chi, M. T. H. (in press). An interactive model of strategic processing. In S. J. Ceci (Ed.), *Handbook of cognitive, social, and neuropsychological aspects of learning disabilities.* Hillsdale, NJ: Erlbaum.

Resnick, L. B. (1982). A developmental theory of number understanding. In H. Ginsburg (Ed.), *The development of mathematical thinking* (pp. 110–151). New York: Academic Press.

Richman, C. L., Nida, S., & Pittman, L. (1976). Effects of meaningfulness on child free-recall learning. *Developmental Psychology, 12,* 460–465.

Rumelhart, D. E. (1981). Schemata: The building blocks of cognition. In R. Spiro, B. Bruce, & W. Brewer (Eds.), *Theoretical issues in reading comprehension* (pp.33–58). Hillsdale, NJ: Erlbaum.

Schneider, W., & Fisk, A. D. (1982). Concurrent automatic and controlled visual search: Can processing occur without resource cost? *Journal of Experimental Psychology: Learning, Memory, and Cognition, 8,* 261–278.

Schneider, W., & Shiffrin, R. M. (1977). Controlled and automatic human information processing: I. Detection, search, and attention. *Psychological Review, 84,* 1–66.

Siegler, R. S., & Robinson, M. (1982). The development of numerical understandings. In H. Reese & L. P. Lipsitt (Eds.), *Advances in child development and behavior* (pp. 241–312). New York: Academic Press.

Siegler, R. S., & Shrager, J. (1984). A model of strategy choice. In C. Sophian (Ed.), *Origins of cognitive skills* (pp. 229–294). Hillsdale, NJ: Erlbaum.

Simon, D. F., & Simon, H. A. (1978). Individual differences in solving physics problems. In R. S. Siegler (Ed.), *Children's thinking: What develops?* (pp. 325–348). Hillsdale, NJ: Erlbaum.

Sternberg, R. J. (1981). A componential theory of intellectual giftedness. *Gifted Child Quarterly, 25*, 86–93.

Sternberg, R. J. (1984). What should intelligence tests test? Implications of a triarchic theory of intelligence for intelligence testing. *Educational Researcher, 13*, 5–15.

Sternberg, R. J. (in press). All's well that ends well, but it's a sad tale that begins at the end: A reply to Glaser. *American Psychologist.*

Sternberg, R. J., & Davidson, J. E. (1983). Insight in the gifted. *Educational Psychologist, 18*, 51–57.

Sternberg, R. J., & Wagner, R. K. (1982). Automatization failure in learning disabilities. *Topics in Learning and Learning Disabilities, 2*, 1–11.

Vernon, P. A. (1983). Speed of information processing and general intelligence. *Intelligence, 7*, 53–70.

4. Creativity Testing and Giftedness

Michael A. Wallach
Duke University

This chapter represents an attempt to put into perspective three decades of research on creativity testing and giftedness. The chapter consists of four general sections. In the first section I consider the growth of evidence showing intelligence testing to offer but a limited window on giftedness. Next I describe the rise of creativity testing as an alternative that is expected to help elucidate giftedness where intelligence testing has shown itself to be limited. In the third section is a discussion of some widespread but dubious practices in the use of creativity tests that have arisen in the wake of their recent popularity. And finally, I suggest that a shift from creativity and intelligence testing toward discipline-centered or field-specific approaches for facilitating giftedness is currently taking place.

The Limitations of Intelligence Testing

To call a person gifted or talented seems, in common sense terms, to refer to that person's unusual accomplishment at something meaningful in its own right—biology or music, sculpture or creative writing. To Whitmore (1981) giftedness referred to exceptional achievement at an intrinsically valuable form of endeavor. Read (1982) noted that the term *gifted* is domain-specific as commonly used, and Feldman (1982) defined giftedness

99

in terms of a person's potential for contributing strongly to any specific field of accomplishment that is valued. It was often assumed that intelligence or academic ability test scores were serviceable indicators for such accomplishment and that something like intellective ability could be assessed as a convenient shorthand for describing the gifted. This assumption persists. It is a common custom to simply use IQ scores above some relatively high level to define giftedness, and to weight heavily small differences in the upper range of scores to make educational selection decisions.

But IQ scores are not criteria for giftedness. Considerable work has demonstrated that, from the middle to the upper end of their range, scores on tests of intellective ability are not good predictors of giftedness. Some investigators seek additional ways of viewing intelligence (e.g., Sternberg & Davidson, 1983) that might improve the ability to predict directly valued accomplishments. The evidence for poor prediction from customary assessments of intelligence in the upper part of the range, briefly reviewed here, gave substance to the misgivings about the use of intelligence testing in identifying giftedness during the 1960s and 70s. I first consider work that relates IQ scores to significant out-of-school accomplishments during the student years. I then consider the relation between IQ scores and occupational accomplishments. I include examples of typical studies from what is an extensive literature on intelligence test score distributions within approximately the upper half of the overall range.

IQ and Out-of-School Accomplishments

In national samples of high school students Walberg (1971) found virtually no correlation between IQ scores and awards or prizes for out-of-school accomplishments in the fields of creative writing, science, music, the visual arts, drama, dance, or in group leadership. (Self-report, which was used in the Walberg study and in most others pertaining to students, has been found to provide acceptable accuracy [Maxey & Ormsby, 1971].) In work by Richards, Holland, and Lutz (1967), intellective ability test scores for high school students were unrelated to similar kinds of talented accomplishments during high school and failed to predict such accomplishments when the students were followed 1 or 2 years into college. On the other hand, exhibiting those accomplishments in high school predicted their continuance in college. Such predictability was specific. For example, earlier attainment in art predicted later attainment in art but not in writing or science, and earlier attainment in creative writing predicted later attainment in writing but not in science or music. Comparable results across a longer time span were reported by Munday and Davis

---

I am grateful to the many researchers represented here for their work. Whatever our agreements and disagreements, better understanding of giftedness should be the ultimate outcome.

(1974), who found ability test scores at the end of high school unrelated to talented accomplishments then or 6 years later, equivalent to 2 years after completion of college, whereas later accomplishment was predictable from earlier accomplishment in the same field.

Using similar methods, numerous other studies have documented the same general picture. Holland and Richards (1965), for example, found ability test scores for college freshmen attending an academically varied range of institutions to show little or no relation to talented out-of-school accomplishments during the years of high school, ranging across fields such as art, music, creative writing, dramatics, science, and leadership. This was true even when the considerations used for defining accomplishment within a domain were quite demanding. On the other hand, the students' ability test scores were related to their academic grades. Wallach and Wing (1969) found similar results for freshmen attending a selective college. Those results were replicated with a broadened ability test score range by Wing and Wallach (1971), who considered all applicants to an institution rather than just matriculants, and by Willingham and Breland (1982), who studied applicants to an academically heterogeneous set of colleges.

Other methods have yielded similar results. Parloff, Datta, Kleman, and Handlon (1968), for example, had scientists judge the novelty and effectiveness of independent research projects conducted out of school by high school students. The considerable quality differences discerned among the projects were unrelated to ability test scores. Morrison (1963) found competence in theater arts in college to be unrelated to intellective ability test scores but predictable from extracurricular involvement in theater during high school. And quality of independent research projects by graduate students in psychology, although found to vary widely when judged in terms of imaginativeness and contribution to knowledge, was reported by Mednick (1963) to be unrelated to ability test scores.

IQ and Occupational Accomplishments

A similar picture has emerged for occupational and professional achievements in the adult years. In work by Taylor and associates (e.g., Taylor, 1978; Taylor & Ellison, 1975), ability test scores were not reliable predictors of quality of scientific accomplishment among industrial scientists and engineers nor of numerous criteria of excellence among physicians. Barron (1963) found no relation between intelligence test scores obtained from adult artists and the judged quality of their artistic work. Similar findings have been reported for architects, research scientists, and mathematicians (Helson & Crutchfield, 1970; MacKinnon, 1968), chemists and mathematicians (Bloom, 1963), and physical and biological scientists (Harmon, 1963). Additional reports on such work for both students and adults can be found in McClelland (1973) and Wallach (1971, 1976a, 1976b, 1983a).

Various criticisms of these failures to validate the relation between intelligence scores and accomplishment have been considered over the years, but the criticisms do not seem to account fully for the failures (see, e.g., Wallach, 1971,1976a,1976b). For example, since the talented attainments studied are rare events, perhaps they are too rare to be predictable from test scores. Yet, as has been seen, they turn out to be predictable from earlier display of similar attainments. Another criticism has been that the range of the test scores used to predict is too restrictive. But the range is great enough that the test scores are found to correlate with academic grades, and score distinctions within this range are used for defining eligibility for educational opportunities. Also, reported correlations between test scores and attainments are sometimes negative rather than positive.

If so much evidence contradicts the existence of a relation between intelligence test scores in their upper ranges and giftedness, how does one explain classic earlier studies by Cox (1926) and Terman and Oden (1947), which seemed to support such a relationship? Cox demonstrated that historical geniuses had unusually high IQs, but she inferred IQ, in the absence of IQ tests, from biographically recorded activities such as, among other things, level of talented attainments in childhood. The biographical evidence used for claiming very high childhood intelligence levels for Mozart, Voltaire, and Goethe, for example, included considerations such as Mozart's composing a minuet at age 5, Voltaire's writing poetry when very young, and Goethe's producing precocious literary work at age 8. Terman and Oden demonstrated that high IQ test scores in childhood were related to talented accomplishments in adulthood. In this case, social class confounded the relationship: The high-IQ children also were socioeconomically superior (McClelland, 1973). Thus, privilege and opportunity differences were sufficient to account for the relationship.

The kinds of results sampled confirm a growing skepticism about the utility of a general ability concept such as intelligence, at least within approximately the upper half of test score ranges, in accounting for talented accomplishments that directly define giftedness. This is not to deny that special abilities might play a role. For example, Chauncey and Hilton (1983) reported on studies by others in which the quality of research scientists' accomplishments failed to relate to differences on a general intelligence test but did relate (to a small degree) to a quantitative ability measure. Particular competencies, such as quantitative skill, could have a direct part in related forms of professional achievement. Overall, however, research has called into question the concept of general intelligence as underlying the presence of giftedness in life contexts (Perkins, 1981).

From Intelligence Testing to Creativity Testing

A major response to the skepticism about IQ as a predictor of giftedness was to fashion another general ability concept—a disposition for creativity. In recent years, it has become widely accepted (e.g., Feldman, 1980; Keating, 1983; Kogan, 1983; Perkins, 1981; Wallach, 1970, 1971) that one form of cognitive functioning in particular is minimally correlated with general intelligence. This ability is known as ideational fluency, or the tendency to generate many ideas or associations, including unusual or original ones, in response to various task requests. Fluency in producing ideas thus became a promising candidate to replace IQ as a general ability that was relevant to direct criteria of giftedness. This work had its origins in the 1950s with Guilford's structure-of-intellect model (e.g., Guilford, 1956; Wallach, 1970), a formulation that included a major distinction between two kinds of operations for producing further information from what is given—convergent and divergent thinking. Although convergent thinking fit the intelligence testing notion of finding a right answer, as in vocabulary, verbal reasoning, and verbal comprehension, divergent thinking involved generating multiple possibilities.

Divergent thinking looked promising as an index for creative ability or potential (Guilford & Christensen, 1973). Typical tests of divergent thinking included items such as naming all the things one can think of that are white and edible, or describing all the possible occupations one can imagine for which a person's clothing would have a bell on it (Guilford, 1975). Other items included naming uses for common objects, problems suggested by particular happenings, or consequences that certain changes might produce. Scores on these tests of ideational fluency were found to have little relation to intelligence test results (see Wallach, 1970).

Guilford devised other kinds of tests as measures of divergent thinking. For example, he used tests of word fluency, in which subjects provide words that start with a given letter; of expressional fluency, in which subjects compose alternative sentences with words whose first letters are specified; and of redefinition, in which subjects break a set to use objects only in customary ways. These tests correlated about as strongly with tests of intelligence as they did with one another. Limiting the repertoire to tests more similar to ideational fluency tended to raise their degree of autocorrelation and reduce their relation to convergent thinking tasks, which, in turn, tended to be autocorrelated. Richards (1976) later confirmed the same point with new administrations of Guilford tests. Ideational fluency tests thus seemed to measure something other than, or in addition to, what is measured by IQ tests, whereas other divergent thinking tests merged more with IQ.

Measuring Ideational Fluency

Further work using a rather wide variety of tasks for tapping divergent thinking led to a progressive narrowing of the divergent thinking definition to ideational fluency and its close relatives. With students from sixth grade to high school, Getzels and Jackson (1962) used divergent thinking tests that included tasks such as giving alternative meanings for words that have more than one definition (e.g., bolt); perceiving essentials, as represented by detecting hidden geometric figures embedded in more complex ones; and giving alternative uses for various common objects. Although their tests have been shown in further analyses (e.g., Wallach, 1970) to correlate with IQ and to do so about as strongly as they correlate with one another, the alternative uses test, which comes closest to tapping ideational fluency, showed more separability from intelligence test scores.

Torrance (1963) developed children's versions of verbal and figural tests for ideational fluency and other measures of divergent thinking. In one test a child is shown a picture of a clownlike figure looking at his reflection in water and is asked to write questions the picture raises, to list causes for the depicted situation, and to list its possible consequences. But some other tasks, such as adding lines to an oval of green paper to make a clever picture, had less to do with ideational fluency. Also, the nonfluency issue of elaboration—scoring for detail and specificity of responses—was included in the Torrance tests. The result was a somewhat heterogeneous set of operations for defining divergent thinking, but they were less heterogeneous than those of Getzels and Jackson.

The evidence from numerous studies (see Wallach, 1970) documented relations between Torrance testing and IQ, thus raising doubts about the separability of the Torrance battery as a whole from IQ. Because overall scores often were used, even though some scores and tests might have less to do with IQ than others, the distinction between intellective ability and Torrance scores was unclear. Although Torrance himself (1975) seems not to mind leaving intelligence and divergent thinking confounded in his battery, considerable further research moved in the direction of concentrating on ideational fluency as a way to operationalize divergent thinking that was minimally related to IQ in its upper ranges while also yielding substantial correlations among different kinds of fluency assessments. Indeed, when separate scoring lets it be teased out, ideational fluency may be what is reliably measured apart from intelligence in the Torrance tests as well (Hocevar, 1979b).

The work of Wallach and Kogan (1965) accelerated the move toward concentrating on ideational fluency as an index of creativity that could be juxtaposed to customary measures of intellective ability. They administered various kinds of tasks to fifth graders and scored number of ideas and their relative uniqueness in the sample. In one task, for example, children listed possible similarities between pairs of named objects, and in another gave multiple possible meanings for various abstract visual patterns. Task appropriateness was an implicit requirement for the responses. The number and average uniqueness of the ideas offered by the children in such tasks turned out to be related variables—the absolute number of ideas left after subtracting unusual ones was correlated with the number of unusual ideas—and to yield consistent orderings of the children across the different tasks. By contrast, within this middle-class sample, correlations with IQ scores were nil. Results on various IQ tests were related to one another and to academic achievement.

As the link between number and unusualness suggests, Ward (1969) also found that unique ideas tend to come later in strings of ideas; this finding was replicated by Hattie (1980), among others. Wallach and Kogan's tasks differed, however, from those used in earlier work on divergent thinking, not only in focusing exclusively on ideational fluency and fluency-related uniqueness of ideas, but also in being administered in ways that were more gamelike than testlike, such as without time pressure. Although both differences could have been responsible for the clearer separation shown in their work between divergent thinking and intelligence, Wallach and Kogan's findings also could have been due to either difference alone.

The Role of Context

Numerous studies with diverse age groups have replicated the separation between IQ and fluency, the latter assessed in ways that minimized testlike aspects. To determine whether a permissive testing context for fluency is necessary in order to show this separation, several studies examined ideational fluency results obtained under testlike rather than permissive conditions. Although some of this evidence seems to confirm the original Wallach and Kogan argument that both a focus on fluency and a gamelike context are necessary for the separation from IQ (Boersma & O'Bryan, 1968; Nicholls, 1971), the preponderance of evidence seems to suggest that context is irrelevant (Wallach, 1971).

By administering Wallach–Kogan type fluency tasks to the same 4-year-olds under testlike and permissive conditions, with tasks and administration conditions counterbalanced, Williams and Fleming (1969) found children's ideational fluency levels to be consistent for the different tasks and administration contexts and to be independent of IQ regardless of context. Sherwood (1969) assessed different sixth graders for fluency in testlike or permissive contexts and found fluency scores for different tasks to be related to one another but not to intelligence scores regardless of context. Whereas both of Sherwood's contexts involved administering tasks to individuals, Kogan and Morgan (1969) fashioned testlike and gamelike contexts in which fluency tasks were administered to groups.

With different fifth graders assigned to each context, fluency tasks in either context again were interrelated but independent of IQ.

More recent evidence further confirms the irrelevance of context (Hattie, 1977). Hattie noted that although the task administration context can affect the absolute scores achieved on ideational fluency tests, it tends not to affect the relative ordering of individuals. In another study, Hattie (1980) demonstrated again that, for ideational fluency and fluency-related uniqueness of ideas on various tasks, different sixth graders whose fluency was assessed under testlike or gamelike conditions tended toward consistency on the fluency-based assessments and different orderings on IQ, regardless of fluency test administration conditions. Ideational fluency thus seems separable from intelligence quite generally, whatever the assessment context for the fluency tasks.

Ideational fluency also may underlie other measures sometimes treated as distinctive. For example, Hocevar (1979a) administered to college students Guilford tests calling for the listing of alternate uses for common objects, titles for stories, and possible consequences of particular situations. He found that originality scores, whether based on statistical infrequency or on qualitative judgments, showed little residual interrelationship across tasks, and minimal residual reliability as well, after ideational fluency was partialed out. The quantity of responses has been found to be related to giving unusual ideas of high quality for children ranging from preschoolers to high school seniors (Milgram, Milgram, Rosenbloom, & Rabkin, 1978; Moran, Milgram, Sawyers, & Fu, 1983). Although distinctions within ideational fluency may prove possible, such as counting only those uses that are less likely to be carried out rather than counting all uses for an object (Harrington, Block, & Block, 1983), the majority of evidence to date suggests that fluency is the active element in most creativity testing that yields a clear difference from orderings on intelligence tests (Kogan, 1983).

Ideational Fluency and Out-of-School Accomplishments

This finding does not, however, demonstrate that creative ability underlies ideational fluency and related measures. Although claims have been made that such assessments account for direct criteria of gifted and talented functioning better than do intelligence test scores within the upper range, the evidence at best seems mixed. Consider some examples. On the positive side, Wallach and Wing (1969) found ideational fluency measures based on Wallach–Kogan tasks to relate to talented out-of-school accomplishments during the high school years, whereas ability test scores showed no such relationships. With Israeli students graduating from high school, Milgram and Milgram (1976) found results similar to those of Wallach and Wing's American sample. In a study of college students,

Milgram and Arad (1981) used a more contrived criterion of talent—the successful and original solving of problems in an artificial laboratory situation. It nevertheless seems of interest that ideational fluency on Wallach–Kogan tasks predicted successful and original problem solving on laboratory tasks—a stringent standard. Intelligence, by contrast, was unrelated both to ideational fluency and problem solving. In another study of college students, Hocevar (1980) again found ideational fluency to be related to out-of-school accomplishments; although intelligence was unrelated to fluency, in this case it was related to accomplishments.

Some comparable outcomes have been reported with children. Singer and Whiton (1971) found ideational fluency, but not intelligence test scores, to predict the judged expressiveness of kindergarteners' art. With a sample that was unusual in that it included children with a lower range of IQ scores, Wallbrown and Huelsman (1975) found ideational fluency to be related to evaluations of a clay sculpture made by third and fourth graders, but not to ratings of two crayon drawings also made by them. Again, IQ was minimally predictive. A follow-up of seventh graders (Howieson, 1981) suggested that ideational fluency-type assessment predicted to a small but significant degree certain forms of talented out-of-school attainments a decade later, at average age 22, whereas IQ did not.

Amabile (1983a) reported that relationships existed between ideational fluency-type assessment and each of two talent criteria—judged quality of collage making and of story telling—for first and second graders. Milgram (1983) found, for children of several age levels and with a broader IQ range than is usually considered, that ideational fluency again seemed to predict original stringent-standard problem solving on laboratory tasks. Intelligence differences contributed little to the relationship. Harrington et al. (1983) found that ideational fluency and IQ assessed at ages of 4 to 5 years each predicted no more than marginally to teacher-evaluated creativity in sixth grade, whereas a more refined fluency measure, which was restricted to imaginative responses, was a better predictor. Because the judgment of the teacher was essentially based on the child's thinking style, however, it may be that both predictor and criterion were assessments of an imaginative thinking style.

Despite these positive results, much of the variation in the criteria of giftedness remains unaccounted for by ideational fluency-type assessment. If ideational fluency has a role in such displays of giftedness as a measure of general creative ability, analogous to but different from general intelligence, it appears to be a small one. Some investigators have questioned whether ideational fluency plays any role at all. Kogan and Pankove (1972), for example, found ideational fluency at fifth and tenth grade to predict talented out-of-school attainments at tenth grade in one school system but not in another. In a follow-up study, considering out-of-school attainments of the same children at the end of high school, Kogan and Pankove (1974) found hardly any predictability from 5th- or

10th-grade ideational fluency to those attainments, but they found some predictability from IQ. Negative results of a study by Cropley (1972), as reanalyzed by Jordan (1975), indicate no predictability on a 7th-grade assessment from either ideational fluency or from IQ to out-of-school attainments examined in the 12th grade.

Gough (1975) was unable to predict the quality of the professional contributions of physical scientists and engineers from information on ideational fluency or from scores on an intelligence test. In a study of art students, Getzels and Csikszentmihalyi (1976) found neither ideational fluency measures nor intelligence tests to predict professional achievement as an artist 5 to 6 years after graduation. Ideational fluency and IQ likewise failed to predict students' artistic achievement as it was evaluated by their instructors while the students were in art school. Finally, Perkins (1981) questions the utility of ideational fluency for predicting gifted accomplishment on the grounds that the poets he studied did not search for alternate ideas while writing poetry, judging from their introspective reports. What they did was more related to the skills of their particular craft.

In short, the evidence regarding connections between ideational fluency and gifted or talented attainments is mixed at best. Something on the order of creative ability may sometimes underlie the display of ideational fluency, but fluency may also be affected by other factors, such as compliance with an authority's request to respond profusely, or an obsessive tendency to proliferate fine-grained distinctions (Wallach, 1971, 1976b, 1983a). To consider fluency a proxy for creative ability probably reflects a desire to think of gifted attainments as products of broad abilities—if not of intelligence, then of creativity. The evidence suggests, however, that this is not the case. Unfortunately, studies are frequently encountered in which results from fluency tests are viewed as being synonymous with creative ability. The logic of such work treats tests that are at best weak predictors of gifted attainments as if the tests were validation criteria in their own right.

The Predictor Becomes the Criterion

In numerous studies, investigators have sought other correlates of ideational fluency-type scores, assuming that they were discovering correlates to creative ability. For example, Bowers and van der Meulen (1970) found "suggestible" college students to earn higher ideational fluency scores and argued from this that suggestibility is a childlike regressiveness conducive to creativity. In a follow-up study, Bowers (1971) found a similar relationship among women but not among men, which was interpreted similarly. In a text on creativity, Lytton (1972) also viewed the connection between suggestibility and ideational fluency as indicating a personality correlate of creative ability. It is possible, however, that compliance with the experimenter's suggestions and not creative ability is the link between suggestibility and output of ideas in these studies.

Compliance is certainly not one of the personality characteristics that is commonly associated with talented achievement. In a study by Taft and Gilchrist (1970), for example, college students who showed talented out-of-school attainments of high quality were found to be rebellious and unconventional. Similarly, Parloff et al. (1968) found the quality of out-of-school scientific research among high school students to be correlated with independence and self-assertiveness. College students who showed outstanding ability for making movies (Domino, 1974) seemed to be less accepting of guidance from others than did students in control groups. Similar results have been found with highly gifted architects (MacKinnon, 1983) and with highly gifted women mathematicians (Helson, 1983). If anything, suggestibility or compliance to authority seems lower in those who display giftedness—the converse of Bowers's findings with the fluency tests. Although nonconformity or independence has been found to be a correlate of gifted attainment, it should not be assumed that nonconformity has been validated as a proxy for giftedness. This has been done, however (e.g., Rimm & Davis, 1980). Nonconformity, like ideational fluency, is multiply determined; equating it with giftedness is misleading.

Teaching Ideational Fluency

Some investigators have tried to raise levels of gifted achievement through instruction. Often, the criterion of efficacy for such instruction is increased scores on ideational fluency-type tests. Clearly, the equivalence of fluency-related scores and creative ability is needed in order to justify this approach. Both Gowan (1977) and Michael (1977) have emphasized that teaching should be designed to enhance abilities thought to be indexed by tests of ideational fluency, because they believed this would strengthen the likelihood of gifted achievement. Gowan considered this approach to be analogous to an athletic coach's teaching in ways that enhance performance at a sport. Although such coaching is closely related to accomplishment in a given sport, training in fluency does not appear to be directly related to gifted accomplishment. The idea of coaching people in order to foster gifted accomplishment may in fact be sound. But such training is strikingly different from, rather than analogous to, teaching to enhance fluency. Yet recommendations for such teaching abound, as the samples in the following paragraphs illustrate.

A number of experimental studies have been carried out to demonstrate that ideational fluency can be increased with training. It has been found that fluency and fluency-related uniqueness of ideas increase when undergraduates are trained to provide different word association responses each time a given stimulus word recurs (e.g., Maltzman, Simon, Raskin, & Licht, 1960). Such enhancement effects are mitigated, however, if even a 2-hour delay intervenes between the training and the test (Maltzman et al., 1960). That general creative ability has been increased seems less likely than other possible interpretations. For example, the training may induce a mental set to try harder or may encourage students to split hairs to come up with fine-grained response differences to the stimulus word, because any difference qualifies. Instilling such sets can raise fluency test scores, but this says nothing about creative ability.

In other studies, it was found that children's responses to creativity tests were affected when they were first shown a model. In a study by Belcher (1975), children were shown a film of a model responding to a uses test and then were given a uses test. Those children showed higher ideational fluency and unusualness scores than did children who did not see the film. As expected, fluency and unusualness were highly correlated. The author suggested that teachers could increase children's scores on such tests by modeling desired responses—ignoring the possible confounding effect of authoritative promptings about the kinds of responses wanted on a test. Similarly, raising creativity test scores by direct reward (e.g., Glover & Gary, 1976; Milgram & Feingold, 1977) may also demonstrate responsiveness to an authority's wishes. Yet, teachers are encouraged to use these procedures to raise test scores, as if raising the scores for any reason will suffice.

In another set of studies (Dansky, 1980; Dansky & Silverman, 1973, 1975), allowing children to play with materials the same as, or similar to, alternate uses test items was found to enhance test scores. Again, however, the relation between the change in scores and the children's creative ability was not demonstrated. Play most likely afforded increased familiarization with varied uses for the test materials or materials like them. Dansky and Silverman (1973) disavowed any claim to having increased the children's creative ability when raising their test scores, yet at the same time they claimed that the alternative uses test is warranted as a test of creative ability.

Experimental manipulation of humor has also been found to affect ideational fluency-type responding (Ziv, 1976). Tenth graders who listened to a recording of a popular comedian before taking a test had higher test scores than those who did not. The author did not claim that creative ability had been increased; but without that implication, demonstrating that test scores can be raised seems pointless. It may be that scores go up because an authority figure shows by playing the record that a wide range of test responses, including humorous ones, are valued and permitted. Learning about factors other than creative ability that enhance creativity test scores might be useful if viewed as confounds, but instead they are viewed as ways to teach creativity.

Extensive work has also been devoted to efforts to raise fluency-related test scores by using long-term manipulations such as creativity training courses. Reese and Parnes (1970) gave high school seniors a 13-week program, 2 classes per week, that included techniques for stimulating alternative ideas and coming up with new uses and improvements. Ideational fluency on the posttests was enhanced over pretest scores in the experimental group relative to a control group. Two years of such course training with college students—four college courses—also produced better scores on ideational fluency-type tests (Noller & Parnes, 1972; Parnes & Noller, 1972; Reese, Parnes, Treffinger, & Kaltsounis, 1976).

A number of explanations for these findings is possible. For example, training effects may reflect responsiveness to what is wanted on the tests, encouragement to try harder on them, and practice with materials similar to the test items. In fact, in the 2-year study, direct accomplishment criteria such as skill at creative writing also were assessed, with little evidence of benefit from the training. In a related vein, Dirkes (1978) recommended having students score their own ideational fluency tests for idea counts and having the teacher recognize improvements—an obvious case in which students would be learning to give teachers what they want.

A third type of work on raising creativity test scores has used broader educational programs in which "open education" is the intervention. The assumption is that open education should benefit creative ability or potential. Again, alternative reasons for why test scores might be higher need to be considered. Perhaps most notably, the values and demands that teachers communicate as to kinds of test responses that are congruent with the emphasis in open classrooms on children's freedom to explore and manipulate diverse materials in alternative ways need to be considered. Recent overviews by Horwitz (1979) and Giaconia and Hedges (1982) suggested that students in open versus traditional education settings do show higher creativity test scores. Among the most careful studies in this area, considerable attention has been given to defining the contrast between the two education settings, whereas the appropriateness of using creativity test scores as outcome measures tends to be taken for granted. A description of three of these more careful studies follows.

In work with second graders, Forman and McKinney (1978) compared matched groups of children in classes that were independently rated as strongly contrasting on a set of characteristics pertinent to open versus traditional education; comparisons were made in each of three school systems serving socioeconomically different clientele. Ideational fluency and fluency-related uniqueness scores were obtained on the Wallach-Kogan tests. In a similar study by Thomas and Berk (1981) with first and second graders, Torrance tests were used as a creativity measure.

Both studies yielded complex patterns of results that were difficult to interpret: open classrooms, traditional classrooms, or neither alternately looked better, depending on type of test, the school system, and the sex of child.

Solomon and Kendall (1976) compared the Wallach-Kogan test scores of fourth graders from carefully contrasted open and traditional classes and extensively assessed a range of personality and other characteristics. Overall there was a trend for children from open classrooms to score higher on ideational fluency and fluency-related uniqueness; however, this trend turned out to be the result of scores for only one subset of children, and they were identified as conformity-prone individuals. These children, who were responsive to suggestions from authorities and wanted approval, would be expected to conform to the norms and values of the type of class they attended. Again, higher fluency scores appear to be a result of responsiveness to demands from authorities.

I have shown in this section that considerable effort has been made based on the belief that ideational fluency and related test scores can be treated as functional equivalents of the kinds of criteria that serve to validate them—gifted achievements of one form or another. Although other reasons for variation in these test scores exist, they have been used as the criterion in studies of their correlates and of ways to enhance such scores. I have argued that casting them in the role of criterion is misguided, even if they possess an element of validity as predictors of gifted attainments, because of their multiply determined nature.

Although some still advocate using fluency-type tests for selection and as outcome measures for evaluating creativity training (e.g., Torrance, 1972, 1975), skepticism is growing. The claims for general creative ability playing a strong role in gifted achievement, like the claims for IQ before it, are hard to sustain in light of such evidence as I have reviewed. When fluency test scores go up, reasons other than enhancement of creative ability offer the most plausible interpretations. These alternatives include responsiveness to what is valued on the test, encouragement toward persistence, and training that teaches to the test (Mansfield, Busse, & Krepelka, 1978; Perkins, 1981; Wallach, 1971). Treffinger (1980), who has been deeply involved in using creativity courses, seems now to have misgivings. Keating (1980) goes so far as to view training that focuses on generating ideas as potentially counterproductive because of its pull away from disciplinary knowledge and standards.

Creativity may be defined most usefully as excellence of work in a particular field and thus as expansion at the field's cutting edge. Note what happens to the problem of teaching to the test when instruction in particular forms of gifted achievement replaces training that is presumed to increase general creative ability. To the extent that a test allows one to demonstrate particular forms of giftedness per se, such as excellence in writing or modern dance, teaching to the test can be a virtue. In short, specific gifted attainments, not general creativity, should be the outcomes that are enhanced by instruction.

Field-Specific Approaches to Giftedness

Increasingly, efforts to foster giftedness and talent are being formulated in field-specific terms. Gardner (1982, 1983) proposed, for example, that there are a number of semiautonomous human competences, which he identified with specific realms: creative writing, musical composing and performance, mathematics, art and architecture, dance and athletics, and political leadership. Similarly, Hocevar (1981) argued that, for reasons including limitations of time and effort, achievement is likely to be domain-specific. Renzulli and Smith (1978) asserted that too much emphasis is often placed on the general cognitive processes of gifted and talented individuals and that more attention should be given to knowledge and skills connected to specific disciplines or fields. Even those still committed to broad cognitive processes seem to be granting increased recognition to the importance of field-specific training (e.g., Wagner & Sternberg, 1984). Differences among disciplines in the nature of gifted achievement are coming strongly into focus, and there are two implications. One is that greater attention is given to pedagogy, with the recognition that much of what is needed for teaching depends on the structure of a particular discipline. Second, it is being recognized that excellence in a given field of accomplishment may offer a better basis for selecting individuals for educational benefits than does testing for such general dispositions as intelligence or creativity.

The Training of Prodigies

Feldman (1980, 1982) found that intense, field-specific instruction played a crucial role in the development of prodigies, contrary to the widely held view that prodigies develop spontaneously. According to Feldman, 8-year-old chess prodigies had systematic, long-term instruction with teachers who led them through a recapitulation of the history of the game over the last century, went move by move over recent tournament games played by the prodigy and others, and built a curriculum from games played by former world champions who had similar styles of play. A 9-year-old violinist received lessons from various teachers in diverse aspects of music, was specifically prepared for violin competitions, and was taught musical composition in a way that recapitulated the history of the discipline. A 6-year-old who was extremely capable at mathematics and physics received weekly tutoring from a mathematician. These prodigies showed extraordinary achievement in a given domain but were similar to age peers in other respects. The training they received was characterized by systematic movement through successive levels of mastery in the discipline, but at a rapid rate. Feldman believes that, although a child must have a proclivity for the field, if the field does not lend itself to instruction and if the instruction is not provided over a long period of intensive practice and with support from parents and others, achievement will not result. He therefore advises that schools provide more carefully sequenced, domain-specific instruction and that students be pointed toward what they seem to do best. Whether the given field be used vocationally or not, Feldman argues that broad benefits result from the discipline of mastering the work of a specific field. What matters is that the instruction be sufficiently expert so that the student is brought to mastery cumulatively and without gaps of knowledge.

There are many examples of the kind of instruction Feldman advocates. Yeatts (1980) gave an account of a novelist who taught writing in classes for the gifted in high school, provided experiences at different kinds of writing, elicited criticism of the novelist's own work in progress, and emphasized the importance of revising and editing. A professional artist had students' pottery work critiqued by an expert in ceramics (Donmoyer, 1983). A music educator emphasized extensive practice and uncompromising evaluation (Durden, 1983). Each of these examples fits the athletic coach model of disciplined immersion in the work and striving to meet standards: Instruction centers on the particular field to be mastered and on the development of particular skills in sequence. And, as in athletics, competitions and awards are sometimes used to help students develop a taste for and knowledge of quality, because they provide relevant standards for comparison (Barone, 1983). This kind of instruction is characterized by the idea that creativity, understood as excellence of accomplishment, is not teachable in a general sense but is expressed through mastery of a particular field of work and hence being able to push at its limits. To become creative is to master a given domain to the point where one's contributions are viewed as advancing that discipline. Although relevant instruction always involves systematic cumulation, it will look very different for different fields.

Prescriptive Instruction

The athletic coach analogy is well exemplified in work by Stanley and his colleagues (e.g., Stanley, 1977), who offered accelerated mathematics instruction to seventh and eighth graders who showed high math proficiency. Their program of acceleration was systematically cumulative to ensure that no knowledge gaps occurred. Thus, summer programs in precalculus mathematics start with diagnostic testing to determine what is and is not known by students, followed by prescriptive instruction that fills in the gaps. As a result, 12- or 13-year-olds can complete 2 years of typical high school mathematics courses in 40 to 48 hours of summer instruction (e.g., Bartkovich & Mezynski, 1981). Math-proficient seventh or eighth graders also seem to do very well in summer college math courses without undue social or emotional strain (e.g., Solano & George, 1976). Such students may also start their undergraduate careers at a younger age and complete PhDs earlier as well. Careful, accelerated instruction matched to a student's field of high proficiency allows that student to move more rapidly to the field's boundaries and thus be in a position to go beyond them (Brandt, 1981; Stanley & George, 1980). As Keating (1980) put it, acceleration at mathematics learning, in moving the learner more rapidly to the discipline's cutting edge, promotes the possibility of creative contributions by encouraging excitement and initiative while minimizing boredom and frustration.

These principles should apply to fields other than mathematics. What seems to matter is being field-specific in defining candidates for the instruction and the nature of that instruction. Retrospective accounts by adults gifted in a particular profession suggest the same process. Interviews of highly accomplished under-35-year-old concert pianists, Olympic swimmers, and research mathematicians (Bloom, 1982; Bloom & Sosniak, 1981) point to the importance of systematic, long-term, mastery-oriented instruction in their fields of achievement. Beginning at an early age and continuing for a decade or longer, intensive instructional resources were brought to bear on the individual's talent area, with individualized diagnoses as to what needed to be learned next, suggestions for appropriate practice, and a time schedule for when the next goal should be achieved to a prescribed standard.

In these accounts and in Feldman's, learners were guided through increasingly sophisticated instruction in their disciplines, and learners' special facilities tended to be restricted to their fields. Performance or contest events had an instructional function as targets toward which preparation was directed and as yardsticks for developing critical standards. Gifted adults cited particular teachers as having been important to them earlier—an observation also made in other retrospective studies (e.g., Chambers, 1973; Zuckerman, 1983). Parents also helped with teaching, which corroborates Albert's (1983a) historical observations on the role of parents in early instruction in a field where later eminence is achieved. Based on studies of the young and on those of eminent adults, the importance of sustained, carefully guided work in a given specialty is becoming clear (Walberg, 1983). Common among various specialties is the idea that creativity is a byproduct of field-specific instruction rather than a teachable skill in its own right.

Identifying Specific Talents

The focus for identifying gifted individuals thus becomes students' specific talents, not their assumed general abilities. As was noted earlier, achievement during adolescence in a given line of endeavor tends to persist, making accomplishment in a particular field a good basis for predicting its continuance. Historical studies of eminence suggest that specialized achievement continues through the years of mature professional work (e.g., Albert, 1983b; Simonton, 1977). Evidence about patterns of activities prior to adolescence also seems to support the idea of domain-specific continuance. In a retrospective study, Segal, Busse, and Mansfield (1980) found that biologists whose research was cited frequently were more likely than were other biologists to have had science-related hobbies as children, particularly biology-related hobbies. Likewise, Walberg and his associates (Walberg, Rasher, & Parkerson, 1979; Walberg et al., 1981) found historically eminent figures to have shown concentrated perseverance as children in what turned out to be their field of later eminence. Research that tracks domain-specific talented achievements from childhood to professional maturity is needed.

Taking the view that creativity is a domain-specific achievement may lead one to reinterpret some earlier findings. Amabile (1983a, 1983b) might have been better advised, for example, to think of judged quality of collage making as pertaining to artistic achievement in particular, rather than as a paradigm for creative achievement in general. Getzels and Csikszentmihalyi (1976) found that art students who pay more attention to the properties of objects to be used in a still life drawing show greater professional success as artists a few years later. This may suggest that stronger devotion to and involvement in the process of doing art tends to maintain itself over time, not that creativity calls for a generalized disposition toward problem finding.

Studies of college admissions decisions suggest that much more emphasis has been placed on small differences within the upper range of intelligence test scores than on direct indications of gifted accomplishments in various domains. For example, in one selective institution (Wallach, 1976a, 1976b; Wing & Wallach, 1971), admissions decisions were found to depend much more heavily on general intelligence criteria than on significant out-of-school accomplishments. Similar results have been reported for nine private colleges (Willingham & Breland, 1982; Wallach, 1983b). Given the low association between intelligence test scores and actual gifted achievements, assessing gifted attainments, for example, by judging actual work samples, deserves more emphasis in selection decisions. One effort in this direction was made by the Educational Testing Service (1983). ETS instituted a national talent search program for which high school seniors submit work samples, such as color slides of art, videotapes of dance or drama performances, or samples of creative writing, which are evaluated by expert judges for the purpose of granting scholarships.

Conclusion and Future Directions

Developmental research on creativity testing as it relates to the study of giftedness seems to be undergoing a needed shift away from the general and toward the specific. Giftedness has been found to be much more domain-specific than was first understood: psychologically different for math than for art, for writing than for leadership. Identifying the gifted and facilitating their development, along with understanding what lies behind their talent, require a closer focus on forms of disciplinary knowledge and competence in their own right.

General ability concepts, creativity as well as intelligence, have proven elusive, perhaps for the good reason that they ignore the particularities that may be most pertinent to giftedness. The evidence does not support viewing creativity as a general ability to be assessed and then to be facilitated by training. Further research using creativity tests as the focus would seem likely to yield the same ambiguities and errors as have been witnessed to date, whether one is looking for correlates of test performance or for ways to raise test scores. This is because of the multiply determined nature of the test responses, which leaves them open to myriad influences having nothing to do with creative ability. Alternatively, creativity may be best understood as what characterizes the work done at the cutting edge of a given field by those who have mastered it.

Having examined the last three decades of research, what is needed in the next three decades? Two major directions seem desirable, both following from the newly emerging focus on the knowledge and skills connected with particular fields or domains of talented accomplishment. One is research on discipline-specific approaches to improving instruction, recognizing that, apart from the importance of cumulative mastery, the nature of effective instruction needs to be understood in relation to each discipline's structure. The other is research across people's life spans for which the trajectory of development for domain-specific accomplishments of various kinds is considered.

References

Albert, R. S. (1983a). Family positions and the attainment of eminence. In R. S. Albert (Ed.), *Genius and eminence: The social psychology of creativity and exceptional achievement* (pp. 141–154). Elmsford, NY: Pergamon Press.

Albert, R. S. (1983b). Toward a behavioral definition of genius. In R. S. Albert (Ed.), *Genius and eminence: The social psychology of creativity and exceptional achievement* (pp. 57–72). Elmsford, NY: Pergamon Press.

Amabile, T. M. (1983a). *The social psychology of creativity*. New York: Springer-Verlag.

Amabile, T. M. (1983b). The social psychology of creativity: A componential conceptualization. *Journal of Personality and Social Psychology, 45,* 357–376.

Barone, T. (1983). Things of use and things of beauty: The Swain County High School arts program. *Daedalus, 112*(3), 1–28.

Barron, F. (1963). *Creativity and psychological health.* Princeton, NJ: Van Nostrand.

Bartkovich, K. G., & Mezynski, K. (1981). Fast-paced precalculus mathematics for talented junior high students: Two recent SMPY programs. *Gifted Child Quarterly, 25,* 73–80.

Belcher, T. L. (1975). Modeling original divergent responses: An initial investigation. *Journal of Educational Psychology, 67,* 351–358.

Bloom, B. S. (1963). Report on creativity research by the examiner's office of the University of Chicago. In C. W. Taylor & F. Barron (Eds.), *Scientific creativity: Its recognition and development* (pp. 251–264). New York: Wiley.

Bloom, B. S. (1982). The role of gifts and markers in the development of talent. *Exceptional Children, 48,* 510–522.

Bloom, B. S., & Sosniak, L. A. (1981). Talent development vs. schooling. *Educational Leadership, 39*(2), 86–94.

Boersma, F. J., & O'Bryan, K. (1968). An investigation of the relationship between creativity and intelligence under two conditions of testing. *Journal of Personality, 36,* 341–348.

Bowers, K. S. (1971). Sex and susceptibility as moderator variables in the relationship of creativity and hypnotic susceptibility. *Journal of Abnormal Psychology, 78,* 93–100.

Bowers, K. S., & van der Meulen, S. J. (1970). Effect of hypnotic susceptibility on creativity test performance. *Journal of Personality and Social Psychology, 14,* 247–256.

Brandt, R. (1981). On mathematically talented youth: A conversation with Julian Stanley. *Educational Leadership, 39*(2), 101–106.

Chambers, J. A. (1973). College teachers: Their effect on creativity of students. *Journal of Educational Psychology, 65,* 326–334.

Chauncey, H., & Hilton, T. L. (1983). Aptitude tests for the highly gifted. In R. S. Albert (Ed.), *Genius and eminence: The social psychology of creativity and exceptional achievement* (pp. 85–98). Elmsford, NY: Pergamon Press.

Cox, C. M. (1926). *The early mental traits of three hundred geniuses.* Stanford, CA: Stanford University Press.

Cropley, A. J. (1972). A five-year longitudinal study of the validity of creativity tests. *Developmental Psychology, 6,* 119–124.

Dansky, J. L. (1980). Make-believe: A mediator of the relationship between play and associative fluency. *Child Development, 51,* 576–579.

Dansky, J. L., & Silverman, I. W. (1973). Effects of play on associative fluency in preschool-aged children. *Developmental Psychology, 9,* 38–43.

Dansky, J. L., & Silverman, I. W. (1975). Play: A general facilitator of associative fluency. *Developmental Psychology, 11,* 104.

Dirkes, M. A. (1978). The role of divergent production in the learning process. *American Psychologist, 33,* 815–820.

Domino, G. (1974). Assessment of cinematographic creativity. *Journal of Personality and Social Psychology, 30,* 150–154.

Donmoyer, R. (1983). The principal as prime mover. *Daedalus, 112*(3), 81–94.

Durden, W. G. (1983). Lessons for excellence in education. *Daedalus, 112*(3), 95–111.

Educational Testing Service. (1983). *1982 annual report.* Princeton, NJ: Author.

Feldman, D. H. (1980). *Beyond universals in cognitive development.* Norwood, NJ: Ablex.

Feldman, D. H. (1982). A developmental framework for research with gifted children. In D. H. Feldman (Ed.), *New directions for child development: No. 17. Developmental approaches to giftedness and creativity* (pp. 31–45). San Francisco: Jossey-Bass.

Forman, S. G., & McKinney, J. D. (1978). Creativity and achievement of second graders in open and traditional classrooms. *Journal of Educational Psychology, 70,* 101–107.

Gardner, H. (1982). Giftedness: Speculations from a biological perspective. In D. H. Feldman (Ed.), *New directions for child development: No. 17. Developmental approaches to giftedness and creativity* (pp. 47–60). San Francisco: Jossey-Bass.

Gardner, H. (1983). *Frames of mind: The theory of multiple intelligences.* New York: Basic Books.

Getzels, J. W., & Csikszentmihalyi, M. (1976). *The creative vision: A longitudinal study of problem finding in art.* New York: Wiley.

Getzels, J. W., & Jackson, P. W. (1962). *Creativity and intelligence: Explorations with gifted students.* New York: Wiley.

Giaconia, R. M., & Hedges, L. V. (1982). Identifying features of effective open education. *Review of Educational Research, 52,* 579–602.

Glover, J., & Gary, A. L. (1976). Procedures to increase some aspects of creativity. *Journal of Applied Behavior Analysis, 9,* 79–84.

Gough, H. G. (1975). A new scientific uses test and its relationship to creativity in research. *Journal of Creative Behavior, 9,* 245–252.

Gowan, J. C. (1977). Background and history of the gifted-child movement. In J. C. Stanley, W. C. George, & C. H. Solano (Eds.), *The gifted and the creative: A fifty-year perspective* (pp. 5–27). Baltimore: Johns Hopkins University Press.

Guilford, J. P. (1956). The structure of intellect. *Psychological Bulletin, 53,* 267–293.

Guilford, J. P. (1975). Creativity: A quarter century of progress. In I. A. Taylor & J. W. Getzels (Eds.), *Perspectives in creativity* (pp. 37–59). Chicago: Aldine.

Guilford, J. P., & Christensen, P. R. (1973). The one-way relation between creative potential and IQ. *Journal of Creative Behavior, 7,* 247–252.

Harmon, L. R. (1963). The development of a criterion of scientific competence. In C. W. Taylor & F. Barron (Eds.), *Scientific creativity: Its recognition and development* (pp. 44–52). New York: Wiley.

Harrington, D. M., Block, J., & Block, J. H. (1983). Predicting creativity in preadolescence from divergent thinking in early childhood. *Journal of Personality and Social Psychology, 45,* 609–623.

Hattie, J. A. (1977). Conditions for administering creativity tests. *Psychological Bulletin, 84,* 1249–1260.

Hattie, J. A., (1980). Should creativity tests be administered under testlike conditions? An empirical study of three alternative conditions. *Journal of Educational Psychology, 72,* 87–98.

Helson, R. (1983). Creative mathematicians. In R. S. Albert (Ed.), *Genius and eminence: The social psychology of creativity and exceptional achievement* (pp. 311–330). Elmsford, NY: Pergamon Press.

Helson, R., & Crutchfield, R. S. (1970). Mathematicians: The creative researcher and the average PhD. *Journal of Consulting and Clinical Psychology, 34,* 250–257.

Hocevar, D. (1979a). Ideational fluency as a confounding factor in the measurement of originality. *Journal of Educational Psychology, 71,* 191–196.

Hocevar, D. (1979b). The unidimensional nature of creative thinking in fifth grade children. *Child Study Journal, 9,* 273–278.

Hocevar, D. (1980). Intelligence, divergent thinking, and creativity. *Intelligence, 4,* 25–40.

Hocevar, D. (1981). Measurement of creativity: Review and critique. *Journal of Personality Assessment, 45,* 450–464.

Holland, J. L., & Richards, J. M., Jr. (1965). Academic and nonacademic accomplishment: Correlated or uncorrelated? *Journal of Educational Psychology, 56,* 165–174.

Horwitz, R. A. (1979). Psychological effects of the "open classroom." *Review of Educational Research, 49,* 71–85.

Howieson, N. (1981). A longitudinal study of creativity: 1965–1975. *Journal of Creative Behavior, 15,* 117–134.

Jordan, L. A. (1975). Use of canonical analysis in Cropley's "A five-year longitudinal study of the validity of creativity tests." *Developmental Psychology, 11,* 1–3.

Keating, D. P. (1980). Four faces of creativity: The continuing plight of the intellectually underserved. *Gifted Child Quarterly, 24,* 56–61.

Keating, D. P. (1983). The creative potential of mathematically precocious boys. In R. S. Albert (Ed.), *Genius and eminence: The social psychology of creativity and exceptional achievement* (pp. 128–138). Elmsford, NY: Pergamon Press.

Kogan, N. (1983). Stylistic variation in childhood and adolescence: Creativity, metaphor, and cognitive styles. In J. H. Flavell & E. M. Markman (Eds.), *Handbook of child psychology: Vol. 3. Cognitive development* (4th ed., pp. 630–706). New York: Wiley.

Kogan, N., & Morgan, F. T. (1969). Task and motivational influences on the assessment of creative and intellective ability in children. *Genetic Psychology Monographs, 80,* 91–127.

Kogan, N., & Pankove, E. (1972). Creative ability over a five-year span. *Child Development, 43,* 427–442.

Kogan, N., & Pankove, E. (1974). Long-term predictive validity of divergent-thinking tests: Some negative evidence. *Journal of Educational Psychology, 66,* 802–810.

Lytton, H. (1972). *Creativity and education.* New York: Schocken.

MacKinnon, D. W. (1968). Selecting students with creative potential. In P. Heist (Ed.), *The creative college student: An unmet challenge* (pp. 101–116). San Francisco: Jossey-Bass.

MacKinnon, D. W. (1983). Creative architects. In R. S. Albert (Ed.), *Genius and eminence: The social psychology of creativity and exceptional achievement* (pp. 291–301). Elmsford, NY: Pergamon Press.

Maltzman, I., Simon, S., Raskin, D., & Licht, L. (1960). Experimental studies in the training of originality. *Psychological Monographs, 74*(6, Whole No. 493).

Mansfield, R. S., Busse, T. V., & Krepelka, E. J. (1978). The effectiveness of creativity training. *Review of Educational Research, 48,* 517–536.

Maxey, E. J., & Ormsby, V. J. (1971). *The accuracy of self-report information collected on the ACT test battery: High school grades and items of nonacademic achievement* (ACT Research Report No. 45). Iowa City, IA: American College Testing Program.

McClelland, D. C. (1973). Testing for competence rather than for "intelligence." *American Psychologist, 28,* 1–14.

Mednick, M. T. (1963). Research creativity in psychology graduate students. *Journal of Consulting Psychology, 27,* 265–266.

Michael, W. B. (1977). Cognitive and affective components of creativity in mathematics and the physical sciences. In J. C. Stanley, W. C. George, & C. H. Solano (Eds.), *The gifted and the creative: A fifty-year perspective* (pp. 141–172). Baltimore: Johns Hopkins University Press.

Milgram, R. M. (1983). Validation of ideational fluency measures of original thinking in children. *Journal of Educational Psychology, 75,* 619–624.

Milgram, R. M., & Arad, R. (1981). Ideational fluency as a predictor of original problem solving. *Journal of Educational Psychology, 73,* 568–572.

Milgram, R. M., & Feingold, S. (1977). Concrete and verbal reinforcement in creative thinking of disadvantaged children. *Perceptual and Motor Skills, 45,* 675–678.

Milgram, R. M., & Milgram, N. A. (1976). Creative thinking and creative performance in Israeli students. *Journal of Educational Psychology, 68,* 255–259.

Milgram, R. M., Milgram, N. A., Rosenbloom, G., & Rabkin, L. (1978). Quantity and quality of creative thinking in children and adolescents. *Child Development, 49,* 385–388.

Moran, J. D., III, Milgram, R. M., Sawyers, J. K., & Fu, V. R. (1983). Original thinking in preschool children. *Child Development, 54,* 921–926.

Morrison, J. (1963). The comparative effectiveness of intellective and non-intellective measures in the prediction of the completion of a major in theater arts. *Educational and Psychological Measurement, 23,* 827–830.

Munday, L. A., & Davis, J. C. (1974). *Varieties of accomplishment after college: Perspectives on the meaning of academic talent* (ACT Research Report No. 62). Iowa City, IA: American College Testing Program.

Nicholls, J. G. (1971). Some effects of testing procedure on divergent thinking. *Child Development, 42,* 1647–1651.

Noller, R. B., & Parnes, S. J. (1972). Applied creativity: The creative studies project. Part III: The curriculum. *Journal of Creative Behavior, 6,* 275–294.

Parloff, M. B., Datta, L., Kleman, M., & Handlon, J. H. (1968). Personality characteristics which differentiate creative male adolescents and adults. *Journal of Personality, 36,* 528–552.

Parnes, S. J., & Noller, R. B. (1972). Applied creativity: The creative studies project. Part II: Results of the two-year program. *Journal of Creative Behavior, 6,* 164–186.

Perkins, D. N. (1981). *The mind's best work.* Cambridge, MA: Harvard University Press.

Read, P. B. (1982). Foreword. In D. H. Feldman (Ed.), *New directions for child development: No. 17. Developmental approaches to giftedness and creativity* (pp. 1–4). San Francisco: Jossey-Bass.

Reese, H. W., & Parnes, S. J. (1970). Programming creative behavior. *Child Development, 41,* 413–423.

Reese, H. W., Parnes, S. J., Treffinger, D. J., & Kaltsounis, G. (1976). Effects of a creative studies program on structure-of-intellect factors. *Journal of Educational Psychology, 68,* 401–410.

Renzulli, J. S., & Smith, L. H. (1978). Developing defensible programs for the gifted and talented. *Journal of Creative Behavior, 12,* 21–29, 51.

Richards, J. M., Jr., Holland, J. L., & Lutz, S. W. (1967). Prediction of student accomplishment in college. *Journal of Educational Psychology, 58,* 343–355.

Richards, R. L. (1976). A comparison of selected Guilford and Wallach-Kogan creative thinking tests in conjunction with measures of intelligence. *Journal of Creative Behavior, 10,* 151–164.

Rimm, S., & Davis, G. A. (1980). Five years of international research with GIFT: An instrument for the identification of creativity. *Journal of Creative Behavior, 14,* 35–46.

Segal, S. M., Busse, T. V., & Mansfield, R. S. (1980). The relationship of scientific creativity in the biological sciences to predoctoral accomplishments and experiences. *American Educational Research Journal, 17,* 491–502.

Sherwood, D. W. (1969). The differential effects of assessment context and scoring method on creativity performance in children (Doctoral dissertation, Duke University, 1969). *Dissertation Abstracts International, 30,* 1888B.

Simonton, D. K. (1977). Eminence, creativity, and geographic marginality: A recursive structural equation model. *Journal of Personality and Social Psychology, 35,* 805–816.

Singer, D. L., & Whiton, M. B. (1971). Ideational creativity and expressive aspects of human figure drawing in kindergarten-age children. *Developmental Psychology, 4,* 366–369.

Solano, C. H., & George, W. C. (1976). College courses and educational facilitation of the gifted. *Gifted Child Quarterly, 20,* 274–285.

Solomon, D., & Kendall, A. J. (1976). Individual characteristics and children's performance in "open" and "traditional" classroom settings. *Journal of Educational Psychology, 68,* 613–625.

Stanley, J. C. (1977). Rationale of the study of mathematically precocious youth (SMPY) during its first five years of promoting educational acceleration. In J. C. Stanley, W. C. George, & C. H. Solano (Eds.), *The gifted and the creative: A fifty-year perspective* (pp. 75–112). Baltimore: Johns Hopkins University Press.

Stanley, J. C., & George, W. C. (1980). SMPY's ever-increasing D_4. *Gifted Child Quarterly, 24,* 41–48.

Sternberg, R. J., & Davidson, J. E. (1983). Insight in the gifted. *Educational Psychologist, 18,* 51–57.

Taft, R., & Gilchrist, M. B. (1970). Creative attitudes and creative productivity: A comparison of two aspects of creativity among students. *Journal of Educational Psychology, 61,* 136–143.

Taylor, C. W., (1978). How many types of giftedness can your program tolerate? *Journal of Creative Behavior, 12,* 39–51.

Taylor, C. W., & Ellison, R. L. (1975). Moving toward working models in creativity: Utah creativity experiences and insights. In I. A. Taylor & J. W. Getzels (Eds.), *Perspectives in creativity* (pp. 191–223). Chicago: Aldine.

Terman, L. M., & Oden, M. H. (1947). *Genetic studies of genius: Vol. 4. The gifted child grows up: Twenty-five years' follow-up of a superior group.* Stanford, CA: Stanford University Press.

Thomas, N. G., & Berk, L. E. (1981). Effects of school environments on the development of young children's creativity. *Child Development, 52,* 1153–1162.

Torrance, E. P. (1963). *Education and the creative potential.* Minneapolis: University of Minnesota Press.

Torrance, E. P. (1972). Can we teach children to think creatively? *Journal of Creative Behavior, 6,* 114–143.

Torrance, E. P. (1975). Creativity research in education: Still alive. In I. A. Taylor & J. W. Getzels (Eds.), *Perspectives in creativity* (pp. 278–296). Chicago: Aldine.

Treffinger, D. J. (1980). The progress and peril of identifying creative talent among gifted and talented students. *Journal of Creative Behavior, 14,* 20–34.

Wagner, R. K., & Sternberg, R. J. (1984). Alternative conceptions of intelligence and their implications for education. *Review of Educational Research, 54,* 179–223.

Walberg, H. J. (1971). Varieties of adolescent creativity and the high school environment. *Exceptional Children, 38,* 111–116.

Walberg, H. J. (1983). Scientific literacy and economic productivity in international perspective. *Daedalus, 112*(2), 1–28.

Walberg, H. J., Rasher, S. P., & Parkerson, J. (1979). Childhood and eminence. *Journal of Creative Behavior, 13,* 225–231.

Walberg, H. J., Tsai, S. L., Weinstein, T., Gabriel, C. L., Rasher, S. P., Rosecrans, T., Rovai, E., Ide, J., Trujillo, M., & Vukosavich, P. (1981). Childhood traits and environmental conditions of highly eminent adults. *Gifted Child Quarterly, 25,* 103–107.

Wallach, M. A. (1970). Creativity. In P. H. Mussen (Ed.), *Carmichael's manual of child psychology, Vol. 1* (3rd ed., pp. 1211–1272). New York: Wiley.

Wallach, M. A. (1971). *The intelligence/creativity distinction.* Morristown, NJ: General Learning Press.

Wallach, M. A. (1976a). Psychology of talent and graduate education. In S. Messick & Associates (Eds.), *Individuality in learning: Implications of cognitive styles and creativity for human development* (pp. 178–210). San Francisco: Jossey-Bass.

Wallach, M. A. (1976b). Tests tell us little about talent. *American Scientist, 64,* 57–63.

Wallach, M. A. (1983a). Creativity and talent. In *Documentary report of the Ann Arbor symposium on the applications of psychology to the teaching and learning of music: Session 3. Motivation and creativity* (pp. 23–29). Reston, VA: Music Educators National Conference.

Wallach, M. A. (1983b). [Review of *Personal qualities and college admissions*]. *American Journal of Education, 91,* 279–282.

Wallach, M. A., & Kogan, N. (1965). *Modes of thinking in young children: A study of the creativity-intelligence distinction.* New York: Holt, Rinehart & Winston.

Wallach, M. A., & Wing, C. W., Jr. (1969). *The talented student: A validation of the creativity-intelligence distinction.* New York: Holt, Rinehart & Winston.

Wallbrown, F. H., & Huelsman, C. B., Jr. (1975). The validity of the Wallach-Kogan creativity operations for inner-city children in two areas of visual art. *Journal of Personality, 43,* 109–126.

Ward, W. C. (1969). Rate and uniqueness in children's creative responding. *Child Development, 40,* 869–878.

Whitmore, J. R. (1981). Gifted children with handicapping conditions: A new frontier. *Exceptional Children, 48,* 106–114.

Williams, T. M., & Fleming, J. W. (1969). Methodological study of the relationship between associative fluency and intelligence. *Developmental Psychology, 1,* 155–162.

Willingham, W. W., & Breland, H. M. (1982). *Personal qualities and college admissions.* New York: College Entrance Examination Board.

Wing, C. W., Jr., & Wallach, M. A. (1971). *College admissions and the psychology of talent.* New York: Holt, Rinehart & Winston.

Yeatts, E. H. (1980). The professional artist: A teacher for the gifted. *Gifted Child Quarterly, 24,* 133–137.

Ziv, A. (1976). Facilitating effects of humor on creativity. *Journal of Educational Psychology, 68,* 318–322.

Zuckerman, H. (1983). The scientific elite: Nobel laureates' mutual influences. In R. S. Albert (Ed.), *Genius and eminence: The social psychology of creativity and exceptional achievement* (pp. 241–252). Elmsford, NY: Pergamon Press.

5. A Cultural Perspective on the Development of Talent

Jayanthi Mistry
Barbara Rogoff
University of Utah

A cultural perspective on talent focuses on how talents develop and are situated in broader sociocultural contexts that encourage specific talents. The term *gifted* is often used synonymously with the term *talented*, but to be consistent with the theme of this chapter we use the term *talented* to avoid evoking connotations of the term *gifted*. We wish to avoid connotations deriving from the psychometric tradition that equate giftedness with high IQ (Feldman, 1982) and assume that it reflects a stable, trait-like characteristic that can be measured and used to predict performance in other situations. *Talent* implies more domain-specific skills and allows for the possibility of a variety of talents (see Tannenbaum, 1983, for discussion of uses of the terms gifted and talented). In this chapter we take the perspective that individual talents develop in domains of practice encouraged by sociocultural contexts varying in what skills are valued and hence fostered and honored. We stress the relationship that exists between the development of specific talents and the sociocultural experience of the individual, and we argue that the assumption of context-free generality in skills is misleading.

A cultural perspective on talent emphasizes different questions and concerns than does most of the research on giftedness among various cultural groups. Research on giftedness has typically dealt with problems of identifying the gifted in different cultural groups (especially among minority groups in the United States) and has therefore grappled with issues such as the cultural bias of intelligence tests. There is often an implicit assumption of a hidden underlying ability or potential, the problem being how to identify and assess it. By contrast, we argue that cultural influences on talent derive from the skills and abilities that are valued or adaptive for functioning in a particular culture. The individual development of specific talents occurs within cultural contexts in which the value of particular talents is stressed and their selective development is arranged for.

In this chapter we present an overview of cross-cultural research on talent, differentiating between two approaches, each with its own set of major questions. First we present research in which psychometric methods are used to assess giftedness and in which the focus is on identifying hidden general skills. This is followed by a discussion, based on cross-cultural research, in which we question the assumption that it is possible under ideal circumstances to attribute underlying capacities to people's performance on tests without concern for the context of that performance. (By context we mean any physical or social feature of an activity that channels behavior.) We then present a culturally based approach to developing talent, including a discussion of research on cultural conceptions of talent and intelligence and of research on the role of sociocultural experience in the development of talent.

Psychometric Testing of Giftedness

Psychometric work on giftedness in different cultural groups has been focused on either of two questions. How can children with promise (i.e., hidden potential) in ethnic and lower social class groups or in less developed countries be identified in order to nurture their potential? What characteristics differentiate gifted from nongifted children? We briefly review the findings of these two lines of research to orient the reader to what has been learned from applying the psychometric approach to different cultural groups. Then we argue that application of Western tests in other cultures may overlook the skills that are valued and nurtured in different cultural groups. Although Western tests may be well suited

Preparation of this chapter was supported in part by PHS National Research Service Award 5-T32-MH 15747 from the National Institute of Mental Health. We are grateful to Judy Skeen for her comments on a previous draft of this chapter.

for analyzing academic and technical skills valued in Western settings, they do not necessarily represent universally valued skills or formats in all cultures. Indeed, to develop a cultural perspective on talent, it may be valuable to examine (rather than to control for) the rich variation found across cultures.

Identifying Individuals Who Have Hidden Potential

In efforts to overcome the bias against disadvantaged groups in traditional psychometric screening methods, some researchers have searched for hidden traces of giftedness among the disadvantaged by modifying testing instruments and procedures to identify hidden talent. Bruch (1971) isolated items from the Stanford-Binet on which Black elementary schoolchildren performed well to develop an abbreviated form of the Stanford-Binet assessing only those abilities on which Blacks proved proficient (e.g., problem-solving skills with visual and auditory content, memory operations, and convergent production). In an attempt to assess the potential of underprivileged groups (in this case, retarded performers), Feuerstein (1979) rejected conventional methods of testing ability as static measures. Instead, Feuerstein assessed the modifiability of an individual's functioning by measuring how much better a child can perform on tasks assessing general intelligence after being given instructions to solve such problems.

Rather than modifying conventional tests and procedures for assessing giftedness, some researchers have advocated obtaining information from a wide range of nontraditional sources to evaluate hidden potential (Bernal, 1980; Draper, 1980; Frasier, 1979; Torrance, 1978). Mercer and Lewis (1977) discussed the System of Multicultural Pluralistic Assessment, which, in addition to being used to measure intellectual and perceptual-visual skills, is used to obtain information from parents about a child's performance of social roles and sociocultural, health, and economic characteristics of the family. Similarly, Kranz (1978) favored identifying talented minority children by obtaining information from teachers and parents and by having a local screening committee (consisting of the teacher of the gifted program, counselor, librarian, and principal) evaluate the information. The committee would rate talents associated with the child's cultural heritage, such as abilities in visual and performing arts, creative thinking, leadership, and academic ability in specific disciplines, as well as general intellectual ability. Many other methods for identifying gifted children among culturally different groups have been suggested. In most cases it is advocated that initial identification be based on characteristics such as ability to learn quickly, leadership, alertness, or curiosity (Holle, 1980) or be based on tests of creativity, high motivation, or talent in visual and performing arts (Torrance, 1977, 1978).

Attempts to identify gifted children in other countries are also based on the goal of identifying potential that can then be nurtured and fulfilled in later adult performance. Hidden potential is seen as a national resource (Gibson & Chennells, 1976; Lowenstein, 1979; Milgram, 1980) that educational programs should identify and nurture. The exchange of information among nations regarding the education of gifted individuals and the nurturance of giftedness has been stimulated by World Conferences on the Gifted and Talented, first held in 1975 (Brickman, 1979; Gibson & Chennells, 1976; Gold, 1982). Educators and government representatives from 24 countries summarized their governments' policies and programs for the gifted in the proceedings of the first World Conference (Gibson & Chennells, 1976). A few detailed descriptions of programs in other countries focusing on the gifted among the disadvantaged are also available (e.g., Smilansky & Nevo, 1979).

Comparing the Gifted From Different Backgrounds

Ethnicity is assumed to affect the pattern of mental abilities, as is suggested by the diverse cognitive strengths that have been identified among American Blacks (e.g., skills in solving problems with visual and auditory content [Bruch, 1971]) or among Mexican Americans (Bernal, 1974). Similarly, a number of cultural groups (Black, Jewish, Chinese, and Puerto Rican) have been found to have distinct performance profiles on verbal ability, reasoning, number, and spatial ability tests, suggesting that different emphases on intellectual functions are cultivated by different groups (Lesser, Fifer, & Clark, 1965).

Researchers of gifted children have also attempted to describe the intellectual and nonintellectual characteristics that differentiate gifted from nongifted children. In terms of personality characteristics, gifted minority children seem to resemble gifted mainstream children. High-achieving Black children living in poverty had personality characteristics that resembled those of high-achieving children from mainstream backgrounds, suggesting that perhaps the way to succeed in the dominant culture is to adopt its success-oriented values and behaviors (Davidson, Greenberg, & Gerver, 1962). Similarly, gifted Asian American children have been described as possessing characteristics such as initiative, enthusiasm, industry, reliability, and regularity in school attendance. When compared with gifted non-Asians, they were even better at getting along with others, especially adults, and were found to be more diligent and industrious (Chen & Goon, 1976).

Gifted children have been found to be superior on social adjustment scales (assessed through standard personality inventories) when compared with nongifted children of the same cultural group. Gifted children in Israel appear to differ from nongifted Israeli children in terms of having a more positive self-concept, internal locus of control, culturally appropriate sex role identity, and less anxiety (Milgram, 1980). Similarly, Taiwanese gifted children have been found to be superior to average

Taiwanese children on self-concept, creativity, and cognitive development, and to have a wider range of interests (Liu, 1982).

In summary, the main concerns within the psychometric approach have been identifying the gifted in different cultural groups and describing their intellectual and nonintellectual characteristics. We now discuss concerns with the validity of using Western tests in research on giftedness among non-Western groups.

Concerns About the Validity of Tests for Giftedness

Many investigators, especially those advising the use of multiple criteria for identifying the gifted, express concerns with the appropriateness of IQ-based assessments to identify gifted children among different cultural groups. This concern is consistent with evidence that testing situations for non-Western cultural groups represent an unusual social and intellectual setting (Rogoff, 1981). Cross-cultural researchers who have supplemented their tests of performance with ethnographic observations have been struck by the fact that people who have difficulty with a particular task in a test may use the skill of interest spontaneously in their everyday activities (Cole, Hood, & McDermott, 1978; Laboratory of Comparative Human Cognition, 1979; Rogoff, 1982; Rogoff, Gauvain, & Ellis, 1984). For example, Micronesian navigators who show extraordinary skills in memory, inference, and calculation in sailing from island to island perform poorly on standard tests of intellectual functioning (Gladwin, 1970). Similarly, people who have difficulty with logical syllogisms in a test situation often can be observed using elegant reasoning in other situations, such as giving hypothetical arguments for not answering logical reasoning problems (Scribner, 1976).

Furthermore, test performance is integrally linked to familiarity of materials and the meaningfulness of the goal of the task. Nonliterate Liberian adults are more successful in classifying bowls of rice than in classifying geometric stimuli differing in color, shape, and number (Irwin & McLaughlin, 1970). American undergraduates respond to requests to sort bowls of rice with the same hesitance and bewilderment shown by Liberian nonliterates who are asked to sort cards decorated with squares and triangles (Irwin, Schafer, & Feiden, 1974), and both groups sort in a manner considered less advanced when tested with unfamiliar materials. It should be noted that familiarity of materials and tasks is intimately related to the organized practices (e.g., major economic activities) of a particular culture.

Such cross-cultural observations of the variability of people's performance in contexts differing in familiarity call into question the practice of interpreting test scores as reflecting a general ability or trait. Tyron (1979) referred to this as the test-trait fallacy. Instead of treating test scores as being indicative of performance or as predicting future performance in the activities observed, people assume that test scores provide measures of stable underlying characteristics of the person that are called traits or abilities. Similarly, Tannenbaum (1983) emphasized the futility of a "quest for traits that are supposed to typify all gifted children" (p. 74) and instead urged that an interest be taken in examining and understanding children's special talents in worthwhile activities.

Another problem with the testing approach is that mainstream Western values and criteria are used to judge talent in other cultural groups. Although multiple selection criteria for identifying talent may provide a partial solution to overcoming the cultural bias of IQ tests, the issue regarding what talent is being tested for remains. In attempts to identify the talented in minority and other cultural groups it is assumed that the gifted will compete well with others in the mainstream culture if only they can be identified through multiple selection criteria and sensitive assessment and if the obstacle of poor environment can be overcome. For example, in a program directed toward gifted children and adolescents from disadvantaged backgrounds in Israel, sensitive measures and procedures are used to identify talent, but the skills that are identified and encouraged are those of the mainstream culture (Smilansky & Nevo, 1979). This program selects children on the basis of educational criteria, social reports, tests, and personal interviews as well as interviews with school and welfare officials. The children participate in a residential school program aimed at taking them out of their disadvantaged setting and then providing academic training. The program claims success based on the fact that the children reach high levels of academic and vocational achievement in the mainstream society.

Criticisms of the testing tradition have at times been countered by the claim that it is the social system rather than the testing instrument that is prejudiced against ethnic and lower social class minorities. Tannenbaum (1983) contended that despite the awareness that multiple talents exist, there has been a preoccupation with academic skills, illustrating the point by arguing that in the post-Sputnik period, the need for technical skills resulted in a national talent hunt for those with science and academic skills but not for those with talent in art or social leadership. Later, when concerns with social justice and egalitarianism in education shifted the focus onto the underprivileged, there was much criticism of using IQ tests for identifying the gifted. In practice, however, intelligence tests continue to be used as the basis for identifying individuals with potential among minority cultural groups (Alvino, McDonnel, & Richert, 1981).

Some educators have been sensitive to the possibility of an implicit application of mainstream Western values even when using multiple selection criteria to identify gifted minority children. For example, Bernal (1979) cautioned against letting programs for gifted minorities become "acculturation" programs, that is, compensatory programs to make the minority gifted student become more like the mainstream gifted student. Others, however, have argued that gifted individuals' contributions to society will be made in terms of the strengths valued by the mainstream culture and hence that identifying skills valued by the mainstream must be emphasized along with culturally valued skills (Witty, 1978). Since technical intelligence is valued in the Western ethnopsychology of intelligence (Lutz & LeVine, 1982), IQ-based criteria for identifying talent may be appropriate within Western cultures. However, other skills and talents that are valued and necessary for functioning in various cultural groups are also ideals against which talent should be assessed and fostered in these cultures.

A Cultural Perspective on Talent

To develop a cultural perspective on talent, we used a distinction offered by the Laboratory of Comparative Human Cognition (1983) that contrasts a model of task- and culture-specific cognitive processing with a model of general intellectual ability. The latter model assumes that experience operates in a general way on central cognitive machinery that in turn guides performance on any task that an individual encounters. This model thus represents a view of development that assumes that personality, behavioral propensities, and abilities are general. In contrast, the model of task and culture-specific processing assumes that an individual develops skills in particular tasks through experience in related activities. Thus, experience in a variety of similar events (usually in culturally central domains of activity or experience) builds skills that are specifically groomed in practiced activities and are applied in related tasks. The cultural perspective on the development of talent that we discuss in this section is based on a task-specific and culture-specific model of cognitive processing. The focus is on how talents develop within a domain and within the context of a specific culture.

The notion of domain-specific cognitive functioning has recently received support from cognitive psychologists who have argued against the unitary nature of cognition (Gardner, 1983) or against general cognitive stages. Children who are highly talented in specific domains such as chess, mathematics, or music perform much like other bright children of their age on both IQ tests and Piagetian tasks (Feldman, 1982). Similarly,

Gardner (1982) hypothesized the existence of relatively independent domains of knowledge or intellect, claiming that

> All normal individuals possess some potential for developing each of the intellectual competences, but individuals differ from one another in the extent to which they can and will realize each competence, even as their cultures and subcultures differ in the extent to which they value disparate intellectual competences. (p. 51)

Gardner further argues that there is flexibility for growth in any domain, and, since humans are particularly flexible organisms, it is important to determine the various ways in which a skill may be expressed, as well as the role of the environmental context in this process. For example, visual intelligence will be exploited in different ways by an engineer, an artist, or a surgeon in a technological society, and in yet different ways by a weaver or an aboriginal tracker in a nontechnological society.

In the remainder of this chapter we elaborate on the connection between culture and talent by addressing these two issues: (a) how variation between cultures in values and belief systems determines what skills are honored and nurtured and (b) how particular talents develop through experience in culturally central domains of activity and in culturally organized learning experiences.

Relation Between Cultural Belief Systems and Valued Skills

Sociocultural values, attitudes, and practices are reflected in indigenous concepts of intelligence. The skills promoted in different cultures fit with diverse cultural ideals of intelligent behavior. Indigenous concepts of intelligence vary widely across cultures, with some behaviors valued at opposite extremes. For example, Ugandan villagers associate intelligence with adjectives such as slow, careful, and active, whereas Ugandan teachers and Westernized groups associate it with speed (Wober, 1972). Such value differences are relevant to performance on tests that often involve an element of speed.

Goodnow (1976) characterized the view of intelligence used to judge performance on cognitive tests in terms of (a) focusing on the task independent of the social context and (b) working for speed, efficiency of moves, unambiguous responses, and mental rather than physical solutions to problems. Similarly, the American ethnopsychology of intelligence values the separation of form from content (i.e., abstract formalism), a technical intelligence separate from social and emotional skills (Lutz & LeVine, 1982). The American view contrasts with the Ugandan view that casts intelligence as knowing how to do and doing the socially appropriate thing. The Ifaluk of the Western Pacific similarly regard intelligence as not only having the knowledge of good social behavior, but also performing it (Lutz & LeVine, 1982). Australian students rate academic skills more highly than do Malay students and stress ability to adapt to new events. Malay students, on the other hand, value social and practical skills, along with speed and creativity (Gill & Keats, 1980). Although Australian and Chinese students are similar in their ratings of the relevance to intelligence of items from Western tests such as the WISC, they differ in judging the difficulty and importance of items. Chinese students reported that having memory for facts is both easy and important, perhaps because memory skills remain important in the heritage of traditional agriculture; the Australians regarded having memory skills as trivial (Chen, Braithwaite, & Huang, 1982).

Although being aware of the differences among definitions of intelligence can sensitize people to the fact that different behaviors may be valued and defined as intelligent by different cultural groups, it is also important to determine the criteria by which people actually evaluate the behavior of other people (Goodnow, 1984; Serpell, 1982). Goodnow (1984) advocates a shift from regarding intelligence as a quality people possess in varying degrees to regarding it as a judgment made by others when observing people's display of intelligent behaviors. Such a shift highlights the role of value judgments by individuals and by cultural groups in defining intelligence and focuses attention on the specific skills (signs of intelligence) on which these judgments are based.

A few researchers have examined how indigenous concepts of intelligence relate to actual cognitive performance. Nonliterate villagers in Botswana have highly differentiated notions of intelligence or shrewdness that adults use in rating children's intelligence. Ratings made by adults accurately predict how well children recall stories, just as grade point average is found to predict academic performance in the United States (Dube, 1982). Similarly, behavioral descriptors used by Mexican American barrio residents to characterize giftedness are useful in discriminating gifted Chicano children from their average peers (Bernal, 1974). Guatemalan preschool-age children's performance on cognitive tests (embedded figures, analogies, memory for design) is congruent with ratings of their "listura" (smartness) by local adults (Klein, Freeman, Spring, Nerlove, & Yarborough, 1976). The adults regarded children who were "listo" as independent and having verbal facility, good memory, alertness, and a high level of physical activity. Klein et al. also replicated the evidence of a relation between adults' conceptions of intelligence and cognitive test performance with a New Jersey sample.

There is conflicting evidence regarding whether performance on tests can be predicted on the basis of children's everyday activities. In one study it was found that rankings made by adults of Guatemalan children's performance of everyday activities was related to how children ranked on cognitive tests (Nerlove, Roberts, Klein, Yarborough,

& Habicht, 1974). However, in another study no correlation was found between Guatemalan children's activities and memory test performance (Rogoff, 1978).

Some of the studies that relate indigenous conceptions of intelligence to performance on adapted Western tests are limited in that informants are not asked to specify the behavioral criteria by which they assessed the children. Experimental instructions may have predisposed informants to assess children on the same dimensions of behavior emphasized by a Western definition of intelligence, which result in findings suggesting that native adults' ratings correspond with Western definitions of intelligence (Serpell, 1982). To avoid this bias, Serpell (1977, 1982) determined which dimensions of behavior are valued in an African community by identifying local situations in which adults would normally assess children's behavior and by asking adults which of a group of children they would call on for help in each situation and why. Capability in specific situations and social responsibility (i.e., cooperativeness and obedience) formed interdependent components of what was valued as intelligence.

Similarly, Kipsigis (Kenyan) parents value a quality (*ng'om*) in their children that is essential to responsible participation in family and social life (Super & Harkness, 1983). The word *ng'om* is universally translated as intelligence by bilinguals, but the word also has connotations of responsibility and obedience. Similarly, the Baoule' of the Ivory Coast also have a term (*n'gloue'le'*) that integrates cognitive as well as social attributes of intelligence (Dasen, 1984). Thus, intelligence implies social and emotional skills as well as cognitive skills in some cultures, and these components of intelligence are also valued and used by people in judging behavior.

Relation Between Culturally Central Domains of Experience and Talents

Research has demonstrated that a connection exists between cultural learning situations and the development of particular talents. The cultural context of learning includes both an institutional level and an interpersonal level (Vygotsky, 1978). At the institutional level, the culture provides organizations, tools, and practices useful to the development of skills facilitating socially appropriate solutions to problems (through institutions such as school and inventions such as literacy). Operating along with such institutional practices is the immediate social interactional context of learning and using skills. Social interaction provides a structure for the development of individual skills, especially as information regarding tools and practices is transmitted through interaction with more experienced members of society. Particular skills are transmitted through cultural patterns of interpersonal relations, which, in turn, are

organized by institutional conventions and by the availability of particular cultural tools.

An emphasis on the cultural context of development may appear to
focus only on the culture's role in individual development, as if each
culture produces certain child-types "like a cookie cutter producing many
gingerbread boys and girls" (Wartofsky, 1983, p. 198). However, a cultural
perspective strives to keep both sides of the dialectic process between
culture and individual development in view, by emphasizing that individuals constitute and produce the culture in which their development
is embedded. The individual child is active in selecting and constructing
relevant features of the environment. Wartofsky (1983) elaborates the
idea, arguing that:

> The child is *not* a self-contained homunculus, radiating outward in
> development from some fixed configuration of traits, dispositions, or
> preformed potencies; and . . . the world, in turn, is not some eternal
> and objective network of causal factors converging on the neonate to
> shape an unresisting, passive blob to its external, pregiven structures.
> To put this positively: the child is an agent in its own *and* the world's
> construction, but one whose agency develops in the context of an
> ineluctably social and historical praxis, which includes both the con-
> straints and potentialities of nature and the actions of other agents.
> Nurture, in short, is both given *and* taken; so is Nature. (p. 188)

In the following sections we examine the role of institutional and
cultural practices that lead to differences between groups in the skills
and talents that are fostered. Then, at the individual level, we raise
questions regarding how social interaction channels individual development.

The Role of Institutional and Cultural Practices

A cultural perspective on talent assumes that experience in culturally
central domains of activity builds skills in those specific domains. Thus,
the talents that are likely to be found in specific cultures will be related
to domains of activity valued and practiced in those cultures. Different
cultural groups may foster various cognitive skills that are adaptive to
the particular environment (Guilmet, 1975; Kleinfeld, 1973) or develop
in the context of culturally central domains of activity. For example, the
ecological demands made by the arctic environment and arctic hunting
may foster a high level of figural abilities among Eskimos (Kleinfeld,
1973) because of the need to be extremely sensitive to visual detail (e.g.,
detecting cracks in the ice or attending to the angle and shape of the
snow to find the way home). Eskimo children and adults score better than
Western groups on tests of figural detail, figural memory, and spatial
abilities when schooling and familiarity with Western institutions are
equalized (Kleinfeld, 1973). Similarly, nonliterate Australian aborigines

are reported to have exceptional spatial skills, which they use in calculating scores in a traditional indigenous card game as well as in other culturally relevant cognitive activities such as expert orienteering (Davidson, 1979). Posner (cited in Ginsburg, 1978) found impressive computation skills among nonschooled children in a cultural group that emphasizes numerical concepts in economic activities, compared with the performance of children in a neighboring nonmerchant cultural group.

Memory skills also vary in their adaptiveness and value in cultures in which different occupational or institutional demands are made on people's memory. African youths show better story recall than do American subjects, possibly because in African cultures storytelling is encouraged, whereas in American society stories may be read or watched on television but may not often be told (Dube, 1982). Other examples of skills promoted in some cultures include the extraordinary skills in memory and inference demonstrated by seafaring Polynesian navigators (Gladwin, 1970) and memory feats performed by singers of epic poetry (Lord, 1965); by African oral historians (Griots), who preserve essential records of history and line of descent (D'Azevedo, 1982); and by Iatmul (New Guinea) elders, whose phenomenal memory for totemic knowledge is required to resolve conflicts between clans over claims to property (Bateson, 1982).

Skills in rapid mental calculation are prevalent in Japan and China, where children are trained in the use of the abacus from an early age and many national contests encourage development of this valued skill. Abacus experts, in fact, calculate by means of a mentally visualized image of the abacus, mentally manipulating it as they would an actual abacus. Their internalization and use of this culturally specific tool leads to more rapid calculations in the absence of the actual abacus (Stigler, Barclay, & Aiello, 1982).

Another example of how cultural values and life-style foster specific skills is provided by a study of a nomadic tribe of magicians and performers, the Qalandar of Pakistan (Berland, 1982). The Qalandar value keen observational skills and the ability to make fine discriminations in contexts such as food sharing, which may be vital for individual or group survival. They also value the ability to disregard unimportant information (*Rokna*) while focusing on the essential demands of each context or task. *Rokna* is a vital skill for the talented and successful magician, who must mislead others by focusing their attention on nonessential features of perceptual displays. When compared with sedentary groups on tests of perceptual disembedding, more Qalandar performed in a manner indicating sensitivity to distinctions between perceived and actual properties of stimuli, perhaps reflecting the significance of this culturally valued ability to focus on important information and disregard nonessential cues.

Although some of these skills may be perfected by only some individuals in these cultures, the fact that these skills are valued in some cultures but not in others supports the point that variation in intellectual skills is to be expected in different contexts. Individual differences within cultures are also to be expected and are likely to result from differences in the specific developmental environments of individuals as well as from genetic differences within the population.

Social Guidance of the Development of Talent

In the preceding section we discussed how the intellectual strengths of various cultural groups are related to culturally central domains of experience or activity. At a different level of analysis we may ask how interactions among people and experience in learning situations structure the development of talents within specific domains. Gardner (1982) stressed the social environment's critical role in giving the individual the will and purpose to develop his or her talents. In a similar vein, Feldman (1982) suggested the need to identify (a) the role of specific environmental experiences such as with teachers, peers, educational materials, and technology in the development of talent; (b) the match between environment and a highly pretuned talent; and (c) the importance of historical and cultural forces in the recognition and development of talent. As an example of the significance of sociohistorical forces and the match between environment and a highly pretuned talent, Feldman (1982) raised the question of whether Einstein's talent and contribution would have been possible if he had been raised as a Buddhist monk, or if Gandhi's leadership and contribution to a country's struggle for freedom would have been possible if he had been raised on a farm in Kansas.

The development of talents through careful and intense nurturing is evident in studies of the environmental circumstances of individuals who have been identified as talented. Gardner (1981) argued that the Indian mathematician Ramanujan was unable to make new contributions to formal mathematics in spite of his talent because he was introduced to the field too late and thus did not benefit from the influence of teachers and exposure to the field. Long periods of training under favorable circumstances has been cited as being essential for the talent and achievement of Olympic swimmers, pianists, and mathematicians in America who attained world class status in their fields before the age of 35 (Bloom, 1982). Bloom claimed that whatever the individuals' special abilities or skills, without favorable and supportive training and circumstances, they would not have been likely to reach high levels of attainment. Similarly, eminent men born between the fourteenth and the twentieth centuries were usually stimulated by the availability of cultural materials and education related to their fields of eminence—at least 60 percent of them were exposed to eminent persons in their fields during childhood (Walberg et al., 1981). By contrast, there also have been individuals like Sequoya, the Cherokee Indian leader, who labored against the obstacles of no formal schooling or assistance and isolation from his family and community, to invent a marvelously simple and logical syllabary for his people, apparently sustained by his earnest desire to serve his nation (Carpenter, 1976). The idea was sparked, however, by his observation that white explorers were able to transmit messages using marks on paper.

Cultures provide their members with structured training or supports for developing skills. For example, the culturally organized artistic environment in which Balinese children grow up supports budding artists or musicians by providing short cuts for learning (Belo, 1955; McPhee, 1955). Ready-made symbolism provides children with a means for handling rich fantasy and ideas in spite of a lack of skill in drawing techniques or styles (Belo, 1955). Children use the artistic forms of heroes and demonic figures from culturally familiar shadow plays to solve their representation problem, giving their fantasies form through these ready-made symbols. The fact that Balinese children's drawings were judged superior to the work of American and European children in an international exhibition supports the idea that the culture's artistic tradition of using conventional symbols may help child artists to overcome obstacles in drawing that might have occurred had they been required to find a symbolic language of their own (Belo, 1955).

The notion that extraordinary skills can be nurtured is also supported by studies of mathematical ability and expert memory skills. Ericsson, Chase, and Faloon (1980) trained a subject with no special memory abilities to increase his digit span from the usual 7 ± 2 digits to 76 or 80 digits. Over 250 hours of practice with an appropriate mnemonic system and retrieval structure enabled the subject to acquire the skill. An extreme emphasis on intellectual attainment and literary analysis in Eastern European Jewish communities involved the children from age 3 in serious study of the scriptures in special schools. Children who were precocious in this learning were treated with great respect by all and were encouraged to devote themselves to this service to the community at community expense (Zborowski & Herzog, 1952). African parents actively encourage their infants to learn certain skills (sitting, walking) and discourage others (crawling). The parents arrange explicit learning situations for the valued skills, and their infants prove to be precocious in these, but not in the less valued skills, (Kilbride, 1980; Super, 1981). Based on the premise that talent is not inborn and that every child acquires skill through experience and repetition, Suzuki (1969) advocated early intensive music training, and described an educational movement called the Talent Education Method in which children struggling to get along in school are trained to become talented in a specific domain, in this case music.

Thus, a cultural perspective on talent views individual development within cultural context. Cultural values, belief systems, and practices are seen as integrally related to what skills are honored and hence nurtured. Furthermore, the notion that individual functioning is derived from cultural activity or practice suggests that the particular culturally guided learning experiences are crucial for understanding the development of an individual's talents.

Conclusions and Future Directions

We have argued that culturally organized practices and activities determine what skills and talents are valued and adaptive for functioning in a particular cultural group. This is supported by evidence of cultural differences in valued skills and talents, related to culturally central domains of activities. A first step in this direction is made by work emphasizing the role of social guidance at the individual level (e.g., Bloom, 1982; Feldman, 1982; Gardner, 1981). Future research should also focus on how talents develop within domains of expertise and within the context of a specific culture. We need a clearer conceptualization of how a novice (child or adult) gains expertise in a particular domain and learns to use the socially provided tools and techniques through which the individual learns the skill regarded as desirable in that context.

Such specific conceptualization and delineation of the process of talent development could follow the lead offered by the context-specific model of cognitive development (Laboratory of Comparative Human Cognition, 1983). Beginning with identification of skills and talents valued within a culture, an investigator identifies domains of activity and situations that foster these, examining how people learn the necessary skills within that context and how individuals transfer those skills to other domains of activity. This approach would also identify the range and nature of overlap between contexts in which transfer takes place and the role of other people in this process.

In addition to clarifying the process of development of a specific skill, this approach could also be used to investigate the sources of individual differences within cultures. Investigating how individuals bring previous experience to bear on performing a task and use society's tools and techniques to learn the skill would clarify how individual differences arise. The issue of individual differences within cultures may result from an inevitable blending of the individual's biological characteristics and social and cultural experiences and practices. This view contrasts with one that would place biological and social influences in opposition.

Adopting the approach that the development of talent occurs within the context of cultural practices and specific experiences in relevant domains of activity would also permit one to examine how developmental processes can be characterized. In developing a talent, does skill grow incrementally, or does the individual's approach to the domain alter qualitatively as new understandings are reached? We suspect that transformations in understanding may be the rule as talents are developed, but this issue requires examination. Feldman's (1982) speculation regarding the possible stage-sequential nature of gaining expertise within specific fields or domains raises similar issues, although Feldman also acknowledges that the utility of stage notions within domains still has to be assessed through research.

Investigators of talent in cultural contexts may benefit from examining studies that focus on the development of everyday cognitive processes within the daily cultural context. The qualitative and quantitative transformations in a person's skill over the course of an event (such as solving a problem or learning a game) or over repeated episodes are often examined through microgenetic analyses. Some examples include Anzai and Simon's (1979) examination of the changes in problem-solving strategies of a subject learning to solve the Tower of Hanoi problem; Lawler's (1981) study of the learning processes involved in a child's mastery of addition through the integration of knowledge based on specific, particular experiences; and Gearhart's (1979) research on changes in children's social planning as they engaged in repeated episodes of playing store. Detailed analyses of practical and functional thinking processes as they are used in day-to-day experiences also provide an understanding of how skills develop. For example, Scribner (1984) described how dairy workers' job experiences provide them with different practice in manipulating numbers and adapting strategies to the job at hand. Chase and Ericsson (1982) analyzed how individuals become skilled in memory performance by learning to use specific retrieval strategies and to index information and speed up these processes through practice. Similarly, through a focus on functional and cultural contexts, cross-cultural researchers described how children learn memory, perceptual, and arithmetic skills (Lancy, 1983; Serpell, 1982).

We have argued that because cultures differ in the skills and talents that are valued, it is important to identify these skills and talents and the domains of activity and situations that foster them. This would allow detailed analyses of how a novice (adult or child) learns necessary skills within a specific domain and how those skills are transferred to other domains of activity. Such analyses would elucidate the developmental processes in learning skills, would explicate the role of society's tools and practices and the role of more experienced people in the learning of talents, and would help researchers to investigate the sources of individual differences in talents within a culture.

References

Alvino, J., McDonnel, R. C., & Richert, S. (1981). National survey of identification practices in gifted and talented education. *Exceptional Children, 48*(2), 124–132.

Anzai, Y., & Simon, H. A. (1979). The theory of learning by doing. *Psychological Review, 86,* 124–140.

Bateson, G. (1982). Totemic knowledge in New Guinea. In U. Neisser (Ed.), *Memory observed: Remembering in natural contexts* (pp. 269–273). San Francisco: Freeman.

Belo, J. (1955). Balinese children's drawing. In M. Mead & M. Wolfenstein (Eds.), *Childhood in contemporary cultures* (pp. 52–69). Chicago: University of Chicago Press.

Berland, J. C. (1982). *No five fingers are alike: Cognitive amplifiers in social context.* Cambridge, MA: Harvard University Press.

Bernal, E. M. (1974). Gifted Mexican American children: An ethnoscientific perspective. *California Journal of Educational Research, 25,* 261–273.

Bernal, E. M. (1979). The education of the culturally different gifted. In A. H. Passow (Ed.), *The gifted and the talented: Their education and development* (pp. 395–400). Chicago: University of Chicago Press.

Bernal, E. M. (1980). *Methods of identifying gifted minority students.* ERIC (Report No. 72). Princeton, NJ: Educational Testing Service, ERIC Clearinghouse on Tests, Measurement and Evaluation. (ERIC Document Reproduction Service No. ED 204 418).

Bloom, B. S. (1982). The role of gifts and markers in the development of talent. *Exceptional Children, 48*(6), 510–522.

Brickman, W. W. (1979). Educational perspectives for the gifted and talented in other countries. In A. H. Passow (Ed.), *The gifted and the talented: Their education and development* (pp. 308–329). Chicago: University of Chicago Press.

Carpenter, I. (1976). The tallest Indian. *American Education, 12,* 23–25.

Chase, W. G., & Ericsson, K. A. (1982). Skill and working memory. *The Psychology of Learning and Motivation, 16,* 210–236.

Chen, M. J., & Goon, S. W. (1976). Recognition of the gifted from among disadvantaged Asian children. *Gifted Child Quarterly, 20,* 157–164.

Chen, M. J., Braithwaite, V., & Huang, S. T. (1982). Attributes of intelligent behavior: Perceived relevance and difficulty by Australian and Chinese students. *Journal of Cross-Cultural Psychology, 13,* 139–156.

Cole, M., Hood, L., & McDermott, R. P. (1978). Concepts of ecological validity: Their differing implications for comparative cognitive research. *The Quarterly Newsletter of the Institute for Comparative Human Development, 2,* 34–37.

Dasen, P. (1984). The cross-cultural study of intelligence: Piaget and the Baoule'. *International Journal of Psychology, 19*(4), 407–434.

Davidson, G. R. (1979). An ethnographic psychology of aboriginal cognitive ability. *Oceania, 49*(4), 270–294.

Davidson, H. H., Greenberg, J. W., & Gerver, J. M. (1962). *Characteristics of successful school achievers from a severely deprived environment.* Mimeo, NY: City University of New York, City College.

D'Azevedo, W. A. (1982). Tribal history in Liberia. In U. Neisser (Ed.), *Memory observed: Remembering in natural contexts* (pp. 258–268). San Francisco: Freeman.

Draper, W. (1980). The creative and gifted minority student: Related research, developmental, and teaching strategies. *The Creative Child and Adult Quarterly, 5*(3), 171–179.

Dube, E. F. (1982). Literacy, cultural familiarity, and "intelligence" as determinants of story recall. In U. Neisser (Ed.), *Memory observed: Remembering in natural contexts* (pp. 274–292). San Francisco: Freeman.

Ericsson, K. A., Chase, W. G., & Faloon, S. (1980). Acquisition of a memory skill. *Science, 208,* 1181–1182.

Feldman, D. H. (1982). A developmental framework for research with gifted children. In D. H. Feldman (Ed.), *New directions for child development: 17. Developmental approaches to giftedness and creativity* (pp. 31–45). San Francisco: Jossey-Bass.

Feuerstein, R. (1979). *The dynamic assessment of retarded performers*. Baltimore, MD: University Park Press.

Frasier, N. M. (1979). Rethinking the issues regarding the culturally disadvantaged gifted. *Exceptional Children, 45*, 538–542.

Gardner, H. (1981, May). Prodigies' progress. *Psychology Today*, pp. 75–79.

Gardner, H. (1982). Giftedness: Speculations from a biological perspective. In D. H. Feldman (Ed.), *New directions for child development: 17. Developmental approaches to giftedness and creativity* (pp. 47–60). San Francisco: Jossey-Bass.

Gardner, H. (1983). *Frames of mind: The theory of multiple intelligences*. New York: Basic Books.

Gearheart, M. (1979). *Social planning: Role play in a novel situation*. Paper presented at the meeting of the Society for Research in Child Development, San Francisco.

Gibson, J., & Chennells, P. (1976). *Gifted children: Looking to their future*. London: Latimer New Dimensions, Ltd.

Gill, R., & Keats, D. M. (1980). Elements of intellectual competence: Judgments by Australian and Malay university students. *Journal of Cross-Cultural Psychology, 11*, 233–243.

Ginsburg, H. (1978). Poor children, African mathematics, and the problem of schooling. *Educational Research Quarterly, 2*, 26–42.

Gladwin, T. (1970). *East is a big bird*. Cambridge, MA: Belknap Press.

Gold, M. J. (1982). World gifted. *Gifted Child Quarterly, 26*(3), 144–145.

Goodnow, J. J. (1976). The nature of intelligent behavior: Questions raised by cross-cultural studies. In L. B. Resnick (Ed.), *The nature of intelligence* (pp. 169–188). Hillsdale, NJ: Erlbaum.

Goodnow, J. J. (1984). On being judged intelligent. *International Journal of Psychology, 19*(4), 391–406.

Guilmet, G. M. (1975). Cognitive research among the Eskimo: A survey. *Anthropologica, 17*(1), 61–84.

Holle, J. (1980). Separate criteria: Identification of gifted children in California. *School Psychology International, 1*(3), 13–14.

Irwin, M. H., & McLaughlin, D. H. (1970). Ability and preference in category sorting by Mano school children and adults. *Journal of Social Psychology, 82*, 15–24.

Irwin, M. H., Schafer, G. N., & Feiden, C. P. (1974). Emic and unfamiliar category sorting of Mano farmers and U.S. undergraduates. *Journal of Cross-Cultural Psychology, 5*, 407–423.

Kilbride, P. L. (1980). Sensorimotor behavior of Baganda and Samai infants. *Journal of Cross-Cultural Psychology, 11*, 131–152.

Klein, R. E., Freeman, H. E., Spring, B., Nerlove, S. B., & Yarborough, C. (1976). Cognitive test performance and indigenous conceptions of intelligence. *Journal of Psychology, 93*, 273–279.

Kleinfeld, J. S. (1973). Intellectual strengths in culturally different groups: An Eskimo illustration. *Review of Educational Research, 43*, 341–354.

Kranz, B. (1978). Multi-dimensional screening device for the identification of gifted/talented children. (Publication No. 9). Grand Forks, ND: Bureau of Educational Research Services. (ERIC Document Reproduction Service No. ED 177 761).

Laboratory of Comparative Human Cognition. (1979). Cross-cultural psychology's challenges to our ideas of children and development. *American Psychologist, 34*, 827–833.

Laboratory of Comparative Human Cognition. (1983). Culture and cognitive development. In W. Kessen (Ed.), *Handbook of child psychology: Vol. 1. History, theory and methods* (4th ed., pp. 295–356). New York: Wiley.

Lancy, D. F. (1983). *Cross-cultural studies in cognition and mathematics.* New York: Academic Press.

Lawler, R. W. (1981). The progressive construction of mind. *Cognitive Science, 5,* 1–30.

Lesser, G. H., Fifer, G., & Clark, D. H. (1965). Mental abilities of children from different social class and cultural groups. *Monographs of the Society for Research in Child Development, 30*(4), Serial No. 102.

Liu, F. (1982). Developmental psychology in China. *International Journal of Behavioral Development, 5,* 391–411.

Lord, A. B. (1965). *Singer of tales.* New York: Atheneum.

Lowenstein, L. F. (1979). Discovering gifted children in a Third World nation. *School Psychology International, 1,* 27–30.

Lutz, C., & LeVine, R. A. (1982). Culture and intelligence in infancy: An ethnopsychological view. In M. Lewis (Ed.), *Origins of intelligence: Infancy and early childhood* (pp. 1–28). New York: Plenum Press.

McPhee, C. (1955). Children and music in Bali. In M. Mead & M. Wolfenstein (Eds.), *Childhood in contemporary cultures* (pp. 70–94). Chicago: University of Chicago Press.

Mercer, J. R., & Lewis, J. F. (1977). *System of Multicultural Pluralistic Assessment (SOMPA).* New York: The Psychological Corporation.

Milgram, R. M. (1980). Gifted children in Israel: Theory, practice, and research. *School Psychology International, 1*(3), 10–13.

Nerlove, S. B., Roberts, J. M., Klein, R. E., Yarborough, C., & Habicht, J. P. (1974). Natural indicators of cognitive development: An observational study of rural Guatemalan children. *Ethos, 2,* 265, 295.

Rogoff, B. (1978). Spot observation: An introduction and examination. *Quarterly Newsletter of the Institute for Comparative Human Development, 2,* 21–26.

Rogoff, B. (1981). Schooling and the development of cognitive skills. In H. C. Triandis & A. Heron (Eds.), *Handbook of cross-cultural psychology: 4. Developmental psychology* (pp. 233–294). Boston: Allyn & Bacon.

Rogoff, B. (1982). Integrating context and cognitive development. In M. E. Lamb & A. L. Brown (Eds.), *Advances in developmental psychology* (Vol. 2, pp. 125–170). Hillsdale, NJ: Erlbaum.

Rogoff, B., Gauvain, M., & Ellis, S. (1984). Development viewed in its cultural context. In M. H. Bornstein & M. E. Lamb (Eds.), *Developmental psychology* (pp. 176–193). Hillsdale, NJ: Erlbaum.

Scribner, S. (1976). Situating the experiment in cross-cultural research. In K. F. Riegel & J. A. Meacham (Eds.), *The developing individual in a changing world* (Vol. 1, pp. 310–321). Chicago: Aldine.

Scribner, S. (1984). Cognitive studies of work. *Quarterly Newsletter of the Laboratory of Comparative Human Cognition, 6*(1), 1–49.

Serpell, R. (1977). Strategies for investigating intelligence in its cultural context. *The Quarterly Newsletter of the Institute for Comparative Human Development, 1*(3), 11–15.

Serpell, R. (1982). Measures of perception, skills and intelligence: The growth of a new perspective on children in third world country. In W. W. Hartup (Ed.), *Review of child development research* (Vol. 6, pp. 392–440). Chicago: University of Chicago Press.

Smilansky, M., & Nevo, D. (1979). *The gifted disadvantaged: A ten year longitudinal study of compensatory education in Israel.* London: Gordon & Breach.

Stigler, J. W., Barclay, C., & Aiello, P. (1982). Motor and mental abacus skill: A preliminary look at an expert. *The Quarterly Newsletter of the Laboratory Comparative Human Cognition, 4*(1), 12–14.

Super, C. M. (1981). Behavioral development in infancy. In R. H. Munroe, R. L. Munroe, & B. B. Whiting (Eds.), *Handbook of cross-cultural human development* (pp. 181–270). New York: Garland.

Super, C. M., & Harkness, S. (1983). *Looking across at growing up: The cultural expressions of cognitive development in middle childhood.* Unpublished manuscript.

Suzuki, S. (1969). *Nurtured by love: A new approach to education.* New York: Exposition Press.

Tannenbaum, A. J. (1983). *Gifted children: Psychological and educational perspectives.* New York: Macmillan.

Torrance, E. P. (1977). *Discovery and nurturance of giftedness in the culturally different.* Reston, VA: The Council for Exceptional Children.

Torrance, E. P. (1978). Dare we hope again? *Gifted Child Quarterly, 22*(3), 292–312.

Tyron, W. W. (1979). The test-trait fallacy. *American Psychologist, 34*(5), 402–406.

Vygotsky, L. S. *Mind in society.* (1978). Cambridge, MA: Harvard University Press.

Walberg, H. J., Tsai, S., Weinstein, T., Gabriel, C. L., Rasher, S. P., Rosecrans, T., Rovai, E., Ide, J., Trujillo, M., & Vukosavich, P. (1981). Childhood traits and environmental conditions of highly eminent adults. *Gifted Child Quarterly, 25*(3), 103–107.

Wartofsky, M. (1983). The child's construction of the world and the world's construction of the child: From historical epistemology to historical psychology. In F. S. Kessel & A. W. Siegel (Eds.), *The child and other cultural inventions* (pp. 188–216). New York: Praeger.

Witty, E. P. (1978). Equal educational opportunity for gifted minority group children: Promise or possibility? *Gifted Child Quarterly, 22,* 344–352.

Wober, M. (1972). Culture and the concept of intelligence: A case in Uganda. *Journal of Cross-Cultural Psychology, 3,* 327–328.

Zborowski, M., & Herzog, E. (1952). *Life is with people.* New York: International Universities Press.

Part 2. Aspects of Giftedness

Aspects of Giftedness

The study of giftedness and its development is not limited strictly to investigating and measuring intellectual processes. The ways in which a gifted person interacts with the social world and the influences of the external environment on the development of talent are also important areas of study. The authors of the chapters in this section discuss giftedness in a social perspective and suggest areas in which research and innovative action might be most useful.

In chapter 6, Paul Janos and Nancy Robinson of the Child Development Research Group at the University of Washington address an issue that has long plagued work with gifted populations: Are highly intelligent people different in ways other than the intellectual? Terman's findings challenged the commonly held belief that the intellectually gifted were likely to be disturbed emotionally or poorly adjusted socially. Janos and Robinson review the more recent literature and conclude that Terman's conclusions have been confirmed. If anything, gifted children tend to be more mature and have fewer behavioral and social problems than do other children, at least until adolescence. Gifted children are also more likely to show personality characteristics such as persistence, energy, and self-sufficiency, to be less concerned with conformity, and to be better able to focus their efforts on tasks important to them. Thus, according to Janos and Robinson, the overall picture of the gifted child is a positive one, particularly when academic opportunities are matched to a child's intellectual capabilities.

Lynn Fox and Jerrilene Washington of The Johns Hopkins University review approaches to educating gifted children in chapter 7. Traditional program models for the gifted generally focus either on enrichment of the curriculum or acceleration of the student through the standard curriculum. In Fox and Washington's view, the most useful approach incorporates both these models and adapts them to the individual situation. Fox and Washington call for more evaluation research and investigations into the nature of special abilities as critical to the design of future gifted programs. In addition, practical problems of implementation—financing, administrative rigidity, lack of qualified teachers, and inadequate identification procedures—must, according to Fox and Washington, be addressed if education of the gifted in America's schools is to be improved.

The identification and education of gifted young people from minority groups is the topic addressed in chapter 8 by Alexinia Baldwin of the State University of New York at Albany. Programs for the gifted in our schools are often seen by minority parents and educators as exclusionary and therefore discriminatory. Baldwin argues for the need to expand our definitions of gifted performance, moving away from reliance on the culturally biased standard IQ test, in order to make such programs inclusive. In addition, Baldwin encourages the active seeking out of talented minority students and the adaptation of curricula to accommodate the intellectually talented but socioeconomically disadvantaged minority student.

The special case of gifted women is addressed in chapter 9. Jacquelynne Eccles of the University of Michigan begins with the recognition that women's achievement patterns are different from those of men and proceeds to describe research on sex differences in educational and occupational attainment. Eccles believes that social patterns of discrimination are not the only, or even the primary, source of these sex differences. Instead, she says, such psychological factors as achievement-related beliefs and gender role schemas are largely responsible for women's educational and occupational performance. The perceived value of any achievement-related task depends upon how well its performance conforms with a person's self-image, versus the potential cost, in terms of time or energy taken from other tasks. Given different socialization histories, men and women will place different values on the same task, leading to sex differences in the allocation of time and energy. Eccles also stresses the role of parents, teachers, and counselors in encouraging gifted young women to make educational and occupational choices that are concomitant with their intellectual abilities.

6. Psychosocial Development in Intellectually Gifted Children

Paul M. Janos
Nancy M. Robinson
University of Washington

The literature on psychological and social development in gifted children is beset with problems of inconsistency in definitions and imprecision of measures, both for giftedness itself (Newland, 1976; Passow, 1981; Renzulli, 1978; Tannenbaum, 1983) and for developmental constructs (Wohlwill, 1973). Definitional problems are discussed throughout Part I of this volume. Our review will deal primarily with studies of subjects characterized as advanced in general intellectual ability (usually operationalized as IQ), because that is the population represented best in the research literature. In most of the studies we will review, subjects have IQs of at least 120 or 130 and are doing well in school; sample IQ means range between 130 and 150. We use the phrase "not identified as gifted" to designate comparison subjects, since that phrase is at least as informative as "average" or "nongifted," and more accurate and positive in tone as well.

A few studies of children explicitly characterized by specific academic aptitude (e.g., mathematical reasoning) or by creativity are included in a special section, as are a few dealing with school groups that were identified by local procedures. Although we recognize the value of nonacademic talents in a thoughtful society (Gardner, 1983), we have omitted studies of children with special talents in the visual, performing, or athletic spheres.

As real as definitional problems are, they proved secondary in importance to the paucity of substantive empirical research of a truly developmental nature. The literature provided few cross-sectional or longitudinal studies and even fewer investigations matching advanced and average children on mental age or any other developmental dimension. Any developmental conclusions that can be drawn from such a literature may be attributed both to the general nature of the questions that have been addressed and to the consistency of answers to these broad questions.

In this chapter, then, we review the information that has accrued over the 60 years since Terman's seminal work (1925). His *Genetic Studies of Genius,* a longitudinal study of 1,528 intellectually gifted children in California, began in 1921 and continues, under the direction of his scientific heirs, to this day (Burks, Jensen, & Terman, 1930; Oden, 1968; Sears, 1977; Sears & Barbee, 1977; Terman, 1925; Terman & Oden, 1947, 1959). The findings from this study have been validated repeatedly by other investigators.

The chapter has been organized around issues that anyone hoping to enhance the well-rounded growth of intellectually gifted children needs to consider, including whether rapid intellectual development is accompanied by rapid psychosocial development, or maturity; whether intellectually gifted children evidence satisfactory psychosocial adjustment, or mental health; whether gifted children exhibit differential personality characteristics; and how intellectual status affects the development of friendships and of intimate attachments. We have also included sections dealing with subsets of the gifted population.

Psychosocial Maturity

Are intellectually gifted children advanced in psychosocial as well as cognitive maturity? Typically, parents and educators are doubtful. Remarks such as "He's bright, but he's still a little kid" or "Skipping grades is harmful because children can't handle the social demands" reflect an assumption that psychosocial status corresponds much more closely to

The unstinting support of the staff of the Child Development Research Group enabled us to write this chapter. The authors would like to extend particular thanks to Gregg Sullivan. Preparation of the chapter was made possible by support from the William H. Donner Foundation.

chronological than to mental age. This assumption is, however, far from proven. In fact, the inference that intellectually precocious children show no advancement in psychosocial domains appears to be untenable. Because inaccurate assumptions still impede the appropriate placement of gifted children in schools (Daurio, 1979), it is important to examine the relevant literature, even though the studies taken individually are subject to profound limitations.

Maturity, a particularly difficult concept to define (Jahoda, 1958), is usually operationalized by investigators by age-referenced checklists or standardized personality inventories and by parent and teacher ratings. Although these sources of data have serious limitations, most investigators find, indeed, that a substantial relationship exists between intelligence and psychological and social maturity. A few studies have focused on more elaborate theoretical constructs, such as social cognitive variables (Shantz, 1983), and these too appear to be related to intellectual level.

Maturity in Social Cognition and Friendships

The literature on social cognitive development among gifted children remains scant and unsatisfying. Two theoretical studies have provided data regarding gifted children's sensitivity to peer behavior. In their ability to predict classmates' sociometric choices (Gallagher, 1958b; Miller, 1956) and in their ability to describe the ease with which classmates learn things (Miller, 1956), intellectually gifted elementary school-age children were found superior to children not identified as gifted.

Many studies of social cognition have employed conceptual tasks with social content, akin to problems that might have been included in intelligence tests, and it is therefore not surprising that bright children do well with them. Social problem solving (Roedell, 1978); perceptual, conceptual, and affective perspective taking (Abroms & Gollin, 1980); social knowledge (Scott & Bryant, 1978); and gender constancy (Miller & Roedell, 1977) have all been examined. These investigations imply that intellectually gifted children are advanced in comparison with age peers, but no comparison groups, other than norms in one study (Roedell, 1978), were examined. Yet the social cognitive variables under consideration did not reliably manifest themselves in social behavior any more consistently among intellectually gifted than among other groups of children (Abroms & Gollin, 1980; Miller, 1956; Roedell, 1978). Most of the existing studies have been with preschoolers; there are few studies even within this age group, and sample sizes have always been tiny. Moreover, comparison samples other than norms are used infrequently.

Miller and Roedell (1977), Abroms and Gollin (1980), and Roedell (1978) each considered relations between intelligence and social cognitive measures, although only within gifted samples. Miller and Roedell investigated the development of gender concepts in seventeen 3- and 4-year-old children (mean Stanford-Binet IQ = 132). They reported a stronger correlation (r = .83) between MA and scores on the Gender Constancy Test (Slaby & Frey, 1974) than between chronological age and gender constancy scores. Abroms and Gollin (1980) studied twenty 3-year-olds with a mean Slosson Intelligence Test IQ of 134. Dependent variables were measured using modified versions of perspective-taking tests in the research literature (Borke, 1971; Flavell, Botkin, Fry, Wright, & Jarvis, 1968; Masangkay et al., 1974; Zahn-Waxler, Radke-Yarrow, & Brady-Smith, 1977). They found that IQ was not significantly correlated with perceptual or conceptual perspective taking at the beginning of the pre-school year, although it was correlated with affective perspective taking. By the end of the year, correlations with IQ had risen sharply and were significant. Mental age was positively correlated with all measures of perspective taking in the autumn and, with the exception of affective perspective taking, continued to be so in the spring. Correlations ranged from .30 to .66.

Roedell (1978) investigated the social interaction skills of a group of intellectually advanced (mean IQ = 138) 3- to 5-year-old children. Three measures of social skills were taken: The Preschool Interpersonal Problem Solving Skills Test (PIPS) (Spivak & Shure, 1974), teachers' responses on the Hahnemann Preschool Behavior Rating Scale (Spivak & Shure, 1974), and observations of ongoing social behavior during free activity time in a preschool. IQ was related only to those measures that involved cognitive aspects of social behavior; for example, children with the highest IQs had more ideas about ways children might solve theoretical social conflicts and had more ideas about ways for children to interact cooperatively. These advanced social cognitive skills were not, however, reflected in the children's behavior.

Moral Judgment

In early research on the character of gifted children and in more recent work on moral judgment within a social-cognitive framework, significant relations with IQ have been found. These studies have not, however, yielded satisfactory predictors of moral behavior. Terman (1925) found that his sample of 643 pre-high school children (mean age = 9.7 years) with IQs above 140 exhibited maturity in moral development. In willingness to claim undeserved accomplishments, choosing between socially constructive and personally gratifying activities, attitudes toward authorities, and rating the seriousness of misbehaviors, they appeared to have reached a stage of moral development normally attained at the age of 13 or 14. Terman's instruments may not appear to be sophisticated by contemporary standards, but evidence of their reliability and validity was reported.

Thorndike (1940) studied how 50 top centile gifted pupils of ages 9 to 12 responded to a checklist of items selected to show an age progression in moral judgment from elementary school through college. He tentatively concluded that the intellectually gifted group had a mature disregard for conventional prohibitions of activities such as playing cards, smoking, and dancing, but tended to be more severe in judging personal antisocial behavior such as screaming, bribery, and lawlessness. The age equivalent of the "emotional quotients" he computed fell much closer to the children's mental ages (approximately 16.0 years for boys and 15.3 years for girls) than to their chronological ages. This study, unfortunately, did not include a comparison group of pupils not identified as gifted.

The Defining Issues Test (DIT) (Rest, 1979), which is derived from Kohlberg's Moral Development Interview (Kohlberg, 1973), provides an estimate of level of moral judgment with psychometric properties superior to those instruments that have been discussed. Tan-Willman and Gutteridge (1981) found that DIT scores for 115 adolescents in a highly competitive Toronto high school (no IQs reported) were 35 percent higher than norms, although their mean level of moral judgment remained at the conventional level. Using the DIT, Janos, Robinson, and Sather (1983) compared 24 markedly accelerated university students, of ages 11 to 18, with typical university students and with two nonaccelerated gifted groups, college-age National Merit Finalists, and gifted high school students. All three groups of intellectually gifted individuals exhibited significantly more advanced moral judgment than did typical university students. Although no adolescent group not identified as gifted was available for comparison, the accelerated and nonaccelerated gifted groups scored substantially higher than a normative sample (Rest, 1979) of senior high school students of comparable age.

Play Interests

Play interests change markedly during childhood and can serve as one index of developmental status. In Terman's (1925) studies, procedures similar to those used to assign mental age levels to IQ test items were employed to estimate age levels for a detailed checklist of activities. Gifted boys and girls 9 or 10 years of age were considerably more mature in their play interests than were control groups of corresponding age. They tended to prefer solving puzzles, chess, and (for girls) charades to playing guessing games, tiddledy-winks, or house. In the Thorndike (1940) study cited earlier, intellectually gifted children manifested a number of mature interests, particularly of a scientific or intellectual type, in addition to enjoying activities typical of their age such as baseball, bicycling, and collecting postage stamps. Among the same children, Thorndike (1939) examined forced-choice preferences on item pairs differentiated by maturity level. On this test, the developmental quotients of the intellectually gifted children were only slightly in advance of expectations based on chronological age norms. An analysis of items showed highest maturity in choices of books to read, future vocations, and things to think about. Aesthetic appeal was more marked for the gifted children than for a group of comparison children.

Although not a direct measure of maturity, a preference for (and acceptance by) older children suggests advancement among many high-IQ children on developmental dimensions, such as play interests, implicated in friendship choices. Parents and teachers report that a much larger percentage of intellectually gifted boys and girls than comparison children prefer older playmates (Painter, 1976; Terman, 1925). A consistent increase in the proportion of gifted children preferring older companions has been observed from grammar school to college, girls preferring them more frequently (Burks et al., 1930).

Maturity in Personality

Studies of the affective maturity of intellectually gifted children are rare. Some are to be found in a later section on personality characteristics. Two previously cited studies offer a few insights. Terman (1925) found no differences between his gifted and comparison samples on teachers' reports of excessive timidity or tendency to worry. In the Thorndike study, the self-reports of the 9- to 12-year-old subjects suggested that they had "sloughed off most of the fears of childhood to about the extent of the junior or senior high school student, without as yet showing much concern for the more mature worries" (1940, p. 592).

Evidence from objective personality questionnaires suggests advanced psychosocial maturity among intellectually gifted youngsters of junior and senior high school age, in comparisons both with samples not identified as gifted (Lessinger & Martinson, 1961; Robinson & Janos, in press) and with norms (Davids, 1966; Haier & Denham, 1976; Weiss, Haier, & Keating, 1974). Lessinger and Martinson (1961), whose study is frequently cited for its norms for high-ability samples, used the California Psychological Inventory (CPI) (Gough, 1969) in a study of 436 gifted junior and senior high school students and 172 comparison students representative of the pupil population of California in 1958 and 1959. The authors concluded that "the maturity of the gifted eighth grade boys was much more closely related to that of the gifted high school boys and to the general adult population than to the general maturity of their age-mates" (p. 573). The same conclusions held for gifted girls and for gifted students in secondary school.

Robinson and Janos (1983) compared the CPI responses of 24 markedly accelerated university students of ages 11 to 18 with other university students and National Merit Finalists an average of 4 years older. Although they were slightly lower in self-confidence and assertiveness than were the college-age students, the accelerated students otherwise responded in a fashion remarkably similar to the older comparison students. A group of youngsters who were qualified for, but did not elect, marked acceleration, evidenced a similar pattern. Unfortunately, the lack of a sample of youngsters not identified as gifted leaves open the question of whether they too would compare favorably with the university students.

Summary

Researchers have measured psychosocial maturity with developmental tests, teachers' reports, and standardized personality inventories. Their studies document consistently that intellectually gifted elementary and high school students are superior to students not identified as gifted both in their ability to make certain kinds of social judgments and in play interests. Relationships that exist between IQ and other social maturity variables, including gender constancy, interpersonal problem solving, and perspective taking have also been documented. The common observation that high-IQ children choose older children as friends also suggests, although indirectly, significant advancement in social maturity. Teachers' reports of developmental data, scant as they are, indicate that intellectually gifted children may be more comparable to agemates on variables tapping the emotional life, but self-reports of fears suggest that they may be more comparable to older children than to agemates. Cross-sectional studies of responses to personality inventories consistently find scores of intellectually gifted children to be more like those of older children than those of agemates not identified as gifted.

The studies that have been reviewed have not, in most cases, been adequately replicated; in them researchers have considered only a restricted segment of the age spectrum and only a few of the constructs and behaviors that contribute to psychosocial maturity. Studies of prosocial and moral behavior, emotional development, and interpersonal intimacy are, for example, sparse or nonexistent. The need for using comparison samples, particularly those that would unravel the influences of intelligence and superior home environment, remains. Particularly glaring is the absence of direct observational data or reports from teachers, who can presumably make reasonable comparative judgments in a way that parents cannot. Although limitations in methodology necessitate using caution in making generalizations, most of the studies suggest that high-ability youngsters are slightly to substantially more mature than are unselected agemates. None of the studies suggests the opposite. Although the degree and breadth of advantage may be difficult to predict, the direction of the difference is not.

The maturity measures are less precise or reliable than are intelligence tests, and they are infused with cultural values to an even greater degree. Yet, the extent to which maturity accompanies high ability bears on one of the most controversial and significant issues in the field: whether to accelerate a child in school to meet his or her intellectual needs. Intellectual and social needs can be fulfilled by presenting advanced material to agemates of comparable ability and interests, but such grouping practices are not always practical, nor may they serve well for highly gifted children or for children with uneven academic abilities. Class placements that are commensurate with psychosocial maturity, on the other hand, can be accomplished easily and economically (Stanley, 1979). Better means of assessing both the maturity of individual gifted children and the maturity demands of specific academic settings are essential to prescribing appropriate academic environments (Robinson & Robinson, 1982).

Psychosocial Adjustment

The concept of psychosocial adjustment, like maturity, is difficult to define (Jahoda, 1958), and the concepts overlap. Here we collect many diverse studies into a loosely defined category connoting one's ability to operate effectively within and constructively beyond the structures imposed by the environment, to respond zestfully to challenge, and to maintain a high degree of relatedness, vitality, and personal satisfaction. In fact, however, the definitions of other authors have tended to be considerably narrower than this. Most investigators have used personality inventories or parent and teacher reports of behavior problems or have examined self-concept or self-esteem. In working with intellectually gifted children there is a clear danger of operating within too restricted a framework. For example, those who believe that adjustment should be conflict free will ignore much of the richness of human personality (Dirkes, 1983; Wallach & Kogan, 1965), and, indeed, some individuals who attain outstanding achievement may simultaneously be seriously disturbed (Andreasen, 1975, 1978; Andreasen & Canter, 1975). Those who believe that all children should model their behavior on the appropriate sex role stereotype will also impute maladjustment where there is none. Despite the possibility of such disagreements, we have, by and large, in this survey, accepted the orientation of the investigators represented with all the ambiguities that result.

Because assessments of adjustment often reflect normative, age-related expectations (Rutter & Garmezy, 1983; Wenar, 1982), deviation from such expectations may affect perceptions of adjustment (Manaster & Powell, 1983). Children who are exceptionally mature or richly expressive may deviate significantly enough from age norms to be evaluated as poorly adjusted. For example, intellectually gifted children tend to prefer older friends (Terman, 1925; Janos, 1983; Janos, Robinson, & Marwood, 1984), but the widely used Child Behavior Checklist (Achenbach

& Edelbrock, 1983) lists the item, "prefers playing with older children," as a behavior problem. Other examples are Kennedy, Cottrell, and Smith's (1963, 1964) and Kennedy and Smith's (1962) reminders that intellectually gifted individuals' significantly higher scores on scales of the Minnesota Multiphasic Personality Inventory, Edwards Personality Preference Scale, and Rotter Incomplete Sentences Test should not be interpreted as indicating greater difficulties in adjustment.

Despite assessment problems, childhood adjustment merits continued attention and possible intervention. For gifted populations, as for those not identified as gifted, positive adjustment in childhood tends to be associated with enhanced school achievement (Milgram & Milgram, 1976) and with adjustment during later years (Oden, 1968; Terman & Oden, 1947, 1959). Sears (1977) and Sears and Barbee (1977), likewise, have shown for members of the Terman gifted sample that, over the life span, family satisfaction and success in marriage were predicted by social and family adjustment during childhood.

A major caveat in this area relates to the backgrounds of gifted individuals, who tend to be relatively advantaged in socioeconomic status, in educational opportunities and other resources, and, generally, in mental health status. That is, it is difficult to estimate the relative contributions of background and intelligence to the adjustment picture. This problem has plagued studies from Terman's onward, and even when efforts are made to match gifted children with others of similar background, one cannot be sure that subtle selective factors have not intruded. Except as otherwise indicated, in the major studies reported here gifted and comparison groups were selected from roughly comparable backgrounds, but because advantaged groups tend to have children with above-average IQs, the confounding has seldom been dealt with adequately.

Preadolescence

The standard—indeed, the repetitive—finding of reviewers is that intellectually gifted preadolescent children tend to show average or superior adjustment (Carroll & Laming, 1974; Getzels & Dillon, 1973; Khoury & Appel, 1977; Miles, 1954; Monks & Ferguson, 1983). Terman was the first to draw this conclusion, which he supported for both preadolescents and adolescents with a wide range of self-report inventories (e.g., Cady's [1923] version of the Woodward Personality Inventory) and character trait ratings by parents and teachers (Burks, Jensen, & Terman, 1930; Terman, 1925). Other studies employing self-report instruments or psychological tests (Janos, 1983; Lehman & Erdwins, 1981; Liddle, 1958; Mensch, 1950; Milgram & Milgram, 1976), parents' responses to behavior checklists (Janos, 1983), parents' ratings of adjustment characteristics (Burks et al., 1930; Terman, 1925), teachers' trait ratings (Hildreth, 1938, Mensch, 1950; Specht, 1919), and teachers' responses to behavior problem checklists (Hitchfield, 1973; Janos, 1983; Ludwig & Cullinan, 1984) have documented the same finding in elementary school children.

The following list shows the broad range of behaviors addressed in the studies finding more favorable psychosocial adjustment in gifted groups:

• trustworthiness under stress, freedom from psychopathic trends, social preferences and attitudes, and diminished tendencies to boast, exaggerate, and cheat (Burks, Jensen, & Terman, 1930; Terman, 1925)

• sense of self-worth, social skills, sense of personal freedom, reduced antisocial tendencies, school relationships, and comfort with oneself and with interpersonal relationships (Lehman & Erdwins, 1981)

• participation in extracurricular activities, sociability, values and interests, and personality characteristics (Pollin, 1983)

• social competence, internalizing and externalizing behavior problems, less inadequacy, immaturity, and socialized delinquency (Ludwig & Cullinan, 1984)

• fewer aggressive and withdrawal tendencies (Liddle, 1958)

• ratings of courtesy, cooperation, willingness to take suggestions, egotism, self-will, domineeringness, sense of humor, and self-assurance (Miles, 1954)

Hitchfield's (1973) longitudinal report on British children is one of the soundest methodologically. She studied a subset of the group investigated by Pringle, Butler, and Davie (1966), which included almost all children born in a single week in 1958 in England, Wales, and Scotland. The mean IQ of the subsample was 131 for boys and 126 for girls, the children were above average on achievement measures, and many were identified as gifted in mathematics, art, and sports. On the Bristol Social Maturity Scales, teachers rated the gifted children as being significantly more stable than a control sample matched for background. The incidence of maladjustment among gifted children was 3 percent at age seven versus 12 percent for controls. At age 11, the incidence was 7 percent for gifted children, although the comparable figure for the control children was not published. Incidence of maladjustment in other British and U.S. samples of normal children range from 6 to 16 percent at age 11 (Achenbach & Edelbrock, 1981; Kastrup, 1976; Pringle et al., 1966; Rutter, Tizard, & Whitmore, 1970).

The results of two studies in other developed Western cultures substantiate these findings. In an American sample, Ludwig and Cullinan (1984) studied 111 pairs of high-achieving, high-IQ (above 125 on an individually administered Otis-Lennon test) and control children in Grades 1 through 5. On the Behavior Problem Checklist (Quay & Peterson, 1975), gifted children showed fewer problems than did classmates. Using a Hebrew translation of the Tennessee Self-Concept Scale (Fitts, 1965), Milgram & Milgram (1976) found in their sample of seventh- and eighth-grade Israeli children that the gifted subjects reported greater feelings of personal adequacy in the family context, were less guarded and defensive, and gave fewer indications of psychological disturbance. They were more consistent and took less extreme positions in describing themselves. The younger gifted students earned lower scores on a criterion-referenced pathology scale, but the older gifted students earned higher scores on a criterion-referenced scale of neuroticism. The intellectually gifted samples at both ages reported less general anxiety and test anxiety than did the comparison group on adaptations of measures devised by Sarason, Davidson, Lighthall, Waite, and Ruebush (1960). Milgram and Milgram noted that both gifted children and children not identified as gifted scored within the normal range on all measures, suggesting that the various statistical differences did not imply pathology.

Although the typical finding is of superior psychosocial adjustment among gifted children, there is some indication that groups identified by parent nomination may appear somewhat more disturbed than comparison children (Freeman, 1979). In Freeman's sample of 70 intellectually gifted British children (mean Stanford-Binet IQ = 147) who were compared with 70 other gifted children (mean IQ = 134), the first group, whose parents had joined the British National Association for Gifted Children, evidenced considerably poorer personal and social adjustment from the perspectives of both teachers and parents. They were described as difficult, particularly sensitive, very emotional, having difficulties with sleep, and having no friends far more often than the second group of children, whose parents had not joined the organization. The finding that boys evidence more behavior problems than girls throughout childhood (Achenbach & Edelbrock, 1981; Eme, 1979) has also been documented among intellectually gifted children (Janos, 1983; Ludwig & Cullinan, 1984). In early adulthood, however, this sharp sex distinction may diminish (Terman & Oden, 1947).

Adolescent- and College-Age Groups

On self-report instruments, typically personality inventories, academically accelerated adolescents appear to be well adjusted (Daurio, 1979; Pressey, 1949; Robinson & Janos, in press). This same finding has been strongly documented among markedly accelerated, mathematically talented adolescents (Daurio, 1979; Haier & Denham, 1976; Pollin, 1983; Weiss, Haier, & Keating, 1974). Yet, in general, the probability of observing more adjustment problems may increase as gifted children enter adolescence. The Milgram and Milgram (1976) study previously cited, for example, suggested somewhat more neurotic behavior among intellectually gifted eighth graders than among comparison students.

Certain studies of intellectually gifted middle and older adolescents also suggest more adjustment difficulties than are found among children not identified as gifted (Chambers & Dusseault, 1972; Mason, Adams, &

Blood, 1968; Mason & Blood, 1966; Pandey, 1977; Tomlinson-Keasey & Smith-Winberry, 1983). It should be noted that these data issue from interpretations of personality inventories rather than from direct observations and that almost all scores earned by gifted children are within the normal range. Cautions have appeared in the literature about interpreting such discrepancies as pathological (Kennedy, Cottrell, & Smith, 1963, 1964; Kennedy & Smith, 1962). Additional caution is mandated by evidence in each of the reports, with the exception of Pandey's, which was obtained in India and may not be representative of youth in the United States, that significant proportions of the subjects may have been academic underachievers, who, as shall be seen later, are especially vulnerable to adjustment problems.

Most studies of intellectually superior, college-age subjects provide strong evidence of favorable adjustment among those who are achieving at a high level (Davids, 1966; Horrall, 1949, 1957; Robinson & Janos, in press; Nichols, 1967; Nichols & Davis, 1964; Pollin, 1983). Warren and Heist (1960), for example, studied 918 college seniors who had received extremely high scores on the National Merit Scholarship Qualifying Test. They concluded, "the gifted are independent, confident, and generally mature in their interactions with the external world . . . . In neither sex is there a higher incidence of emotional disturbance or adjustment difficulties among the gifted than is found in the general college population" (p. 336). For students of undistinguished achievement, even if not designated as underachieving, the adjustment picture may be less impressive. Gifted students who do not attend college, or attend academically nonchallenging colleges, have been ignored in the literature but presumably constitute a particularly high-risk group.

Self-Concept and Self-Esteem

A number of studies have been focused specifically on variables addressing self-perception (e.g., self-concept, self-esteem, self-confidence), all of which are associated with psychological adjustment (Brownfain, 1952; Fitts, 1972; Lipsitt, 1958; Powell, 1948; Taylor & Coombs, 1952). Investigators whose roots are in contemporary developmental psychology recognize that differentiated aspects of self-perception must be assessed (Dweck & Elliot, 1983; Kelly & Colangelo, 1984). Harter (1981, 1983), for example, focuses on aspects of cognitive, social, and physical development; competence; and general self-worth. Yet, most of the extant studies with gifted children limit themselves to reporting global summary scores. Such studies are difficult to interpret and, not surprisingly, inconsistent. Results tend to vary, too, according to the comparison group selected.

Intellectually gifted children of elementary school through high school age sometimes appear to evidence higher self-concept and self-esteem than do children not identified as gifted (Janos, 1983; Karnes & Wherry,

1981; Ketcham & Snyder, 1977; Maddux, Scheiber, & Bass, 1982; Tidwell, 1980). All of these studies, however, determined superiority in self-esteem by comparing the Piers-Harris Children's Self-Concept Scale (Piers & Harris, 1969) scores of intellectually gifted children with the norms listed in the Piers-Harris manual. Data presented by Coleman and Fults (1982) suggest that these norms may significantly underestimate the scores of middle-class children not identified as gifted. When scores on other measures are examined (Bracken, 1970; Glenn, 1978; Tidwell, 1980), or in direct Piers-Harris comparisons between intellectually gifted subjects and subjects not identified as gifted (Coleman & Fults, 1982; Klein & Cantor, 1976; Maddux et al., 1982; Stopper, 1978), the purported superiority of intellectually gifted children often, but not always (Lehman & Erdwins, 1981; O'Such, Twyla, & Havertape, 1979) disappears. Tidwell (1980), for example, found that although 1,593 10th-grade gifted students (mean Stanford-Binet IQ = 137) exceeded norms on scales of the Piers-Harris Self-Concept Scale, their mean self-esteem score (the affective aspect of self-concept) on the Coopersmith Self-Esteem Scale was within the normal range.

Sex may moderate the differences in self-esteem between intellectually gifted children and children not identified as gifted. Kelly and Colangelo (1984) found that intellectually gifted junior high school males participating in a gifted program scored higher on global self-concept and on academic and social self-concepts as measured, respectively, by the Tennessee Self-Concept Scale and the Academic Self-Concept Scale (Brookover, Patterson, & Thomas, 1962). Gifted females did not score similarly higher than females not identified as gifted in their sample. These sex differences in relative superiority do not necessarily imply that intellectually gifted girls have lower self-concepts than gifted boys. Mills (1984) found that mathematically gifted girls and boys scored essentially the same on both a self-concept scale derived from an adjective checklist and a self-esteem inventory.

In a few studies evidence of lower self-concept and self-esteem among intellectually gifted children has been found. Klein and Cantor (1976) observed that an intellectually gifted kindergarten through fourth grade sample exhibited lower self-concept than did children not identified as gifted, although low self-concept among the comparison children was also frequent. Other studies of specific aspects of self-concept do not always favor the gifted. Milgram and Milgram (1976), for example, administered an Israeli version of the Tennessee Self-Concept Scale. They observed that, although intellectually gifted seventh graders demonstrated a higher degree of personal worth and self-confidence than did comparison students, the reverse was true of eighth graders, and comparison children had a more positive physical self-concept at both grade levels.

Two groups of investigators compared academic self-concept with aspects of self-concept thought to be less influenced by intellectual ability.

Ross and Parker (1980) found that the academic self-concept of 147 intellectually gifted fifth through eighth graders was significantly higher than their social self-concept, and more so for eighth graders than for children in lower grades. Winne, Woodlands, and Wong (1982) found that intellectually gifted children scored higher than learning disabled children on academic self-concept subscales, although learning disabled children significantly exceeded gifted on physical and social subscales.

Contemporary investigators, fortunately, are beginning to turn to more complex models to predict self-esteem. For example, in 284 female high school sophomores identified as gifted and talented, Hollinger (1983) observed that those who described themselves as more androgynous on the Personal Attributes Questionnaire (Spence, Helmreich, & Stapp, 1974) had higher self-perceptions of social competence and self-esteem on the Texas Social Behavior Inventory (Helmreich, Stapp, & Ervin, 1974). Hollinger determined that it was the combination of expressiveness (femininity) and instrumentality (masculinity), rather than instrumentality alone, that accounted for her findings. Lack of a comparison group prevents determining how the gifted group might have differed from one not identified as gifted.

Franks and Dolan (1982) proposed that the relation between giftedness and self-concept is mediated primarily by achievement. The evidence supporting this model can hardly be considered compelling, although some support might be inferred from the studies cited previously, in which academic self-concept was significantly higher than other aspects of self-concept (Ross & Parker, 1980; Winne et al., 1982). Additional circumstantial support is provided by evidence that underachieving children typically exhibit poor self-concepts (Anastasiow, 1964; Mehta, 1968; Thiel & Thiel, 1977).

Feeling different from other children may be a significant component of self-concept. In Freeman's (1979) study, for example, the single question "Do you think your child feels different from other children?" proved to be the most discriminating of the 217 variables in the study. Parents of 52 percent of the poorly adjusted children said "Yes." Intellectually gifted children actually do often feel different from children not identified as gifted (Kaplan, 1983). Among a group of intellectually gifted 6- to 10-year-olds asked whether they perceived themselves as different from agemates, the 37 percent who said that they did scored lower than those who said they did not on 4 of the 6 Piers-Harris scales, although, paradoxically, these children usually reported their differences as being superior in some way to other children's (Janos, Robinson, & Fung, in press).

Children in Gifted Programs. Although in general we have omitted discussion of educational issues, self-concept and self-esteem have so frequently been examined with respect to special programs for the intellectually gifted that we mention a few here. It has usually been hypothesized either that special programs place children among a reference group with whom it is more difficult to compare favorably, or that labeling and educational segregation produce in children a sense of difference from agemates. Barbe (1957), for example, polled more than 400 graduates of the Cleveland Major Work classes, of whom 45 percent felt that the attitudes of other students toward Major Work students and lack of social contacts with students not identified as gifted were negative aspects of their experience. In contrast, hypotheses linking higher self-esteem with special programs may also be proposed.

Not surprisingly, consistency is not a distinguishing characteristic of the special program literature. In two studies in which children in gifted programs were compared with gifted children not in such programs, it was found that self-concept and self-esteem were lower among the special program students (Rodgers, 1979; Stopper, 1978), whereas in four similar studies no differences were found (Evans & Marken, 1982; Karnes & Wherry, 1981; Kolloff & Feldhusen, 1984; Maddux et al., 1982). In three studies comparing children in programs for the gifted with high achieving mainstream students (Coleman & Fults, 1980; Fults, 1980) or with norms (Stopper, 1978) superior self-concept and self-esteem were found among the mainstreamed or normative students. In two other studies comparing students in programs for the gifted to norms (Ketcham & Snyder, 1977; Maddux et al., 1982) no such differences were found. Kelly and Colangelo (1984) found that gifted students exhibited higher self-esteem than did students not identified as gifted. Coleman and Fults (1982) found that self-concept and self-esteem of gifted middle school age children rose sharply after they left the special program; this appears to provide partial support for the negative association of self-concept with certain types of special programs. No one, as far as we know, has examined the specific aspects of special programs that may be associated with higher or lower self-esteem nor, indeed, the goals those programs were trying to accomplish.

Summary

Most assessments of general psychosocial adjustment show that intellectually gifted children and adults are at least comparable to those not so designated, except possibly in adolescence, when more adjustment problems are occasionally noted. Intellectual advancement may, however, be associated with multiple personal and social difficulties if it becomes the overriding determinant of relationships with parents, teachers, and other children. The mixed findings from the relatively extensive self-concept research are perhaps the best indicators of what happens when investigation is more highly focused. The need to define dependent and independent variables and comparison groups more precisely and to consider the impact of moderating variables is strongly evident in this literature. Investigators do not consistently find gifted children to be above or below children of average intelligence in self-esteem, even in areas directly related to their gift, that is, in academic self-concept. Many factors other than giftedness influence self-concept and self-esteem, including age, sex, sex role identification, and participation in special programs. Investigators need to increase the sophistication of their conceptualizations accordingly.

Patterns in Personality: The Cultivation of the Gift

Certain personality characteristics are invaluable assets in developing intellectual talents (Barron & Harrington, 1981). Bloom (1982), for example, found in the lives of world class concert pianists, Olympic swimmers, and research mathematicians, an "unusual willingness to do great amounts of work . . . to achieve at a high level . . . great competitiveness . . . and a determination to do their best at all costs" (p. 572). Characteristics such as these have even begun to enter into the definition of giftedness. Renzulli (1978), for example, cites as the sine qua non of giftedness the following triad of qualities: above average ability, creativity, and *task commitment* (emphasis ours). Tannenbaum (1983) adds to the list of non-intellective traits requisite for excellence in any worthwhile field of endeavor the following: impulse control, tolerance for ambiguity and complexity, venturesomeness, and openness to experience.

Few authors have posited hypotheses derived from developmental theories in which intellectual level plays a significant role in the development of talent, and even fewer have attended to systematic age changes. Even theories regarding the development of achievement motivation (Dweck & Elliot, 1983; McClelland, Atkinson, Clark, & Lowell, 1953) have been overlooked. These theories suggest that parents who start independence training early acquaint their children with more situations that display achievement-related features and higher standards of excellence (Trudewind, 1982). Both achievement motivation and the more general effectance motivation (Harter, 1981) have, moreover, been noted to correlate with IQ (Pearlman, 1984). Data consistent with the model were found by Norman (1966), who observed correlations between independence demands and values of parents, measured by the Survey of Interpersonal Values (Gordon, 1960), and achievement patterns in intellectually gifted sixth-grade children (IQs > 130). He noted that parents' encouragement of general independence was probably not as important as the specific fostering of independent achievement.

Heckhausen (1982) pointed to one prerequisite for the development of achievement motivation: "First, the child should attend to the outcome in a way that leaves no doubt that the outcome is recognized as self-produced" (p. 601). The personality variable of locus of control relates directly to this prerequisite. In fact, intellectually gifted individuals of junior high and high school age appear to have internalized to a greater degree than individuals not identified as gifted a sense of control over the outcomes of their actions (Fincham & Barling, 1978; Tidwell, 1980), although in one study this was true only of the outcomes that were perceived as desirable (Milgram & Milgram, 1976).

People who have internalized a strong sense of control over what happens to them may consequently exhibit strong personal autonomy. Ratings of parents and teachers and self-reports document repeatedly that intellectually gifted individuals at all ages exhibit the following characteristics.

- self-sufficiency (Hollingworth & Rust, 1937)
- independence (Bachtold, 1968; Blaubergs, 1978; D'Heurle, Mellinger, & Haggard, 1959; Freeman, 1979; Nichols, 1967; Smith, 1964; Warren & Heist, 1960)
- autonomy (Blaubergs, 1978; Griggs & Price, 1980; Hogan, 1980; Hogan, Viernstein, McGinn, Daurio, & Bohannon, 1977; Kennedy et al., 1964; Nichols, 1967; Viernstein, 1976; Viernstein & Hogan, 1975)
- dominance and individualism (Nichols, 1967; Werner & Bachtold, 1969)
- self-direction (Griggs & Price, 1980)
- nonconformity (Lucito, 1964)

For this last characteristic, the gifted show a lesser tendency to conform although they typically do conform to reasoned expectations and engage in cooperative relationships. Boys appear to exhibit all of these characteristics more than do girls (Werner & Bachtold, 1969), although among those achieving noteworthy adult success, the pattern is similar for males and females (Blaubergs, 1978). Not only do gifted children exhibit independence, but they feel comfortable exercising it, where appropriate (Hays & Rothney, 1961; Stewart, 1979).

Activities and Interests

Interests are quite distinct from motivations, but they may be helpful in predicting the crystallization of talent, and they provide a measure of the breadth and depth of sustained, concentrated, personal intent. Broad and intense interests are commonly observed among intellectually gifted children. Terman (1925) and Thorndike (1939), for example, documented stronger and more mature intellectual, play, occupational, and reading interests among elementary and junior high school age intellectually gifted boys and girls. The children made many more collections, including collections of a scientific nature, and expressed greater interest in abstract subjects (e.g., literature) than in practical subjects (e.g., penmanship). The boys in Terman's sample showed increasingly strong scientific interests, and girls showed increasingly strong literary and domestic interests (Burks et al., 1930). As adults, the 150 "most successful" men in Terman's intellectually gifted sample had stronger, broader, and more intellectual interests than the 150 "least successful" (Terman & Oden, 1947).

Similarly, Warren and Heist (1960) concluded that the attribute most sharply differentiating highly talented college students from other college students on the California Personality Inventory (Gough, 1969) was a strong disposition toward intellectual activity. Specifically, the groups differed in their interest in reflective and abstract thought and working with ideas and concepts. The Warren and Heist (1960) conclusions were essentially the same as those obtained in the personality inventory studies of National Merit Scholars by Nichols and Davis (1964) and Nichols and Astin (1966). They have also been extended to younger samples of mathematically talented individuals, who show a strong interest in careers in mathematics and science (Fox & Denham, 1974).

Energy and Enthusiasm

Not necessarily marshalled by interests, but certainly available for their development, are energy (Miles, 1954; Terman, 1925), enthusiasm (Halpin, Payne, & Ellett, 1975; Hunt & Randhawa, 1980) and vigor (Carter, 1958) superior to that of children not identified as gifted. The energy referred to by Miles (1954) was reported in studies both of physical health and school behavior, whereas in Terman's study it referred to physical energy rated by parents. Nichols and Astin (1966) commented on "the sense of vitality that is such a striking characteristic of the questionnaire responses" (p. 680) of their college-age intellectually gifted sample.

Enthusiasm and vigor imply at least as much mental as physical energy. Mental energy is exhibited in the capacity to do a great deal of hard work to achieve goals and overcome obstacles (Freehill & McDonald, 1981; Galton, 1892). Parents and teachers rate intellectually gifted children as having more willpower and perseverance than children not identified as gifted (Burks et al., 1930; Terman, 1925). Terman and Oden (1947) also reported that in childhood the most successful men had been rated much higher on perseverance than had been the least successful men. Differences in persistence favor the gifted from nursery school (Lamson, as cited in Miles, 1954) through junior high school (Cooperative Research Group on Supernormal Children, 1981; Franks & Dolan, 1982; Griggs & Price, 1980). Persistence, perseverance, striving, and sacrificing for goals are perhaps even more characteristic at college age (Nichols & Astin, 1966) and later, especially among "successful" females (Blaubergs, 1978).

Mental and physical energy contributes to people's success in developing and fulfilling high aspirations. Terman's (1925) checklist of occupational preferences indicated that, even as young as age 11, 48 percent of gifted versus 25 percent of comparison males said they were "most likely to follow" a career in the professions. This difference did not obtain for females; both gifted and comparison groups chose the professions 37 percent of the time. "Ambition" was common throughout the lifespan in the Terman gifted sample (Goleman, 1980), In other samples it has been manifested as higher motivation and competitiveness (Wittek, 1973).

It is no surprise that energetic, independent people with a wide range of interests and high aspirations seek new experiences. At all ages, intellectually gifted individuals appear to express their independence through curiosity, experimentation, exploration, and risk taking more often than individuals not identified as gifted (Cooperative Research Group on Supernormal Children, 1981; Davids, 1966; Hunt & Randhawa, 1980; Payne, Halpin, Ellett, & Dale, 1975). In David's (1966) study, intellectually gifted adolescent girls presented themselves as seeking novel experiences, avoiding routine, and enjoying challenging situations even more than gifted boys.

Sociability

The focus on intellectual development that one might expect to find among intellectually gifted children may also be implicated in variations along the continuum of introversion and extroversion (Eysenck, 1967). D'Heurle et al. (1959) reported a balance between these tendencies in their third grade sample. The balance appears to move toward the introverted end of the spectrum as development proceeds, either because gifted children change in that direction as they grow, or because samples selected at those ages tend to recruit the more introverted children. Berndt, Kaiser, and Van Aalst (1982), for example, found 248 academically gifted 14-to-17-year-olds to be more socially introverted on the whole. Haier and Denham (1976) found their mathematically talented sample of seventh- and eighth-grade boys to be less extroverted than a sample of the American college population. Warren and Heist (1960) found their National Merit Scholar sample to be slightly less socially oriented on the Allport-Vernon-Lindzey Social Scale, although the reverse was true on the Omnibus Personality Inventory. National Merit students have reported themselves to be less friendly, sociable, easygoing, obliging, or cooperative, and teachers and peers have concurred with these evaluations (Nichols, 1967; Nichols & Davis, 1964).

Summary

In an attempt to create focus in a disorganized body of literature, we have intentionally limited our discussion of personality to a small number of characteristics that bear directly upon the development of intellectual talent. Intellectually gifted individuals with high achievement patterns exhibit all of these characteristics: having broad and mature sets of interests, including depth in a few of them; working hard and continuously to overcome obstacles; having high standards of quality; being willing to wait for deferred rewards; and having the self-sufficiency necessary to pursue goals they find important, even if their choices are not always validated by parents or friends. These characteristics appear to become stronger as the gifted grow older and are perhaps of necessity most marked among those who emerge as successful young adults. Possibly because of increasing focus on intellectual development, gifted children may become somewhat more introverted in adolescence and young adulthood.

Many intellectually gifted people do not, of course, exhibit high achievement. Consequently, these findings must be cautiously generalized. Furthermore, many individuals who are not identified as gifted in childhood or youth come to be so identified later in life, largely because they, too, exhibit these personality characteristics. Renzulli's emphasis on task commitment, cited earlier, seems on target in this context.

The apparent coherence in the personality structure of intellectually gifted children is, like most of the other inferences drawn from this review, based on a collection of basically nondevelopmental findings. Longitudinal and cross-sectional studies of the development of achievement motivation and delay of gratification, and in other areas in which developmental models already exist, may be the most fruitful areas in which to extend the investigations. Whether or not introversion increases as the nature of intellectual demands changes over time also requires longitudinal investigation. Research may also profitably tackle, we believe, questions about the development of the abilities to set attainable goals, derive energy from successful attainment of them, and cope with the disappointment associated with failure.

Interpersonal Relations

Parents, friends, and community affect maturity, psychosocial adjustment, and talent-fostering personality characteristics in intellectually gifted children (Newland, 1976). We start the discussion of their influence with background factors largely determined by social status, move into the quality of relationships with parents, and then turn attention to the child in the peer group.

Family Factors

High levels of education, occupation, and income, and harmonious marital relationships are observed consistently among parents of intellectually gifted children, and they often predict the children's superiority on psychological and social variables such as creativity (Aldous, 1975; Barbe, 1956; Getzels & Jackson, 1961), interests (Frierson, 1965), and psychological maturity (Monks & Ferguson, 1983; Nichols & Davis, 1964). The most successful men from Terman's study came from higher socioeconomic classes, and their families had histories of higher education and higher status occupations, were more stable, and provided more supervision and psychological and financial support to the children for pursuing their abilities and interests (Oden, 1968). Frierson (1967), comparing gifted elementary school children from more and less advantaged homes, found that the former group had more favorable attitudes toward school and read more and better quality books after school. Although it has been argued that such background characteristics provide much of the explanation for the variance between groups of differing ability levels (Bonsall, 1955; Davidson, 1943), other studies have provided evidence that intelligence level is independently determinative (Nichols & Astin, 1966; Nichols & Davis, 1964; Terman, 1925).

Parents who spend time with their children, facilitate their interests, answer their questions, and provide a warm, supportive base for intellectual exploration are likely to foster psychosocial maturity and adjustment. This is the kind of interaction parents of intellectually gifted children seem to offer (Roedell, Jackson, & Robinson, 1980). McGehee and Lewis (1940) studied teachers' estimates of the attitudes of parents toward 45,000 children in 36 states. The majority of gifted boys (66%) and girls (61%) had the advantage of parental attitudes rated as "superior" compared with only 20 percent of the normative groups of boys and 23 percent of the girls. Parents appear to encourage socially desirable and developmentally appropriate behavior (Torrance, 1963). Pressuring the child is not commonly observed. For example, Terman (1925) reported that, of 396 parental respondents, only 19.3 percent encouraged their children to "forge ahead" in school, 71.3 percent allowed their children to go at their own pace, and 9.4 percent held their children back. Although computations were not made for comparison children, Terman concluded that the large majority of children in his sample were not subjected to "hothouse" environments.

Wolf (1974) and Trotman (1977) asked mothers how they encouraged their children's learning. Their questionnaire identified specific activities that encouraged achievement motivation, language development, and provisions for general learning. With mothers of fifth graders (Wolf, 1974) and ninth graders (Trotman, 1977), much stronger correlations were found between these process variables and the children's IQs than between social status and IQ. Longstreth (1978) cautioned that bright children may elicit growth-fostering behavior from parents, but Tannenbaum (1983) sensibly concluded that the interchange is probably mutual.

The effects of family relations on personality were considered in the study by D'Heurle et al. (1959). For at least six years they studied an entire class of 76 children who were, in 1950, in the third grade of the Laboratory School at the University of Chicago. The median IQ exceeded the 90th percentile. Extensive personal and social data were collected, including laboratory observations, ability and achievement tests, projective tests, and numerous questionnaire and interview responses from parents, children, and teachers. Those children who achieved well in all areas appeared to adopt parental standards and be secure and confident with them and with other adults, although subtle negative behavior toward the parents, particularly the mother, was also observed. The children were socially competent, although somewhat competitive with siblings and agemates.

D'Heurle et al. (1959) also classified groups by performance on the Primary Mental Abilities battery (PMA) (Thurstone, 1938). Children who scored high on all subscales were outwardly independent, self-confident, and aggressive. Their parents were judged to be overprotective and demanding of high achievement, and the children were somewhat dependent on them. These children had, however, also internalized parental standards.

The above data suggest that how parents socialize their children to achieve can substantially affect personality characteristics and relations with adults and other children. In a brief review of student achievement and home environment, Morrow and Wilson (1961) reported that parents of high achievers of elementary, high school, and college age tend to use more praise and approval, show more interest and understanding, report feeling closer to their children, convey a greater sense of belongingness, and identify more with their own parents. Other work has shown that children with a desire to achieve had mothers who valued early independence in their children (Winterbottom, 1954); Terman, of course, had observed that the parents of the most successful men had encouraged initiative and independence (Goleman, 1980). Receiving warmth from the mother appeared important for inspiring achievement in males in the study of Mensa members by Groth (1974). McGillivray (1964) found that parents of high-achieving children tended to have high ambitions for them and that they were, in general, aware of their children's interests.

Peer Relations

Few studies in the literature identify the peers of intellectually gifted children by any variable other than age. This is unfortunate, because "peerness" rests largely in the degree to which the complexity of children's behavior is matched (Hartup, 1978; Lewis & Rosenblum, 1975). Our review revolves around the question of whether being socially at ease and establishing compatible friendships is made more difficult by having high intellectual ability.

Even with peers defined only by age, moderately gifted schoolchildren appear to manage quite well, both in studies employing sociometric measures (Gallagher, 1958a, 1958b; Gallagher & Crowder, 1957; Grace & Booth, 1958; Miller, 1956) and in those employing ratings by parents and teachers (Duncan & Dreger, 1978; Gallagher & Crowder, 1957; Janos, 1983). There is, however, no linear relation between IQ and sociometric ratings in groups representing a wide range of intellectual ability (Bonney, 1943; Grossman & Wrighter, 1948). Austin and Draper (1981) suggest that once a certain threshold of ability is reached, incremental gains in peer adjustment are small, and that at elevated levels of IQ, actual decreases may appear.

Intellectually gifted children report liking other children and enjoying play with them (Janos, Marwood, & Robinson, in press; Terman, 1925), although they may show less interest in competitive games than do other children (Terman, 1925). In the Janos, Marwood, and Robinson study, the majority of 79 primary grade gifted children reported that they were as friendly as other children. Most children reported that they played with other children on a daily basis, and this was verified by the majority of parents. Ninety-four percent of the children reported having at least one really good, close friend. High-IQ fourth-grade children have been found to choose other high-IQ children as friends more frequently than they choose children not identified as gifted (Miller, 1956), but Gallagher (1958b) found among a similar age group little tendency for the intellectually bright children to choose other bright children as friends.

Gifted children of junior high school age show a somewhat less marked tendency than other children to restrict playmates to the same sex (Terman, 1925), although best friends at the elementary age are almost always of the same sex (Janos, Marwood, & Robinson, in press). Among Terman's sample, interest in the opposite sex increased abruptly for boys at ages 13 to 14, whereas the interest of girls was uniformly high (Burks et al., 1930).

Gifted children tend to be more popular throughout childhood than children not identified as gifted (Burks et al., 1930; Gallagher, 1958a, 1958b, 1975; Grace & Booth, 1958; Heber, 1956), although not as a linear function of IQ (Burks et al., 1930; Hollingworth, 1942; Terman, 1925), and perhaps not during adolescence for girls (Austin & Draper, 1981). Burks et al. (1930), for example, reported that gifted children at age 14, who were an average of 2 years younger than their high school classmates, were nevertheless as popular as ordinary 16-year-olds.

Although intellectually gifted children were, in the Terman sample, somewhat more often than control children considered queer or different, the number of children so regarded was quite low (Terman, 1925). These children are, of course, indeed different, at least intellectually, and they are perceived that way by themselves (Janos, Fung, & Robinson, in press), their parents (Freeman, 1979), and their peers. There is strong evidence from the ratings of parents and teachers, however, that, in general, the peer relations of intellectually gifted children are satisfactory, although not necessarily superior to those of children not identified as gifted (Barbe, 1964; Bracken, 1970; Janos, 1983; Lehman & Erdwins, 1981). In the Janos (1983) study, for example, both parents and teachers rated a sample of 79 intellectually gifted children as being well within the normative range on the social skills scale of the Personality Inventory for Children (Wirt, Lachar, Klinedinst, & Seat, 1977).

Monks and Ferguson (1983) took a developmental approach in discussing the friendships of intellectually gifted children. They noted that, among the Terman sample, the most successful compared to the least successful men were rated as being friendlier and as having better social relationships. Yet as young adolescents, the most successful group rated themselves as more different from their classmates, as being at a social and physical disadvantage relative to classmates, and as having more difficulty entering into social activities and making friends. The authors related these difficulties to the accelerated academic status of the most successful individuals, which placed them among peer groups who valued characteristics they did not yet have, such as athletic prowess and freedom from certain parental restrictions. Later, when the factors that determine social acceptance emphasized achievement-related variables, the quality of peer relations improved substantially.

Summary

In this section we have covered relationships with adults, particularly parents, and with peers, and have attempted to describe the generally positive tenor of both that characterizes most intellectually gifted children. Gifted children typically enjoy favorable home backgrounds and the informed and attentive parenting that predisposes them toward making strong, if occasionally ambivalent, attachments and exerting themselves to meet reasonable demands. This attitude of trust and cooperation seems to transfer to relationships with other adults and with peers, and to elicit from them supportive and friendly responses. Intelligence, then, appears to be an advantage in successfully relating to others, at least at moderate elevations of IQ. As shall be seen in the following section, for children with extremely high IQs, the picture may be significantly altered.

In the area of peer relations, it seems to us that the question of whether high intellectual ability makes it more difficult for people to feel socially at ease and establish compatible friendships has been addressed only indirectly. For example, no studies have examined how peer interactions of children at different IQ levels are affected by the number of intellectually similar peers available for interaction. No studies involving gifted children have examined qualitative differences in the relationships among children of markedly discrepant IQs. These and many other questions that focus on social relations in which intelligence is theoretically implicated should be entertained by future investigators.

Subsets of the Gifted Population

The generalizations in the preceding sections do not apply equally to subsets of the gifted and talented population. For example, differences in the degrees of giftedness, in creativity, in areas of cognitive strength, and in academic achievement all introduce important qualifications.

Highly Intelligent Children

Individuals of extraordinarily superior general intellectual ability (Robinson, 1981), operationalized as having attained IQs at least four standard deviations above the mean on the Stanford-Binet, have been segregated for special attention in investigations by Burks et al. (1930); Feldman (1984); Hollingworth (1926, 1931, 1942); Janos (1983); Jenkins (1943); Selig (1959); Terman and Oden (1947); and Zorbaugh, Boardman, and Sheldon (1951). All of these, with the exception of the Selig study, have involved interview procedures and contact with individual children and their families for a number of years. Although based on relatively small numbers of children, and subject to the biases of the participant-observer investigators, the studies offer interesting developmental insights.

Hollingworth's studies of children with IQs above 180 are acknowledged as ground-breaking in this field, and her insights—like Terman's—have been strongly substantiated by subsequent investigations. The results of the studies suggest that a substantial minority of children of very superior intellectual ability suffer from a variety of psychosocial difficulties, including being bullied by older classmates, having play interests that agemates cannot share, and being required to tolerate unreasonable restrictions. The estimate derived from the literature is that psychosocial difficulties are present in at least 20 to 25 percent of school-age children of very superior intellectual ability (Burks et al., 1930; Janos, 1983; Selig, 1959), versus 5 to 7 percent in a representative (e.g., non-parent-referred) sample of children of moderate intellectual superiority (Hitchfield, 1973) or 6 to 16 percent in representative samples of average children (Achenbach & Edelbrock, 1981; Kastrup, 1976; Pringle et al., 1966; Rutter et al., 1970). The estimated percentages of highly gifted children having difficulties in the various studies were 21 percent (Janos, 1983), 36 percent by one criterion and 71 percent by another in Burks et al. (1930), and 55 percent (Selig, 1959).

A combination of stressors (Khoury & Appel, 1977; Manaster & Powell, 1983) complicates life for highly gifted children. Many experience unusual emotional distance from or closeness to their parents (Albert, 1978) and extraordinary intellectual demands (Bloom, 1982; Fowler, 1981). Albert detailed the picture:

> A complicated, tense parent-child relationship helps the eminent-to-be person learn to cope with tensions, complexity, and a sense of being quite special to usually one, but sometimes both, parents. . . . In cases where the eminent-to-be person is highly scientific or mathematically gifted, he or she is likely to describe their parent–child relationship as one of distance than of hostility; where the gifts are more artistic, the child is likely to have been extremely involved with one or both parents. (Albert, 1980, p. 737)

Outside of the family, there are usually few children with whom to play comfortably (Hollingworth, 1942; Zorbaugh et al., 1951). For example, Hollingworth (1942) mentioned that the children she knew with IQs above 180 typically strove to play with other children but were defeated by differences in interests and vocabulary. Zorbaugh et al. (1951) reported that the emotional energy of their subjects was "increasingly absorbed within themselves." As children, very bright individuals attempt to affiliate with other children, but since they may prefer to make friends of similar mental age (Miller, 1956; O'Shea, 1960), often they end up with no friends or few friends with whom they may play relatively infrequently (Hollingworth, 1942; Janos, 1983; Janos, Marwood, & Robinson, in press; Jenkins, 1943).

Freeman (1979) suggested that intellectually gifted children feel a moral obligation to society to fulfill their potential. If so, it may be most acute for highly intelligent children. As a group these children typically fail to meet this obligation, at least in terms of creative intellectual or artistic achievement (Dvorak, 1923; Feldman, 1984; Zorbaugh et al., 1951). It is not clear whether this is a problem of unreasonable expectations on the part of parents, teachers, and investigators, or whether it is indeed a problem of translating abilities into achievements. Terman and Oden (1947) did not seem to find any problem, for they concluded that, in adulthood, subjects with the highest IQs in childhood had accomplished more than subjects who had IQs considerably lower. After examining the files of the 26 Terman subjects scoring above 180 IQ, Feldman concluded that "there is the disappointing sense that they might have done more with their lives" (1984, p. 522). Performance pressure may indeed be more severe for this group than for other able people.

A significant minority of high-IQ children appear to experience social difficulties throughout their development. Hollingworth (1942) found difficulties to be "particularly acute" at ages 4 through 9. At the mean age of nearly 15 years (range 8–21) for boys and nearly 14 years for girls (range 8–16), Burks et al. (1930) found a definite tendency for children scoring above IQ 170, who were typically accelerated in school, to be rated as less well socially adjusted than less gifted subjects. As adults, apparently much of the tension may be reduced or resolved, but as Zorbaugh et al. (1951) pointed out, the resolution may have been at the expense of creative productivity.

For the highly gifted, the discrepancy between the child's abilities and the ordinary school environment, with its peer group of same-age children, is so strong that maladjustment is very likely. Programs that have attempted to provide a more "optimal match" (Robinson & Robinson, 1982) between ability level and educational challenge for highly gifted children, such as the Study of Mathematically Precocious Youth at Johns Hopkins University (Keating, 1976; Stanley, 1979) and the Early Entrance Program at the University of Washington (Robinson, 1983), have typically reported evidence of positive psychological and social adjustment (Daurio, 1979; Pollin, 1983; Robinson & Janos, in press). Such acceleration generally is accompanied by familial support and sensitivity, so that environmental support mechanisms are multiple.

Domains of Talent

There appear to be subtle differences in adjustment patterns among the artistically and scientifically gifted (Andreasen, 1975, 1978; Andreasen & Canter, 1975; Juda, 1949; Roe, 1951a, 1951b, 1952). A higher than average percentage of writers and artists, for example, have been observed to exhibit overt psychopathology, such as severe depression and alcoholism (Andreasen, 1975, 1978; Andreasen & Canter, 1975; Juda, 1949), whereas eminent scientists appear to exhibit more disruptions in interpersonal intimacy (Roe, 1951a, 1951b, 1952). Results of retrospective studies suggest that differences in adult adjustment are foreshadowed by differences in childhood (McCurdy, 1960; Yoder, 1894), as difficulties of this type often are. It also seems possible to us that they are precipitated by the intense demands of the creative process. Both questions provide springboards for future research.

Differences in verbal and mathematical talent have been documented repeatedly in the achivment patterns of children during childhood (D'Heurle et al., 1959) and early adolescence (McGinn, 1976). It remains an open question whether different social and personality patterns are associated with these cognitive differences. Although researchers in the Study of Mathematically Precocious Youth have reported separately on the personality correlates of verbally (McGinn, 1976) and mathematically (Haier & Denham, 1976) talented children, researchers have also made direct comparisons of lesser levels of talent. Gifted children who are characterized as scientific and analytically ingenious appear to differ from those characterized as literary and interpretative at elementary school

(D'Heurle et al., 1959; Miles, 1954), high school (Mills, 1983; Payne, Halpin, & Ellett, 1973; Silverblank, 1973; Viernstein, Hogan, & McGinn, 1977) and college age (Reynolds, 1975). For example, using the Sixteen Personality Factor Questionnaire (16PF, Cattell & Eber, 1969), Payne et al. (1973) concluded that academically talented students are characterized by practical learning, rapid mastery of intellectual tasks, and not allowing tension to interfere with school work. Artistically talented students, on the other hand, were characterized as being interested in working with ideas with more current, realistic, practical, and concrete consequences.

In the D'Heurle et al. (1959) study of third graders, the reading-talented children appeared to be more introspective, more anxious, and less communicative, and they were less popular with peers, whereas arithmetic achievers tended to be more aggressive, independent, self-confident, and competitive. This picture appears to hold true also for mathematically talented children during early and middle adolescence (Haier & Denham, 1976; Weiss et al., 1974).

Gifted Underachievers

It is beyond the scope of this chapter to examine in detail the roots of problems among underachieving, intellectually gifted youngsters. The favorable conclusions drawn in the review in the previous section are not likely to apply to this group. Krouse and Krouse (1981) argued that underachievement must be viewed as a complex interaction among three factors: weakness in specific academic skills, such as reading, note-taking, mathematics, and taking exams; deficiencies in behavioral self-control skills, such as self-monitoring and scheduling study time; and interfering affective factors, including test anxiety and personality maladjustment.

Underachievement in gifted children may be viewed variously from either the perspective of chronological age (i.e., achievement below regular school grade) or of mental age (i.e., achievement below that expected for ability level or special school placement). Although either of these is likely to reflect underlying problems and constitutes a failure to reach one's potential, there is remarkable lack of clarity in the research literature on a definition of underachievement in children of high ability.

A major portion of the research on intellectually gifted underachievers has, moreover, been restricted to describing personal maladjustment. Underachieving students fare badly in most comparisons with achieving gifted children at all age levels. Some of the adjustment variables on which gifted underachievers have been found to compare unfavorably are as follows:

• maturity (Hecht, 1975; Newland, 1976; Newman, Dember, & Krug, 1973; Raph, Goldberg, & Passow, 1966)

- emotional adjustment (Champaign Community Unit Schools, 1961; Faunce, 1968; Hecht, 1975; Horrall, 1957; Pringle, 1970; Raph et al., 1966)
- social adjustment (Bricklin & Bricklin, 1967; Whitmore, 1980)
- personality characteristics (Easton, 1959; Janos, Robinson, & Sanfillipo, 1985; Norfleet, 1968)
- self-concept (Anastasiow, 1964; Colangelo & Pfleger, 1979; Dean, 1977; Kanoy, Johnson, & Kanoy, 1980; Mehta, 1968; Raph et al., 1966; Saurenman & Michael, 1980; Shaw, 1961; Thiel & Thiel, 1977; Whitmore, 1980)
- motivation (Simono, 1967; Uhlinger & Stephens, 1960)
- conflict with environment (Otop, 1977; Shaw & Grubb, 1958)

Gurman's (1970) claim that family interaction is largely involved in the underachieving syndrome is well supported. Intellectually gifted underachievers are distinctly different from achieving gifted children in both family characteristics and social relations (Dowdall & Colangelo, 1982; Janos, Robinson, & Sanfillipo, 1985; Norman, 1966; Pringle, 1970; Uhlinger & Stephens, 1960). Parents' focusing on achievement is usually constructive but may inspire unconscious resistance (D'Heurle et al., 1959). Parents who are rigid and controlling may exacerbate difficulties in communication about educational decisions and generate conflict (Hays & Rothney, 1961). The outcomes of such conflict can be destructive (Kennedy & Wilcutt, 1963), as the famous cases of Winifred Stoner and William James Sidis attest (Montour, 1977). Both of these outstanding childhood prodigies came to naught as adults, seemingly because their parents had poorly met their emotional and social needs. Even where the outcomes are not so tragic, inappropriate expectations can produce underachievement (Hattwich & Stowell, 1930).

Pringle's (1970) study provided detailed treatment of some of these family issues. Pringle studied 103 intellectually gifted school-age children with a variety of problems (typically including underachievement). Although parents were well educated and the majority were professional or nonmanual workers, less than half of the homes were judged to have a happy and harmonious atmosphere. Even in these homes, above average cultural and social opportunities, including leisure activities, were provided by only a minority of parents. Pringle felt that discipline by parents seemed sensible in only one case out of four, and that inconsistent handling was most prominent in professional homes. Their children's educational progress was of concern to almost all parents; however, their children's emotional development appeared to be of little importance to a sizable minority. Pringle concluded that intellectual ability was probably by itself insufficient to compensate for inadequate support and interest shown by parents.

The literature pertaining to intellectually gifted underachievers emphasizes that, in addition to the personal and family deficits, inadequacies in educational approaches to gifted students may contribute to low achievement (Freeman, 1979; Whitmore, 1980). Such deficiencies may include dull and meager curricula (Hildreth, 1966; Strang, 1951), excessive emphasis by institutions on grades and external evaluation (Sears & Sherman, 1964), and petty school rules and teachers' disbelief in a child's competence (Freeman, 1979).

All of these difficulties of underachieving intellectually gifted children have been known (Gallagher & Rogge, 1966) and unsuccessfully addressed for years (Dowdall & Colangelo, 1982). Underachievement in gifted children has many sources, and the broad findings of unsupportive backgrounds, conflicted familial and extrafamilial relationships, poor personal adjustment, and inadequate educational provisions reflect both cause and effect. The assumption that all gifted children should achieve well at academic tasks is probably itself flawed. Since "systematic, large-scale research involving the identification of and educational intervention with young gifted underachievers remains unaccomplished" (Whitmore, 1980, p. 172), we can only suggest that, should such research be attempted, it would appear advisable to orchestrate multiple interventions, as was suggested by Krouse and Krouse (1981), simultaneously focusing on altering the structure of the school system and the patterns of family interaction. Whitmore (1980) suggested some possibilities for action in the school system, and Gurman (1970) suggested others for family interaction.

The Highly Creative, Intellectually Gifted

The personality characteristics of creative individuals have been competently reviewed by Barron and Harrington (1981) and by Dellas and Gaier (1970), to which the reader is referred for breadth and depth of coverage in this important area. In this section, we discuss only those findings regarding creative people who are also intellectually gifted, omitting those studies in which intelligence was not assessed. We examined whether our earlier conclusions can be generalized to this group, or whether significant alterations in the picture of general psychosocial development are required. It is important to note, however, that above IQ 120, creativity and intellectual advancement are not highly correlated (Guilford, 1962; Wallach & Kogan, 1965). It is, indeed, unfortunate that the rubric "gifted" has been applied to both (Albert, 1980), for within the permutations of high and low performance on measures of these distinct traits runs the broadest possible range of individual differences.

There exists a moderate degree of overlap between the personality characteristics of intellectually gifted children and those descriptive of highly creative persons. Barron and Harrington (1981) identified a fairly stable set of "core characteristics" of creative people, which included "high valuation of aesthetic qualities in experience, broad interests, attraction to complexity, high energy, independence of judgment, autonomy, intuition, self-confidence, ability to accommodate apparently opposite or conflicting traits in one's self-concept, and a firm sense of one's self as creative" (p. 453). Dellas and Gaier (1970) arrived at a similar set: independence in attitudes and social behavior, dominance, introversion, openness to stimuli, wide interests, self-acceptance, intuitiveness, flexibility, and social poise together with an unconcern for social norms. Broad interests, high energy, autonomy, self-confidence, introversion, self-acceptance, and social poise, as has been seen, are commonly found among intellectually gifted children and youths. The characteristics with little apparent overlap between intellectual giftedness and creativity seem to be independence of judgment, intuition, flexibility, tolerance for ambiguity, unconcern for social norms, and a firm sense of oneself as creative.

Several studies have contrasted the personality characteristics of intellectually gifted children with those of intellectually gifted children who are also creative. Wallach and Kogan (1965), for example, measured in a relatively playful context the ability of 151 fifth-grade children to generate unique and plentiful associates appropriate to the task. They found that the correlations among 10 creativity measures derived from the children's responses were of the same magnitude as correlations among 10 measures of intelligence and that the correlation across domains was low. They composed four groups of children within each sex: those high or low in both creativity and intelligence and those high in one and low in the other. The groups were rated on behavioral dimensions by trained classroom observers prior to the assessments of creativity and intelligence. High interrater reliability was obtained.

The highly intelligent and highly creative fifth-grade children showed high self-confidence, high interest in academic work, and popularity with peers. The group was also high in disruptive, attention-seeking behavior, which was interpreted by Wallach and Kogan as being an indication that these children, bored by classroom routines, may have been eager to propose divergent ideas. These children showed by far the greatest ability to range beyond the physical and into the realm of affective content. In contrast, children high in intelligence but low in creativity also showed confidence and concentration on academic work but, although they were sought out by others, they were somewhat cool and aloof. They showed the lowest level of anxiety of the four groups, but were unwilling to take chances or express affective associations and were intolerant of unlikely, unconventional ideas.

The finding regarding differences in level of anxiety among these groups has not been replicated. Flescher (1963) compared 28 sixth-grade children with IQ scores above 130 who were not in the top quartile on a set of creativity measures with 24 children whose IQs were also above

130 but who did have creativity scores in the top quartile. No differences were found between the groups on either the General or the Test Anxiety Scales for Children (Sarason et al., 1960).

High academic achievement in a conventional educational setting may, indeed, be the province of the less creative, intellectually gifted student. Hogan and Weiss (1974) compared a group of 54 Johns Hopkins University Phi Beta Kappans with 61 Johns Hopkins classmates with high scores on the Intellectual Efficiency scale of the California Personality Inventory, who were regarded by the authors as being academically inclined, and with 87 unselected Hopkins undergraduates. In comparison with the other two groups, the Phi Beta Kappans were stable, stodgy, and unoriginal, but they showed unusual conscientiousness, industry, dependability, and attention to the rules of the academic game.

Nichols (1964) suggested that mothers' childrearing attitudes may contribute to the differences in creativity observed at the college level. He studied the correlations between mothers' attitudes and creativity in a sample of 796 male and 450 female National Merit Finalists. Mothers' authoritarian attitudes as measured by the Parental Attitudes Research Instrument (Schaefer & Bell, 1958) were negatively correlated with originality and creativity of children, which was measured by a variety of personality inventories and creativity attribute scales. Children of authoritarian mothers, especially males, did, however, achieve higher grades in school and receive more favorable ratings by teachers on emotional stability, maturity, dependability, and intellectual leadership. All of the correlations were, however, minuscule, and valuable only in suggesting further questions for research.

The literature that simultaneously assessed the relations between intellectual and creative giftedness and psychosocial characteristics consists, as far as we can determine, of the meager scattering of studies reported in this section, most of which are more than 20 years old. We have illustrated that success in conventional educational settings tends to accrue to those who exhibit less creativity. Of particular interest is the question of whether creative talents in high academic achievers can sprout even after being buried for the protracted years of convergent thinking that is mandated by the traditional educational system.

Conclusions and Future Directions

Sixty years of research with intellectually gifted children has barely scratched the surface as far as psychological and social development are concerned. Overall, one is left with the impression that growth in these areas transpires basically as it does for children at large, but that normal development is pervasively moderated by high ability. Unless we undertake to untangle these interactions, gifted children will continue to run the risk of remaining seriously underserved.

One is tempted to conclude that, as a group, moderately gifted children who are making good use of their potential mature more rapidly than their age peers in almost every aspect of development, although not to the same extent that they outstrip them in intellectual development. The data hardly warrant such a sweeping conclusion. Ground has been broken in some areas, of course, including social cognition, moral cognition, interests and attitudes, play activities, and personality. Yet studies of comparative changes over time are essentially nonexistent. To satisfy the theoretical interest in differential rates of development, studies with instrumentation and control groups adequate to detect such differences are needed.

When it comes to considerations of psychological adjustment, the case seems to be clear-cut. In most studies, moderately gifted children compare favorably with their age-mates, whether the variables are broad-band, such as overall ratings of behavior problems, personality characteristics, or social relationships, or whether the focus is more specific, as on self-concept and self-esteem, family relations, and friendships. Being intellectually gifted, at least at moderate levels of ability, is clearly an asset in terms of psychosocial adjustment in most situations. Environmental variables, such as poorly conceived or implemented educational programs, may, of course, alter this reassuring picture.

Several aspects of this generally positive portrait warrant special attention:

1. The notion that gifted children are destined to be unhappy and isolated has been firmly laid to rest. Positive psychological adjustment is the general theme for the group as a whole, although individual differences are at least as great among intellectually gifted as among average children. Positive adjustment enhances the resources available to intellectually gifted children for learning and other productive enterprises.

2. The personality characteristics that most consistently differentiate gifted from average individuals relate to sustained intent and concentrated effort. Interests tend to be defined earlier and to be more intense and more mature from preschool age through adulthood. Gifted children tend to approach what they do with energy, focus, perseverance, enthusiasm, vigor, and commitment. At the same time, especially as they head into adolescence, they appear to gain some freedom from interpersonal constraints on their development, with greater self-sufficiency, autonomy, dominance, individualism, and a lesser tendency to conform. Many exhibit greater curiosity, experimentation, and risk-taking, as well as creativity and originality. At the same time, during adolescence, some gifted individuals do experience greater vulnerability in self-esteem and general adjustment.

3. Maturity in intellect tends to be accompanied by maturity in personal and social growth. As a group, gifted children contradict the widely

held notion that, aside from being bright, they are better characterized by their chronological age than by their mental age. Using either chronological age or mental age alone to predict levels of functioning in widely diverse areas of competence is, of course, likely to prove frequently fallible. Nevertheless, the fact is that many bright children are also socially mature; they seek older friends and exhibit social understanding and interests typical of older individuals. The degree and dimensions of this resemblance need further exploration, as do ways of assessing individual differences in order to provide an optimal environment for each child. Clearly there is no empirical justification for assuming that one's classmates and friends should invariably be one's agemates.

4. Familial influences on the development of intellectual giftedness are poorly described in the literature despite their central role. Although the general picture of familial relationships suggests that such children are cherished by parents, special stresses exist in a substantial percentage of families. This is an area ripe for further exploration.

5. Findings regarding favorable personal and social adjustment emanate from studies of moderately rather than extremely gifted children. The most highly talented are the most vulnerable, probably because they are exceedingly "out of sync" with school, friends, and even family. These children, few in number though they are, have great potential for remarkable insights and significant achievements and deserve the best opportunities we can devise in order to develop motivational and personal strength and momentum. Although they need to be recognized as being individuals who have worth independent from their productivity, highly intelligent children too frequently disappoint our expectations for creative intellectual or artistic achievement. They may become superficially adjusted but sacrifice possibilities for outstanding fulfillment and significant, socially valued contributions. These are, in our opinion, problems of clinical proportions, but research devoted to exploring them pales in comparison with that devoted to virtually any other maladaptive set of behaviors.

6. Highly creative, gifted individuals may also be at risk for psychopathology, although the evidence for this difference is clearer with adults than with children. Although the differences are merely suggestive, problems of the "creative" in areas of verbal/subjective talent are more frequently associated with conflict, disruption, attention seeking, and impulsivity, whereas creative people in the quantitative/scientific fields may be more overcontrolled and socially withdrawn. Conventional schools tend to reward the less original students and may, indeed, exacerbate the problems of some creative children.

7. Underachievement in gifted individuals is a tragic waste for them and for the rest of us. There is a complex but well-documented portrait of intractable problems, inappropriate upbringing, negative school behavior, low motivation, and lack of focus. Surprisingly few interventions

have been tried with this group, yet the picture is firmly established for many children by early adolescence.

This review suggests several paths for action. Fitting academic opportunities to intellectual abilities is logically mandated. Although gifted children are demanding in the sense that they "use up" curricula more quickly than others, they are likely to benefit from coherent programs grounded in specific intellectual objectives that are simultaneously flexible enough to incorporate and to encourage student-initiated extensions. For exceedingly precocious, creative, and underachieving gifted children, standard solutions to meeting the needs of gifted children may not be sufficient.

Aside from their families, the most critical resource for such individuals may be informed school psychologists and counselors who are able to match children's special needs with existing resources, such as teachers who are not easily intimidated, class settings that can provide more advanced opportunities and appropriate challenges, out-of-school resources, and mentors. Counselors can help children evaluate their own situations and sort out "difference" from "deviance." Skilled psychologists are also needed to work with parents to develop appropriate expectations and means of meeting the needs of family and child. At present, school counselors, school psychologists, or child–clinical psychologists who have any training in working with this group are rare.

Throughout this chapter, we have mentioned many neglected areas of research. The correlation of intelligence with social class is well established, yet many authors have failed to take into account the social backgrounds of their subjects. Will some of the truisms fall apart when close matches for family background—not simply gross measures such as parental occupation—are employed? What can investigators discover about highly intelligent children who come unexpectedly from backgrounds of low social status as concerns both the source of their advancement and the difficulties that may arise in conflict with their environment? What are the special stresses of adolescence that cause a dip, for some intellectually gifted children, in their psychosocial adjustment and feelings of self-worth?

Still another area warranting attention is the effect of gifted individuals on those around them. In what ways does the child elicit patterns of support or criticism from parents? What are the effects on siblings who are not themselves as intellectually gifted? On teachers who may be ill prepared for the special demands? On classmates to whom they may furnish leadership and ideas—or destructive competition?

Possible programs of intervention with gifted children follow naturally from the findings reported in this chapter. For example, are there discussions or support groups or other services that would help parents deal with these unusual children? Are there teachable social skills that would help intellectually gifted children deal in socially positive ways with their realistic sense of being different from other children? Are there means of softening the pangs of adolescence? And, in terms of its frequency of occurrence and tragic outcome, are there ways in which parents and teachers can help to motivate youngsters whose lack of zest and effort make them settle for less than their best?

Although intervention may be appropriate for many gifted children, their families, and their teachers, the overall maturity and favorable adjustment of most gifted children suggest that they also need to engage in their own decision making. These children are, by definition, in some ways more competent than are their age peers. Many of them are more competent than are other children to manage their lives effectively, given a supportive context. This is not by any means to recommend a laissez-faire approach to rearing intellectually gifted children, but merely to emphasize their need to be respected in their goals and motivations, to be encouraged without being robbed of autonomy, energy, and self-direction by well-meaning but misplaced intrusion.

Finally, it is time for developmental psychologists to recognize the relevance of this special group of children to the development of all. Applications to the National Institutes of Health, the National Science Foundation, and other mainstream research funding sources for projects focusing on gifted children are very few. Part of the reason may be that in the past few decades researchers have attended to broad themes of development rather than to individual differences. Yet, there are clearly bands of investigators in similar fields who value those exceptions for the light they shed on mainstream developmental phenomena.

This is an opportune time for action. There is clamor for excellence in education, and there is no group more capable of responding to opportunity than gifted children. The opportunity can be presented effectively only, however, if there are psychologists able and willing to become involved.

References

Abroms, K. I., & Gollin, J. B. (1980). Developmental study of gifted preschool children and measures of psychosocial giftedness. *Exceptional Children, 46*(5), 334–341.

Achenbach, T. M., & Edelbrock, C. S. (1981). Behavioral problems and competencies reported by parents of normal and disturbed children aged 4–16. *Society for Research in Child Development Monographs, 46*(1, Serial No. 188).

Achenbach, T. M., & Edelbrock, C. S. (1983). *Manual for the child behavior checklist and revised behavior profile.* Burlington, VT: Authors.

Albert, R. S. (1978). Characteristics and suggestions regarding giftedness, familial influence, and attainment of eminence. *Gifted Child Quarterly, 22*, 201–211.

Albert, R. S. (1980). Genius. In R. H. Woody (Ed.), *Encyclopedia of clinical assessment* (Vol. 2). San Francisco: Jossey-Bass.

Aldous, J. (1975). Search for alternatives: Parental behaviors and children's orig-
inal problem solutions. *Journal of Marriage, 37*(4), 711–722.
Anastasiow, N. (1964). A report of self concept of the very gifted. *Gifted Child
Quarterly, 8*(4), 177–178.
Andreasen, N. C. (1975). The creative writer: Psychiatric symptoms and family
history. *Comprehensive Psychiatry, 15,* 123–131.
Andreasen, N. C. (1978). Creativity and psychiatric illness. *Psychiatric Annals,
8*(3), 23–45.
Andreasen, N. C., & Canter, A. (1975). Genius and insanity revisited. In R. Wirt,
G. Winokur, & M. Roff (Eds.), *Life history research in psychopathology* (Vol.
4). Minneapolis: University of Minnesota Press.
Austin, A. B., & Draper, D. C. (1981). Peer relationships of the academically gifted:
A review. *Gifted Child Quarterly, 25*(3), 129–134.
Bachtold, L. M. (1968). Interpersonal values of gifted junior high school students.
Psychology in the Schools, 5(4), 368–370.
Barbe, W. B. (1956). A study of the family background of the gifted. *Journal of
Educational Psychology, 47,* 302–309.
Barbe, W. B. (1957). What happens to graduates of special classes for the gifted?
Ohio State University Educational Research Bulletin, 36, 13–16.
Barbe, W. B. (1964). The adjustment of gifted children in special classes. *Gifted
Child Quarterly, 8*(1), 32–35.
Barron, F., & Harrington, D. (1981). Creativity, intelligence, and personality.
Annual Review of Psychology, 32, 439–476.
Berndt, D., Kaiser, C., & Van Aalst, F. (1982). Depression and self-actualization
in gifted adolescents. *Journal of Clinical Psychology, 38*(1), 142–150.
Blaubergs, M. S. (1978). Personal studies of gifted females: A review and com-
mentary. *Gifted Child Quarterly, 22,* 539–547.
Bloom, B. S. (1982). The role of gifts and markers in the development of talents.
Exceptional Children, 48, 510–522.
Bonney, M. (1943). R stability of social, intellectual, and academic status in grades
2–4. *Journal of Educational Psychology, 34,* 88–102.
Bonsall, M. (1955). The temperament of gifted children. *California Journal of
Educational Research, 6,* 162–165.
Borke, H. (1971). Interpersonal personal perceptions of young children: Egocen-
trism or empathy? *Development Psychology, 6,* 263–269.
Bracken, B. (1970). Comparison of self-attitudes of gifted children and children
in a non-gifted normative group. *Psychological Reports, 47,* 715–718.
Bricklin, B., & Bricklin, P. (1967). *Bright child, poor grades.* New York: Delacorte.
Brookover, W., Patterson, A., & Thomas, S. (1962). *Self-concept of ability and
school achievement.* East Lansing, MI: Michigan State University, Office of
Research and Publications.
Brownfain, J. J. (1952). Stability of the self-concept as a dimension of personality.
Journal of Abnormal and Social Psychology, 47, 597–606.
Burks, B. S., Jensen, D. W., & Terman, L. M. (1930). *Genetic studies of genius:
Vol. 3. The promise of youth: Follow-up studies of a thousand gifted children.*
Stanford, CA: Stanford University Press.
Cady, V. (1923). The estimation of juvenile incorrigibility. *Journal of Delinquency
Monograph,* No. 2, 140.
Carroll, J. L., & Laming, J. R. (1974). Giftedness and creativity: A Review. *Gifted
Child Quarterly, 18,* 85–96.
Carter, T. (1958). The play problems of gifted children. *School Sociology, 86,* 224–
225.
Cattell, R., & Eber, H. (1969). *Handbook for the 16 Personality Factor Question-
naire.* Champaign, IL: Institute for Personality and Ability Testing.

Chambers, J., & Dusseault, B. (1972). Characteristics of college age gifted. *Proceedings of the 80th Annual Convention of the American Psychological Association, 7*(2), 527–528.

Champaign Community Unit Schools. (1961). Factors associated with underachievement and overachievement of intellectually gifted children. *Exceptional Children, 28,* 167–175.

Colangelo, N., & Pfleger, L. (1979). Academic self-concept of gifted high school students. In N. Colangelo & R. Zaffran (Eds.), *New voices in counseling the gifted.* Dubuque, IA: Kendall/Hunt.

Coleman, J., & Fults, E. (1982). Self-concept and the gifted classroom: The role of social comparisons. *Gifted Child Quarterly, 26,* 116–120.

Cooperative Research Group of Supernormal Children. (1981). Summary of a year's research on supernormal children. *Acta Psychologica Sinica, 13*(1), 35–41.

Daurio, S. P. (1979). Educational enrichment versus acceleration. In W. George, S. Cohn, & J. Stanley (Eds.), *Acceleration and enrichment: Strategies for educational change.* Baltimore: Johns Hopkins University Press.

Davids, A. (1966). Psychological characteristics of high school male and female potential scientists in comparison with academic underachievers. *Psychology in the Schools, 3,* 79–87.

Davidson, H. H. (1943). *Personality and economic background: A study of highly intelligent children.* New York: Kings Crown Press.

Dean, R. (1977). Effects of self concept on learning with gifted children. *Journal of Educational Research, 70*(6), 315–318.

Dellas, M., & Gaier, E. (1970). Identification of creativity. *Psychological Bulletin, 73*(1), 55–73.

D'Heurle, A., Mellinger, J., & Haggard, E. (1959). Personality, intellectual, and achievement patterns in gifted children. *Psychological Monographs, 73*(13, Serial No. 483).

Dirkes, M. A. (1983). Anxiety in the gifted: Plusses and minuses. *Roeper Review, 6*(2), 68–70.

Dowdall, C., & Colangelo, N. (1982). Underachieving gifted students: Review and implications. *Gifted Child Quarterly, 26*(4), 179–185.

Duncan, J., & Dreger, R. (1978). Behavior analysis and identification of gifted children. *Journal of Genetic Psychology, 133,* 43–57.

Dvorak, H. (1923). The mental tests of a superior child. *Mental Hygiene, 7,* 250–257.

Dweck, C., & Elliot, E. S. (1983). Achievement motivation. In E. M. Hetherington (Ed.), *Handbook of child psychology: Vol. 4. Socialization, personality, and social development* (4th ed., pp. 643–691). New York: Wiley.

Easton, J. (1959). Some personality traits of underachieving high school students of superior ability. *Bulletin of the Maritime Psychological Association, 8,* 34–39.

Eme, R. (1979). Sex differences in childhood psychopathology: A review. *Psychological Bulletin, 86,* 574–595.

Evans, E., & Marken, D. (1982). Multiple outcome assessment of special class placement for gifted students: A comparative study. *Gifted Child Quarterly, 26*(3), 126–132.

Eysenck, H. (1967). Intelligence assessment: A theoretical and experimental approach. *British Journal of Educational Psychology, 77,* 81–98.

Faunce, P. (1968). Personality characteristics and vocational interests related to the college persistence of academically gifted women. *Journal of Counseling Psychology, 15*(1), 31–40.

Feldman, D. H. (1984). A follow-up of subjects scoring above 180 IQ in Terman's "Genetic Studies of Genius." *Exceptional Children, 50,* 518–523.

Fincham, F., & Barling, J. (1978). Locus of control and generosity in learning disabled, normal achieving, and gifted children. *Child Development, 49*(2), 530–533.

Fitts, W. (1965). *Manual for the Tennessee self-concept scale.* Nashville, TN: Counselor Recording and Tests.

Fitts, W. (1972, June). The self concept and behavior: Overview and supplement. *Dede Wallace Center Monograph,* Serial No. 7.

Flavell, J., Botkin, P., Fry, C., Wright, J., & Jarvis, P. (1968). *The development of role-taking and communication skills in children.* New York: Wiley.

Flescher, R. (1963). Anxiety and achievement of intellectually gifted and creatively gifted children. *Journal of Psychology, 56,* 251–268.

Fowler, W. (1981). Case studies of cognitive precocity. *Journal of Applied Developmental Psychology, 2,* 319–369.

Fox, L., & Denham, S. (1974). Values and career interests of mathematically and scientifically precocious youth. In J. Stanley, D. Keating, & L. Fox (Eds.), *Mathematical talent: Discovery, description, and development* (pp. 140–176). Baltimore: Johns Hopkins University Press.

Franks, B., & Dolan, L. (1982). Affective characteristics of gifted children: Educational implications. *Gifted Child Quarterly, 26*(4), 172–178.

Freehill, M., & McDonald, J. (1981). Zeal: Essential to superior intellectual achievements. *Gifted Child Quarterly, 25*(3), 123–127.

Freeman, J. (1979). *Gifted children.* Baltimore: University Park Press.

Frierson, E. C. (1965). A study of differences between gifted children from upper and lower status communities. *Science Education, 49,* 205–210.

Frierson, E. C. (1967). A study of selected characteristics of gifted children from upper and lower socioeconomic backgrounds. *Dissertation Abstracts, 28*(2-A), 495.

Fults, E. (1980). The effect of an instructional program on the creative thinking skills, self-concept, and leadership of intellectually and academically gifted elementary students. *Dissertation Abstracts International, 41,* 2931A.

Gallagher, J. J. (1958a). Peer acceptance of highly gifted children in elementary school. *Elementary School Journal, 58,* 465–470.

Gallagher, J. J. (1958b). Social status of children related to intelligence, propinquity, and social perception. *Elementary School Journal, 58,* 225–231.

Gallagher, J. J. (1975). *Teaching the gifted child.* Boston: Allyn & Bacon.

Gallagher, J. J., & Crowder, T. (1957). The adjustment of gifted children in the regular classroom. *Exceptional Children, 23,* 306–312, 317–319.

Gallagher, J. J., & Rogge, W. (1966). The gifted. *Review of Educational Research, 36*(1), 37–54.

Galton, F. (1892). *Hereditary genius.* London: Macmillan.

Gardner, H. (1983). *Frames of mind: The theory of multiple intelligences.* New York: Basic Books.

Getzels, J. W., & Dillon, J. T. (1973). The nature of giftedness and the education of the gifted child. In R.M.W. Travers (Ed.), *Second handbook of research on teaching.* Chicago: Rand McNally.

Getzels, J., & Jackson, P. (1961). Family environment and cognitive style: A study of the sources of highly intelligent and of highly creative adolescents. *American Sociological Review, 26*(3), 251–360.

Glenn, P. (1978). The relationship of self concept and IQ to gifted students' expressed need for structure. *Dissertation Abstracts, 38*(7-A), 4091.

Goleman, D. (1980). 1528 little geniuses and how they grew. *Psychology Today, 14*(2), pp. 28ff.

Gordon, L. (1960). *SRA manual for the Survey of Interpersonal Values.* Chicago: Scientific Research Association.

Gough, H. G. (1969). *Manual for the California Psychological Inventory.* Palo Alto, CA: Consulting Psychologists Press.

Grace, H., & Booth, N. (1958). Is the "gifted" child a social isolate? *Peabody Journal of Education, 35,* 195–196.

Griggs, S., & Price, G. (1980). A comparison between the learning styles of gifted versus average suburban junior high school students. *Roeper Review, 3,* 7–9.

Grossman, B., & Wrighter, J. (1948). Intelligence, social status, and personality among 6th grade subjects. *Sociometry, 11,* 346–355.

Groth, N. (1974). The relationship of the affective needs of a sample of intellectually gifted adults to their age, sex, and perceptions of emotional warmth to their parents. *Dissertation Abstracts, 35*(1–A), 286.

Guilford, J. (1962). Creativity: Its measurement and development. In S. Parnes & H. Harding (Eds.), *A source book for creative thinking.* New York: Scribner.

Gurman, A. (1970). The role of the family in underachievement. *Journal of School Psychology, 8*(1), 48–53.

Haier, R., & Denham, S. (1976). A summary profile of the non-intellectual correlates of mathematical precocity in boys and girls. In D. Keating (Ed.), *Intellectual talent: Research and development* (pp. 225–241). Baltimore: Johns Hopkins University Press.

Halpin, G., Payne, D., & Ellett, C. (1975). Life history antecedents of current personality traits of gifted adolescents. *Measurement and Evaluation in Guidance, 8*(1), 29–36.

Harter, S. (1981). A model of mastery motivation in children: Individual differences and developmental change. In W. Collins (Ed.), *Aspects of the development of competence: The Minnesota Symposia on Child Psychology* (Vol. 14). Minneapolis, MN: University of Minnesota Press.

Harter, S. (1983). Developmental perspectives on the self-system. In E. M. Hetherington (Ed.), *Handbook of child psychology: Vol. 4. Socialization, personality, and social development* (4th ed., pp. 275–385). New York: Wiley.

Hartup, W. (1978). Children and their friends. In H. McGurk (Ed.), *Issues in childhood social development* London: Methuen.

Hattwick, B., & Stowell, M. (1930). The relation of parental over-attention to children's work habits and social adjustments in kindergarten and the first six grades of school. *Journal of Educational Research, 30,* 169–176.

Hays, D., & Rothney, J. (1961). Educational decision-making by superior secondary school students and their parents. *Personnel and Guidance Journal, 40,* 26–30.

Heber, R. (1956). The relation of intelligence and physical maturity to social status of children. *Journal of Educational Psychology, 47,* 1158–1162.

Hecht, K. (1975). Teacher rating of potential dropouts and academically gifted children: Are they related. *Journal of Teacher Education, 26,* 172–175.

Heckhausen, H. (1982). The development of achievement motivation. *Review of Child Development Research, 6,* 600–669.

Helmreich, R., Stapp, J., & Ervin, C. (1974). The Texas Social Behavior instrument: An objective measure of self-esteem or social competence. *JSAS Catalog of Selected Documents in Psychology, 4,* 79.

Hildreth, G. H. (1938). Characteristics of young gifted children. *Journal of Genetic Psychology, 53,* 287–262.

Hildreth, G. (1966). *Introduction to the gifted.* New York: McGraw-Hill.

Hitchfield, E. (1973). *In search of promise: A long-term national study of able children and their families.* London: Longman.

Hogan, R. (1980). The gifted adolescent. In J. Adelson (Ed.), *Handbook of adolescent psychology* (pp. 536–559). New York: Wiley.

Hogan, R., Viernstein, M., McGinn, P., Daurio, S., & Bohannon, W. (1977). Verbal giftedness and sociopolitical intelligence. *Journal of Youth and Adolescence, 6*, 107–116.

Hogan, R., & Weiss, D. (1974). Personality correlates of superior academic achievement. *Journal of Counseling Psychology, 21*(2), 144–149.

Hollinger, C. (1983). Counseling the gifted and talented female adolescent: The relationship between social self-esteem and traits of instrumentality and expressiveness. *Gifted Child Quarterly, 27*(4), 157–162.

Hollingworth, L. S. (1926). *Gifted children: Their nature and nurture.* New York: Macmillan.

Hollingworth, L. S. (1931). The child of very superior intelligence as a special problem in social development. *Mental Hygiene, 15*, 3–16.

Hollingworth, L. S. (1942). *Children above 180 IQ. Stanford-Binet: Origin and development.* Yonkers, NY: World Book.

Hollingworth, L. S., & Rust, M. (1937). Application of the Bernreiter to highly intelligent adolescents. *Journal of Psychology, 4*, 287–293.

Horrall, B. (1949). Relationships between college aptitude and discouragement-buoyancy among college freshmen. *Journal of Genetic Psychology, 74*, 185–243.

Horrall, B. (1957). Academic performance and personality adjustment of highly intelligent college students. *Genetic Psychology Monographs, 55*, 3–83.

Hunt, D., & Randhawa, B. (1980). Personality factors and ability groups. *Perceptual and Motor Skills, 50*(3), 902.

Jahoda, M. (1958). *Current concepts of positive mental health.* New York: Basic Books.

Janos, P. (1983). *The psychosocial adjustment of children of very superior intellectual ability.* Unpublished doctoral dissertation, Ohio State University.

Janos, P., Fung, H., & Robinson, N. (in press). Perceptions of deviation and self-concept within an intellectually gifted sample. *Gifted Child Quarterly.*

Janos, P., Marwood, K., & Robinson N. (in press). Friendship patterns of highly intelligent children. *Roeper Review.*

Janos, P., Robinson, N., & Sanfillipo, S. (1985). *Patterns of underachievement in students markedly accelerated in college.* Manuscript in preparation.

Janos, P., Robinson, N., & Sather, K. (1983). *The performance of a sample of markedly accelerated students on a developmental scale of moral judgment.* Unpublished manuscript.

Jenkins, M. D. (1943). Case studies of Negro children of Binet IQ 160 and above. *Journal of Negro Education, 12, 159–166.*

Juda, A. (1949). Relations between highest mental capacity and psychic abnormalities. *American Journal of Psychiatry, 106*(4), 296–307.

Kanoy, R., Johnson, B., & Kanoy, K. (1980). Locus of control and self-concept in achieving and underachieving bright elementary students. *Psychology in the Schools, 17*, 395–399.

Kaplan, L. (1983). Mistakes gifted young people too often make. *Roeper Review, 6*(2), 73–77.

Karnes, F. A., & Wherry, G. N. (1981). Self-concepts of gifted students as measured by the Piers-Harris Children's Self-Concept Scale. *Psychological Reports, 49*, 903–906.

Kastrup, M. (1976). Psychic disorders among pre-school children in a geographically delimited area of Arhus Country, Denmark. *Acta Psychiatrica Scandinavica, 54*, 29–42.

Keating, D. P. (Ed.) (1976). *Intellectual talent: Research and development.* Baltimore: Johns Hopkins University Press.

Kelly, K., & Colangelo, N. (1984). Academic and social self-concepts of gifted, general, and special students. *Exceptional Children, 50*, 551–553.

Kennedy, W., Cottrell, T., & Smith, A. (1963). Norms of gifted adolescents on the Rotter Incomplete Sentence Blank. *Journal of Clinical Psychology, 19*(3), 314–315.

Kennedy, W., Cottrell, T., & Smith, A. (1964). EPPS norms for mathematically gifted adolescents. *Psychological Reports, 14*(2), 342.

Kennedy, W., & Smith, A. (1962). A high performance MMPI scale for adolescents. *Psychological Reports, 11*(2), 494.

Kennedy, W., & Wilcutt, H. (1963). Youth–parent relations of mathematically gifted adolescents. *Journal of Clinical Psychology, 19*(4), 400–402.

Ketcham, B., & Snyder, R. (1977). Self-attitudes of gifted students as measured by the Piers-Harris Children's Self-Concept Scale. *Psychological Reports, 40*, 111–116.

Khoury, T., & Appel, M. (1977). Gifted children: Current trends and issues. *Journal of Clinical Child Psychology, 6*(3), 13–20.

Klein, P., & Cantor, L. (1976). Gifted children and their self-concept. *Creative Child and Adult Quarterly, 1*(2), 98–101.

Kohlberg, L. (1973). *Collected papers on moral development and moral education.* Cambridge, MA: Harvard University Press.

Kolloff, P., & Feldhusen, J. (1984). The effects of enrichment on self-concept and creative thinking. *Gifted Child Quarterly, 28*(2), 53–58.

Krouse, J., & Krouse, H. (1981). Toward a multimodal theory of academic underachievement. *Educational Psychologist, 16*(3), 151–164.

Lehman, E., & Erdwins, C. (1981). Social and emotional adjustment of young intellectually gifted children. *Gifted Child Quarterly, 25*(3), 134–138.

Lessinger, L., & Martinson, R. (1961). The use of the California Psychological Inventory with gifted pupils. *Personnel and Guidance Journal, 39*, 572–575.

Lewis, M., & Rosenblum, M. (1975). *Friendship and peer relations.* New York: Wiley.

Liddle, G. (1958). Overlap among desirable and undesirable characteristics in gifted children. *Journal of Educational Psychology, 49*, 219–223.

Lipsitt, L. (1958). A self-concept scale for children and its relation to the children's form of the manifest anxiety scale. *Child Development, 29*, 463–472.

Longstreth, L. E. (1978). A comment on "Race, IQ, and the Middle Class," by Trotman: Rampant false conclusions. *Journal of Educational Psychology, 70*, 469–472.

Lucito, L. (1964). Independence-conformity behavior as a function of intellect: Bright and dull children. *Exceptional Children, 31*, 5–13.

Ludwig, G., & Cullinan, D. (1984). Behavior problems of gifted and non-gifted elementary school girls and boys. *Gifted Child Quarterly, 28*(1), 37–40.

Maddux, C., Scheiber, L., & Bass, J. (1982). Self-concept and social distance in gifted children. *Gifted Child Quarterly, 26*(2), 77–82.

Manaster, G., & Powell, P. (1983). A framework for understanding gifted adolescents' psychological maladjustment. *Roeper Review, 6*(2), 70–73.

Masangkay, Z., McCluskey, K., McIntyre, C., Sims-Knight, J., Vaughn, B., & Flavell, J. (1974). The early development of inferences about the visual percepts of others. *Child Development, 45*, 357–366.

Mason, E., Adams, H., & Blood, D. (1968). Further study of personality characteristics of bright college freshmen. *Psychological Reports, 23*(2), 395–400.

Mason, E., & Blood, D. (1966). Cross validation study of personality characteristics of gifted college freshmen. *Proceedings of the 74th Annual Convention of the American Psychological Association*, 283–284.

McClelland, D., Atkinson, J., Clark, R., & Lowell, E. (1953). *The achievement motive.* New York: Appleton-Century-Crofts.

McCurdy, H. G. (1960). The childhood pattern of genius. *Horizon, 2*, 33–38.

McGehee, W., & Lewis, W. (1940). Parental attitudes of mentally superior, average, and retarded children. *School and Society, 51*, 556–559.

McGillivray, R. (1964). Differences in home background between high-achieving and low-achieving gifted children. *Ontario Journal of Educational Research, 6*(2), 99–106.

McGinn, P. (1976). Verbally gifted youth: Selection and description. In D. Keating (Ed.), *Intellectual talent: Research and development* (pp. 160–183). Baltimore: Johns Hopkins University Press.

Mehta, P. (1968). The self-concept of bright, underachieving male high school students. *Indian Educational Review, 3*(2), 81–100.

Mensch, I. M. (1950). Rorschach study of the gifted child: A survey of the literature. *Journal of Exceptional Children, 17*, 8–14.

Miles, C. C. (1954). Gifted children. In L. Carmichael (Ed.), *Carmichael's manual of child psychology* (3rd ed.). New York: Wiley.

Milgram, R., & Milgram, N. (1976). Personality characteristics of gifted Israeli children. *Journal of Genetic Psychology, 129*, 185–194.

Miller, J., & Roedell, W. (1977). *Sex-role development in intellectually gifted preschoolers.* Unpublished manuscript, University of Washington, Child Development Research Group, Seattle.

Miller, R. (1956). Social status and socioeconomic differences among mentally superior, mentally typical, and mentally retarded children. *Exceptional Children, 23*, 114–119.

Mills, C. (1983, April). *Personality characteristics of gifted adolescents and their parents: Comparisons and implications for achievement and counseling.* Paper presented at the annual meeting of the American Educational Research Association, Montreal, Canada.

Mills, C. (1984, April). *Sex differences in self-concept and self-esteem for mathematically precocious adolescents.* Paper presented at the annual meeting of the American Educational Research Association, New Orleans, LA.

Monks, F., & Ferguson, T. (1983). Gifted adolescents: An analysis of their psychosocial development. *Journal of Youth and Adolescence, 12*(1), 1–18.

Montour, K. (1977). William J. Sidis, the broken twig. *American Psychologist, 32*(4), 265–279.

Morrow, W., & Wilson, P. (1961). Family relations of bright high-achieving and under-achieving high school boys. *Child Development, 32*, 507–510.

Newland, T. (1976). *The gifted in socioeducational perspective.* Englewood Cliffs, NJ: Prentice-Hall.

Newman, J., Dember, C., & Krug, O. (1973). He can but he won't. *Psychoanalytic Study of the Child, 28*, 83–129.

Nichols, R. (1964). Parental attitudes of mothers of intelligent adolescents and creativity of their children. *Child Development, 35*, 1041–1049.

Nichols, R. (1967). The origin and development of talent. *Phi Delta Kappan, 48*, 492–496.

Nichols, R., & Astin, A. (1966). Progress of the merit scholars: An eight-year follow-up. *Personnel and Guidance Journal, 44*, 673–686.

Nichols, R., & Davis, J. (1964). Some characteristics of students of high academic aptitude. *Personnel and Guidance Journal, 42*, 794–800.

Norfleet, M. (1968). Personality characteristics of achieving and underachieving high ability senior women. *Personnel and Guidance Journal, 46*(10), 976–980.

Norman, R. (1966). The interpersonal values of parents of achieving and nonachieving gifted children. *Journal of Psychology, 64*(10), 49–57.

Oden, M. (1968). The fulfillment of promise: Forty-year follow-up of the Terman gifted group. *Genetic Psychology Monographs, 77*, 3–93.

O'Shea, H. (1960). Friendship and the intellectually gifted child. *Exceptional Children, 26,* 327–335.

O'Such, K., Twyla, G., & Havertape, J. (1979). Group differences in self-concept among handicapped, normal, and gifted learners. *The Humanist Educator, 18,* 15–22.

Otop, J. (1977). Sources of school failure in gifted pupils as revealed by teachers' ratings. *Polish Psychological Bulletin, 8*(2), 107–113.

Painter, E. (1976). *Comparison of achievement and ability in children of high intellectual potential.* Unpublished master's thesis, London University, London, England.

Pandey, A. (1977). Adjustment between bright and average intermediate adolescents: A comparative study. *Indian Educational Review, 12*(4), 86–90.

Passow, A. (1981). The nature of giftedness and talent. *Gifted Child Quarterly, 25*(1), 5–11.

Payne, D., Halpin, G., & Ellett, C. (1973). Personality trait characteristics of differentially gifted students. *Psychology in the Schools, 10*(2), 189–195.

Payne, D., Halpin, G., Ellett, C., & Dale, J. (1975). General personality correlates of creative personality in academically and artistically gifted youth. *Journal of Special Education, 9*(1), 105–108.

Pearlman, C. (1984). The effects of level of effectance motivation, IQ, and a penalty/reward contingency on the choice of problem difficulty. *Child Development, 55,* 537–542.

Piers, E., & Harris, D. (1969). *Manual for the Piers-Harris Children's Self-Concept Scale.* Nashville, TN: Counselor Recordings and Tests.

Pollin, L. (1983). The effects of acceleration on the social and emotional development of gifted students. In C. Benbow & J. Stanley (Eds.), *Academic precocity: Aspects of its development* (pp. 160–179). Baltimore: Johns Hopkins University Press.

Powell, M. (1948). Comparisons of self-ratings, peer ratings, and expert ratings of personality adjustment. *Educational and Psychological Measurement, 8,* 225–234.

Pressey, S. (1949). Educational acceleration: Appraisal and basic problems. *Ohio State University Bureau of Educational Research Monographs,* (Serial No. 31).

Pringle, M. L. K. (1970). *Able misfits.* London: Longman.

Pringle, M., Butler, R., & Davie, R. (1966). *11,000 seven-year-olds.* London: Longman.

Quay, H., & Peterson, D. (1975). *Manual for the Behavior Problem Checklist.* Unpublished mimeo, University of Miami, FL.

Raph, J., Goldberg, M., & Passow, A. (1966). *Bright underachievers.* New York: Columbia University Press.

Renzulli, J. S. (1978). What makes giftedness? Reexamining a definition. *Phi Delta Kappan, 60,* 180–184, 261.

Rest, J. (1979). *Manual for the Defining Issues Test.* Minneapolis: University of Minnesota.

Reynolds, C. (1975). Correlates of mental ability among somewhat superior American adolescents. *Dissertation Abstracts, 35*(10–A), 6519–6520.

Robinson, H. B. (1981). The uncommonly bright child. In M. Lewis & D. Rosenblum (Eds.), *The uncommon child* (pp. 57–81). New York: Plenum.

Robinson, H. B. (1983). A case for radical acceleration: Programs of the Johns Hopkins University and the University of Washington. In C.P. Benbow & J. C. Stanley (Eds.), *Academic precocity: Aspects of its development* (pp. 139–160). Baltimore: Johns Hopkins University Press.

Robinson, N., & Janos, P. (in press). The psychological adjustment of youngsters in a program of marked academic acceleration. *Journal of Youth and Adolescence.*

Robinson, N. M., & Robinson, H.B. (1982). The optimal match: Devising the best compromises for the highly gifted student. In D. Feldman (Ed.), *New directions for child development: Developmental approaches to giftedness and creativity* (No. 17, pp. 79–95). San Francisco: Jossey-Bass.

Rodgers, B. (1979). *Effects of an enrichment program screening process on the self-concept and other-concept of gifted elementary children.* Unpublished doctoral dissertation, University of Cincinnati, OH.

Roe, A. (1951a). A psychological study of eminent biologists. *Psychological Monographs, 65*(14, Serial No. 331).

Roe, A. (1951b). A psychological study of eminent physical scientists. *Genetic Psychology Monographs, 43,* 121–235.

Roe, A. (1952). A psychologist examines 64 eminent scientists. *Scientific American, 187*(5), 21–25.

Roedell, W. C. (1978, August). Social development in intellectually advanced children. In H. B. Robinson (Chair), *Intellectually advanced children: Preliminary findings of a longitudinal study.* Symposium conducted at the Annual Convention of the American Psychological Association, Toronto, Canada.

Roedell, W., Jackson, N., & Robinson, H. (1980). *Gifted young children.* New York: Columbia University, Teachers College.

Ross, A., & Parker, M. (1980). Academic and social self concepts of the academically gifted. *Exceptional Children, 47*(1), 6–10.

Rutter, M., & Garmezy, N. (1983). Atypical social and personality development. In E. M. Hetherington (Ed.), *Handbook of child psychology: Vol. 4. Socialization, personality, and social development* (4th ed., pp. 775–911). New York: Wiley.

Rutter, M., Tizard, J., & Whitmore, K. (Eds.). (1970). *Education, health, and behavior.* London: Longman.

Sarason, S., Davidson, K., Lighthall, F., Waite, R., & Ruebush, B. (1960). *Anxiety in elementary school children.* New York: Wiley.

Saurenman, D., & Michael, W. (1980). Differential placement of high achieving and low achieving gifted pupils in grades 4, 5, and 6 on measures of field independence, creativity, and self-concept. *Gifted Child Quarterly, 24,* 81–85.

Schaeffer, E., & Bell, R. (1958). Development of a parent attitude research instrument. *Child Development, 29,* 339–361.

Scott, E., & Bryant, B. (1978). Social interactions of early-reading and non-reading kindergarten students with high intellectual ability. *Catalog of Selected Documents in Psychology, 8,* 95.

Sears, P., & Barbee, A. (1977). Career and life satisfactions among Terman's gifted women. In J. C. Stanley, W. C. George, & C. H. Solano (Eds.), *The gifted and creative: A fifty-year perspective* (pp. 28–66). Baltimore: Johns Hopkins University Press.

Sears, P., & Sherman, V. (1964). *In pursuit of self-esteem.* Belmont, CA: Wadsworth.

Sears, R. (1977). Sources of life satisfactions of the Terman gifted men. *American Psychologist, 32*(8–A), 119–128.

Selig, K. (1959). Personality structure as revealed by the Rorschach technique of a group of children who test at or above 170 IQ on the 1937 revision of the Stanford Binet. *Dissertation Abstracts, 19,* 3373–3374.

Shantz, C. (1983). Social cognition. In J. H. Flavell & E. M. Markman (Eds.), *Handbook of child psychology: Vol. 3. Cognitive development* (4th ed., pp. 495–555). New York: Wiley.

Shaw, M. (1961). *The interrelationship of selected personality factors in high ability underachieving school children* (Project 58–M1). Sacramento: California State Department of Public Health.

Shaw, M., & Grubb, J. (1958). Hostility in able high school underachievers. *Journal of Counseling Psychology, 5,* 263–266.

Silverblank, F. (1973). Selection of selected personality factors between students talented in English and students talented in mathematics. *California Journal of Educational Research, 24*(2), 61–65.

Simono, R. (1967). Observed expressions of the achievement needs of gifted students. *Psychology in the Schools, 4*(2), 174–176.

Slaby, R., & Frey, K. (1974). Development of gender constancy and selective attention to same-sex models. *Child Development, 46,* 849–856.

Smith, D. (1964). *Personal and social adjustment of gifted adolescents* (Research Monograph No. 4). Washington, DC: Council for Exceptional Children.

Specht, L. (1919). A Terman class in Public School No. 64, Manhattan. *School and Society, 9,* 393–398.

Spence, J., Helmreich, R., & Stapp, J. (1974). The personal attributes questionnaire: A measure of sex role stereotypes in masculinity and femininity. *Journal Supplement Abstract Service Catalog of Selected Documents in Psychology, 4*(43), No. 617.

Spivak, G., & Shure, M. (1974). *Social adjustment of young children.* San Francisco: Jossey-Bass.

Stanley, J. C. (1979). Identifying and nurturing the educationally gifted. In W. C. George, S. J. Cohn, & J. C. Stanley (Eds.), *Educating the gifted* (pp. 172–183). Baltimore: Johns Hopkins University Press.

Stewart, E. (1979). *Learning styles among gifted/talented students.* Ann Arbor, MI: University Microfilms.

Stopper, C. (1978). *The relationships of the self-concept of gifted and non-gifted elementary school students to achievement, sex, grade level, and membership in a self-contained academic program for the gifted.* Unpublished doctoral dissertation, University of Pennsylvania.

Strang, R. (1951). Mental hygiene of gifted children. In P. Witty (Ed.), *The gifted child.* Lexington, MA: Heath.

Tan-Willman, C., & Gutteridge, D. (1981). Creative thinking and moral reasoning of academically gifted secondary school adolescents. *Gifted Child Quarterly, 25*(4), 149–154.

Tannenbaum, A. J. (1983). *Gifted children: Psychological and educational perspectives.* New York: Macmillan.

Taylor, C., & Coombs, A. (1952). Self-acceptance and adjustment. *Journal of Consulting Psychology, 16,* 89–91.

Terman, L. M. (1925). *Genetic studies of genius: Vol. 1. Mental and physical traits of a thousand gifted children.* Stanford, CA: Stanford University Press.

Terman, L. M., & Oden, M. H. (1947). *Genetic studies of genius: Vol. 4. The gifted child grows up: Twenty-five years' follow-up of a superior group.* Stanford, CA: Stanford University Press.

Terman, L. M., & Oden, M. H. (1959). *Genetic studies of genius: Vol. 5. The gifted group at mid-life: Thirty-five years' follow-up of the superior child.* Stanford, CA: Stanford University Press.

Thiel, R., & Thiel, A. (1977). A structural analysis of family interaction patterns and the underachieving gifted child. *Gifted Child Quarterly, 21,* 267–275.

Thorndike, R. (1939). Responses of a group of gifted children to the Pressey interest-attitudes test. *Journal of Educational Psychology, 30,* 588–594.

Thorndike, R. (1940). Performance of gifted children on tests of developmental age. *Journal of Psychology, 9,* 337–343.

Thurstone, L. L. (1938). *Primary mental abilities.* Chicago: University of Chicago Press.

Tidwell, R. (1980). A psycho-educational profile of 1593 gifted high school students. *Gifted Child Quarterly, 24*(2), 63–68.

Tomlinson-Keasey, C., & Smith-Winberry, C. (1983). Educational strategies and personality outcomes of gifted and non-gifted college students. *Gifted Child Quarterly, 27*(1), 35–40.

Torrance, E. P. (1963). What kind of a person do you want your gifted child to become? *Gifted Child Quarterly, 7*(3), 87–91.

Trotman, F. K. (1977). Race, IQ, and the middle class. *Journal of Educational Psychology, 69,* 266–273.

Trudewind, C. (1982). The development of achievement motivation and individual differences: Ecological determinants. *Review of Child Development Research, 6,* 669–704.

Uhlinger, C., & Stephens, M. (1960). Relation of achievement motivation to academic achievement in students of superior ability. *Journal of Educational Psychology, 51,* 259–266.

Viernstein, M. (1976). Origence, intelligence, and interpersonal effectiveness as determinants of humanistic precocity. *Dissertation Abstracts, 37*(2–B), 1044.

Viernstein, M., & Hogan, R. (1975). Parental personality factors and achievement motivation in talented adolescents. *Journal of Youth and Adolescence, 4*(2), 183–190.

Viernstein, M., Hogan, R., & McGinn, P. (1977). Personality correlates of differential verbal and mathematical ability in talented adolescents. *Journal of Youth and Adolescence, 6,* 169–178.

Wallach, M., & Kogan, N. (1965). *Modes of thinking in young children: A study of the creativity-intelligence distinction.* New York: Holt, Rinehart & Winston.

Warren, J., & Heist, P. (1960). Personality attributes of gifted college students. *Science, 132,* 330–337.

Weiss, D., Haier, R., & Keating, D. (1974). Personality characteristics of mathematically precocious boys. In J. C. Stanley, D. P. Keating, & L. H. Fox (Eds.), *Mathematical talent: Discovery, description, and development* (pp. 126–140). Baltimore: Johns Hopkins University Press.

Wenar, C. (1982). Developmental psychopathology: Its nature and models. *Journal of Child Clinical Psychology, 11*(3), 192–201.

Werner, E., & Bachtold, L. (1969). Personality factors of gifted boys and girls in middle childhood and adolescence. *Psychology in the Schools, 2,* 177–182.

Whitmore, J. R. (1980). *Giftedness, conflict, and underachievement.* Boston: Allyn & Bacon.

Winne, P., Woodlands, M., & Wong, B. (1982). Comparability of self-concept among learning disabled, normal, and gifted students. *Journal of Learning Disabilities, 15,* 470–475.

Winterbottom, M. (1954). *The relation of childhood training in independence to achievement motivation.* Unpublished doctoral dissertation, University of Michigan, Ann Arbor.

Wirt, R., Lachar, D., Klinedinst, J., & Seat, P. (1977). *Multidimensional description of child personality.* Los Angeles, CA: Western Psychological Services.

Wittek, M. (1973). Reflections of the gifted by the gifted on the gifted, grades five, six, and seven. *Gifted Child Quarterly, 17*(4), 250–253.

Wohlwill, J. (1973). *The study of behavioral development.* New York: Academic Press.

Wolf, R. (1974). The measurement of environments. In R. H. Moos & P. Insel (Eds.), *Issues in social ecology: Human milieux.* Palo Alto, CA: National Press Books.

Yoder, A. H. (1894). Study of the boyhoods of great men. *Pedagogical Seminary, 3,* 134–156.

Zahn-Waxler, C., Radke-Yarrow, M., & Brady-Smith, J. (1977). Perspective-taking and prosocial behavior. *Developmental Psychology, 13,* 87–88.

Zorbaugh, H., Boardman, R., & Sheldon, P. (1951). Some observations on highly gifted children. In P. Witty (Ed.), *The gifted child.* Lexington, MA: Heath.

7. Programs for the Gifted and Talented: Past, Present, and Future

Lynn H. Fox
Jerrilene Washington
The Johns Hopkins University

Issues Concerning Programs for the Gifted and Talented

Educational programs for the gifted are often spoken of as being "qualitatively differentiated"; however, this term has not been well defined. Indeed, not all experts in the field of gifted education agree on the specifics of programs that are best suited to academically gifted students. Disagreements usually involve four issues: the definition of giftedness, goals of programs for the gifted, the importance of a specific instructional mode, and the proper environment for learning.

Definition of Giftedness. Conceptual and operational definitions of giftedness influence people's choices of program model. Students who are selected on the basis of scores on a group test of global intelligence may require a different program from one designed for students who are selected on other criteria, such as scores on difficult tests of mathematics, evidence of creativity, or student self-nomination. Thus, for example, programs designed for the gifted by Stanley (1980) differ from those designed by Renzulli (Renzulli, 1977) or Tannenbaum (Tannenbaum & Baldwin, 1983) because all three define their target populations in very different ways. (For a more detailed discussion of these issues see Fox, 1981a.)

Program Goals. The goal or primary purpose of programs for the gifted is also widely debated and the issues of concern are related only in part to definitions of giftedness. For some educational planners, the acceleration of the students' progress through the basic curriculum is a rational goal. To others, acceleration is not considered necessary or even desirable, and the focus is upon enriching the students' experiences by a variety of means such as special field trips or projects, internship experiences, supplemental topics added to the basic curriculum, time out for self-exploration, or special courses in creative problem solving. In addition to the acceleration issue is the concern by some for nonacademic outcomes such as opportunities for social and intellectual interaction with peers or opportunities to interact with truly gifted adult role models. Some advocate a return to the classical educational models that emphasize the humanities and stress classical languages as well as modern foreign languages. There are educators who emphasize the importance of learning specific bodies of content, sometimes described as "product oriented," and those who stress "process" as opposed to content. These process educators are generally concerned with trying to teach general problem-solving strategies and creative thinking.

Instructional Models. Controversy over modes of instruction and curriculum models can be traced to two sources. The first is the general lack of definitive research in which various instructional methods or curriculum models are compared among samples of gifted students. The other source of disagreement is related to philosophies about psychosocial goals. For example, diagnostic testing with prescriptive instruction will invariably lead to acceleration for the able student and is likely to focus on products rather than processes, whereas independent study projects are less likely to result in systematic acceleration and are compatible with both process and product models. When systematic empirical research evidence is lacking, educators are likely to be guided by their philosophical position.

Environment. Controversies over learning environments tend to center around charges of elitism generated when gifted students are homogeneously grouped in special classes or special schools or given field trips or extra equipment such as computers. Additional considerations are logistical and economic. Hiring specialists to conduct "pull-out" classes for enrichment is more expensive than allowing students to move to a more advanced class with older students or individualizing students' instruction within the regular heterogeneously grouped class.

For the purpose of this chapter, "program for the gifted" is used loosely to encompass a wide variety of means of providing learning experiences for children of above-average general intellectual or specific academic aptitude. In some cases the discussion is also relevant to non-academic abilities such as art and music. A program can be at any administrative or geographic level; for example, it can be a national program or one in a particular classroom.

In some programs the focus is on manipulating or enriching the basic school curriculum. Some model programs emphasize special instructional techniques or changes in the rate of instruction of the basic curriculum. Others are concerned primarily with altering the learning environment for gifted students by grouping or by using special equipment such as computers. Although it is not possible to describe every existing program prototype in detail, some relevant program parameters are described in this chapter.

This chapter begins with a brief summary of the history of the gifted child movement in the United States. Most of the chapter is focused on descriptions of more generalized models of curriculum or instruction; a few examples of some existing programs that have been evaluated or at least reported descriptively in the literature are included. This will be followed by our speculations about education of the gifted in the future, and a discussion of a few practical and administrative concerns such as staff training and special populations. The conclusion focuses on questions for future research.

Programs: The Past

Education for the gifted and talented in the 1800s is not well documented and is probably best characterized as private school training and training by parents and tutors for such luminaries as John Stuart Mill and Thomas Edison (Van Tassel-Baska, 1981). In the 1900s the development of the intelligence test and the pioneering work of the psychologists and researchers Terman and Hollingworth led to greater recognition of individual differences in learning and the creation of numerous special programs (Van Tassel-Baska, 1981). For example, between 1912 and 1918, rapid-advancement classes were found in many large cities such as New York and Chicago, and individualized education plans were used in San Francisco, California; Winnetka, Illinois; and Louisville, Kentucky. Although these programs might be considered accelerative, enrichment approaches were introduced in cities such as New York where Special Opportunity Classes were formed to provide enrichment through specialized instruction in the history and evolution of civilized man.

Other enrichment approaches in the early 1920s include the Cox Experimental Classes in Columbus, Ohio; the Cleveland Major Work Classes; and Stedman's class at the University Elementary School of the University of California at Los Angeles in which individualized and seminar work were provided for the gifted. Yet no universal standards or mandate for gifted programs developed out of these early efforts. Witty (1975) postulated three reasons for the sporadic nature of program development during the first half of the twentieth century: the small numbers of students identified as gifted in many communities, the fear of developing an intellectually elite group, and the assumption of many educators that the gifted could take care of themselves.

During the 1950s the concern over Sputnik led to financial support for the National Defense Education Act and other funding for programs designed to identify, develop, and educate gifted and talented students in the sciences, mathematics, and foreign languages (Pannwitt, 1978; Van Tassel-Baska, 1981). Homogeneous grouping, acceleration, honors classes, and the program that is now the Advanced Placement Program of the College Entrance Examination Board were established (Pannwitt, 1978). The National Merit Scholarship Fund and many specialized high schools were developed (Pannwitt, 1978; Witty, 1981). Many state departments of education developed programs for the gifted, for example, the Mentally Gifted Minors Program in California, the Governor's School in Georgia, Demonstration Centers for Teaching the Gifted in Illinois, and the model for the education of the gifted in Connecticut (Pannwitt, 1978). These types of programs were influenced by the research and writings of Torrance (1965) and of Guilford (1965) and therefore included some emphasis on the assessment of and practice or teaching of creative thinking and problem-solving skills.

During the 1960s many programs for the gifted and talented dissolved as the national interest shifted to disadvantaged and handicapped populations. Only a few research studies and programs thrived. The Presidential Scholars Program and the National Achievement Scholarship Fund for Negro Students were among the few new programs developed at the national level (Pannwitt, 1978).

In 1971 Sidney Marland, then U.S. Commissioner of Education, was mandated by Congress to study, report, and recommend methods of improving the education of gifted and talented students. His report (1972) led to the creation of the Office of Gifted and Talented and some funding for assistance to states with the enactment of the Special Projects Act of 1974. The National/State/Leadership Training Institute was then funded to conduct workshops and develop a variety of materials for use by state and local education agencies.

With the authorization of the Elementary and Secondary Education Act (ESEA) in 1978, Congress shifted gifted and talented education out of Special Projects and into Part A of Title IX—Additional Programs.

Under the Grants Consolidation enacted by Congress in 1981, funds for education of the gifted and talented merged with 29 other programs under Chapter Two. This shift reduced the federal role as a catalyst in gifted and talented education.

Today the federal government leaves to each state the decision as to whether or not programs for the gifted should be mandated as part of special education as opposed to being permitted within basic educational programs. Federal guidelines are vague enough to allow a multitude of interpretations and thus many different program prototypes.

Programs: The Present

By 1978, 42 states had either laws, regulations, or at least guidelines for gifted and talented education (Karnes & Collins, 1978). Much of the current thinking about gifted education for the 1980s has its roots in the ideas of the 1972 report by Marland to Congress. The Marland Report called for programs to have three basic characteristics: (a) a differential curriculum that denotes high-level cognitive concepts and processes; (b) instructional strategies that accommodate the learning styles of the gifted and talented for the specific curriculum content; and (c) special grouping arrangements and a variety of administrative procedures appropriate or necessary for delivering services to particular children. In this section of the chapter these three characteristics described as critical by the Marland Report will be discussed in terms of theories, research, and practice.

Curriculum

There are numerous books and articles describing how to differentiate curriculum for the gifted (Gallagher, 1975; Kaplan, 1974, 1979; Khatena, 1982; Maker, 1982a, 1982b; Tannenbaum, 1983). Many school systems develop their own handbooks or curriculum guides for gifted and talented students after drawing ideas from the more generalized discussions provided in the professional literature. Although these handbooks may incorporate ideas from several general curriculum models or psychological theories, Renzulli (1980) noted that the typical guide at some point utilizes either Bloom's Taxonomy of Educational Objectives (Bloom, 1956) or Guilford's Structure of Intellect model (Guilford, 1967).

Thus, references to high-level thinking skills are usually translated into the stages of analysis, synthesis, and evaluation in Bloom's hierarchical taxonomy. Guilford's model has been adapted by Meeker (1969) to produce testing and teaching materials and has been related to teacher and student behaviors to generate lesson plans for a variety of content areas by Williams (1970). Taba's (1962) work on sequential questioning techniques used by teachers to guide students' intellectual discoveries is also discussed in some program literature. A few programs also try to incorporate activities addressing the affective components of the learning process based on Krathwohl's Taxonomy of Affective Educational Objectives (Krathwohl, Bloom, & Masia, 1964).

Curriculum guides for the gifted are often sprinkled with activities aimed at improving creative thinking or creative problem solving. In some cases separate curriculum models have been developed such that creative problem solving becomes a subject unto itself despite the lack of evidence that creativity is a teachable skill. An excellent overview of major theories as they apply to curriculum and instruction has been prepared by Feldhusen and Treffinger (1980). Maker (1982b) believes that current programs for the gifted have been strongly influenced by the Parnes Creative Problem Solving Model (Parnes, 1972). Certainly the work of Torrance (1965, 1977) on testing for creativity and future problem-solving games and simulations has influenced many of today's programs. There are now national and international Future Problem-Solving Bowls or competitions evolving from his work.

Instructional Models

Perhaps the two best known and most comprehensive program models for gifted education, including unique procedures for identifying and assessing student needs as well as specific strategies for instruction, are the Enrichment Triad developed by Renzulli and his colleagues (Renzulli, 1977) and the Hopkins accelerative models developed by Stanley and his associates (Benbow & Stanley, 1983a; Keating, 1976; Stanley, George, & Solano, 1977; & Stanley, Keating, & Fox, 1974). In the early years of the development of these two models, they appeared to be at opposite extremes with respect to acceleration and enrichment. More recently, however, the constituents of the two programs have begun to talk about both approaches, albeit with different terms and emphases. Both are complex models and are in constant flux as the researchers experiment with new ideas and evaluate ongoing projects.

The Enrichment Triad. The Enrichment Triad instructional program consists of three levels or types of activities. The first two levels are not limited to gifted students but are proposed as generally enriching for all students. Type I activities include general exploration of topics of interest to the student that are not covered in the basic curriculum. Type II activities emphasize problem-solving strategies and creative thinking.

Type III activities are generally intended for gifted students. The assumption is that students are identified as gifted on the basis of Renzulli's three-ring model of giftedness (1978). Thus, a gifted student should possess three clusters of traits: above-average ability in some area, creative potential, and task commitment. Typically the focus of the type III activity is upon enrichment rather than on acceleration of students in the core curriculum. The model does necessitate compacting the learning of the basics, however, so that students will have the time to pursue special projects. The range of acceptable projects is limited only by one's imagination. This model seems to be popular with classroom teachers who want a means of providing enrichment to a handful of students in a heterogeneous group. It is sometimes adopted by entire schools or school systems. In these cases there may be a special teacher who conducts a "pull-out" program in a resource room. Efforts are under way to evaluate the program in several school systems. In most cases, the success of the program will depend upon the skill and training of the teachers who are responsible for directing the students' independent studies.

The Accelerative Model. The Hopkins model had its roots in the creation of the Study of Mathematically Precocious Youth (SMPY) in 1971 (Benbow & Stanley, 1983b; Fox, 1974a; Keating & Stanley, 1972; Stanley, Keating, & Fox, 1974). Since that time a number of parallel or complementary projects have emerged at Hopkins, including the Intellectually Gifted Child Study Group, the Study of Verbally Gifted Youth, and the Center for Talented Youth (CTY). Because of the amount of overlap among the groups they are often referred to collectively as the Hopkins model, and a number of replications of some of these projects have been undertaken at several other major universities.

Like the Enrichment Triad, the Hopkins programs are based on a unique conceptual and operational definition of giftedness. Students who are first screened on in-grade measures of achievement take the difficult Scholastic Aptitude Test intended for high school students while they are in Grade 7 or earlier in some cases. Students who participate in the formal talent searches are counseled by mail about a variety of educational opportunities ranging from summer enrichment classes to programs leading to radical acceleration and early admission to college.

Two instructional strategies pioneered at Hopkins were the fast-paced and enriched-class concepts (Fox, 1974b, 1981a) and the diagnostic testing-prescriptive instruction (DT-PI) model for the mathematically gifted using peer tutors (Stanley, 1980). In the fast-paced classes, students are given master teachers, often college instructors, who pace and run the class along the lines of a college course. There are lectures and a tremendous amount of home study. Although the actual class hours for meeting are greatly reduced, typically to 3 hours a week, students may cover as much as 2 years of mathematics work in 1 year. In a few cases classes have been known to cover the entire precalculus curriculum beginning with algebra in 2 years, meeting only on Saturday mornings. When the method was translated into the verbal areas, somewhat less acceleration occurred, but some fairly dramatic results were found in the study of languages including German, Latin, and Chinese.

Perhaps the most dramatic examples of students' acceleration of learning are in the gains some students are able to make with the aid of mentors in intensive summer school sessions (Stanley, 1980). Peer tutoring is, of course, not new, but so often the focus has been upon remediation of the slower student. In the Hopkins model the mentor is typically another gifted child who is a few years older and is also a product of the DT-PI program.

To date, the fast-paced class concept has been replicated successfully in a number of public schools and school systems (Fox, Brody, & Tobin, 1985). The tutor model is newer and has not yet been widely embraced. As was mentioned earlier, replication efforts are in progress at several universities. Indeed, the programs at Hopkins are perhaps the best researched of any existing model. An 8-year follow-up of students is reported in the most recent book to come out of the project. Most special classes were carefully evaluated and some have been or are in the process of being studied longitudinally (Benbow & Stanley, 1983a).

It appears that students can indeed benefit from the intensive and telescoped educational experiences provided by the SMPY and CTY programs at Hopkins. Many of the students from these programs eventually go to college early. Those who do not, often enter college with advanced standing. So far the negative social or emotional consequences of this acceleration that were predicted by critics have not emerged. Most of the early entrants to college have outstanding records and go on to graduate school.

Programs for the gifted are sometimes criticized for their piecemeal approach, in which enrichment units are inserted into a standard curriculum package. This criticism is certainly not applicable to either the Hopkins or Enrichment Triad or Revolving Door Models described here. These are perhaps the most representative of the few efforts to organize a comprehensive approach to curriculum and instruction.

Delivery Systems

The delivery of an educational program for the gifted and talented can take many different forms. A variety of program options should be designed and implemented because no single program concept can effectively and efficiently meet the varied educational needs of all gifted and talented students in all subjects. The choice of a specific method may sometimes depend upon logistical and economic considerations such as available staff and space, transportation problems, and funding. Some delivery systems are accelerative by their nature and others are not. Some require special teachers and the homogeneous grouping of students and some do not. Thus, delivery systems are tied to the philosophical and social goals of programs as well as to practical considerations. A number of these delivery systems are described in the following section. More

detailed discussion and analysis of the components of these program prototypes and the logistical and philosophical arguments concerning them
are found in Cox (1982), Cox and Daniel (1983a), Feldhusen (1983), Feldhusen and Kolloff (1978), Fox (1979, 1981b), and Khatena (1982).

Special Schools. In 1901, the first special school for the gifted and
talented was founded in Massachusetts (Tannenbaum, 1983). Soon after,
the cities of Baltimore and New York initiated similar schools. Such
schools were sometimes run more like colleges than traditional public
schools and provided a wide variety of courses and flexible scheduling.
Such schools can be expensive and are often criticized as being elitist
programs that isolate gifted students. Partly to counter these criticisms,
two compromises or variations on the special schools have been used: the
magnet school, and the satellite school-within-a-school approach.

In the magnet school program, one high school may become designated as the school for the sciences and engineering, whereas another
becomes a center for creative and performing arts, and so forth. This
approach is now being used by the city schools in Houston and Cincinnati
and by the states of New York and North Carolina (Cox & Daniel, 1983c).

In the satellite or school-within-a-school, the gifted and talented population receives instruction from special teachers in specific subjects, and
participates with the total school for social events and nonacademic subjects. At the extreme there might be learning centers for only one subject.
The learning center or laboratory approach can also be used within one
school building, in a portion of a building, in a classroom, or in a portion
of a classroom. Students attend special programs at such centers on a
part-time basis. These centers can be used for accelerated study of basic
material or for enrichment projects or seminars. A full description of the
use of learning centers in one city in Iowa is provided by Khatena (1982).

Continuous-progress and nongraded schools may provide a comprehensive approach to education for all children. In the nongraded school,
no labels are used to designate a student's placement in the traditional
age and grade system. The gifted students simply move ahead in the
program as they demonstrate mastery of content and skills. Such schools
necessitate cooperation among staff and teams and large amounts of planning time (Cox, 1982). The Learning Research and Development Center
at the University of Pittsburgh and the Plano Independent School District
in Texas use the continuous progress approach, and the Chesapeake Demonstration School in Virginia and the Los Angeles Elementary Laboratory
School of the University of California use the nongraded model.

At present, most public schools for the gifted are located in large
urban or suburban school systems, with the exception of the state-wide
program in North Carolina and Louisiana where there are some residential public schools for gifted students. Many private schools consider
themselves to have a very gifted student body but only a few advertise
themselves specifically as schools for the academically and intellectually

gifted. These include the Calasanctius School in Buffalo, New York, and the Roeper City and Country School in Bloomfield Hills, Michigan (Cox & Daniel, 1983c; Gerencser, 1979; Karnes & Peddicord, 1980).

Concurrent Enrollment in High School and College. There are a number of ways in which students may acquire high school and college credits simultaneously. It is often possible for a student to be a full-time high school student but supplement his or her program with college courses taken in the evenings, on weekends, in the summers, or by correspondence during the regular school year. Few colleges actually require a high school diploma for admission if a student's scores on an admission test are very high, and indeed many colleges actively recruit high school students for special credit programs (Benbow & Stanley, 1983b; Fox & Stanley, 1977).

The International Baccalaureate has recently been organized to provide an opportunity for concurrent enrollment in high school and college and to facilitate admission to colleges and universities throughout the world (Cox & Daniel, 1983a; Karnes & Chauvin, 1982a, 1982b). Approximately 120 colleges and universities in the United States accept International Baccalaureate course credits for college credit. Houston's Bellaire High School began offering this program in 1980, for example, and the Armand Hammer College in New Mexico bases its curriculum on this program.

Special Classes. Perhaps the most common method of providing for the gifted is by means of homogeneously grouped classes for either acceleration or enrichment. Classes can embody all the advantages of a special school without creating as many administrative or logistical problems. An added advantage is that students need not be gifted in every subject area in order to participate. For example, students might be able to accelerate their studies radically in science and mathematics but remain in less advanced classes in language arts or social studies.

One well-known program with a long history of success is the Advanced Placement Program (APP) in which students can earn high school credit and try for college credit by examination at one of the 650 colleges and universities that accept APP courses (Cox, 1983). Although students may prepare for the examinations on their own or with a tutor, until recently most high schools encouraged juniors and seniors to take the examinations only if they had had a course offered at their high school. Unfortunately, many high schools have too few students or too few qualified teachers to offer the full array of available courses. Too often access to these courses has been difficult for the truly brilliant younger student.

In the past decade the work of the Study of Mathematically Precocious Youth and its related associates at The Johns Hopkins University, Duke University, and some local school systems has led to the availability of accelerated courses in the lower grades and greater access to APP and college courses for younger students. Many school systems offer enriched classes at either or both the elementary and secondary levels. In some instances students are pulled out of a regularly scheduled class one or more days a week and given supplemental work in the same subject, work in an entirely different subject area, or an independent study project. The benefits of such practices are often difficult to assess and thus their value is often debated (George, Cohn, & Stanley, 1979). Some feel that enrichment courses in such areas as statistics, logic, creative writing, or career education should not be limited to the academically able, whereas others feel that such programs are elitist, or are wasted play time.

Scheduling accelerated or enriched classes may present a problem, or there may be too few students in a particular school to justify a separate class. Computer and media technology may solve these problems in the future, but at present school systems may try to offer systemwide classes after regular hours or on weekends. In a few states there are residential summer camps, sometimes called Governor's Schools, in which enriched classes are offered. One example of such a program is the Maryland Center for the Performing Arts where students talented in music, dance, drama, and the visual arts can spend a 2-week period of intensive study in the summer. Accelerated summer programs are also currently being offered by a number of colleges and universities, many based on the Hopkins model.

Administrative Arrangements for Acceleration. It appears that intellectually or academically gifted students can accelerate their progress through the traditional school experience in several different ways. One method is early admission to kindergarten. Objections are often raised to this practice, and many states try hard to discourage it, despite the lack of evidence of harmful social and emotional effects of early school admission (Daurio, 1979). The major barrier to early entrance seems to be the lack of adequate screening procedures to identify those who should enter early (Maddux, 1983). The emergence of preschool programs for the gifted, such as the Astor Program in New York, the Child Development Center of the University of Washington, and the preschool program for the handicapped gifted at the University of Illinois, may provide the necessary vehicle to screen and prepare students for early admission to kindergarten or first grade (Fox, 1979; Karnes & Peddicord, 1980; Van Tassel-Baska, 1981).

Early admission to college without a high school diploma is relatively simple at some institutions of higher education, provided that the applicant has outstanding test scores. At other colleges and universities, early admission is almost impossible. In some states the high school diploma is automatically granted upon a student's successful completion of the freshman year of college. Clearly there are only small numbers of students who are so brilliant and accelerated in their knowledge in most areas to warrant radical acceleration to college at age 14 or or even younger (Robinson, 1983). There are, however, a few for whom this may indeed be the best solution. Some students have found that it is easier and more practical financially to enter college with advanced standing rather than early. In this situation a student graduates from high school at the expected or near expected time but has already earned 1 or even 2 years of college credit.

Double promotions or grade-skipping was not uncommon in the early part of this century but is rarely practiced today. The arguments against such a practice seem to be based on concerns about alleged social or emotional harm despite the lack of empirical evidence. Other critics warn about the dangers of having students miss important blocks of curriculum. Although this might be a problem in some content areas, it seems likely that such omissions could be readily assessed by testing and some instruction in order to fill any small gaps that may be found.

Recently the idea of subject-matter acceleration has been gaining advocates, perhaps at least in part due to the research and writings from the Hopkins projects. Students might advance their knowledge in one or more subject areas beyond the available offerings for their grade or age level and move ahead to the next level class with older students, work with a tutor, study independently, and so forth. Such students are accelerated only in the subjects in which they are most talented rather than being advanced a whole year in every area. Of course this is frequently done with no fuss in reading in the elementary years. Until recently, however, it was difficult for a child in the middle school grades to move ahead in just one subject such as mathematics.

In the 1940s and 1950s, some of the large urban school systems, such as those in New York and Baltimore, offered telescoped programs in which students could complete the 3 years of a junior high school program in 2 years or complete a year of college while in high school. Although there are few programs of this type in operation, it is still possible for many enterprising students to complete all the requirements for high school graduation in 3 years rather than 4 years.

Independent Study. There are two general types of independent study projects: the systematic study of a course on one's own or perhaps with the use of a programmed instruction-type textbook and self-directed study of a topic that may or may not be related to a specified course of study at the school. Although independent study may work well when a student is trying to learn elementary skills such as arithmetic operations, it does not appear to be the best method for learning material that involves creativity and higher level thinking skills. A slight variation of the typical independent study project is to have students take college courses by correspondence. One high school in Kansas has a special teacher to work with whole classes of high school students who are taking a variety of college courses by correspondence.

Self-directed independent study projects probably have great value for students who wish to explore topics of special interest in far greater depth than they otherwise could. Without some basic training and skills in research or close guidance and supervision, however, some students' projects degenerate into exercises in busywork or play. Treffinger (1975) has developed a model by which students are trained to become self-directed students before they attempt ambitious projects.

Mentorships, Tutorials, and Internships. The differences among mentorships, tutorials, and internships are subtle. The mentor model utilizes an older expert or gifted person as a role model and informal teacher. Ideally a relationship of trust and sharing develops between mentor and student. The mentor concept seems to have a long history and is reported in biblical as well as historical and literary documents. The current vogue is to identify a student's interests and then try to place the student in a nonschool setting such as an office, scientific laboratory, or hospital, where the student can observe and assist the adult mentor in the work setting (Lambert & Lambert, 1982).

Although the tutor, like the mentor, may be a potential role model and form a close relationship with the student, this aspect is secondary to the tutor's role. The tutor has a more formal instructional role, guiding the learner through a predetermined course of study in a systematic way in a one-on-one relationship. In the internship arrangement, the focus is often more explicitly upon a set of experiences for the learner in a work setting than upon a relationship with a specific person. Internships are required in many graduate and professional schools, and some undergraduate colleges provide internship experiences in congressional or executive government offices. Opportunities for younger gifted students are now being offered by some school systems and private groups. In some areas internships in the visual and performing arts have been provided by grants from the National Endowment for the Humanities.

Cox and Daniel (1983b) describe some exemplary internship programs, such as Project Matchmaker in Polk County, Florida, the Illinois Governmental Internship Association, and the Creative and Performing Arts Programs in Dallas, Texas. Such programs need careful planning and continual monitoring and, with the exception of didactic tutoring in specific curricula, are difficult to evaluate, especially since the effects of the experience may not really emerge until the student is ready to make educational and career choices.

Programs: The Future

Although it is intellectually stimulating, speculating about the nature of gifted and talented education in the coming years usually raises the question of whether or not education for the gifted will or should be considered necessary. Indeed, projections for gifted education in the year 2000 are likely to be made contingent upon expected trends in education as a whole. Programs for the gifted are only rarely the trendsetters. More typically they evolve as an afterthought to other changes in curriculum or instruction for the typical student. Three current educational topics that are likely to affect the nature of gifted education over the next decade and beyond are telecommunications, the use of personal computers in the home and classroom, and the call for excellence in education, especially in mathematics and science education. We discuss each of these topics very briefly and only in terms of the ways in which they might enhance educational opportunities for the gifted.

Telecommunications

The term *telecommunications* encompasses a variety of instructional uses of telephones and televisions at home or in classrooms. Two fairly standard models in operation for a variety of populations have only recently been suggested for gifted students (Fox, 1981b). One of these is conducting seminars by conference telephone calls. Although used occasionally by some colleges and for hospitalized or homebound students in some school systems, the use of telephone seminars with young gifted students has not been reported in the literature. Yet the advantage is clear: telephone seminars allow gifted students to interact with one another and with stimulating lecturers in ways not otherwise possible because of geographic or temporal constraints. For example, many schools have too few students of near age and ability to form a special class, but by phone a few students could become part of a larger class based miles away.

This logic applies to the use of televised courses as well. Suppose a high school had only one or two students who needed an advanced course in calculus, English literature, or Spanish. Such students could take courses in which televised lectures were supplemented with interactive computer programs, telephone conferences, or mail correspondence for teacher–pupil interaction and grading of papers. This is not done very extensively for high schools and much less for elementary schools. Nonetheless, these uses of modern technology could overcome many of the nagging barriers to programs for the gifted such as too few students, lack of teachers, lack of money to pay for special teachers, and conflicts in schedules. Since such programs are expensive to produce, at least initially, they are not likely to gain wide acceptance for the gifted unless they demonstrate potential for use with the general school population or other special populations.

Microcomputers in the Home and in Classrooms

Microcomputers can be used directly for instruction or as a tool for record keeping and the management of instruction for individuals or groups. There are thousands of instructional software packages available in a wide variety of subjects and at several levels; some are specifically targeted for gifted students. Most have not been evaluated, allowing only broad generalizations about what is available. There are three major categories of software packages: drill and practice of skills; programmed instruction of content, much like old programmed instruction books of the early 1960s; and simulations or games in which there is some learning by discovery or induction from playing the games or doing the simulation activities.

These latter types are the most creative and probably suitable only for use by children with above average intellectual aptitude. How much the children learn from this material as opposed to similar intellectual activities presented as group activities in a class is not known. Probably the primary advantage of putting logic puzzles, simulations, and questioning or discovery-type activities on microcomputer is the ease of use by many students with little need for direction by teachers.

The advantages of drill and skill programs also lie in the flexibility of the schedules of teachers and students and in the fact that a bright child might move through a program more rapidly than other classmates. The better programs usually can be controlled by teachers (or sometimes by the students themselves) to adjust for individual differences in beginning levels of knowledge or speed of learning.

The use of computerized packages of content may work well for some but not necessarily all gifted students. If a student has partial knowledge of a subject, he or she may become bored by being forced to move lock-step through a series of questions. Most programs do not allow the student to skim or start in the middle and jump about to specific pieces as easily as one can in a textbook. The programs do, however, provide a sort of private tutor such that some gifted children might work by themselves on material too advanced for the rest of their classmates.

The two most important long-range advantages of microcomputers for gifted students may be the earlier opportunity for bright students to learn about computers and computer languages, and the possibility for greater individualization of instruction for students within any class or school. The record keeping and related management functions provided by many commercial programs may enable a teacher to handle more easily a roomful of students who are all at different points in the instructional sequence. The one-on-one tutor capability also provides more tutorial opportunities for individual children. Some educators, however, fear that this will create a generation of gifted children who have been taught almost solely by robots.

The Call for Excellence in American Education

Just as the fear of Russian domination of the heavens led to curriculum reform in the 1960s, new comparisons of the United States with Russia, Japan, and China have led to a fear of the United States' loss of supremacy in technological innovation and world economic leadership. It is too soon to say what will be done in the 1980s, but discussions and reports, such as the one by the National Commission on Excellence in Education (1983), seem to focus on the lack of qualified teachers, especially in mathematics and science, and upon the limited range of course offerings in the high schools. Improvements in the preparation of teachers, the addition of more advanced courses, or the upgrading of existing ones should certainly benefit the academically able, but unless support for special programs for the academically talented are included in the reform efforts, the needs of the most gifted students will not be met.

Recognition of Special Needs Populations

Objections to special programs for gifted students have sometimes been raised because the programs were seen as elitist—geared to middle- and upper-class white males. Over the past 20 years there has been a slow but steadily growing movement toward the expansion of the populations served by gifted programs through the use of multicultural approaches to identifying talent (Fox, 1981a). This trend has been concerned with the rural and urban poor and ethnic groups in the population such as Hispanics and Blacks. More recently, attempts have been made to include gifted, physically handicapped students who are learning disabled in programs for the gifted (Fox, Brody, & Tobin, 1983; Maker, 1977). Greater diversity in students' backgrounds may well necessitate major changes to ideas about programs in many schools. In some cases gifted students with special problems such as learning disabilities will need classes designed specifically to remediate problem areas such as writing, simultaneously challenging the student in other areas such as mathematics. It may be desirable, however, to include culturally different gifted children in the regular gifted program and provide support services to the children and teachers as they are needed. Decisions for placing students with special handicapping conditions in programs can probably be best made on a case-by-case basis.

Although gifted girls have rarely been purposely excluded from gifted programs, they have not always participated as fully or benefited as much as the boys have in many programs. For example, many girls have chosen not to enroll in advanced mathematics, computer, or physics classes in high school, and fewer gifted women than men pursue their education beyond the bachelor's degree in many areas (Fox & Zimmerman, in press). Many teachers and counselors now realize that in the past they held different expectations for girls and boys and may not have provided equal support and encouragement for participation in gifted programs. In the future, the addition of more counseling and career education components to gifted programs may help young women understand the complexities of the choices that they face, such as the problems of combining careers and motherhood.

Trends

Historically, more rhetoric than dollars has been put forth to address the needs of the gifted and talented. Concerns about elitism, the idea of the "rich get richer," and pressure for other special student interest groups such as the disadvantaged or handicapped tend to push programs for the gifted to a low-priority position in most public schools. Often, even when programs are provided, they are of the type that is superficially enriching or that is done haphazardly (Renzulli, 1980).

There are, however, three trends that bespeak of continued or increased support for the academically able student (although not necessarily for those gifted in nonacademic areas). First, the push for greater individualization of instruction by supporters of the handicapped, could, if applied to all students, allow the able to move rapidly through the basic elementary and secondary school curriculum. This is likely to happen if teachers embrace, rather than shun, the use of technology such as microcomputers.

The dangers of a student's completing all the school offerings at age 12 are offset by the second, possibly saving, trend for gifted education: the greater interest and involvement of private and public institutions of higher education in the education of younger gifted children. Many of the best programs available to bright children today are those being offered by colleges and universities such as The Johns Hopkins, Purdue, and Duke. Indeed, one can find some summer programs for gifted children on a college campus in almost every state. Since these programs typically generate revenues for the host college as well as serve as recruitment programs for bringing talented students to the colleges as full-time students later, these programs are likely to be continued for quite a while, or until the colleges again become overcrowded.

A third trend, which may help to dispel objections to programs for the gifted on the basis of elitism, is the increasing effort to use multicultural approaches to identify students, the increasing awareness of the special needs of women, interest in physically handicapped gifted students, and the acknowledgment of the existence of learning disabled, gifted people (Fox, Brody, & Tobin, 1983; Fox & Zimmerman, in press; Maker, 1977).

Administrative Concerns

Since there are few data comparing the effectiveness of one program model to another, the choice of a specific program for a school or school system often depends on a variety of economic, logistical, and political factors. Ideally, a school system should offer a wide variety of options to meet the individual needs of many students who are identified as gifted and talented. Indeed, Feldhusen (1983) has argued for an eclectic but comprehensive approach to the education of the gifted. In his model there is a range of activities including acceleration and enrichment or process and product activities. By contrast, many schools offer little or nothing for gifted students.

Gallagher (1975) reported that educators explain the paucity of programs for the gifted and talented by the lack of funds allocated at the federal, state, and local levels. Although it is true that there never is much money earmarked for activities in the area of the gifted, and although it is also true that some alternatives suggested for gifted education such as special residential schools or summer residential camps are expensive, the real barriers to good programs for the gifted are probably rigidity, apathy, and ignorance on the part of educators and the general public. Many programs can be offered for the gifted with little cost; such options may, however, require flexibility and creativity in planning and scheduling.

Consider some of the practical problems that school administrators are likely to face when trying to provide a smorgasbord of educational experiences. First, there is sometimes a problem with getting enough qualified teachers. This is particularly acute in the areas of advanced science and mathematics courses. Even when teachers are available who know their subject matter well, they may not be knowledgeable about the characteristics of the gifted students. Indeed, until very recently undergraduate training in education did not include coursework in the area of exceptional children. Even if a teacher has had such a course it may have included very little on the gifted. Although some colleges and universities offer graduate courses or degree programs in the area of gifted education, the numbers of teachers enrolled in these programs remains small. It is sometimes possible to overcome these problems by having college teachers work with secondary school gifted students and having high school teachers work with younger gifted children. In the long-term analysis it would seem desirable to upgrade teachers' knowledge of content and their understanding of the nature and needs of the gifted as well as developing teams of master teachers who are trained to teach and counsel gifted children and their parents. This would take time and money.

A second real barrier to providing opportunities to the gifted are inflexible rules about matters such as high school graduation requirements, teacher certification, transportation, and room schedules. A few examples might help illustrate these kinds of problems. Consider the case of a high school for the performing and visual arts in one large city where the teachers and mentors were professional artists and performers who, because they did not have the typical undergraduate education courses required for certification, could not be paid as teachers. Another school system tried to have a city-wide after-school accelerated mathematics course. It took months to get permission for the students to ride the bus to the center—even though bus transportation to that center was already being provided for a city-wide band program. In another example, one brilliant student was not awarded his high school diploma until after he graduated from college because he failed to progress through the rigid lockstep sequence of courses prescribed by his school. The idiosyncratic problems presented by gifted students are difficult to deal with but certainly not impossible. What is needed is an attitude of facilitation and creative problem solving rather than a conservative demand for the preservation of the status quo.

Another problem confronting gifted education is often an over-zealous reaction to a program model. Once an idea has taken shape, it is often overused. If a model worked for a small group of carefully chosen gifted students, it must then work for everyone in the system. Related to this is the problem of too loose a screening and identification procedure. Children who are chosen on the basis of a measure of intelligence are often assumed to be gifted equally in all subject areas and accelerated or enriched despite the fact that they may have an uneven profile of abilities. In the extreme case a gifted student may actually be learning disabled in reading. Students who are identified as gifted on any one measure may in fact differ widely from each other on other independent skills. Even when children have almost identical ability profiles, they may differ in terms of interest, motivation, and preferred learning modes. Not everyone likes to work in groups, and not everyone likes to work independently. Some students are eager to accelerate their progress in school and others are not. Such individual differences in interests and personalities should be considered.

Finally, when administrators initiate programs for the gifted, they are sometimes shocked to encounter apathy or even hostility from some parents and teachers. Some people sincerely believe that gifted students really are advantaged and can learn on their own. Also, many are opposed to programs in which students are homogeneously grouped because they see this as the formation of an elitist group of the white middle class. Ironically, failure to provide gifted programs is probably hardest on children from disadvantaged homes, whose parents may not have the education or resources to supplement the school's program with enrichment activities.

Some models for gifted education require the involvement of other school personnel besides the classroom teacher. Full-time coordinators may be needed. Often the success of the program depends upon the commitment of the principal so that the necessary resources can be available and changes in the usual scheduling procedures can be facilitated. At present, few counselors are involved in programs for the gifted. The assumption that gifted students need no counseling is false, but few models of how counseling and instruction may go hand in hand have been provided. Some special problems arise when children must learn to understand that they are different from other children in their school, may have different academic requirements to meet, and in some instances face isolation. For discussions of the kinds of counseling programs that might be desirable for the gifted, the reader is referred to Colangelo and Zaffrann (1979). Ideally, programs for the gifted should be carefully monitored by a team of experts. Stanley (1980) has proposed the longitudinal teaching team approach to ensure continuous and logical planning for individual children.

Too often the excuse for not providing special programs for gifted learners is the lack of funds. Yet often the needs of a sizable number of children could be met with relatively little cost if there were more administrative flexibility. Perhaps the key concept is the recognition of individual differences and the accommodation of them within the existing structures of today's educational system. No single program prototype will be perfect for all children who are gifted. Every child deserves an educational program that develops his or her talents with a minimum of anxiety, frustration, and boredom. Many options must be available, and everyone involved—students, teachers, administrators, and parents—must dare to take a few risks, try some new ways of doing things, and not allow old rules and habits to prevent creative problem solving in the schoolhouse.

Conclusions and Future Directions

There are no universal definitions for terms such as "qualitatively differentiated curriculum for the gifted," "most effective instructional strategy for the gifted," "ideal program model for the gifted," or "best learning environment for the gifted." Lack of consensus stems from philosophical differences among educators, lack of empirical evidence about the merits of particular programs, and perhaps the illusive nature of giftedness and the wide range of individual differences that may exist within any group so labeled.

Although philosophical issues such as the arguments for or against liberal arts programs versus early specialization in technical training cannot be readily resolved by research, it is clear that there is a dearth of empirical information about the outcomes or effects of most program models. Even though there is a large body of research on instruction, including aptitude–treatment interaction, most research does not address the basic problems of the highly gifted. Very few programs for the gifted have used sophisticated evaluation procedures.

In order to nurture the gifted and talented student, we must understand more about the nature of special abilities. Thus, it appears that efforts should be directed toward the study of the gifted and talented in order to provide better information about their specific educational needs. Following are some examples of specific research questions that would help to guide educators in providing more effective programs for gifted children.

1. Information Processing. Do individuals who are considered to be gifted in a particular area such as language, mathematics, or visual arts process information in their area of strength differently from or faster than people not considered gifted in that area?

2. Cognitive Development. Do students with high intelligence test scores need less concrete or manipulative experience at the Piagetian stages of preoperational and operational thought than do their peers?

3. Social Development. What are the harmful and beneficial outcomes of grouping students with their intellectual peers as opposed to their chronological peers in school and play settings?

4. Learning and Teaching. What is the most effective method for teaching basic arithmetic computation to bright children?

5. Assessment of Intellectual and Social Growth. What are the possible cognitive and affective outcomes of programs such as mentorships and internships and how can these effects be measured or studied?

6. Sex Differences. Are there important differences between males and females in the organization and functioning of the brain that will affect the ways in which they learn some skills or ideas or that suggest that they need to be taught in different ways?

These examples are but a very few of the thousands of research questions that might be formulated. For example, Gage (1979) has argued for a merging of the two traditional approaches to research on teaching such that instructional strategies be studied within a hierarchial framework and characteristics such as high aptitude become one of the six levels of the hierarchy. Thus, one might compare the learning of spelling by poorly motivated but verbally gifted students in each of several different learning environments or by different methods. Similarily, one could also generate numerous hypotheses about the development of special abilities and then repeat all the questions separately for such specific subgroups as American Indians, learning disabled gifted, or disadvantaged gifted in rural settings.

Until the results of such research are available, most decisions about the education of the gifted are likely to be made on the basis of logistical, economic, or social or philosophical considerations, or simply in response to the current educational fad. In a world that is becoming increasingly complex, in part due to advances in science and technology, there is a tremendous need for people to become technically educated. There are some potential dangers in the rush toward new technology, however.

Technology should not be allowed to overpower the need for preserving cultural heritage and for continuing to allow for innovation and creation in the visual and performing arts. Nor should the psychological needs of scientifically gifted children be ignored. Imagine such children learning by themselves, perhaps at home with a microcomputer, without the benefit of guidance from and interaction with mentors who can teach moral and social values and compassion along with logic and technology. Finally, the need to identify and nurture those whose interests and talents lie in the areas of the social sciences must not be overlooked. Society will need brilliant minds to help create, shape, and regulate social structures in ways that enhance the quality of life in dimensions beyond the new technologies. As our society heads into the twenty-first century, it can ill afford to continue its laissez-faire attitude toward the education of the gifted and the talented.

References

Benbow, C. P., & Stanley, J. C. (Eds.). (1983a). *Academic precocity: Aspects of its development*. Baltimore: Johns Hopkins University Press.

Benbow, C. P., & Stanley, J. C. (1983b). Constructing educational bridges between high school and college. *Gifted Child Quarterly, 27*, 111–113.

Bloom, B. S. (Ed.). (1956). *Taxonomy of educational objectives: Handbook 1. Cognitive domain*. New York: David McKay.

Colangelo, N., & Zaffrann, R. (Eds.). (1979). *New voices in counseling the gifted*. Dubuque, IA: Kendall/Hunt.

Cox, J. (1982). Continuous progress and nongraded schools. *G/C/T, 25*, 15–21.

Cox, J. (1983). Advanced placement: An exemplary honors model. *G/C/T, 26*, 47–51.

Cox, J., & Daniel, N. (1983a). Options for the secondary level g/t student (Part II). *G/C/T, 27*, 25–30.

Cox, J., & Daniel, N. (1983b). The role of the mentor. *G/C/T, 29*, 54–61.

Cox, J., & Daniel, N. (1983c). Specialized schools for high ability students. *G/C/T, 28*, 2–9.

Daurio, S. P. (1979). Educational enrichment versus acceleration: A review of the literature. In W. C. George, S. J. Cohn, & J. C. Stanley (Eds.), *Educating the gifted: Acceleration and enrichment* (pp. 13–16). Baltimore: Johns Hopkins University Press.

Feldhusen, J. F. (1983). Eclecticism: A comprehensive approach to education of the gifted. In C. P. Benbow & J. C. Stanley (Eds.), *Academic precocity: Aspects of its development* (pp. 192–204). Baltimore: Johns Hopkins University Press.

Feldhusen, J. F. & Kolloff, M. B. (1978). A three-stage model for gifted education. *G/C/T 4*, 3–5, 53–57.

Feldhusen, J. F., & Treffinger, D. J. (1980). *Creative thinking and problem solving in gifted education*. Dubuque, IA: Kendall/Hunt.

Fox, L. H. (1974a). Facilitating educational development of mathematically precocious youth. In J. C. Stanley, D. P. Keating, & L. H. Fox (Eds.), *Mathematical talent: Discovery, description, and development* (pp. 47–69). Baltimore: Johns Hopkins University Press.

Fox, L. H. (1974b). A mathematics program for fostering precocious achievement. In J. C. Stanley, D. P. Keating, & L. H. Fox (Eds.) *Mathematical talent: Discovery, description, and development* (pp. 101–125). Baltimore: Johns Hopkins University Press.

Fox, L. H. (1979). Programs for the gifted and talented: An overview. In A. H. Passow (Ed.), *The gifted and the talented: Their education and development* (pp. 104–126). Chicago: University of Chicago Press.

Fox, L. H. (1981a). Identification of the academically gifted. *American Psychologist, 36*, 1103–1111.

Fox, L. H. (1981b). Instruction for the gifted: Some promising practices. *Journal for Education of Gifted, 4*, 246–254.

Fox, L. H., Brody, L., & Tobin, D. (Eds.). (1983). *Learning disabled/gifted children: Identification and programming*. Baltimore: University Park Press.

Fox, L. H., Brody, L., & Tobin, D. (1985). The impact of early intervention programs upon course-taking and attitudes in high school. In S. Chipman, L. Brush, & D. Wilson (Eds.), *Women and mathematics: Balancing the equation* (pp. 249–274). Hillsdale, NJ: Erlbaum.

Fox, L. H., & Stanley, J. C. (1977). A university responds to the plight of the gifted. *Journal of the Maryland Association for Higher Education, 1*, 2–5.

Fox, L. H., & Zimmerman, W. (in press). Gifted women. In J. Freeman (Ed.), *The psychology of gifted children*. New York: Wiley.

Gage, N. L. (1979). The generality of dimensions of teaching. In P. L. Peterson & H. J. Walberg (Eds.), *Research on teaching: Concepts, findings, and implications* (pp. 264–288). Berkeley, CA: McCrutchan.

Gallagher, J. J. (1975). *Teaching the gifted child*. Boston: Allyn & Bacon.

George, W. C., Cohn, S. J., & Stanley, J. C. (Eds.). (1979). *Educating the gifted: Acceleration and enrichment*. Baltimore: Johns Hopkins University Press.

Gerencser, S. (1979). The Calasanctius experience. In A. H. Passow (Ed.), *The gifted and talented: Their education and development* (pp. 127–137). Chicago: University of Chicago Press.

Guilford, J. P. (1967). *The nature of human intelligence*. New York: McGraw-Hill.

Kaplan, S. N. (1974). *Providing programs for gifted and talented: A handbook*. Ventura, CA: Ventura County Superintendent of Schools.

Kaplan, S. N. (1979). *Inservice training manual: Activities for developing curriculum for the gifted/talented*. Ventura, CA: Ventura County Superintendent of Schools.

Karnes, F., & Chauvin, J. (1982a). Almost everything that parents and teachers of gifted secondary school students should know about early college enrollment and college credit by examination, *G/C/T*, Sept./Oct., 39–42.

Karnes, F., & Chauvin, J. (1982b). A survey of early admission policies for younger than average students: Implications for gifted youth. *Gifted Child Quarterly, 26*, 68–73.

Karnes, F. A., & Collins, E. C. (1978). State definitions on the gifted and talented: A report and analysis. *Journal for the Education of the Gifted. 1*, 44–62.

Karnes, F. A., & Peddicord, H. Q. (1980). *Programs, leaders, consultants and other resources in gifted and talented education*. Springfield, IL: Charles C Thomas.

Keating, D. P. (Ed.). (1976). *Intellectual talent: Research and development*. Baltimore: Johns Hopkins University Press.

Keating, D. P., & Stanley, J. C. (1972). Extreme measures for the exceptionally gifted in mathematics and science. *Educational Researcher, 1*, 3–7.

Khatena, J. (1982). *Educational psychology of the gifted*. New York: Wiley.

Krathwohl, D. R., Bloom, B. S., & Masia, B. B. (1964). *Taxonomy of educational objectives: Handbook 2. Affective domain*. New York: David McKay.

Lambert, S. E., & Lambert, J. W. (1982). Mentoring: A powerful learning device. *G/C/T, 25*, 12–13.

Maddux, C. D. (1983). Early school entry for the gifted: New evidence and concerns. *Roeper Review, 5*, 15–17.

Maker, C. J. (1977). *Providing programs for the gifted handicapped.* Reston, VA: Council for Exceptional Children.

Maker, C. J. (1982a). *Curriculum development for the gifted.* Rockville, MD: Aspen.

Maker, C. J. (1982b). *Teaching models in education of the gifted.* Rockville, MD: Aspen.

Marland, S. P., Jr. (1972). *Education of the gifted and talented: Report to the Congress of the United States by the U.S. Commissioner of Education.* Washington, DC: U.S. Government Printing Office.

Meeker, M. N. (1969). *The structure of intellect: Its interpretation and uses.* Columbus, OH: Charles E. Merrill.

National Commission on Excellence in Education. (1983). *A nation at risk: The imperative for educational reform.* Washington, DC: U.S. Government Printing Office.

Pannwitt, B. (1978). Who are the gifted and talented? *Curriculum Report, 8*, 1–2.

Parnes, S. J. (1972). *Creativity: Unlocking human potential.* Buffalo, NY: D. O. K.

Renzulli, J. S. (1978). What makes giftedness? Reexamining a definition. *Phi Delta Kappan, 60*, 180–184, 261.

Renzulli, J. S. (1980). Will the gifted child movement be alive and well in 1990? *Gifted Child Quarterly, 24*, 3–9.

Renzulli, J. S. (1977). *The enrichment triad model: A guide for developing defensible programs for the gifted and talented.* Mansfield Center, CT: Creative Learning Press.

Robinson, H. B. (1983). A case for radical acceleration: Programs of the Johns Hopkins University and the University of Washington. In C. P. Benbow & J. C. Stanley (Eds.), *Academic precocity: Aspects in its development* (pp. 139–159). Baltimore: Johns Hopkins University Press.

Stanley, J. C. (1980). On educating the gifted. *Educational Researcher, 9*, 8–12.

Stanley, J. C., George, W. C., & Solano, C. H. (Eds.). (1977). *The gifted and creative: A fifty-year perspective.* Baltimore: Johns Hopkins University Press.

Stanley, J. C., Keating, D. P., & Fox, L. H. (Eds.). (1974). *Mathematical talent: Discovery, description, and development.* Baltimore: Johns Hopkins University Press.

Taba, H. (1962). *Curriculum development: Theory and practice.* New York: Harcourt, Brace & World.

Tannenbaum, A. J. (1983). *Gifted children: Psychological and educational perspectives.* New York: Macmillan.

Tannenbaum, A. J., & Baldwin, A. (1983). Giftedness and learning disability: A paradoxical combination. In L. H. Fox, L. Brody, & D. Tobin (Eds.), *Learning disabled/gifted children* (pp. 11–36). Baltimore: University Park Press.

Torrance, E. P. (1965). *Gifted child in the classroom.* New York: Macmillan.

Torrance, E. P. (1977). Creatively gifted and disadvantaged gifted students. In J. C. Stanley, W. C. George, & C. H. Solano. *The gifted and the creative: A fifty-year perspective* (pp. 173–196). Baltimore: Johns Hopkins University Press.

Treffinger, D. J. (1975). Teaching for self-directed learning: A priority for the talented and gifted. *Gifted Child Quarterly, 19*, 46–59.

Van Tassel-Baska, J. (1981). *An administrator's guide to the education of gifted and talented children.* Washington, DC: National Association of State Boards of Education.

Williams, F. E. (1970). *Classroom ideas for encouraging thinking and feeling.* Buffalo, NY: D. O. K.

Witty, P. (1975). The education of the gifted and creative in the U.S.A. In W. B. Barbe & J. S. Renzulli (Eds.), *Psychology and education of the gifted* (pp. 39–47). New York: Irvington.

8. Programs for the Gifted and Talented: Issues Concerning Minority Populations

Alexinia Y. Baldwin
State University of New York at Albany

It is not easy to separate the issues concerning gifted minority individuals from those issues that are a part of the total concept of education for the gifted. These issues evolve from both philosophical and pragmatic considerations related to all aspects of developing programs for the gifted, from defining the population to evaluating efforts to meet the needs of this population. Gifted students have often been referred to as the other minority, so I view this chapter as one that deals with "the other minority's minority."

In this chapter the other minority's minority are those gifted individuals who might not be identified or have an opportunity to develop their full mental capacities due to such interacting variables as cultural diversity, socioeconomic deprivation, or geographic isolation. These interacting variables can occur singularly or in combination, as is shown in Figure 1. These variables can affect people's ability to recognize exceptional mental abilities among minority children because these exceptional abilities are often expressed in behaviors that deviate from those traditionally accepted as indicators of excellence in ability. The inability

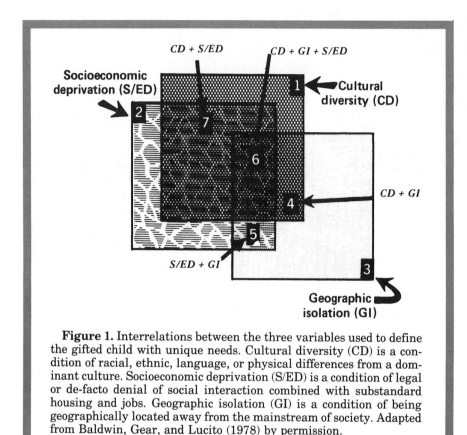

Figure 1. Interrelations between the three variables used to define the gifted child with unique needs. Cultural diversity (CD) is a condition of racial, ethnic, language, or physical differences from a dominant culture. Socioeconomic deprivation (S/ED) is a condition of legal or de-facto denial of social interaction combined with substandard housing and jobs. Geographic isolation (GI) is a condition of being geographically located away from the mainstream of society. Adapted from Baldwin, Gear, and Lucito (1978) by permission.

to recognize these abilities also affects the type of educational programs designed for this population of gifted children.

The Issues

The issues that are presented in this chapter are those that affect all American minority populations—Blacks, Hispanics, American Indians, Asian Americans, and Mountain Dwellers, to name a few. With the recent arrival, for example, of many Vietnamese and Haitians, the schools have had to focus on the educational needs that are specific to these popula-

The opportunity to teach a class of Black gifted boys and girls in Birmingham, Alabama gave impetus to my ideas in this chapter. I gratefully acknowledge the assistance of editors Frances Degen Horowitz and Marion O'Brien and the anonymous reviewer who commented on the draft of this chapter.

Requests for reprints should be sent to Alexinia Y. Baldwin, Department of Program Development and Evaluation, ED 309 State University of New York at Albany, 1400 Washington Avenue, Albany, NY 12222.

tions. The United States is made up of many different cultural groups. As historians have noted, the rate of change in the economic status, educational development, and social acceptance among the various groups has been uneven. Smilansky and Nero (1975) observed that as each society passes through processes of modernization, groups within the society mature as they work toward relative social equilibrium. To achieve equilibrium each group must experience supportive and interactive opportunities. Without these opportunities a maturational crisis will occur.

One perspective on the problems associated with identifying and nurturing minority gifted children is that the research and literature on minorities has been focused more on deficits than on strengths. The effects of such a focus have been exacerbated by a lack of educational and social support for minorities within the society and the existence of negative stereotypes about groups whose physical appearance or social mores make them clearly different from the majority. In the United States, Hispanics, Black Americans, and American Indians have the lowest proportionate representation in organized educational programs for the gifted. This has resulted in a backlash against policies related to education for the gifted in some urban centers with large minority populations. This backlash is manifested in a continuing mistrust among many minorities in the concept of giftedness, because they see this concept as another way of excluding those students who do not present the classic intelligence or achievement profile that is equated with giftedness.

Recently interest in issues related to educational planning for gifted children of minority groups has increased. A search of dissertation documents as of October 1983 on the topic of gifted minorities showed that the eight dissertations recorded for the years 1980–1982 represented 36 percent of all dissertations on this subject since 1956. One may speculate that one of the reasons for the upsurge of interest is that an increased number of minority group investigators are interested in finding answers about themselves as gifted individuals and about those members of their minority groups who might also be gifted. The increase in the number of advanced degrees that have been awarded in the field of education of the gifted and strong reactions to psychological reports that have hypothesized an inherent deficit in the intellectual abilities of minorities may be contributing to a heightened awareness of the dearth of information that specifically relates to minority individuals. It is likely that this has resulted in more attempts to isolate variables that affect the functioning levels of minority students.

Several recent research programs are relevant to the topic. Out of concern for the lack of Mexican Americans in programs for the gifted, Mercer (1971) has designed an identification instrument that takes into account the effects of the total environment on a child. Research by Guilford (1967) and by Meeker and Meeker (1979) has shown that individuals process information in many different ways and at varying levels of proficiency. These researchers have introduced a larger pool of abilities that can be used to develop a profile of an individual's exceptional ability to process information.

Additionally, there has been an attitudinal change among people in centers for research and development, in institutions of higher education, and in professional organizations about the uniqueness of behavioral and environmental variables within and among the various minority groups. There has been a challenge to develop validated educational processes that will enhance the mental development of future generations of minorities. Credibility has developed about the viability and legitimacy of specific research on minorities. These changes have had international implications, which are reflected in the concern for discovering and nurturing talent in developing countries. Finally, there has been a growing appreciation of the fact that a solution to the knotty problems of developing appropriate educational challenges for the gifted of minority groups will benefit educational practices for all children. As Passow (1977) has stated, "Ironically, concern for the disadvantaged [minority] has triggered opposition to what had become established and accepted practices for the gifted" (p. 51).

The Assumptions

There is an urgent need for accelerating the development of theoretical concepts and recommendations for appropriately meeting the educational needs of gifted individuals who come from minority groups. Changes in attitudes toward the innate capabilities of minorities is an important consideration for those who will subsequently resolve the issues addressed in this chapter, because attitudes establish the philosophy or mind set for approaching the problems and questions presented by these issues. A start in this direction would be the acceptance of the following three assumptions:

1. Giftedness exists in all human groups, and this giftedness does not manifest itself in a manner that can be genetically ascribed to that group. Culture and environment play important roles in a person's developing a penchant for certain activities and skills, but highly developed specific behaviors associated with a particular group do not provide the basis for assuming that these represent the innate capacities of the group.

2. Techniques other than usual standardized tests can be used to identify the gifted.

3. Behaviors that may be unique or special to a cultural group can serve as accurate indicators of high-level capacity to conceptualize and organize phenomena.

The issues that I present in this chapter are based on the acceptance of these three assumptions. These issues are organized around the discussion of three basic themes: defining the population of gifted children, setting goals for educating these children, and determining the most effective instructional system and evaluating the process and the product of the planned program. The largest share of the discussion is devoted to the first theme because of the central importance of identification strategies and the many unsolved problems related to this topic.

Defining the Population of Gifted and Talented Minority Children

Defining Giftedness

Our society's definition of giftedness has changed during the last three decades—from one based on a single IQ score to a multidimensional definition in which the significance of above-average ability in any human endeavor is recognized. The writings of Davis in the 1940s and 1950s with his "Davis-Eells Games" (cited in Eells et al., 1951), of Witty, with his theory of the need for multidimensional identification (1951), of Torrance (1960), of Getzels and Jackson (1962), and of many others, represent a definite trend toward recognizing the many facets of giftedness. The general educational community did not embrace giftedness as a multiply defined concept, however, until the federal government legitimized this view by defining giftedness in its legislation as including general academic abilities, special academic abilities, visual and performing arts, leadership ability, and psychomotor ability. Although there has been a broader acceptance of the multidimensionality of giftedness, there are still many people who equate giftedness only with standard IQ scores that range above 130.

It is important to differentiate between a definition of giftedness that refers to a philosophical notion of a characteristic of human beings and one that might be used to provide an organizational convenience within a school or school district. Due to constraints of space and finances, school districts make pragmatic decisions regarding the exceptional abilities for which special programs will be designed. A district might decide to include only 3 percent of its school population in programs for the gifted even though more than 3 percent of their students may be qualified. Another school might choose to have a program that emphasizes the sciences. In this case, those children who are gifted in music, arts, or other areas will not be accommodated. When a program for the gifted is advertised, those children who are selected are dubbed "gifted"; many people will then not consider those who are not selected as being gifted. This misconception has unfortunately fueled the contention that programs for the gifted are elitist.

In view of the fact that each community might define giftedness to suit its organizational needs, it is imperative that researchers refer to a philosophical notion of giftedness in making generalizations about this area. In an effort to clarify the meaning of giftedness, Renzulli (1979) has presented an operational definition of giftedness (derived from historical information and research data), which states that the gifted individual is one who should bring three clusters of behavior to bear upon any phenomena: above average ability, task commitment, and creativity. Clark (1983), drawing heavily upon brain research, has stated, "Intelligence is defined . . . as total and integrated brain functioning, which includes cognition, emotion, intuition, and physical sensing" (p. 6).

In an attempt to integrate these and earlier definitions of giftedness, I will use a definition of giftedness that involves the presence of or the capacity for high ability, task commitment, and creative problem-finding ability in the cognitive, psychosocial, psychomotor, or creative areas either singularly or in combination. Figure 2 illustrates the integration of the elements of this definition.

The cognitive area includes learned capabilities in specific academic areas such as math and science. It also includes scores on IQ tests. The creative area refers primarily to the graphic and performing arts. The psychomotor area includes physical abilities related to body movement and manual dexterity. The psychosocial area includes leadership abilities and a large array of social skills. The three clusters—task commitment, above average ability, and creativity—are brought to bear upon each of the areas. Task commitment means that an individual commits energy and time to an area of interest. Above average ability refers to evidence of ability in any of the areas, which ranks above the average according to accepted local, national, or international norms. Creativity involves the ability to sense, to be intuitive, to feel, and to use these abilities in problem finding and problem solving.

According to my definition, the capacity for high ability is important in defining giftedness. This part of the definition is particularly critical when referring to minorities because it underscores the fact that interacting variables that affect so many minorities can influence the display of the capacity for giftedness. This definition of giftedness can be applied to (a) abilities that are phenomenally high and intense regardless of environment, (b) abilities that are high and can be served through appropriate school activities, and (c) potential abilities that can be enhanced through proper educational planning. Gardner's (1983) recent proposals about the existence of multiple intelligences and the qualitative and quantitative evidence reported by researchers in education of the gifted support such an integrated definition. Many generic questions about the nature of giftedness remain to be asked. Is giftedness biologically rooted, and are the biological bases the same for all populations? Are the concepts *talented* and *gifted* synonymous? Is there a potential for giftedness in

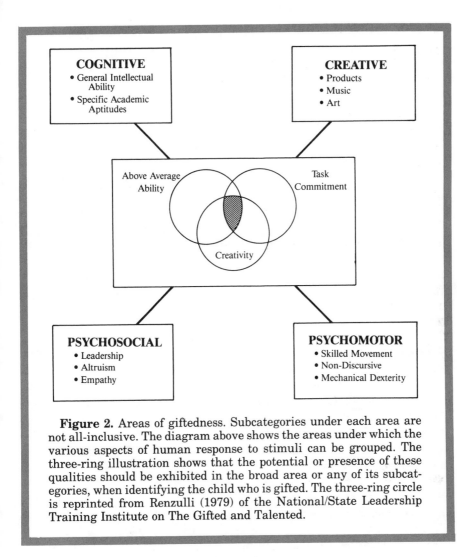

Figure 2. Areas of giftedness. Subcategories under each area are not all-inclusive. The diagram above shows the areas under which the various aspects of human response to stimuli can be grouped. The three-ring illustration shows that the potential or presence of these qualities should be exhibited in the broad area or any of its subcategories, when identifying the child who is gifted. The three-ring circle is reprinted from Renzulli (1979) of the National/State Leadership Training Institute on The Gifted and Talented.

some area for every individual? Is the definition of giftedness one that can be applied in the same manner to all minority groups? Questions that relate to defining giftedness relate to identifying the gifted as well.

Identifying the Gifted in Minority Populations

Identifying gifted children from minority groups has posed one of the most challenging problems in the education of the gifted. Standardized testing procedures are known to be fraught with inconsistencies, and this is especially true when applied to minority populations, which range widely across socioeconomic levels. The children from minority groups who are most often selected for programs for the gifted are likely to come from middle class environments or to have been particularly resilient in the face of adverse circumstances. Many have come from social or economic groups that have adjusted to the expectations of a nonminority population.

Central to the issue of successfully identifying giftedness in those children who come from cultures or circumstances different from the majority social norm is an understanding of the variables that influence the functioning level of these children. Minorities exhibit many behaviors that represent their making adaptive responses to environmental circumstances. It is very important that the dimensions of these behaviors be understood in terms of giftedness. Table 1 gives a broad perspective of the behaviors that might be indicative of exceptional mental ability that should be developed in an environment that is rich and stimulating.

The list of descriptors in Table 1, along with the correlated columns on external and internal deficits and possible environmental causality, are derived from notations made by me as a teacher and later verified or culled from the literature on children who are experiencing the effects of cultural diversity, socioeconomic deprivation, and geographic isolation. The columns called "Exceptional Characteristics to Look For" and "Intellectual Processing Ability Indicators" are based on the work of Guilford (1967) and on three taxonomies of educational objectives (Bloom, 1977; Harrow, 1972; Krathwohl, Bloom, & Masia, 1969). The contents of the last column of this table, "Horizontal/Vertical Program Adaptation," are derived from my experiences within the classroom and from recommendations made by Kaplan (1974), Sato (1973), and Torrance (1971). The items shown in Table 1 can be used to develop identification techniques that involve analyzing evidenced behavior that could then be described along a continuum of exceptional ability.

Little empirical evidence exists to support the use of such techniques; however, there have been some reports of identification procedures in which some of the concepts suggested by the information presented in Table 1 were followed. For example, Hilliard (1976) used the literature on behavioral styles (Cohen, 1971; Shapiro, 1965) as the basis for his argument that behavioral styles are a vehicle through which intelligence is expressed, and if these styles could be clarified, more information regarding the ability of the child could be garnered. Hilliard cited behavioral styles found in music, religion, and language among the Afro American group. A prescreening instrument was used for minority students of the California school system. The gifted students tended to show the following characteristics: alertness, energy, confidence, humor, expressiveness, experimentation, social control, verbal creativity, attention-seeking, sympathy, and risk-taking.

Boothy and Lacoste (1977) observed that "standardized assessment procedures tend only to identify as gifted, those children who are reflective, field independent, analytic, and have an internal locus of control" (p. 9). They suggested that along with the expansion of the definition of giftedness, that the "mainstream culture's philosophy underlying that definition must be expanded" (p. 9). These authors have boldly proposed that traits such as field dependence, impulsivity, global processing, and external locus of control be included as part of the identification process. Their rationale for this proposal is that these traits are recognized and accepted in the inner city among minorities as being in many instances a sign of giftedness that is synonymous with survival. They have also suggested that "there be a compromise between the integration of the minority gifted into the mainstream of logical thought and the presentation of the unique conceptual style of the minority child" (p. 9) as a viable set of styles that should be developed.

In a comparable analysis of Mexican Americans, Bernal and Reyna (1974) noted that this group places high value on cognitive and linguistic abilities, pragmatic alertness, sensitivity to others, leadership ability, interpersonal skills, and bilingual fluency. Thus, efforts to identify the gifted among Mexican Americans should include considering those exceptional abilities in behaviors that are valued and considered important by that population. In their studies of creativity, Torrance (1971) and his colleagues have investigated several of the factors noted by Hilliard and by Bernal and Reyna and concluded that children of minority populations perform on creativity tests as well as those from any other group. Although White children surpassed Black children in the verbal measures on the creativity tests, there were no significant differences on scores of figural fluency, flexibility, and originality; and in some cases minority groups surpassed white groups.

Davis (1978) has presented a strong argument for what he calls "community-based identification" of the gifted among minority children. His basic premise is that minority pupils' interactions within the community often reveal abilities of a superior nature that might be overlooked in the school. Davis designed a developmental framework for community leaders (Black and White) to use as a nomination schedule for children entering programs for the gifted. This concept fits well with the spirit of the assumptions presented at the beginning of this chapter. However, the results of longitudinal research needed to evaluate this type of identification are not yet available.

Following the implementation of the California Education Codes that used nontest methods for identifying giftedness, there was an increase in the number of students from minority and low-level socioeconomic groups included in programs for the gifted. The change in the composition of the classes for the gifted caused some concern among educators regarding the students' feelings of alienation, self-concept, and school adjustment. As a result, Tidwell (1979) collected psychoeducational information on 193 Black, Asian, White, and Hispanic American 10th-

Table 1
The Most Common Descriptors for Children Affected by Cultural Diversity, Socioeconomic Deprivation, and Geographic Isolation

Descriptors	External and Internal Deficit	Possible Environmental Causality
1. Outer locus of control rather than inner locus of control	1. Inability to attend to task without supervision	1. Discipline does not encourage inner locus of control. Child is given directions. Tradition dictates strict adherence to directions
2. Loyalty to peer group	2. Inability to externalize behavioral cues	2. A need to belong: empathy for those in similar situation
3. Physical resiliency to hardships encountered in the environment.	3. Inability to trust or consider beauty in life	3. Environment dictates need to survive. Anger and frustration increase animalistic desire to survive. Alternatives, solutions are forced
4. Language rich in imagery and human rich with symbolism; persuasive language	4. Perhaps only avenue of communication; standard language skills not used	4. A need to use subterfuge in environment to get message across; a lack of dominant language skills; a need to fantasize through language; acute awareness of environment due to its effect on individual
5. Logical reasoning; planning ability and pragmatic problem-solving ability	5. Opinions disallowed in school situation	5. Early responsibility related to survival
6. Creative ability	6. Lack of directed development of ability	6. Need to use items of environment as substitute, e.g., dolls, balls out of tin cans; wagons, sleds out of packing boxes; dolls out of corn husks
7. Social intelligence and feeling of responsibility for the community: rebellious regarding inequities	7. No opportunity to exercise behavior in community without censorship	7. Social reforms needed to help community; high regard for moral obligation to fellow human; religious influence, tradition, survival dictates awareness of social elements related to survival
8. Sensitivity and alertness to movement	8. Lack of training and development	8. Need to excel, toughness of environment, family emphasis on physical prowess to substitute for lack of educational input

Note. Adapted from Baldwin, Gear, & Lucito (1978) by permission.

Table 1—Continued

Exceptional Characteristics To Look For	Intellectual Processing Ability Indicators	Horizontal/Vertical Program Adaptation
1. Academic: good memory	1. Convergent production of semantic units	1. Contract activities; directed level development; counseling for trust–skill development
2. Psychosocial: sense of humor; intuitive grasp of situations; understanding of compromise	2. Affective behavior: possible indication of convergent production of behavioral units or classification	2. Group activity, debating, counseling seminars, philosophy, logic, process and skill development
3. Creative: tolerance for ambiguities, insight, inventiveness, revolutionary ideas	3. Divergent production	3. Creative activities, counseling mentor relationship; process/skill development
4. Creative: fluency, flexibility, ability to elaborate, originality. Academic: good memory, ability to think systematically	4. Divergent production of semantic classifications, systems relations, and transformations; fluency of thought; evaluation of behavioral implications	4. Writing and speaking emphases. Debating, rhetoric analysis, contemporary and historical literary comparisons, literary product development
5. Thinks in logical systems, uncluttered thinking, insightfulness, understanding cause and effect	5. Systems analysis, decision-making skills	5. Exposure to systematically developed strategies for solving problems, logic
6. Flexibility of thinking, fluency, special aptitudes in music, drama, creative writing	6. Divergent production of symbolic transformation, flexibility of thought	6. Special classes in creative aptitudes, independent study, mentor, process and content skills development
7. Intuitive grasp of situations, sensitiveness to right and wrong	7. Affective domain: Kohlberg's upper levels of moral development	7. Leadership seminars, community service participation, counseling, historical antecedents, process and content skills
8. Hand–eye coordination, physical stamina, skilled body movements	8. Divergent production, convergent production of behavioral implication	8. Special developmental classes, Olympic participation, physical culture classes

grade students who were identified for programs for the gifted by these nontest methods. Five self-report affective instruments were administered to the students to determine the students' self-concepts, locus of control, and attitudes toward school.

> The results indicated that with regard to the variable of self-concept, this sample of gifted students obtained (1) general self-concept scores higher than those of the general population; (2) academically related self-concept scores that were positive; and (3) self-esteem scores higher than those of the reported norm groups. (Tidwell, 1979, p. 8)

Tidwell's analyses of findings regarding each of the groups indicated that there was a significant difference in self-concept scores ($p < .01$) among students from different racial backgrounds, with the Black group having a high mean score and the Asian Americans a low mean score. Hispanic students displayed greater internal locus of control than did the other groups. According to Tidwell:

> The pattern of results indicating a significantly higher self-concept for the Black gifted students is consistent with the findings of several researchers . . . At the same time, however, this finding is contradictory with the finding of those who contend that no self-concept differences exist between the various racial groups . . . or those who maintain that the self-concepts of Blacks are actually lower than those from other racial groups. (Tidwell, 1979, p. 10)

Tidwell's research was limited to volunteers and to pupils who were perhaps nominated by teachers because they exhibited the very characteristics that the researcher was examining. Broad generalizations from this research cannot be made; however, these findings should give more insight into the types of behaviors that can be listed among the indicators of giftedness.

A review of the high school and college performance of a group of 25 Black students who would not have been selected for classes of the gifted by using single-standard criteria was reported in the *Phi Delta Kappan* (Baldwin, 1977). As fourth graders these children did not have the required IQ scores for acceptance into the gifted program. They had been selected through the use of recommendations of teachers, interviews, and scores on individual and group IQ tests and achievement tests. Greater reliance was placed upon the recommendations of teachers and the responsiveness shown by the children during the interview than on IQ scores. Students were asked to talk about the activities they participated in away from school. They also answered a series of questions related to their ambitions for the future. These children were obviously not selected in the traditional manner, yet they performed satisfactorily in the gifted program and excelled in high school and college courses. This finding adds credence to the importance of paying attention to alternate ways of selecting minorities.

Meeker (1978) suggested that a cognitive assessment instrument for gifted, disadvantaged minority children should not discriminate against those whose lack of formal English skills would cause them to score poorly on the Binet or WISC. To this end Meeker has been involved in investigating the cognitive abilities of Navajo Indians. Her analysis of data from the Structure of Intellect Learning Abilities test (SOI-LA; Meeker and Meeker, 1979) showed that those children who exhibited high-level abilities in the subtests of the SOI-LA had high levels of auditory memory. This ability is highly correlated with success in mathematics (Meeker, 1969). It would therefore be anticipated that these students would score consistently high in mathematics, yet not score particularly high on the Binet, which requires visual memory, an attribute that is most highly related to language arts (Meeker, 1969).

The Navajo children also showed low semantic ability, high figural ability, and, surprisingly, very low classification skills in the figural dimension. Meeker attributed the latter, which, according to Guilford (1967) is the basis of concept information, to the fact that the Navajo language is a spoken, sparse, aurally learned language with a minimum of, or no words for, classification. Such knowledge gained from research about particular groups can be used in designing identification instruments specifically for those groups.

Renzulli and Smith (1977) have discussed the need to recognize the minority gifted and have shown through their research in the inner city that peer nominations were quite accurate in identifying these minority gifted students. Peer nomination was included in their case study approach to identification. Renzulli's "Revolving Door" concept (Delisle, Reis, & Gubbins, 1981) provides for a large pool of students to be selected for an organized enrichment program within a school. Theoretically, such a policy should widen the net of potentially gifted students to include more minorities. In actuality, the evidence from oral comments of Delisle, Reis, and Gubbins indicate that this has not occurred, which points out the need for considering the training and attitudes of those people who are responsible for selecting children for gifted programs. Renzulli's model is one that should be considered viable as long as attention and training for use of criteria other than that which is called "standard" is given.

Claims of cultural bias in tests have also prompted the need for finding alternative means of identifying gifted minority individuals. In an effort to draw attention to problems of standardized tests, Williams (1970) developed what he called the "BITCH" test with items definitely biased to a particular cultural population. People outside of that culture had no chance to pass his test with a credible score. Although his approach is not recommended for wide adoption, Williams's demonstration of cultural bias in testing was effective.

In his article, "Concepts of Culture-Fairness," Thorndike (1974) illustrated the importance of looking further than the mean differences of the major or minor group in determining the fairness of a test. He stated that

> Fairness of a test relates to fair use . . . one definition of fair use states that a common qualifying score may be used with two groups if the regression line based on one group does not systematically over- or under-predict criterion performance in the other . . . an alternative definition would specify that the qualifying scores on a test should be set at levels that will qualify applicants in the two groups in proportion to the fraction of the two groups reaching a specified level of criterion performance. (p. 35)

The use of either of these definitions of fair use of test results requires that anyone wishing to employ a test with minority populations ought to first make the kind of analysis suggested by Thorndike.

The extensive analysis of test results of different populations by Jensen (1969) has been relentlessly reviewed, supported, and rejected with equal fervor. As a result, the task of suggesting or developing more effective assessment strategies for gifted minorities becomes one to be pursued with vigor. The most recent effort on the part of psychometricians to develop a culture-free test has been that by Kaufman and Kaufman (1983). Their test battery is currently being investigated to determine if it is a culture-free instrument.

Another identification strategy is exemplified by the Baldwin Identification Matrix (Baldwin, 1984; Baldwin & Wooster, 1977). It involves an array of assessment techniques for the areas of giftedness described in Figure 2: cognitive, psychosocial, psychomotor, creative (products), task commitment (motivation), and creativity (process). Objective and subjective identification techniques for each of these areas can be selected by the school district. A supplemental checklist of behaviors is included for each area of the definition. The checklists are filled out by the teacher, the parents, or another person in the inter- and intraschool community. The information derived refers to the ability scores of children who are above the average in that school district, state, or other large organizational group. The matrix items provide a total profile and provide concrete substantiation for the basic philosophy that each of the areas included contributes to a useful definition of giftedness. The format can be thought of as valuable for the identification process with all populations, reinforcing Passow's (1977) claim that the development of techniques for selecting children of minority groups will enhance the advances in identification techniques for all gifted children.

The Baldwin Identification Matrix has been used to increase the numbers of the minority students in programs for the gifted (Blackshear, 1979; Dabney, 1980; Long, 1981). Blackshear, for example, worked with the District of Columbia school system to develop norms for the overwhelmingly Black population in city schools, including items on the matrix that were specifically appropriate for that school system. McBeath, Blackshear, and Smart (1981) evaluated the identification process used in the District of Columbia. The 205 students identified for the program were compared with a random sample of 205 students who were not selected for the program. The items used on the matrix involved informal creative thinking tests, reading and mathematics tests, school grades, and nominations from peers, parents, and teachers. The first analysis indicated that the highest contributor to the selection process was a combination of nominations from peers, parents, and teachers. The next level of analysis indicated that the next combination of variables contributing to the identification procedure was peer nominations, mathematics, and parent nominations. A comparison of students who were continued in the program for the gifted from 1978 to 1981 and those who did not remain showed that the variable contributing most to those who stayed was creative thinking.

At a conference on special education for Black exceptional children, Dabney (1983) reported on the use of multiple criteria in selecting gifted Black adolescents using an adaptation of the Baldwin Identification Matrix. After 4 years of study, she had found that among the children identified as gifted, high-level leadership skills appeared to be predictive of success both in the program and in college entry. Her study was based on data gathered from a new public high school program for the potentially gifted child that was started with a ninth-grade class.

A nondiscriminatory identification model for minority students was developed by Long (1981) to be used with minority Black students in Rome, Georgia. Local norms were used for this study with the intent of revising these norms every 3 years. The following items were used with the Baldwin matrix: mental ability tests, nonverbal tests, achievement tests (reading and math), and teacher rating scales (leadership potential, learning characteristics, motivation, creativity). Analysis of data led Long to recommend that: (a) local norms on group mental ability tests and reading and math should be established and (b) the Raven's Progressive Matrices should be considered for use in a matrix design because it eliminates bias and "therefore gives consideration to the disadvantaged gifted as well as the advantaged gifted" (p. 7). Long concluded that the model designed for this school district was nondiscriminatory.

The Alonzo Bates Academy in Detroit is a public school for gifted children that was established in 1981 in a school region that consisted largely of minorities. This school has used a system of identification and program planning that has been highly accepted by the community: the Baldwin Identification Matrix format for identification, including tests of creativity, achievement records, and nominations by parents and teachers for selection. An evaluation of the selection process and curriculum is presently being done. The findings of the research should be extremely significant considering the fact that the school's enrollment is predominantly minority.

A number of other identification strategies related to gifted minority individuals have been reported. Stallings (1972) has developed an environmentally based procedure for identifying gifted children of different cultures. His technique involves using pictures of familiar buildings and other objects from the children's district or community in order to eliminate unfamiliarity with items used for ascertaining complex reasoning abilities as a variable that influences responses. Bruch (1972) developed a version of the Binet that was designed to allow for differences in cultures. Mercer (1971) developed the System of Multi-Pluralistic Assessment (SOMPA) that is designed to accommodate the variables that might affect the functioning level of the child. The SOMPA IQ scores of many of the students qualified them for the established "cutoff score" needed for entry into a program for gifted students. The validity of many of the identification strategies described here is the object of extensive current investigation. Eventually, the data may help to indicate which one or several are the most useful. Continued research in this area is very important.

Variables Affecting Success in Identifying Gifted Minority Children

It is widely recognized that useful strategies for identifying gifted minority children must be designed with an understanding of the factors that may influence the functioning level of minority children. These have sometimes been referred to as intervening environmental factors, and they are found more frequently in lower classes than in middle classes. These factors are drawn from those suggested originally by Metfessel (1965) and from interviews with people who worked with children from minority groups.

1. Parents who cannot speak English and thus cannot converse with their children may be unable to foster English language skills.
2. A home environment that lacks toys and other playthings may not stimulate cognitive and developmental skills.
3. A lack of conversation in the home may deny children the opportunity to listen to the discussion of topics and learn the art of participating in dialogue.
4. Cultural attitudes that emphasize having respect for elders may make minority children appear to be cowardly and backward.
5. The type of discipline given by parents may not encourage children to develop an inner locus of control, which may lead to a lack of self-motivation and problem-solving skills.

6. The pragmatic nature of activities in the home may actively discourage fantasy as a way for children to explore possibilities or to develop flexibility in thinking.

7. The traditions of the minority group may supersede the commonly accepted practices of the majority, leading to misconceptions about the abilities of the children.

8. The tradition of oral history might affect the interest of children in minority groups in reading to secure more information.

9. An environment that is focused on survival may force children to accept mature responsibilities in order to satisfy immediate needs rather than to pursue education.

10. Standard, out-of-school experiences such as visiting museums, libraries, exhibit halls, and zoos may be limited for minority children.

11. The attitude of parents that school does not supersede the family may lead to children's having a lack of concern or respect for school regulations.

12. A noisy and over-stimulating home environment may cause children to tune out auditory stimuli, thus seriously undermining the development of listening skills.

13. Prejudices against minorities that may exist in the community may have a negative effect upon minority members' self-concepts.

14. Minority children's use of their native language, which may be rich in imagery, may interfere with their learning the precise vocabulary of standard school language.

15. Environmental isolation may limit children's interactive skills, which may be important for developing leadership skills.

16. Social behaviors that are traditional for a minority group may be misunderstood in social situations in which standard behaviors are emphasized as being indicative of intelligence.

The foregoing factors might be considered to interfere with the acquisition of skills deemed important for success in school. In some cases the acquisition of substitute nonstandard behavior can mask exceptional ability. These intervening factors are not entirely negative in their effects. Some children are resilient enough to use these variables as stepping stones toward the development of their abilities. Understanding the characteristics of these individuals or the circumstances that might be common factors in their lives may offer some insight into the identification of gifted minority individuals. Understanding how the intervening factors help mask giftedness in the affected individuals should lead to the development of more selective assessment techniques for identifying gifted minority children.

It is important to analyze tests and their purposes before using them. It is also important that test results be interpreted in light of special knowledge about the groups being tested, and this involves paying attention to the presence of intervening factors that may serve to bias test results with respect to long-term prediction. Rosenbach (1979) has argued that "most claims of 'test bias' are basically unfounded." He takes the position that what we really have is "a situation where tests are accurate predictors of school success (grades, scores on achievement tests) but where school success, in turn, is not very predictive of success outside of school" (p. 6). The implications of Rosenbach's analysis are tremendous if schools are intended to prepare individuals for success in society.

Most recent reports evaluating the status of education in the United States recommend a no-nonsense approach by reasserting strict adherence to established high achievement-level indicators. One interpretation of these recommendations could mean that there will be little tolerance for creative planning for the selection of children as gifted who do not present standard, appropriate test profiles. In the implied criticism here, it is not suggested that assessment should not be rigorous; rather, proper techniques must be adopted in order to identify exceptional ability among minority groups. The traditional standardized assessment techniques are not always appropriate and no single common ability descriptor has been found that is generalizable for all gifted minority students. The idea of multidimensional screening, which includes the use of objective and subjective data, has been growing. Continued research on the effectiveness of this technique is needed.

It is known that achievement norms that have been set for a particular school district's identification process have resulted in more minority students being included in gifted programs. However, information on the subsequent manifestation of giftedness by these individuals is needed. Teachers' attitudes toward the lack of standard indices of giftedness among minority students have affected their ability to reliably recommend the gifted minority students in their classes. It is obvious that research on these issues and on the nature of gifted indices for different minority groups is sorely needed.

Setting Goals and Objectives for Programs for Gifted Minority Students

Designating program goals for gifted minority children is an essential task if the needs of these children are to be met. Among educators of the gifted, there is much talk about qualitatively different curricula for all gifted children, but very often a curriculum (the plan or goals we hope to achieve) is confused with instructional activities for the student. (A full discussion of these issues appears in Chapter 7 of this volume.) Curriculum goals should derive from a philosophical stance about attitudes, concerns, and beliefs regarding the specific area, the client group (in this case, gifted minority), and the purpose of education in general. If, for instance, the philosophy of a school district or program is based on values that support the assimilation of subcultures into the American culture, then the goals of the curriculum will be designed to reflect this plan.

In my opinion, the philosophy required to accommodate the needs of the gifted minority population includes a rational acceptance and respect for differences. It should include a belief in the value of cross-cultural experiences for all children. It should embrace the three assumptions listed in the introduction of this chapter and should emphasize the importance of all aspects of giftedness.

Concerns for curriculum are related to interpretations of the meanings placed on qualitatively different curricula for the gifted and a misconception that another, different curriculum should be planned for the gifted minority individual. Those professionals involved in clarifying issues related to education of the gifted agree that curriculum for the gifted should be qualitatively different. *Qualitatively different* is a term that has been difficult to define or operationalize. Many people have interpreted it as more pages of math or two reports instead of one. It is important for planners to realize that the concept of qualitative difference as applied to programs for the gifted requires goals that involve the basics planned for all children and then an extension of these basics in a variety of ways. Although gifted minority children may have some deficits in some areas, it is important to remember that these children have the basic capacity to learn.

Curriculum goal setting for these children should include sequencing content to provide vertical development in areas in which students have deficits, while at the same time expanding or enriching content through goals that ensure qualitative differences. Goals should also be set for expansion horizontally in the areas in which a student has strengths. This means that vertical progression is not remediation but attention to skill development that involves an enrichment of concepts. In this sense, the movement through content is upward (acquiring increasingly difficult concepts) and outward (enlarging and enriching the understanding of these concepts). Concept acquisition can be "telescoped," making progression from weaknesses to strengths much faster and consonant with a child's ability. I agree with Maker (1982), that this content should be more abstract and varied, and the scope and sequence of the material should be differentiated; therefore, as is suggested for all gifted students, a differentiated curriculum for gifted minority students embodies "a high level of cognitive and affective concepts and processes beyond those normally provided in the regular curriculum of the local educational agency" (Office of Education, 1976, pp. 18665–18666).

For the minority individual, the subject matter of the content should include material that is related to the background of the student. For example, a history or music curriculum could be modified to explore the parallel changes of the structure of jazz and the socioeconomic climate of this country during particular times in history. Thus, significant parallels can be explored while students learn about the musical concepts related to jazz and the historical events of this nation. Leadership profiles of political leaders along with historical struggles of minorities can be used as means of developing critical thinking skills.

Preplanned curriculum goals and objectives are considered by some to be contradictory to the concept of giftedness because goal setting is viewed as being too structured to meet the needs of gifted children. However, goal setting eliminates the hit or miss approach to meeting these needs. For gifted children, many of the listed goals would be the basic or minimum accomplishment to be expected. Careful attention to goal setting is important for gifted minority children who may have deficits in skills relevant to the tasks with which they are involved. The functioning behaviors of gifted minority children will often be quite different from the textbook descriptions of gifted children. This fact and these differences require understanding as well as creative and indepth planning.

Operationalizing Goals and Objectives

Operationalizing goals is a difficult task. The process of goal setting for gifted children, and gifted minority children in particular, requires co-operative planning on the part of all of the school personnel with whom a child will be in contact. The various organizational patterns used for meeting the needs of the gifted make this task more difficult. Pull-out programs, self-contained classes, and resource teachers are a few of the ways in which schools organize programs for educating the gifted. Without the proper cooperation and goal setting, a gifted child can become the beneficiary of a program that is uncoordinated and poorly planned. A total planning scheme with the various options cannot be included here, but the reader is referred to Maker (1982) and Baldwin, Gear, and Lucito (1978).

There are two basic elements to be considered in curriculum planning. First, it is important to develop an analysis of the total skill profile of gifted minority students. As has been noted, some gifted minority students will come to the learning environment with deficits in certain areas. These deficits are often in academic areas, but may be found also in such areas as creativity or social awareness. The task, then, is to develop curricula with goals that take into account diagnosed strengths and weaknesses, being mindful that these children have the capacity to learn, but that they need the skills and attitudes that will allow them to unlock their potential. Second, it is important to develop evaluative criteria that will accommodate each student's differing levels of ability and experience yet accomplish the specific objectives of the curriculum. If a teacher has planned or is aware of the minimum requirements to be achieved, he or she can select the most effective strategies. The word *minimum* here is used to imply that preplanned evaluative criteria cannot specify the outer limits a gifted child is capable of attaining. Significant progress toward these outer limits ought to be the continuing goal of every teacher.

The resolution of issues related to curriculum for gifted minorities is largely dependent upon the logical development of theoretical models that can be used to generate research to evaluate curriculum designs. Ward (1961) has developed a comprehensive general theory of differentiated curriculum for the gifted. However, Ward's model has not been examined in relation to its appropriateness for minority gifted children. This needs to be done, and, if the model proves not entirely applicable to minorities, alternative procedures should be developed.

Another research issue related to curriculum involves questions about the most appropriate curriculum for minority students. Should there be, for example, a curriculum that is based on a theme of leadership because minorities are among those people who have few leadership role models? Fuchigami (1978) has suggested that a leadership framework is needed from kindergarten through 12th grade that "will be superior to any curriculum currently available to minority gifted children" (p. 71). Although it is generally acknowledged that research on curricula for the gifted is needed, there is an even greater need to consider appropriate curriculum adaptations for gifted minority students.

Developing Instructional Systems and Evaluating Product and Process

The instructional system, which is the "how" of the three basic themes of this chapter, refers to the techniques used to achieve planned goals and objectives. This system, sometimes called the delivery system, includes teaching strategies, the behavior of teachers, the organization of the environment, and the evaluation of products and processes. It is important again to note the fact that planning the delivery system for gifted minority individuals involves the same attention to the myriad of educational models as is required for planning systems for nonminority gifted students.

Teaching Strategies

According to Newland (1976), a good teaching method

> depends upon the particular constellation of factors at any given time: the nature of the social situation in which the learning is occurring or is to occur, a composite of the characteristics of the pupils doing the learning (what they bring to the learning task in terms of their potentialities, their prior learnings, their motivation, and their social-emotional adjustments). (p. 154)

A teacher's instructional strategies can be, for example, didactic, autocratic, inductive, or facilitative. Questioning and discussion techniques should provide students an opportunity to explore divergent and higher level thought processes. Activities that will provide learning experiences can take place through projects, field trips, tutors, contracts, or methodically assigned classwork. Additional ideas for prototypical activities can be found in Baldwin, Gear, and Lucito (1978) and Maker (1982). Frasier and McCannon (1981) have suggested activities such as bibliotherapy—the use of stories or biographies of high-achieving minority individuals—to develop the self-concept of minority gifted individuals. The combination of activities and teaching strategies chosen will be dependent upon the students' needs and the restrictions of the environment. A teacher of gifted minority children must have what is desired of all teachers of the gifted: excellent training in education of the gifted and successful teaching experience. But, in addition, it is imperative that the teacher appreciate, know, respect, and understand the heritage of the children in the classroom.

The organizational environment is an important aspect of the total program provided for gifted children in general and minority gifted children in particular. Some examples of organizational patterns are learning centers developed by teachers and students, multilevel or self-contained class groups, mentors in and outside of school, resource rooms, and internships. Evaluation of the specific goals for a particular unit or subject area has been discussed as part of the curriculum and instructional section of this chapter. The evaluative criteria used for curriculum planning involve summative evaluation but can also represent formative evaluation for a total program for gifted minorities. The issues under evaluation are related to the products and the processes of all aspects of the program that have been designed to meet the needs of gifted minority children.

Evaluating Products and Processes

The first product of the program for the gifted that should be evaluated is the child, whose attitudes about the program, basic skills acquired, weaknesses overcome, strengths developed, motivation, and self-concept should be assessed. These evaluations should be done according to the particular goals set for the child.

The second set of products to be evaluated are those produced by the child. These products can be of the kind called Type III by Renzulli (1977), which involve the child in developing an idea that addresses a particular problem. The idea should be original and one that can be presented to some consumer (an audience, the general public, etc.) for its use. There can also be products that are a part of the lesson outcomes for which the teacher and student have set evaluative guidelines.

The third type of product to evaluate is associated with teachers: curriculum, the plan for the teaching strategies, and the organizational pattern selected for the program. Finally, the fourth set of products to evaluate involves the attitudes about the programs of parents, other teachers of the school, and the administrative staff. Changes in attitude toward including minorities in a program for the gifted, using alternative identification techniques, and the interschool communication about the program are some examples of evaluative concerns.

The process aspect of evaluation refers to processes used by teachers and students in reaching the desired outcomes of the program. Processes for the teacher include the selection of teaching styles or models, the quality of the selections, and the relations of these selections to the needs of the student and the content being presented. Processes for the student include the use of various processes in completing the program objectives, such as brainstorming, scientific discovery methods, and research techniques. Also included are evaluating the processes used to institute a program and evaluating the process of the involvement of the community, parents, and other faculty of the school.

Techniques for evaluating programs, products, and processes can involve the use of instruments that are standardized or those that are subjective and designed by teachers or students. A list of tests that can be used for evaluative purposes can be found in Maker (1982), and a format for evaluating programs for the gifted can be found in Renzulli's (1975) guidebook for evaluating programs for the gifted and the talented. Renzulli articulated some important problems associated with evaluating programs for the gifted, and these problems are intensified when evaluating programs for the minority gifted students. The problems arise from the need to evaluate a program that is highly individualized because students are at varying levels of skills and capacities. The students are also above the average; therefore, large-scale standardized testing does not adequately assess the changes that took place as a result of the educational program planned. A combination of techniques should be used, with standardized testing being only one strategy. If the program uses a profile such as that suggested by the Baldwin Matrix, another profile can be made that would show the changes.

It is important to note here that the evaluative data for gifted minority children will possibly show large gains during the first evaluative period. Subsequent gains might not be as high unless skill development is still needed for "catch-up" purposes. It is expected that the level of gains will stabilize as students become adjusted to a program.

Conclusions and Future Directions

The purpose of this chapter has been to address the issues related to developing programs for gifted minority children. These issues have been presented as having three themes: (a) defining population, including issues of defining giftedness and identifying gifted minorities; (b) deciding on goals and objectives (curriculum); and (c) deciding on the proper instructional system and evaluating the products and process of educational programs. The issues and problems have been presented as outgrowths of three basic assumptions: that giftedness does not manifest itself in a manner that can be genetically ascribed to any group, that techniques other than the usual standardized tests can adequately identify gifted minorities, and that behaviors that might be unique to a culture can be accurate indicators of high-level capacity to conceptualize and organize phenomena.

Throughout the chapter, I have pointed out the inextricable relation between the concerns about the education of gifted children in general and about the education of gifted minority children in particular. An awareness of these concerns is extremely important, and, although there are special considerations that must be applied to gifted minority children, there is no reason to think that an entirely separate conceptualization is needed for programs for gifted minorities. Planners for gifted minorities should be concerned with these unique elements: positive attitudes toward cultural differences; an awareness of cultural and ethnic history and traditions; the availability of resources related to minorities, (including books and media as well as human resources); how flexible an organization is in accommodating programs for gifted minorities; and high levels of knowledge of behavioral manifestations of conceptual capacity. If these elements are combined with the qualitatively different strategies required for all gifted students, the needs of gifted minority students will be met.

I have included in the discussion of each issue some problems out of which research questions can be generated for future development. All of these are important problems. The most immediate problem, however, is identifying minority gifted children by techniques other than the typical ones, by validating some techniques that already exist and developing others. Furthermore, model programs that have adequately accommodated gifted minorities and are exportable should be evaluated and shared among school districts.

Gifted minority individuals represent an important untapped source of human potential. It is imperative that attention be given to discovering and developing this potential. We cannot at this time in history risk the possible loss of an opportunity to enrich the lives of these children, nor risk the loss of their potential contributions to humankind.

References

Baldwin, A. (1984). *The Baldwin Identification Matrix 2 for the Identification of the Gifted and Talented: A handbook for its use.* New York: Trillium Press.

Baldwin, A., & Wooster, J. (1977). *Baldwin Identification Matrix Inservice Kit for the Identification of Gifted and Talented Students.* Buffalo, NY: D.O.K.

Baldwin, A. Y. (1977). Tests do underpredict: A case study. *Phi Delta Kappan, 58*(8), 620–621.

Baldwin, A. Y., Gear, G., & Lucito, L. (Eds.) (1978). *Educational planning for the gifted: Overcoming cultural, geographic, and socio-economic barriers.* Reston, VA: Council for Exceptional Children.

Bernal, E., & Reyna, J. (1974). *Analysis of giftedness in Mexican-American children and design of a prototype identification instrument: Final report* (Contract No. OEC-47-062113-307). Austin, TX: Southwest Education Development Laboratory.

Blackshear, P. (1979). *A comparison of peer nomination and teacher nomination in the identification of the academically gifted, black, primary level student.* Unpublished doctoral dissertation, University of Maryland, College Park.

Bloom, B. S. (Ed.). (1977). *Taxonomy of educational objectives: Handbook 1. Cognitive domain.* New York: David McKay.

Boothy, P., & Lacoste, R. J. (1977). *Unmined gold: Potentially gifted children of the inner city* (Report No. UDO-018171). San Antonio, TX: University of Texas. (ERIC Document Reproduction Service No. ED 154 076)

Bruch, C. B. (1972). *The ABDA: Making the Stanford-Binet culturally biased for black children.* Unpublished manuscript, University of Georgia, Athens.

Clark, B. (1983). *Growing up gifted* (2nd ed.). Columbus, OH: Charles E. Merrill.

Cohen, R. (1971). *The influence of conceptual role-sets on measures of learning ability. Race and intelligence.* Washington, DC: American Anthropological Association.

Dabney, M. (1980). *The black adolescent: Focus upon the creative positives.* Paper presented at the annual meeting of the Council for Exceptional Children, Philadelphia, PA. (ERIC Document Reproduction Service No. ED 189 767)

Dabney, M. (1983, July). *Perspectives and directives in assessment of the black child.* Paper presented at the meeting of the Council for Exceptional Children, Atlanta, GA.

Davis, P. (1978). *Community-based efforts to increase the identification of the number of gifted minority children.* Ypsilanti, MI: Eastern Michigan College of Education. (ERIC Document Reproduction Service No. ED 176 487)

Delisle, J., Reis, S., & Gubbins, E. (1981). The revolving door identification and programming model. *Exceptional Children, 482,* 152–156.

Eells, K., Davis, A., Havighurst, R., Herrick, V., & Tyler, R. (1951). *Intelligence and cultural differences.* Chicago: University of Chicago Press.

Frasier, M., & McCannon, C. (1981). Using bibliotherapy with gifted children. *Gifted Child Quarterly, 25*(2), 81–85.

Fuchigami, R. Y. (1978). Summary, analysis, and future directions. In A. Baldwin, G. Gear, & L. Lucito (Eds.), *Educational planning for the gifted: Overcoming cultural, geographic, and socio-economic barriers* (pp. 65–76). Reston, VA: Council for Exceptional Children.

Gardner, H. (1983). *Frames of mind: The theory of multiple intelligences.* New York: Basic Books.

Getzels, J. W., & Jackson, P. W. (1962). *Creativity and intelligence: Explorations with gifted students.* New York: Wiley.

Guilford, J. P. (1967). *The nature of human intelligence.* New York: McGraw-Hill.

Harrow, A. (1972). *Taxonomy of the psychomotor domain: A guide for developing behavioral objectives.* New York: David McKay.

Hilliard, A. G. (1976). *Alternative to IQ testing: An approach to the identification of the gifted "minority" children* (Report No. 75-175). San Francisco, CA: San Francisco State University. (ERIC Document Reproduction Service No. ED 147 009)

Jensen, A. (1969). How much can we boost IQ and scholastic achievement. *Harvard Educational Review, 39,* 1–123.

Kaplan, S. (1974). *Providing programs for the gifted and talented: A handbook.* Ventura, CA: Office of the Superintendent of Ventura County Schools.

Kaufman, A., & Kaufman, N. (1983). *Kaufman Assessment Battery for Children (K-ABC).* Circle Pines, MN: American Guidance Service.

Krathwohl, D., Bloom, B., & Masia, B. (Eds.). (1969). *Taxonomy of educational objectives: Handbook 2. Affective Domain.* New York: David McKay.

Long, R. (1981, April). *An approach to a defensible non-discriminatory identification model for the gifted.* Paper presented at the meeting of the Council for Exceptional Children, New York, NY.

Maker, J. (1982). *Curriculum development for the gifted.* Rockville, MD: Aspen Systems Corporation.

McBeath, M., Blackshear, P., & Smart, L. (1981, August). *Identifying low income, minority gifted and talented youngsters.* Paper presented at the annual meeting of the American Psychological Association, Los Angeles, CA. (ERIC Document Reproduction Service No. ED 214 328)

Meeker, M. (1969). *The structure of the intellect: Its interpretation and uses.* Columbus, OH: Charles E. Merrill.

Meeker, M. (1978). Nondiscriminatory testing procedures to assess giftedness in Black, Chicano, Navajo, and Anglo children. In A. Baldwin, G. Gear, & L. Lucito (Eds.), *Educational planning for the gifted: Overcoming cultural, geographic, and socio-economic barriers* (pp. 17–26). Reston, VA: Council for Exceptional Children.

Meeker, M., & Meeker, R. (1979). *SOI Learning Abilities Test* (rev. ed.). El Segundo, CA: SOI Institute.

Mercer, J. R. (1971, September). *Pluralistic diagnosis in the evaluation of black and chicano children: A procedure for taking sociocultural variables into account in clinical assessment.* Paper presented at the meeting of the American Psychological Association, Washington, DC.

Metfessel, N. (1965). *Twenty correlates of creative thinking.* Los Angeles: University of Southern California.

Newland, T. E. (1976). *The gifted in socio-educational perspective.* Englewood Cliffs, NJ: Prentice-Hall.

Office of Education. (1976). Program for the gifted and talented. *The Federal Register, 41,* 18665–18666.

Passow, A. H. (1977). The gifted and the disadvantaged. In J. Miley, I. Sato, W. Luche, P. Weaver, J. Curry, & R. Ponce (Eds.), *Promising practices: Teaching the disadvantaged gifted and talented* (pp. 51–57). Ventura, CA: Office of the Superintendent of Ventura County Schools.

Renzulli, J. (1975). *A guidebook for evaluating programs for the gifted and talented.* Ventura, CA: Office of the Superintendent of Ventura County Schools.

Renzulli, J. (1977). *The enrichment triad model: A guide for developing defensible programs for the gifted and talented.* Mansfield Center, CT: Creative Learning Press.

Renzulli, J. (1979). *What makes giftedness? A reexamination of the definition of the gifted and the talented.* Ventura, CA: Office of the Superintendent of Ventura County Schools.

Renzulli, J., & Smith, L. (1977). Two approaches to identification of gifted students. *Exceptional Children, 43,* 512–518.

Rosenbach, J. (1979). Instrumentation for assessing culturally different: Some conceptual issues. In L. K. Novak (Chair), *Instrumentation: Applications to exceptionality.* Symposium conducted at the meeting of the Council for Exceptional Children, Dallas, TX.

Sato, I. (1973). *Group summary for work conferences on the culturally different gifted child.* Unpublished manuscript, National/State Leadership Training Institute on the Gifted and the Talented, Los Angeles, CA.

Shapiro, D. (1965). *Neurotic styles.* New York: Basic Books.

Smilansky, M., & Nero, D. (1975, March). A longitudinal study of the gifted disadvantaged. *Educational Forum, 39,* 272–294.

Stallings, C. (1972). Gifted disadvantaged children. *National Leadership Institute Teacher Education/Early Childhood.* Storrs, CT: University of Connecticut.

Thorndike, R. (1974). Concepts of culture-fairness. In R. Tyler & R. Wolf (Eds.), *Crucial issues in testing* (pp. 35–45). Berkeley, CA: McCutchan.

Tidwell, R. (1979). *A psycho-educational profile of gifted minority group students identified without reliance on aptitude tests.* Los Angeles, CA: University of California. (ERIC Document Reproduction Service No. ED 177 231)

Torrance, E. P. (1960). The Minnesota studies of creative thinking in the early school years. *University of Minnesota Research Memorandum (No. 59-4).* Minneapolis, MN: University of Minnesota Bureau of Educational Research.

Torrance, E. P. (1971). Are the Torrance tests of creative thinking biased against or in favor of "disadvantaged groups"? *Gifted Child Quarterly, 15,* 75–80.

Ward, V. (1961). *Educating the gifted: An axiomatic approach.* Columbus, OH: Charles E. Merrill.

Williams, R. L. (1970). Black pride, academic relevance, and individual achievement. *The Counseling Psychologist, 2*(1), 18–22.

Witty, P. (Ed.). (1951). *The gifted child.* Lexington, MA: Heath.

9. Why Doesn't Jane Run? Sex Differences in Educational and Occupational Patterns

Jacquelynne S. Eccles
University of Michigan

Despite recent efforts to increase the participation of women in advanced educational training and high-status professional fields, women in general, and gifted women in particular, are still underrepresented in many high-level educational and occupational settings. The persistence of these patterns has attracted the interest of social scientists and public policy makers. The possibility that sex differences in educational and occupational choices may reflect differential use and development of human potential has raised special concern. In particular, social scientists and policy makers alike have worried that both the individual and society may be suffering from the underdevelopment and under-use of the intellectual talents of women. The fact that gifted women, compared to their male peers, are underrepresented at the higher levels of educational training and occupational status is especially worrisome since these women clearly have sufficient intellectual talent to participate fully in these educational and vocational settings. Many factors, ranging from outright discrimination to the subtle and not-so-subtle processes of gender role socialization, contribute to this discrepancy in participation rates among gifted men and women.

Discussing all possible mediating variables is beyond the scope of a single chapter; thus I focus on the set of social and psychological factors that I and my colleagues have found to be important mediators of achievement-related behaviors. The chapter begins with a review of sex differences in achievement patterns among the gifted. In subsequent sections, I present a model that accounts for these differences, review the available evidence to support the hypotheses generated by the model, discuss the role of socialization in perpetuating these sex differences, suggest needed research, and suggest educational interventions that might help ameliorate the situation.

In any discussion of sex differences in achievement the problems of societal influence on the very definitions of achievement as well as on the assessment of the differential worth of various forms of achievement must be acknowledged. Defining achievement itself, much less defining appropriate or ideal ways of using one's talents, is a value-laden enterprise at best. Evaluating the meaning and consequences of sex differences on any particular criterion of achievement is equally value laden. Too many social scientists have adopted a male standard of ideal achievement when judging the value of achievements by women (see Parsons & Goff, 1980). Using this standard, they have focused on the question, "Why aren't women more like men?" As a consequence, very little systematic, quantitative information has been gathered regarding more stereotypically female-typed achievements, such as the academic accomplishments of one's offspring or of one's pupils or one's contributions to local organizations.

Even less qualitative information has been gathered regarding the meaning of various achievement-related activities to either gifted men or women. As a result, very little is known about the ways in which gifted women think they express their intellectual talents. Defining achievement in terms of typically male-typed activities inevitably leads to the question, "Why aren't the women achieving at the same levels as the men?" instead of the question, "Why do gifted women choose particular achievement arenas?" Nonetheless, while acknowledging this value bias, it is still instructive to compare men and women on the set of activities assumed to be indicators of achievement by the culture at large. The reader is forewarned, however, that these indicators do favor men. To balance this bias, particular attention will be focused, whenever possible, on the reasons gifted women provide to explain the achievement-related choices they make.

Preparation of this manuscript was funded in part by grants from the National Institutes of Mental Health and the National Institute of Child Health and Development.

Research on Sex Differences Among the Gifted

In reviewing the educational and occupational patterns of gifted men and women, I have relied heavily on two sets of data: the longitudinal data compiled on Terman's gifted population and the cross-sectional and longitudinal data being compiled by researchers at Johns Hopkins University who are studying mathematically and verbally precocious children. I have supplemented these studies with general statistics on the occupational and educational advancement of extremely bright males and females.

Terman's Gifted Population

In 1921, Terman began a longitudinal study of approximately 1,450 gifted boys and girls 7 to 15 years old. The original sample contained 831 males and 613 females. These individuals have been recontacted several times; extensive demographic, intellectual, and social-developmental data were gathered at each contact. Because the researchers have been able to relocate approximately 80 percent of the original sample at each new wave of data collection, this longitudinal study provides the richest and most complete set of data available on the life-span development of gifted males and females. Although bound by its historical period, it provides the best data available for comparing the educational and occupational patterns of gifted males and females.

Even though striking educational and vocational differences characterize this sample of gifted males and females, there are some important similarities that should also be noted (Terman 1925, 1930; Terman & Oden, 1947). First, although the girls had a slight edge over the boys on measures of social adjustment during childhood, these males and females have scored approximately the same on a variety of measures of social adjustment at each wave of testing, especially during the adult years. In addition, both the males and the females scored as well as did normative samples on measures of social adjustment and maturity. Second, the males and females received approximately the same grades during high school. When a difference emerged for either grades or teachers' ratings of academic performance, the girls performed slightly better than the boys, despite the fact that the boys scored slightly higher than the girls on timed achievement tests in math, history, and science. In college, the women did as well, if not better, than the men in all courses except science and math courses. Third, the males and females were graduated from

Table 1
Most Common Undergraduate and Graduate Majors of Men and Women in the Terman Study: 1940

Major	Undergraduate		Graduate	
	Female	Male	Female	Male
Biological Sciences	6%	10%	9%	17%
Education	9%	1%	19%	6%
Engineering	<1%	15%	<1%	8%
Letters	36%	9%	28%	6%
Physical Sciences	5%	17%	4%	13%
Social Sciences	37%	40%	32%	18%
Other	6%	8%	7%	32%
Total Number of Students	388	523	218	356

Note. Percentage figures are rounded to the nearest whole number. They represent the percentage of the total within each column. Some of the graduate students were in their graduate programs at the time these data were gathered. Data are derived from Terman and Oden (1947).

both high school and college at approximately the same age. And, finally, these males and females were equally likely to enter college upon leaving high school.

Sex differences in the educational patterns of Terman's sample emerged for the first time when the sample was in college. Table 1 summarizes the fields in which these men and women obtained their college degrees (not all of the original sample graduated from college). These men and women specialized in very different fields of study at both the undergraduate and graduate levels (Terman & Oden, 1947). These differences reflect sex stereotypes still held today, particularly with regard to the fields of education, engineering, and the physical sciences.

In addition to these differences in field of study, sex differences also emerged in length of study. Although the men and women were equally likely to earn bachelor's degrees (71% of the men and 67% of the women had graduated from college by 1960), the men were more likely than the women to complete graduate degrees. For example, by 1960, 40 percent of the original male sample and only 24 percent of the original female sample had obtained advanced degrees (Oden, 1968). Furthermore, the men obtained higher and more prestigious degrees than did the women. For example, by 1960, 87 men and only 20 women had obtained PhDs (Oden, 1968). Similarly, by 1945, 126 men compared to only 8 women had received either a law degree or an MD (Terman & Oden, 1947). The women were also less likely than the men to complete graduate degrees once they had entered graduate school. For example, in 1945 only 10 percent of the male graduate students had failed to obtain a degree; in comparison, of the students who had entered graduate programs, fully 23 percent of the female graduate students had failed to obtain their graduate degrees in the same time period. Finally, although men and women were equally likely to obtain financial assistance for their first year of graduate training, a higher percentage of the male graduate students continued to receive financial support for two or more years (Terman & Oden, 1947). As a consequence, the men received three times as much financial assistance for graduate training as did the women.

Differences in occupational patterns are even more extreme. The most striking difference lies in the percentage of men and women who reported having an occupation. From 1940 to 1960, more than 99 percent of the men were either employed full time or retired from full-time employment. In contrast, during this same period, only 36 to 49 percent of the women were employed full time (Oden, 1968; Terman & Oden, 1947). Not surprisingly, the vast majority of the unemployed women were housewives, many of whom remained unemployed even after their children had grown and left home.

There are also marked sex-stereotypic differences in the occupational attainment of the fully employed men and women. The occupations of the fully employed men and women from Terman's sample in 1960 are summarized in Table 2. As was true each time the sample was surveyed, the gifted women were less likely to be employed than were the men (42% versus 97%). The men and women also differed in the occupations they held. The women were more likely than the men to be employed in traditionally female fields (education and administration below the college level, library science, social work, and high-level clerical and accounting). In contrast, the men were more likely than the women to be employed in traditionally male fields (law, science and engineering, and executive and managerial). In general, the men also held more prestigious positions than did the women. A similar pattern characterized this population of gifted men and women when they were surveyed in 1945.

In addition, the gifted men in Terman's sample earned a great deal more money than did the gifted women. For example, in 1959, the median annual income for the men was $13,464, with a range from $5,000 to more than $300,000. Twenty percent of the men earned in excess of $25,000. In contrast, the median annual income for the fully employed women was $6,424 and ranged from $2,800 to only $28,000. Even the single, professional women did not match their male peers in terms of occupational attainment and income, although they generally fared better than their married counterparts (Oden, 1968).

It is clear from these data that the gifted women in the Terman sample achieved less in terms of educational and vocational attainment

Table 2
Occupations of Men and Women of the
Terman Study Who Were
Employed Full-Time in 1960

Profession	Men		Women	
	In each occupation: N	Percent	In each occupation: N	Percent
Professional and Semiprofessional				
Lawyer, Judge	77	10%	2	<1%
College or University Faculty	54	7%	21	8%
Teaching and Administration (below four-year college level)	32	4%	68	27%
Scientist, Engineer, Architect	107	15%	2	<1%
Physician, Clinical Psychologist	42	6%	8	2%
Author, Journalist	17	2%	11	4%
Nurse, Pharmacist, Lab Technician	0		6	2%
Librarian	0		15	6%
Government Work (military and federal agencies)	18	2%	0	
Social Work, Welfare Personnel	0		14	6%
Arts and Entertainment	21	3%	4	2%
Other Professional	29	4%	8	2%
Business				
Executive and Managerial Positions	179	24%	23	9%
High-level Clerical and Accountant	61	8%	54	21%
Real Estate, Insurance, Investments, Small Business	40	5%	7	3%
Public Relations, Promotions, Advertising	15	2%	5	2%
Skilled Trades and Agriculture	27	4%	0	
Miscellaneous	14	2%	5	2%
Totals	733		253	

Note. Percentages are based on the number of full-time employed individuals within each sex. Percents are rounded to the nearest whole number. Data are based on Oden (1968) and reflect employment status in 1960. Total population in 1960: males 759; females 597. Percent of the sample employed full-time: males 97%; females 42%.

than did their gifted male peers. To get a more complete picture of the achievements of this group of gifted women, it is also of interest to compare them with a more typical group of college-trained women. In 1940, at approximately the same time that Terman and Oden gathered their data, Babcock surveyed the status of American college graduates. Sixty-six percent of the female college graduates were employed; 25 percent were housewives (Babcock, 1941). In addition, 78 to 84 percent of the employed female graduates were in the professions, primarily in education. In comparison to this general sample of college-educated women, Terman's gifted women were less likely to be employed and, if employed, were more likely to be clerical and office workers. Thus, the occupational status of the gifted women in Terman's sample was lower than that of both their gifted male peers and the general population of college-educated American women at that point in history.

A somewhat different picture emerges for educational attainment. Although the gifted women in Terman's sample were less likely than their gifted male peers to have earned advanced degrees, a higher percentage of the gifted women obtained advanced graduate degrees than did female college graduates drawn from the general population (27 percent versus 12 percent; Greenleaf, 1937).

Explaining the Difference Between Men's and Women's Attainments

The results from the Terman studies clearly indicate that the gifted women achieved less than did the gifted men in terms of both educational and occupational advancement. But did they make less use of their intellectual talents? As I noted earlier, this is primarily a question of values. The accomplishments of the gifted men are easy to document. They were highly successful vocationally. Furthermore, the number of distinctions that these men had won by 1960 is quite impressive (see Table 3) and much greater than the number won by their gifted female peers. In contrast, the majority of the gifted women invested a large portion of their time and energy into their families. As a consequence, their educational and vocational attainments are less notable than those of their male peers. But have these women contributed less? The gifted men and women themselves provide one answer to this question. In 1960, they were asked to rate the extent to which they had lived up to their intellectual promise. Although the unemployed housewives gave a slightly lower rating than the professional women, both groups of gifted women were quite positive in their response to this question. In addition, as a group, the men and women were equally positive in their responses (Oden, 1968). In general, then, in 1960 these gifted women were fairly satisfied with their use of their intellectual talents. Apparently, at that point in history they viewed their contributions to their families and to their communities as positively as their male peers viewed their vocational success.

More recent interviews suggest that some of these women now have more regrets about their high levels of investment of both time and energy in their families coupled with their relatively low levels of investment in their own professional development (Sears, 1979). When asked to rate

Table 3
Numbers of Men and Women in the Terman Study Who Were Recipients of Outstanding Honors and Recognition by 1960

Honor	Men	Women
Elected to Phi Beta Kappa[1]	88	78
Elected to Sigma Xi[1]	77	17
Graduated from College with Honors	159	117
Who's Who in America	46	2
American Men of Science	81	12
Dictionary of American Scholars	10	5
International Who's Who	6	0
Elected to Political Office[2]	26	3
Appointed to Political Position[2]	18	4

Note. Numbers are estimates based on self-reports; relevant information was not available for all individuals. Data are derived from Oden (1968) and Terman and Oden (1947).
[1]Elected at college graduation
[2]These figures were not tabulated by the researchers. They are estimates based on mention of position in Oden (1968).

their level of satisfaction with several areas of their lives, the gifted women were less satisfied than the gifted men with their occupational development, more satisfied than the gifted men with their friendships and the cultural richness of their lives, and equally satisfied with their family life and general joy of living. In addition, when asked how they would have structured their lives differently, substantially fewer of the gifted women would have chosen the homemaker role as primary and substantially more would have chosen a career.

This shift in satisfaction with their life decisions has undoubtedly been stimulated by the shifting cultural norms regarding women's family and occupational roles. The decision to invest time and energy in one's family rather than in an occupation was consistent with the gender role norms of the late 1930s and early 1940s. In addition, given the difficulty these women had retaining financial support for their graduate training and the probable discrimination they would have faced if they had sought out high-level professional employment, the types of jobs readily available to these women were quite limited. Investing time in one's family and community may well have seemed a more interesting alternative than working in a less than satisfying job. But, women have been reevaluating gender role norms for the past 15 years. In addition, employment and educational opportunities for gifted women have expanded substantially over the last 30 years. Consequently, when asked to reconsider the decisions they made 30 to 40 years ago, the cost of these decisions in terms of their own development is likely to have become more salient since 1960. Furthermore, the direct benefits gained by their families may seem less salient now that their children have left home and most of their husbands have retired.

But what was the value to society of these women's commitments to their families and communities? To provide an objective answer to this question, it is necessary to measure these women's contributions using criteria of accomplishment that are not based on the dominant, male-typed value system. Many of these gifted women spent their lives rearing and educating children (approximately 80 percent were either teachers or homemakers or both). Comparing how these children fared intellectually, educationally, and vocationally with children reared and educated by less intellectually talented women would provide one indicator of these women's contributions. If the children of gifted mothers benefited on these criteria by their mothers' staying home, then their mothers' decision to use their intellectual talents at home would represent a substantial contribution to society and one that ought to be recognized and rewarded. Likewise, if the students of gifted teachers learned more and developed higher motivation to continue learning than did students of the average teacher, then the commitment of gifted women to educating youth would also be an important contribution to society and one that society should be willing to pay for.

In fact, society may be paying a rather heavy price now for not recognizing the contributions that gifted and talented women were making to public education. There is now a shortage of math and science teachers. In the past, a sizable percentage (10 to 12 percent of Terman's sample) of gifted women with math and science skills went into elementary and secondary education both because they wanted to teach children and because teaching fit well with their own family plans. Cultural change has encouraged these gifted women to seek out more prestigious and better paying jobs in industry and higher education.

Data relevant to some of these hypotheses may be available in the Terman data set. Many of the offspring of the original gifted sample were given the Stanford-Binet Intelligence Test. These data are summarized only briefly in the reports of the Terman study. For example, sex-of-child comparisons are reported in both Oden (1968) and Terman and Oden (1947); in each case the male and female children scored equally well. What is needed is a comparison of the children's scores broken down by the sex of the gifted parent and by the employment status of the mother. Such a comparison would provide an estimate of the benefit children of gifted mothers derive from having a gifted mother as well as from having a gifted mother who stayed at home during some or all of their childhood years.

But whatever the benefits of having a gifted mother, the influence of children on their gifted mothers' occupational achievements is quite clear. For example, between 1940 and 1945, the percentage of gifted women employed dropped from 49 to 36 largely because of the birth of children (Terman & Oden, 1947). Furthermore, of the 30 women who had attained outstanding vocational achievements outside the home, 25 had no children (Oden, 1968).

In summary, the gifted women in Terman's sample achieved less than their gifted male peers both educationally and vocationally. In large part, this differential pattern reflects the impact of gender role socialization on these men's and women's definitions of the appropriate roles of mothers and fathers. Gifted mothers made vocational choices that meshed well with their desire to spend a lot of time with their children. It is also important to note that even the single, professional women did not attain the same levels of occupational status as their gifted male peers. Clearly, then, factors other than motherhood also limited the vocational attainments of Terman's gifted women. I discuss some of these social and psychological factors later in the chapter.

The Johns Hopkins Study of the Gifted

Over the past 15 years, Stanley and his colleagues at Johns Hopkins University have been studying mathematically and verbally precocious children. During this period, several thousand junior high school aged children drawn from regional and national talent searches have been given aptitude tests and questionnaires tapping attitudes, career plans, interests, and values. Many of these children have been or are currently being retested in order to chart their educational development.

Perhaps the most interesting aspect of the data emerging from these studies is their similarity to the findings of the Terman studies, especially given the social changes that have occurred during the last 50 years. Just as was true in the Terman study, fewer females than males have emerged as being gifted in mathematics in each of the Johns Hopkins studies. Furthermore, the boys in the Johns Hopkins samples have consistently scored higher than the females on the SAT-Math test (the test used by the Johns Hopkins team to assess mathematical talent). Finally, the girls have scored as well as the boys on the SAT-Verbal test (the test used to assess verbal talent). Thus, as was true of the Terman sample, giftedness in math is more common and more extreme among boys. In contrast, verbal precocity appears to be more equally distributed between the sexes (Benbow & Stanley, 1980, 1983; Fox & Cohn, 1980).

The pattern of sex differences in educational pursuits is also quite similar across the two studies despite the lapse of 50 years. In fact, differences that were not apparent until college in the Terman sample are evident in the Johns Hopkins samples by junior high school. This difference is best characterized in terms of the underrepresentation of girls in "extra" educational settings, especially settings associated with math and science. The Johns Hopkins teams have consistently found gifted girls to be less likely than gifted boys to enroll in accelerated or special programs (Benbow & Stanley, 1982b; Stanley, 1976), to respond positively to an invitation to join a gifted program (George & Denham, 1976; Stanley, 1976), and to enter college early (Stanley, 1976). In addition, in follow-ups of the boys and girls who enrolled in the Johns Hopkins Summer Enrichment courses, the girls were less likely to remain on an accelerated math track (Fox & Cohn, 1980), were enrolled in fewer math and science courses (Benbow & Stanley, 1982a), and expressed less interest in majoring in science or engineering in college than did the boys (Benbow & Stanley, 1984). These differences exist despite the fact that these girls, like the girls in the Terman study, did just as well as the boys in their high school math and science courses.

Conclusions Drawn From the Johns Hopkins and the Terman Studies

As is true for the population at large (Eccles [Parsons], 1984), gifted females do not achieve as highly as do gifted males either educationally or vocationally. They are less likely to seek out advanced educational training, and, even when they do, they do not enter the same fields as do their male peers. They are overrepresented in the fields of education and literature and underrepresented in science, math, and engineering. Most importantly, they are, in fact, underrepresented in almost all advanced educational programs and in the vast majority of high-status occupations. Gifted women are less likely to have a professional career than their male peers, and even those who choose to have a profession tend to select occupations that have lower status, require less education, are more compatible with family time schedules, and make fewer demands on one's off-the-job time and on one's family.

One might argue that the underrepresentation of females in the sciences is a natural consequence of the pattern of sex differences on the aptitude measures taken by both Terman and the Johns Hopkins team. This is an unwarranted conclusion for several reasons. First, both of these studies focused on gifted children. Thus, even though the females may have less math aptitude than their male peers, they certainly have sufficient aptitude to make important contributions to science as well as to other professions. Second, although aptitude differences were positively related to the subsequent mathematical training of gifted boys in the Johns Hopkins programs, differences in aptitude were unrelated to the gifted girls' decisions regarding both enrollment in subsequent accelerated math classes (Fox & Cohn, 1980) and intended college major (Benbow & Stanley, 1984). Furthermore, the sex differences in high school math enrollment and in intended college major were significant even with the differences in math aptitude controlled (Benbow & Stanley, 1982a, 1984).

Finally, although it is not yet known what the males and females in the Johns Hopkins study will do as adults, the Terman study certainly suggests that gifted females are not participating in the professional world as much as they could given their exceptional intellectual talents. Recent data on the ratio of men to women receiving advanced degrees indicate that this pattern of underrepresentation even in language and education fields is still evident. For example, even though education is the field most often selected by women in general, as well as by gifted women, women received only 35 percent of the doctorates in education awarded in 1977 (National Center for Educational Statistics [NCES], 1979). Similarly, women received only 39 percent of the doctorates in letters, 22 percent of the doctorates in social science, 9 percent of the doctorates in computer science, 10 percent of the doctorates in physical science, 13 percent of the doctorates in mathematics, and 3 percent of the doctorates in engineering. Although not all PhD recipients would be classified as gifted, they certainly are intellectually talented. These recent figures suggest that the pattern of sex differences in the educational development of today's intellectually talented individuals is similar to, although somewhat less extreme than, the pattern reported by Terman and Oden in 1947.

Given these results, it is quite likely that social forces and personal beliefs have a large influence on the sex-differentiated educational and vocational patterns of gifted individuals. And, although institutional barriers and discriminatory practices undoubtedly account for some of the differences (Vetter, 1981), psychological processes are also important (see Eccles [Parsons], 1984; Eccles & Hoffman, 1984). These processes are the focus of the remainder of this chapter. I discuss neither the potential causal impact of differences in aptitude on achievement patterns nor the possible causes of sex differences in performance on aptitude tests. I do not omit these topics because differences in aptitude are unimportant. Rather, although such differences may contribute, in part, to the disproportionately large numbers of men in math- and science-related fields, they do not account for the low percentages of gifted women who seek out advanced educational training of all types and who aspire to high-status, time-costly occupations.

Second, given that differences in aptitude do not account for all the variation in the educational and vocational choices of men and women, it is important that the basis of women's decisions be understood in order to advance general knowledge of achievement motivation and vocational decisions among the gifted. Third, given the instability of marriage as a primary means of financial support for women and their children, it is imperative that females prepare themselves for adult occupations that will be both rewarding and financially adequate. Finally, given the previous assumption, I wish to focus attention on those variables that are amenable to intervention so that gifted females can make wise career decisions in terms of both their personal development and their future financial autonomy.

Psychological Influences on Educational and Vocational Choices

Although few theories exist that explain sex differences in the educational and vocational choices of gifted individuals in particular, many theories have been proposed to explain such sex differences in the general population. Reviewing all of these is beyond the scope of this chapter. Instead, I explore the possible origins of the sex-differentiated achievement pattern found among the gifted within the context of a general model of achievement-related choices developed by my colleagues and me over the past several years (Eccles et al., 1983; Meece, Eccles, Kaczala, Goff, & Futterman, 1982). Given the importance attached to gender role by many investigators in this field (e.g., Fox & Cohn, 1980; Nash, 1979), special attention will be paid to the ways in which gender role socialization may be affecting gifted individuals' educational and occupational decisions.

Although the model is assumed to be general and applicable to non-gifted as well as to gifted individuals, the fact that gifted individuals have more than sufficient intellectual talent to succeed at most educational and vocational pursuits increases the potential importance of motivational and attitudinal influences on gifted students' achievement-related decisions. It also increases the probability that sex differences in these decisions are mediated by sex differences in social experiences and psychological variables.

A Model of Achievement-Related Choices

Over the past 15 years, my colleagues and I have studied the motivational and social factors that influence long- and short-range achievement goals and behaviors such as career aspirations, vocational and avocational choices, course selections, persistence on difficult tasks, and the allocation of effort across various achievement-related activities. Given the striking differences in the educational and vocational patterns of intellectually able, as well as gifted, males and females, we have been particularly interested in the motivational factors underlying their educational and vocational decisions. Frustrated with the number of seemingly disconnected theories set forth to explain sex differences in these achievement patterns, we

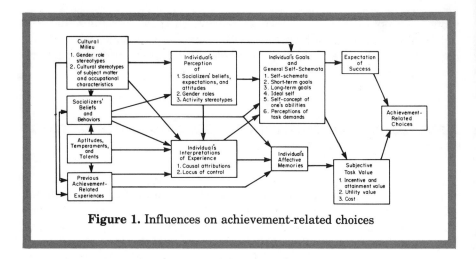

Figure 1. Influences on achievement-related choices

developed a comprehensive theoretical framework to guide our research endeavor.

Drawing upon the theoretical and empirical work associated with decision making, achievement theory, and attribution theory (see Atkinson, 1964; Crandall, 1969; Weiner, 1974), we have elaborated a model of achievement-related choices. This model, depicted in Figure 1, links educational, vocational, and other achievement-related choices most directly to two factors: the individual's expectations for success and the importance or value the individual attaches to the various options that he or she perceives as being available. The model also specifies the relations among these beliefs and cultural norms, experiences, aptitudes, and those personal beliefs and attitudes that are commonly assumed to be associated with achievement-related activities by researchers in this field (Eccles et al., 1983). In particular, the model links achievement-related beliefs, outcomes, and goals to causal attributional patterns, to the input of socializers (primarily parents and teachers), to gender role beliefs, to self-perceptions and self-concept, and to one's perceptions of the task itself. Each of these factors is assumed to influence both the expectations one holds for future success at various achievement-related tasks and the subjective value one attaches to these options. These expectations and values, in turn, are assumed to influence choice among achievement-related options.

For example, let us consider course enrollment decisions. The model predicts that people will be most likely to enroll in courses that they think they will do well in and that have high task value for them. Expectations for success depend on the confidence the individual has in his or her intellectual abilities and on the individual's estimations of the difficulty of the course. These beliefs have been shaped over time by the individual's experiences with the subject matter and by the individual's subjective interpretation of those experiences (e.g., does the person think that her or his successes are a consequence of high ability or lots of hard work?). The value of a particular course is also influenced by several other factors: Does the person like doing the subject material? Is the course required? Is the course seen as being instrumental in meeting one of the individual's long- or short-range goals? Have the individual's parents or counselors insisted that the course be taken or, conversely, have other people tried to discourage the individual from taking the course? Does the person have fears associated with the material to be covered in the course?

Three features of our model are particularly important for understanding sex differences in the educational and vocational decisions of gifted individuals. The first of these is our focus on achievement-related choices as the outcome of interest. We believe that individuals continually make choices, both consciously and nonconsciously, regarding how they will spend their time and effort. Many of the most significant sex differences among the gifted (e.g., in vocational aspirations) occur on achievement-related behaviors that involve the element of choice, even if the outcome of that choice is heavily influenced by socialization pressures and cultural norms. Conceptualizing sex differences in achievement patterns in terms of choice takes one beyond the question "Why aren't gifted women more like gifted men?" to the question "Why do gifted women and men make the choices they do?" Asking this latter question, in turn, legitimizes the choices of both gifted men and women and suggests several new variables as possible mediators of the sex differences we observe in gifted individuals' achievement patterns. By legitimizing the choices of both men and women, we can look at sex differences from a choice perspective rather than a deficit perspective.

Conceptualizing sex differences in achievement-related behaviors in terms of choice highlights a second important component of our perspective, namely, the issue of what becomes part of an individual's field of possible choices. Although individuals do choose from among several options, they do not actively, or consciously, consider the full range of objectively available options in making their selections. Many options are never considered because the individual is unaware of their existence; others are not considered because the individual has inaccurate information regarding either the option itself or the individual's possibility of achieving the option. For example, a girl may have inaccurate information regarding the full range of activities an engineer can do or inaccurate information regarding the financial assistance available for advanced educational training. Still other options may not be seriously considered because they do not fit in well with the individual's gender role schema. Assimilating the culturally defined gender role schema can have such a powerful effect on one's view of the world that activities classified as part of the opposite sex's role are rejected, often nonconsciously, without any serious evaluation or consideration.

Research has provided some support for this hypothesis. By age five, children have clearly defined gender role stereotypes regarding appropriate behaviors and traits (Huston, 1983; Williams, Bennett, & Best, 1975). In addition, children appear to monitor their behaviors and aspirations in terms of these stereotypes (e.g., Montemayor, 1974; see Eccles & Hoffman, 1984 and Huston, 1983, for recent reviews). Consequently, it is likely that gender roles influence educational and vocational choices through their impact on individuals' perceptions of the field of viable options, as well as through their impact on expectations and subjective task value.

Understanding the processes that shape individuals' perceptions of the field of viable options is essential to understanding the dynamics leading gifted men and women to make such different achievement-related decisions. Yet there is very little evidence regarding these processes and their link to important achievement-related choices. Socialization theory provides a rich source of hypotheses, few of which have been tested in gifted populations. For example, one effect of role models may be to make people aware of novel options and options that are not generally considered by people of their sex. Parents, teachers, and school counselors can also influence students' perceptions of their field of options through the information and experiences they provide to students. Parents can directly affect both the options actually available to their children (e.g., by providing or withholding funds for a college education) and the options seriously considered (e.g., by mandating, encouraging, ignoring, and discouraging various options). Finally, peers can affect the options seriously considered by either providing or withholding support for various alternatives. The effects of peers can be both direct (e.g., laughing at a girl when she says she is considering becoming a nuclear physicist) and indirect (e.g., anticipating that one's future spouse will support one's occupational commitments).

It should be clear from these examples that social agents can either encourage or discourage gifted students from considering gender role stereotypic options. Unfortunately, social agents typically influence students to consider options that are consistent with gender role stereotypes. The possible mechanisms underlying these effects are discussed in more detail further on.

The third important feature of our perspective is the explicit assumption that achievement-related decisions, such as the decision to enroll in an accelerated math program or to major in education rather than law or engineering, are made within the context of a complex social reality that presents each individual with a wide array of choices, each of which has both long-range and immediate consequences. Furthermore, the choice is often between two or more positive options or between two or more options that each have both positive and negative components. For example, the decision to enroll in an advanced math course is typically made in the context of other important decisions, such as whether to take advanced English or a second foreign language, whether to take a course with one's best friend or not, or whether it is more important to spend one's senior year working hard or having fun. Too often theorists have focused attention on why gifted, capable women do not select the high-status achievement options rather than asking why they select the options they do. This approach implicitly assumes that complex choices, such as career and course selection, are made independently of one another; for example, it is assumed that the decision to take advanced math is based primarily on variables related to math. We explicitly reject this assumption, arguing instead that it is essential to understand the psychological meaning of the roads taken as well as the roads not taken if we are to understand the dynamics leading to the differences in men's and women's achievement-related choices.

Consider, as an example, two junior high school students: Mary and Barbara. Both young women enjoy mathematics and have always done very well. Both have been identified as gifted in mathematics and have been offered the opportunity to participate in an accelerated math program at a local college during the next school year. Barbara hopes to major in journalism when she gets to college and has also been offered the opportunity to work part time on the city newspaper doing odd jobs and some copyediting. Mary hopes to major in biology in college and plans a career as a research scientist. Taking the accelerated math course involves driving to and from the college. Since the course is scheduled for the last period of the day, it will take the last two periods of the day as well as 1 hour of after-school time to take the course. What will the young women do?

In all likelihood, Mary will enroll in the program because she both likes math and thinks that the effort required to take the class and master the material is worthwhile and important for her long-range career goals. Barbara's decision is more complex. She may want to take the class but may also think that the time required is too costly, especially given her alternative opportunity at the city paper. Whether she takes the college course or not will depend on the advice she gets at home and from her counselors. If they stress the importance of the math course, then its subjective worth to her will increase. If its subjective worth increases sufficiently to outweigh its subjective cost, then Barbara will probably take the course despite its cost in time and effort.

In summary, we assume that achievement-related choices, whether made consciously or nonconsciously, are guided by the following: (a) one's expectations for success on the various options considered, (b) the relation of perceived options both to one's short- and long-range goals and to one's core self-identity and basic psychological needs, (c) the individual's gender role schema, and (d) the potential cost of investing time in one activity rather than another. All of these psychological variables are influenced by one's experiences, by cultural norms, and by the behaviors and goals of one's socializers and peers. Each of these variables and their relation to the achievement-related decisions of gifted men and women are discussed in more detail in the following sections; the psychological constructs are discussed first, followed by a discussion of the socialization influences on these psychological variables. Evidence documenting both the sex differences on the variables and the link of these sex differences to the achievement-related decisions of gifted men and women is presented. It should be noted, however, that very little of this evidence exists. Although there are sound theoretical reasons for suggesting these links, much of the essential empirical work remains to be done.

Expectations for Success

Expectations for success and confidence in one's abilities to succeed have long been recognized by decision and achievement theorists as important mediators of behavioral choice (e.g., Atkinson, 1964; Bandura, 1977; Lewin, 1938; Weiner, 1974). There have been numerous studies demonstrating the link between expectations and a variety of achievement-related behaviors including educational and vocational choices among both average and gifted populations. For example, Hollinger (1983) documented a fairly strong relation between gifted girls' confidence in their math abilities and their aspirations to enter math-related vocations such as engineering and computer science. Similarly, Terman (1925) found a positive relation between gifted students' subject matter preferences and their ratings of the ease of the subject for themselves. But are expectations influenced by gender roles and do males and females differ in their expectations for success at various academic subjects and in various occupations? The answers to these questions are not clear for either average or gifted populations.

Gender Roles and Expectations

Since females are typically stereotyped as being less competent than males, incorporating gender role stereotypes into one's self-concept could lead girls to have less confidence than do boys in their general intellectual abilities. This, in turn, could lead girls to have lower expectations for success at difficult academic and vocational activities. It could also lead girls to expect to have to work harder in order to achieve success at these activities. Evidence from several sources suggests that either of these beliefs could deter girls from selecting demanding educational or vocational options, especially if these options are not perceived as being especially important or interesting. Consequently, these beliefs might account, in part, for the relatively low numbers of gifted women in high-status occupations.

Gender stereotyping of particular occupations and academic subjects could further exacerbate the situation. Many educational programs and vocational options are gender stereotyped in this culture. Most high-status professions, especially those associated with math, science, technology, and business, are thought to be male activities. In contrast, teaching below the college level, working in clerical and related support-type jobs, and excelling in language-related courses are thought to be female activities by both children and adults (for reviews see Eccles & Hoffman, 1984; Huston, 1983). Incorporating these beliefs into one's self-concept could lead girls to have lower expectations for success in male-typed activities such as engineering and higher expectations for success in female-typed activities such as elementary school teaching. This pattern of differential expectations could lead gifted girls to select female-typed activities over male-typed activities, despite the fact that they have exceptional talent in math and science.

Evaluating these predictions is difficult. Researchers have tended to study students of average or slightly above average intellectual ability. Few relevant studies of gifted individuals exist, and those that do present a mixed picture. For example, Fox (1982) found that highly motivated gifted girls have lower self-confidence than equally highly motivated gifted boys. Similarly, Terman (1925) found that gifted girls were more likely to underestimate their intellectual skills and knowledge, whereas gifted boys were more likely to overestimate theirs. In contrast, Tidwell (1980) found no sex differences on measures of general self-concept. Tidwell (1980) and Tomlinson-Keasey and Smith-Winberry (1983) found no sex differences on measures of locus of control (a construct often linked to self-confidence and personal efficacy beliefs, e.g., Bandura, 1977).

There is also little evidence to support the hypothesis that gifted girls are less confident of their math and science ability than are gifted boys. For example, Benbow and Stanley (1982a) found no substantial sex difference in gifted students' estimates of their math and science competence. Similarly, although Terman's (1925) gifted students preferred courses that they thought were easier for them, the boys and girls did not differ in their perceptions of the ease of mathematics. Finally, Schunk and Lilly (1982) found no sex difference in gifted children's expectations for success on a laboratory math task.

Given this mixed set of results, it is not clear that gifted girls are typically less confident of their intellectual abilities than are gifted boys. Although it is true that the differences, when they are found, do support this conclusion, any differences that exist are quite small. Furthermore, the mediating role of these sex differences in explaining the discrepancy between men's and women's educational and vocational choices has not been demonstrated. Although students' expectations have been measured, the link of these expectations to sex differences in academic and vocational choices has typically not been assessed. Furthermore, my own data (gathered on high-ability high school students) suggest that sex differences in the value attached to both math and English are more critical mediators of sex differences in course enrollment decisions than are sex differences in students' estimates of their math and English abilities (Eccles, Adler, & Meece, 1984). These results are discussed in more detail later.

It is possible, however, that researchers have been assessing the wrong expectancies. Typically, students are asked to report on their confidence about succeeding on an upcoming task or course. They are not asked how confident they are that they could succeed in particular professions or in particular advanced training programs. They are also not asked how much effort they think it will take to succeed in various professions or advanced training programs. It could be that gifted girls are less confident than gifted boys of their prospects for success in these more abstract activities. It is also possible that gifted girls are as confident as gifted boys in their ability to succeed, but that they assume that it will take more effort to succeed than do their male peers. As I noted earlier, either of these beliefs could mediate a sex difference in the educational and vocational decisions of gifted individuals, especially given the gender stereotyping of high-status occupations. Clearly, more research is needed before these hypotheses can be evaluated.

It is also possible that the critical expectancy beliefs are neither the absolute expectation one has for success in a particular field nor the perception one has of the absolute amount of effort it will take to succeed in a particular field; instead, the critical beliefs may be the relative expectations one has for success across several fields and the perceptions one has of the relative amounts of effort it will take to succeed in various fields. If gifted females think it will take more effort to succeed as an engineer or a doctor than as an elementary school teacher, journalist, or nurse, they may opt for the more female-typed occupations, especially if they place high importance on having a career that is compatible with their anticipated family roles. These hypotheses have yet to be evaluated.

Causal Attributions and Expectations

Causal attributions are often linked to self-confidence, expectations, and achievement behaviors (e.g., Dweck & Licht, 1980; Eccles et al., 1983; Weiner, 1974). The possibility that sex differences in causal attributions might mediate sex differences in achievement behaviors, especially in the motivation to persist despite difficulty and failure, has been suggested by several psychologists (e.g., Bar-Tal, 1978; Dweck & Licht, 1980; Nicholls, 1975; Parsons, Ruble, Hodges, & Small, 1976). However, as is true for expectations and self-confidence in general, the pattern of sex differences on measures of causal attributions is equivocal, the hypothesized mediating effect of these sex differences on achievement choices is not clear, and very few studies have been done on gifted students (Cooper, Burger, & Good, 1981; Eccles Parsons, 1983; Eccles, Adler, & Meece, 1984; Frieze, Whitley, Hanusa, & McHugh, 1982; Parsons, Meece, Adler, & Kaczala, 1982).

One interesting sex difference has emerged for mathematical tests and course grades. Girls, especially girls of high ability, rank acquired skill, diligence, and effort as more important causes of their math success than do boys of equal attainment. In contrast, the boys rate natural talent as a more important cause of their math success. (Eccles et al., 1983; Eccles et al., 1984; Parsons, Meece, Adler, and Kaczala, 1982; Wolleat, Pedro, Becker, & Fennema, 1980). This pattern of differences may have important consequences for students' decisions regarding future involvement with mathematics and interest in math-related professions. People who view consistent effort (or skill and knowledge acquired through consistent effort) as the important determinant of their success in mathematics may avoid future courses if they think future courses will be more difficult, demanding even more effort for continued success. The amount of effort students can or are willing to expend on any one activity has limits, and if students already believe that they are working very hard to do well in math, they may conclude either (a) that their performance will deteriorate in the more difficult future math courses because they are trying as hard as they can at present, or (b) that the amount of effort necessary to continue performing well is just not worthwhile. As I noted earlier, either of these beliefs would be sufficient justification for avoiding both future math courses and math-related careers, especially for students who do not place high subjective value on math.

The same limits would not apply to students who view ability rather than effort as the relatively more important determinant of success in math. High levels of math ability should guarantee continued success with little or no increment in one's efforts. If this analysis is correct, then girls should be less likely than boys to enroll in advanced math courses and to aspire to math-related technical fields. This is, in fact, the case in both average and gifted populations. Unfortunately, the relevant attributional data have not been gathered on gifted students. In the one study in which causal attributions for a laboratory math task were assessed, no significant sex differences were found among the gifted subjects (Schunk & Lilly, 1982). Clearly, more research is needed before the role played by causal attributional patterns in shaping sex differences in gifted students' educational and vocational decisions can be evaluated.

Although Hollinger (1983) clearly demonstrated a link between confidence in one's math abilities and gifted girls' math-related vocational aspirations, the mediating role of expectations and self-confidence in fostering sex differences in the educational and occupational choices of the gifted has yet to be demonstrated. More studies are needed, especially studies designed to assess the causal relations between variables related to self-concept and actual educational and vocational choices.

Values as Mediators of Achievement-Related Choices

Value is the second major component of our expectancy/value model of achievement-related choices. This component predicts that decisions regarding course enrollments, college majors, and occupation are influenced by the value individuals attach to the various achievement-related options they believe are available to them. Furthermore, subjective value is hypothesized to have at least as much influence as expectations for success on educational and vocational choices. Finally, given the probable impact of gender role socialization on the variables assumed to be associated with subjective task value, sex differences in the subjective value of various achievement-related options are predicted to be important mediators of sex differences in achievement-related choices in both typical and gifted populations. Our own data support these hypotheses.

In a longitudinal study of the math course enrollment decisions of high-aptitude, college-bound students, sex differences in students' decisions to enroll in advanced mathematics were mediated primarily by sex differences in the value the students attached to mathematics (Eccles et al., 1984). More specifically, the girls were less likely than the boys to enroll in advanced mathematics primarily because they felt that math was less important, less useful, and less enjoyable than did the boys. Similar results linking sex differences in course choice to sex differences in the subjective task value of various course or major choices have been reported by Katz, Norris, and Halpron (cited in Humphreys, 1984) and by Zerega and Walberg (1984).

Since *value* can mean many different things and since it has received so little systematic attention until recently, I would like to elaborate on our interpretation of value and its link to achievement-related choices before reviewing the empirical literature. Like others (e.g., Crandall, Crandall, Katkovsky, & Preston, 1962; Raynor, 1974; Spenner & Featherman, 1978; Stein & Bailey, 1973), we assume that task value is a quality of the task that contributes to the increasing or declining probability that an individual will select it. We have defined this quality in terms of three components: (a) the utility value of the task in facilitating one's long-range goals, (b) the incentive value of engaging in the task in terms of more immediate rewards, and (c) the cost of engaging in the activity.

Incentive and Attainment Value

Incentive value can be conceptualized in a variety of ways, two of which are particularly relevant to the issue of sex differences in the educational and vocational choices of gifted individuals. On the one hand, incentive value can be conceptualized in terms of the immediate rewards, intrinsic or extrinsic, an individual derives from performing a task. For example, studying mathematics is intrinsically rewarding to those individuals who enjoy solving mathematical problems; studying mathematics can also yield extrinsic rewards, particularly if one's parents or teachers provide praise or privileges for doing well in mathematics. To the extent that gifted boys either find mathematics and the physical sciences more enjoyable or are rewarded more by their parents and teachers for doing mathematics and science, gifted boys should place more value on mathematics and science than do gifted girls. In turn, gifted boys should be more likely to enroll in math and science courses and to enter math-related occupational fields.

Incentive value can also be conceptualized in terms of the needs and personal values that an activity fulfills. As they grow up, individuals develop an image of themselves. This image includes (a) conceptions of one's personality and capabilities, (b) long-range goals and plans, (c) schema regarding the proper roles of men and women, (d) instrumental and terminal values (Rokeach, 1973), (e) motivational sets, (f) ideal images of what one should be like, and (g) social scripts regarding proper behavior in a variety of situations. Those parts of an individual's self-image that are central or critical to self-definition should influence the value that the individual attaches to various educational and vocational options; these differential values, in turn, should influence the individual's achievement-related choices (Eccles et al., 1984; Markus, 1980; Parsons & Goff, 1980). For example, if being a good athlete is a central part of an individual's self-image, then that individual should work at being a good athlete. Similarly, if helping other people is a central part of an individual's image, then that person should place higher value on helping occupations than on nonhelping occupations.

Essentially, I am arguing that personal needs, self-images, and values operate in ways that both reduce the probability of engaging in those activities or roles perceived as inconsistent with one's central values and increase the probability of engaging in roles or activities perceived as consistent with one's definition of self. More specifically, my colleagues and I believe that individuals perceive tasks in terms of certain characteristics that can be related to their needs and values. For example, a difficult task that requires great effort for mastery may be perceived as an achievement task; if it also involves pitting one's performance against others, it may be perceived as a competitive task. Other tasks may be perceived in terms of nurturance, power, or aesthetic pleasure. Participating in a particular task will require demonstrating the characteristics associated with the task. Whether this requirement is seen as an opportunity or a burden will depend on the individual's needs, motives, and personal values, and on the individual's desire to demonstrate these characteristics both to him- or herself and to others.

In summary, this model forms the basis for making the following propositions:

1. Individuals seek to confirm their possession of those characteristics that are central to their self-image.

2. Various tasks provide differential opportunities for such confirmation.

3. Individuals will place more value on those tasks that either provide the opportunity to fulfill their self-image or at least are consistent with their self-image and long-range goals.

4. Individuals will be more likely to select tasks with high subjective value than those with lower subjective value.

To the extent that gifted males and females have different self-images, they will place different values on various educational and vocational options, and, in turn, they will differ in their educational and vocational choices.

Perceived Cost

The value of a task also depends on a set of beliefs that can best be characterized as the cost of participating in the activity. Cost is influenced by many factors, such as anticipated anxiety, fear of failure, and, of particular importance in the discussion of long-term educational and vocational choices, the loss of time and energy for other activities. People have limited time and energy. They cannot do everything they would like; they must choose among activities. To the extent that one loses time for activity B by engaging in activity A and to the extent that activity B is high in one's hierarchy of importance, then the subjective cost of engaging in A increases. Alternately, even if the attainment value of A is high, the value of engaging in A will be reduced to the extent that the attainment value of B is higher and to the extent that engaging in A jeopardizes the probability of successfully engaging in B.

Gender Roles and Task Value

This analysis has a number of important implications for our understanding of sex differences in the educational and vocational choices of gifted individuals. Because socialization shapes individuals' goals and values, men and women should acquire different values and goals through the process of gender role socialization. Through their potential impact on subjective task value, these role differences in value structure can affect educational and vocational choices in several ways.

Gender role socialization could lead men and women to have different hierarchies of core personal values (such as their terminal and instrumental values; Rokeach, 1973). Consequently, tasks embodying various characteristics should have different subjective values for men and women. For example, both boys and girls stereotype mathematicians and scientists as being loners who have little time for their families or friends, because they work long hours in a laboratory on abstract problems that typically have limited immediate social implications (Boswell, 1979). If the analysis developed in the previous section is correct, such a profession should hold little appeal to someone who rates social values highly and thinks it is very important to devote time and energy to one's family— typically a female trait (Fox & Denham, 1974). Thus, gifted females should be less likely than gifted males to aspire to a career as a mathematician or scientist.

Several studies provide support for the hypothesized link between personal values and achievement-related choices. Dunteman, Wisenbaker, and Taylor (1978), for example, studied the link between personal values and selection of one's college major using a longitudinal, correlational design. They identified two sets of values that both predicted students' subsequent choice of major and differentiated the sexes. The first set (labeled *thing-orientation*) reflected an interest in manipulating objects and understanding the physical world; the second set (labeled *person-orientation*) reflected an interest in understanding human social interaction and a concern with helping people. Students who were high on thing-orientation and low on person-orientation were more likely than other students to select a math or a science major. Not surprisingly, the females were more likely than the males to be person-oriented and to major in something other than math or science. In contrast, the males were more likely than the females both to be thing-oriented and to major in math and science.

Similarly, in a study of mathematically talented children, Fox and Denham (1974) found a relation between interest in mathematics and scores on the Allport-Vernon-Lindsey Scale of Personal Values. Interest in math and science was related to high scores on the theoretical, political, and economic scales and to low scores on the social value scale. Again, the females were less likely than the males both to endorse the math- and science-related values and to aspire to math- and science-related careers.

Men and women could also differ in the density of their goals and values. There is some evidence suggesting that men are more likely than women to exhibit a single-minded devotion to one particular goal, especially their occupational goal. In contrast, women in both gifted and typical populations seem more likely than men to be involved in, and to value, competence in several activities simultaneously (Baruch, Barnett, & Rivers, 1983; Fox, Pasternak, & Peiser, 1976; Maines, 1983; McGinn, 1976; Terman & Oden, 1947). For example, in his study of doctoral students in mathematics, Maines (1983) asked the students what they worried about. The men were concerned most about their professional status and about their mentors' estimates of their professional potential, whereas the women were concerned most about the impact of their graduate training on their families and their other interests. They felt that graduate training was taking too much time and energy away from other activities that they valued just as much as their graduate training. This discrepancy could reflect differing density patterns for the hierarchy of goals and personal values held by these men and women. That is, the women appeared to place high attainment value on several goals and activities; in contrast, the men appeared more likely to focus on one main goal: their professional development. If this is true, then the psychological cost of engaging in their primary goal in terms of time and energy lost for other important goals would certainly be less for these men than for their female colleagues.

Gender role socialization could also lead men and women to place different values on various long-range goals and adult activities. The essence of gender roles (and of social roles in general) is that they define the activities that are central to the role. In other words, they define what one should do with one's life in order to be successful in that role. If success in one's gender role is a central component of one's identity, then activities that fulfill this role should have high value, and activities that hamper efforts at successfully fulfilling one's gender role should have lower subjective value. Gender roles mandate different primary activities for men and women. The established role of women is that of supporting their husbands' careers and raising their children; the role for men is that of competing successfully in the occupational world in order to support their families. To the extent that a gifted woman has internalized this cultural definition of the female role, she should order the importance of various adult activities differently than her gifted male peers. In particular, she should rate the parenting and the spouse-support roles as more important than a professional career role, and she should be more likely than her gifted male peers to resolve life's decisions in favor of these family roles. In contrast, gifted men, like men in general, should rate family and career roles as being equally important. In fact, since they can fulfill their family role by having a successful career, gifted men, like men in general, should expect these two sets of roles to be compatible. Consequently, aspiring to a high-status, time-consuming career should have high subjective value to gifted men, not only because of the rewards inherent in these occupations, but also because they fulfill the male gender role mandate.

Similarly, gender roles can influence the definition one has of successful performance of those activities considered to be central to one's identity.

Consequently, the ways in which men and women conceptualize the requirements for successful task participation and completion may differ. If so, then men and women should approach and structure their task involvement differently even when they appear on the surface to be selecting a similar task. The parenting role provides an excellent example of this process. If males define success in the parenting role as an extension of their occupational role, then they may respond to parenthood with increased commitment to their career goals and with emphasis on encouraging competitive drive in their children. In contrast, if women define success in the parenting role as being highly involved in their children's lives, they may respond to parenthood with decreased commitment to their career goals. Furthermore, if staying home with her children and being psychologically available to them most of the time are central components of a gifted woman's gender role schema, then involvement in a demanding, high-level career should have reduced subjective value precisely because it conflicts with a more central component of her identity.

Finally, gender roles could affect the subjective value of various educational and vocational options indirectly through their influence on the behaviors and attitudes of the people gifted individuals are exposed to as they grow up. If, for example, parents, friends, teachers, or counselors provide gifted boys and girls with different feedback on their performance in various school subjects, with different advice regarding the importance of various school subjects, with different information regarding the importance of preparing to support oneself and one's family, or with different information regarding the occupational opportunities that the student should be considering, then it is likely that gifted boys and girls will develop different estimates of the value of various educational and vocational options. Similarly, if the males and females around the gifted children engage in different educational and vocational activities, then gifted boys and girls should develop different ideas regarding which activities they are best suited for.

The analysis developed in this section suggests that the educational and occupational differences between gifted men and women result, in part, from sex differences in gender role definition and in the structure of one's hierarchy of values and interests. These differences are assumed to be the result of differential socialization experiences and the internalization of culturally defined, and readily observable, gender roles. More specifically, this analysis suggests that the differential involvement of gifted men and women in math- and science-related occupations may result, in part, from differences in their interest patterns and their personal values (for example, being thing-oriented versus being person-oriented). Furthermore, this analysis suggests that the differential involvement of gifted men and women in high-status, time-consuming occupations that require long periods of preprofessional training may result, in part, from differences in men's and women's psychological investments in their family roles versus their professional roles. These gender differences in psychological investment in family versus professional roles are assumed to result from a complex set of both psychological and sociological forces including the internalization of gender roles, the individual's assessment of which jobs and roles are realistically available, and both overt and subtle forms of discrimination operating in educational and occupational institutions. Consequently, women may choose to limit their investment in the professional role because they want to maximize their investment in their family role or because they think that their opportunities in the professional role are restricted by discriminatory forces beyond their control, or both (see Astin, 1984; Callahan, 1979; Frieze & Hanusa, 1984; Sears, 1979; Vetter, 1981, for a discussion of the external barriers to success gifted women face within the professions).

An adequate test of these hypotheses not only requires demonstrating a sex difference in interest patterns and value hierarchies; it also requires demonstrating the proposed causal link between these beliefs and the educational and vocational choices gifted men and women make. By and large, these causal links have not been assessed in either gifted or more typical populations. Thus, as was true for expectations of success, the essential research has yet to be done. Even though the causal relations implicit in this analysis have not been adequately studied, however, several large-scale studies of the gifted have assessed sex differences in personal values and interests. In general, the data are consistent with the analysis in this section.

Before turning to these studies, it is important to note that the analyses outlined in this and previous sections have implications for individual differences within each sex as well as for sex differences. Thus, for example, we would predict that gifted women who enter a scientific profession will be more likely to endorse a thing-orientation than gifted women who enter other professions; similarly, gifted women who choose to become school teachers should be more person-oriented than the gifted women who go into engineering. Finally, a gifted woman who seeks out a traditional male occupation and exhibits a male-like career pattern should have less of a traditional gender role orientation than the gifted woman who seeks out a more traditional female occupation and a more traditionally female career pattern. Several studies support these predictions for both gifted and more moderately talented women (e.g., Callahan, 1979; Frieze & Hanusa, 1984; Helson, 1980; Luchins & Luchins, 1980).

Sex Differences in the Values and Interests of the Gifted

In both the Terman study and the studies being conducted at Johns Hopkins University, interests, values, and goals have been assessed for a large number of gifted individuals. These studies suggest that differences between gifted boys and girls are evident from an early age. Although gifted boys and girls appeared more similar in their values and interests than comparison groups of boys and girls drawn from the general population, the gifted girls in both studies had more stereotypically feminine interest patterns than did the gifted boys. When asked their favorite school subjects, the girls rated English, foreign languages, composition, music, and drama higher than did the boys. In contrast, the boys rated the physical sciences, physical training, and U.S. history higher than did the girls (Benbow & Stanley, 1984; George & Denham, 1976; Terman, 1925, 1930). The sex differences in interest in mathematics were typically weak if present at all.

Similarly, when asked their occupational interests and anticipated college major, girls rated domestic, secretarial, artistic, biological science, medical, and social service occupations and training higher than did the boys. The boys expressed more interest than the girls in high-status and business-related occupations in general, and in the physical sciences, engineering, and the military in particular (Benbow & Stanley, 1984; Fox, Pasternak, & Peiser, 1976; Terman, 1925, 1930). Finally, when asked their leisure time activities and hobbies, similar differences in interest patterns emerged. At all ages, the females reported liking and spending more time than the boys reading, writing, and participating in a variety of activities related to arts and crafts, domestic skills, and drama. The males reported spending more time engaging in sports, working with machines and tools, and being involved with scientific, math-related, or electronic hobbies (Fox, 1976; McGinn, 1976; Terman, 1925, 1930; Terman & Oden, 1947).

Gender stereotypic patterns of differences also emerged on tests of personal values, occupational values, and personality traits. The Allport-Vernon-Lindsey Scale of Values was given to many of the children who participated in the studies at Johns Hopkins. The gifted girls typically scored higher than the gifted boys on scales that tapped social and aesthetic values, whereas the boys typically scored higher than the girls on scales that tapped theoretical, economic, and political values (Fox, 1976; George & Denham, 1976; McGinn, 1976). Similarly, on the Strong-Campbell Interest Inventory, the girls scored higher than the boys on social and aesthetic interests. Both boys and girls, however, scored equally high (and quite high) on investigative interests (Fox, Pasternak, & Peiser, 1976; George & Denham, 1976; McGinn, 1976).

It is also of interest to note that the boys evidenced a more unidimensional set of interests on the Strong-Campbell tests; that is, they scored high on investigative interests and low on most other interests. In contrast, the girls scored higher than average on several interest clusters (McGinn, 1976). A similar discrepancy emerged when gifted boys and girls were asked to rate several occupations on a Semantic Differential Scale. The boys gave positive ratings only to traditional male scientific and mathematical professions; they rated the female professions and the homemaker role quite negatively. The girls, on the other hand, gave both male- and female-typed professions positive ratings, and they gave the homemaker role as positive a rating as that which they gave their most preferred professional occupations.

A similar pattern emerged from the most recent data from the Terman sample (Sears, 1979). The gifted men and women were asked to rate how important each of six goals were to them in making their life plans during early adulthood. Men rated only one area (occupation) as being more important; in contrast, the women rated four areas as being more important (family, friends, richness of one's cultural life, and joy in living). These data suggest that the gifted women desired a more varied or multifaceted type of life. One other pattern characterized the responses of these gifted men and women. Consistent with our hypothesis, the men rated family and occupation as of equal importance, whereas the women rated family as more important than occupation.

Summary

There are clear differences in the interests and values of gifted males and females. Furthermore, these differences reflect gender-stereotyped patterns: females are more likely to hold social and aesthetic values, and males are more likely to hold scientific values. In addition, females rate the homemaker role as positively as they rate professional activities, and they rate a good family life as more important to their life satisfaction than a successful career. These results are consistent with the analysis linking values to sex differences in educational and vocational choices. Additional support for this hypothesis comes from a recent report by Benbow and Stanley (1982a). Gifted girls in their study were less likely than gifted boys to take advanced mathematics in part because they liked language-related courses more than they liked mathematics courses. In addition, in their gifted samples, Benbow and Stanley (1984) found weak but consistent positive relations between liking biology, chemistry, and physics and having plans to major in these areas. In their study, the possibility that sex differences in subject area interests might contribute to sex differences in anticipated college major was not assessed (or if it was assessed, the data were not presented).

Thus, although there is some support for the hypothesis that sex differences in values have an impact on gifted students' educational and vocational choices, this hypothesis has not been adequately tested. In most studies documenting sex differences in interest patterns, personal values, and goals and aspirations, the mediating role of these differences in educational and vocational decisions has not been assessed. Longitudinal studies exploring the possible causal links between values and achievement-related choices are needed. More information is also needed on the relation between gender role schema and personal values and interests. Finally, more information is needed on the origin of sex differences, as well as individual differences, in values.

The Influences of Parents, Teachers, and Counselors on Educational and Vocational Choices

As I noted earlier, sex differences in educational and vocational choices are undoubtedly shaped in part by differential socialization experiences. Several studies have documented the importance of social support from parents, teachers, and counselors in the lives of women who make nontraditional educational and occupational choices (Barnett & Baruch, 1978; Casserly, 1980). Perhaps gifted girls make rather traditional educational and occupational choices because they receive inadequate social support for alternative choices. It is to this issue that I now turn. Before discussing specific studies, however, a general overview of the ways in which social agents can influence achievement-related choices is useful.

Social agents can influence educational and occupational choices through a variety of subtle and blatant means (for a full discussion see Eccles & Hoffman, 1984). Through their power as role models, social agents provide the information that shapes children's stereotypes of appropriate occupations for males and females as well as children's broader view of the educational and vocational options available to them. It seems reasonable to assume that gifted children, like more typical groups of children, are exposed to a gender role biased set of role models. To the extent that this is true, gifted males and females should develop gender role stereotyped beliefs regarding appropriate educational and occupational choices.

Social agents can indirectly affect educational and vocational choices through their influence on children's self-concepts, personal values, and preferences. For example, parents have ample opportunity to comment on their children's academic performance, and these comments influence their children's self-concepts. Parsons, Adler, and Kaczala (1982), for example, found that parents who attributed their children's good math grades to hard work tended to have children with lower confidence in their math ability than parents who attributed their children's good math grades to ability. Furthermore, the parents of high-ability girls were more likely than the parents of high-ability boys to make such an attribution. Not surprisingly, then, the high-ability girls in this sample had less confidence in their math ability than the high-ability boys. Whether a

ECCLES

similar bias characterizes parents of gifted children has yet to be determined.

Social agents can also influence children's view of the educational and vocational world through explicit and implicit messages they provide as they counsel children. Social agents, especially parents and school personnel, give children information about the occupational world and the need to prepare themselves for that world. To the extent that these messages are gender role stereotyped, boys and girls will internalize different views of the occupational world, different ideas about their potential involvement in that world, and different ideas regarding the need to be able to support themselves. Each of these differences has implications for the educational and vocational decisions of gifted, as well as more typical, males and females.

Peers also take part in this process. Students discuss with their friends the options they are considering; the opinions and reactions they receive from peers are often gender role stereotyped (see, for example, Frieze & Hanusa, 1984; Kavrell & Petersen, 1984; Tresemer, 1976). Since peer acceptance is so important during the adolescent years (Kavrell & Petersen, 1984), the gender role bias in adolescents' reactions to each other's plans may limit the educational and vocational options considered seriously by gifted females at a time when very important achievement-related decisions are being made. Fear of peer disapproval could also lead gifted girls either to drop out of or to refuse to participate in special programs for the gifted.

Social agents can influence the educational and vocational decisions of gifted individuals more directly by actively structuring the options that are offered to gifted boys and girls. For example, entry into accelerated or special programs depends on being identified as gifted by school personnel. To the extent that the process of identification is sex-biased, gifted girls and boys may differ in the opportunities they are offered to develop their skills. Parents can also either limit or broaden their children's educational and vocational options by the economic, as well as psychological, support they provide for various options. Families with limited resources are generally more willing to invest these resources in their sons than in their daughters (see Eccles & Hoffman, 1984). If a similar preference characterizes families with gifted children, then gifted males will have more opportunities for special and advanced training. Such differences, if they exist, not only limit girls' options directly, but can also limit the development of gifted girls' preferences because they restrict the range of experiences gifted girls are exposed to. Computer camps are an excellent example of this latter process; boys outnumber girls at computer camps by at least a factor of 4 (Kiesler, Sproull, & Eccles, in press). Clearly, parents are spending more money sending their sons rather than their daughters to computer camp. Why this might be so has yet to be determined. But the long-term implications of this difference for the future educational and vocational decisions of math-talented boys and girls should be clear; since math-talented girls are having less opportunity to develop their computer skills, an interest in computing, and confidence in their ability to master the computer, they will be less likely than math-talented boys to enroll in computer courses and to enter computer science professions.

Several mechanisms of influence have been suggested in this section. Few of the hypotheses suggested have been tested directly in typical, much less gifted, populations. There is evidence, however, for differential treatment of gifted males and females by social agents, and this literature is reviewed in the next section.

Parents

In both the Terman and the Johns Hopkins studies, the parents of gifted boys and girls acknowledged their children's general intellectual talents. The sex of the gifted child did not affect the parents' estimates of the children's general intelligence; it did, however, affect parents' estimates of their children's specific skills. For example, parents in Terman's study rated the boys higher than the girls on math and mechanical ingenuity; they rated the girls higher than the boys on drama, music, and general dexterity. Since this pattern of sex differences also characterized the children's performance on standardized skill tests, the direction of causality for these data is not clear. The parents' estimates may have reflected the differences they were observing in their children, or the parents may have helped to create the behavioral differences through differential socialization practices (Terman, 1925).

Gender role bias in parental beliefs is more clear on other measures. Parents in the Johns Hopkins studies were asked their occupational aspirations for their children. The majority of the parents of girls (between 89 and 94 percent in one study) expected their daughters to follow the traditional occupational pattern for females of working for a while and then taking time out to raise their children (Brody & Fox, 1980; Fox, 1982). The parents were also more likely to expect their sons to enter math-related or scientific fields (Brody & Fox, 1980) and to provide their sons with math- and science-related toys, kits, and books (Astin, 1974). Finally, parents of daughters reported noting giftedness in their children at a later age than did parents of sons (Fox, 1982) and were often quite surprised when informed that their daughters might be gifted (Fox, personal communication). Thus, although parents have a generally positive attitude toward their daughters' intellectual talents, they do not appear to be encouraging their daughters to develop these talents in occupational pursuits. And, in many cases, they appear to underestimate their daughters' talents.

Teachers and Counselors

The data on teachers are quite mixed. On the one hand, Terman (1927, 1930) found teachers to be quite positive toward both gifted boys and girls, and to rate gifted girls more positively than gifted boys in terms of their performance and competence on most subjects and on deportment. In addition, boys were more often reported as being weak in at least one subject. On the other hand, both Terman (1927) and Fox (1982) found that teachers were less likely to identify girls as gifted or to recommend them for accelerated educational programs. Furthermore, to the extent that teachers held negative stereotypes of gifted children, their stereotypes of gifted girls were more negative than were their stereotypes of gifted boys (Solano, 1977). Finally, when teachers were found to treat boys and girls differently in the classroom, these differences were most marked among the brightest students (Brophy & Good, 1974; Parsons, Kaczala, & Meece, 1982).

Fox (1976) found evidence of active resistance on the part of some teachers to continued accelerated math training for the girls who had participated in the Johns Hopkins Summer Accelerated Math Program. Furthermore, the presence or absence of teacher and counselor support was the major factor distinguishing between the girls who continued and the girls who chose to drop back into a more traditional math program. Similarly, in their study of female mathematicians, Luchins and Luchins (1980) found that 80 percent of the females, as compared to only 9 percent of the males, had encountered active discouragement from continuing their math training; this discrepancy was especially pronounced during the college years.

Evidence regarding the role of counselors is sparse. In general, counselors have not been found to be especially encouraging of nontraditional educational and occupational choices for either boys or girls (see Eccles & Hoffman, 1984), even among gifted students. For example, counselors have been found to actively discourage gifted girls from continuing their accelerated math training programs (Fox, 1976). Likewise, more than a quarter of the gifted adults interviewed by Post-Kammer and Perrone (1983) reported that their high school counseling had been poor or inadequate. Benbow and Stanley (1982b) found that less than 12 percent of the gifted students they identified in their talent search were participating in any special programs. And girls were less likely than boys to be among the few who did receive these special opportunities: only 6 percent of the girls compared to 11 percent of the boys were in special programs.

These results are especially disturbing given the growing body of evidence that teachers and counselors can be an important source of encouragement for gifted girls. Several studies have demonstrated the positive effect of supportive teachers and of well-designed classroom intervention programs on gifted and talented girls' educational and vocational plans (e.g., Brody & Fox, 1980; Callahan, 1979; Casserly, 1980; Fox, 1976; Fox, Benbow, & Perkins, 1983; Sloat, 1984; Tobin & Fox, 1980; Tomlinson-Keasey & Smith-Winberry, 1983). Casserly (1980) identified the 20 school districts in the United States that had the best record of enrollment by talented females in their advanced placement (AP) courses in math and science. She interviewed students, teachers, and counselors at these schools regarding the factors that they believed accounted for the high participation rates of the female students in these courses. Several themes emerged rather consistently across the districts: early placement in a curricular track that leads automatically to the AP courses; high proportions of females in the classes from the beginning of the tracking sequence; active efforts to allow female friends to stay together in these courses; active support of the females' interests, confidence, and, perhaps most importantly, participation in class activities; active recruitment of younger females into the courses by the AP teachers and by the older female students; active career counseling by AP teachers within their classes; and creative, noncompetitive instruction in the AP classes.

Casserly's study clearly suggests that supportive teachers can play an important role in encouraging gifted and talented females to develop their math and science skills and to consider seriously careers in math and science. Other studies provide support for this hypothesis. For example, women in nontraditional fields often cite the positive influence of a supportive teacher on their career goals (Barnett & Baruch, 1978; Boswell, 1978; Luchins & Luchins, 1980). Casserly's study also indicates that early acceleration may be important.

Several studies suggest that adolescent gifted girls are less attracted to special programs, particularly in math and science, than are adolescent gifted boys. (Fox, 1976; Fox, Benbow, & Perkins, 1983; Tobin & Fox, 1980). In contrast, accelerated programs begun in elementary school have at least as many female as male participants. Furthermore, both girls and boys enrolled in such programs retain their accelerated status throughout high school and are graduated at an earlier age than their nonaccelerated peers without any apparent deleterious effects on their intellectual and social development (cf., Callahan, 1979).

Finally, Casserly's study points to the importance of instructional strategies themselves. The AP teachers in her study were especially likely to include career counseling in their courses; to use noncompetitive teaching strategies; to include applied concerns drawn from fields such as engineering, design, medicine, and architecture; to stress the creative components of math and science rather than facts and word problem sets; and to be actively committed to nonsexist education. Observational studies of science teachers suggest that a similar set of characteristics differentiates teachers who produce high levels of interest in science among their female students from teachers who do not (Kahle, 1984).

Further support of the importance of these characteristics is provided by Fox (1976). Concerned with the low participation rates of gifted girls in the special program being offered at the Johns Hopkins University for gifted children, these researchers designed a special math class to attract females. This class incorporated many of the "girl-friendly" principles uncovered by Casserly (1980) and Kahle (1984): It was taught by women who used cooperative learning strategies and included career guidance, and all of the students were female. The class was successful in increasing the participation rates of gifted female students, but longitudinal follow-ups indicate that the long-range impact of this experience was minimal, suggesting that one-shot interventions may not be effective in producing lasting change. Girl-friendly practices may need to be a continuing part of gifted girls' educational experiences (Brody & Fox, 1980).

Studies from a variety of sources suggest that girl-friendly practices are not typical, especially in math and science classrooms. Many teachers use competitive, motivational strategies, especially in junior and senior high school math and science classes (Brush, 1980), and few include career counseling in their courses (Parsons, Kaczala, & Meece, 1982). Substantive increases in the number of teachers using girl-friendly practices will depend on incorporating sex equity instruction into teacher and counselor education programs, into educational inservice training programs, and into higher education's affirmative action programs.

Future Directions for Research

Throughout this chapter, I have noted weaknesses in the research literature on gifted females. In summary, I recommend areas in which continued research is particularly needed.

General Problems

Sparsity is the most glaring problem in the research literature on gifted females. The research base also suffers at times from the lack of a coherent theoretical framework. As a consequence, studies tend to be isolated from one another and tend to focus on limited subsets of variables, making integration of the field difficult. Systematic programs of research that are guided by a comprehensive theoretical framework are needed. I have outlined one such framework; it could be used to design systematic programs of research on the processes that influence the development and maintainence of sex differences in the educational and vocational choices of gifted individuals. As I have noted throughout this chapter, very few of the hypotheses implicit in this framework have been adequately tested.

The existing research literature also suffers from a problem common to many studies on sex differences in achievement behaviors, namely, the failure to assess the impact of the variable under study on males' and females' achievement-related behaviors. Much existing research provides descriptions of sex differences on variables assumed to influence achievement-related behaviors but fails to test whether these differences are actually responsible for the sex differences in achievement-related behaviors. For example, Benbow and Stanley (1980) reported a significant sex difference in gifted seventh-grade students' scores on the SAT and concluded that this difference is responsible for differential enrollment in advanced math courses. Such an inference is not warranted on logical grounds and has not been supported by subsequent empirical study.[1] Researchers need to exercise great caution in extrapolating beyond their data to make causal inferences regarding the possible long-range implications of sex differences obtained on putative mediating variables. Without the appropriate longitudinal studies, it is simply not known whether a particular variable mediates sex differences in achievement-related choices and behaviors or not.

Longitudinal Studies of Psychological Development and Socialization

There is a clear need for comprehensive, longitudinal, multiple-wave studies of the processes and variables that shape the educational and vocational choices of gifted males and females. Because such studies rely on multivariate regression procedures, causality cannot, strictly speaking, be determined. But by including all those variables that might have a significant longitudinal effect, such studies can be used to assess the probable relative importance of various factors as they operate in the natural setting. Furthermore, by measuring all the relevant variables at several points in time, researchers can statistically model the interrelations among the variables under study.

To accomplish this goal, a comprehensive study should include measures of the following socialization variables: parents' attitudes, parents' occupations and activities, parents' plans for their children's educational development, teachers' behaviors and attitudes, childrens' participation in special programs, and the attitudes and advice of both school counselors and peers. Equally important are the following attitudes and beliefs of students: perceptions of peer reactions to various educational and vocational options, gender role beliefs, self-concept, personal values, long-range goals and aspirations, career orientation versus family or community orientation, thing- versus person-orientation, stereotypes of var-

---

[1]In a subsequent follow-up of a subset of these students, sex remained a significant predictor of course enrollment patterns even after the sexes were equated statistically for their scores on the SAT (Benbow & Stanley, 1982).

ious educational and occupational options, anxieties, and the subjective value attached to various educational and occupational options. If such measures were gathered in several waves across the secondary school and college years, researchers could begin to assess how parents and teachers influence the attitudes and beliefs of gifted students and how these beliefs, in turn, influence the early educational and vocational choices of gifted females and males. Researchers could also begin to assess how parents, teachers, counselors, and peers directly affect the educational and vocational options that are considered by gifted females and males.

Some longitudinal research efforts are currently underway. For example, the gifted students originally identified in the Johns Hopkins Talent Searches are being followed up as they move through high school and into college. Small subgroups of these students were given an extensive battery of questions tapping many of the constructs outlined in the previous paragraph, but the psychological data available on most of the students is much more limited. To date, predictive equations based on the available data have accounted for only a small portion of the variance in gifted students' course enrollment and college major decisions (between 10 and 20 percent of the variance in high school enrollment in advanced math courses, Benbow & Stanley, 1982a; and between 1 and 7 percent of the variance in anticipated college major, Benbow & Stanley, 1984). The low predictive power of these findings is cogent evidence of the need for more broad-based, theoretically oriented studies.

Studies of Adult Development

More extensive longitudinal and biographical studies are also needed to unravel the factors that influence the educational and vocational behavior patterns of the gifted across their life spans. Such studies need to focus on issues such as (a) the internal and external factors that either inhibit or facilitate gifted women's, as well as gifted men's, occupational development; (b) the shifting priority patterns of gifted men and women across their life spans; (c) the internal and external factors that lead some gifted women to change their priorities substantially in either a traditional or nontraditional direction; (d) the benefits to both gifted women and society of their committing time and energy to their families and communities; and (e) the kinds of support that are necessary to allow gifted women of various ages to move into the occupational world at levels commensurate with their talents.

Longitudinal studies of this magnitude are very expensive and require the commitment of either a team of researchers or a research institute. The Terman data bank is one source of existing data that is being used to explore some of these issues. Given the major changes that have occurred over the last 20 years in this culture's gender roles, however, new life-span longitudinal studies focusing on the upcoming generations of gifted women need to be initiated.

Developing and Evaluating Effective Educational Programs for Gifted Girls

More information is needed on the most effective kinds of educational and counseling programs for gifted boys and girls. Gifted girls may show low participation in certain enrichment-type and accelerated programs for math and science during the secondary school years because they find such programs less appealing than do gifted boys or gifted boys' parents (Callahan, 1979). Very few studies have examined whether a particular program is more attractive to, or more effective with, boys or girls. One such study demonstrated that different types of math enrichment programs are needed to attract equal numbers of gifted boys and girls (Fox, Benbow, & Perkins, 1983). More research is needed on the types of programs that would be most effective in facilitating the development of gifted females' talents.

Effective Counseling Programs

Little is known about the most effective means of providing gifted boys and girls with sufficient information on which to base wise educational and vocational decisions. If society's goal is to get gifted women to consider a wider range of occupational options, including such traditionally male fields as math, engineering, and the physical sciences, then current counseling practices are not adequate. The forces operating to maintain gender-stereotyped decisions are ubiquitous. Effective reeducation designed to counter these forces will require comprehensive, long-term counseling programs that involve as many of the relevant social agents as possible, for example, programs that involve parents and the community as well as teachers and counselors in providing gifted girls with alternative role models, alternative educational and vocational experiences, more detailed information on the educational and vocational options available and on the prerequisites for entry into these opportunities, active encouragement to take advanced placement courses in math and science as well as in English and foreign languages, more extensive information on the need to prepare oneself for financial independence, more extensive information on the ways one can integrate family plans with various traditional and nontraditional occupations, and support for making nontraditional choices. Field-based experimental studies are needed to test the effectiveness of such alternative counseling procedures.

Identifying the Gifted

The processes involved in identifying children as gifted and talented and recommending them for either accelerated education or special programs are not well understood. Very little is known about the criteria, other than standard IQ scores, that parents, teachers, and counselors use to judge students' giftedness. It may be that gifted females are more likely to go unnoticed than gifted males. Furthermore, the research reviewed earlier in this chapter suggests that gifted females may be more likely than gifted males to ignore or underrate their own talents, thereby participating passively in their own invisibility. Both of these processes need to be studied and alternative remediation strategies need to be evaluated.

Adult Education and Occupational Supports

The sparsity of high-quality adult education and training programs is yet another factor that may be inhibiting the occupational development of gifted women. Educational and occupational training systems are now designed to mesh well with the life patterns of men. They also tend to operate on the implicit assumptions that late entry into professions such as medicine, law, or the sciences and less than complete devotion to one's profession are bad ideas. Both of these assumptions need to be evaluated empirically because they serve to discriminate against gifted women's entry into and advancement in high-status professions. In addition, educational and occupational support programs that are specifically designed for gifted women who have life patterns different from those of gifted men need to be developed and evaluated. Such programs should be responsive to the fact that the educational and occupational patterns of many gifted women are influenced by their desire to spend significant amounts of time raising their children. This priority should be acknowledged as being legitimate and the assumption that late entry into educational or occupational training programs signifies lack of commitment should not be made.

Conclusion

As is true for all men and women, gifted men and women differ in their educational and occupational patterns in a gender-stereotypic fashion. In this chapter I have explored why this might be true and have outlined a research agenda to study these hypotheses. Gender role beliefs and schema seem to be especially important influences in that they affect both expectations for success and the subjective value individuals attach to participation in various educational, occupational, and family-related pursuits. The beliefs and behaviors of parents, teachers, counselors, and peers are also critical. These socialization agents appear to lack confidence in gifted girls' ability or motivation to succeed at demanding educational programs. They do little to foster gifted girls' perception of these programs as valuable and important, to help gifted girls evaluate the relative importance of careers and family as well as the absolute importance of economic independence, or to provide gifted girls with accurate and detailed information about the educational and occupational options available to them. Given the omnipresence of gender role prescriptions regarding appropriate life choices for females, parents, teachers, and counselors must actively encourage gifted girls to develop nontraditional roles.

References

Astin, H. S. (1984). Academic scholarship and its rewards. In M. W. Steinkamp & M. L. Maehr (Eds.), *Women in science* (pp. 259–280). Greenwich, CT: JAI Press.

Atkinson, J. W. (1964). *An introduction to motivation.* Princeton, NJ: Van Nostrand.

Babcock, F. L. (1941). *The U. S. college graduate.* New York: Macmillan.

Bandura, A. (1977). Self-efficacy: Toward a unifying theory of behavior change. *Psychological Review, 84,* 191–215.

Bar-Tal, D. (1978). Attributional analysis of achievement-related behavior. *Review of Educational Research, 48,* 259–271.

Barnett, R. C., & Baruch, G. K. (1978). *The competent woman.* New York: Irvington.

Baruch, G., Barnett, R., & Rivers, C. (1983). *Life prints.* New York: McGraw-Hill.

Benbow, C. P., & Stanley, J. C. (1980). Sex differences in mathematical ability: Fact or artifact? *Science, 210,* 1262–1264.

Benbow, C. P., & Stanley, J. C. (1982a). Consequences in high school and college of sex differences in mathematical reasoning ability: A longitudinal perspective. *American Educational Research Journal, 19,* 598–622.

Benbow, C. P., & Stanley, J. C. (1982b). Intellectually talented boys and girls: Educational profiles. *Gifted Child Quarterly, 26,* 82–88.

Benbow, C. P., & Stanley, J. C. (1983). Sex differences in mathematical reasoning ability: More facts. *Science, 222,* 1029–31.

Benbow, C. P., & Stanley, J. C. (1984). Gender and the science major: A study of mathematically precocious youth. In M. W. Steinkamp & M. L. Maehr (Eds.), *Women in science* (pp. 165–196). Greenwich, CT: JAI Press.

Boswell, S. (1979). *Nice girls don't study mathematics: The perspective from elementary school.* Paper presented at the meeting of the American Educational Research Association, San Francisco, CA.

Brody, L., & Fox, L. H. (1980). An accelerated intervention program for mathematically gifted girls. In L. H. Fox, L. Brody, & D. Tobin (Eds.), *Women and the mathematical mystique* (pp. 164–178). Baltimore: Johns Hopkins University Press.

Brophy, J. E., & Good, T. (1974). *Teacher-student relationships: Causes and consequences.* New York: Holt, Rinehart & Winston.

Brush, L. (1980). *Encouraging girls in mathematics: The problem and the solution.* Boston: ABT Books.

Callahan, C. M. (1979). The gifted and talented woman. In A. H. Passow (Ed.), *The gifted and talented: Their education and development. The seventy-eighth yearbook of the National Society for the Study of Education.* Chicago: The University of Chicago Press.

Casserly, P. (1980). *An assessment of factors affecting female participation in advanced placement programs in mathematics, chemistry, and physics.* In L. H. Fox, L. Brody, & D. Tobin (Eds.), *Women and the mathematical mystique* (pp. 138–163). Baltimore: Johns Hopkins University Press.

Cooper, H. M., Burger, J. M., & Good, T. L. (1981). Gender differences in the academic locus of control beliefs of young children. *Journal of Personality and Social Psychology, 40,* 562–573.

Crandall, V. C. (1969). Sex differences in expectancy of intellectual and academic reinforcement. In C. P. Smith (Ed.), *Achievement-related behaviors in children* (pp. 11–45). New York: Russell Sage Foundation.

Crandall, V. J., Crandall, V. C., Katkovsky, W., & Preston, A. (1962). Motivational and ability determinants of young children's intellectual achievement behavior. *Child Development, 33,* 643–661.

Dunteman, G. H., Wisenbaker, J., & Taylor M. E. (1978). *Race and sex differences in college science program participation.* Report to the National Science Foundation. North Carolina: Research Triangle Park.

Dweck, C. S., & Licht, B. G. (1980). Learned helplessness and intellectual achievement. In J. Garber & M. E. P. Seligman (Eds.), *Human helplessness: Theory and applications.* New York: Academic Press.

Eccles, J., Adler, T. F., Futterman, R., Goff, S. B., Kaczala, C. M., Meece, J. L., & Midgley, C. (1983). Expectations, values and academic behaviors. In J. T. Spence (Ed.), *Achievement and achievement motivation* (pp. 75–146). San Francisco: Freeman.

Eccles, J., Adler, T. F., & Meece, J. L. (1984). Sex differences in achievement: A test of alternate theories. *Journal of Personality and Social Psychology, 46,* 26–43.

Eccles, J., & Hoffman, L. W. (1984). Sex roles, socialization, and occupational behavior. In H. W. Stevenson & A. E. Siegel (Eds.), *Research in child development and social policy.* (Vol. 1, pp. 367–420). Chicago: University of Chicago Press.

Eccles Parsons, J. (1983). Attributional processes as mediators of sex differences in achievement. *Journal of Educational Equity and Leadership, 3,* 19–27.

Eccles (Parsons), J. (1984). Sex differences in mathematics participation. In M. W. Steinkamp & M. L. Maehr (Eds.), *Women in science,* (pp. 93–138). Greenwich, CT: JAI Press.

Fox, L. H. (1976). Sex differences in mathematical precocity: Bridging the gap. In D. P. Keating (Ed.), *Intellectual talent: Research and development* (pp. 183–214). Baltimore: Johns Hopkins University Press.

Fox, L. H. (1982). *The study of social processes that inhibit or enhance the development of competence and interest in mathematics among highly able young women: Final report.* Washington, DC: National Institute of Education.

Fox, L. H., Benbow, C. P., & Perkins, S. (1983). An accelerated mathematics program for girls: A longitudinal evaluation. In C. P. Benbow & J. Stanley (Eds.), *Academic precocity: Aspects of its development* (pp. 113–131). Baltimore: Johns Hopkins University Press.

Fox, L. H., & Cohn, S. J. (1980). Sex differences in the development of precocious mathematical talent. In L. H. Fox, L. Brody, & D. Tobin (Eds.), *Women and the mathematical mystique* (pp. 94–111). Baltimore: Johns Hopkins University Press.

Fox, L. H., & Denham, S. A. (1974). Values and career interests of mathematically and scientifically precocious youth. In J. C. Stanley, D. P. Keating, & L. H. Fox (Eds.), *Mathematical talent: Discovery, description, and development.* (pp. 140–175). Baltimore: Johns Hopkins University Press.

Fox, L. H., Pasternak, S. R., & Peiser, N. L. (1976). Career-related interests of adolescent boys and girls. In D. P. Keating (Ed.), *Intellectual talent: Research and development.* (pp. 242–261). Baltimore: Johns Hopkins University Press.

Frieze, I. H., & Hanusa, B. H. (1984). Women scientists: Overcoming barriers. In M. W. Steinkamp & M. L. Maehr (Eds.), *Women in science* (pp. 139–164). Greenwich, CT: JAI Press.

Frieze, I. H., Whitley, B., Hanusa, B. H., & McHugh, M. (1982). Assessing the theoretical models for sex differences in causal attributions for success and failure. *Sex Roles, 8,* 333–343.

George, W. C., & Denham, S. A. (1976). Curriculum experimentation for the mathematically talented. In D. P. Keating (Ed.), *Intellectual talent: Research and development* (pp. 103–131). Baltimore: Johns Hopkins University Press.

Greenleaf, W. J. (1937). *Economic status of college alumni* (Bulletin No. 10). Washington, DC: U. S. Office of Education.

Helson, R. (1980). The creative woman mathematician. In L. H. Fox, L. Brody, & D. Tobin (Eds.), *Women and the mathematical mystique* (pp. 23–54). Baltimore: Johns Hopkins University Press.

Hollinger, C. L. (1983). Self-perception and the career aspirations of mathematically talented female adolescents. *Journal of Vocational Behavior, 22,* 49–62.

Humphreys, L. G. (1984). Women with doctorates in science and engineering. In M. W. Steinkamp & M. L. Maehr (Eds.), *Women in science* (pp. 197–216). Greenwich, CT: JAI Press.

Huston, A. C. (1983). Sex-typing. In E. M. Hetherington (Ed.), *Handbook of child psychology: Vol. 4. Socialization, personality, and social development* (4th ed.). New York: Wiley.

Kahle, J. (1984). *Girl-friendly science.* Paper presented at the meeting of the American Association for the Advancement of the Sciences, New York.

Kavrell, S. M., & Petersen, A. C. (1984). Patterns of achievement in early adolescence. In M. W. Steinkamp & M. L. Maehr (Eds.), *Women in science* (pp. 1–36). Greenwich, CT: JAI Press.

Kiesler, S., Sproull, L., & Eccles, J. (in press). Poolhalls, chips, and war games: Women in the culture of computing. *Psychology of Women Quarterly.*

Lewin, K. (1983). *The conceptual representation and the measurement of psychological forces.* Durham, NC: Duke University Press.

Luchins, E. H., & Luchins, A. S. (1980). Female mathematicians: A contemporary appraisal. In L. H. Fox, L. Brody, & D. Tobin (Eds.), *Women and the mathematical mystique* (pp. 7–22). Baltimore: Johns Hopkins University Press.

Maines, D. R. (1983). *A theory of informal barriers for women in mathematics.* Paper presented at the meeting of the American Educational Research Association, Montreal, Canada.

Markus, H. (1980). The self in thought and memory. In D. M. Wegner & R. R. Vallacher (Eds.), *The self in social psychology.* New York: Oxford University Press.

McGinn, P. V. (1976). Verbally gifted youth: Selection and description. In D. P. Keating (Ed.), *Intellectual talent: Research and development* (pp. 106–182). Baltimore: Johns Hopkins University Press.

Meece, J. L., Eccles Parsons, J., Kaczala, C. M., Goff, S. B., & Futterman, R. (1982). Sex differences in math achievement: Toward a model of academic choice. *Psychological Bulletin, 91,* 324–348.

Montemayor, R. (1974). Children's performances in a game and their attraction to it as a function of sex-typed labels. *Child Development, 45,* 152–156.

Nash, S. C. (1979). Sex role as a mediator of intellectual functioning. In M. A. Wittig & A. C. Petersen (Eds.), *Sex-related differences in cognitive functioning: Developmental issues* (pp. 263–381). New York: Academic Press.

National Center for Educational Statistics. (1979, September). Proportion of degrees awarded to women. *Chronicle of Higher Education.*

Nicholls, J. G. (1975). Causal attributions and other achievement-related cognitions: Effects of task outcomes, attainment value, and sex. *Journal of Personality and Social Psychology, 31,* 379–389.

Oden, M. H. (1968). The fulfillment of promise: 40 year follow-up of the Terman gifted group. *Genetic Psychology Monographs, 77,* 3–93.

Parsons, J. E., Adler, T. F., & Kaczala, C. M. (1982). Socialization of achievement attitudes and beliefs: Parental influences. *Child Development, 53,* 310–321.

Parsons, J. E., & Goff, S. B. (1980). Achievement motivation: A dual modality. In L. J. Fyans (Ed.), *Achievement motivation: Recent trends in theory and research* (pp. 349–373). New York: Plenum.

Parsons, J. E., Kaczala, C. M., & Meece, J. L. (1982). Socialization of achievement attitudes and beliefs: Classroom influences. *Child Development, 53,* 322–339.

Parsons, J. E., Meece, J. L., Adler, T. F., & Kaczala, C. M. (1982). Sex differences in attributional patterns and learned helplessness? *Sex Roles, 8,* 421–432.

Parsons, J. E., Ruble, D. N., Hodges, K. L., & Small, A. W. (1976). Cognitive-developmental factors in emerging sex differences in achievement-related expectancies. *Journal of Social Issues, 32,* 47–61.

Post-Kammer, P., & Perrone, P. (1983). Career perceptions of talented individuals: A follow-up study. *Vocational Guidance Quarterly, 31,* 203–211.

Raynor, J. O. (1974). Future orientation in the study of achievement motivation. In J. W. Atkinson & J. O. Raynor (Eds.), *Motivation and achievement.* Washington, DC: Winston Press.

Rokeach, M. (1973). *The nature of human values.* New York: Free Press.

Schunk, D. H., & Lilly, M. W. (1982). *Attributional and expectancy change in gifted adolescents.* Paper presented at the meeting of the American Educational Research Association, New York.

Sears, P. S. (1979). The Terman genetic studies of genius: 1922–1972. In A. H. Passow (Ed.), *The seventy-eighth yearbook of the National Society of the Study of Education.* Chicago: University of Chicago Press.

Sloat, B. F. (1984). *Women in science: A university program of intervention, outreach, and research.* Paper presented at the Second International Interdisciplinary Congress on Women, Groningen, The Netherlands.

Solano, C. H. (1977). Teacher and pupil stereotypes of gifted boys and girls. *Talents and Gifts, 19,* 4.

Spenner, K., & Featherman, D. L. (1978). Achievement ambitions. *Annual Review of Sociology, 4,* 373–420.

Stanley, J. C. (1976). Use of tests to discover talent. In D. P. Keating (Ed.), *Intellectual talent: Research and development* (pp. 3–22). Baltimore: Johns Hopkins University Press.

Stein, A. H., & Bailey, M. M. (1973). The socialization of achievement orientation in females. *Psychological Bulletin, 80,* 345–366.

Terman, L. M. (1925). *Genetic studies of genius: Vol. 1. Mental and physical traits of a thousand gifted children.* Stanford, CA: Stanford University Press.

Terman, L. M. (1930). *Genetic studies of genius: Vol. 3. The promise of youth: Follow-up studies of a thousand gifted children.* Stanford, CA: Stanford University Press.

Terman, L. M., & Oden, M. H. (1947). *Genetic studies of genius: Vol. 4: The gifted child grows up: Twenty-five years' follow-up of a superior group.* Stanford, CA: Stanford University Press.

Tidwell, R. (1980). Gifted students' self-images as a function of identification procedure, race, and sex. *Journal of Pediatric Psychology, 5,* 57–69.

Tobin, D., & Fox, L. H. (1980). Career interests and career education: A key to change. In L. H. Fox, L. Brody, & D. Tobin (Eds.), *Women and the mathematical mystique* (pp. 171–191). Baltimore: Johns Hopkins University Press.

Tomlinson-Keasey, C., & Smith-Winberry, C. (1983). Educational strategies and personality outcomes of gifted and nongifted college students. *Gifted Child Quarterly, 27,* 35–41.

Tresemer, D. (1976). The cumulative record of research on "fear of success." *Sex Roles, 2,* 217–236.

Vetter, B. M. (1981). Women scientists and engineers: Trends in participation. *Science, 214,* 1313–1321.

Weiner, B. (1974). *Achievement motivation and attribution theory.* Morristown, NJ: General Learning Press.

Williams, J. E., Bennett, S., & Best, D. (1975). Awareness and expression of sex stereotypes in young children. *Developmental Psychology, 11,* 635–642.

Wolleat, P. L., Pedro, J. D., Becker, A. D., & Fennema, E. (1980). Sex differences in high school students' causal attributions of performance in mathematics. *Journal of Research in Mathematics Education, 11,* 356–366.

Zerega, M. E., & Walberg, H. J. (1984). School science and femininity. In M. W. Steinkamp & M. L. Maehr (Eds.), *Women in science* (pp. 37–50). Greenwich, CT: JAI Press.

Part 3. Reflections on the Study of Giftedness

Reflections on the Study of Giftedness

The previous sections of this book have clearly indicated the need for empirical research and developmental perspectives on giftedness. Some of the issues raised, however, have philosophical as well as empirical roots, suggesting that solutions to problems of investigating giftedness may themselves require creativity as well as scientific rigor. In this section, authors explore approaches to studying the development of the gifted from diverse and innovative points of view.

Whether there can be giftedness in the socioemotional as well as intellectual arena is the subject treated by Howard Gruber of the University of Geneva, Switzerland, in chapter 10. When the world faces moral crises, are there people who are especially capable of assuming moral responsibility? Or is it the obligation of all creative and intelligent individuals to take an ethical stand? Although rarely addressed in the research literature, such issues are critical to our understanding of the psychological aspects of famine relief, human rights obligations, and war and peace. Through historical analysis, Gruber provides insight into the degree to which gifted scientists have assumed moral responsibility, and proposes several approaches to creative thinking about human survival.

In chapter 11, Lloyd Humphreys of the University of Illinois defines giftedness psychometrically, as being represented by the upper end of the intelligence continuum. From this perspective, giftedness is seen not as a fixed, unitary trait, but as a complex and dynamic repertoire that is subject to a variety of developmental influences. In Humphreys' view, how gifted young peple are educated is vitally important for the realization of intellectual potential. He proposes an approach based on the homogenous grouping of gifted students and individualized curriculum materials, combined with an increase in societal rewards in the form of scholarship aid to gifted students.

In chapter 12, Doris Wallace of Bank Street College sets forth an outline of the major components of the evolving systems approach to the study of giftedness. She differentiates between the concept of giftedness, which is typically applied to children and represents precocity, and its adult counterparts, creativity and productive, innovative work. Through case studies of highly creative adults, Wallace attempts to understand the nature of giftedness and creativity and to trace the processes by which individuals come to live a creative life.

In chapter 13, Edward Zigler and Ellen Farber of Yale University propose that students of giftedness have much to learn from past research with the retarded. Issues of definition and assessment, conflict over the causes of differences in intellectual ability, and the role of socioemotional factors in atypical development are all of concern to investigators of retarded and gifted populations alike. According to Zigler and Farber, recognizing the similarities in retarded and gifted groups may allow researchers who work with the gifted to resolve some troublesome questions and move ahead to study the truly unique aspects of giftedness.

In the final chapter of this section, Patrick DeLeon of the U.S. Senate Staff and Gary VandenBos of the University of Bergen suggest some approaches to focusing the attention of policymakers on issues important to research with gifted populations and the solution of problems associated with educational programs for the gifted. The authors review the history of public policy with regard to gifted children and find that it reflects our democratic nation's ambivalent attitude toward exceptional talent. In general, however, DeLeon and VandenBos believe that the area of giftedness has developed a strong core of support among professionals and the public and that advocacy efforts are therefore more likely to succeed today than they were 25 or even 10 years ago.

10. Giftedness and Moral Responsibility: Creative Thinking and Human Survival

Howard E. Gruber
University of Geneva, Switzerland

> To struggle against war is therefore to act according to the logic of
> life against the logic of things, and that is the whole of morality.
> (Piaget, 1918)

The Country of the Blind

The gift of Midas brings him to grief, for if everything he touches turns
to gold, what is there to eat or drink, whom to caress? The escape route
from Plato's cave is not taken. The long-enchained inhabitants of the
grotto do not wish to see the world outside. The explorer's journey has
been in vain. The erstwhile liberator is killed. A great gift is futile when
its owner is not appropriately connected to the world.

   This is also the theme of a number of H. G. Wells's stories. In *The
Invisible Man,* the person with an extraordinary gift moves in an ordinary

world, which defeats him. In *The Country of the Blind,* an ordinary person finds himself in an unusual world. It is the person–world connection that must be appropriate. The meaning and value of a gift depends on that relationship. To understand it, we psychologists must study both person and world.

In the country of the blind, so the saying goes, the one-eyed man is king. Not so, says Wells. In the fable he creates, a sighted person falls into a forgotten valley, where all the people are blind. He sees his opportunity. Here he will be king and master. But the people have mastered the world they live in, and they do not understand his. They defeat his aspirations. As they are kind, they wish to make him one of them. Their skillful surgeons propose to cut away those worse than useless pulpy fluttering malformations he calls "eyes."

My first goal in this chapter is to examine the concept of moral responsibility. Is there a domain of moral responsibility (in which someone might be gifted or creative) that might have the same epistemological standing as, for example, the domain of mathematics or music? How does moral responsibility differ from moral judgment, which has been the main target of investigations in the field of moral development? Is it helpful to think of this domain as being located in a social-historical space rather than in the individual as Feldman (1980) has suggested for other domains? Or is it more useful to think of moral responsibility as a frame of mind or special sort of intelligence of the kind that Gardner (1983) has recently proposed? Does it make sense to say that some people are morally gifted?

My second goal is to raise some questions about the relevance of moral responsibility to all gifted and creative individuals. Does being gifted or creative impose a special moral responsibility on an individual? Does it equip him or her better to handle both normal and special responsibilities? Do gifted and creative people feel such moral responsibility? How does moral responsibility develop?

All statements about what *ought* to be done imply that something *can* be done. When one steps outside of well-charted, rule-governed situations, what ought to and can be done can only be discovered by persistent creative

This chapter is an outgrowth of the Conference on Research Needs in the Study of the Development of Extraordinary Moral Responsibility, held at Yale University, November 10–12, 1983. The Conference was jointly sponsored by the Social Science Research Council (SSRC) and the Bush Center for Child Development and Social Policy of Yale University. I thank Peter B. Read of SSRC, Edward Zigler, Director of the Bush Center, and David Feldman, Chairman of the SSRC Committee on Giftedness and Creativity, for their cooperation. I especially acknowledge the collaboration of Sam Nash of the New Haven Board of Education in organizing the Conference and the participation of David Bakan, Michael Basseches, Ann Colby, William Damon, Henry-Lewis Gates, Carol Gilligan, Edmund W. Gordon, Aaron Hershkowitz, Martin L. Hoffman, George B. Hogenson, Robert Holt, Sharon Lynn Kagan, Georg Lind, Fayneese Miller, Bruce M. Russet, Victor Saraiva, Gloria Small, Robert J. Sternberg, Elliott Turiel, Doris B. Wallace, and Helen Weinreich-Haste. I take sole responsibility, however, for the ideas expressed in this chapter.

efforts. Such efforts must necessarily be made within some framework and be governed by some point of view (see Gruber, 1985).

In this chapter I describe some individuals who have acted within the framework of the Judeo-Christian ethic, placing primary value on human life, condemning mass destruction of human populations as immoral, and treating the survival of the human species as one of a small number of ultimate goods. I describe these individuals in order to clarify the general idea of extraordinary moral responsibility. This choice does not imply that any specific formula exists for deciding who is morally responsible.

Having made the distinction between moral reasoning and moral responsibility, it remains for psychologists to discover how to identify and nurture the gift of extraordinary moral responsibility. It will be important to do so in forms that respond to the great moral issues of our age, among which the greatest is the prevention of a nuclear holocaust. It might be said that this statement is a value judgment and has no place in a scientific discussion of giftedness and creativity. Let me address those two points separately.

First, of course it is a value judgment to say that preventing a nuclear holocaust is society's greatest moral issue. But calling the statement a value judgment is an inappropriate response and betrays what clinicians call "inappropriate affect." Consider the statement, "The Nazis should not have killed six million Jews." That is a value judgment, but no one says so because the values in question are universally accepted.

Second, in doing scientific work, researchers try to free their statements from the constraints of any particular set of values, in large part by becoming more aware of their own points of view, always searching for wider, more universal frameworks in which to house their knowledge. At the same time, no one can escape his or her personal construction of the historical context in which he or she lives. Every great scientific idea that is now universally accepted—the nature of heavenly bodies, the shape of the earth, the origin of species—has passed through a period in its history when it seemed to be primarily a moral question or to be inseparable from moral questions. Looked at in this historical perspective, the feeling that something is a value judgment, rather than disqualifying it as a scientific issue, might rather be a good clue that here is a promising problem for us to tackle.

For my own part, I write from within the framework of the same ethic that impelled the young Piaget to write, "To struggle against war is therefore to act according to the logic of life against the logic of things, and that is the whole of morality" (Piaget, 1918/1977). I do not try either to escape from or reexamine that framework. But I do recognize that the idea of extraordinary moral *responsibility*, as distinct from moral *reasoning*, is relatively new to and unexplored by psychologists. Exploring the idea brings into prominence questions about the relation between value systems and the study of giftedness and creativity.

Psychologists who have written about moral development have been concerned predominantly with how a good person reasons about moral issues, not about how a good person acts to make a better world. Is the first kind of morality more "psychological" than the second? In spite of its subtitle, "The Changing Status of Children: Rights, Roles and Responsibilities," a special issue of the *Journal of Social Issues* is almost entirely concerned with what adults can do for children. Only one author, Takanishi (1978), mentions an alternative conception of "children as redeemers of the social order." Must each person go through a long period of unalloyed dependency, growing up to taking responsibility only upon reaching young adulthood? Are there perhaps some morally precocious young people who need not or cannot wait so long? If they exist, how would a developmental theory of giftedness and creativity apply to them? My old copy of the *Boy Scout Handbook* quoted the Athenian Boy's Oath, "to leave my city fairer than I found it." Contemporary editions omit it. Was that idea once appropriate for children, but not now?

In my own efforts to relate the fields of moral development and giftedness, and at the Yale Conference on Research Needs in the Study of the Development of Extraordinary Moral Responsibility, two different ideas have been considered: first, that there might actually be a domain of moral giftedness and creativity, and second, that creative achievement in other domains is related to the problem of moral responsibility as it is experienced by creative people.

Although the first idea engenders interesting discussion, there is considerable controversy about it and not even the beginnings of a research approach. Considering the amount of recent ethological literature on the phenomenon of altruism, it is at least reasonable to broach the question of whether a domain of moral giftedness exists. If stages of development in moral reasoning can be entertained as a plausible idea, then some people might be considered precocious in this regard; if moral responsibility were also somehow connected with maturity of moral reasoning, an argument in favor of the idea of moral giftedness would have a foundation. Rejecting the idea of moral giftedness might entail rejecting some of these presuppositions.

The second idea involves analyzing the relation between moral responsibility and giftedness. It seems reasonable and defensible to propose that a successful, creative person is in a good position to assume moral responsibility. He or she has proven ability in some domain and is a member of a special community that may be relevant to the moral issues at stake. He or she has earned some degree of eminence and influence that may actually make it possible to affect the course of events. For example, some of the physicists who were involved in the early development of nuclear weapons saw the moral relevance of their scientific work, and engaged in a prolonged search for ways of applying their special knowledge to some moral purposes. In the case of psychology, it seems evident that practically all modern thinking about war and peace, military strategy, and the possibility of peace is permeated with psychological assumptions. As a result, psychologists may be in a good position to use their professional knowledge and creativity to increase the chances of the survival of our species.

For these reasons, therefore, the way in which some scientists and other creative people become motivated to take responsibility for great social issues is itself an important psychological question. At one extreme, one might argue that giftedness is general and that a person who is creative in one domain ipso facto is well equipped to deal with great moral issues and, consequently, has the obligation to do so. Taking a more moderate position, one might argue only that a person who is creative in one domain is in a good position to assume moral responsibility, that sometimes he or she becomes aware of this possibility, and that it is incumbent upon psychologists who are interested in giftedness to understand how this comes about.

These are the psychological questions that underlie this chapter. I cannot hope to answer them all. I do explore them, and in order to help me, I discuss two groups of gifted and creative people. One group comprises those physicists who have been faced with the deep moral problem posed by their role in the invention of nuclear weapons, with special attention to their early responses in the 1930s and 1940s. In the other, I examine the idea of moral responsibility as it applies to the working lives of three distinguished psychologists: William James, B. F. Skinner, and Charles Osgood.

The choice of these subjects reflects a third goal I had in writing this chapter: to link the topics of morality and giftedness and creativity to today's imperative need to reduce the threat to the survival of our species. To some readers this may seem to be a far-fetched set of connections, and so I will deal with this issue before turning to the other matters.

Linking Giftedness and Creative Thinking With Moral Responsiblity and the Threat to Human Survival

Ecological Considerations

There is now widespread agreement that psychologists must work out a more sophisticated understanding of the environments in which behavior and development occur. Brunswik (1956, 1957) gave this position its most profound examination. Recently, Bronfenbrenner (1977) has urged an ecological approach to developmental psychology.

There are two quite distinct ways in which the threat of nuclear war forms a part of our contemporary life space. First, nuclear war is an objective threat, attested to and agreed upon by experts of so many kinds and persuasions that it hardly needs documentation. Second, the threat is phenomenally present or subjectively real in the sense that information and discussion about it is very widespread in many sources of public information. In the press, the recent recognition of the danger of a "nuclear winter" has been widely disseminated. The film *The Day After* was shown on a national television network. The film *War Games*, shown in movie theaters across the country, depicts a gifted adolescent who, in playing with his computer, penetrates the most secure military computer network and comes close to triggering a full-scale nuclear war. It is to be expected that many gifted and creative individuals will be well informed about public concerns for the survival of our species. Even a Sunday newspaper supplement, *Parade Magazine*, carried Carl Sagan's (1983b) analysis of the threat of a nuclear winter to 50,000,000 readers. Sagan and his colleagues have calculated that a moderate-scale nuclear war would throw up enough smoke and dust to screen out the sun's rays and produce a three-year period of darkness with temperatures throughout the northern hemisphere remaining steadily at about $-25°C$. There is no way of keeping this kind of information from young people. A thoughtful youngster might justifiably wonder, "What is the point of cultivating my talents?"

In 1977 a task force of the American Psychiatric Association was formed to study "the psychological effects on children and adolescents of living in a world where thermonuclear disaster is a constant threat." One of the members, John Mack of the Harvard University Medical School summed up the results: "Children are aware of the threat of nuclear war and live in fear of it." He cited more detailed evidence of the way in which young people are shaping their life plans with these fears as a major consideration (Mack, 1981). Lifton and Falk (1982) have also given an excellent account of the historical and developmental course of such fears. They concluded, "Questions arise among the young about adults' capacity to keep them, and the world, alive" (p. 55).

Attitudes Toward Science and Public Policy

It cannot be said that there is perfect agreement among psychologists that in their role as psychologists they should concern themselves with such broad issues. At one extreme, perhaps, is the position advocated by the American Psychological Association's ad hoc Committee on Public Affairs, recommending that the wider the issue the less the American Psychological Association should do (Tyler, 1969). Presumably, since the extermination of our species is the widest possible issue, it would get zero attention.

In sharp contrast to this is the position of Psychologists for Social Responsibility, an association that devotes most of its energy to involving psychologists in stopping the arms race. Three gifted and creative former presidents of the American Psychological Association are among the members of the Advisory Board: Jerome Bruner, Carl Rogers, and M. Brewster Smith. Later on in this chapter, I discuss the career of Charles Osgood, another gifted psychologist and former APA president, who has long made survival of the human species a professional concern.

It is not my purpose in this chapter to explain the behavior of all the individuals I mention. But in mentioning them I do want to establish a kind of "existence theorem": It is possible for someone to be an excellent scientist—or otherwise gifted and creative person—and still find time for steady, demanding involvement on behalf of what he or she feels is a moral responsibility, both inside and outside the domain of his or her creative work. Beyond the profession of psychology, there are other scientists concerned and willing to engage in the issue of human survival with all the aid possible of scientific and professional tools and organizations. For example, in 1982 an assembly of presidents of scientific academies and other scientists from all over the world presented a "Declaration on Prevention of Nuclear War" to the Vatican. After outlining the dangers, the Assembly appealed

> To scientists, to use their creativity for the betterment of human life, and to apply their ingenuity in exploring means of avoiding nuclear war and developing practical methods of arms control. To religious leaders and other custodians of moral principles, to proclaim forcefully and persistently the grave human issues at stake so that these are fully understood and appreciated by society. (Conference on Nuclear Warfare, 1982, p. 449)

Thus, although there is no unanimity on the issue, there is strong support for the idea that creativity and morality can be linked in scientific and professional approaches to eliminating the threat of species extermination.

There are many relevant historical precedents, but perhaps the most pertinent is the official American reaction to the Soviets' launching the Sputnik satellite in October 1957, the first such achievement by any country. Admiration was coupled with dismay that our feared rival had stolen a technological march on us and had gotten ahead in science education. This event sparked a wave of expansion in science education and increased support for the education of the gifted. Social and technological change do sometimes beget changing psychoeducational needs, attitudes toward creativity, and decisions about the kind of creativity needed.

The Idea of Moral Responsibility

One does not read very far in the literature of moral development without rediscovering (a) that most of it is concerned with moral reasoning or judgment, not action (Weinreich-Haste & Lock, 1983) and (b) that neither levels of development in moral reasoning nor any other verbal measures of morality are good predictors of moral action (Straughan, 1983). Mischel and Mischel (1976) concluded that only about 10 percent of the variance in moral behavior could be predicted from tests of moral reasoning; obviously that limitation in predictive power runs in both directions.

It may be psychologically interesting to find ways of improving such predictions or, alternatively, of explaining the low values obtained. But scientists who feel some sense of urgency about facing the threat to species survival need to take another approach to studying the development of moral responsibility. It might help to identify and understand those unusual people who do want to be effective, who are morally responsible, rather than studying the typical course of development. In psychological research, a time-honored strategy for attacking a general problem is to study some atypical cases. To this end, let me first sketch a hypothetical, idealized, very full and demanding version of a morally gifted person who is faced with the threat of nuclear war. The ideal morally gifted person would exhibit the following four characteristics.

1. Moral Reasoning and Universalism. A morally gifted individual would have to exhibit the universalism that is considered to be characteristic of the higher stages of moral reasoning (Kohlberg, 1973; Weinreich-Haste & Lock, 1983). In some historical contexts there may be valid arguments, residues of cultural relativism, against insisting on universalism. But any universalist moral standard, such as "the greatest good for the greatest number," necessarily presupposes that species survival is an ultimate good. A morally gifted person who is facing the threat of nuclear war cannot escape recognizing that the fate of all humankind is joined: Nuclear winter for one is nuclear winter for all.[1]

---

[1]Kohlberg described the higher stages of moral development as follows: "Postconventional, autonomous, or principled level. At this level, there is a clear effort to define moral values and principles which have validity and application apart from the authority of the group or persons holding these principles, and apart from the individual's own identification with these groups ... Stage 6. *The universal ethical principle orientation.* Right is defined by the decision of conscience in accord with self-chosen *ethical principles* appealing to logical comprehensiveness, universality, and consistency. These principles are abstract and ethical ... they are not concrete moral rules like the Ten Commandments ... These are universal principles of *justice*, of the *reciprocity* and *equality* of human *rights*, and of respect for the dignity of human beings as *individual persons*" (1982, p. 282). It is noteworthy that in 1969 (when Kohlberg first made this statement) it was still possible to emphasize individual rights in formulating the universalist ideal of the highest stage of moral development. In 1984, the point that individual human rights presuppose the continued existence of humanity as a species has become salient. This transformation in the conception of the highest stage of moral development entails a corresponding change in the conception of moral giftedness.

2. Cognition and Moral Responsibility. A person cannot act in a morally responsible way unless he or she is well informed about the world in which action must take place. For example, the recently available information about nuclear winter makes much clearer the need for a universalistic ethic concerned with species survival as an ultimate good and as an indispensable criterion for moral action. The fact that no matter where the bombs explode, the fate of our species is the same disposes once and for all of any application of "just war" doctrines to nuclear warfare. The person who does not know enough to understand this is simply not in the game and can hardly begin to be morally responsible.

But knowledge is not enough. The person who is extraordinarily morally responsible in relation to the issue of nuclear war must be capable of living with the knowledge of potential horror, and of making it a basis for positive action. This kind of cognitive-affective control may be a rare trait; there is reason to believe that the more typical response to such knowledge is either repression or avoidance. (Janis & Feshback, 1953). In his study, "Imagining the Real," Lifton has recently elaborated his idea of psychic numbing and applied it to the reactions of children and adolescents to the danger of nuclear war (Lifton & Falk, 1982).

3. Initiative. A person who is morally gifted would take steps to resist the blandishments and distractions of everyday life in order to free energies for the cause in question. Being morally responsible means more than moral responsiveness, more than waiting at the ready for Kitty Genovese to cry out for help. It means envisioning a need, looking for something to do about it, and doing it.

4. Moral Passion. In the literature on moral development almost no attention is given to moral feeling, notwithstanding some valuable works such as those by Gilligan (1982) and Hoffman (1980). When cognitive psychology was being invented, in the century or so between the rationalist Descartes and the empiricist Hume, everyone who wrote about the Understanding, including those two, stressed the impossibility of clear thought without strong passions. "The Reason is, and ought to be, the Slave of the Passions" (Hume, 1777).

In studying moral giftedness today, there is a special need for examining anew the relation between cognition and emotion. To be a morally gifted person requires having a commitment to prolonged, steady work. This simply cannot be maintained without continued access to the feelings that will sustain it. It is significant that when a wide array of leaders—relatively cool diplomats (George Kennan), scientists (Lewis Thomas), and soldiers (Field Marshal Lord Michael Carver)—speak of the threat of nuclear extinction, they speak with great emotion (see Kennan, 1981; Thomas, 1981). They do not "lose their cool," they use their warmth. For brevity, I give only one example—Carver's closing words in an article on no first use of nuclear weapons. Carver, who was Chief of the Defense Staff of the United Kingdom from 1973 to 1976, wrote, "no human being has yet faced the terrible decision of ordering the first use of a nuclear weapon, when he knew that those against whom it is to be fired can, and almost certainly will, retaliate in kind. Let us hope that no being will give that order. If he did, he would not be human" (Carver, 1983).

In summary, a person who displays extraordinary moral responsibility has high levels of moral reasoning, concern for issues of great import, strong moral passion and courage, and a propensity to translate thought and feeling into effective action. This is a person who takes moral initiatives, rather than only responding to situations that are thrust upon her or him.

This description is intended as an idealization in order to clarify a concept rather than to describe accurately any actual person. Much of the rest of the chapter is an examination of a few individuals who may have approached this ideal in ways connected with the issue of war and peace. I have chosen physicists as one group to consider because many of them have sensed that their work might lead to the destruction of their species. I have chosen psychologists as another group, because I am a psychologist, and because I believe that psychologists have much to contribute toward achieving nuclear disarmament.

Moral Responsibility and the Role of the Creative Individual in History

Any discussion of moral responsibility rests on an assumption that human beings, individually and collectively, can affect the course of history. If history is an impersonal force not under our control, there can be no effective way for people to change it, and the concept of moral responsibility is meaningless or at best a delusion. In that case my argument should come to a halt now.

B. F. Skinner has recently taken an interesting position on the role of the individual in history (Skinner, 1981). He argued for recognition of "selection by consequences" as a "causal mode found only in living things, or in machines made by living things," and proposed that this idea be applied at three levels: to organic evolution, individual learning, and cultural change. At the third level he suggested a mysterious "we" who can "introduce new forms of behavior . . . But having done these things we must wait for selection to occur." He concluded his argument with a remark on the role of the individual in history: "So long as we cling to the view that a person is an initiating doer, actor, or causer of behavior, we shall probably continue to neglect the conditions which must be changed if we are to solve our problems" (Skinner, 1981, p. 504).

If Skinner is right, efficient operant conditioning would be the most favorable way of producing social change, and this would have definite implications for any discussion of giftedness. Unfortunately, our species will have little or no opportunity to experience the benefits of operant conditioning in regard to nuclear war. A different gift must be exploited: vision, or the ability to imagine possible futures without experiencing them.

A small group of gifted and creative physicists who were at the center of research leading up to the destruction of Hiroshima and Nagasaki accepted this visionary function and its role in history. To be sure, there were many brilliant physicists who did not exercise this visionary function in the moral domain, some even denying moral responsibility for the consequences of their work. My aim is neither to insist upon nor deny the occurrence or even prevalence of such cases, but to point out the existence of those physicists who did vigorously seek out moral responsibility.

Throughout the 1930s, a series of developments in physics brought the age of nuclear warfare closer. As early as 1935, Irène and Frédéric Joliot-Curie received the Nobel Prize for chemistry for their discovery of artificial radioactivity. On that occasion, Frédéric Joliot-Curie said, "scientists who can construct and demolish elements at will may also be capable of causing nuclear transformations of an explosive character" (Jungk, 1958, p. 48).

Even earlier, in October 1933, Leo Szilard, a Hungarian physicist, had begun to sketch the features of a chain reaction. By 1935, he was frightened enough to begin to urge his colleagues toward a policy of secrecy and restraint regarding research that might lead to the use of nuclear weapons. In 1938 and 1939, further research made it clear to the Olympian few of modern physics that the making of nuclear weapons was indeed feasible. Szilard, now joined by Enrico Fermi and others, renewed efforts to persuade scientists to stop working in this direction. They failed. As it became clear that physicists everywhere would understand the potential of nuclear weapons, the same inner circle changed their goal. Now the aim was to develop the bomb before the Nazis got it. In this aim they succeeded.

Much later, Heisenberg, who stayed in Germany throughout the war, said, "In the summer of 1939 twelve people might still have been able, by coming to mutual agreement, to prevent the construction of atom bombs." Jungk, from whom I take this account, added, "He himself and Fermi, who were undoubtedly included among the twelve, ought then to have taken the initiative. But they let the opportunity go by. Their powers of political and moral imagination failed them . . . They never succeeded in achieving thought and action appropriate to the future consequences of their invention" (Jungk, 1958, p. 81).

Skinner could certainly take these events as support for his position on the futility of personal agency. If he is right, then institutional forces that are moving toward nuclear war must stumble on until they teach us their terrible lesson of consequences. But past failures of moral imagination do not mean that there is no such thing, nor that successes are impossible.

I have called this section "Moral Responsibility and the Role of the Creative Individual in History." But the affirmation of individual creativity is no denial of human solidarity and collaboration. One can believe, as I do, in individual human greatness without subscribing to the great man theory of history (Gruber, 1983). All sorts of collaboration are possible and necessary. Collaboration made the bomb. The kind of gift that will be needed if humanity is to survive must include the ability of very different people to work together. People who work for a common goal need not be similar; it is more likely that they must be different. A large and complex problem requires a variety of talents, including the skills for pooling them effectively.

There is an odd feature of the early history of nuclear fission that brings out this point. Frederick Soddy was one of the great pioneers in the study of radioactivity. In 1921 he received the Nobel Prize for work on isotopes. In 1909 he wrote a popular book, *Interpretation of Radium*. The physicists and chemists of that early day already had some idea of the immense energy of the atom, and of its potential for good or evil. The prescient H. G. Wells read Soddy's book, thought about the energy in the atom, and, in 1910, wrote *The World Set Free*, a short, tract-like novel about science out of control, the perfection of a nuclear chain reaction, an atomic war, and the destruction of civilization. The optimistic title comes from the aftermath. Enough of humanity survives to build a World Republic in which "the vast mass of people [expressed] a long smothered passion to make things. The world broke out into making, and at first mainly into aesthetic making" (p. 285). This was after the "catastrophe of the atomic bombs which shook men out of cities and businesses and economic relations, shook them also out of their old established habits of thought" (p. 287). After reading this book in the mid-1930s, Leo Szilard came to believe that atomic bombs could actually be built.

So Wells, the literary man, listened to the scientist Soddy. Then the scientist Szilard listened to the literary man. This coupling of scientific and literary imaginations almost worked to prevent or delay the manufacture of nuclear weapons. (I have pieced this story together from several sources: Jungk, 1958; Lifton & Falk, 1982; Wells, 1910; West, 1984.)

Domains of Giftedness

It is not necessary to decide whether moral responsibility constitutes a unitary domain of giftedness, any more than does music or physics. Perhaps the only serious treatment of the history of any domain in which personality, ability structures, intradisciplinary history, and social history are all considered together is *Born Under Saturn* by Wittkower and Wittkower (1969). Their findings led them to argue "most strongly against the existence of a timeless constitutional type of artist" (p. 293). If such is the case for the domain of art, why not expect something similar for the domain of moral responsibility? Such an approach does not diminish the importance of studying the social function and organization, media, history, and contents of any domain—and the changing psychological requirements imposed by these historical conditions. To demand that the properties of a domain be timeless and unchanging is to adopt an ahistorical Platonism that would probably destroy the whole field of social science.

To take another tack, anyone hoping to find a unitary domain with a unique and stable factor structure would expect to find certain correlations among abilities. For example, it is often pointed out that mathematicians (and mathematical physicists like Einstein) are frequently good performing musicians. But I know of no case in which a great mathematician was also a great musician. Many great composers have also been great instrumentalists—not a combination found among mathematicians who play music. This does not mean that music loses its status as a domain, rather, that the domain of music is a social-historical fact and a realm into which different people move in different ways.

Music and poetry also seem related, but there are, I think, no great musicians who are also great poets. On the other hand, at least one great visual artist, William Blake, was also a great poet. And a few great poets have also written great prose, notably John Milton. Shakespeare's sonnets alone would make him great, as of course would his plays, but he wrote no prose that we know of.

Thus, whether or not domains of giftedness are unitary, it is evident that at this level of very high achievement there are at least some cases of great work in more than one domain. But there is little reason to argue, in the cases I have cited, that creative achievement in one domain imposed the responsibility of work in another field. Matters stand a little differently in the field of moral responsibility. A case can be made for the claim that creative people in every domain could use both their eminence and their mastery of a field in the cause of human survival.

At least two Nobel prizes reflect such a dual capacity. Linus Pauling received the 1954 Nobel prize in chemistry for his work on the nature of the chemical bond and the 1962 Nobel peace prize for his part in the campaign for an atmospheric test ban treaty. Bertrand Russell received the 1950 Nobel prize, not for *Principia Mathematica*, but for his "philosophical works . . . or service to moral civilization" (Clark, 1976, p. 512). The Nobel committee was clearly aware of Russell's long career as a pacifist.

A few years later, in 1955, Russell drafted the famous Einstein–Russell statement calling on all nations to renounce the use of nuclear weapons, a move that gave great impetus to the involvement of eminent scientists in the effort. The underlying raison d'être for the statement and for assembling Nobelists and other eminent signatories was the belief that eminence in one domain, such as in science, imposes moral responsibility on the individual that may require activity in other domains.

Moral Responsibility and Psychology

The psychology of morality has not always had a comfortable place in general and developmental psychology. Even William James, who thought and wrote much on the subject, gave only 4 pages in his 1,400-page *Principles of Psychology* (1890/1950) to a section on "Aesthetic and Moral Principles" and concluded, "An adequate treatment of the way in which we come by our aesthetic and moral judgements would require a separate chapter, which I cannot conveniently include in this book" (1890/1950, vol. 2, p. 675). In an important and pioneering collection of papers on developmental psychology (Barker, Kounin, & Wright, 1943), the subject received scant treatment—a mention in passing in a chapter on personality development.

Piaget's seminal work, *The Moral Judgment of the Child* (1932/1965), is the starting point for almost all modern research on moral development. But Piaget himself became generally dissatisfied with his early work (from the 1920s to the 1930s) on the egocentrism of childhood. He included in this category his work on moral judgment and referred to it very little in his later years (see Gruber, 1982b). In the Festschrift celebrating his 70th birthday (Bresson & deMontmillon, 1966), there was only one brief reference to *The Moral Judgment of the Child* and in that for his 80th birthday, none. Important and excellent discussions and surveys of Piaget's work sometimes fail to mention this topic altogether (e.g., Boden, 1980; Voyat, 1982). In Geneva, in the early 1980s, there is no work in progress on moral development.

The page is by no means completely blank. James did do seminal work on the subject of moral development in *The Varieties of Religious Experience* (1902/1958), written more than a decade after *Principles* was finished. His near contemporary (and in his time equally luminous), James Mark Baldwin, did not neglect the subject (Baldwin, 1897; see also various chapters in Broughton & Freeman-Moir, 1982). Piaget's work did not spring unannounced from his fertile brow, but was part of a significant Genevan tradition. He did write *Moral Judgment*, and he did open the path to Kohlberg's influential work.

My point is not that there has been total neglect of the psychology of morality but rather that this great domain of human experience has only recently begun to find its stable place in scientific psychology. There are probably three main reasons for this. First, under the severe tutelage of positivist philosophy, many social scientists strove for decades for a value-free social science. Today that impossible and undesirable dream has been almost shattered by the whole enterprise of the modern sociology of knowledge. Second, in more recent years, when the time might have been ripe for a new upsurge of interest in moral issues, the "cognitive revolution" has in many quarters prevented the study of moral issues from taking on its own special character. Indeed, both Piaget and Kohlberg themselves have mainly applied the Piagetian insights of cognitive-development psychology and genetic epistemology to this domain. Their finding, that there are striking parallels between stage-wise development of moral judgment and stage-wise cognitive development, is the main result, and it is always reported with the clear implication that cognitive development controls moral development. Third, the psychology of affectivity and the psychology of aesthetic experience are both still extremely weak. It is my guess that a mature psychology of morality cannot develop without an understanding of how values become infused with moral passion. The scientific tools to carry out that task do not yet exist.

It should be added here that important special aspects of the moral domain have occupied the attention of some psychologists over the past 50 years. During and just after the Hitler regime in Germany (1933–1945), there were some significant attempts to explain the rise of fascism, such as Fromm's *Escape From Freedom* (1941), and that Americanized empirical outcropping of the Frankfurt School, *The Authoritarian Personality* (Adorno, Frenkel-Brunswik, Levinson, & Sanford, 1950). In the latter work, the authors studied a large panel of American subjects and attempted to explain how people with a certain character structure might be susceptible to authoritarian political movements. But there has been no thorough attempt to connect that work with the holocaust literature and with knowledge of moral development. Psychologists' reflections on evil are no less disjointed than their grasp of moral responsibility.

At the end of World War II, a group of distinguished psychologists published *Human Nature and Enduring Peace* (Murphy, 1945), including a psychologists' manifesto to the effect that war is not inevitable, not inscribed in "human nature." There has always been a steady flow of work about the psychology of aggression and war, although not large in amount compared to research such as that on discrimination learning in the rat. Throughout the 1950s, 60s, and 70s, various egalitarian movements (especially those for racial equality and women's rights) were reflected in increased psychological interest in justice morality. Now, in the 1980s, the threat of nuclear war looms ever larger, and there are renewed attempts to understand the moral issues involved in making war and making peace. It is notable that authors of important papers on this subject tend to treat nations as though they were individuals: Nations have ideals, they make assumptions about other nations, they repress unpleasant thoughts, and they believe in their own rightness.

It is certainly useful to examine the shared belief system underlying the justification of war and strategies that may lead to war. But so far, as psychologists, we have neglected the point that social change is made by social movements, that effective movements require effective leaders and devoted participants who give their best efforts to the cause—in short, people who take responsibility. (At present, both the search for peace and the arms race are treated in the media mainly as a set of cognitive dilemmas having to do with outguessing and outgunning the other side— but not by too wide a margin, because that might provoke aggressive action.) If peace is a moral imperative for which people must struggle, then psychologists need to understand the emergence, development, and functioning of those unfortunately too few who take on extraordinary moral responsibility.

Developmental Theory and Giftedness

The most prominent theories of developmental stages are ill suited for explaining extraordinary moral responsibility. They are, rather, intended to explain the normal or species-typical course of development that has evolved in a relatively stable environment. Focusing attention either on species-typical or culture-wide accomplishments, they draw on the embryological metaphors of regular, highly predictable, stage-wise development within a stable environment. This may well be appropriate for understanding species-typical development. But the study of giftedness and creativity focuses not on the typical but on the atypical and innovative. Here, the metaphors of "creative evolution" (Bergson, 1911) and Darwin's insistence on evolutionary divergence (Gruber, 1978) may be more appropriate.

Let us consider the general form of most stage theories. Each stage depends strictly on its predecessors. The occurrence of the later stages therefore implies the previous occurrence of the earlier ones. Thus, A $\subset$ B $\subset$ C $\subset$ D $\subset$ E $\subset$ F. In such celebrated sequences as Freud's, Piaget's and Erikson's stage theories, only a single line of development is considered; they are *unilinear stage theories*. But the general form of argument, which might be called *backward implication*, can be modified to permit multilinear developmental pictures.

The geneticist-embryologist Waddington (1957) advanced the notion of *homeorhesis*: A given developmental pathway is guaranteed by a number of constraints on development that stabilize it. In Waddington's metaphor of the "epigenetic landscape," these constraints operate much like the sides of a valley, down which a ball is rolling or a stream is flowing; minor deviations may occur, but the slopes act as a regulating mechanism, and in the main, movement follows the contour of the bottom. Waddington used this model to explain both the extremely regular course of species-typical development and the occasional major deviations that open up new "valleys" or developmental pathways. Piaget made use of the idea of homeorhesis, but only to explain the regular appearance of a single developmental pathway. In effect, he postulated an epigenetic landscape with only one valley and very steep sides. To deal with a rapidly changing world in which our species can adapt and survive, psychologists need to conceptualize development as being open and capable of producing totally new adaptations to totally new conditions (see Gruber, 1982a).

Evolutionary divergence lies at the heart of Darwin's theory. His discovery of the explanation of the evolutionary necessity of divergence may be as important as the theory of natural selection itself. His image of a diverging and irregularly branching pattern of development contrasts with the unilinear theories just described. To be sure, these two kinds of models do not necessrily contradict each other. One might be relevant from conception to birth or to a certain age; the other might be relevant in the time beyond. But it remains the case that in psychology this second kind of model has hardly been elaborated. Werner (1948) made a good start in that direction, but his ideas lie fallow now.

Corresponding to the contemporary theoretical emphasis on species-typical aspects of moral development, the same stress can be found in empirical studies. A survey that I have made of recent volumes of *Child Development* and *Developmental Psychology* (1978–1982) reveals that almost no attention is given to individual differences or exceptional cases. Even when variability data are given or when an exceptional response is mentioned, variability is treated as stemming from errors of measurement or from a flaw in the hypothesis, not as a subject with its own intrinsic worth.

In *Beyond Universals* (1980), Feldman has argued that developmental theory must concern itself neither with species-typical behavior alone nor with unique, idiosyncratic behavior alone, but with both. Moreover, he has argued, developmental theory will remain weak and incomplete until it can deal with the transitions between unique and universal psychological characteristics.

Feldman's current work (in press) on child prodigies represents an important exception to this leveling or averaging treatment of developmental issues. This work focuses on exceptional children who satisfy a very high criterion level in the fields of chess, music, writing, and science. In a recent conversation Feldman has informed me that in the course of his search for prodigies in these fields he also discovered several cases of children who invite the description "morally exceptional." In one instance a child expressed his moral gifts by protecting another gifted child, who was gifted in more readily recognized domains, against the collective persecution to which children in school often subject the exceptional child.

Although developmental psychologists who are concerned with moral development have not addressed themselves to the individual case or to the exceptional person, there are various other contexts in which information is available. For example, in *Their Brothers' Keepers*, Friedman (1978) studied Christians in Nazi-occupied Europe who risked their own and their families' lives to help endangered Jews. Kren, a historian, and Rappoport, a psychologist, gave a reflective account of resistance to extermination of self and others in *The Holocaust and the Crisis of Human Behavior* (1980). Gaylin, a psychiatrist, described five cases in detail in his *In the Service of Their Country: War Resisters in Prison* (1970). I add to this list Goodman's (1981) study, *Death and the Creative Life*; although she did not address herself to the particular issue of moral responsibility, her panel of 22 creative artists and scientists reveal their concerns with issues and perspectives that stand outside themselves and their own work.

Those works deal with people's struggles against established powers that are seen as committing large-scale human devastation. These are the records of people outside the "Establishment." They are interesting and important because in the historical situation we confront—as in all situations requiring creative innovation—there must be some presumption against the established way of doing things. But an equally interesting, and in some ways perhaps more important, panel of exceptional cases comprises those individuals who succeed inside an established order and then reconsider its assumptions and their commitments. These are people with certified gifts, expertise, and eminence.

I now turn to an examination of three such cases within the profession of psychology: William James, B. F. Skinner, and Charles Osgood. As will become apparent, far from representing similar patterns or points of view, these men reveal the diverse ways in which moral responsibility may be expressed.

William James

James's classic essay *The Moral Equivalent of War*, appeared in 1910, when he was 68 years old, but its period of gestation extended over his lifetime. His father was a devout and active Swedenborgian, who published 13 books in defense of his faith. A man of inherited wealth, he was able to publish all the books at his own expense; this was also a necessity, for they did not sell. He never had to work for a living, and this may be reflected in his theological preoccupations—primarily a man's personal relation with his God, redemption, and salvation. Anderson (1980) has described a stage theory that appears in Henry James's father's theology:

In the first step God establishes man, but in such a way that man has no connection to the divine. In this state man is utterly selfish, and it is impossible for him to attain salvation through moral action or by following ecclesiastical rules. The second step is the experience of "vastation" [something like crisis, emptying, moratorium]. Vastation is the preliminary to the third step, redemption, the process by which man gives up his selfishness and becomes unified with society and with God. (p. 85)

This movement from destructive egocentricity to constructive and redemptive sociality can be seen also in Piaget's early poem, "The Mission of the Idea" (1915/1977), and of course, in James's *Moral Equivalent of War*.

William James experienced considerable paternal pressure to become a scientist, more specifically one who would justify his father's theology with the tools of science. Eventually, he conceded far enough to study medicine, biology, and physiology at Harvard and at several places in Europe. These studies led, after some detours, to his teaching of anatomy and physiology, psychology, and philosophy at Harvard, beginning in 1873. It is James's resistance and his detours that are pertinent to the topic of this chapter.

During the years 1855 to 1860 he traveled to Europe, lived in Geneva, and studied painting both abroad and at home. He certainly could draw beautifully. All this led to a protracted double conflict. The son had trouble choosing between art and science, and he had even more trouble in communicating to his father his unwillingness to embrace Swedenborgian theology. William finally decided for science, but it is not clear to what extent he was capitulating to paternal pressure and to what extent he was choosing the field in which he felt his greater talents lay.

During the years 1867 to 1872 (age 25 to 30) William suffered a profound crisis in which he could do little work, although he does seem to have studied a great deal. His difficulty was a crisis of will: how to believe in personal efficacy, how to decide that anything was worth doing, and how to do it? Then he read the French philosopher Charles Renouvier, and on April 30, 1870, recorded in his diary, "I think that yesterday was a crisis in my life." He embraced Renouvier's definition of free will: "the sustaining of a thought *because I choose to* when I might have other thoughts." And he exclaimed, "My first act of free will shall be to believe in free will" (cited in Perry, 1948/1964, p. 121).

Early in this period of darkness, in January 1868, James wrote a letter to his friend, Thomas Ward, in which he outlined two major currents of thought that were to preoccupy him for years to come: "the thought of having a will," and the idea of "belonging to a brotherhood of men" that would enable him to "contribute to the weal of the species" through the exercise of his will (Anderson, 1980, p. 122).

The long chapter, "Will," in *The Principles of Psychology* does not appear until Chapter 26. In fact, most of it had already appeared in essays published in 1880 and 1888. The chapter covers a wide spectrum. At one extreme is the baffling question of how the movement of a finger could be construed as purposeful, and at the other extreme, the concept of personal heroism. Of the latter he wrote:

> When a dreadful object is presented, or when life as a whole turns up its dark abysses to our view, then the worthless ones among us lose their hold on the situation altogether, and either escape from its difficulties by averting their attention, or if they cannot do that, collapse into yielding masses of plaintiveness and fear . . . But the heroic mind does differently. To it, too, the objects are sinister and dreadful, unwelcome, incompatible with wished-for things. But it can face them if necessary, without for that losing its hold upon the rest of life. The world thus finds in the heroic man its worthy match and mate . . . He can *stand* this Universe . . . He must be counted with henceforth; he forms a part of human destiny. (James, 1890/1950, Vol. 2, p. 579).

From 1895 to 1904, James was especially concerned about American imperialism. He wrote ten letters to the press criticizing American colonialism in Venezuela and the Philippines. His 1904 address at the 13th Universal Peace Congress foreshadowed his 1910 essay, *The Moral Equivalent of War*. He served for a time as vice-president of the Anti-Imperialist League.

The freshness of *The Moral Equivalent of War* is preserved today. In this pacifist document James attributed great human qualities to the antagonist, the "war party." He took for granted that there are extraordinary people and energies on the other side, and that these must be enlisted if peace is to prevail. James gave a quick sketch of the history and horrors of war and summed up:

> Modern war is so expensive that we feel trade to be a better avenue to plunder; but modern man inherits all the innate pugnacity and all the love of glory of his ancestors. Showing war's irrationality and horror is of no effect upon him. The horrors make the fascination. War is the *strong* life . . . Our ancestors have bred pugnacity into our bone and marrow, and thousands of years of peace won't breed it out of us . . . At the present day, civilized opinion is a curious mental mixture. The military instincts and ideals are as strong as ever, but are confronted by reflective criticisms which sorely curb their ancient freedom. (James, 1910, pp. 312–314)

Thus, in spite of James's insistent Darwinism and biological determinism, another intellectual note was added—civilized reflection.

James sought conciliation and continued: "Pacifist though I am, I will refuse to speak of the bestial side of the war-régime . . . and consider only the higher aspects of militaristic sentiment . . . intrepidity; contempt of softness, surrender of private interest, obedience to command" (pp. 316–323). James's solutions are as follows:

> Pacifists ought to enter more deeply into the aesthetical and ethical point of view of their opponents . . . this is my idea . . . instead of military conscription a conscription of the whole youthful population to form for a certain number of years a part of the army enlisted against *Nature* . . . Great indeed is Fear; but it is not, as our military enthusiasts believe and try to make us believe, the only stimulus known for awakening the higher ranges of men's spiritual energy. (pp. 320–328)

James's remedy (a sort of spiritual forerunner of the Peace Corps) seems inadequate today, but has it ever been tried on a wide-enough scale?

Woodward (1980) has written an excellent account of the way in which James's work on the will affected the later history of the ideas of purpose, teleology, feedback, and motivation in American psychology. But James's work was not simply a chapter in the science of a largely cognitive psychology; it grew out of his early moral concerns and fed into his later moral and social thought. The 1910 essay and its history show how a central moral concern, coupled with an idea of the morally effective person, permeated the thinking of one of the founders of modern psychology.

B. F. Skinner

Although I do not agree with much of Skinner's psychology, I recognize that he has been an intensely moral psychologist for many years, striving to put his scientific thinking to social use. *Walden II* (Skinner, 1948) was an immensely popular book and led to the establishment of an intentional community with the same name. I have already referred to his use of a mysterious "we" standing above individuals. Similarly, in *Walden II* Skinner resorted to a directing personality who stood outside the system of positive reinforcement. *Beyond Freedom and Dignity* (Skinner, 1971) also received great critical attention, much of it negative.

It is of some interest in connection with the theme of this chapter that Skinner (1938) decried both the theoretical place and the practical use given to the idea of negative reinforcement. Surely Skinner or one of his disciples would view the rapidly developing failure of the MAD strategy (Mutually Assured Destruction) of nuclear deterrence as an unhappy vindication of his critique of punishment.

In his autobiography Skinner (1976) stated that he read Bertrand Russell's *Philosophy* (1927) while floundering in his "Dark Year," just after graduating from college. It was Russell's clear and enthusiastic account that led Skinner to J. B. Watson and started him toward his lifelong career as a behaviorist. A little later the same year, he read an article in the *New York Times Magazine* in which Pavlov was praised to the skies. This tipped the balance, moving him away from his unpromising start as a writer and toward graduate work in psychology. (Skinner's youthful efforts as a writer have recently been described by Coleman [1984], whose account I read after writing this chapter. The picture Coleman gives is consonant with what I have written.)

Little social conscience or public morality is evident in Skinner's younger years. In his autobiography there are long accounts of various practical jokes, odd jobs, and his adolescent sexual worries. He characterized his college years as "intellectual vandalism"—probably a little overdrawn. Those were years of prosperity and self-satisfaction for middle-class America, and Skinner was a member of an upwardly mobile family. His social concerns came later. From his own account, *Walden II* did not come out of any long-abiding prior commitment. At a dinner party in 1945 (when he was 41 years old) he had a conversation about what could come after the war, which led to the idea for the book. Then, in 1948, "to my surprise, I began to write *Walden II*" (Skinner, 1967). In 1977 Skinner summed up his position on the controversy generated by that book:

> *Walden II* was an early essay in the design of a culture. It was fiction, but I described a supporting science and technology in *Science and Human Behavior* (1953). . . . I returned to the issue in *Beyond Freedom and Dignity* in 1971. Unfortunately, that title led many people to believe that I was opposed to freedom and dignity. I did, indeed, argue that people are not in any scientific sense free or responsible for their achievements, but I was concerned with identifying and promoting the conditions under which they *feel* free and worthy . . . . There is a further goal: what lies beyond freedom and dignity is the survival of the species, and the issues I first discussed in *Walden II* have become much more pressing as the threat of a catastrophic future becomes clearer. Unfortunately, we move only slowly toward effective action. (pp. 380–381)

Skinner is an interesting case because he came late to his expressions of social concern and because, as the embodiment of tough-minded empiricism in psychological science, he still found time to write his utopian novel and other reflections on large human problems. Until they know much more about it psychologists should expect surprises in their studies of the development of moral responsibility.

Charles E. Osgood

On June 10, 1963, President John F. Kennedy announced a "Strategy for Peace." He found something to praise the Russians for and declared that the United States was stopping all atmospheric tests of nuclear weapons, and would not resume them unless another country did so first. On June 15th, Soviet Premier Kruschev announced that the Soviet Union was stopping the production of strategic bombers. On August 8th, the United States, Great Britain, and the Soviet Union signed a partial test ban treaty (agreeing not to test nuclear weapons in the atmosphere, in outer space, or under water). A thaw in the cold war seemed under way. The sociologist Amitai Etzioni called this "The Kennedy Experiment" (1967; see also Osgood, 1980). In his *Autobiography*, Osgood, after recounting these facts, remarked, "But then, on November 22, 1963, the Kennedy Experiment came to an abrupt end in Dallas, Texas" (1980).

The story has a place in Osgood's *Autobiography* because in 1962 he had published his book, *An Alternative to War or Surrender*, in which he had proposed the strategy of Graduated and Reciprocated Initiatives in Tension Reduction (GRIT). It was a fitting idea for a cognitive behaviorist like Osgood to propose negotiation through actions rather than through the long and often dismal process of negotiation through words. What Osgood proposed was the strategy of announcing and carrying out a small but clearcut act in the direction of disarmament or tension reduction and waiting for the other side to react. This process, he argued, could lead to a general winding down of the arms race.

Osgood had sent his book to Kennedy in 1962, together with other papers on the same subject. No one, including Osgood, would suggest that a single source of influence could determine the complex decisions at stake. But a clearly reasoned argument in favor of a particular strategy may help a group that is considering a move in the same direction to clarify its thinking. After all, strategies do arise out of thought and argument.

Osgood did not become involved in efforts toward arms control and disarmament through a direct path. In 1958, Osgood was 42 years old, already a very distinguished psychologist. He had published his massive and influential *Method and Theory in Experimental Psychology* in 1953 and *The Measurement of Meaning* in 1957. In 1958, he spent a fellowship year at the Center for Advanced Study in the Behavioral Sciences at Stanford University. His plan was to write a book to be called *Method and Theory in Psycholinguistics*. That book never got written. Osgood's office at the Center lay between that of the cognitive psychologist, George Miller, and that of the psychiatrist, Jerome Frank. The latter had already begun to bring his professional expertise and other gifts to bear on the problems of war and peace. He and Osgood joined forces at the Center in organizing seminars on the threat to survival of the human species in the nuclear age. This work led eventually to Osgood's book on GRIT.

There is nothing much in Osgood's early life to suggest that his work would take this direction. His boyhood certainly fits the description of that of any gifted youngster. He read science fiction and had a wide-ranging interest in jazz (he still plays a mean piano). Giving up early aspirations to be a novelist-journalist, he committed himself to becoming a scientific psychologist. After studies at Dartmouth and Yale, he did a stint in the Air Force, where his main duties were research for the improvement of gunnery training. After that he had an almost meteoric career at Yale University and the Universities of Connecticut and Illinois, the latter at which he has remained for many years. He began publishing psychological articles as an undergraduate and has worked steadily in psycholinguistics, social psychology, and some branches of experimental psychology.

In his *Autobiography*, he describes his work under three themes: Theme I—"Meaning in Individuals"—is essentially an attempt to apply a liberalized, cognitivized Hullian behavior theory to the problem of the meaning of words. Theme II—"Meaning Across Cultures"—is a massive, international attempt to elaborate the idea of a multidimensional semantic space that could account for all meaning in all languages. Theme III—"Meaning for Human Survival"—is the effort for world peace described above (Osgood, 1980).

Theme I dominated his efforts in the 1950s, and Theme II in the 1960s. Theme III did not appear actively until 1958 and has been very important but intermittent ever since. Osgood's personal ambivalence about making a full commitment to Theme III is shown in two parts of his *Autobiography*. In 1963, when he was preparing his presidential address to the American Psychological Association, he knew that everyone expected him to make a speech about international affairs. After much hesitation he spoke "On Understanding and Creating Sentences," restricting himself to pressing issues in psycholinguistics (cited in Osgood, 1980).

Somewhat ruefully and a little puzzled about himself, Osgood ended his *Autobiography* with a confession:

> One might think that, as my estimated probabilities for the survival of Mankind in the nuclear age go down (as they have been doing over the past few years), my urge to give highest priority to writing *Mankind 2000?* should go up. But just the reverse has been the case. As prospects for Mankind's survival go down, the more I feel driven— like an artist getting ready to "paint his last picture"—to write my last scientific contribution, *Toward an Abstract Performance Grammar*, regardless of whether anyone will be around to read it. It is as if I, too, am subject to a selfish egoism that, under stress, takes precedence over altruism. (Osgood, 1980, p. 387)

Osgood, in spite of his conflicts has not done at all badly, has he? He has given much of his time and energy, proposed an original idea for tension reduction, and found many platforms from which to expound it. He has used his mind and his eminence well. From the whole tone of his *Autobiography* it is clear that he thinks of himself as an effective human being, and he thinks that individuals can have some effect on the course of history. And yet, when faced with this most urgent question of all, like most of us, he has held his energy in check and has worried about that, too.

"Ought" Implies "Can" Implies "Create"

Any "ought" statement necessarily implies "can": It makes no sense to say that something ought to be done unless it can be done. But how do we know what can be done? In the realm of difficult, intractable problems, such as the threat to species survival, only protracted, vigorous, and creative work can be expected to reveal the full range of the possible. Creative work almost always takes a long time (Gruber, 1981; Westfall, 1980).

If Piaget and Inhelder's (1955/1958) description of adolescent intellectual development is even approximately right, that is the time of life when the real becomes a special case of the possible. At least for some, it is no longer necessary to be a prisoner of either the past or the present. But this surge in capacity for abstract and visionary thought is not instantly translated into effective creative work. Nor does a fruitful and impassioned integration of moral responsibility and creativity necessarily follow.

Psychologists have not produced a very clear picture of the course of moral responsibility as it becomes interwoven with other features of the creative person's career. Lehman (1953) studied the age of creative achievement in many fields of endeavor. In general, he found that both first and major achievements in mathematics and in the natural sciences come rather early in life, somewhat later in the life sciences, and even later in literature.

Lehman's results suggest that achievement in the ethical realm comes, not very late, but somewhat later than in other fields. The picture is actually quite variable. James's concern with moral responsibility was lifelong, but his public productive achievements in this realm came rather late; Osgood and Skinner made their ethical concerns public in their 40s. Piaget's early passionate involvement with moral issues, as a public scientific concern, seems to have diminished or gone underground by about his 40th year (Gruber, 1982b).

A striking phenomenon has recently appeared in American life, a special sort of retirement syndrome typified by men like Rickover, MacNamara, and Colby. Once out of the military institutions in which they enjoyed eminence and power, they come to the fore with deep misgivings about the chance of avoiding catastrophic nuclear war. Thus, although the visionary function, and the distinction between the real and the possible, may become pronounced in adolescence, their expression in the moral domain displays an extremely variable pattern.

Different Ways of Thinking About Peace

Future research on morality, giftedness, and creativity must deepen understanding of the different ways of thinking and acting about the moral imperative of peace. It would be helpful to approach this task in as detached a spirit as possible, bearing in mind that there is not one right way. Let us compare three different ways of thinking about the threat to human survival. Each of them might have positive or negative consequences, depending on how it is employed.

Worst Case Thinking. One approach to moral issues is to dwell on extreme cases and their consequences, such as the firestorms produced by a nuclear war, the "nuclear winter" recently brought to public attention by Sagan and others (Ehrlich, 1984; Sagan, 1983a; Turco, Toon, Ackerman, Pollack, & Sagan, 1983), or the consequences of a limited nuclear war under a particularly unfavorable confluence of other circumstances. When Herman Kahn wrote *On Thermonuclear War* (1961) and introduced the phrase, "thinking the unthinkable," his intention was to increase the credibility of the United States' nuclear deterrent: He was endorsing and justifying the MAD (Mutually Assured Destruction) strategy. In contrast, when men like George Kennan (former U.S. Ambassador to the Soviet Union) or Nick Humphrey (British ethologist who made a celebrated appearance on BBC-TV) confess their enormous pain and difficulty in imagining the consequences of nuclear war, they are thinking about the unthinkable. They are not contemplating waging nuclear war or pretending to be prepared to wage it—they are opposing it and opposing the MAD strategy that might engender it.

Utopian Thinking. A second way of thinking about moral issues is to imagine some ideal end state and try to construct imaginatively what it might be like in all its detail, without much concern about how to reach the goal. Utopias are ways of making basic allegiances and premises clear, so that one person's Utopia is always another's prison. Even the idea of a world without war has its detractors. William James, too, thought that the institution of war did in fact evoke some of humankind's noblest qualities. Rather than sacrifice these, in *The Moral Equivalent of War* he proposed a Utopian arrangement that would let us eat our cake of peace and have our savage splendor. Boulding (1982) has argued that many people find it hard to work for peace because they have lost hope; they can no longer imagine a peaceful world. She has invented the ingenious device of workshops in which the participants are asked to imagine momentarily a world without armaments, then to imagine what the immediately preceding state of affairs would be like, and so on back to the present.

Systems Thinking. In his book, *The New Utopians*, Boguslaw (1965) argued that some social systems thinking is a modern form of utopianism. The particular form that I have in mind here is intended to be a contrast to the previously mentioned heuristics. Instead of imagining a drastic change in the world, one imagines a set of minimal changes that may accomplish a large and important result, but without upsetting anyone's apple cart. Some combination of improved hot line, cautious application of Osgood's GRIT idea, and mutually agreed peaceful surveillance (MAPS) might represent an application of this strategy. But it must be remembered that MAD is also put forth as an application of global systems thinking or, if not global, at least joined in by the two superpowers.

Each of these heuristics has the following characteristics. It is a general strategy that can be applied in more than one way and with varying outcomes. It delineates a form of idealization or limiting case. The thinker has the option of restricting her- or himself to dwelling in the limiting case, or of using it as a point of departure for further, possibly more realistic, thought.

In applying this line of thinking to the present concern with giftedness and creativity, one key point leaps into view. There is no reason to think that the same people will be good at or be invested in all three approaches. True, it is believed (on rather slender evidence) that a great abstract artist will also be a good, but not necessarily great, realistic painter. Picasso's early representative art is striking because it is Picasso's—but we do not laud him as though he were another Rembrandt.

If this line of thought has merit, it leads to the conclusion that there is no single turn of mind that can be labeled "moral giftedness," but rather a number of different ways of thinking, all of which could be useful if harnessed to the common goal. Then the gift needed is the human solidarity to mobilize the gifts we all have for that great moral purpose, the survival of our species.

References

Adorno, T. W., Frenkel-Brunswik, E., Levinson, D. J., & Sanford, R. N. (1950). *The authoritarian personality.* New York: Harper.

Anderson, J. W. (1980). *William James's depressive period (1867–1872) and the origins of his creativity: A psychobiographical study.* Unpublished doctoral dissertation, University of Chicago, IL.

Baldwin, J. M. (1897). *Social and ethical interpretations in mental development.* New York: Macmillan.

Barker, R. G., Kounin, J. S., & Wright, H. F. (Eds.). (1943). *Child behavior and development.* New York: McGraw-Hill.

Bergson, H. (1911). *Creative evolution.* London: Macmillan.

Boden, M. A. (1980). *Jean Piaget.* New York: Viking Press.

Boguslaw, R. (1965). *The new utopians.* Englewood Cliffs, NJ: Prentice-Hall.

Boulding, E. (1982, June). *Imaging a world without weapons.* Workshop conducted at the meeting of the Social Scientists and Nuclear War, City University of New York.

Bresson, F., & deMontmillon, M. (Eds.). (1966). *Psychologie et épistémologie génétique: Thèmes Piagetiens.* Paris, France: Dunod.

Bronfenbrenner, U. (1977). Toward an experimental ecology of human development. *American Psychologist, 32,* 513–531.

Broughton, J. M., & Freeman-Moir, D. J. (1982). *The cognitive-developmental psychology of James Mark Baldwin: Current theory and research in genetic epistemology*. Norwood, NJ: Ablex.

Brunswik, E. (1956). *Perception and the representative design of psychological experiments* (2nd ed.). Berkeley, CA: University of California Press.

Brunswik, E. (1957). Scope and aspects of the cognitive problem. In H. E. Gruber, K. R. Hammond, & R. Jessor (Eds.), *Contemporary approaches to cognition* (pp. 5–31). Cambridge, MA: Harvard University Press.

Carver, L. M. (1983). No first use: A view from Europe. *Bulletin of the Atomic Scientist, 39,* 22–26.

Clark, R. W. (1976). *The life of Bertrand Russell*. New York: Knopf.

Coleman, S. R. (1984). B. F. Skinner's other career. *History of Psychology Newsletter, 16,* 14–22.

Conference on Nuclear Warfare. (1982). *Declaration on prevention of nuclear war. Science, 218,* 448–449.

Ehrlich, A. (1984). Nuclear winter: A forecast of the climatic and biological effects of nuclear war. *Bulletin of the Atomic Scientists, 40,* 1S–16S.

Etzioni, A. (1976). The Kennedy experiment. *Western Political Quarterly, 20,* 361–380.

Feldman, D. H. (1980). *Beyond universals in cognitive development*. Norwood, NJ: Ablex.

Feldman, D. H. (in press). *Nature's gambit: Child prodigies and the development of human potential*. New York: Basic Books.

Friedman, P. (1978). *Their brothers' keepers*. New York: Holocaust Library/Schocken Books.

Fromm, E. (1941). *Escape from freedom*. New York: Farrar and Rinehart.

Gardner, H. (1983). *Frames of mind: The theory of multiple intelligences*. New York: Basic Books.

Gaylin, W. (1970). *In the service of their country: War resisters in prison*. New York: Viking Press.

Gilligan, C. (1982). *In a different voice: Psychological theory and women's development*. Cambridge: Harvard University Press.

Goodman, L. (1981). *Death and the creative life*. New York: Springer.

Gruber, H. E. (1978). Darwin's "Tree of Nature" and other images of wide scope. In J. Wechsler (Ed.), *On aesthetics in science* (pp. 121–140). Cambridge, MA: M.I.T. Press.

Gruber, H. E. (1981). On the relation between "Aha!" experiences and the construction of ideas. *History of Science, 19,* 41–59.

Gruber, H. E. (1982a). On the hypothesized relation between giftedness and creativity. In D. Feldman (Ed.), *New directions for child development: Developmental approaches to giftedness and creativity* (pp. 7–29). San Francisco: Jossey-Bass.

Gruber, H. E. (1982b). Piaget's mission. *Social Research, 49,* 239–264.

Gruber, H. E. (1983). History and creative work: From the most ordinary to the most exalted. *Journal of the History of the Behavioral Sciences, 19,* 4–15.

Gruber, H. E. (1985). From the epistemic subject to the unique creative person at work. *Archives de Psychologie, 53,* 167–185.

Hoffman, M. L. (1980). Moral development in adolescence. In J. Adelson, (Ed.), *Handbook of adolescent psychology* (pp. 295–343). New York: Wiley.

Hume, D. (1777). *A treatise of human nature*.

James, W. (1910). *The moral equivalent of war* (Leaflet No. 27). Association for International Conciliation. (Also published in *McClure's Magazine* and in *The Popular Science Monthly,* 1910)

James, W. (1950). *The principles of psychology* (Vols. 1–2). New York: Dover. (Original work published 1890)

James, W. (1958). *The varieties of religious experience: A study in human nature.* New York: Mentor. (Original work published 1902)

Janis, I. L., & Feshback, S. (1953). Effects of fear-arousing communications. *Journal of Abnormal and Social Psychology, 48,* 78–92.

Jungk, R. (1958). *Brighter than a thousand suns: A personal history of the atomic scientist.* New York: Harcourt Brace Jovanovich.

Kahn, H. (1961). *On thermonuclear war.* Princeton, NJ: Princeton University Press.

Kennan, G. F. (1981, June). A modest proposal. *New York Review of Books,* 14–16.

Kohlberg, L. (1973). The claim to moral adequacy of a highest stage of moral development. *Journal of Philosophy, 70,* 630–646.

Kohlberg, L. (1982). Moral development. In J.M. Broughton & D. J. Freeman-Moir, *The cognitive-development psychology of James Mark Baldwin: Current theory and research in genetic epistemology.* Norwood, NJ: Ablex.

Kren, G. M., & Rappoport, L. (1980). *The holocaust and the crisis of human behavior.* New York: Holmes & Meier.

Lehman, H. C. (1953). *Age and achievement.* Princeton, NJ: Princeton University Press.

Lifton, R. J., & Falk, R. (1982). *Indefensible weapons: The political and psychological case against nuclearism.* New York: Basic Books.

Mack, J. E. (1981). Psychological trauma. In R. Adams & S. Cullen (Eds.), *The final epidemic: Physicians and scientists on nuclear war* (pp. 21–34). Chicago: Educational Foundation for Nuclear Science.

Mischel, W., & Mischel, H.N. (1976). A cognitive social-learning approach to morality and self-regulation. In T. Lickona (Ed.), *Moral development and behavior.* New York: Holt, Rinehart and Winston.

Murphy, G. (1945). Human nature and enduring peace. *Third Yearbook of the Society for the Psychological Study of Social Issues.* Boston: Houghton Mifflin.

Osgood, C. E. (1953). *Method and theory in experimental psychology.* New York: Oxford University Press.

Osgood, C. E., Suci, G. J., & Tannenbaum, P. H. (1957). *The measurement of meaning.* Urbana: University of Illinois Press.

Osgood, C. E. (1962). *An alternative to war or surrender.* Urbana: University of Illinois Press.

Osgood, C. E. (1980). Autobiography: Focus on meaning in individual humans, across human cultures, and for survival of the human species. In G. Lindzey (Ed.), *A history of psychology in autobiography* (Vol. 7, pp. 335–393). San Francisco: Freeman.

Perry, R. B. (1964). *The thought and character of William James.* New York: Harper and Row. (Original work published 1948)

Piaget, J. (1965). *The moral judgment of the child.* New York: Free Press. (Original work published 1932)

Piaget, J. (1977a). Biology and war. In H. E. Gruber & J. Voneche (Eds.), *The essential Piaget* (pp. 38–41). New York: Basic Books. (Original work published 1918)

Piaget, J. (1977b). The mission of the idea. In H. E. Gruber & J. Voneche (Eds.), *The essential Piaget* (pp. 26–37). New York: Basic Books. (Original work published 1915)

Piaget, J., & Inhelder, B. (1958). *The growth of logical thinking from childhood to adolescence.* New York: Basic Books. (Original work published 1955)

Russell, B. (1927). *An outline of philosophy.* New York: New American Library.

Sagan, C. (1983a). Nuclear war and climatic catastrophe: Some implications. *Foreign Affairs, 62*, 257–292.

Sagan, C. (1983b, October 30). The nuclear winter. *Parade.*

Skinner, B. F. (1938). *The behaviour of organisms.* New York: Appleton.

Skinner, B. F. (1948). *Walden II.* New York: Macmillan.

Skinner, B. F. (1953). *Science and human behavior.* New York: Macmillan.

Skinner, B. F. (1967). Autobiography. In E.G. Boring & G. Lindzey (Eds.), *History of psychology in autobiography* (Vol. 5).

Skinner, B. F. (1971). *Beyond freedom and dignity.* New York: Knopf.

Skinner, B. F. (1976). *Particulars of my life.* New York: Knopf.

Skinner, B. F. (1977). The experimental analysis of operant behavior. *Annals of the New York Academy of Sciences, 291*, 374–382.

Skinner, B. F. (1981). Selection by consequences. *Science, 213*, 501–504.

Soddy, F. (1909). *Interpretation of radium.*

Straughan, R. (1983). From moral judgment to moral action. In H. Weinreich-Haste & D. Lock (Eds.), *Morality in the making: Thought, action and the social context* (pp. 125–140). New York: Wiley.

Takanishi, R. (1978). Childhood as a social issue: Historical roots of contemporary child advocacy movements. *Journal of Social Issues, 34*, 8–29.

Thomas, L. (1981, September). Unacceptable damage. *New York Review of Books,* pp. 3–5.

Turco, R. P., Toon, O. B., Ackerman, T. P., Pollack, J. B., & Sagan, C. (1983). Nuclear winter: Global consequences of multiple nuclear explosions. *Science, 222*, 1, 283–292.

Tyler, L. (1969). An approach to public affairs: Report of the ad hoc Committee on Public Affairs. *American Psychologist, 24*, 1–4.

Voyat, G. E. (1982). *Piaget systematized.* Hillsdale, NJ: Erlbaum.

Waddington, C.H. (1957). *The strategy of the genes.* London: Allen and Unwin.

Weinreich-Haste, H., & Lock, D. (Eds.). (1983). *Morality in the making: Thought, action and the social context.* New York: Wiley.

Wells, H. G. (1910). *The world set free.* London: Odhams Press.

Wells, H. G. (1911). *The country of the blind.* London: Nelson.

Werner, H. (1948). *Comparative psychology of mental development.* Chicago: Follet. (Original work published 1926)

West, A. (1984). *H. G. Wells: Aspects of a life.* New York: Random House.

Westfall, R. S. (1980). Newton's marvelous years of discovery and their aftermath: Myth versus manuscripts. *Isis, 71*, 109–121.

Wittkower, R., & Wittkower, M. (1969). *Born under Saturn: The character and conduct of artists.* New York: Norton.

Woodward, W. R. (1980). William James' psychology of will: Its revolutionary impact on American psychology. In J. Brozek (Ed.), *Exploration in the history of American psychology.* Lewisburg, PA: Bucknell University Press.

11. A Conceptualization of Intellectual Giftedness

Lloyd G. Humphreys
University of Illinois

This is a conceptual account of the nature of intelligence and of intellectually gifted children. I shall not attempt to review the literature concerning practice and research. Rather I shall provide a framework for developing programs for the gifted, understanding research on the gifted, and planning future research. The account is a traditional one of the individual differences genre. It is a direct descendant of the factor theories initiated by Spearman (1904) and of the tests developed by Binet and Simon (1905). I also draw heavily on my own theoretical and empirical contributions to the literature. The latter, in considerable number, have been made possible by Project Talent (Flanagan et al., 1962).

Within the domain of experimental cognitive psychology, there is considerable interest in individual differences. Knowledge of components in problem solving and of processes underlying cognitive behaviors is potentially relevant to an understanding of gifted individuals, but this knowledge has added very little to that understanding up to this point in time. In any event, that literature is left to others.

Dimensions of giftedness other than the intellectual will not be treated directly in this chapter. Athletes, musicians, and graphic artists can perform at gifted levels, but the talents involved are not primarily intellectual. There are small positive correlations among measures of individual differences in abilities, skills, and proficiencies in a wide range of talents that cover a much broader domain than the intellectual, but the determinants of these correlations are largely unknown. It is uncertain whether there is any causal significance in these small correlations, but it is noteworthy that desirable traits do tend to covary.

Other problem areas relevant to giftedness have also not been researched adequately. I shall of necessity make assertions that are supported only by my theoretical approach. If not always characterized as hypotheses, these assertions should be interpreted as such. Assertions involving values, on the other hand, are not directly researchable. Mine are unabashedly meritocratic.

The Centrality of Intelligence to Giftedness

The fundamental basis for intellectual giftedness is a high level of general intelligence. A person can be described as being narrowly gifted intellectually, such as being gifted only in mathematics or only in the mathematics of probability, but the basis for a person's level of attainment is his or her high general intelligence.[1] If a mathematically gifted group is first selected, it is of course true that the group's mean score on a test of general intelligence will be somewhat closer to the population mean than is its level of mathematical attainment. On the other hand, if a group is first selected in terms of its level of general intelligence, the group's scores in mathematics and in every other type of attainment will be closer to the population mean than will level of general intelligence. If such selection, either for narrow or general attainment, is made from a largely unselected population, the correlations among the several measures will be high and regression toward the mean on the measure not used for selection will be small. Among the various kinds of intellectual giftedness there is a great deal of communality.

A Definition of Giftedness

No a priori statement can be made about the size of the upper tail of a distribution of attainment that represents giftedness. The size of this tail depends on the needs of those who wish to use the description for some social purpose. The designation *gifted* can be applied to the highest one-tenth or the highest one-tenth to the fourth power.

---

[1] In people who have organic pathologies of the central nervous system, there is evidence for a good deal of specificity in intellectual functioning. I have not considered this literature in the present account because there is no reason to believe that development in the normal person is related to the patterns of behavior revealed following cerebral insult.

If there were some qualitative change that takes place in people with high levels of intelligence, one could define gifted less arbitrarily, but differences appear to be entirely ones of degree. When the two intellectual measures, or when the intellectual measure and the social criterion, have adequate ceilings and floors for measurement purposes, most regressions of X on Y and Y on X appear to be approximately linear.

In contrast, there is a qualitative change in the other tail of the distribution. There is an excess of very low scores in the lower tail and most of these are accompanied by organic involvement, which in turn, frequently has a genetic basis. When people represented by the lower tail are removed from the distribution, the frequencies of scores that are two or more standard deviations below the mean drop more nearly to those expected. For a valid diagnosis of mental retardation, it is essential to use organic etiology in addition to measures of intelligence and adaptivity. The three criteria can be used to place a child unequivocally in a diagnostic category. As will become clear later, behavioral measures of individual differences are not sufficiently stable over time to support such placement at either end of the distribution of intelligence. On the basis of this reasoning, there is no category of giftedness. One does not diagnose a condition. One merely cuts a frequency distribution at some arbitrary and convenient point in the upper tail at a given point in time.

Early Studies of the Gifted

The definition of giftedness as being represented by the upper end of a frequency distribution is highly traditional. It dates at least from the landmark studies of Cox (1926), Terman (1925), and Terman and Oden (1947, 1959). A closer look at Cox's retrospective study of the data on the early development of people whose attainments as adults were considered to be at the genius level is of interest because the data are not as well known as those derived from Terman's follow-up studies of high-scoring children. Also, Cox's results were recently misinterpreted, even maligned, in a popular but highly biased book by Gould (1981).

Cox assembled biographical data concerning those people of genius in her sample and asked trained examiners of the Stanford-Binet to evaluate the ability of her subjects to pass the age-graded items of the test at given chronological ages. For those who have administered and scored the protocols of a substantial number of tests, this is not an impossible task. Measurement error in the resulting IQs may be relatively large for individuals, but Cox was concerned with group trends. A more important problem was the sparse amount of biographical data available on various individuals in the sample, and Cox obtained a measure of this. She called this a measure of reliability, but it did not lead to the usual random measurement error. The procedure used in estimating IQs ensured that no one for whom little information was available would receive a high

IQ. Judges assigned an average IQ to everyone at the outset and proceeded from there. Thus, mean IQs of her gifted adults were either underestimated by the relative absence of early data or, at least, if one assumes that absent data indicated absent precociousness, not inflated.

In a follow-up, Terman's gifted group had high attainment as adults, on the average, but there was also substantial variability in the adult criterion information. High intelligence may be a necessary condition for high intellectual attainment, but other individual difference variables are involved. There are also important situational factors, labelled "luck" by Jencks (1972), that affect adult attainment. Examples are the availability of higher education and the quality and variety of the offerings. Family connections also fall in this category.

Intelligence and Educational Level

Perhaps the most convincing evidence for the centrality of intelligence in giftedness is so commonplace that its importance is often neglected. Being in a position to make a gifted contribution to society depends very largely on education, and education depends very largely on intelligence. (The argument is the same if "is associated strongly with" is substituted for "depends very largely on.") Intelligence test scores predict graduation from high school, application for admission to four-year colleges, acceptance into college, graduation from college, application to graduate or professional school, acceptance into graduate or professional school, and graduation from such schools. Furthermore, across the full range of talent, the predictions from intelligence tests are more accurate than are those from any other trait.

The relation between intelligence and educational level would be substantially higher than it is now if it were not for the wide range of academic standards among educational institutions. Among the high schools in Project Talent, a random sample of all of the nation's high schools, the variance of the mean scores on the intelligence composite of the 10th grade students was more than one-third of the total variance (Humphreys, Parsons, & Park, 1979, 1984). The high schools differed more in mean intelligence of the students than in mean socioeconomic status of the families. Similar data are not available for the nation's four-year colleges, but the variability is probably even greater than it is among high schools. There are a number of four-year colleges, for example, who select almost 100 percent of their regular admission students from the top 10 percent of the intelligence distribution. There are equivalent differences among graduate and professional schools, but even so the mean of these students is very high relative to the full range of talent. Further variability is introduced by the standards for the different academic disciplines. There is probably no higher scoring group of students than the graduate students in physics in a premier institution.

Intelligence and Occupation

The best data on the distribution of intelligence across occupations with the test data being obtained prior to entrance into the occupation, are from the Project Talent 11-year follow-up (Rossi, Bartlett, Campbell, Wise, & McLaughlin, 1975). Although a discriminant analysis of the data has not been published, inspection of the profiles indicates that the first and largest by far discriminant function defined by the cognitive tests depends on across-the-board differences in level of profile, or general intelligence. A unit-weighted composite of the tests that discriminate most sharply among occupations would produce individual differences not distinguishable from those obtained on a standard test of intelligence. It is not as apparent how the second discriminant would be defined, but it would probably represent differences among occupations associated with the verbal-numerical-educational and mechanical-spatial-practical major group factors of Vernon (1960). This discriminant would distinguish between lawyers and engineers as well as between clerks and mechanics. The third discriminant would probably be the more familiar verbal-quantitative distinction represented in the Scholastic Aptitude Test and in the Graduate Record Examination. The relatively weak third discriminant across the full range of talent is useful for undergraduate and graduate student selection and guidance because prior educational selection has restricted the variance of the general factor on which the first discriminant is based. Self-selection on the general factor in the decision to apply to a particular institution also enhances this effect.

Intelligence in Factor Studies

In any table of intercorrelations of cognitive measures obtained across a wide range of talent, there is evidence for a large general factor. Of course, there is evidence for the presence of group factors as well, but factor by factor these are typically small relative to the general factor in their respective contributions to variance. The latter is revealed basically by the ubiquitous positive correlations among cognitive measures, and can be computed by using oblique rotations and factoring in two or more orders as necessary. Humphreys (1962) adopted the hierarchical model from Vernon (1960) and has found no reason for discarding it (Humphreys, in press).

Humphreys, Parsons, and Park (1979) published evidence for the importance of the general factor that went beyond the variability of school means mentioned previously. They computed the intercorrelations of the means of 59 tests and 20 descriptive indices of the schools from which they were able to define four orthogonal factors. Only one of the factors bore a resemblance to one of Thurstone's (1938) primary mental abilities. This one was defined by tests similar to those loaded on his Perceptual Speed factor. Such tests involve the rapid identification of same and different among stimuli presented visually, but in individual data the scores contain little general factor variance. Differences among high schools on these measures may be associated with the racial composition of the school.

My colleagues and I (Humphreys et al., 1979) found that the largest contribution to variance of high school means was made by a factor general to the tests and to some of the school variables. Measures such as teaching salaries, rate of college attendance, and per capita pupil expenditures have modest loadings on this general intellectual factor. The remaining two factors—one describing rural schools and one parochial schools—were best and almost solely described by the school indices. According to analyses of intercorrelations based upon individual students, those tests that appear to be the best measures of intelligence had loadings in the school data of trivial size on all but the general factor. The investigators attempted to define other factors in the school means that could be identified as primary mental abilities, but without success. If such factors were important in demographic or curricular differences among schools, they should have appeared in the analysis. We therefore concluded that the important determinant of who goes where to high school, over and beyond rural residence or religious affiliation, is general intelligence.

Summary

In this section I have defined the intellectually gifted as those who have high levels of general intelligence, and I have begun to justify this conception. Intelligence is very general. It is reflected in the intercorrelations of cognitive tests, but more importantly, it is reflected in the ways in which we have organized our society. Intelligence test scores are highly related to the high school and college attended, to the amount of education attained, and to the occupation that a person selects. I also maintain that there is no diagnostic category of giftedness that is independent of a given stage of development. I shall return to this point in the next section.

The Nature of Intelligence

It is not imperative that the definition of a psychological construct follow common usage, nor that the definition precede research and measurement. One can start from the empirical correlates of a measuring instrument that has achieved an important place in both research and application. Physicists could measure both voltage and amperage before theory concerning the nature of electricity was well developed. Physics represents a more useful model for a psychologist than does cultural heritage.

Those who reject current intelligence tests as measures of a capacity or potential, the construct derived from our cultural heritage, embrace a conception of the trait that cannot be measured or inferred from measurements. Such conceptions are useless in either basic or applied science. On the other hand, many who accept present tests as being valid, or largely valid, have the same basic notion, derived from the same source, concerning the nature of intelligence. Present measures of intelligence, although invalid for the common conception of the trait, have many desirable attributes. Among these attributes are the correlates described in the preceding section. There is merit in bringing the construct of intelligence into line with well-established measurement operations and their socially important correlates.

A Definition of Intelligence

My definition of intelligence has been developing for many years, but has changed relatively little from the one I gave in 1971. Intelligence is the repertoire of knowledge and skills, categorized as intellectual or cognitive, available to a person at a particular point in time. A consensus of those who construct and do research with intelligence tests is the basis of this categorization. The Stanford-Binet and the various Wechsler tests sample the repertoire and help to define the consensus. Similarities of the items in these tests to the items in the 1905 Binet-Simon test also illustrate the consensus. Although there has been relatively little change to date, a consensus should change over time as data accumulate. Broad though it is, general intelligence is probably defined somewhat too narrowly. Piagetian tasks belong in the consensus (Humphreys & Parsons, 1979a) along with measures of academic achievement (Humphreys, Rich, & Davey, in press). The inclusion of these items provides a measure with a higher loading on Spearman's general factor than on the standard Wechsler test alone. That is, a broadening of the consensus would increase the construct validity of an intelligence test.

An important aspect of this definition is that intelligence is the repertoire, not the score on a test. It is not even the score on what I have called a standard test. Language in all of its manifestations is a very important part of that repertoire. It is obvious that a repertoire largely in Spanish cannot be tested by questions and answers that require knowledge of English. It is not so obvious that bilingual children may have repertoires that, in a sense, do not speak to each other. Bilingual children should be tested in both languages, and the final score should allow for success in either language. The conditions of measurement, including rapport between the examiner and subject, are also important in obtaining a valid assessment of the repertoire.

Comprehension of language is close to the core of this conception of intelligence. A test of reading comprehension that is labeled "achievement" is a more valid measure of the repertoire than an offbeat intelligence test supposedly measuring information processing. The reading comprehension test is highly fallible, however, in the early grades. It continues to be highly fallible for a small percentage of individuals who have a specific reading disability. For these people, an orally administered intelligence test in the appropriate language or languages is essential. A substantial discrepancy between aural and visual comprehension of language does occur. In these cases the former is a more valid measure of the repertoire. A few people can be highly intelligent but be able to read only haltingly.

Intelligence as Phenotype

Intelligence is a behavioral phenotypic trait. The behavior can be assessed by tests or can be evaluated by raters who know the subject well. Intelligence differs from traits of physique in being behavioral and therefore not as readily isolatable. Like traits of physique, intelligence changes with age. Intelligence is dependent on both maturation and experience, but this does not set it apart from many traits of physique. Unfortunately, however, there is presently no metric for the measurement of intelligence that allows one to describe the changes that take place during development in the way one describes growth in height. With the switch to deviation IQs that are defined in terms of an individual's distance from the mean of his or her age group, the mental age scale was abandoned. In no sense is an IQ a measure of absolute intelligence; it is a measure of relative intelligence. A ratio scale of measurement for intelligence comparable to the ratio scale of length for height is certainly not feasible and probably not possible, but a quasi-interval scale that would reflect intellectual growth as a thermometer reflects temperature is technically feasible.

The lack of such a scale leads to conceptual errors in research. It is highly misleading, for example, to correlate IQs with any measure that shows growth over time in a sample that is heterogeneous with respect to chronological age. For example, computing a correlation between IQs and grade placement scores in a sample of children varying in age results in an underestimate of the relationship. As a matter of fact, the correlation is smaller than the one that would be obtained after converting grade placement to a metric that reflects achievement relative to chronological age. Relative scores can be compared to other relative scores, and growth scores to growth scores, but the two should not be mixed.

For the description of giftedness, however, the mental age scale or its conceptual equivalent is unnecessary. Here there is no doubt about the appropriateness of a metric that reflects attainment relative to a group that is homogeneous in chronological age. Similar scales for physical measurements are equally desirable, but the computation of a score that reflects relative height does not convert phenotypic height into a capacity or rate of growth. Nor is an IQ a measure of capacity or rate of growth. Instead it represents merely the relative size of the intellectual repertoire within a group that is homogeneous with respect to chronological age.

Substrates for Intelligence

The intellectual repertoire is acquired, but the learning is by a biological organism. The genetic mechanism is a producer of individual differences par excellence in all plant and animal species, and there is every reason to believe that there are genetic contributions to individual differences in phenotypic intelligence in humans. It is unwise, however, to specify a precise amount that the genes contribute to individual differences in intelligence because genetic and environmental determinants are so intertwined during development. My preference is to recognize that intelligence has in some unknown degree both a genetic and an environmental substrate and to accept the limitations, if any, that a lack of precise apportioning of variance imposes on the interpretation and use of intelligence test scores. A careful look at the limitations resulting from the inability to pinpoint the size of the genetic contribution reveals very few problems (Humphreys, 1978). Most hereditarians and environmentalists believe that accepting the predominance of one or the other would lead automatically to diametrically opposed social and personal consequences, but such beliefs are fallacious. Inferences from test scores require sound empirical research. It is helpful if there is also a theoretical framework that ties together the empirically based generalizations, but this is quite different from "theory," based on wishful or fearful thinking, that disregards research findings.

The Temporal Dimension

Intelligence is defined in terms of the repertoire available at a particular point in time. This aspect of the definition is critical to the interpretation and use of intelligence test scores. At no point in time during development can one obtain an estimate of a fixed capacity or potential from the score on an intelligence test. As intelligence grows, relative standing changes.

Conventional wisdom states that measured intelligence during the preschool years is not stable because the preschool tests are inadequate. However, during the school years intelligence does supposedly stabilize. Unfortunately, relatively high levels of stability of obtained scores from year to year during the public school period have been interpreted as if the lack of a perfect relationship were due entirely to error. Correlations between two tests administered one year apart do not become unity when allowance is made for the measurement error present at each occasion.

The obtained and corrected coefficients also become progressively smaller as the amount of time between the initial and the final test increases. The matrix of intercorrelations of an intelligence test administered on several occasions has the highest correlations adjacent to the principal diagonal (from one year to the next), and the lowest correlation is the one based on the two most remote occasions.

This pattern was first described by Anderson (1939, 1940). He obtained near zero correlations between gains in mental age from year to year and mental age at the beginning of the year. He interpreted the observed stability of intelligence as being the expected characteristic of a part–whole correlation. For example, the mental age of a child at 7 includes the mental age of that child at 6 to which an uncorrelated increment has been added. As uncorrelated increment follows uncorrelated increment, correlations between IQs obtained early and IQs obtained later must decrease.

Roff (1941) replicated Anderson's findings in full, yet the belief in the stability of intelligence persisted as well as the interpretations of intelligence as capacity or potential. How can one infer a fixed capacity from an intelligence test score when the expected gain during the coming year cannot be predicted from the current level?

Guttman (1955) coined the term *simplex* to describe matrices showing this pattern, although he did not apply his model to learning or to developmental phenomena. I did the latter (Humphreys, 1960). Intercorrelations of observed scores are called *quasi-simplex* matrices. A true simplex requires that certain quantitative relationships exist among true scores that can only be estimated. These relationships will hold if the correlations between initial true score and the subsequent true score gain are uncorrelated.

I have summarized more recent data (Humphreys, in press). In three different sets of data originally gathered by three different investigators at different periods of time and using different measures of intelligence, reasonably good fits were obtained to the simplex model. The best fit was found for a constant sample of more than 1,300 white boys and girls for an intellectual composite of tests designed to be as parallel as possible from the 5th to the 11th grades (Humphreys & Parsons, 1979b). The poorest fits were obtained for separate samples of approximately 600 boys and 700 girls at maximum, but with the actual sample size varying from one occasion to another (Humphreys, Davey, & Park, 1984). In these data, also, different group tests were used from year to year. In the third set of data, reasonably good fits were obtained from 9 months to 15 years for individual intelligence tests in correlations for which a constant sample size was again not feasible (Humphreys & Davey, 1984). In these three sets of data the fit of the simplex was perfectly correlated with the degree of suitability of the data for model fitting.

Even the data sets that showed the poorest fits to the model provided approximate fits. For one thing, residuals appeared more or less at random as compared to the patterning of residuals when intercorrelations of height were analyzed in the same fashion. There are determinants of adult height that affect growth during the period of sexual maturation in a fashion that is not congruent with the simplex model. Secondly, the model fitting for intelligence provided estimates of reliabilities and true score stabilities that were generally congruent with those obtained in the better data.

The various analyses provide a basis for the following conclusions:

1. True score stabilities over only a half-year period are only moderate in size (.75) during the first two years.

2. Stabilities from year to year reach a high level (.96 to .97) early in the grade school period and remain at that level during high school.

3. The data are congruent with the hypothesis that tests from year one through 17 are measuring the same construct. The assumption that people are changing is tenable.

4. The stability of true scores for any two occasions between the first and the 12th grades is approximated by .96 to .97 raised to the power of the number of years separating the occasions.

True score stabilities are estimated to be between .69 and .76, the 9th powers of .96 and .97, respectively, for beginning first grade through the 9th grade. Assuming that the reliability of the intelligence test score at each occasion is .95, a generous estimate, the obtained score stabilities become .66 and .72 for the two true score stability assumptions. In Wilson's (1983) data, the correlation between Wechsler test scores at 6 and 15 is .69 for 246 cases. Thus my approximation produces a value quite close to a relatively stable computed value.

One might still conclude that intelligence is relatively stable, rather than relatively unstable, over long time periods even if it is not fixed. For present purposes, however, the degree of instability is important. If 145 in the Wechsler metric is the cutting score for describing a child as gifted in the first grade, a child at that level is expected in the typical school system to drop to about 130 at the end of the 12th grade. The standard deviation of individual IQs about this expected mean will be about 12. A small number of such children will show a gain, most will lose, and rarely a child will be below 100 at 18. Thus, to describe a child as gifted, one must specify the point during development at which the description is applied.

Intelligence and Learning

Although it is by no means certain that the seeming independence of true score gains and earlier true score level is determined entirely by the learning mechanism—polygenic determinants could certainly have similar effects—there are other reasons as well to look at the principles of learning in conjunction with the growth of intelligence. All responses to questions and problems posed on intelligence tests are based on past learning.

The intellectual repertoire is gradually and slowly acquired from birth onward. After the first few years, the repertoire is highly though imperfectly stable from year to year, yet change in the ordering of individual differences proceeds continuously. Some unknown amount of the variance of change, as well as the variance of status at a particular point in time, is associated with learning. The conditions of learning should have something to do with increases in intelligence as measured by a scale that can reflect growth and with changes in relative intelligence, the IQ.

In order to put the effects of learning on intelligence in perspective, it is necessary to consider the size of the intellectual repertoire at any age after early infancy. Change does not take place rapidly because the repertoire becomes large at a very early age. It continues to grow, largely without loss, so that an annual increment is relatively small in comparison to its base. Anderson (1939, 1940) used the analogy of the part–whole correlation as described earlier to explain the degree of stability of intelligence over short time intervals. Training experiments designed to affect intelligence have to be continued over extended intervals of time if the experimenter is to have much chance of obtaining statistically significant effects on IQ in the sample sizes used in most experiments.

It also goes without saying that the experimenter must know the important variables that produce intellectual gains and be able to manipulate them with sufficient impact to stand out above the myriad systematic effects produced by variables not under experimental control. Home, neighborhood, school, particular classroom and teacher, immediate peer group, and anatomical-physiological changes that a person experiences all have their effects. The change in IQ during any one period of time represents a summation of many influences.

Summary

Intelligence has been defined as a repertoire of acquired behaviors. There is, however, a genetic substrate for this repertoire as well as an environmental one. As a repertoire it is a phenotypic trait. Furthermore, it is incorrect to discuss a repertoire as if it were an entity. Referring to intelligence as "it," as I have just done, can be misleading. Such references are merely a verbal convenience. As is true of other phenotypic traits such as height, intelligence grows during development. An IQ is a measure not of intelligence but of relative intelligence. A standard measure of the growth of intelligence has been neglected since the switch to deviation IQs.

Intelligence is not fixed either in the growth sense or in the relative sense. High but imperfect stability of IQs from year to year becomes much lower stability over longer intervals of time. A gifted child can be identified at a particular point in time, but that child's score several years earlier or later is expected to regress toward the mean of the population. There is also a substantial amount of variability about the expected score. These effects are enhanced only slightly by the measurement error in the scores present at a particular point in time.

Relative intelligence does change over time, but the determinants of change are largely unknown. There may be genetic as well as environmental causes. Research on the effects of learning on intelligence must consider the size that intellectual repertoires reach early in development. Change does not occur readily for the excellent reason that large repertoires change slowly as increments are added.

The Development of Narrower Abilities

It is the thesis of this analysis that narrower cognitive abilities develop from a base that is appropriately called general intelligence. The available research does not point uniformly in this direction, but there may be reasons over and beyond the typical small samples for the lack of consensus. If abilities differentiate over time with learning and experience, they would be expected to do so slowly and gradually. One would also not expect the differentiation to occur at the same time for all abilities. Furthermore, one would expect the genetic contribution to individual intellectual differences to be to the general factor.

The Differentiation Hypothesis

An attractive hypothesis is that differentiation occurs in much the same order as the levels found in Vernon's (1960) hierarchy for the intellectual domain. Vernon's model placed Spearman's general factor at the top of the hierarchy. At the next level are the major group factors of verbal-numerical-educational and mechanical-spatial-practical. Minor group factors at the third level, such as verbal, numerical, memory, inductive reasoning, and spatial factors, include those that Thurstone (1938) called primary. Although Vernon did not describe further levels in the hierarchy, further levels can be found. This version of the differentiation hypothesis suggests that the two major group factors form early in development. Both maturation and learning are involved in early differentiation, but learning becomes increasingly important for the lowest and narrowest factors in the hierarchy. Differences among chemistry, physics, geology, and engineering measures of attainment are obviously produced during postsecondary education.

Support for this idea is furnished by the report of Atkin et al. (1977), who factored the longitudinal data from the ETS Growth Study (Hilton, Beaton, & Bower, 1971). Samples were large and, in addition, use of the same samples of boys and girls over four occasions further controlled sampling error. The conclusions do not depend on the choice of rotational program, but are clearly apparent in the size of the latent roots of the successive principal factors extracted from matrices in which squared multiple correlations were introduced as estimates of communalities. The size of a latent root has a one-to-one relationship with the size of a factor. Among 16 cognitive tests there were two sizable latent roots in the fifth-grade data. Roots three and four became appreciably larger at grades 7 and 9, and by grade 11 a fifth root became significant. Factors were, therefore, becoming differentiated.

The two highly oblique factors at grade 5 separated the six Scholastic Tests of Educational Progress and the two School and College Aptitude Test subscores from the eight subtests of the Test of General Information. A separate quantitative factor could have been defined at grade 5 somewhat arbitrarily, but poorly. At grades 7 and 9 the four factors, still highly oblique, were verbal comprehension, quantitative, mechanical-science information, and cultural-aesthetic information. The fifth factor at grade 11 was defined by social science information. At each grade level the intercorrelations for the first-order factors defined a general factor that did not shrink appreciably in size over time. The measures in the ETS data were insufficient to distinguish clearly between major and minor group factors as was required by the hierarchical model.

Heritability of Narrow Abilities

Although there are reports of differential degrees of heritability among narrow abilities, typically of the primary mental ability variety, there is again no consensus. It is the thesis of this conceptualization that most of the differences in heritability that have been reported are a function of sample size and of the limited amount of information used. The genetic methodology in which the maximum amount of information in twin resemblance correlations is used indicates that there are no dependable differences in the heritabilities of a very heterogeneous set of information, academic achievement, and aptitude tests. To the extent that there is a genetic contribution to individual intellectual differences, it appears to be to the general factor.

I reached this conclusion (Humphreys, 1974) using an analysis of all the between-twin and within-twin intercorrelations among 40 measures from Project Talent. Within-twin correlations are used as standard. For each member of a twin pair, all r_{ij} are computed. When i equals j, the correlation becomes the standardized variance of i. Between-twin correlations involve computing all r_{ij}, but the score of a first twin is correlated with the score of a second twin. When i equals j, the correlation represents the between-twin correlation for the same variable, but there are 39 between-twin correlations involving different variables. The usual twin study compares the size of the between-twin correlations for a single variable for monozygotic and dizygotic twins.

An attractive alternative to the usual analysis is to compare the ratios of mean between-twin to mean within-twin correlations based on the remaining 39 variables. If heritability of a given variable is equal to 1.0, the ratio of between- to within-twin correlations should equal 1.0 for monozygotic twins and .5 for dizygotic twins in the absence of assortative mating. Both assortative mating and environmental influences can drive the .5 upward. Environmental influences can drive the 1.0 downward. A genetic contribution requires an appreciable difference between these ratios for the two types of twins.

For both male and female monozygotic twins in the Project Talent sample, the means of more than 40 very heterogeneous tests of the ratios based on the other 39 tests were close to .9. For dizygotic female twins the same mean of the 40 tests were somewhat greater than .7; for dizygotic male twins, somewhat greater than .6. There is no genetic explanation for this difference, but for both sexes the differences in ratios for the two types of twins is compatible with a genetic contribution to individual differences. More importantly for present purposes, the variability in the size of these ratios about their respective means appears to be entirely random. If there is a genetic contribution to the covariances among tests that define several different group factors as well as a general factor, this genetic contribution appears to be as large for various kinds of specialized information—the Bible, mechanics, farming, home economics—as for traditional intellectual measures—vocabularly, abstract reasoning, spatial visualization, arithmetic reasoning. Common to these heterogeneous tests is the general factor; therefore, the potential genetic contribution appears to be primarily to the general factor.

Relation Between Cognitive and Noncognitive Abilities

Narrow cognitive abilities may develop out of a general factor and a common genetic substrate, but there are positive correlations among intelligence and desirable noncognitive traits as well. For example, it has been known for many years that height and intelligence are positively correlated (Tanner, 1966). The usual value cited for this correlation among adults is .20, but the relationship is not determined by a common genetic (within-family) substrate. Husen (1959) applied the between-twin, within-twin methodology to this problem and was able to reject the genetic hypothesis unequivocally. Between-twin correlations were slightly smaller than the within-twin for both types of male twins in his samples, but the ratio did not even vary in the expected direction for the dizygotic twins.

Husen opted for an explanation in terms of joint environmental effects on height and intelligence, especially during the prenatal period of development. Jensen (1980) opted for a different sort of genetic explanation from the one presumably responsible for the positive intercorrelations of cognitive tests. Jensen's explanation requires joint assortative mating for height and intelligence. These traits would be independent of each other if mating were random, but if people who are tall and bright tend to mate with those who are also tall and bright, positive correlations between the otherwise independent traits can be produced. In contrast, if mating were random, various cognitive measures would still be intercorrelated to the extent that there is a genetic contribution to the variances of those measures.

Might the within-family genetic explanation also be inappropriate for the small correlations between intelligence and neuromuscular coordination, musical pitch, and even simple reaction time? The research required to answer this question has not been done. Correlations between traits for which there is no necessary genetic basis, particularly when the traits are as different as are height and intelligence, convey important information about the determinants of both traits. The developmental model would differ for narrow cognitive and narrow noncognitive traits under these circumstances.

Summary

High general intelligence is indeed basic to intellectual giftedness. Although the evidence is not conclusive, it is a viable hypothesis that there is differentiation of cognitive factors from a common general ability during development. It also appears plausible that the differentiation takes place in accordance with Vernon's hierarchical model of intelligence with the major group factors being first to diverge followed by narrower and narrower factors lower in the hierarchy.

Although the data are not conclusive, it is also a viable hypothesis that the potential contribution of genetics to individual cognitive differences is restricted to the general factor of intelligence. When general factor variance is controlled statistically in such measures as mathematical and verbal abilities, the residual variability may be entirely environmental in origin.

Noncognitive traits can also be positively correlated with general intelligence, but the genetic causes of excellence in neuromuscular coordination, reaction time, and pitch discrimination may have nothing to do with a person's intelligence. Height is positively correlated with intelligence, but the causes differ from those that produce the positive intercorrelations of cognitive measures.

Implications of This Conceptualization for Intellectual Giftedness

In developing this conceptualization thus far I have been primarily concerned with intelligence in general. There has been little attention paid to giftedness per se. There are, however, important implications for the gifted and for programs for them. Early in this exposition it was stated that giftedness was not a condition to be diagnosed. It was, instead, defined as that portion of the high tail of the distribution of intelligence falling beyond some arbitrary cutoff at a particular point in time. The percentage of gifted individuals in a population depends on the needs of the definer. The number of people who fall within the segment of the distribution selected depends on the particular time in their development that the designation of gifted is bestowed.

Regression Toward the Mean

If a group of children is described as being gifted at age 6, most of them can also be described as being gifted at age 7. The mean at age 7 and the variability around that mean will, however, be somewhat different than would be expected in terms of the random error in the measurements made at the two ages. The mean at age 7 will show slightly more regression and the variability around that mean will be somewhat greater than anticipated on the basis of the respective reliabilities. But this is only the beginning. There is further regression and further heterogeneity with each passing year. By age 18, using observed scores rather than the estimated true scores assumed in the theoretical discussion, the gifted 6-year-olds will probably have regressed 40 percent to 50 percent toward the 18-year-old mean.

Did Terman's gifted group regress less than this? It is difficult to determine. The ages of those in the group at first test was greater than 6. Norms for the various tests used were not dependable, let alone equated. The sample was also doubly selected: by teachers' nominations and by the Stanford-Binet. Finally, the people in the group were selected and followed; they were not merely described.

It also follows that not all those in a group of 18-year-old gifted students were gifted throughout their development. The further back in time one looks for other test scores, the greater is the expected regression. Statistically, regression is bidirectional. Anecdotal accounts of individuals with high intellectual attainment as adults who were only average in intelligence in the early grades may well be true, but these accounts do not deny the tie between high intelligence and high levels of adult attainment in our society. The age at which measurements are made is critical. Cox's study (1926) of people of genius contained two estimates of IQ during development. On average, the earlier estimate was lower than the later one. This is, of course, the outcome anticipated although it is not congruent with a fixed intelligence. From the present point of view, some number of the IQs estimated to be average in Cox's study would reflect the absence of early precocity rather than the absence of information about children who are supposed to be precocious.

Measures of Other Traits

Would the formation of a composite of general intelligence and other, noncognitive traits increase the stability of the definition of giftedness? It is possible statistically that the answer to this question is "yes," but it is not possible to specify the trait or traits that should be added. It is also highly probable that the trait or traits, if they can be found, would only slow down the rate of change. Some would wish to add task commitment, creativity, or both to the definition of gifted, but are measures of these traits more stable than measures of IQs? My guess is that change in these traits is more rapid over time. A composite that included them might therefore be less stable.

On the basis of present evidence, it seems probable that every human trait showing increases or decreases in the group mean over time will also show nonrandom changes in the ranking of individuals. Correlations between measures obtained on adjacent occasions will be higher than correlations between measures obtained on remote occasions. All such matrices, after correction for measurement error, will not have the properties of a perfect simplex, but there will be a family resemblance.

As was mentioned earlier, it is possible to diagnose a condition of mental retardation when one finds low intelligence, a low evaluation of adaptive behavior in the individual's environment, and a known biological etiology. A child with Down's syndrome at age 6 will still be a Down's syndrome youth at age 18. It is not possible, however, to diagnose a condition of mental retardation on the basis of behavioral evidence alone. One's best bet, an actuarial prediction, is that a child without biological involvement testing low at age 6 will test substantially higher at age 18. Similarly, a child whose adaptive behavior rating is low at age 6 and who is biologically unimpaired will probably have a substantially higher rating at age 18. These expectations follow directly from the idea that individual differences are not stable over time. The intercorrelations of adaptive behavior ratings over prolonged time spans have not been computed, but the only question concerns the degree of instability. It is also unknown whether a composite of the two measures, intelligence and adjustment, would be more or less stable than the former alone.

Stability Following Intervention

The discussion thus far has assumed that a gifted group has been described by a particular set of measurements, but has not been given special treatment. The data that have been gathered and analyzed have been samples of school children who were not specially selected and provided with a special program. It is not known what effects on stability of relative intelligence special programs have for children at either end of the intellectual continuum, but learning and motivational principles provide a basis for speculation.

Assume that a group of gifted children are placed in a special classroom in which the curricular materials, the methods of instruction, and the methods and content of examinations are selected to challenge the individual children. Also, so that they can perceive the competitive level of the group in which they are placed, the children are made aware of the changing levels of attainment of the class as they mature and learn. It is obvious that the curricular materials and methods of instruction must be pitched at an appropriate level well above the chronological ages of the children. It is not so obvious that mastery and criterion-referenced tests are typically not sufficiently challenging to provide adequate feedback to gifted children. Norm-referenced tests pitched at the gifted level will provide the feedback concerning the group performance required to promote competition and high achievement.

Under these circumstances, change in the rank-order of individuals within the group will continue, but it is hypothesized that the expected regression over successive occasions of measurement will be about the mean of the selected group. In contrast, if the gifted group had been left in a heterogeneous classroom, the data on stability of unselected groups show that the regression would have been toward the lower mean. Not only is evidence concerning this hypothesis lacking, it has not been recognized as a possibility.

It would also follow that the best situation in which to promote intellectual growth is for a child to (a) be below average in a group but not so far below that competition is out of the question, (b) have an ego that can tolerate more failures than successes relative to the performance of the rest of the group, and (c) have good study habits and the time and energy to work hard intellectually.

Intervention programs require that participants be reevaluated frequently. Gifted 6-year-olds may or may not qualify as being gifted later in their educational career, and some who do not qualify early will qualify later. If an educational system could be devised that would provide intellectually challenging and motivating curricular materials, tutorial methods, and assessments of progress for each child, grouping for intervention purposes would not be necessary. Up until very recently in the United States, however, the overall trend has been in the reverse direction. Humanistic education had an egalitarian component. Racial integration increased classroom heterogeneity. In part the push in education to replace norm-referenced tests with criterion-referenced and mastery tests was similarly motivated. Such tests hide individual differences among above-average children. There may be here an explanation for the decreasing number of high-ability students at the high end of the distributions of SAT verbal and mathematics scores.

The Development of Narrow Giftedness

The assumption in this conceptualization is that environmental determinants are responsible for the development of narrow intellectual abilities on the basis of a child's general intelligence. A child who is gifted mathematically is also gifted more generally. It appears to be quite difficult at times, on the other hand, to convert a generally gifted child to being gifted in mathematics. One constraint may be chronological age. If abilities can be acquired as a child ages, a parallel conclusion for disabilities would seem to follow. Remediation should start at age 6, not wait until the student is through high school. A second constraint may be the importance of the social milieu in which learning takes place. More is involved than reinforcement contingencies for the individual learner in the mathematics portion of the school day or the mathematics homework at night. Parents, siblings, peers, and the media are all involved.

The large ratio of 11 and 12-year-old boys to girls having extreme scores (in their age group) on mathematics aptitude of the SAT has been the subject of speculation and controversy in recent years (Benbow & Stanley, 1980, 1981; Pallas & Alexander, 1983). In this debate an important possible basis for the difference in proportions of mathematically gifted boys and girls has been neglected. Differences in the tail of a distribution can arise from a difference in variance as well as from a difference in means. By the end of high school boys have a higher mean and a larger standard deviation than girls on achievement tests in mathematics, but there is no appreciable difference in means in grade school or early in junior high school (Hilton, Beaton, & Bower, 1971). Much has been made of this equality of means, but the debaters have not noted that boys in the same study were more variable than girls as early as the fifth grade. Furthermore, the difference in variability is not restricted to mathematics. For example, boys are more variable than girls on all subtests except listening in the Scholastic Tests of Educational Progress. In addition, the difference in variances is independent of the direction of the difference in means; the difference in writing is as large as the difference in mathematics. Are highly intelligent boys encouraged to work harder and to work more frequently beyond their classroom assignments than are girls?

Summary

In this section I have expanded on the relative instability of the designation of intellectual giftedness. One's expectation is that a person who is measured at the gifted level at any chronological age will have been lower on the same scale at an earlier age and will also be lower at a more advanced age. Although it is conceivable that other measures could be added to intelligence to form a composite measure of giftedness that would be more stable than intelligence alone, it is highly improbable that any behavioral measure would remain fixed during growth and development. It is also probable that measures of temperament and so-called creativity would be less stable than general intelligence.

It is possible, on the other hand, that intervention programs have effects on the stability of giftedness that are not predictable from studies of stability in the typical school situation. It is hypothesized that the members of a group who are given special treatment will continue to show instability of relative intelligence, but that the group as a whole may not regress toward the mean of the population from which they were selected.

Narrow giftedness is presumed to arise on the basis of high intelligence, but it may still be difficult to convert a generally gifted child to being gifted in a narrower domain such as mathematics. If specific abilities can be acquired, it is plausible that disabilities can also be acquired. The social milieu in which learning takes place can inhibit the acquisition of a particular form of narrow giftedness.

Giftedness and the Social Structure

A widely used argument against implementing special education programs for gifted students is that the criteria used for selection are strongly biased in favor of the children of majority white, upper-middle-class parents. Thus, programs for the gifted are seen as being programs for the children of economically privileged families. It is easy to demonstrate that this criticism is overdrawn. Critics have either not looked at or have disregarded the objective information that requires modification of their exaggerated claims.

Intelligence and Socioeconomic Status

Table 1 presents the scatter-plot of the relation between the intelligence composite and the socioeconomic status (SES) composite used in Project

Table 1
Scatterplot in Relative Frequencies of Intelligence and Socioeconomic Status for a Sample of 9th-Grade Boys

		Socioeconomic Status From the Lowest Level (1) to the Highest Level (7)							
		1	2	3	4	5	6	7	Total
Intelligence From the Lowest Level (1) to the Highest Level (9)	9	*	0010	0066	0136	0102	0012		0326
	8		0005	0056	0251	0373	0226	0025	0936
	7	*	0021	0149	0498	0554	0232	0022	1476
	6	0002	0044	0273	0655	0582	0196	0014	1766
	5	0007	0090	0402	0728	0511	0121	0009	1868
	4	0010	0133	0476	0683	0376	0072	0006	1756
	3	0013	0155	0409	0488	0240	0046	0003	1354
	2	0007	0060	0146	0159	0078	0014	0001	0465
	1	*	0005	0015	0018	0013	0002		0053
	Total	0039	0513	1936	3546	2863	1011	0092	1.0000

*Nonzero frequency, but less than .00005. Decimal points have been omitted elsewhere.

Note. This table reveals the relative frequency with which the 63 possible combinations of SES and intelligence occurred in the sample of more than 40,000 ninth-grade boys. Only three combinations had zero frequencies. One can note, for example, that only .0012 out of a total of .0326 at the highest level of intelligence were from the highest level of SES. The families at this level of SES contributed only a little more than 3 percent of the most intelligent children. Based on data from Project Talent, cited in Flanagan et al. (1962).

Talent (Shaycoft, 1967) for 44,423 ninth-grade boys. Although the data were obtained in 1960, there is every reason to believe that there has been little if any change in the degree of this relationship.

Project Talent obtained a stratified random sample of the nation's high schools, including the ninth grades in junior high schools. Thus the individuals in this scatter plot are representative of the U.S. ninth-grade population with the exception of the small number of dropouts that occur in prior grades. Social classes and minorities are represented in accordance with their numbers in the population. Scores on the talent intelligence composite, including tests of reading comprehension, arithmetic reasoning, and abstract reasoning, would have correlated highly with the total Wechsler IQ if the latter had been available. The SES composite included the wide range of information required by the standard sociological index of class status, including parents' education, income, occupation; housing; and books and appliances in the home. The measurement scales for both composites were highly arbitrary with respect to the zero and units of measurement; in this presentation, the intervals have been coded digitally. A "1" represents the lowest interval on both continua.

The correlation of intelligence and SES across this wide range of talent is very close to .40. This is at the top of the range of correlations typically found in samples of reasonable size for these two variables. Both regressions are linear throughout most of the range, but the small deviations from linearity at the extremes are probably not functions of too little ceiling or floor for the respective scales of measurement. Thus they require explanations.

The regression of intelligence on SES flattens at both ends of the distribution. The children of parents at level 7 of SES score below the linear expectation, and the children of parents at level 1 score above that expectation. Level 7 may represent inherited wealth and, therefore, more generational regression toward the mean. Level 1 may represent a larger proportion of families headed by a lone woman. Although there were fewer such families in 1960 than there are today, poverty very generally accompanies death of the father, accident to the father, divorce, desertion, and illegitimacy. The mix of these causes has changed since 1960, but the effect is the same.

The regression of SES on intelligence flattens at the low end of the intelligence scale. The mean SES of level 1 intelligence is actually somewhat higher than the mean at level 2. A possible explanation is that a middle class child of low intelligence is more apt to be promoted into the ninth grade and to remain in school long enough to be given that promotion than a lower class child at the same level of intelligence. Middle class parents probably abandon hope less readily, provide more help to their children, and place more pressure on teachers and principals than do lower class parents.

If gifted is defined as being at level 9 on the intelligence composite, which includes the top 3.3 percent, gifted children cover the range of socioeconomic status from level 2 through level 7. Only the lowest .4 percent of families is not represented. The largest number of gifted children are in level 5, which is just above the middle category of SES. Levels below 5 contain almost 70 percent as many gifted as do levels above 5. Percentages of gifted people are larger for families at the upper end of the SES scale, but for purposes of forming social policies, sheer number is the more important. If family income had been substituted for the broader measure of social status, the correlation with intelligence would have been smaller, and larger numbers of gifted children would have been found in the middle range of income.

With both individual intelligence and family status being less than completely stable during development of the child, there is no reason to expect that the relation between those variables is fixed at the .40 level. In addition to some variability in the size of the correlation between intelligence and SES associated with instability of both measures during development, there is the usual effect on correlations of the range of talent in the population. Applicants for admission to college are more restricted in range than are ninth-grade students.

In the population of college applicants that today includes large numbers of minorities who, on average, are lower than the majority white population on measures of both intelligence and SES, the same correlation is in the .20 to .30 range. It is likely to be lower still as a function of the reduced range of talent among the applicants for admission to a particular institution. In the late sixties, in a blaze of egalitarian sentiment, at least one faculty senate voted to admit a substantial percentage of applicants by a lottery in order to increase the representation of students from disadvantaged families. It was later discovered that the correlation between the admissions test and family income and occupation among applicants was nearly zero. Thus the lottery could not have helped reach the goal desired. It is not unique, of course, for a faculty to establish policy on the basis of sentiment without regard to data. Even the small amount of nonlinearity in the data did not conform to the prevailing expectation that disadvantaged students could not possibly compete on the biased test. Applicants from high-income families who had low scores were actually more heavily represented in the applicants than the proportional expectation. Conversely, applicants from the same level of family income with high scores were underrepresented. Some selection in terms of entrance test did occur at the high end of the socioeconomic scale.

Environmental Privilege or Genetic Superiority

It is obvious from Table 1 that gifted intelligence in the ninth grade is not simply the result of economic and social privilege. The gifted children who were born into the most unlikely environments, as gauged by the usual indicants of privilege, cannot be explained by measurement error. Environmentalists must look at subtler factors in the home than level of SES. On the other hand, a correlation of .4 between these measures of privilege and children's intelligence is highly congruent with genetic expectation. The genetic hypothesis would predict a higher correlation between parents' intelligence and child's intelligence, and the correlation involving midparent IQ (the average IQ of two parents) is indeed .55 to .60.

The fit of the genetic hypothesis to the data cannot be used as conformation of the hypothesis, and the lack of an adequate environmental theory and of measures of the more complex and subtle environmental determinants required cannot be used to reject that explanation. Obtaining definitive answers in the absence of experimental controls is also an unlikely prospect. The absence of definitive answers, however, is not as critical for social policy formation as the debaters of nature verses nurture believe it to be. The highly emotional debate about the possible genetic contribution to individual and group differences in intelligence has actually obscured a number of important issues.

The Importance of Phenotype

People's behavior is governed by their phenotypic traits. The phenotypic intelligence of lower class children may be lower than their genotypic intelligence but unless a behavioral phenotype can be modified, the hypothesis concerning genotype is merely of academic interest. The effects of environment contribute to variances in behavioral phenotypes, and phenotypes are not necessarily quickly and easily changed. If phenotype can be changed, there are some pertinent questions. What variables produce change in the desired direction? How much change can be expected? What will it cost in time, money, and other resources? Does the time during development at which change is attempted have a bearing on the answers to these questions?

I evaluate intellectual handicaps in the same fashion as I do physical ones. If a Glen Cunningham can overcome the handicap of a severe leg burn and become a champion miler, I am delighted, but he should not be placed on the track team only because his time in the mile is fast relative to his handicap. A woman who has been inspired by newly acquired attitudes to aspire to an engineering degree, but who has had only two years of mathematics and no physical science in high school, should be required to obtain the necessary prerequisites. If she enrolls, and succeeds, I am again delighted, but her performance should not be judged on norms relative to her lack of high school preparation. There is only one standard of excellence in group comparisons. To describe a child from a poor family as being gifted on the basis of a separate table of norms and discover that he or she cannot compete with others in the gifted group helps neither that child nor the group. Such children should be given opportunities and be encouraged to achieve as much as possible, but the learning program should be designed for the child's phenotypic intellectual level.

Giftedness and Race

At this point in the nation's history, Blacks are, on average, less intelligent as defined herein than are Whites. Because standard deviations are approximately equal when tests have adequate numbers of items of appropriate difficulty levels for both races, the ratio of White to Black children at various intellectual levels increases predictably with distance above the White mean. Black children are found at all intellectual levels, but any objective definition of giftedness will qualify a smaller percentage of Black children as being gifted in the school-age population.

The causes of the intelligence difference between American Blacks and American Whites are not known. There is insufficient evidence to reject the genetic hypothesis, but there is also insufficient evidence to reject the environmental hypothesis. Whatever the causes may be, according to the reports of the National Assessment of Educational Progress,[2] the gap seems to be closing only among 9-year-old Black and White children. There have been no gains for Black 17-year-olds. At age 13 there has been a small gain. Beyond age 17 the gap appears to be as large on the Graduate Record Examination, Law School Aptitude Test, and Medical College Aptitude Test as it is at the time of college entrance. Blacks need higher levels of intellectual achievement in order to achieve proportional representation in higher education, business, and the professions. Affirmative action at age 18 and beyond in the form of lower standards for blacks is not achieving the intellectual gains required.

Putting First Things First

In all of the controversy about the nature of intelligence and the tests that measure intelligence that has gone on in recent years, it is interesting that a traditional democratic goal has been neglected. We are not rewarding individual merit as it is measured by present tests nearly as well as we could and should. A well-documented conclusion of Jencks (1972) has received little notice. If college entrance were based entirely on test scores and grades, the current advantage of middle-class over working-class children would be reduced by a third. Every study of college-going shows that family income is almost as highly correlated with this criterion as is measured intelligence. The correlation between college-going and family income is also higher than the validity of the family income variable for predicting academic achievement of the offspring. By the mid-seventies a smaller percentage than in 1961 of highly intelligent students, especially from middle income families, was entering four-year colleges.

Postsecondary education has been busily pricing itself out of the market for families below the highest quartile. Can costs be cut? Can more ways be found to provide financial support for college-going? Over and beyond scholarship support, could more part-time work be provided on campus, supplanting full-time employees as necessary? Could we back away from rampant egalitarianism and provide scholarship help only for high-ability students who are also in financial need?

Financial help is only a part of the problem; the rest is more difficult. Attitudes of working-class children will have to be modified, and the modification may well require major changes in the reward systems we have established in our society. The financial rewards in a good many

---

[2]The National Assessment of Educational Progress has been funded since about 1970 by the U.S. Office of Education and more recently by the Department of Education. The original contract was with the Education Commission of the States, Denver, Colorado. A large number of reports have been published periodically by the latter organization covering the major areas of academic achievement in 9-, 13-, and 17-year-olds.

occupations, for which college training is not required and in which the individual differences in performance have little relation to social needs, are higher than in other occupations that do require four or more years of college and in which individual differences in performance affect the national welfare. Such judgments are difficult, but a consensus can be obtained.

If we are now awarding as many degrees in higher education as the society demands, some would argue that there is no cause for concern. However, society needs to fill its leadership roles with the best people available. This represents a selfish need of the body politic, not merely an application of democratic ideology. In order to accomplish this, the class structure has to be sufficiently fluid, and effective mechanisms must be available. Possessing a credential is a woefully inadequate guide to quality. Quality of performance at the conclusion of four years in college is more a function of the quality of the students who enter than it is of the exposure to higher education. There is also a correlation between the quality of the entering students and the level of expectation for their academic achievement that attenuates the worth of the credential. We need to increase student quality by abolishing a means test, the ability of the family to pay, for entrance into higher education. Anything else represents a short-sighted national policy. Furthermore, the desired change can be effected without worrying about a possible middle-class bias in college entrance and academic achievement tests.

Conclusion

In this chapter I have defined intellectual giftedness as an arbitrarily defined percentage of people at the high end of a phenotypic, behavioral dimension of intelligence. As is true of many other phenotypic traits, intelligence so defined is not fixed. It is not a capacity. As children grow in intelligence, their relative intelligence (IQ) can and does change. The expectation for the direction of change is toward the population mean, either forward or backward in time. Over the time span of one year change is small, but it becomes quite substantial during, for example, the usual period of schooling.

High general intelligence is a necessary, but not sufficient, condition for the development of narrow giftedness such as in mathematics. To the extent that there is a genetic component to variance, the contribution appears to be to the general factor and not to the narrow ability after the latter has been residualized following control of general factor variance. High general intelligence is a necessary, but not sufficient, condition for high intellectual achievement, but other important human qualities are also involved. In contrast to the narrow intellectual abilities there is no reason to believe that the important motivational or temperamental traits share the genetic substrate for intelligence. The other traits required for high achievement are probably no more stable, and may well be less, than general intelligence. There is no way of selecting children at age 6 who will be equally gifted as adults.

On the other hand, it might be possible to increase the stability of the designation of gifted through environmental manipulation. If educational programs for the gifted were widespread, of high quality, initiated in the first grade, and continued for the following 16 years, it is possible that stability would be increased for the selected and specially treated group. Individual variability from year to year might still be pronounced, but regression might be toward the initial mean of the gifted group. There are, however, no adequate longitudinal data on the long-term affects of continuing gifted programs.

When admission to gifted programs is based entirely on standard intelligence tests reliably administered and scored, the largest number of gifted children are found in families in the middle range of social status. The percentage of gifted children does vary with family status, but one finds gifted children of every age at all levels of socioeconomic status. The correlation between the social status of families and children's intelligence is positive, but not as high as many have assumed. There are also nonzero correlations between certain demographic groups and intelligence as herein defined, but all groups are represented at any given objectively defined gifted level. At this point in our history the proportions are unequal.

Differences in phenotypic intelligence do have consequences for individuals and for society. Insisting on having proportional representation of relevant demographic groups in all gifted programs reduces the intellectual quality of the programs or makes effective participation in high-quality programs impossible for some of those who were selected only because a goal or quota needed to be met. This conclusion also applies to all levels of the socioeconomic distribution. The dull children of high-status families who enter higher education and occupations of high prestige in greater numbers than their attainments warrant have a similar depressing effect. As long as high-ability students, as measured by present tests, are being overlooked in substantial numbers, it is incongruous to give higher priority to possible test bias than to programs that would facilitate access to educational opportunities.

References

Anderson, J. E. (1939). The limitations of infant and preschool tests in the measurement of intelligence. *Journal of Psychology, 8,* 351–379.

Anderson, J. E. (1940). The prediction of terminal intelligence from infant and preschool tests. In *Thirty-ninth yearbook* (Part 1, pp. 385–403). Chicago: National Society for the Study of Education.

Atkin, R., Bray, R., Davison, M., Herzberger, S., Humphreys, L. & Selzer, U. (1977). Ability factor differentiation, grades 5 through 11. *Applied Psychological Measurement, 1*, 65–76.

Benbow, C. P., & Stanley, J. C. (1980). Sex differences in mathematical ability: Fact or artifact? *Science, 210*, 1262–1264.

Benbow, C. P., & Stanley, J. C. (1981). Mathematical abilities: Is sex a factor? *Science, 212*, 118–119.

Binet, A., & Simon, T. (1905). Methodes nouvelles pour le diagnostic du niveau intellectuel des anormaus. *Anée Psychologique, 11*, 191–244.

Cox, C. M. (1926). *Genetic studies of genius: Vol. 2. The early mental traits of 300 geniuses.* Stanford: Stanford University Press.

Flanagan, J. C., Dailey, J. T., Shaycoft, M. F., Gorham, W. A., Orr, D. B., & Goldberg, I. (1962). *Design for a study of American youth.* Boston: Houghton Mifflin.

Gould, S. J. (1981). *The mismeasure of man.* New York: Norton.

Guttman, L. (1955). A generalized simplex for factor analysis. *Psychometrika, 20*, 173–192.

Hilton, T., Beaton, A., & Bower, C. (1971). *Stability and instability in academic growth: A compilation of longitudinal data* (Final Rep., Research No. 0-0140). Washington, DC: U.S. Office of Education.

Humphreys, L. G. (1960). Investigations of the simplex. *Psychometrika, 25*, 313–323.

Humphreys, L. G. (1962). The organization of human abilities. *American Psychologist, 17*, 475–483.

Humphreys, L. G. (1971). Theory of intelligence. In R. Cancro (Ed.), *Intelligence: Genetic and environmental influences* (pp. 31–42). New York: Grune & Stratton.

Humphreys, L. G. (1974). The misleading distinction between aptitude and achievement tests. In D. R. Green (Ed.), *The aptitude-achievement distinction* (pp. 262–273). Monterey: CTB/McGraw-Hill.

Humphreys, L. G. (1978). Relevance of genotype and its environmental counterpart to the theory, interpretation and nomenclature of ability measures. *Intelligence, 2*, 181–193.

Humphreys, L. G. (in press) General intelligence: An integration of factor, test, and simplex theory. In B. Wolman (Ed.), *Intelligence.* New York: Wiley.

Humphreys, L. G., & Davey, T. C. (1984). Continuity in the development of intelligence from one year to 17. Unpublished manuscript.

Humphreys, L. G., Davey, T. C., & Park, R. K. (1984). A correlational analysis of standing height and intelligence. Unpublished manuscript.

Humphreys, L. G., & Parsons, C. K. (1979a). Piagetian tasks measure intelligence and intelligence tests assess cognitive development, *Intelligence, 3*, 369–382.

Humphreys, L. G., & Parsons, C. K. (1979b). A simplex process model for describing differences between cross-lagged correlations. *Psychological Bulletin, 86*, 325–334.

Humphreys. L. G., Parsons, C. K., & Park, R. K. (1979). Dimensions involved in differences among school means of cognitive measures. *Journal of Educational Measurement, 16*, 63–76.

Humphreys, L. G., Parsons, C. K. & Park, R. K. (1984). Errata. *Journal of Educational Measurement, 21*, ii.

Humphreys, L. G., Rich S., & Davey, T. C. (in press). A Piagetian test of intelligence. *Developmental Psychology.*

Husen, T. (1959). *Psychological twin research.* New York: Free Press.

Jencks, C. (1972). *Inequality*. New York: Basic Books.

Jensen, A. R. (1980). *Bias in mental testing*. New York: Free Press.

Pallas, A. M., & Alexander, K. L. (1983). Sex differences in quantitative SAT performance: New evidence on the differential coursework hypothesis. *American Educational Research Journal, 20*, 165–182.

Roff, M. (1941). A statistical study of the development of intelligence performance. *Journal of Psychology, 11*, 371–386.

Rossi, R., Bartlett, W., Campbell, E., Wise, L. & McLaughlin, D. (1975). *Using the talent profiles in counseling: A supplement to the* Career Data Book. Palo Alto, CA: American Institutes for Research.

Shaycoft, M. F. (1967). *The high school years: Growth in cognitive skills*. Pittsburgh, PA: American Institutes for Research and University of Pittsburgh.

Spearman, C. (1904). General intelligence, objectively determined and measured. *American Journal of Psychology, 15*, 201–293.

Tanner, J. M. Galtonian eugenics and the study of growth: The relation of body size, intelligence test score, and social circumstances in children and adults. *The Eugenics Review, 58*, 122–135.

Terman, L. M. (Ed.) (1925). *Genetic studies of genius: Vol. 1. Mental and physical traits of a thousand gifted children*. Stanford: Stanford University Press.

Terman, L. M., & Oden, M. H. (1947). *Genetic studies of genius: Vol. 4. The gifted child grows up: Twenty-five years' follow-up of a superior group*. Stanford: Stanford University Press.

Terman, L. M., & Oden, M. H. (1959). *Genetic studies of genius: Vol. 5. The gifted group at mid-life: Thirty-five years' follow-up of the superior child*. Stanford: Stanford University Press.

Thurstone, L. L. (1938). *Primary mental abilities*. Chicago: University of Chicago Press.

Vernon, P. (1960). *The structure of human abilities* (rev. ed.). London: Methuen.

Wilson, R. S. (1983). The Louisville twin study: Developmental synchronies in behavior. *Child Development, 54*, 298–316.

12. Giftedness and the Construction of a Creative Life

Doris B. Wallace
Bank Street College

Interest in gifted young people is fundamentally directed toward the future. The extensive literature on identifying the gifted, on educational programs for the gifted, and on advice to teachers and parents of gifted children represents visions of these children's hoped-for future as creative adults. But giftedness in childhood is different from creativity in adulthood. John Curtis Gowan, former editor of the *Gifted Child Quarterly*, has emphasized this point:

> "Giftedness represents only potentiality, the major variable is *crea-tivity*. We should redefine giftedness therefore as the . . . potential to become creative" (1977, p. 21).

The clear implication is that creativity develops. Behind this idea lies an unsolved developmental puzzle: Gifted children do not necessarily grow up to become creative adults, and creative adults were not necessarily gifted children (Gruber, 1982). Neither Einstein nor Hegel distinguished himself at school. This is not to deny that there are some gifted children who become creative adults, Mozart being one of the most famous examples. On the other hand, in spite of the fact that Terman called his work *Genetic Studies of Genius*, his longitudinal sample of 1,000 high-

IQ children selected in 1925, who are now well past middle age, has not produced a single truly illustrious individual.

On the Conceptual Differences Between Giftedness and Creativity

Let us examine some of the differences between child giftedness and adult creativity at a conceptual level. First, the term *gifted* is usually applied to children; it is the accepted label for describing children who have unusual talent. *Creative*, in its serious sense, is more often applied to adults. Being gifted implies that a person has been "given" a gift, for example, unusual musical or mathematical ability, rather than the person producing or developing something through his or her own effort. Creativity has a quite different connotation. Second, being creative refers not to a state but to sustained, purposeful action. Third, the gift that gifted children have is arresting and unusual because of its unexpectedly early appearance, that is, its precocity. Precocity is part and parcel of giftedness in childhood; the unusually early performance of some well-recognized function that usually appears later or is typically associated with maturity is a hallmark of giftedness. Giftedness is surprising because a child is performing like, or better than, an adult. Creativity is surprising because it produces phenomena the world has not seen before.

These distinctions, as well as some relationships that exist between the two concepts, can usefully be seen as a set of figure-ground relationships. In the case of giftedness, child status is the ground and giftedness is the figure. In the case of creativity, great ability is the ground and original or innovative work is the figure. But giftedness and creativity can both be subsumed within a larger category, "extraordinariness." This term emphasizes the potential relationship between the two concepts, rather than the distinctions between them. It follows then that if extraordinariness is the ground, giftedness and creativity are figures in a common conceptual space. These distinctions and relationships are outlined in Table 1.

Both concepts represented in Table 1 include an expanded idea of giftedness. For the creative adult, his or her abilities have become a means, an integrated, seasoned instrument, for organizing and living a purposeful creative life. For the child, the gift in question is still to be developed and its formal structures mastered. Moreover, it must be integrated into the psychological system of the still developing child. Mastery is not enough. The child must settle difficult questions of identity

I thank Margery B. Franklin, Howard E. Gruber, and Edna K. Shapiro for their most helpful comments.

Table 1
A Comparison of Two Concepts of Extraordinariness

	Gifted Child	Creative Adult
Basic premise	Possession of gift	Purposeful action leading to product(s)
Criterion	Precocity: early appearance of recognized forms	Novelty: appearance of previously unknown forms
Figure	Gift	Creative work
Ground	Child status	Great ability
Common conceptual space	Extraordinariness	Extraordinariness

and elaborate a set of purposes that will enable him or her to put this mastery to work. In other words, one cannot describe the object of inquiry without considering its functions and its fate. This is teleology with a vengeance.

In this chapter, I grasp this teleological nettle deliberately by examining a particular approach to the study of highly creative adults. I refer to this approach as the *evolving systems approach*, a term originated by Gruber (1980). This approach is used to study recognized creative individuals, and it focuses, in each case, on the development of a particular aspect of the creative work and life. Several authors have described and exemplified some of the principles and techniques of this approach (e.g., Franklin, 1983; Gruber, 1981a, 1981b; Keegan & Gruber, 1983), and a book is currently underway in which a comprehensive description of the evolving systems approach and case studies that exemplify its different aspects (e.g., studies of Galileo, Wordsworth, Darwin, and Piaget) are presented (Wallace & Gruber, 1985).

Some of the approaches and techniques that have been developed for studying highly creative adults can usefully be brought to bear on the study of giftedness in children. If giftedness in childhood is to lead to creativity in adulthood, then understanding more about adult creativity will expand one's understanding of giftedness. That is, knowledge of later states or stages is important in examining what has gone before. It is helpful to look back and forth. Theories of child development are permeated with presuppositions of what lies ahead—for example, when the capacities of children at a given stage of development are described in terms of the capacities not yet present but still to come in the succeeding stage or stages (Shapiro & Wallace, 1981). Understanding how creative adults actually do their work and lead their lives can lead to a different way of looking at gifted children and young people. Knowledge of the adult can provide clues about what to look for earlier in the life history. This heuristic for solving difficult problems by working backwards from the desired end-state has been described by Polya (1957).

The evolving systems approach is a case study approach to creative work. The case study method is used not only because highly creative individuals are unique (as everyone is), but also because it is their uniqueness that virtually defines their creativity. The way in which Leonardo or Newton were unlike other people is precisely what they are known and remembered for. Even when one considers extremely creative people who were living at the same time and working in the same field, such dissimilarity is apparent. Pissarro (1830–1903), Degas (1834–1917), Monet (1840–1926), Renoir (1841–1919), and Van Gogh (1853–1890) were all painting at the same time and are familiar to people as members of the impressionist and postimpressionist movement. But just as impressive as their collectivity are the striking differences in the work of these artists.

Another reason for studying highly creative individuals is that when available knowledge of a complex phenomenon is still relatively primitive, it is extremely useful to study clear and indisputable instances of it. Doing so maximizes the variable of interest. One may also want to understand the creativity of everyday life or the kind of creativity that does not reach the greatest heights. Focusing on very high levels of creativity prepares the way for such work.

The detailed study of a single case has often accompanied the development of theory in psychology (Garmezy, 1982; Shapiro & Wallace, 1981). Some familiar examples are Watson's conditioning and deconditioning fear of a white rabbit in the boy Albert; Ebbinghaus's use of himself as subject in his memory experiments; Freud's seminal case studies of hysteria, of Little Hans and others; and the intensely interesting and marvelous record that Stratton kept of his own response over several weeks to an inverted retinal image. All these studies, and there are many others, had profound effects in their respective fields.

Mystery and Measurement: Two False Moves

Serious case studies of creative work that go beyond biography are still quite rare. Emphasis on objectivity and measurement can be found in some quarters and insistence on the mystery of creativity in others. This has left the field of case studies open mainly to clinically oriented writers who, rather than demystifying creativity, intensify the mystery by relegating the major processes to the unconscious. But most research in creativity has been experimental and psychometric (Barron & Harrington, 1981). Furthermore, traditional wisdom, coupled perhaps with its popular appeal, has kept creativity mysterious and elusive.

We have for centuries learned that to understand creativity is somehow out of our reach. Plato, in his dialogue *Ion*, asserted that the poets received their work like a bolt from the blue "possessed by a spirit not their own" (1920, p. 6). He described them as creating not by rational means but by irrational inspiration. The changing meanings and historical contexts of the idea of the unconscious long before the growth of psychoanalytic theory in the twentieth century has been traced by Whyte (1962), who documented the recurrent notion, also held by creative artists and scientists such as Milton, Dryden, Newton, and Goethe, that the unconscious is the source of the creative imagination.

In the twentieth century, psychoanalytic theory first relegated creativity entirely to the unconscious. Here, not only the wellspring of creativity, but sometimes its content, are hidden from the creator (for example, in Freud's monograph on Leonardo [1916/1964]). Creativity can become knowable only through the interpretation of psychoanalysis. Although this kind of reconstruction details the causes and origins of the creative work, it does not give an individual's productions and achievements integrity in their own right, but rather reduces them deterministically to universal mind.

More recent psychoanalytic theory has tempered the absolutist and reductionist notion that creative work is the product of a defense mechanism sublimating unconscious drives. For example, Kris (1952, 1967) saw creativity as a process that moves among the realms of conscious rational thought, preconscious fantasy and daydreams, and unconscious drives. Kris evoked Plato's description in his discussion of poetic inspiration as a process in which the poet (sometimes by the poet's own description) writes poetry involuntarily and passively, as if possessed by some outside force. Kris believed that states of inspiration in creative work are "dominated by the ego and put to its own purposes" (1952, p. 302), but he also saw inspiration as the process that drives the unconscious toward consciousness.

Kris's "regression in the service of the ego" thus allows for the intrusion of drive-determined (primary process) material, but controlled by the ego in the interests of the creative product. Current psychoanalytically oriented theorists such as Arieti (1976) and Rothenberg (1979) also emphasize the interplay of conscious with unconscious processes in creativity, but they give greater credence to the creative achievements. Biber

(1984) provided a thoughtful discussion of psychoanalytic and other theories of creativity. (A detailed and thorough account of psychoanalytic theories of creativity can be found in Slochower [1974].)

There is another line of thought in which creativity is conceived of as a series of essential traits or properties that, if they could be identified, would unlock the mystery and enable scientists to measure and predict creativity. The abstracted measurement of personality attributes, such as the need for autonomy (MacKinnon, 1963; Taylor & Barron, 1963) or of cognitive capacities such as divergent thinking (Guilford, 1967; Guilford & Hoepfner, 1971; Torrance, 1966), are examples of this way of thinking. These investigators often recognized that creativity is not unidimensional: Guilford's influential divergent thinking construct includes ideational fluency and flexibility among other dimensions. Nevertheless, the hope of such work is to discover a few simple and general principles that will explain and predict creativity.

In contrast, there is now a perceptible trend toward demystifying giftedness and creativity without sacrificing the investigation of uniqueness and complexity of each creative person (Feldman, 1980; Gruber, 1980, 1981a; Perkins, 1981). Although the investigators representing this trend do not reject the role of preconscious and unconscious processes, their focus is on close examination of conscious ones. At the same time, the case study method is gaining wider respectability as a method for developing knowledge in psychology (Denenberg, 1982; Hudson, 1975; Kazdin, 1982; Runyon, 1982) and is being strongly recommended for the study of giftedness and creativity (Bamberger, 1982; Feldman, 1982; Gardner, 1982).

The Evolving Systems Approach

In the evolving systems approach, there are three guiding ideas: The creative individual is unique, developmental change is multidirectional, and the creative person is an evolving system. The necessary uniqueness of the creative person argues against psychometric approaches and other efforts to reduce psychological description to a fixed set of dimensions. The creative person is not conveniently "far out" along some well-charted path: He or she is unique in unexpected ways. Indeed, it may never be possible to make more than a few crude generalizations about ways in which all creative people are alike, for example, that almost all of them work hard. Nevertheless, the methods of approach and techniques of study are widely applicable and have already yielded some across-case findings.

Unfortunately, the prevailing image of psychological change in developmental theory is one of unilinear, predictable, and irreversible growth in accordance with a species-general standard. For those using the evolving systems approach, however, development is not restricted to a unilinear standard pathway, but is a process in which many alternative pathways are possible. An evolving system does not operate as a linear sequence of cause–effect relationships but displays, at every point in its history, multicausal and reciprocally interactive relationships both among the internal elements of the system and between the organism and its external milieu.

Thus, the evolving system of the creative person is multicausal, unpredictable (i.e., unique), and irreversible. It is unpredictable in the sense that one cannot know exactly what the next work of art will be that an artist will create, nor can one forecast the next revolutionary theory in art or science. Predictability may be a false god. Nontrivial novelty cannot be predicted. Biologists could never have known how to predict the evolution of the ostrich; but once faced with the ostrich and informed about its systematic place in an evolving biosphere, they could hope to understand its evolutionary significance. In the study of creativity, as in the study of evolutionary novelty, as an alternative to the methodological battle cry of prediction and control, I propose a two-part approach: careful, analytic description of each case and efforts to understand each case as a unique, functioning system.

With this as brief background, I now turn to a discussion of some of the central features of the evolving systems approach. In particular, I discuss (a) the historical, personal, and material context in which creative work evolves; (b) the goal of phenomenological reconstruction of the creative person's own experience; and (c) the evolving organization of purpose displayed by the creative person, as manifested in his or her network of enterprise.[1]

The Context of Creative Work

Context is a modern preoccupation. To see not just things themselves but things in their context is a complex and rich idea with many different expressions, from those of ecologists, to the perceptual laws of Gestaltists, to the surrealist paintings of Magritte. In the evolving systems approach,

---

[1]Space does not allow description of two other features of the evolving systems approach. One is that of reconstructing the actual movement from step to step in the making of a creative product. The interested reader should consult Gruber (1981a), Arnheim (1962), Wertheimer (1959), or Armstrong (1980). Armstrong's *Closely Observed Children* shows well how individual children can be taken seriously and how their creative work in the area of their central concerns can be observed and understood. The second feature not discussed in this chapter is the ensembles of metaphors that a creative person uses both to integrate thoughts and to construct ideas. This matter has been dealt with by Gruber (1981a, 1981b), Wallace (1982), and Osowski (1985). The key point is not metaphoric fluency or precocity, but the way in which metaphors function in the process of creative construction.

context is like a series of frames: a particular project of a creative person, the opus of which it is a part, the creative work as a whole, the creative life, and the social and historical period. At any given moment, the context can shift as the focus of attention of the creative person, as well as that of the investigator, moves among these frames.

A fundamental initial finding and, by now, a presupposition of those using the evolving systems approach is that creative work proceeds and evolves over long periods of time. The context for the work is therefore the life history in its social setting as it is experienced by its creator. As I have stated, a creative person is a system in the process of continual change. Even though a thoroughgoing examination or description of the whole system is an ideal that will probably never be reached, the whole system must be taken into account when any part of that system is examined. When this is not done, when a part or parts of the system are studied without reference to the whole, then the nature of isolated parts is distorted. This follows from the systemic assumption that the parts of the system are interconnected.

Although the idea that creative work evolves in a context over time seems self-evident, most studies of creativity ignore context altogether. For example, to ask a creative scientist to complete a mathematical series, a figure, or a verbal analogy, or to provide the greatest possible number of uses for a brick—no matter how interesting or enjoyable the task may be—is to ask that he or she perform a task that is not only trivial compared to those faced in research, but also one that is decontextualized and, in that sense, meaningless. The scientist's own work demands complex and widely ranging knowledge and skills, such as knowledge of the work of others and the ability to develop and grasp theory, to make predictions, to ask the right questions, to review and connect disparate facts or observations, to devise experiments, and to discover fallacies and discrepancies. These processes take place in a context and on a time scale that psychometric research cannot begin to approximate. Creative thinking does not occur in a vacuum. As Hudson (1966) has pointed out, the operations that are brought to bear when a person is in the process of creative work are not only complicated but also depend on huge accumulations of experience and on the fact that the person cares intensely about the work. Consider, for instance, Watson's (1968) account of the long, intense, tortuous, and competitive struggle to define the structure of DNA.

Although cognitive and personality tests have proliferated in the past three decades, there are almost no serious validation studies relating authentic creative work to psychometric test scores. Vinacke (1974), Barron and Harrington (1981), and Mansfield and Busse (1981) among others, have criticized psychometric measurement of creativity on these grounds. Through such tests one may find out roughly how bright a person is or whether he or she has a high divergence score (i.e., can produce many uncommon uses for a common object). But one is likely to miss completely the set of interests around which the creative person's world revolves and the critical mass of knowledge, skills, aspirations, and purposes that he or she has developed. In the evolving systems approach the orientation is to studying how someone does something that he or she is extraordinarily good at—the hallmark of the highly creative person.

This orientation leads to a focus primarily on the person in the process of working. Recently, investigators such as Rothenberg (1979) and Perkins (1981) have also done this by studying poets writing poems. Much earlier, Patrick (1935, 1937) studied poetic and artistic composition in the laboratory setting in order to verify the four-stage process put forward by Wallas (1926)—preparation, incubation, illumination, and verification. Some comments from Patrick's subjects—for example, that the poetic "idea" may be present in the poet's mind over many months or years, even during the incubation period—and certainly Rothenberg's study of the creation of a single poem point up the long evolution of creative work, even though the poem might be short.

The context to be considered is manifold. Often the particular work and thought being studied is part of a larger opus, the latter being itself an element in the work of a creative lifetime and part of a complex organization of purpose. At another level, the individual self, life, and time are contextual elements in the system that penetrate the development of the work being examined.

Biography: The Life Versus the Work

The evolving systems approach, in which a person's mature, creative work is the focus, is to be distinguished from biography, which, in a different way, renders the life of an individual set off by the two events, birth and death. The biographer attempts to capture the *person* and to reconstruct that person's life as it was lived. This, too, is in part a psychological task. Consider, for example, Edel's (1959) description of the responsibility of the literary biographer: "To catch the flickering vision behind the metaphor, to touch the very pulse of the hand that holds the pen . . . to discover the particular mind and body that drove the pen in the creative act" (p. 56).

Strictly speaking, the biographer's formal responsibility is to give an accurate factual account of the life and, through artistry, to convey what the person was like as a human being. There may be extremely few available facts, as for Shakespeare, or a superabundance, as for recent presidents of the United States. For some, the biography is seen as the vehicle for describing the ordinariness of extraordinary people—for telling us how they do the things that we all do—"going about their daily

affairs, toiling, failing, succeeding, eating, hating, loving" (Woolf, 1932/
1959, p. 261).

The problem is that, although the biography is written because of the
achievements of a person, focusing on the personality and on the ordinary
things often leads to neglect of the achievements. For example, Bedford's
(1974) 700-page biography of Aldous Huxley is almost entirely concerned
with Huxley's life when he was not writing. No attempt was made, in this
interesting book, to describe Huxley's thought and work—precisely the distinction that has brought him to our attention in the first place.

Kramer (1977) has called attention to this kind of omission in literary
biography: "The biographer proceeds on the assumption which nowadays
seems to be shared by the reader, that it is possible to give a true account
of a writer's life without giving an account of his writings" (p. 3). It is as if
the biographer's tacit assumption in these cases is that the reader already
knows the work and that it somehow speaks for itself, whereas the biographer's responsibility is to reveal the private and personal life about which
the reader knows much less. This focus can dichotomize the work and life
as if they were separate and unconnected domains. Although this should
not lead us to overlook what the biographer does do—often extremely well—
there is a responsibility, at minimum, to recognize that reconstructing the
life without the work tells only half the story, or even less. Of course, not
all biographies are of this order. Two classic exceptions are Ellmann's *James
Joyce* (1959) and Boswell's *Life of Johnson* (1791/1859).

Autobiography can fall prey to the same kind of problem. A case in
point is the contrast between two books by Bertrand Russell. His long autobiography (1967, 1968, 1969) is full of personal and social detail but give
little idea of the man thinking; his small book, *My Philosophical Development* (1959), focuses entirely on the growth of his thought and work.

Making a Creative Life

There is evidence that the purposeful organization of creative work plays
a vital or dominant role in how a creative life is organized and lived. The
necessity for making living arrangements that support the creative work
often emerges clearly, especially in the lives of women, because convention and expectation militate against them. Woolf has argued this extensively in *A Room of One's Own* (1929/1957). Special domestic
arrangements that are invisible in men's lives become the centerpiece in
women's. Wollstonecraft's long struggle to find a suitable social and emotional setting for her work is a good case in point, and Showalter (1977)
as well as Olsen (1978) have shown that many women writers did not
and do not lead conventional lives as wives and mothers. Indeed, four of
the greatest English women novelists of the nineteenth century—Jane
Austen, Emily Bronte, Charlotte Bronte, and George Eliot—did not have
children.

The lives of creative men often have a different cast. Until he married, Wordsworth's intensely close, intimate relationship with his sister Dorothy provided a niche for his work, not only because she ran his household unobtrusively and well so as to give the greatest possible rein to his work, but also because she was an understanding, encouraging, and admiring companion, and sometimes a kind of collaborator and transducer of experience for him. Wordsworth often tried his poetry out on Dorothy, and he used her notebooks of their shared experiences (Jeffrey, 1983). She wrote a prose description of the same daffodils (seen when she and her brother were on a walk together) that Wordsworth transmuted in his famous poem *The Daffodils*.

Darwin, at the age of 29, was in the fine flush of discovery. At the same moment he was also in the throes of a decision about marriage. Just as he was working out the theory of evolution, as is recorded in his celebrated notebooks, he scribbled some other notes headed "This is the Question":

> If *not* marry TRAVEL? Europe—yes? America????? If marry-means limited—Feel duty to work for money. London life, nothing but Society, no country, no tours, no large Zoolog; collect., no books.

To marry, on the other hand, meant

> Children—(if it please God)—constant companion (friend in old age) who will feel interested in one, object to be beloved and played with . . . Forced to visit and receive relations *but terrible loss of time.* (Barlow, 1958, pp. 232–233)

Darwin was working out a conception of himself and his plans that would not only allow room for work and marriage but would also allow his personal life to be organized to support his work.

It is clear from case study work that context is not simply a given condition but one that a person shapes and controls. A creative individual, with greater or lesser difficulty, fashions a personal context, an ecological niche that provides the fullest opportunities for the realization of creative work. Making these arrangements becomes part of the person's long-term organization of purpose and creative life.

Another facet of the context to be taken into account is the social-historical time and place in which a creative person lived and worked. Like biography and autobiography, the evolving systems approach entails historical reconstruction, irrespective of whether the person being studied is alive or dead. One looks back at a person's achievements and reconstructs how they were achieved. Fromm (1980) has said that every society has its own social filters through which only certain ideas, concepts, and experiences can pass. Those that cannot pass through this social filter are "unthinkable" and also therefore "unspeakable." The creative thinker, in Fromm's formulation, is faced with the problem of having and expressing new concepts that do not yet exist for most people in contemporary thought or language. One could say that the Inquisition pressured Galileo to deny his belief in the Copernican theory because it was considered unthinkable, and that the initial reception of Freud's theory of infantile sexuality was so hostile because people thought Freud's theory was unspeakable. The reasons for Darwin's long delay in publishing *The Origin of the Species* may have been due to his anticipation of similar reactions.

A creative thinker's products, according to Fromm, must be a "blend of what is truly new and the conventional thought which it transcends" (Fromm, 1980, p. 3). Such a person may be able to think the thoughts that contemporary society considers unthinkable, but he or she is still a part of that society. Like any good historian, the investigator understands this dynamic. In their historical analysis of the "character and conduct of artists," Wittkower and Wittkower (1963) warned that when analysis is historically naive, historical situations and the meaning of art in history can be entirely distorted. In his vitriolic attack on psychohistory, Stannard (1980) argued that psychohistory violates the most important achievement of modern historians—their increasing recognition that life in the past was fundamentally different, both socially and cognitively, from our own.

It is taken for granted, then, that the creative person being studied is part of a social and historical milieu. He or she is neither completely independent of this environment nor entirely subject to it. Furthermore, the same is true of the investigator. The investigator is a product of history just as the subject of the case is. Being aware of this opens the possibility of being able to transcend it (at least to a degree) and to appreciate the differences between one's own society and its outlook and those of the period at issue. The further back in time, the greater some of these differences will probably be. What was unthinkable in the past is often commonplace in the present. But being aware of them makes it more possible to avoid both ethnocentrism and what Runyon (1982) called *temporocentrism,* the habit of judging other times and periods by the standard and practice of one's own time and the tendency to see one's own time as inherently superior to other times. The capacity to rise above one's own social and historical situation depends on the sensitivity with which one recognizes one's involvement. Increasing knowledge and familiarity with the case and its context makes this more possible and more likely.

A Phenomenological Perspective: The Importance of Point of View

In order to understand how creative work proceeds, it is not enough to study the process from the outside, governed only by one's own perspective. It is necessary to try to enter the mind of the person being studied in order to reconstruct the framework and problems that he or she was developing. This is what I mean by a phenomenological perspective. To do this entails being as free as possible of prior assumptions. Unlike those who use traditional empirical research conventions, by which one begins with a hypothesis to be tested, introduces an experimental task or situation, and analyzes the subject's response to see if the hypothesis is confirmed or not, those who use the evolving systems approach try to "let what is there speak" (MacLeod, 1964, p. 65), that is, to deal with ideas "gathered from" experience rather than "forced into" experience, in Dewey's words (1917).

Part of the task, in gathering from the person's experience, is to understand what the person was doing from his or her point of view. The issue of point of view is especially critical because the hallmark of a creative artist or scientist is the creation or discovery of something novel and valuable, and constructing a new point of view accompanies this process. When Darwin, as a young naturalist, set off on the *Beagle* voyage, he lived in a world in which the prevailing catastrophist theory of the earth's evolution was being challenged. The first volume of Lyell's *Principles of Geology* (1830) had just been published. Lyell maintained that geological change was not the result of a series of physical catastrophes, such as floods, produced by divine intervention. Lyell's theory—later called uniformitarianism—was that, according to natural laws, the earth had evolved through slow geological change that had always operated and would always operate. Lyell's hypotheses left room for occasional divine intervention to effect the creation of new populations of organic beings to inhabit the earth.

One can say now that it was not a very great departure from Lyell's steady state geological theory to Darwin's steadily evolving natural order. But "making that small shift and expunging the Creator from the process of change were the twin tasks that were to become Darwin's life work" (Gruber, 1981a, p. 100). To make this small shift and develop his new evolutionist point of view was a long undertaking. When Darwin joined the *Beagle* on her circumnavigation voyage he was not an evolutionist. This point of view evolved gradually as a result of what he read, observed and thought about during the five-year voyage. It was only some months after his return, in 1837, that he had become a confirmed evolutionist.

Richardson, the novelist who pioneered the stream of consciousness genre in the English novel, is an example in another realm (Wallace, 1982). An important minor novelist who had a major influence on the English novel, Richardson began writing her life's work, the autobiographical novel *Pilgrimage,* in 1912 when she was 39. She wanted to write a novel that depicted life as it is actually experienced—immediately and subjectively. Richardson was rebelling against the literary realism of her time in which, although minute descriptions were provided, novelists felt their characters from the outside—as Pritchett (1949) said, "like miniatures from a height." Richardson, a feminist, associated literary realism with male forms of novel writing, tied to linear, sequenced, dramatic action and plot. This "masculine realism," as she called it, was, in her view, an inaccurate depiction of life as experienced—especially as experienced by women—and it had never captured the psychologically real. But although Richardson knew she wanted to write a new kind of novel, she intended at first no fresh departure in method. It was only after protracted and unsatisfactory struggles with conventional narrative form that she realized that a new method of writing was essential for what she wanted to do.

In order to render experience in its immediacy, she had to remove the author as an intrusive presence who "told" the reader what to think and feel. The first book of *Pilgrimage, Pointed Roofs,* was published in 1915. Richardson's achievement was by no means precocious. At 39, she was in her early middle age when she began writing the first book of *Pilgrimage.* It was written in a new form, which came to be known as the stream-of-consciousness genre. Richardson scrupulously avoided all the familiar expository anchors such as descriptions of place and time and sequenced dramatic action, explained and interpreted by a ubiquitous author. In *Pointed Roofs,* events are registered or reflected upon, often through interior monologue, only by the main character, whose mind is the sole filter through which the novel flows. In 1915 Richardson gave her astonished readers a wholly new experience. Ten years later, the stream of consciousness had become an accepted form, through the novels of Joyce, Woolf, Proust, and others.

The construction of a new point of view is part and parcel of the creative process; it develops slowly, demands mastery in one or several domains, requires thorough and wide-ranging knowledge of the work of others and a vision not only of what one needs to do but also of the skills to do it. An investigator studying the work and thought of a creative person strives to understand the development of this new perspective phenomenologically. The person who can do this well possesses a powerful psychological tool, a special kind of objectivity. But objectivity is not only a matter of assembling phenomenological facts. Getting such facts right is indispensable, but even more important is getting the right facts. Deciding what is significant includes having the capacity to rise above the limited vision of one's own social-historical situation, which, as I have said, partly depends on the ability to recognize the extent of one's involvement in it. Of course, gathering the phenomenological data is not the whole of the task. These data must also be subjected to disciplined critical analysis, judgment, and interpretation. The investigator cannot drown, as it were, in the experiential data of the case.

Hand in glove with this phenomenological perspective goes the decision that it is not only the ultimate creative product or products that are closely examined. Notebooks, diaries, journals, and the like are equally important. Then it is possible to reconstruct the thinking that preceded, accompanied, and culminated in the creative products, often omitted in the products themselves. Gruber's (1981a) study of Darwin's notebooks over the two-year period (1837–1839) during which Darwin constructed the theory of evolution is a case in point. Holmes's (1974, 1984) painstaking reconstruction, from laboratory notebooks, of the experiments of scientists such as Bernard gives a far more accurate and fine-grained picture of the evolution of scientists' ideas than is provided by their own publications, which do not describe the false starts, failures, detours, and struggles, that is, the actual processes and course of scientific discovery.

To take a phenomenological perspective is essentially a psychological idea, and psychologists have made use of it in very different ways. The growth of psychoanalytic theory relied on the phenomenological data that each case presented. When Freud treated his cases of hysteria (Freud & Breuer, 1895/1966), he paid careful attention to how the patients perceived their own experiences and their meaning for them. But although he relied on this phenomenological material as the basic data, by itself it was only the way into the case, the raw material for interpretation. The most important part of the interpretation centered on what the patient "experienced" but did not realize or understand at the time, that is, on unconscious drives outside the patient's conscious experience. Freud used the patient's point of view as a point of departure for his analysis and interpretation of the case. Thus, one could say that he used phenomenological material rather than a phenomenological perspective.

Another psychologist for whom a phenomenological approach was, for a time, indispensable, is Piaget. In his early work, Piaget took the child's point of view as a path toward finding out how children think. In order to ask a child a question like "Where do dreams come from?" one must be able to pick out that question because children will have an answer to it and because the answer will reveal the structure of the child's thought. Asking this kind of question is an example of finding the right facts or knowing what is significant. It also entails being able to clear the mind of possible prior assumptions, for example, that because children do not know where dreams come from, they have no thoughts about it.

Of course, it was Piaget, too, who saw that the ability to take another's point of view was a developmental achievement. Like Freud, Piaget used a phenomenological approach to gather raw material. For both, this was a preliminary step in procedure toward what they saw as the more important goal of interpreting and abstracting this material to build or confirm a universal theory built on prediction and causal relations.

It is tempting to evoke a famous story about a quite different kind of scientist who, on occasion, had what could be called phenomenological fantasies. When Einstein was 16, 7 years before he published his famous paper on relativity, he began to be "in a certain state of being puzzled" (Wertheimer, 1959, p. 214). He was thinking about the relative velocity of light and asked himself what would happen if one were riding on the beam. He was imagining himself physically entering into the phenomena as a way of thinking about them more effectively. He wanted to change his position or point of view with respect to the beam of light, experiencing it directly. It was also Einstein who said, "If atoms could talk, I would surely listen." In spite of the fact that Einstein was dealing with physical and mathematical entities that are far from being able to experience anything subjectively, he wanted—playfully but also seriously—to inject himself into their midst as if they were living organisms. Behind the playfulness, or the irony, of these imaginary events is an understanding that a phenomenological perspective is a powerful intellectual tool.

The Organization of Purpose

An overall purpose is central to the work of a creative person and is part of the motivation to go on working for long periods or for a lifetime (Ferrara, 1984; Gruber, 1980, 1981b). As this process is set in motion, ideas and enterprises proliferate and the means for achieving the overall purpose become both more numerous and more complex. Organization is needed to order this work, to set subsidiary goals, and to work in a way that is of maximum benefit to the individual's working economy as a whole. Perkins (1981) has put it well: "Discovery depends not on special processes but on special purposes" (p. 101).

In examining the working life, it is useful to map a person's enterprises and trace the course and relative weight of those enterprises. An enterprise is a set of projects and tasks that endures over time. In the vocabulary of the evolving systems approach, the map of enterprises is known as a network. The network of enterprise represents a creative individual's organization of purpose as a whole and provides a survey of that person's work activities over time or over the life (Ferrara, 1984; Gruber, 1981b). Charting a network of enterprise is a way of understanding the internal relations of different streams of work—a macrocosmic, simplified view of a system.

A network has a double purpose: (a) it provides an overview of the patterns of continuity and relationships that exist among enterprises, by showing the course of the work as a whole over years or decades of the working life in a simplified form; and (b) it serves as a counterpoint to the detailed and hermeneutic examination of "texts" such as a person's notebooks, critical comments, autobiographical accounts, correspondence, and creative products.[2]

---

[2]*Hermeneutics* is the art of textual interpretation and was, in its beginnings, tied only to theology and jurisprudence. Hermeneutics has now penetrated history and literary criticism. It is gaining increasing attention as a process in social science, where the interpretation of texts, including the responses of subjects, is critical (see, for example, Dallmayr & McCarthy, 1977).

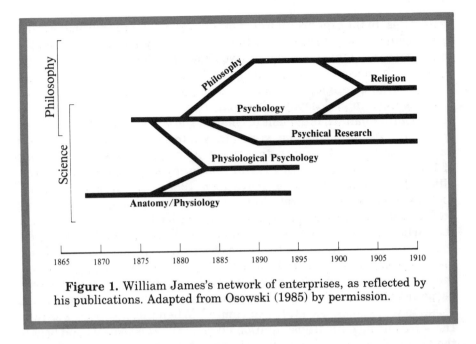

Figure 1. William James's network of enterprises, as reflected by his publications. Adapted from Osowski (1985) by permission.

Mapping a network of enterprise means marshaling and summarizing facts gleaned from intimate knowledge of a person's texts, life, and time line. It is a task performed standing "outside" the case; it provides an aerial map, so to speak, of the development of an individual's work enterprises over time. But each such network also represents aspects of the structure of a given person's knowledge. It entails that person's understanding of what is possible and his or her consciousness of current activities and future plans.

A person's enterprises can be mapped in different ways, for example, as a network of subject matter domains or as a series of themes in the person's work that may cut across subject matter domains or indicate the complexity of a single domain. A person's work creates enterprises composed of the things that he or she is trying to do, the tasks and projects that he or she sets out to accomplish. By tracking these, one can represent the creative purposes of the individual.

Perhaps the most common pattern of creative work is that there is a simultaneity of enterprises. A creative person is usually active in more than one enterprise at a time, although not necessarily with the same degree of intensity. The multiple, simultaneous enterprises of William James, for example, are clearly in evidence in Figure 1. The enterprise of psychology in James's work is a central, unifying one, holding the fabric of his enterprises together. As can be seen, it is also the single enterprise that falls within philosophy and science. This is in part because in the nineteenth century philosophy and psychology were not yet separate fields. In the organization of James's work there is a striking pattern of branching and interweaving. Physiological psychology represents a convergence of James's work in psychology on the one hand, and his activities in anatomy and physiology on the other. Similarly, his interest in religion and religious experience emerged as a separate enterprise from his work in philosophy and psychology.

A similar pattern is evident in Charles Darwin's work. When Darwin was on the *Beagle* voyage he wrote many hundreds of pages of notes on geology, zoology, and various other topics. After the voyage, in the spring of 1836, the development of Darwin's enterprises is represented in the different notebooks that he kept (Gruber, 1983). As can be seen in the highly simplified schematization of Figure 2, Darwin began the *Red Notebook* in 1836. It contains geological notes primarily, but it also includes the earliest notes on evolution. By mid-1837 Darwin had differentiated these enterprises, beginning the *A Notebook,* entirely devoted to geology, and at the same time, the *B Notebook,* which contained his first notes on the transmutation of species. When the B notebook was full, Darwin began the *C Notebook* in which he continued his transmutation notes and began to write about the evolution of mind. When this notebook was full, Darwin continued his transmutation notes in the *D Notebook,* and began the M and N series, which dealt with topics concerning human evolution, such as the expression of emotions and the continuity between *Homo sapiens* and other animals. Figure 2 shows this branching in Darwin's enterprises as well as their simultaneity. The development of differentiation and specialization is striking and occurred when an enterprise had proliferated to the point where it demanded separate status.

A second feature that a network of enterprise reveals is continuity. By organizing work in distinctive enterprises, it becomes possible to put tasks down and resume them without always starting from zero; the paraphernalia of naming and filing, and the separate social and professional networks corresponding to the different tasks support this twin need for differentiation and stabilization. The tasks are of long duration because a creative person characteristically takes up hard problems. If they were easier, many people would solve them, and they would solve them faster. But sometimes an enterprise continues over time for practical reasons—such as the need to earn money—as was the case for Richardson.

Figure 3 shows the ebb and flow of Richardson's writing enterprises as represented by her publications (Wallace, 1985). Richardson's work extends over five decades, from 1900 to about 1950. Although her major project was her autobiographical novel *Pilgrimage*, this was not her only writing enterprise. She wrote and published a great many essays, short stories and sketches, book reviews, commentaries, and other books, and also did translations from French and German. Her enterprises are shown here categorized by genre: short pieces of nonfiction, such as book reviews and commentary; short pieces of fiction, such as short stories and sketches;

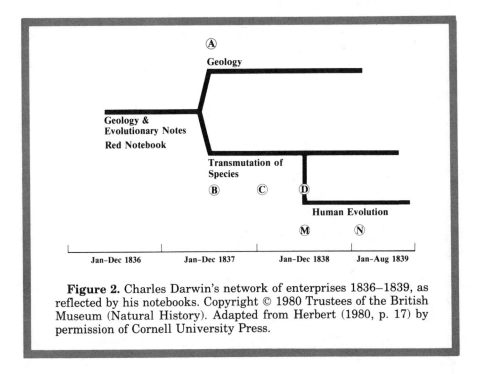

Figure 2. Charles Darwin's network of enterprises 1836–1839, as reflected by his notebooks. Copyright © 1980 Trustees of the British Museum (Natural History). Adapted from Herbert (1980, p. 17) by permission of Cornell University Press.

and two enterprises concerned with longer term work—her 13-book novel *Pilgrimage* and the writing and translating of book-length nonfiction works.

In the first decade of the century, Richardson wrote mostly book reviews and short pieces of fiction. It is as if these enterprises were simultaneously a way into the literary world and a way of practicing beginning to write. But it was also something she could still do toward the end of her career when she was in her seventies. At points in her life when her resources were limited she chose simpler tasks. Hyperbolically, we may speak of heroes as doing the "impossible," but we really mean that what they do is difficult or impossible for others. Choosing the possible must surely be a necessary part of a creative organization of purpose.

Figure 3 shows that in the two decades between 1911 and 1930 these two enterprises of Richardson's were interdependent: Great activity in writing reviews meant relatively less activity in writing short stories. These two enterprises fulfilled important functions for Richardson. They connected her with the literary community of her time and enabled her to practice her craft in varied fiction and nonfiction media, to air and refine her opinions about literature and other topics, and to promote and celebrate what she admired in the books of other writers such as Henry James, Aldous Huxley, H. G. Wells, and James Joyce.

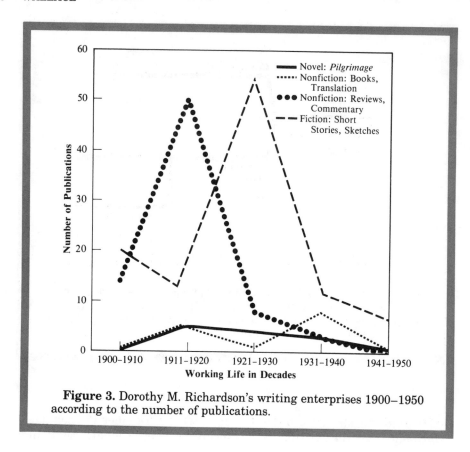

Figure 3. Dorothy M. Richardson's writing enterprises 1900–1950 according to the number of publications.

Accompanying the dynamic of these two enterprises was the stable activity of writing the thirteen books of *Pilgrimage,* which she continued for almost 40 years. Although the course of the novel in Figure 3 necessarily has a low frequency relative to the numerous publications in the journal-writing categories, it is also a more complex and taxing enterprise. Intermittently and over many years, Richardson also worked as a translator, earning a high reputation. Her motive for doing this was to earn money to support her other writing, a task and motive she had in common with many women writers, of whom two of the best known are Mary Wollstonecraft and George Eliot. (Indeed, it could be said that for many creative women, the network of enterprise should be differentiated to show those activities that result from their choice not to derive their identity or economic safety entirely through men, and for those who have families, to include long-term energy-demanding enterprises, such as childbirth and childrearing.) Although Richardson's struggle for money took time and energy, she chose to earn this money by doing something that was related to her other work and interests. Translation was done alongside other work and was put to good use in her larger organization of purpose. But whereas Richardson's translation work was something that she did and dropped as a money-earning enterprise, her writing of the novel continued over four decades.

The simultaneity and continuity that is evident in the enterprises of James, Darwin, and Richardson can provide certain advantages. Resuming work on an enterprise after a lapse means that the fruits of the work on other enterprises can be applied to the work at hand; techniques learned or refined, or knowledge gained in one enterprise, may be turned to advantage in another. Such patterns also suggest that a task or project undertaken in one enterprise becomes an interruption in another and the person is moved to resume work in the interrupted enterprise. Interruptions of this kind have well-known dynamic effects in short-term laboratory situations (Lewin, 1935). The concept of network of enterprise permits the application of the same line of thought on the scale of the life history. A theory of the organization of purpose is needed that deals at once with deep absorption in a single task—an absorption that Köhler (1971) compared with being in love—and management of parallel and sometimes interrelated projects.

Examining a network of enterprise makes clear that purpose is critical and central in the cognitive and affective organization of a creative adult. The organization of purpose includes a high aspiration level that finds reality in the working enterprises and a set of long-term goals that are never finished and that are designed not to be finished.

Conclusion

A critical problem and concern is whether gifted children will develop into creative adults. I have argued that a conception of the gifted child must be different from that of the creative adult. Furthermore, understanding more about gifted children and their potential development is predicated on understanding adult creativity. It then becomes possible to look backwards at the child with some clarity about the conditions necessary for living a creative adult life. In turn, we can begin to look for the emergence or development of these conditions. The first stage we could examine in such backward looking is adolescence.

I have discussed three issues in this chapter that can be extrapolated in order to examine gifted adolescents: First, creative work takes place in a context, and that context cannot be ignored. Second, a phenomenological perspective is critical to understanding the developmental course of creative work. Third, mapping a network of enterprise reveals a long-term organization of purpose.

What is known about the context of the gifted adolescent? I have suggested that the highly creative adult becomes something like a marginal person—part of the society but outdistancing it. Such a person may not be at home in the world as others know it, but in his or her privately constructed world it is another story. The gifted adolescent is doubly marginal. On the one hand, there is the move away from the family and parental control—a normal passage for most adolescents. But gifted children may also be leaving, or have outgrown, a complex and considerable system that supports the gift—a network of parents, teachers, and mentors. Up to this point, the gift has organized the life. Now the adolescent is faced with the task of beginning to shape the life to organize the gift. Virtually nothing is known about how this process of self-construction develops. What are the contexts that support or inhibit it?

It is necessary to do the hard phenomenological work of reconstructing the world of the gifted adolescent from her or his point of view. Family life may have been centered on the child's future much more explicity and significantly than is the case for other children. Many resources may have been mobilized to support and exploit the gift: Family decisions, such as where to live, may have been made with the child in mind, and finances may have been used to an unusual degree to invest in the child's future (Feldman, 1980). However supportive the parents and others are, the adolescent may feel especially indebted to them and acutely aware of the responsibility he or she has accrued to continue to work so that the gift may bear mature fruit. How does the gifted child's reaction to this responsibility affect his or her development?

Not all gifted children realize their gifts in adulthood. Bamberger's (1982) study of failed musical prodigies provides important leads that need to be pursued further. Does the break that she describes occur in other domains? What are the factors that contribute to or lessen the likelihood of failure? To what extent is this issue related to the domain of the gift, to the individual personality, and to social values?

A network of enterprise represents a deep commitment and long-term purposes. The network is a set of options being chosen, an evolving process. The enterprises are self-selected rather than imposed. When children are in school, their enterprises are chosen for them. How does a child move from a controlled school and family situation to the construction of a creative life? When are the necessary commitments made? What is the nature of the network of enterprises of gifted adolescents? How do they differ from those of other adolescents? How do they differ from those of creative adults?

Finally, as we who wish to maximize human development learn how better to mobilize our resources to understand and assist in the transformation of early gifts into adult creativity, we should ask the urgent question, "What is it all for?" Like other carriers of fire, creative people can create or they can destroy. How can we meet our greatest responsibility—helping them to make the right choice?

References

Arieti, S. (1976). *Creativity, the magic synthesis.* New York: Basic Books.

Armstrong, M. (1980). *Closely observed children.*London: Writers and Readers.

Arnheim, R. (1962). *The genesis of a painting: Picasso's Guernica.* Berkeley, CA: University of California Press.

Bamberger, J. (1982). Growing up prodigies: The midlife crisis. In D. H. Feldman (Ed.), *Developmental approaches to giftedness and creativity* (pp. 61–77). San Francisco, CA: Jossey-Bass.

Barlow, N. (Ed.) (1958). *The autobiography of Charles Darwin, 1809–1882.* London: Collins.

Barron, F., & Harrington, D. M. (1981). Creativity, intelligence, and personality. *Annual Review of Psychology, 32,*439–476.

Bedford, S. (1974). *Aldous Huxley, a biography.* New York: Knopf.

Biber, B. (1984). *Early education and psychological development.* New Haven, CT: Yale University Press.

Boswell, J. (1895). *The life of Samuel Johnson, L.L.D.*(Vols. 1–2). London: Routledge, Warner, & Routledge. (Original work published 1791).

Dallmayr, F. R., & McCarthy, T. A. (Eds.) (1977). *Understanding and social inquiry.* Notre Dame, IN: University of Notre Dame Press.

Denenberg, V. H. (1982). Comparative psychology and single-subject research. In A. E. Kazdin & A. H. Tuma (Eds.), *Single-case research designs.* San Francisco, CA: Jossey-Bass.

Dewey, J. (1917). The need for a recovery of philosophy. In *Creative intelligence: Essays in the pragmatic attitude.* New York: Holt.

Edel, L. (1959). *Literary biography.* Bloomington, IN: Indiana University Press.

Ellmann, R. (1959). *James Joyce.* New York: Oxford University Press.

Feldman, D. H. (1980). *Beyond universals in cognitive development.* Norwood, NJ: Ablex.

Feldman, D. H. (1982). A developmental framework for research with gifted children. In D. H. Feldman (Ed.), *Developmental approaches to giftedness and creativity* (pp. 31–45). San Francisco, CA: Jossey-Bass.

Ferrara, N. (1984). *Network of enterprise and the individual's organization of purpose.* Unpublished doctoral dissertation, Rutgers University, NJ.

Franklin, M. B. (1983). Imaginary worlds take shape: a study of creative work in sculpture. *Leonardo, 16*(3), 212–216.

Freud, S. (1964). *Leonardo da Vinci and a memory of his childhood.* New York: Norton. (Original work published 1916)

Freud, S., & Breuer, J. (1966). *Studies on hysteria.* New York: Avon Books. (Original work published 1895)

Fromm, E. (1980). *Greatness and limitations of Freud's thought.* New York: New American Library.

Gardner, H. (1982). Giftedness: Speculations from a biological perspective. In D. H. Feldman (Ed.), *Developmental approaches to giftedness and creativity* (pp. 47–60). San Francisco, CA: Jossey-Bass.

Garmezy, N. (1982). The case for the single case in research. In A. E. Kazdin & A. H. Tuma (Eds.), *Single-case research designs.* San Francisco, CA: Jossey-Bass.

Gowan, J. C. (1977). Background and history of the gifted-child movement. In J. C. Stanley, W. C. George, & C. H. Solano (Eds.), *The gifted and the creative: A fifty-year perspective* (pp. 5–27). Baltimore: Johns Hopkins University Press.

Gruber, H. E. (1980). The evolving systems approach to creativity. In S. Modgil & C. Modgil (Eds.), *Toward a theory of psychological development* (pp. 269–299). Windsor, England: NFER Publishing.

Gruber, H. E. (1981a). Cognitive psychology, scientific creativity, and the case study method. In M. Grmek, R. S. Cohen, & G. Cimino (Eds.), *On scientific discovery: The Erice lectures, 1977.* Dordrecht, Holland: Reidel.

Gruber, H. E. (1981b). *Darwin on man: A psychological study of scientific creativity* (2nd ed.). Chicago, IL: University of Chicago Press.

Gruber, H. E. (1982). On the hypothesized relation between giftedness and creativity. In D. H. Feldman (Ed.), *Developmental approaches to giftedness and creativity* (pp. 7–29). San Francisco, CA: Jossey-Bass.

Gruber, H. E. (1983). History and creative work: From the most ordinary to the most exalted. *Journal of the History of Behavioral Sciences, 19,* 4–14.

Guilford, J. P. (1967). *The nature of human intelligence.* New York: McGraw-Hill.

Guilford, J. P., & Hoepfner, R. (1971). *The analysis of intelligence.* New York: McGraw-Hill.

Herbert, S. (Ed.). (1980). *The red notebook of Charles Darwin.* London and Ithaca: British Museum (Natural History) and Cornell University Press.

Holmes, F. L. (1974). *Claude Bernard and animal chemistry: The emergence of a scientist.* Cambridge, MA: Harvard University Press.

Holmes. F. L. (1984, August). *Laboratory notebooks and scientific creativity.* Paper presented at the meeting of the American Psychological Association, Toronto, Canada.

Hudson, L. (1966)., Contrary imaginations. London: Methuen.

Hudson, L. (1975). *Human beings.* Garden City, NY: Anchor Books.

Jeffrey, F. R. (1983). *The thinker as poet: A psychological study of the creative process through an analysis of a poet's worksheets.* Unpublished doctoral dissertation, Rutgers University, NJ.

Kazdin, A. E. (1982). Single case experimental designs in clinical research and practice. In A. E. Kazdin & A. H. Tuma (Eds.), *Single-case research designs.* San Francisco, CA: Jossey-Bass.

Keegan, R. T., & Gruber, H. E. (1983). Love, death, and continuity in Darwin's thinking. *Journal of the History of the Behavioral Sciences, 19*(1), 15–30.

Köhler, W. (1971). The obsessions of normal people. In M. Henle (Ed.), *The selected papers of Wolfgang Köhler* (pp. 398–412). New York: Liverright.

Kramer, H. (1977, December 25). Writing writers' lives. *The New York Times Book Review,* p. 1.

Kris, E. (1952). *Psychoanalytic explorations in art.* New York: International Universities Press.

Kris, E. (1967). Psychoanalysis and the study of creative imagination. In *Selected papers of Ernst Kris.* New Haven, CT: Yale University Press.

Lewin, K. (1935). *A dynamic theory of personality: Selected papers.* New York: McGraw-Hill.

Lyell, C. (1830). *Principles of geology: Being an inquiry how far the former changes of the earth's surface are referable to causes now in operation* (Vol. 1). London: John Murray.

MacKinnon, D. W. (1963). Creativity and images of the self. In R. W. White (Ed.), *The study of lives: Essays in honor of Henry Murray.* New York: Atherton.

MacLeod, R. B. (1964). Phenomenology: A challenge to experimental psychology. In T. W. Wann (Ed.), *Behaviorism and phenomenology.* Chicago, IL: University of Chicago Press.

Mansfield, R. S., & Busse, T. V. (1981). *The psychology of creativity and discovery.* Chicago: IL: Nelson-Hall.

Olsen, T. (1978). *Silences.* New York: Delacourt Press/Seymour Lawrence.

Osowski, J. (1985). *Metaphor and the organization of knowledge: A case study of William James.* Doctoral dissertation, Rutgers University, NJ. Manuscript in preparation.

Patrick, C. (1935). Creative thought in poets. *Archives of psychology.* No. 178.

Patrick, C. (1937). Creative thought in artists. *Journal of Psychology, 4,* 35–73.

Perkins, D. (1981). *The mind's best work.* Cambridge, MA: Harvard University Press.

Plato. (1920). Ion; or of the Iliad. In E. Rhys (Ed.), *Five dialogues of Plato bearing on the poetic inspiration* (Everyman ed.). New York: Dutton.

Polya, G. (1957). *How to solve it: A new aspect of mathematical method.* Garden City, NY: Anchor Books.

Pritchett, V. S. (1949). *The living novel.* London: Chatto and Windus.

Richardson, D. M. (1976). *Pilgrimage* (Vols. 1–4). New York: Popular Library.

Rothenberg, A. (1979). *The emerging goddess: The creative process in art, science, and other fields.* Chicago, IL: University of Chicago Press.

Runyon, W. M. (1982). *Life histories and psychobiography.* New York: Oxford University Press.

Russell, B. (1959). *My philosophical development.* London: Allen & Unwin.

Russell, B. (1967, 1968, 1969). *The autobiography of Bertrand Russell* (Vols. 1–3). London: Allen & Unwin.

Shapiro, E. K., & Wallace, D. B. (1981). Developmental stage theory and the individual reconsidered. In E. K. Shapiro & E. Weber (Eds.), *Cognitive and affective growth: Developmental interaction.* Englewood Cliffs, NJ: Erlbaum.

Showalter, E. (1977). *A literature of their own.* Princeton, NJ: Princeton University Press.

Slochower, H. (1974). The psychoanalytic approach: Psychoanalysis and creativity. In S. Rosner & L. E. Abt (Eds.), *Essays in creativity.* Croton-on-Hudson, NY: North River Press.

Stannard, D. E. (1980). *Shrinking history: On Freud and the failure of psychohistory.* New York: Oxford University Press.

Taylor, C. W., & Barron, F. (1963). *Scientific creativity: Its recognition and development.* New York: Wiley.

Torrance, E. P. (1966). *Torrance tests of creative thinking: Norms-technical manual.* Personnel Press.

Vinacke, W. E. (1974). *The psychology of thinking.* New York: McGraw-Hill.

Wallace, D. B. (1982). *The fabric of experience: A psychological study of Dorothy M. Richardson's "Pilgrimage."* Doctoral dissertation, Rutgers University, NJ.

Wallace, D. B. (1985). Organization of purpose and feminine realism in the work of Dorothy M. Richardson. In D. B. Wallace & H. E. Gruber (Eds.), *Creative people at work: 12 cognitive case studies.* Manuscript in preparation.

Wallace, D. B., & Gruber, H. E. (Eds.). (1985). *Creative people at work: 12 cognitive case studies.* Manuscript in preparation.

Wallas, G. (1926). *The art of thought.* New York: Harcourt Brace.

Watson, J. D. (1968). *The double helix.* New York: New American Library.

Wertheimer, M. (1959). *Productive thinking.* New York: Harper Torchbooks.

Whyte, L. L. (1962). *The unconscious before Freud.* Garden City, NY: Anchor Books.

Wittkower, R. & Wittkower, A. (1963). *Born under Saturn: The character and conduct of artists. A documented history from antiquity to the French revolution.* New York: Norton.

Woolf, V. (1957). *A room of one's own.* New York: Harcourt Brace Jovanovich. (Original work published 1929)

Woolf, V. (1959). *The common reader* (2nd series). London: Hogarth Press. (Original work published 1932)

13. Commonalities Between the Intellectual Extremes: Giftedness and Mental Retardation

Edward Zigler
Ellen A. Farber
Yale University

The deviant or atypical individual has always been of special interest to psychologists. Intellectual deviance in particular has intrigued many scientists and drawn them to work with retarded and developmentally disabled children. In fact, over the past three decades the study of mental retardation has advanced from a relatively moribund state to a methodologically sophisticated and theoretically diverse discipline in its own right. Rapid progress on the scientific, educational, and political fronts testifies to the devotion of considerable resources to the futures of retarded children. For example, the National Institute of Child Health and Human Development was charged at its inception to take a leading role in funding mental retardation research. Education has moved from remote institutional settings to special, mainstreamed, and even regular classrooms under the supervision of highly trained specialists. Retarded individuals are now accorded the same equal access and legal rights as are all non-handicapped citizens.

The substantial attention lavished on the lower end of the intellectual continuum remains unequaled. No parallel effort has been directed toward unraveling the mysteries of the opposite end of the scale, intellectual giftedness. This relative lack of interest is not particularly surprising inasmuch as mental retardation is generally viewed as a social problem in need of a solution. Giftedness is instead viewed as a privilege bestowed upon a chosen group, and it does not command social intervention. Retarded children are considered deserving of help because their lack of intelligence makes them incapable of helping themselves. Gifted children are assumed to be enviably adept at fending for themselves by virtue of their giftedness.

The differential interest in the two ends of the intellectual spectrum may also be related to the egalitarian ethos of a democracy. Aiding retarded individuals to function as much as possible like nonretarded people is a goal consistent with this ethos. Optimizing the development of intellectually gifted children is a far different matter. The specter is raised of creating an elite group of intelligentsia forever separated from the social mainstream.

Despite the apparent lack of social commitment, in recent years a burgeoning interest has developed in intellectual giftedness. As evidence on this point note that (a) the American Psychological Association is publishing this volume, (b) a committee on the gifted has been created by the Social Science Research Council, (c) hearings on the gifted child were held by a Senate subcommittee in 1983, and (d) there is a proliferation of university-based summer programs for gifted elementary and high school students. The causes of this resurgence of social and scientific interest in giftedness probably involve several timely factors. For one, although the study of mental retardation has been characterized by a rather steady effort over the past three decades (Maloney & Ward, 1979), concern with the gifted has waxed and waned. Gifted children have been periodically rediscovered, as in the months following the Soviet's Sputnik feat, with a temporary flurry of activity by social scientists (see Tannenbaum, 1979).

It is possible that over the years these efforts have produced a critical mass of ideas sufficient to precipitate the recent increased concern with the phenomenon of intellectual giftedness. There are also workers in today's generation who complain that the social sciences have now spent an inordinate amount of effort on children who display attenuated school performance, whereas the effort devoted to gifted students is neither

Preparation of this manuscript was supported by Research Grant HD 03008 from the National Institute of Child Health and Human Development. The authors thank Sally Styfco for her valuable editorial assistance.

comparable nor commensurate with the number of individuals involved. These workers have demanded equity in the intellectual inquiry; parents have demanded equity in academic opportunity.

Perhaps the most compelling explanation for the renewed interest in giftedness lies in the political Zeitgeist. Somewhat suddenly, the ascendancy of the United States as a scientific and technological power is no longer taken for granted. The rapid progress of other nations in military, industrial, and intellectual spheres has brought the United States to the stark realization that it has rested on its laurels too long. At the same time, national and state commissions on education have been decrying serious flaws in the schooling of our youth. Large numbers of students are reading below grade level and are graduating from high school as functional illiterates; SAT scores showed a dramatic drop for a troubling number of years; and colleges and businesses have often had to lower their standards for recruits. Even worse, American students are repeatedly found to be behind children in other industrialized nations, particularly in math and the sciences. These facts have fostered a serious commitment to upgrade the educational system for all American children. Now may be the time for the recalcitrant acknowledgment that gifted children, though few in number, represent a significant force in determining our nation's future technological status and position as a world power.

Present knowledge of intellectual giftedness clearly is not sufficient if psychologists and educators are to develop appropriate educational techniques. However, we need not waste time rediscovering the wheel. The course of the study of mental retardation appears to offer many lessons that can be used to study the opposite end of the intellectual spectrum. Theoretical and historical issues and problems found in the literature on retardation appear to be applicable to the gifted group. Methodology that has been perfected in the mental retardation field also may be adaptable. Our goal in this chapter is to examine these commonalities and to determine how issues relating to retarded people may be employed to illuminate parallel issues relating to those of superior intellect.

History and Myths Concerning Giftedness and Retardation

Popular interest in both intellectually subnormal and intellectually gifted people predates the rise of the formal disciplines that became the social sciences. Both groups were commonly feared because they were thought to be strange and different beings. In fact, the literature is replete with references to both intellectual classes being freaks of nature. In this regard, it is interesting to note that half a century ago Hollingworth (1926) referred to retarded people as "unfortunate deviates" and to gifted people as "fortunate deviates."

The explanations advanced to account for both types of individuals often involved similar mystical or extrahuman forces. In some societies retarded people were thought to be possessed by divine spirits (Zigler, 1968). Luther felt that they were possessed by the devil and that exorcism and drowning were the only effective solutions. The abilities of gifted people to produce impressive accomplishments were also thought to come from supernatural intervention. As Ashby and Walker (1968) explain, the term *gifted* implies that one has received a gift and, because it is bestowed from birth, it must come from God. Similarly, it is not uncommon to hear parents of a retarded child ascribe their plight to God's will as His way of testing their faith and religious commitment.

Another historical similarity between retardation and giftedness is that both groups have been the subject of strong and widely held stereotypes. Many of the myths upon which these stereotypes are based still linger despite considerable evidence to the contrary. For example, the following quotation is from an address given in 1912 by Walter Fernald, who was one of the nation's leading figures in the area of mental retardation:

> The social and economic burdens of uncomplicated feeblemindedness are only too well known. The feebleminded are a parasitic, predatory class, never capable of self-support or of managing their own affairs. The great majority ultimately become public charges in some form. They cause unutterable sorrow at home and are a menace and danger to the community. Feebleminded women are almost invariably immoral and . . . usually become carriers of venereal disease or give birth to children who are as defective as themselves. . . . Every feebleminded person, especially the high-grade imbecile, is a potential criminal, needing only the proper environment and opportunity for the development and expression of his criminal tendencies. (Quoted in Davies & Ecob, 1959, pp. 47–48)

The negative stereotype surrounding retarded individuals has abated somewhat in very recent years. The image of the warm and loving Down's syndrome child and the increased interaction between retarded and non-retarded people as a result of social mainstreaming may be causes or effects of this more positive attitude. Still, the negative tone resurfaces often, as when residents of areas where halfway houses are proposed protest the introduction of the retarded element into their neighborhoods.

Perhaps surprisingly, the stereotypes applied to gifted people have also been largely negative. Back in 1895, Babcock listed the potential outcomes for a person unlucky enough to be born with "degenerate genes," among whom he included the gifted:

First, and most prominent in the order of frequency is an early death. Second, he may swell the criminal ranks. Third, he may become mentally deranged and ultimately find his way into a hospital for the insane. Fourth, and least frequently, he startles the world by an invention or discovery in science or by an original composition of great merit in art, music or literature. He is then styled a genius. (Quoted in Prentky, 1979, p. 2)

The theme of mental derangement has been long lived. Throughout history there has been a popular belief that geniuses in particular pay a price for their creative intellect in madness and emotional instability. This view is based on striking instances of psychopathological ailments among the ranks of the gifted. Sir Francis Galton, for example, suffered nervous symptoms throughout life and had two breakdowns. Gregor Mendel had several breakdowns or depressions, and Charles Darwin was plagued by a chronic and mysterious illness that depleted his energies and made him unable to sleep. Isaac Newton and Michael Faraday, two of the greatest physicists in history, both became psychotic, although each eventually recovered his sanity. The lives of such greats as Van Gogh, Blake, da Vinci, Socrates, Kant, and Poe all had their dark aspects.

The individuals listed here all attained a degree of eminence that earned them the label of genius. The connection between genius and madness remains a possibility worthy of further investigation. However, no such relation has been found for giftedness in general. Several studies of personality traits in gifted individuals have shown no evidence of an inordinately high incidence of maladjustment. The most notable study was that of Terman (1925; Terman & Oden, 1947, 1959), which should set to rest many of the popular stereotypes about gifted individuals. In 1922 Terman reported the results of an initial study of 1,470 children with IQs of 135 or over. They were for the most part in grades 3 to 8 and averaged 11 years old when they were selected. In comparison with a control group of average intelligence, members of the gifted group were found to be more socially poised, more outstanding in educational accomplishments, and less prone to headaches, nervousness, tics, and stuttering. Members of the gifted group were remarkably well adjusted. Follow-up studies were made every 5 to 10 years; the last one was done in 1972, when these individuals were entering their sixties. Their social adjustments were again found to be as satisfactory as in the general population.

Terman's study also contained evidence shattering the myth that a brilliant mind must be housed in a small and fragile body. The children in his gifted group were taller, heavier, and more active in play than were their average-IQ peers. Still, the image persists of the puny, bespectacled prodigy beset by a host of physical shortcomings. The opposite stereotype has long been applied to retarded people: the immense but illiterate "Moose" comic-strip type, or the strong "bull" laborer who speaks in monosyllables if at all. These conceptions are in direct opposition to the facts. For example, a characteristic feature of Down's syndrome is small stature. Individuals whose retardation is caused by other organic disorders are often afflicted by added physical handicaps and health problems. Mildly retarded persons are frequently from the lower socioeconomic classes where malnutrition and poor health care can threaten normal growth and development. The truth is that individuals across the intelligence spectrum come in a variety of shapes, sizes, and degrees of robustness. Nature is not evenhanded: It does not endow the mind and take from the body or vice versa.

Problems With Definition

We have alluded to a subtle but substantial difference between genius and giftedness. This distinction brings us to a basic conceptual problem that has hampered the study of both retarded and superior intelligence— namely the problem of definition. Without clear definitions there is no way of calculating the prevalence of either retardation or giftedness, making it impossible to allocate resources fairly or to plan programs to serve these groups. Scientific knowledge also suffers, since the specific population studied by one researcher may not meet the same parameters as another researcher's sample. Findings are thus not readily generalizable, and considerable investigative effort is denied the impact it should have.

The seriousness of the definitional void is immediately suggested by a glance at the nomenclature used to describe levels of intellect. Retarded individuals have been grouped along various dimensions such as idiot versus moron, custodial versus educable, and profound versus mild. Although the groups in each set maintain some distinction, there are so many sets that the literature has become a muddled sea of jargon. Terms for the gifted are not so numerous, but they completely fail to discriminate because they are used interchangeably. Labels such as genius, prodigy, fast learner, precocious, creative, and brilliant have all become synonymous with intellectual giftedness. The study of both high and low intelligence has been hurt deeply by the confusion of terms because they ultimately confuse thought. The most provocative illustration is the label "exceptional," which has been used to describe both retarded and gifted children.

One reason for the complex lexicon in the study of intelligence is that the topic legitimately falls within the interests of genetics, education, psychology, neurology, sociology, and anthropology, among others. Each of these disciplines has its own circumscribed language. For example, educators refer to trainable or academically talented children, whereas psychologists refer to moderately retarded or high-IQ groups. There is a lesson to be learned here from the biological sciences, which have long used standard Latin terms so that knowledge can be shared on interdisciplinary and international planes. Although we do not necessarily suggest the use of Latin, we are entering a plea for a consistent nomenclature.

The study of mental retardation is considerably more sophisticated than that of giftedness, and some of the definitional issues already identified and addressed may help direct workers in the latter field. For one, there has been an effort to adopt and define terms that differentiate retarded individuals on the basis of severity (mild, moderate, severe) or on the basis of etiology (organic, familial). The requirements of these classes are widely published so that they are becoming familiar to the various professions.

An official and detailed definition of mental retardation was offered in 1959 (see Heber, 1961) by the American Association on Mental Deficiency (AAMD). The effort spurred so much controversy that the definition has since been revised twice (Grossman, 1973, 1983), and further refinements have been suggested (see Zigler, Balla, & Hodapp, 1984). The important point is that the search for a quantitatively precise definition of mental retardation has triggered a great deal of theoretical and philosophical discourse that can only help to enrich future efforts. First we will examine the content of this debate in the field of mental retardation and then attempt to apply relevant insights to parallel problems in the study of giftedness.

Characteristics Used to Define Mental Retardation

There is no question that the most distinctive feature of mental retardation is inadequate cognitive functioning. Long before formal psychometrics were used to assess intelligence, a lack of age-appropriate skills in learning and caring for oneself identified retarded individuals. With the development of intelligence tests, greater reliance was placed on IQ scores as an indicator of retardation. But exactly what IQ score is sufficiently low to reflect a deficit in intellectual capacity? For many years there was general agreement that the retarded population comprised the bottom 3 percent of the IQ distribution. Then in 1959 the AAMD defined mental retardation as being indicated by test scores more than one standard deviation below the mean, or by an IQ lower than 85. In 1973 the Association again shifted the IQ criterion, this time to two standard deviations below the mean, or an IQ below 70. These seemingly simple changes meant that in less than two decades the number of Americans identified as being retarded increased from 6 million (3%) to over 30 million (IQ < 85) and then decreased to about 5 million (IQ < 70).

The changes in cutoff points for designating retardation indicate that there is nothing in the nature of the phenomenon to indicate where the defining line should be. The same is true of giftedness. In terms of IQ, giftedness has been variously defined by scores over 125, over 140, over 180, and as the top 2 to 4 percent of the population. To further confuse the matter, a small number of individuals in the gifted group may qualify as geniuses. However, superlative intelligence is not their ultimate defining feature. One could undoubtedly find many faculty and students at the nation's top universities who have exceptionally high IQs, but there would probably not be a genius among them. To be a true genius an exceptional pattern of basic talent must bring transcendent accomplishment that retains value over the course of time.

This discussion suggests that IQ scores—whether high or low—are not very reliable predictors of behavior. Theorists have thus sought other dimensions to complete their definitions of both retardation and giftedness. We will now examine some of these dimensions and evaluate their usefulness in the scientific enterprise.

It is not very unusual to find two retarded individuals with the same low IQ, one of whom is married, employed, and involved in the community and the other of whom requires constant supervision in an institutional setting. These striking differences in social competence translate into strikingly different responsibilities placed upon the individual and upon society. Hence there have long been efforts to classify as retarded only those who fail both intellectually (academically) and socially. These efforts were formalized in 1973 when the AAMD included deficits in adaptive behavior in their official definition of mental retardation. That is, to be designated as retarded an individual must have an IQ below 70 and fail to meet certain age-appropriate social demands. This was a noble attempt to acknowledge the importance of nonintellectual factors such as motivation and effort in determining social competence. However, the inclusion of such nonquantifiable and controversial phenomena has detracted from the utility of this extremely consequential definition.

In a recent questioning of the AAMD definition, Zigler et al. (1984) pointed out some of the vagaries of the social adaptation concept. For example, social expectancies change with age and with social situations, making it possible for an individual to be considered adapted at some times and places but not at others. A low-IQ child who fails in school would be charged with a deficit in adaptive behavior and labeled retarded. With some remedial instruction the child might do better and be entitled to shed the label. Meanwhile this same child may have functioned adequately outside of school, so the label was appropriate only for the length of the school day. (So much has been said of the "6-hour retarded child" that some have suggested abandoning the retardation label altogether, e.g., Mercer, 1973.) Zigler et al. (1984) concluded:

> Social adaptation is not an enduring trait, and it leads to a classification system that allows individuals to flit from category to category.
> . . . Although the definition of intelligence may remain elusive, work-

ers are light years away from agreeing on the ultimate defining feature of social adaptation; and because social adaptation is so far from basic definition, measures to assess it necessarily lack validity. Such a vague foundation for such an important classification system is inadequate and unacceptable. (pp. 226–227)

Characteristics Used to Define Giftedness

The study of giftedness has likewise been plagued by definitions that are too broad and lack reliable assessment techniques. In defining giftedness, one dimension that is invariably included is superior intelligence. Many workers feel that the truly gifted person has more than this, however, and have embellished the definition to include creativity and various specific talents (see Renzulli, 1978). One such definition was adopted by the United States Office of Education, which recognizes gifted students as those who show demonstrated achievement or potential in any one of six areas (Marland, 1972). These include general intellectual ability, specific academic aptitude, creative or productive thinking, leadership ability, visual and performing arts talent, or excellent psychomotor ability, a category that was subsequently dropped (Fox, 1981). This multifaceted definition of giftedness, like that of retardation, is not easily operationalized, nor does it yield a homogeneous group for educational or research purposes.

The adoption of such an inclusive and vague definition in the 1970s makes one wonder if earlier scientific efforts in this field were ignored. In 1921, when Terman began his classic longitudinal study, he attempted to locate children who, regardless of their intellectual ability, showed exceptional talent in any of the following areas: music, art, mechanical ingenuity, and inventiveness. After a short time these efforts were discontinued for two reasons. First, the devices then available for measuring the specific talents lacked validity and necessitated obtaining the judgments of teachers and others. The judgments, however, had poor interrater reliability and were found to be influenced by personal factors such as attractiveness and effort. Secondly, almost without exception, children who showed unquestionable talent also qualified for the study on the basis of general intelligence (Stanford–Binet IQ of 140 or higher). Thus the time spent in looking for special talent was largely wasted effort (Goodenough, 1956).

In another milestone work on giftedness done in 1926, Hollingworth attempted to distinguish the elements of talent and genius. She wrote, "One who shows a wonderful capacity for mental perfection is called a 'genius'. In general 'talent' means a remarkable ability falling short, however, of the superlative" (p. 3). In a later discussion, Hollingworth suggested that the word *talent* be confined to specialized aptitudes, such as those in music or art, which she thought to be basically unrelated to general intelligence. Thus Hollingworth saw exceptional talents or aptitudes as being something akin to Spearman's s factors. She viewed giftedness as being defined essentially by general intelligence (the g factor).

The controversy over whether giftedness involves specialized or pervasive ability comes to a head for the trait of creativity. Some argue that creativity is an essential component of intellectual giftedness and should be included in the definition. However, in several studies of individuals with high IQs, surprisingly few were judged to be highly creative. Getzels and Jackson (1962) found little overlap between high IQ and high creativity groups when they tested an intellectually superior population of students in a private high school. Torrance (1962) found that only 30 percent of the elementary school students he tested scored within the top 20 percent on both IQ and creativity tests. In fact, Wallach and Kogan (1965a) succeeded in constructing several tests of creativity that correlate positively with one another but not at all with traditional IQ tests.

Of course, intelligence tests were designed to assess academic ability, and creativity may play only a small part in academic performance. McNemar (1964) further suggested that the low correlations found between creativity and intelligence are due to faulty experimental designs. In selecting individuals who have distinguished themselves in creative performance, the studies examine a very narrow range of creativity. These individuals usually have IQs over 120, making the range of intelligence narrow as well. Correlations between creativity and intelligence are thus computed on restricted ranges of the two traits. Barron (1961) found that the correlation between intelligence and creativity over the whole range of ability was approximately $+.40$, but that among individuals with IQs over 120 it was only $+.10$. As a whole, the research suggests that a moderately high level of intelligence is necessary for creative work but that beyond that point being more or less intelligent does not determine the level of a person's creative ability (MacKinnon, 1968).

Another twist in the intelligence–creativity debate centers on the uses of general creative talent. For example, among those with high intelligence, creativity is an important variable in predicting success outside of school (Wallach & Wing, 1969). Children with high intelligence and creativity have been found to be confident, able, and sociable, whereas those with considerable creativity but less outstanding intelligence were not so well adjusted (Wallach & Kogan, 1965b). From a theoretical standpoint, Feldman (1982) saw creativity as an outgrowth of giftedness and not a separate ability. Thus real-life creativity could be considered the end result—the optimal use of one's potential. There is only limited evidence that tests of divergent thinking predict real-life creative accomplishments (e.g., Torrance, 1975). This suggests that creativity may be better used as an outcome measure rather than a predictive variable.

A Tentative Solution to Defining Giftedness and Mental Retardation

The difficulty in resolving a place for creativity in the definition of giftedness is analogous to the problem of including adaptive behavior deficits in the definition of mental retardation. Both criteria are ill defined and evade reliable measurement. Efforts to develop viable tests of the constructs continue, but to date there are no rigorous or even generally accepted definitions of the traits such tests attempt to assess. The intelligence variable, by contrast, presents no such dilemma to the extent that one is satisfied with the definition that intelligence is simply what standard IQ tests measure.

Given the state of the art, Zigler et al. (1984) proposed that mental retardation be defined on the basis of IQ scores alone. This suggestion is not all that revolutionary in spite of the AAMD's formal requirement of a low IQ accompanied by adaptive behavior deficits. In the everyday practice of those working with retarded individuals, exclusive reliance on IQ scores to define retardation is routine. Smith and Polloway (1979) found that most researchers use IQ as the sole criterion for identifying samples of retarded people, a practice that the editor of the official AAMD journal accepts "with some regret" (Robinson, 1980, p. 107). Similarly, physicians and psychologists primarily employ the IQ when making diagnoses of retardation, a practice that many criticize (e.g., Adams, 1973) but that continues nevertheless. Professionals probably avoid social adaptation indicators for the reasons we have mentioned. Although social competence is extremely important, mental retardation must be conceptualized in terms of actual cognitive functioning in order for the condition to make any practical or scientific sense.

Measurement of dimensions of giftedness is also not as well developed as that of intelligence. In fact, the field has not changed significantly in the 60 years since Terman began his study. Psychologists are still not in a position to assess reliably many of the concepts theorists like to include in definitions of giftedness, such as creativity, task commitment, and certain talents (Renzulli, 1978). Thus it may be that IQ is currently the most adequate tool for defining giftedness. Again, this does not mean that noncognitive aspects are unimportant, but only that their inclusion would seriously compromise a precise operational definition of the gifted classification. Creativity and other talents, as well as superior intelligence, remain important branches of study, but maintaining them as separate research areas with overlapping populations appears to be the most fruitful course at this point in time.

It must be noted that there may be little relation between IQ and many measures of everyday functioning. Individuals with low IQs vary widely in social competence, just as people with high IQs vary in the expression of their talents. This can be explained largely by the personality and motivational factors shaped by each person's unique socialization history. For example, the retarded child who is babied and catered to may never have the opportunity or desire to develop independence. The gifted child whose talents are unappreciated or viewed as troublesome may bow to pressures to conform and become an apathetic underachiever. There are simply too many nonintellective determinants of behavior to expect the IQ to be a very robust indicator of everyday functioning. Making the IQ score central to the definitions of mental retardation and giftedness is predicated only on the view that the behavioral sciences currently have no better measure by which to assess intellectual ability.

Explanations for Intellectual Differences

A narrow operational definition of retardation and giftedness does not imply a narrow approach to the study of the intellectual extremes. The causes and potential outcomes of more or less intelligence are the subjects of raging controversies whose diversity must be considered. In this case, the theories concerning the nature and origins of intelligence have been applied with equal fervor to both ends of the IQ distribution. We briefly examine some of these philosophies to show how each leads to a uniform conception of the retarded and gifted groups, although these conceptions differ from one another depending upon the theory on which they are based.

Developmental Versus Difference Theories

An elemental question is whether retarded and gifted people differ quantitatively (have more or less of something like the *g* factor), as developmental theorists maintain, or differ in kind (have qualitatively different cognitive processes) from the majority of the population, which is of average intelligence, as the difference theorists claim. Difference theorists maintain that retarded children of similar developmental levels differ in cognitive performance because of intrinsic differences over and above intellectual slowness (see Zigler & Balla, 1982). The qualitative difference position is encountered most dramatically in early studies that placed retarded children in a position on the phylogenetic scale somewhere between monkeys and nonretarded children (see Zigler, 1968). More recently their defects have been attributed to lack of cognitive differentiation, rigidity, inadequate neurons or neurological functions, and unknown structural phenomena.

Developmental theorists first draw a distinction between organic and familial retarded classes. Individuals who have organic problems such as genetic disorders or brain damage are viewed in much the same way that difference theorists view all retarded people. That is, their cognitive functioning is indeed different because of faulty intellectual apparatus. Although these individuals are found across the entire IQ distribution (some even within the average and above-average range), for the most part their IQs are between 0 and 50, much lower than could be explained by accepted polygenic theories of intelligence. However, the majority of the retarded population have no evidence of organic brain dysfunction and have IQs between about 50 and 70. Developmental theorists consider this familial retarded group as normal in the sense that they fall within the normal distribution of intelligence dictated by the gene pool. Although their rate of intellectual development (IQ) is slower than that of nonretarded children, developmental theorists believe that the cognitive processes at their disposal are the same. Thus their cognitive performance should be similar to that of nonretarded children of equivalent developmental level if motivational factors are controlled.

A parallel controversy in the field of giftedness concerns whether the superior capabilities of gifted children are the result of their ample intelligence or of qualitatively different cognitive powers. Difference theorists are likely to argue the latter case; that is, the nature of the gifted child's thinking is of an entirely different structure, and it is not within the capacity of those with average intellectual potential. That Sir Francis Galton could read and write fluently at the age of 5 would not signify merely accelerated development, but an awesome ability to learn that in no way resembles the learning processes of the average 5-year-old.

Developmental theorists could logically extend the two-group approach to mental retardation to the opposite end of the intelligence scale. Most polygenic explanations of intelligence predict a normal IQ distribution of approximately 50 to 150. That is, given the basic diversity of the species, most naturally occurring genetic combinations and environmental interactions could account for IQs of between three standard deviations below and three above the population mean, or nearly all cases. Thus familial retarded people (IQs 50–70) and intellectually superior people (IQs 130–150) are integral ends of the normal intelligence curve. Those with IQs below 50 or above 150 require a different explanation.

Unlike organically retarded people, gifted individuals cannot be divided into separate groups on the basis of the etiology of their giftedness. However, it may be possible that they differ among themselves in other ways such as in neurophysiological functioning or cognitive style. It has been argued (Hollingworth, 1942) that there is an "optimum intelligence" between IQ 125 and 155 and that too much intelligence may present a serious obstacle to normal psychological development.

Nature Versus Nurture

The developmental position relies heavily on the assumption that heredity is an important determinant of intelligence, an assumption now supported by substantial evidence (see Thiessen, 1972; Willerman, 1979). It must be emphasized, however, that an individual does not inherit an IQ, but rather a collection of genes referred to as the genotype for intelligence. The actual expression of this genotype, called the phenotype, is influenced by environmental experiences. Genes set the upper and lower limits of the phenotype, but the environment determines where in this reaction range the final IQ value will fall. The current nature–nurture controversy is reducible to the single issue of how wide the range of reaction is. Those who favor environmental explanations (e.g., Hunt, 1971) argue for a wide reaction range of 50, 70, or even 100 IQ points. Those who acknowledge genetic determinants assert that the reaction range is more narrow, generally around 25 points (e.g., Cronbach, 1975).

An interesting empirical question is whether the reaction range is the same for all genotypes. A central theme of this chapter is that both retardation and giftedness can be explained by the same conceptual model. This leads us to hypothesize that the reaction ranges for different genotypes are approximately the same. We go a step further and assert that it would be just as difficult for environmental intervention to raise a genotype for an IQ of 60 to a phenotypic expression of 100 as it would be to change a 100 IQ genotype to 140. This viewpoint reflects the growing disillusionment with the "naive environmentalism of the 60's" (see Scarr, 1981). Put most succinctly, retarded children cannot be made normal. Producing genius, which has become something of a cottage industry in recent years, is likewise destined to be a futile effort.

The error in overestimating the power of the environment to alter intelligence is obvious. Not all retarded children come from impoverished and deprived environments, nor do all geniuses hail from wealthy homes filled with expensive environmental enrichment. The fact of the matter is that organic retardation is equally prevalent across the economic spectrum. Although familial retardation is more common in the lower classes, it is certainly not confined there. And, although the incidence of giftedness may be higher in the higher economic stratum, the absolute number of gifted people will be greater in the lower classes because of their larger memberships.

The backgrounds of many geniuses are equally revealing. Galton grew up in advantaged circumstances, but many eminent people were not so fortunate. The father of Isaac Newton was a humble farmer who died before his son was born. Martin Luther and John Knox were sons of peasants. Louis Armstrong was a neglected child whose father deserted the family and whose mother was "out on the town." As a child he was caught firing his stepfather's revolver and was placed in the New Orleans

Colored Waifs Home for Boys, where he was taught to play an instrument. These and many other biographies refute the myth that children will fulfill their exceptional talents only if their abilities are recognized early and if they grow up in advantaged homes in which parents diligently cultivate their child's gift.

This discussion is not meant to depreciate the importance of the environment in determining the ultimate expression of an individual's innate abilities. Interventions such as Head Start and the Milwaukee and Abecedarian Projects have proven that children at risk for retardation are not doomed to a life of intellectual inadequacy (see Zigler & Seitz, 1982). Similarly, there is no question that a gifted child will have a better chance to excel if his or her talents are purposefully guided. Although heredity may largely dictate a person's potential, how much of that potential is actualized is clearly an environmental matter.

The Whole Child

Gifted and retarded children, like everyone else, are complex human beings with physical, emotional, and social aspects. Unfortunately, these aspects of personality are often overlooked in favor of the more interesting focus on atypical intelligence. Yet personality is more influential than an IQ score in predicting success or adaptation. For example, Weaver (1946) studied the adjustment of 8,000 retarded people inducted into the U.S. Army during World War II. The median IQ of those who adjusted successfully was 72. Those who did not adjust had a median IQ of 68, an insignificant difference. Windle (1962) also found that motivational and personality factors rather than IQ differentiated between retarded individuals who were successful in life and those who were not. The same conclusion was reached by Terman, who found that not all of the gifted children he studied became outstanding adults. Some failed in college, some drifted aimlessly from job to job, and some committed crimes. The average IQ of those adults considered most successful was 139, whereas those who were least successful had an equally potent average of 133.

What determines who will and who will not make a successful adjustment? To answer this question, one must realize that both retarded and gifted children have socialization experiences that differ from the norm because of their level of cognitive functioning. There are two main factors to consider. First, these children's unique cognitive abilities lead them to experience their social and physical environments differently from other children. The range of activities that they are capable of, limited in the case of retardation and expanded in the case of giftedness, and their oft-repeated experiences in these activities—failure for the retarded and success for the gifted—lead to the development of unique perceptions of the world. Second, both low- and high-IQ children are treated differently from other children by their parents, peers, and teachers. These situations suggest that there are certain stresses inherent in being gifted or retarded that are likely to affect personality and hence adjustment.

The Age Factor

An obvious source of social problems arises from the difference between mental age (MA) and chronological age (CA) that results from delayed or accelerated intellectual development. With increasing age the absolute difference in intellectual level between retarded, average, and gifted children increases because the abilities of those with lower IQs develop at a slower rate, and the abilities of those with higher IQs develop at a faster rate. Hence retarded children eventually find themselves far behind their agemates and gifted children far ahead. However, when children are compared with children of the same ability (the typical research design), age seems to be an advantage to retarded and a disadvantage to gifted children. Kohlberg (1969) argued that certain behaviors involved in cognitive development (e.g., role-taking ability) are influenced by the sheer number of exchanges that an individual has had with the environment. Because retarded children are older than nonretarded children of the same MA, they supposedly have had more of these exchanges. In one study it was found that retarded children performed more adequately than MA-matched nonretarded children, who in turn did better than younger bright children (Brown, 1973). However, most of the research on this topic does not show the CA variable to have much influence on cognitive performance (see Weisz, Yeates, & Zigler, 1982).

On the other hand, CA is unquestionably a determinant of physical development and capabilities. These in turn are likely to influence certain psychological behaviors. For example, retarded children may be at the same stage of physical development as are their nonretarded peers, although they are at a much lower intellectual stage. Based on their physical appearance, others may expect from retarded children certain behaviors that they are incapable of producing, and this may lead to inordinate numbers of failure experiences. The MA–CA gap may be a positive motivational source as well. Age roles are a part of socialization to which everyone is exposed through observation and social expectancies. As long as retarded people have the intellectual ability to perform age-appropriate behaviors, they are highly motivated to do so. Such achievements can become evidence of their normalcy and self-worth.

At the other end of the continuum, the superior mind of the gifted child often results in others viewing age-appropriate behavior as immature. For example, a 3-year-old might be conversant in three languages but not yet have the physical dexterity to tie his or her shoes. Not only might adults become impatient with the intellectually gifted child of normal physical development, but the child is likely to become frustrated by the inability to carry out certain actions. In studies of the effects of retardation, an increasing number of investigators are using both CA- and MA-matched controls. We should consider using similar control groups to further our understanding of the psychological effects of giftedness.

Coping Strategies

Another unusual stress with which retarded and gifted individuals have to cope is their awareness of being perceived as freaks. Both intellectual groups may employ defense mechanisms that become a hindrance to optimal functioning. Most common is denial of the existence of their atypical intellectual status. In a study of retarded people released from a state hospital, Edgerton (1967) noted the ingenious and strenuous efforts the former residents employed to deny their retardation and to pass as normal and competent in society. He observed that in a desperate search for self-esteem, former patients strived to cover themselves with a protective cloak of competence. Gifted individuals, on the other hand, may adopt a cloak of incompetence to camouflage their unusual intellectual abilities. When asked by peers how she always made As, a very bright child known to the authors responded, "I cheat." This child obviously thought her peers would think better of her if she boasted no extraordinary talent. Another dramatic indicator of very bright children's efforts to escape their intellectual deviance can be found in the number of underachieving gifted children whose academic performance is well below that indicated by their intellectual capacity (Raph, Goldberg, & Passow, 1966).

The following passages, one from a previously institutionalized retarded person and one from a gifted student, highlight the significant stress wrought by peer pressure and the difficulty encountered in attempting to fit into the social mainstream.

> The best way to get by with outsiders (normal people outside the hospital) is just to keep your mouth shut. You know if you just keep your mouth shut you won't say nothing foolish—if you talk you're just gonna say the wrong thing. (Edgerton, 1967, p. 163)

> Eventually, I began to withdraw more and more each day. I wouldn't talk . . . I did have friends but I couldn't match their standards all the time. Though I tried desperately to make jokes, talk the same slang, enjoy the same pastimes, it didn't always run smoothly. I'd hit bumps and just have to admit to myself just how phony it was. It was a bore. I got bored with my very closest friends and that left no one to confide in. (National Student Symposium, 1978, p. 27)

Thus retarded people may adopt a cloak of competence, and gifted people may adopt a cloak of incompetence. Neither group, however, is always successful at denying their atypical status.

The atypical social experiences of intellectually atypical persons may also lead to more general and pervasive response styles. There is a substantial body of evidence (reviewed by Balla & Zigler, 1979) that shows that due to peculiar social histories many retarded people develop traits such as high needs of social reinforcement, strong social approach and avoidance tendencies, permeating fear of failure, and learned helplessness. Motivational factors such as these have a forceful influence on behavior and can attenuate performance much more than can impoverished cognitive ability. With sensitive intervention many of these problems can be overcome, enabling an individual to achieve at a level commensurate with his or her ability.

Gifted children may also have social and cognitive experiences that make them vulnerable to personality difficulties. They may be hypersensitive to stimuli in the external world or be frequently faced with situations that offer insufficient stimulation. The result is that they may become solitary, self-centered, restless, or resistant. But, although brilliant individuals can create problems for themselves, they bring to the solution of these problems tremendous intellectual resources. In fact, Terman found that those in his gifted group who suffered serious psychological difficulties made remarkably quick recoveries. Terman and Oden concluded that "superior intelligence does not appear to be a causal factor in mental disorders as found in this group but seems, rather, to have helped those affected to overcome their difficulties" (1947, p. 108). Of course, this group did represent a highly selected sample. It is likely that children who appeared maladjusted were not chosen for the original sample. A reasonable conclusion is that there is probably as broad a variation in mental health among gifted and retarded persons as among the population in general. Investigators should concentrate on determining the particular difficulties experienced by these groups and the specific conditions that determine the development of adaptive or maladaptive coping strategies (Altman, 1983).

Educational Philosophies

Nowhere is concern with the whole child more important than in the educational arena. Schooling is much more than academic learning. It also involves the social and emotional training that ultimately shapes a person and the place he or she will assume in society. To this point this chapter has been focused on the similarities between the retarded and gifted groups. These comparisons end when the subject of education is reached. The basis for the differences in educational philosophies appears to be differential interest in total development versus cognitive development in the intellectual haves and have nots.

The earliest attempts to educate retarded children were made with the goal of making these students normal. When it became evident that this was impossible, retarded children were either denied schooling or offered special education in separate schools. These were usually residential institutions, which meant that a child was separated not only from peers but from family and society as well. Education eventually moved back into public schools, but still it remained in separate special classrooms. In the past two decades this isolationist approach has undergone a complete reversal. The current philosophy is based on normalization, in an attempt to grant retarded people an environment that is as close to the norm as possible. Thus, whenever possible retarded children are educated in the academic mainstream. Sometimes this means full-time placement in regular classrooms; another possibility is partial mainstreaming, where academic courses are taught in special classes but for noncore subjects special students join their nonretarded peers. This academic revolution has proceeded without scientific evidence that it benefits retarded children academically or socially. The future direction of education for retarded people thus remains uncertain.

Exactly the opposite approach has characterized the training of gifted children. Almost without exception their schooling has taken place in regular graded classrooms. When special treatment was offered, it usually took the form of accelerating gifted children to a grade offering activities commensurate with their intellectual abilities. Both choices have their problems. In regular classes the work may not challenge the superior student, resulting in boredom, disinterest, and frustration. Acceleration through the grades places the intellectually advanced child at a social disadvantage. Most recent academic trends seem to be toward removing the gifted child from the academic mainstream. Programs for Talented and Gifted Students (TAGS) are multiplying in many areas. Often they are token programs in which the TAGS child leaves the regular classroom for only a few hours per week to receive special tutoring. Secondary TAGS students may leave their school altogether to attend classes at local colleges. Again, more research is needed to determine what type of education is best for gifted children, not only in terms of their academic development, but also in terms of their developing healthy, well-rounded personalities. To ignore the social and emotional needs of gifted and retarded people and to focus strictly on their cognitive capacities or incapacities limits their growth and potential contributions to society.

References

Adams, J. (1973). Adaptive behavior and measured intelligence in the classification of mental retardation. *American Journal of Mental Deficiency, 78,* 77–81.

Altman, R. (1983). Social-emotional development of gifted children and adolescents: A research mode. *Roeper Review, 6,* 65–68.

Ashby, W. R., & Walker, C. C. (1968). Genius. In P. London & D. Rosenhan (Eds.), *Foundations of abnormal psychology* (pp. 201–225). New York: Holt, Rinehart & Winston.

Balla, D., & Zigler, E. (1979). Personality development in retarded persons. In N. R. Ellis (Ed.), *Handbook of mental deficiency* (2nd ed., pp. 143–168). Hillsdale, NJ: Erlbaum.

Barron, F. (1961). Creative vision and expression in writing and painting. Presented at the Conference on The Creative Person, Berkeley Institute of Personality Assessment and Research, University of California.

Brown, A. L. (1973). Conservation of number and continuous quantity in normal, bright, and retarded children. *Child Development, 44,* 376–379.

Cronbach, L. J. (1975). Five decades of public controversy over mental testing. *American Psychologist, 30,* 1–14.

Davies, S. P., & Ecob, K. G. (1959). *The mentally retarded in society.* New York: Columbia University Press.

Edgerton, R. B. (1967). *The cloak of competence.* Berkeley: University of California Press.

Feldman, D. H. (1982). A developmental framework for research with gifted children. *New Directions for Child Development, 17,* 31–45.

Fox, L. H. (1981). Identification of the academically gifted. *American Psychologist, 36,* 1103–1111.

Getzels, J. W., & Jackson, P. W. (1962). *Creativity and intelligence: Explorations with gifted students.* New York: Wiley.

Goodenough, F. (1956). *Exceptional children.* New York: Appleton-Century-Crofts.

Grossman, H. J. (Ed.) (1973). *Manual on terminology and classification in mental retardation* (Rev. ed.). Washington, DC: American Association on Mental Deficiency.

Grossman, H. J. (Ed.) (1983). *Manual on terminology and classification in mental retardation* (3rd ed.). Washington, DC: American Association on Mental Deficiency.

Heber, R. (1961). A manual on terminology and classification in mental retardation. *American Journal of Mental Deficiency, 65,*(Suppl. 3).

Hollingworth, L. S. (1926). *Gifted children: Their nature and nurture.* New York: Macmillan.

Hollingworth, L. S. (1942). *Children above 180 IQ. Stanford-Binet: Origin and development.* New York: World Book.

Hunt, J. M. (1971). Parent and child centers: Their basis in the behavioral and educational sciences. *American Journal of Orthopsychiatry, 41,* 13–38.

Kohlberg, L. (1969). Stage and sequences: The cognitive-developmental approach to socialization. In D. Goslin (Ed.), *Handbook of socialization theory and research* (pp. 347–480). Chicago: Rand McNally.

MacKinnon, D. W. (1968). Creativity. In D. L. Sills (Ed.), *International encyclopedia of the social sciences* (Vol. 3, pp. 434–442). New York: Macmillan.

Maloney, M. P., & Ward, M. P. (1979). *Mental retardation and modern society.* New York: Oxford University Press.

Marland, S. P., Jr. (1972). *Education of the gifted and talented: Report to the Congress of the United States by the U.S. Commissioner of Education.* Washington, DC: U.S. Government Printing Office.

McNemar, Q. (1964). Lost: Our intelligence? Why? *American Psychologist, 19,* 871–882.

Mercer, J. R. (1973). *Labeling the mentally retarded.* Berkeley: University of California Press.

National Student Symposium on the Education of the Gifted and Talented. (1978). *On being gifted.* New York: Walker.

Prentky. R. A. (1979). Creativity and psychopathology: A neurocognitive perspective. In B. Maher (Ed.), *Progress in experimental personality research* (Vol. 9, pp. 1–39). New York: Academic Press.

Raph J. B., Goldberg, M. L., & Passow, A. H. (1966). *Bright underachievers*. New York: Teachers College Press.

Renzulli, J. S. (1978). What makes giftedness? Reexamining a definition. *Phi Delta Kappan, 60,* 180–184, 261.

Robinson, N. (1980). Editor's note: Terminology, classification, and description in mental retardation research. *American Journal of Mental Deficiency, 85,* 107.

Scarr, S. (1981). *Race, social class and individual differences in IQ*. Hillsdale, NJ: Erlbaum.

Smith, J. D., & Polloway, E. A. (1979). The dimension of adaptive behavior in mental retardation research: An analysis of recent practices. *American Journal of Mental Deficiency, 84,* 203–206.

Tannenbaum, A. J. (1979). Pre-Sputnik Post-Watergate concern about the gifted. In A. H. Passow (Ed.), *The gifted and the talented: Their education and development* (pp. 5–27). Chicago: University of Chicago Press.

Terman, L. M. (1925). *Genetic studies of genius: Vol. 1. Mental and physical traits of a thousand gifted children*. Stanford, CA: Stanford University Press.

Terman, L. M. & Oden, M. H. (1947). *Genetic studies of genius: Vol. 4. The gifted child grows up*. Stanford, CA: Stanford University Press.

Terman, L. M., & Oden, M. H. (1959). *Genetic studies of genius: Vol. 5. The gifted group at mid-life*. Stanford, CA: Stanford University Press.

Thiessen, D. (1972). *Gene organization and behavior*. New York: Random House.

Torrance, E. P. (1962). *Guiding creative talent*. Englewood Cliffs, NJ: Prentice-Hall.

Torrance, E. P. (1975). Predictive validity of the Torrance tests of creative thinking. In J. Dissinger & C. Arnold (Eds.), *Studies in the psychological foundations of exceptionality*. Monterey, CA: Brooks/Cole.

Wallach, M. A., & Kogan, N. (1965a). *Modes of thinking in young children: A study of the creativity-intelligence distinction*. New York: Holt, Rinehart & Winston.

Wallach, M. A., & Kogan, N. (1965b). A new look at the creativity–intelligence dimension. *Journal of Personality, 33,* 348–369.

Wallach, M. A., & Wing, C. W., Jr. (1969). *The talented student: A validation of the creativity–intelligence distinction*. New York: Holt, Rinehart & Winston.

Weaver, T. (1946). The incidence of maladjustment among mental defectives in military environment. *American Journal of Mental Deficiency, 51,* 238–246.

Weisz, J., Yeates, K., & Zigler, E. (1982). Piagetian evidence and the developmental-difference controversy. In E. Zigler & D. Balla (Eds.), *Mental retardation: The developmental-difference controversy* (pp. 213–276). Hillsdale, NJ: Erlbaum.

Willerman L. (1979). *The psychology of individual and group differences*. San Francisco: Freeman.

Windle, C. (1962). Prognosis of mental subnormals. *American Journal of Mental Deficiency, 66,* (Suppl. 5).

Zigler, E. (1968). Mental retardation. In P. London & D. Rosenhan (Eds.), *Foundations of abnormal psychology* (pp. 519–556). New York: Holt, Rinehart & Winston.

Zigler, E., & Balla, D. (Eds.) (1982). *Mental retardation: The developmental-difference controversy*. Hillsdale, NJ: Erlbaum.

Zigler, E., Balla, D., & Hodapp, R. (1984). On the definition and classification of mental retardation. *American Journal of Mental Deficiency, 89,* 215–230.

Zigler, E., & Seitz, V. (1982). Social policy and intelligence. In R. Sternberg (Ed.), *Handbook of human intelligence* (pp. 586–641). New York: Cambridge University Press.

14. Public Policy and Advocacy on Behalf of the Gifted and Talented

Patrick H. DeLeon
U.S. Senate Staff
Gary R. VandenBos
University of Bergen, Norway

National-level policy attention on any given issue generally rises and falls from one year to the next. This is certainly true with regard to federal policy debates related to the education of gifted and talented children. Tannenbaum (1979) has described national concern for the gifted as being twin peaks of interest separated by a deep 12- to 18-year valley of neglect. He argues that no other special group of children has been alternately embraced and repelled with so much vigor by educators and laypeople alike as have the gifted. Gallagher (1979) has also described Americans' apparent love–hate relationship with the gifted, which he sees as being deeply rooted in American cultural beliefs and experiences— related to our historical battle against an aristocratic elite and our commitment to egalitarianism.

Policy deliberations on any specific topic always take place within the broader context of other policy debates and the overall social climate of the nation. It is, thus, important to consider the policy discussions and decisions related to the gifted in the context of other social issues that compete for public attention and limited resources, as well as the major political and social trends of the times. Tannenbaum (1979) has provided such a review, with particular attention to the broad social events of the last 30 years. We will not duplicate that effort, other than making occasional reference to a given event or trend that is relevant to understanding events in the national discussions related to the gifted or that is helpful in illustrating an aspect of the policy process.

In the present chapter, we review national-level policy deliberations and legislation over the past 30 years as they relate to gifted and talented children. We then offer our observations about the evolution of these efforts, what they illustrate about policy and research developments, and how we see the current state of affairs. We then turn to considerations of advocacy efforts—organizing at the local level, the role and importance of state-level public interest advocacy on behalf of the gifted, and other issues related to effective advocacy.

National Policy Regarding the Gifted

There is a long history of local attention to and professional interest in the gifted and talented. Among early efforts, William Harris in St. Louis is frequently cited for his pioneering efforts, in the 1860s, to develop and implement a systematic approach to the education of gifted students. There are many examples of local programs or schools for exceptional children, some of which were short-term experiments and others that have long histories of achievement. The National Society for the Study of Education published important volumes on the education of the gifted in 1920 and 1924, but it did not publish another until 1958 (Passow, 1979).

Traditionally, most federal initiatives are begun as a result of a specific congressional directive. That is, authorization committees that have jurisdiction over a particular program area first hold extensive hearings; subsequently the issues are debated on the floors of both houses of Congress. A bill is then enacted into public law, which usually not only defines the overall purpose of the program, but also establishes quite specific legislative guidelines for implementation. The following year, the relevant department may submit a detailed budget to the appropriations committees to request the necessary resources to fulfill the expressed will of Congress.

In 1931, however, a special Section on Exceptional Children and Youth was established within the U.S. Office of Education on the Administration's own initiative, without any express legislative direction.

Subsequently, shortly after World War II, during Congressional hearings on the importance of providing federal support for scientific training and research in order to maintain and enhance our technological position in the world and to maintain a strong defense, the probability of there also being a clear "national interest" in supporting the gifted was expressly raised. These hearings ultimately resulted in the passage of the National Science Foundation Act (NSFA, 1950).

At approximately the same time, the Educational Policies Commission (1950) published a report that was expressly critical of the lack of attention being paid to the education of the gifted. Wolfe (1954) reported that fewer than one-half of the top 25 percent of high school graduates completed a college education, and even among the top 5 percent of high school graduates only 60 percent completed college. Policy attention was slowly beginning to build during the 1950s regarding the importance to the nation of educating its brightest and most talented students at all educational levels. When the Soviet Union launched the world's first satellite in 1957, it crystallized public attention on the status of education in the United States.

On September 2, 1958, the Congress declared that an "educational emergency" existed, and the National Defense Education Act (NDEA) was passed. The law linked federal involvement in education to national defense, and it also affirmed that states and local communities still had the primary responsibility for and control of public education. In the next four years almost one billion dollars became available to train teachers for service in public elementary and secondary schools in order to strengthen instruction in modern foreign languages as well as in science and mathematics, to provide grants to states to assist in establishing testing programs for identifying those with special ability and for providing specialized guidance counseling services for them, and to provide various other activities central to improving education.

Research and professional interest related to "giftedness" and "gifted children" also exploded at this time. Albert's (1969) data reveal that the number of citations listed in the *Psychological Abstracts* under these two terms in the six years after the launch of the first satellite (1957–1962) exceeded the total number of citations listed for the previous thirty years (1927–1956).

Services for gifted and talented students, funded through monies from NDEA, escalated during the 1959–1963 period to an all-time high (Zettel, 1982). Goldberg (1965) reported that, according to a national survey conducted by the National Education Association, almost 80 percent of secondary schools were making some type of special services available for their gifted students. Others (cf. Tannenbaum, 1979), however, maintained that there really was no way of knowing precisely what percentage of our schools were truly offering programs that would meet the special educational and counseling needs of the gifted. Many of the special "crash" programs established during this time had disappeared by the mid-1960s, being either discontinued or merged into the general educational curriculum.

Advocates for the gifted and talented, however, working through the Council for Exceptional Children and other public interest groups, continued to call for an expanded long-term role for the federal government in the education of the nation's most talented students. In 1969, identical federal bills were introduced in both houses of the Congress. These initiatives would have established a federal definition of gifted and talented children, provided support to the states to upgrade and expand educational programs for gifted students through amendments to several federal educational improvement funding programs, and directed the U.S. Commissioner of Education to conduct a study to determine the unique needs of the gifted and to suggest how the federal government might best allocate its resources to meet those needs. These proposals were not enacted as a separate law. They were, however, passed, in a modified form, as section 806 of Public Law 91-230 (An Act to Extend Programs of Assistance for Elementary and Secondary Education, and for Other Purposes, 1970), but without any new funding or new funding mechanism. In retrospect, it is clear that the most significant components of this legislation, in terms of future impact on policy, were the provision requiring a report to Congress on the status of and need for the education of the gifted and the determination by the Congress of the United States that gifted and talented youth were a federal concern.

The Marland Report

In late 1971, the then-Commissioner of Education, Sidney P. Marland, Jr., submitted to Congress his report of a national assessment of the status of educational programs for the gifted and talented (Marland, 1972). Included in the report was the following definition of gifted students:

> Gifted and talented children are those, identified by professionally qualified persons, who by virtue of outstanding abilities are capable of high performance. These are children who require differentiated educational programs and/or services beyond those normally provided by the regular school program in order to realize their contribution to self and society. Children capable of high performance include those with demonstrated achievement and/or potential ability in any of the following areas, singly or in combination: general intellectual ability, specific academic aptitude, creative or productive thinking, leadership ability, visual and performing arts, and/or psychomotor ability. (p. 2)

It was suggested that, by this definition, a minimum of 3 to 5 percent of the school-aged population would qualify as gifted and talented students.

Summarized here are the major findings and conclusions of the Marland Report (modified from Zettel, 1982):

1. Existing services to the gifted do not, in general, reach a large number of students, and significant subpopulations (such as minorities and disadvantaged) are strikingly underserved.
2. Special programming for the gifted is a low priority at all levels of government.
3. State and local governments look to the federal government for leadership in the education of the gifted.
4. The federal role in services to the gifted is all but nonexistent.
5. Less than half of the states enacted legislation supporting education of the gifted.
6. Even where such state legislation for the education of the gifted exists, there is little genuine programming.
7. Identification of gifted students is hampered by apathy and hostility among educational personnel as well as by the lack of economic resources.
8. An enormous individual and social loss exists because the talents of the gifted are undiscovered and undeveloped.
9. Gifted students cannot excel without assistance.
10. Gifted students can be harmed when their opportunity to function at the maximum of their ability is restricted through deprivation of appropriate educational resources.
11. Such deprivation is equal to or greater than that suffered by any other population with special needs.
12. Services to the gifted can and do produce significant and measurable outcomes.
13. Special services for the gifted also benefit other populations in need.
14. A conservative estimate of the number of gifted students, in 1970, was between 1.5 and 2.5 million children.

Legislative Proposals

Shortly after the Marland Report was presented to Congress, several bills designed to enhance the education of the gifted were introduced in both houses of the 93rd Congress (1973–1974). The recommendations contained in these bills were ultimately incorporated, in a highly modified form, as a section of the Education Amendments of 1974. This section included

1. Establishment of an Office of Gifted and Talented in the U.S. Office of Education;
2. Authorization of an annual appropriation of up to $12.25 million;

3. A program of grants for training, research, and demonstration projects related to the gifted;

4. A program of grants to state and local educational agencies for support of the education of the gifted; and

5. Establishment of a national clearinghouse on information related to the education of the gifted and talented.

Not included, because of legislative compromises, was proposed authorization for up to a quarter of a billion dollars, over three years, for the support of programs related to giftedness. To the frustration of many advocates for the gifted, only $2.5 million was appropriated in 1975 for the support of federal efforts on behalf of the gifted and talented (and the appropriation remained at that level for several years before increasing slightly).

In the 95th Congress (1977–1978), specific legislative proposals to improve federal support of education for the gifted and talented were again introduced in both houses of Congress. These bills proposed lower authorization levels than those initially proposed in the 93rd Congress (1973–1974), but they proposed levels that were considerably higher than the then-current appropriation levels. The emphasis was on support to state and local educational agencies. Unfortunately, the previous clear commitment to research related to giftedness had weakened. The proposed Gifted and Talented Children's Education Act, which finally passed as Title IX-A of the Education Amendments of 1978, included authorization levels that started at $25 million in fiscal year 1979 and increased to $50 million in fiscal year 1983. The act was primarily a discretionary state grant program, with limited additional authority for the U.S. Commissioner of Education to fund demonstration projects, training, and research related to giftedness. Appropriations, in fact, increased from $3.8 million in 1978 to $6.2 million in 1980; President Carter proposed continuing the latter level, although the Congress ultimately provided $5.652 million in fiscal year 1981.

Since 1980: The Reagan Administration

The 1980 presidential election was viewed by many politicians and political scientists as providing the American people with a clear choice between two contrasting views on the appropriate role for the federal government to play in a number of areas, including education. The Democratic platform, for example, proclaimed:

> The Democratic party is strongly committed to education as the best hope for America's future. We applaud the leadership taken by a Democratic President and a Democratic Congress in strengthening federal programs for education. In the past four years: Federal aid to education has increased by 73 percent—the greatest income increases in such a short period in our history. . . . Over the next four years, we

pledge to continue our strong commitment to education. We will continue to support the Department of Education and assist in its all-important educational enterprise that involves three out of ten Americans. (*Congressional Record*, 1980, H10457).

In seemingly sharp contrast, the Republican platform stated:

Next to religious training and the home, education is the most important means by which families hand down to each new generation their ideals and beliefs. It is a pillar of a free society. But today, parents are losing control of their children's schooling . . . Because federal assistance should help local school districts, not tie them up in red tape, we will strive to replace the crazyquilt of wasteful programs with a system of block grants that will restore decisionmaking to local officials responsible to voters and parents . . . and encourage(s) the elimination of the federal Department of Education. (*Congressional Record*, 1980, S10383).

Although the platforms of both parties contained express commitments to continue to target federal support for the disadvantaged and the handicapped, neither platform mentioned the "gifted and talented" in any manner whatsoever.

When President Reagan was elected to office and the Republicans regained control of the U.S. Senate for the first time in nearly 30 years, many of the underlying educational principles espoused throughout the Republican Party's platform were soon incorporated into public law. For example, the Education Consolidation and Improvement provisions of the Omnibus Budget Reconciliation Act of 1981 consolidated 20 formerly separately appropriated programs into a single, Chapter 2 block grant for state and local educational agencies, simultaneously repealing the authorization statutes of more than 40 categorical programs. This was viewed by many as a compromise from the President's original proposal, which would have entirely eliminated the U.S. Department of Education. This consolidation was also actively supported by the Democratic-controlled House of Representatives.

The expressed purposes for this consolidation may have seemed most reasonable; for example, it was intended to (a) vest greater power for program administration with state education agencies, (b) reduce the paperwork associated with federal programs, and (c) place responsibility for the design and implementation of programs with local boards of education and school personnel involved in school operation. Nevertheless, for those concerned with our nation's educational programs, it is highly significant that the federal funds ultimately made available for educational initiatives were drastically diminished. For example, in comparison with the total fiscal year 1980 funding level of the antecedent programs ($805 million), the fiscal year 1982 funding for the Chapter 2 block grant was $470 million—a decrease of 42 percent.

Although the specific appropriations line item for the gifted and talented initiative may have been eliminated, the underlying authority for state and local educational agencies to expend federal monies in this area was maintained. For example, specific mention of "gifted and talented" or "children who give evidence of high performance capability" was included in the statute's authorized activities for two of the three program subchapters—the Educational Improvement and Support Services subchapter (Section 577[2]) and the Special Projects subchapter (Section 582[3][A]). Furthermore, the Statement of Purpose accompanying the Special Projects subchapter (Section 581) also included a specific reference to "gifted and talented."

Under the current statute, each state is required to submit a formal application to the Secretary of Education in order to obtain federal funds. A number of assurances are to be included in the application, which must be renewed at least every three years. Essentially, however, the federal requirements are of a procedural nature, rather than representing an effort to establish program priorities. Each state, for example, must establish a state advisory committee. Local education agencies, which are to receive 80 percent of a state's allocation, must file applications with their state officials indicating how their federal funds will be expended among the approved activities (i.e., they must submit a formal plan). It is quite clear that the Congress intended to give these local agencies complete discretion in allocating their Chapter 2 funds. There is no requirement that the block grant funds be spent on any specific programmatic initiative.

In 1982, the Administration closed its Office of Gifted and Talented within the U.S. Department of Education, causing one U.S. Senator to proclaim that "the Federal Government now plays virtually no role in helping schools provide opportunities for the gifted and talented" (*Congressional Record*, 1983, S14211). The U.S. Department of Education is, however, collecting aggregate information on how the block grant funds are being used, and their most recent figures indicate that approximately six million dollars was spent in 1983 for the gifted and talented. This is slightly more than was previously available under the categorized approach.

The Call for Excellence in Education

It is perhaps highly symbolic of our nation's underlying ambivalent feelings toward the gifted and talented that, during media coverage of the far-reaching report of the National Commission on Excellence in Education (1983) entitled *A Nation at Risk: The Imperative for Educational Reform*, the gifted and talented were mentioned but not highlighted. Without question this document has been the source of numerous education-oriented policy debates; during the 1984 presidential election year, it has managed to essentially set the educational agenda for aspiring politicians. Yet, in spite of the fact that the National Commission addressed the issue of the gifted and talented on at least six distinct occasions, to our knowledge this has never been effectively reflected in any of the public debates.

For example, the Commission cited as an indicator of the risk that we as a nation are facing that "over half the population of gifted students do not match their tested ability with comparable achievement in school" (p. 8). In citing the severe shortage of certain kinds of teachers, the Commission expressly enumerated "specialists in education for gifted and talented"; yet again, this has not been emphasized by the media. Similarly, the Commission not only cited a special need to allocate funds to develop textbooks in certain "thin-market" areas such as those for the gifted and talented, but the Commission explicitly recommended that the federal government, in cooperation with states and localities, should help meet the needs of "key groups of students such as the gifted and talented . . . [which] include both national resources and the Nation's youth who are most at risk" (National Commission on Excellence in Education, 1983, p. 32).

Following up on *A Nation At Risk*, a number of prestigious organizations have issued similar calls for increased public attention and commitment to our educational programs. The gifted and talented have continued, however, to receive only token public attention. For example, the Carnegie Foundation, under the leadership of former U.S. Education Commissioner Ernest Boyer, released a report entitled *High School: A Report on Secondary Education in America*. In this report Boyer stated that "Today, gifted and talented students are often overlooked. Teachers and administrators just assume they'll 'make it,' 'blossom on their own.' Nothing could be further from the truth" (1983, p. 236). The Foundation further recommended that every high school should have special arrangements for gifted students, and that in large urban areas, magnet schools in the arts or sciences should be developed for gifted and talented students. There was also a call for a network of residential academies in science and mathematics throughout the nation. Yet, very little, if any, media attention was given to this aspect of the report.

Similarly, the National Task Force on Education for Economic Growth, created by the Education Commission of the States and chaired by Governor James Hunt of North Carolina, released its report entitled *Action for Excellence: A Comprehensive Plan to Improve Our Nation's Schools*. This report stressed the importance of increased partnership beween public schools and industry and specifically recommended that "Every state and local school system must expand its programs or develop new ones to identify academically gifted students early in their school careers and to provide a curriculum that is rigorous and enriching enough to challenge talented young people" (Education Commission of the States, 1983, p. 40).

Yet again, very little media attention was focused on these recommendations for the gifted and talented. The National Science Foundation also issued a report on the quality of our nation's elementary and secondary schools. Their panel was co-chaired by former Cabinet member William T. Coleman and called for a presidentially appointed National Education Council, as well as for a distinct federal role in encouraging and financing exemplary schools (or programs) in mathematics, science, and technology in each community throughout the nation. Throughout this report, however, it was clear that the prime focus was to be on improving education for all Americans, not on giving special attention to the gifted. For example, according to the report: "We have too long regarded mathematics and science as the exclusive domain of a talented elite—a preserve for only the gifted . . . While increasing our concern for the most talented, we must now also attend to the need for early and sustained stimulation and preparation for *all* students" (National Science Foundation, 1983). In essence, although the mid-1980s saw the release of a number of far-reaching and well-documented educational policy reports, those whose primary concern is the gifted and talented really did not receive much overt support or public recognition for their concern.

Current Status of Policy Regarding the Gifted

Yet, as the pendulum now seems to have swung away from a special focus on the gifted and talented, there is every reason to believe that eventually it will, as if by natural course, swing the other way. The National Commission on Excellence also pointed out that "more and more schools are also offering advanced placement programs and programs for gifted and talented students, and more and more students are enrolling in them" (1983, p. 34). During its deliberations on the fiscal year 1984 appropriations bill for the U.S. Department of Education (P.L. 98–139), the Senate Appropriations Committee noted the finding of the National Commission on Excellence regarding the "unique needs of gifted children" and stated that "there are a number of pressing issues which must be addressed as to the most effective means to capitalize upon this truly national resource." It further indicated that it would explore this issue during its fiscal year 1985 budget hearings (S. Rep. No. 247, 98th Cong., 1st Sess. 130, 1983). The following year, during its deliberations on the fiscal year 1985 appropriations bill, the Senate Appropriations Committee again raised this issue. In doing so, it expressly urged the Department of Education to collect information comparing expenditures targeted for the gifted and talented under the Chapter 2 block grant program, as compared to expenditures under the antecedent categorical program (S. Rep. No. 544, 98th Cong., 2d Sess. 155, 1984).

Historically, proponents of children's programs per se have felt that Congress has not been as responsive to their unique needs as it should be. The various federal initiatives that affect children do fall under the jurisdiction of a wide range of congressional committees, depending upon the type of program involved (e.g., education, nutrition, social welfare). As an institution, Congress has focused on individual programs rather than on the beneficiary population. The same is true of programs for the elderly; however, special or select committees on aging have been established by both legislative bodies, and the Senate Committee on Aging has now been in existence for more than 20 years.

In the closing days of the 97th Congress (1981–1982), and again at the beginning of the 98th Congress (1983–1984), the House of Representatives established a Select Committee on Children, Youth, and Families. In the 98th Congress (1983–1984), the Senate established two related caucuses: one on children and one on the family. The expressed mission of the Senate Children's Caucus is to provide a focus for a comprehensive review of the range of issues affecting children. In November 1983, a special policy forum was held by the Caucus to explore "the impact of federal budget cuts and rule changes on efforts to identify and educate highly talented children, especially minority, poor, and handicapped children" (Dodd, 1983). At that time, testimony was received from a wide range of concerned individuals including school administrators, public officials, university researchers, the private business community, and a number of gifted and talented children. Although the Children's Caucus does not have any explicit legislative authority (i.e., it cannot "report forth" actual bills for consideration by the full Senate), by providing this public forum for eliciting information on the gifted, it may very well have served as an important catalyst for subsequent recommendations by the legislative committees with appropriate jurisdiction. One should never underestimate the long-term consequences of having elected officials focus expressly on a particular topic. The ideas raised in a public hearing such as this often lead directly to future legislative activity.

In February 1984, the Science and Public Policy Seminar, which is held for Capitol Hill staff by the Federation of Behavioral, Psychological, and Cognitive Sciences, presented a seminar on gifted and talented students featuring James Gallagher, former Associate Commissioner of Education and the first Chief of the Bureau of the Handicapped of the U.S. Office of Education. The seminar highlighted the truly exemplary program at the North Carolina School of Science and Mathematics. This was the political initiative of Governor James Hunt and, even in its planning stages, it was warmly endorsed by noted scientists and mathematicians across the nation, including a number of Nobel laureates. The residential school is supported by public funds and provides the best students in the state with the opportunity to experience advanced training in advanced technology. It serves as a lighthouse or flagship for high technology, and, as such, it has provided an innovative way of upgrading science and mathematics teaching throughout the state of North Carolina. Although established by the state legislature, it has a history of being actively supported by banks and other elements of private industry.

Although no formal legislative action specifically targeted for the gifted and talented is expected in the near future at the national level, legislation will be pending during the 99th Congress in the U.S. Senate and the House of Representatives that would again establish an identifiable 25 to 50 million dollar program for the gifted and talented, as well as reestablish the Office of Gifted and Talented in the U.S. Office of Elementary and Secondary Education and require a formal report to the Congress on departmental plans for advancing opportunities for gifted and talented children, including legislative recommendations.

During the latter part of the 98th Congress, the Congress enacted Public Law 98–511, the Education Amendments of 1984. Included in this bill was the express authority under the Indian Education Act for consideration to be given, in calculating the cost per student for budgetary purposes, to establishing "special programs for gifted and talented students" for contract schools and schools within the Bureau of Indian Affairs. This provision was enacted with little fanfare and should not be viewed as being a major breakthrough. Furthermore, the Department of Interior's Fiscal Year 1986 budget request does propose establishing several model gifted and talented projects. During the closing hours of the 98th Congress, the Human Services Reauthorization Act was enacted, which clearly proclaimed a federal role in enhancing the overall quality of education. Again, although it was not specifically focused on the gifted and talented, this bill included a provision designated as "the talented teachers act," which authorized scholarships for the brightest students in high school who have agreed to enter the teaching profession, as well as a program for outstanding teachers presently in the classroom to advance themselves professionally. Authorization was also included for the construction of a new Center for Excellence at a prominent university to be used as a national research and training resource.

Perhaps during the 99th Congress the advocates of gifted and talented programs will be successful in capitalizing upon the unique federal responsibility for Native American peoples. In the early days of the 99th Congress, a number of bills were again introduced on behalf of the gifted and talented. Of interest in both the House and Senate this time were bills that specifically stressed the importance of the federal government's fulfilling its responsibility to gifted and talented Native Americans. It is presently too early to tell what ultimately will evolve; however, we are confident that the pendulum will swing and that the gifted and talented will receive greater legislative recognition in the foreseeable future.

There are a few recent events that are encouraging and that suggest that public awareness of the educational needs for gifted children may soon receive renewed attention. In a recent national study the Sid W. Richardson Foundation explored what programs exist for "able learners," examined their comparative effectiveness, and assessed their adaptability to various environments. From its four-year investigation, a series of recommendations on how schools can better serve able learners was developed. The full report (Cox, Daniel, & Boston, in press) will be published in the fall of 1985, and it may well help to generate renewed public attention regarding the education of gifted students. It is hoped that similar interest may be generated within health care professions by a recent task force report released by the American Association for Gifted Children entitled "Reaching Out to the Gifted Child: Roles for the Health Care Professions" (Hayden, 1985).

Assessing the Evolution of Federal Policy

Does the history of our national policy deliberations related to giftedness suggest a pattern of continuing attention, stubborn inattention, or an ebb and flow of interest and dedication? There certainly is much about which some may feel frustrated. Over and over there were moments of high hopes and rising expectations of major legislative success mandating large funding, significant educational programs, and important training and research initiatives. Repeatedly these dreams were not fully realized. However, the conclusion that national policymakers have shown stubborn inattention and total unyielding inaction is, we believe, unwarranted.

Progress has been made. First, the National Defense Education Act gave general attention to the improvement of our educational system, although it did not pay explicit attention to the most talented of our best students. About a decade later, however, further progress was made through the Elementary and Secondary Education Amendments of 1969, which required that a systematic national assessment be made to explicitly address the educational needs of the most gifted students, and the determination by Congress that a true federal responsibility exists. Then the Educational Amendments of 1974 legislatively established the Office of Gifted and Talented in the U.S. Office of Education. This was a big step toward improving the status of gifted programs. Finally, in 1978, the Gifted and Talented Children's Education Act was passed (as Title IX-A of the Education Amendments of 1978)—a national legislative bill directly, explicitly, and solely addressing this special population. Should the conclusion be "ebb and flow" or "continued attention"? We favor the latter conclusion.

From 1954 through 1980, national policy changed in a continuing positive and accelerating manner. The language and focus of the relevant legislation for the gifted became increasingly more explicit and targeted. Legislative authority for an administrative unit to address the gifted and talented was granted. Categorical funding for projects related to the gifted were established, and the level of funding slowly increased. A separate legislative bill solely addressing the education of the gifted was passed. This is the most typical pattern of policy evolution.

The events since the beginning of the Reagan Administration must be considered separately. The election of Reagan reflected a major shift in our nation's policy, as well as an apparent major shift in our nation's view of the fundamental role of government per se. Between 1954 and 1980, progress on behalf of the gifted and talented was slow, and the level of resources committed to address the documented needs of the gifted, in the eyes of many, had been grossly inadequate. But progress was made.

Advocates on behalf of the gifted must not be so disappointed that they terminate their efforts or initiate hostile and ineffective interchanges with policymakers. Expectations that arose about the prospects for specialized elementary and secondary education of the truly gifted when the National Science Foundation Act and the National Defense Education Act were enacted were excessive. The younger gifted were not the central focus of the NSFA, nor were the extremely gifted the real focus of the NDEA. Instead, the primary goal of the NDEA was the general improvement of our nation's overall educational systems, with some special attention to the brighter of our students. Nevertheless, these initiatives did stimulate considerable professional interest among educators in the gifted as a topic for further exploration, especially in the area of curriculum development.

The events of 1981 represent a major shift in federal policy, but that change itself was independent from national policy regarding the gifted per se. The change emerged from broader political issues—issues about the roles of the federal government, how it carried out its functions, and its overall priorities. Federal policy related to the gifted and talented was affected significantly. But these changing policies were not directed specifically at the gifted or at advocacy efforts on their behalf. Although we advocates for gifted education need to adjust to the changed situation, reshape our approach, and strengthen our advocacy efforts, we should not become discouraged or angry. We are better organized today, and our efforts have broader and more fundamental support than they did 20 years ago.

The future is bright. For example, in the 98th Congress (1983–1984), 13 members of the U.S. Senate reported that their previous occupation was education related; by comparison, only one Senator indicated that he possessed a health background. It is very rare for the Congress to have such an intimate knowledge of any one subject (DeLeon, Frohboese, & Meyers, 1984). Thus there is considerable potential for significant change as those interested in the gifted become active participants in the political/ public policy process.

There is also increased interest in the gifted and talented within the professional community. The 1983 American Psychological Association—

American Psychological Foundation (APA–APF) National Media/Book Award went to James Webb for his publication entitled *Guiding the Gifted Child* (Webb, Meckstroth, & Tolan, 1983), and the June 1984 issue of APA's recently acquired magazine, *Psychology Today*, featured the gifted and talented. Nevertheless, it should be remembered that our nation has a long history of considering education as being primarily the responsibility of local and state government. The historical source of educational funding has been the local property tax. The judiciary has been most reluctant to find any substantive right to quality education beyond that being provided by local or state authorities (see *San Antonio Independent School District v. Rodrigues*, 1973). Accordingly, those interested in furthering the federal presence in this area—and in particular, on behalf of the gifted—must be able to demonstrate a logical federal interest or nexus.

During the Sputnik era, national defense and national pride provided such a linkage. Today, with the growing awareness of the international nature of our economy and the deepening public concern regarding the federal deficit, a primarily economic-oriented rationale may very well evolve as being the key. Suggestions to this effect are contained in many of the educational policy reports referred to earlier in this chapter, as well as in the obvious efforts by a broad range of education advocates to encourage the private business community to take a more active leadership role in developing our educational policies. As advocates, we must realize that the central policy issue is not that as individuals the gifted deserve greater attention, but instead that it is in our nation's best interest that as a class, their future potential contributions to our economy be enhanced.

State-Level Support for the Gifted

Prior to 1960, only six states had legislation explicitly addressing the gifted (Jackson, 1979). In these states, either a legislative definition of gifted had been enacted or categorical funds for the education of the gifted had been authorized, or both. The vast majority of states, obviously, lacked explicit public policy regarding the gifted. Public advocacy organizations and parent groups that were strongly dedicated to the provision of specialized educational services for the gifted were also rare prior to the 1960s. Well-organized statewide advocacy groups were relatively uncommon, and national-level advocacy appears to have been led by a highly active and dedicated few. There is little evidence of broad-scale public interest and support for programs for the gifted in the 1950s. It should not be surprising, therefore, that many of the programs developed in the early 1960s for the gifted and talented were short-lived. Lacking a state legislative mandate, organized and vocal community support, and informed educational administrators, it is predictable that such services would soon be merged into general educational programs or discontinued once external federal economic support and pressure vanished, diminished, or shifted.

Policy at the federal level is influenced by state policy. The reverse is also true. In short, just as policy decisions at the national level are influenced by competing or co-occurring policy debates, policy deliberations at one level of government interact with policy development at other levels of government. People sometimes overlook these obvious facts when they are attempting to influence policy formation or to understand why a particular policy succeeded or failed (DeLeon, Forsythe, & VandenBos, in press).

National-level advocacy must be supported by state and local advocacy. Elected federal officials are more responsive to the expressed views (or silence) of their constituents (even if they are only partially informed ones) than they are to the informed opinions of experts from another state or district (DeLeon, 1983). It is not that elected officials are nonresponsive to the views, opinions, and advice of experts, it is just that they are more responsive to those who elected them (and might reelect them) than they are to nonvoters. Although a few national public advocates and professional leaders might be able to succeed, in some circumstances, in getting a major piece of federal legislation passed, it will generally not be maintained and expanded unless it gains public support at the state and local levels, with state and local supporters communicating their views to their elected national representatives.

Today, there is clearly much broader and more extensive support, both in state legislation and public interest, for services to the gifted (Jackson, 1979). The innovative North Carolina School of Science and Mathematics has already been noted. The advisory panel for the former U.S. Office of the Gifted and Talented recently completed a national planning effort for the gifted (Gallagher, Weiss, Oglesby, & Thomas, 1983) that involved three separate surveys: a nationwide survey of 1,200 administrators, teachers, and parents; a survey of state directors of programs for gifted education; and a survey of local program directors representing a variety of educational strategies. Although it was reported that almost half of the gifted and talented students were receiving no special education, there was great diversity among the states in the number of gifted pupils being served as well as in the amount of funds being allocated. More than half of the respondents wanted the federal government to continue to play a catalytic role in providing resources for training, research, development, and demonstration projects, with the actual program decisions to be made at the local and state level.

There was little support for increased federal control per se. In the 1980–1981 school year, approximately $150 million was identified as

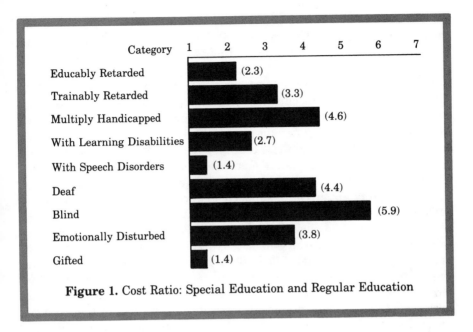

Figure 1. Cost Ratio: Special Education and Regular Education

being spent by states on public school programs for gifted education, although the additional incremental expenditures per gifted student to provide appropriate specialized programming is far lower than that for any other major category of exceptional child, except for those with speech problems (Kakalik, Furry, Thomas, & Carney, 1981). The existence of these data should provide those in public policy positions and those who are concerned with the gifted with the necessary background information required to develop long-term, and thereby more effective, priorities and policies. Professional educators and public administrators are much more knowledgeable today about the unique needs of the gifted and about effective strategies for addressing these needs. Yet, as we pointed out in discussing the handling by the media of the recommendations inherent in *A Nation At Risk* and the educational reports of the mid-1980s, our society is still demonstrably ambivalent about the gifted and talented.

By 1980, 39 states had enacted legislation defining gifted and talented children (Zettel, 1982). The majority of these are modelled after (or identical to) the definition presented by Marland (1972). High general intellectual ability and superior academic aptitude are descriptions nearly universally included in such state legislation, and most also include creative and productive thinking. The areas of leadership, visual and performing arts, and psychomotor ability are included in fewer legislative definitions of giftedness (Zettel, 1979). Thus, most states have adopted a definition of giftedness that is somewhat more narrow than the Marland definition.

There is additional evidence of state-level commitment to the education of the gifted and talented (Zettel, 1982): 38 states make explicit financial allocation for gifted education, 42 states have a full-time government administrative coordinator for gifted education, and 44 states have regulations or guidelines for the screening and identification of the gifted. Seventeen states currently either require or suggest the use of individualized education programs (IEPs) for gifted students. The total annual 1979–1980 allocation for gifted education for those 38 states making such funding commitments totaled over $121 million (Zettel, 1980), and slightly over 750,000 gifted elementary and secondary students were served by state-mandated and state-supported educational programs for the gifted and talented. State-supported educational services to the gifted reportedly doubled between 1975 and 1980, in terms of both financial allocations and number of persons served (Zettel, 1982). The Council of State Directors of Programs for the Gifted conducted a survey and reported in July 1984 that 1,052,108 public school children were being served by programs for the gifted and talented (2.7% of public school enrollment). This growth in state-level commitment is the result of the efforts of state and local public advocacy groups. By the mid-1970s, state or local parent advocacy groups for the gifted and talented existed in at least 36 states (Zettel, 1979).

These figures relating to the present commitment of state government to the educational needs of the gifted are encouraging. They do not, however, mean that the state-level commitment is adequate to the need. Similarly, the present situation does not imply that federal involvement in gifted education is no longer necessary. What these data do imply is that there is, today, a much broader commitment to gifted education by the general public, as well as by state government, than existed 25 years ago. We believe this will make renewed progress on national policy related to giftedness easier, and it will assure that future federal legislation and funding are more appropriately implemented.

Research Initiatives

In a field that is in as much flux as is that of the gifted and talented, quality research can make a significant difference in the evolution of relevant public policies. To the concerned public official there simply does not appear to be any consensus within the field at this point in time. It is therefore necessary for those concerned with the gifted to provide leadership and at least to suggest a reasonable course of action. Research programs must be developed that will both solve immediate questions and, of equal importance, shape the course of future discussion. The following are some of the issues that must be addressed.

• How can one objectively determine who is gifted and talented? What is meant by this? What objective or behavioral measures can be utilized or should be developed? In short, what is the target population?

• What truly unique needs do these individuals possess? For example, are there special emotional or counseling needs for the child, for his or her parents, or for any siblings?

• What special curriculum modifications should be developed? Are there any particular subject matters that should receive priority, or should a priority be given to cognition per se?

• What models are most effective and for what types of children; should there be special magnet schools, special classes within the regular school program, or summer sessions? How do these differ at different age levels?

• What about the truly special gifted and talented, that is, those who are also physically handicapped, or members of minority groups? How can the programs that are already in place for these individuals be adapted for a subset of their gifted, or should they be?

• What information would be useful in order to decide what percentage of an agency's budget (such as that of the National Institute of Education or the U.S. Department of Education) should be expended on the gifted? For example, what types of initiatives should NIE be urged to pursue? Or, to what extent should federal funds be earmarked for exemplary programs or teacher continuing education programs?

One must understand that in the eyes of many policymakers, and undoubtedly also in the eyes of many educators, there is the potential for a fundamental conflict between equity and excellence. Not only is it easy for individuals to misunderstand the unique needs of the gifted, but when one looks at the broader picture, there are so many pressing educational needs. One can thus reasonably ask, "Why spend limited resources on those who will do well enough on their own; is it not their parents' responsibility?" It is exactly because of questions such as this that quality research is important. It is needed in order to demonstrate what can be done and at what cost. The reality is that today the Counselor to the President on Scientific Affairs is not calling for additional resources for the gifted. Nor are teachers' unions doing so. Instead, the latter, for example, are focusing upon issues such as merit pay. Teachers are professionals, and research must be conducted in order to give their unions credible and professional reasons to speak out on behalf of the gifted. There are many types of research that must be conducted: programmatic research, basic cognitive and curriculum research, developmental research, and psychosocial research. As the research knowledge base evolves, however, those concerned with the gifted and talented must also ensure that it is systematically brought to the attention of public policymakers, so that truly informed decisions can be made.

Advocacy Efforts and Public Awareness

There is a wide variety of advocacy groups that work at the national level in support of the gifted and talented. The American Association for Gifted Children and the National Association for Gifted Children are both "specialty" advocacy groups that are specifically concerned with giftedness. The Council for Exceptional Children is also a major national advocacy group that addresses itself to advocacy on behalf of all "exceptional" children, including physically or mentally handicapped and gifted children. Other advocacy groups that are concerned with more general children's issues, such as the Children's Defense Fund, engage at times in advocacy efforts on behalf of the gifted. A range of educational groups, such as the National Council of Parents and Teachers and the National Association of State Boards of Education, as well as professional associations such as the American Psychological Association, the Society for Research in Child Development, and the Committee on the Gifted of the Social Science Research Council engage in advocacy efforts on behalf of the gifted. Similarly, there have been a number of television shows aired by public television and the National Association of Broadcasters that are oriented toward the gifted and talented. Recently, for example, a program called "Child's Play: Prodigies and Possibilities" was aired on the PBS documentary series, NOVA (Mendelsohn, Whittlesey, & Buckner, 1985). Shows such as this greatly assist in developing a popular consensus favorable toward targeting other educational efforts.

This list, a very partial one, may seem impressive; it seems almost as if everyone were advocating on behalf of the gifted. But each of the advocacy groups sees giftedness within the context of its own broader or related interests. The presence and involvement of these groups, whose interests are not expressly identical to those whose advocacy efforts are solely for the gifted, sometimes generate concern among the prime advocates for the gifted. The fear is that although these other groups have good intentions, they may inadvertently dilute the efforts of those groups whose primary concern is advocacy for the gifted. Nevertheless, each type of group is important to successful advocacy for the gifted, because each expands the number of voices calling for action, and each helps to place the policy issues within a broader context.

No single advocacy group is the best one through which to work. Individuals who are extremely active advocates often belong to and work through several different advocacy groups, each of which is primarily active around one or another particular issue of perspective. For example, a psychologist who is interested in research on giftedness might also be the parent of a gifted child and engage in advocacy efforts related to the gifted through the American Psychological Association, the Society for Research in Child Development, and the Council for Exceptional Children. We all, as individuals, have multiple interests and can advance these different personal interests through several associations. When our varied interests overlap, frequently we can persuade seemingly diverse associations to work together toward a common goal.

Effective advocacy involves getting as many different groups as possible (voices and voters) involved in supporting a legislative initiative. Associations that have different primary objectives are, after all, interested in different aspects of what is important for the gifted. For example, associations involving teachers or educational administrators can be convinced to support legislation related to the gifted, because they will support credible legislation that increases funding for education. The APA and various guidance and counseling associations will generally support legislation that includes specialized psychological or counseling services for the gifted. Educational, behavioral, and cognitive research societies will support legislation when a section provides support for research related to giftedness and to enhancing the ability of the gifted to utilize their potential to the fullest. When many apparently diverse special interest groups support a bill, policymakers are impressed and responsive. For them, it means that a consensus exists so that no one should be mad that the "wrong" decision was made and that the proposed action should be viewed positively by many different segments of potential voters. Most effective advocacy groups not only engage in independent initiatives, but also participate in coalitions addressing related legislation.

There is an additional reason for advocates for the gifted to work with other groups. It is sometimes important to neutralize political forces that have what appears to be a valid social policy basis (as opposed to a professional self-interest reason) for opposing or challenging particular policy initiatives. For example, in periods of tight budget (which seems to be always), some opponents of gifted education will claim that the limited funds available should go to those with the greatest need (usually considered to be groups such as the handicapped, minorities, and other disadvantaged populations). The arguments that opponents put forward range from "The gifted already have some advantages by virtue of their high intelligence, and you just want to make them elite" to "The gifted are so bright and able that they can get along well on their own." Such arguments continue to be raised in policy deliberations at all levels (Gallagher, 1983; Tannenbaum & Neuman, 1980). Any advocate for the gifted must be prepared to address this issue. Some counter this argument by pointing out that 10 to 15 percent of high school dropouts are gifted students who are bored and (by being allowed to drop out of high school) are lost as highly creative members of society. It can also be claimed that the gifted can suffer psychological harm by being deprived of the opportunity to utilize their abilities fully. Finally, it is sometimes useful to show that a spillover of improved general instruction often occurs when specialized instruction is developed for gifted students. These are valid points, but they must be backed up with examples and data because the information to support these responses has not been widely disseminated. Accordingly, without concrete examples, state and national policymakers may be inclined to believe that these points are probably not valid. The material presented in this book may help to convince them otherwise.

Advocates for the gifted should also be aware of other strategies for weakening the "serve the disadvantaged first" claims. One way is to incorporate into the proposals related to gifted education provisions for giving special attention to selected disadvantaged groups. For example, it is not uncommon to specify that a given percentage of slots in a program for the gifted children will be reserved for gifted minority group students or for gifted handicapped students (and include in the screening programs special selection efforts focused on these groups). This approach, of course, fits quite well with the general argument that all exceptional (handicapped, disadvantaged, minority, as well as gifted) children should have educational programs that are tailored to their unique educational needs.

Resources for Organizing Advocacy Efforts

A variety of resources are available to assist individuals and groups who wish to begin advocacy for specialized services for the gifted at the state and local levels. Useful information on the most current trends can be obtained from the specialized national advocacy groups concerned with the gifted: American Association for Gifted Children (New York City), National Association for Gifted Children (Hot Springs, Arkansas), and the Council for Exceptional Children (Reston, Virginia). The ERIC (Education Resources and Information Center) Clearinghouse on Handicapped and Gifted Children, operated through the Council for Exceptional Children, and the National/State Leadership Training Institute on the Gifted and the Talented (Ventura County, California) both provide resources, clearinghouse functions, and planning efforts for advocating for and implementing gifted programming. The U.S. Office for Gifted and Talented unfortunately no longer exists; it was disbanded in 1982 as part of the federal reorganization and the consolidation of federal funding. Local telephone directories may list local chapters of national gifted organizations, and a letter to a state's department of education should elicit information on statewide activities on behalf of the gifted. The National Association of State Boards of Education has also been active in providing resources to assist the development of such advocacy efforts.

There are many practical publications available for people who wish to organize and operate a local advocacy group. These publications include suggestions, for example, on how to approach and interact with local and state educational administrators, a procedure that can be quite sensitive (Aubrecht, 1981; Kraver, 1981; Mitchell, 1981; Siewert, 1981). Tannenbaum and Neuman (1980) have provided an excellent brief but detailed "getting ready" list of organizational issues and steps that should be addressed in the first few meetings of a local advocacy group. They also offer a series of especially helpful suggestions about managing anger and frustration, as well as how to spread the work around so that everyone is involved at a maximum level of individual participation (thereby avoiding burnout).

It is very important for concerned individuals, and especially concerned parents, to realize that it is usually not by chance that one's personal interest, such as the advancement of the gifted, has not been receiving sufficient priority. Those who establish public policy, whether in education or in any other area, are constantly faced with more requests (or demands) than they can possibly fulfill. Successful policymakers are professional politicians. As such, they must continue to do the impossible—to forge workable compromises that overtly conflicting parties can view as being reasonable and appropriate. Policymakers have little time to explore issues in any depth; instead, they must constantly respond to matters that are viewed as being of pressing urgency in an immediate and timely fashion.

For those of us concerned with the gifted, as a practical matter, this means that we must see to it that our agenda becomes one of a policymaker's concerns. We must strive to establish a visible presence, and having done this, to be able to provide the policymaker with reasonable alternatives that can be readily implemented. It is not enough merely to complain. We must truly realize and appreciate the significance of the fact that policymakers at all levels of government frequently do not understand the specifics of our concerns. It is therefore our responsibility to make clear to them what can be done and how this can be accomplished over a reasonable period of time. We must understand that being right or having a pressing need is not sufficient to effect change. There are many other equally concerned citizens, for example, those concerned with the elderly, who are vying for their fair share of limited resources. In their view, their case is undoubtedly at least equally meritorious. Furthermore, their case may even be more compelling to a politician. For example, not only do the elderly vote, but more importantly, their requests have visible results. If one establishes a center or a meals on wheels program, one can immediately see concrete results. An identifiable number of senior citizens are more active, healthier, and considerably happier. What is the comparable situation with the gifted? What is the tangible and immediate consequences of providing increased funding for them?

Accordingly, in developing grass roots support for projects targeted for the gifted, it would be especially useful from the public official's vantage point if truly broad-based support could be demonstrated—for example, support from groups that traditionally have not involved themselves in the issue, such as the local chamber of commerce, the university faculty senate, and the local psychological association. Similarly, we must not underestimate the extent to which the media (television, radio, and print) play a major role in shaping an elected or appointed official's perception of pressing needs. Reporters and editorial writers from the media are themselves professionals who are always very interested in learning of pressing community needs and concerns. Their interest should be cultivated, and they should be informed of what in fact can be done (DeLeon & VandenBos, 1984). Perhaps, for example, a special public policy forum could be established in which representatives from the media, local political officials, and gifted children and their parents systematically interact. Nothing is as impressive to a politician as are success and tangible evidence of what can be done. An advocacy organization must ensure that everyone is kept actively involved. Achievable long- and short-term goals must be established. The political process and the public policy process are one. They are evolutionary in nature; they are forever ongoing, with no real beginning and no real end (DeLeon, O'Keefe, VandenBos, & Kraut, 1982).

Conclusions

In this chapter we have reviewed the evolution of educational policy deliberations during the past several decades regarding gifted and talented children, at both the state and national levels. In our judgment, considerable progress has been made; however, there is clearly much more to be done. We feel that it is especially important that those concerned with the gifted and talented become personally more active in the political and public policy process. It is necessary for those whose primary concern is the gifted to exert leadership and to actively suggest to our public officials what the priorities and the future course of action in this area should be. Research agendas, in particular, must be developed that will provide answers to a wide range of immediate concerns and, at the same time, point to areas of further exploration during the next decade. Our nation's educational resources are finite, and there are many more compelling needs than can be met. For the gifted, given the possible public misperception of a conflict between "equity" and "excellence," it is especially critical that documented evidence be generated as to what can and should be done. There is considerable potential at both the local and national level for substantial additional progress to be made in the foreseeable future; however, this will occur only if those concerned with the gifted and talented persist in their efforts to become a viable part of the public policy and political process.

References

An Act to Extend Programs of Assistance for Elementary and Secondary Education and for Other Purposes, Pub L. No. 91-230, § 84 Stat. 121 (1970).

Albert, R. S. (1969). Present day status of the concept and its implications for the study of creativity and giftedness. *American Psychologist, 24*, 743–753.

Aubrecht, L. (1981). Organizing for advocacy: Making it work on the state and local level. In P. B. Mitchell (Ed.), *An advocate's guide to building support for gifted and talented education* (pp. 31–41). Washington, DC: National Association of State Boards of Education.

Boyer, E. L. (1983). *High school: A report on secondary education in America*. New York: Harper & Rowe.

Congressional Record, July 31, 1980, *126*, Part 16, S10383.

Congressional Record, October 1, 1980, *126*, Part 22, H10457.

Congressional Record, October 19, 1983, *129*, S14211.

Cox, J., Daniel, N., & Boston, B. (in press). *Educating able learners: Programs and promising practices*. Austin: University of Texas Press.

DeLeon, P. H. (1983). The changing and creating of legislation: The political process. In B. Sales (Ed.), *The professional psychologist's handbook* (pp. 601–620). New York: Plenum Press.

DeLeon, P. H., Forsythe, P., & VandenBos, G. R. (in press). Federal recognition of psychology in rehabilitation programs. *Rehabilitation Psychology*.

DeLeon, P. H., Frohboese, R., & Meyers, J. C. (1984). Psychologist on Capitol Hill: A unique use of the skills of the scientist/practitioner. *Professional Psychology: Research and Practice, 15*, 697–705.

DeLeon, P. H., O'Keefe, A. M., VandenBos, G. R., & Kraut, A. G. (1982). How to influence public policy: A blueprint for political activism. *American Psychologist, 37*, 476–485.

DeLeon, P. H., & VandenBos, G. R. (1984). Public health policy and behavioral health. In J. D. Matarazzo, S. M. Weiss, J. A. Herd, N. E. Miller, & S. M. Weiss (Eds.), *Behavioral health: A handbook of health enhancement and disease prevention* (pp. 150–163). New York: Wiley.

Dodd, C. J. (1983, November 9). Press statement on the Senate children's caucus hearings on the gifted and talented.

Education Amendments of 1974, Pub. L. No. 93-380, § 88 Stat. 484 (1974).

Education Amendments of 1978, Pub. L. No. 95-561, § 92 Stat. 2143 (1978).

Education Commission of the States. (1983). *Action for excellence: A comprehensive plan to improve our nation's schools*. Denver: A. B. Hirschfeld Press.

Educational Policies Commission. (1950). *Education of the gifted*. Washington, DC: National Education Association.

Gallagher, J. J. (1979). Issues in education for the gifted. In A. H. Passow (Ed.), *The gifted and the talented: Their education and development* (pp. 28–44). Chicago, IL: University of Chicago Press.

Gallagher, J. J. (1983, September 22). *Gifted and talented students*. Science and Public Policy Seminar presented at the meeting of the Federation of Behavioral, Psychological, and Cognitive Sciences, Washington, DC.

Gallagher, J. J., Weiss, P., Oglesby, K., & Thomas, T. (1983). *The status of gifted/ talented education: United States surveys of needs, practices, and policies.* Ventura, CA: Office of the Superintendent of Ventura County Schools.

Goldberg, M. L. (1965). Educating the talented. *White House conference on education: A milestone for educational progress.* Washington, DC: Senate Subcommittee on Education.

Hayden, T. (1985). *Reaching out to the gifted child: Roles for the health care professions.* New York: American Association for Gifted Childen.

Jackson, D. M. (1979). The emerging national and state concern. In A. H. Passow (Ed.), *The gifted and the talented: Their education and development* (pp. 45–62). Chicago: University of Chicago Press.

Kakalik, J., Furry, W., Thomas, M., & Carney, M. (1981). *The cost of special education.* Santa Monica, CA: RAND Corporation.

Kraver, T. C. (1981). Parent power: Starting and building parents organizations. In P. B. Mitchell (Ed.), *An advocate's guide to building support for gifted and talented education* (pp. 24–30). Washington, DC: National Association of State Boards of Education.

Marland, S. P., Jr. (1972). *Education of the gifted and talented: Report to the Congress of the United States by the U.S. Commissioner of Education.* Washington, DC: U.S. Government Printing Office.

Mendelsohn, J., Whittlesey, R., & Buckner, N. (Producers). (1985). *Child's play: Prodigies and possibilities* [Film]. Boston, MA: Documentary Guild.

Mitchell, P. B. (Ed.). (1981). *An advocate's guide to building support for gifted and talented education.* Washington, DC: National Association of State Boards of Education.

National Commission on Excellence in Education. (1983). *A nation at risk: The imperative for educational reform.* Washington, DC: U.S. Government Printing Office.

National Defense Education Act of 1958, Pub. L. No. 85-864, § 72 Stat. 1580 (1958).

National Science Foundation. (1983). *Educating Americans for the 21st century: A plan of action for improving mathematics, science, and technology education for all American elementary and secondary students so that their achievement is the best in the world by 1995.* Washington, DC: Author.

National Science Foundation Act of 1950, Pub. L. No. 81-507, § 64 Stat. 149 (1950).

Omnibus Budget Reconciliation Act of 1981, Pub. L. No. 97-35, § 95 Stat. 357 (1981).

Passow, A. H. (1979). Perspective on the study and education of the gifted and talented. In A. H. Passow (Ed.), *The gifted and the talented: Their education and development* (pp. 1–4). Chicago, IL: University of Chicago Press.

Siewert, R. (1981). Knowing what you want and getting it. In P. B. Mitchell (Ed.), *An advocate's guide to building support for gifted and talented education* (pp. 42–49). Washington, DC: National Association of State Boards of Education.

Tannenbaum, A. J. (1979). Pre-Sputnik to Post-Watergate concern about the gifted. In A. H. Passow (Ed.), *The gifted and the talented: Their education and development* (pp. 5–27). Chicago: University of Chicago Press.

Tannenbaum, A. J., & Neuman, E. (1980). *Reaching out: Advocacy for the gifted and talented.* New York: American Association for Gifted Children.

Webb, J. T., Meckstroth, E. A., & Tolan, S. S. (1983). *Guiding the gifted child.* Columbus, OH: Ohio Psychology Publishing Company.

Wolfe, D. (1954). *America's resources of specialized talent.* New York: Harper and Row.

Zettel, J. J. (1979). State programs for educating the gifted and talented. In A. H. Passow (Ed.), *The gifted and the talented: Their education and development* (pp. 63–74). Chicago, IL: University of Chicago Press.

Zettel, J. J. (1980). *Gifted and talented education for a nationwide perspective.* Reston, VA: The ERIC Clearinghouse on Handicapped and Gifted Children.

Zettel, J. J. (1982). The education of gifted and talented children from a federal perspective. In J. Ballard, B. A. Ramirez, & F. J. Weintraub (Eds.), *Special education in America: Its legal and governmental foundations* (pp. 51–64). Reston, VA: Council for Exceptional Children.

Epilogue. Perspectives on Research and Development

Frances Degen Horowitz
Marion O'Brien
University of Kansas

It is commonly acknowledged that when a child is retarded or functioning below normal, the possible contributions that the individual might have made if he or she had been normal creates a sense of loss. When a child who is talented or gifted performs at a level significantly below his or her potential, however, society is generally unaware of how much it has been deprived, for we do not know how to measure loss on the continuum from normal to superior and extraordinary. A basic scientific interest in understanding the nature of giftedness and talent need only be justified by the desire to know what we do not know; the quest for such knowledge forms the essence of unfettered scientific inquiry. A basic social interest in giftedness and talent, however, is justified in terms of society's need to have at its disposal all the human resources possible so that the goals of society may be more effectively and creatively fulfilled.

Regrettably, neither the scientific nor the social bases for expanding our knowledge of giftedness and talent appear to have provided sufficient impetus to stimulate the funding of programmatic research on these topics at a level that promises significant progress in the foreseeable future. Traditionally, the best and most creative behavioral scientists have not always turned their talents to the study of the gifted. The reasons for this are unclear, though the availability of funds to support such work is undoubtedly one factor. But there must be others. There has not been much theoretical development of ideas related to the gifted and the talented, and, with some exceptions, no large bodies of data have been collected in order to illuminate the genesis of giftedness or to detail the components of giftedness and how they function. Stimulating these kinds of interests and efforts is among the major purposes of this volume.

The chapters that this book comprises represent what is known about the gifted and the talented from a developmental perspective. As one author after the other stresses, this volume is equally a testament to what is not known. It becomes quite apparent by the end of the volume that the development of giftedness in poorly understood. As Grinder makes clear in his historical review (chapter 1) and as DeLeon and VandenBos's social policy analysis reveals (chapter 14), concern for the gifted has been largely episodic and typically related to educational policy and practice; it is often acknowledged that more is needed in order to provide a better understanding of how, why, and when giftedness and talent develop and flourish and how these qualities are ultimately expressed in highly productive lives. The commitment to research, either in the form of resources or in the form of programmatic interest among a large cadre of behavioral scientists, has not followed, however.

Perhaps the general status of developmental theory and research has not been ripe for focusing upon the most basic research questions that need to be addressed in this area. There are good indications from the reviews of this volume that a period of potential scientific fruitfulness may be imminent. Several lines of work appear to be coalescing into similar hypotheses that are testable, given the tools of investigation at hand. In this epilogue, we consider giftedness and talent from the viewpoint of developmental theory and models, discuss some of the recurring themes related to giftedness that have emerged in this volume, and then focus on some questions that might most profitably constitute the research agenda for expanding our basic knowledge of giftedness and talent.

Giftedness and Talent in Developmental Theory

Giftedness and retardation, as Humphreys (chapter 11) and Zigler and Farber (Chapter 13) note, are two ends of the developmental continuum. Neither figures prominently in the major developmental theories, although theorists have not ignored them totally. Indeed, it was Zigler's challenge to the Lewinian notion of retardation, as exemplifying a rigidity of life-space boundaries, that broke open the entire effort to understand the role of social and motivational factors as they influence the level of functioning of retarded individuals. Zigler has now developed a theory about the behavior of retarded individuals that essentially places the cultural-familial retardate on the low end of the normal continuum for intelligence by which social and motivational factors determine the functional behavioral level of the individual. When these social and motivational factors are systematically employed in structured educational or behavior modification programs, retarded individuals can be helped to make considerable progress in their behavioral performances. Might giftedness and talent be similarly conceived in the context of this kind of social-learning theory as being at the high end of the continuum?

Intellectual giftedness, most typically, is defined in terms of an arbitrary cutoff point on the continuum of performance on intelligence tests. What determines that performance is a mixture of genetic and environmental influences; the exact nature of the contribution of each is presently unknown. As with the retarded, however, social and motivational factors based on environmental experience are probably important ingredients. Baldwin (chapter 8) and Mistry and Rogoff (chapter 5) might take issue with this definitional approach, arguing, in the case of minorities in the United States and for cross-cultural analyses, that culture plays a major role in determining not only what is highly prized but also what calls forth the recognition of extraordinary performance. It may be that Sternberg's superordinate componential theory of giftedness (see Sternberg & Davidson, chapter 2), with its reference to metacomponents, performance components, and knowledge-acquisition components, will provide a general theoretical template for the culture-specific substantive characteristics of behavior that can be ranged on a continuum from low (retarded) to high (gifted).

Yet it is clear that none of these conceptualizations relates very directly to the major theories of development. Giftedness, like retardation, is classified as being an "individual difference" phenomenon and as such as been lodged within psychometrics rather than within developmental theory. Developmental theorists have not, however, entirely ignored the question of the gifted. Gesell, for instance, studied the individual growth careers of 84 infants and children (Gesell, Amatruda, Castner, & Thompson, 1939) and noted the highly individualized patterns involved in the expression of giftedness. For some infants there was an early and easily detectible superiority, others evidenced superiority only later, and for a few early superiority was not followed by later evidence of giftedness.

Aware of the imprecision of measurement and of the paucity of psychologists' knowledge of child development at that time, Gesell was cautious in interpreting his observations. Still, he held fast to his basic faith that with increased understanding of the nature of individual growth patterns and of the principles guiding development, it would eventually be possible to make accurate predictions of superiority from observing infants:

> In spite of its obscurities and its ambiguities, infancy is prophetic. This child is not a creature of circumstance. He is part and parcel of the great stream of life. He is biologically father to the man. And the infant is father of the child. Adulthood is not added into infancy: It inheres in infancy. Because of the inherent continuity in the life cycle, there is ample scope for progressive prediction in the consecutive study of infant behavior. (Gesell et al., 1939, p. 21)

Such a point of view is not shared by contemporary students of infant behavior, nor by many of the major developmental theorists. Piagetian theory, limited mostly to cognitive development, can be seen as accounting for giftedness largely in terms of individual differences in rate of development, with rate being determined by inherent individual differences and possibly by selective environmental experience. Freudian theory (which, interestingly, receives little mention in this volume) has traditionally been more focused on the manner in which creativity and special gifts play a role in the psychodynamic functioning of personality rather than with the genesis of giftedness. Freudians regard the expression and perhaps the full development of giftedness and creativity as being forms of sublimated sexual energy, although they have also been interested in the relationship of creative acts to be the psychodynamic structuring of personality. It is possible to use Freudian theory to interpolate some of the developmental implications for the fostering of giftedness and special talents, although there appears to have been little systematic theoretical use of Freudian ideas in the mainstream study of the gifted.

Similarly, the theoretical framework for considering the gifted offered by behaviorists and social learning theorists involves the general principles and assumptions that underlie the behavioristic approach to developmental phenomena—the cumulative, somewhat linear progression in the acquisition of skills, determined in large part by the history of reinforcement experienced by the individual. That some individuals learn more easily and more quickly and go further is, similar to the Piagetian point of view, an individual difference characteristic that may have part of its base in organismic variables and part of its base in environmental variables. The history of reinforcement will determine which skills are acquired. The social definitions of reinforcers will provide for cultural specificity in what is valued and ultimately in what is regarded as gifted. This analysis is not unlike Baldwin's (chapter 8) analysis of giftedness in minority individuals, and it is certainly compatible with Mistry and Rogoff's (chapter 5) discussion of the cultural determinants of the definition of giftedness. Even Humphreys's (chapter 11) highly culturally bound definition of intelligence is not at odds with such an analysis. He regards the history of reinforcement as being an important determinant of performance on intelligence tests. Changes in reinforcement patterns may account for some of the instability of intelligence test performances across the life span.

It is clear that a strong theoretical framework for considering the phenomenon of giftedness does not exist. In part, this may be because the major developmental theories (with the exception, perhaps, of behaviorism) no longer hold sway in providing an encompassing intellectual arch from which hypotheses and experiments are systematically derived. The knowledge base for child development has, in many ways, outstripped psychologists' grand theoretical schemes; theory is more focused on particular topics and behavioral domains. Few of these mini-theory approaches provide a model into which the genesis, development, and maintenance of giftedness fits easily. Wallace (chapter 12) recognizes this when she advocates a case study strategy for learning more about the gifted. She uses an evolving systems analysis in which creative work is viewed as being a process that extends over a long period of time, within a context of time, place, and situational factors. The particular confluence of these factors serves to nurture the expression and development of creativity. The case study approach, combined with an evolving systems approach, is profitably employed by Wallace to illuminate some of the nurturing elements. Her analysis is compatible with the fundamental assumption expressed by a number of authors in this volume that even if giftedness and talent have biological and genetic roots, their development and realization require a functional environment, opportunity for practice, and, in many cases, systematic learning experiences. Still, this is not developmental theory writ large. Perhaps such a theoretical framework is premature, or perhaps the lack of a theoretical framework for understanding giftedness and talent is merely an exemplar of the current state of affairs with respect to the availability of an integrating theory of development or a generic model of development.

An Environment–Organism Model

A developmental model that might serve as a generic frame for considering giftedness has been proposed (Horowitz, 1978, 1982, 1984), and its implications are in the process of being explored (Horowitz, 1985). The model is conceptually uncomplicated, although the combinations and permutations it permits enable a large number of diverse phenomena to be encompassed. Using the model, questions such as those related to continuity and discontinuity in development can be considered in terms of processes rather than with respect to particular phenomena. A diagrammatic representation of this model is shown in Figure 1. Its two major dimensions are environmental variables and organismic variables; the surface of the model represents the level of developmental status at any

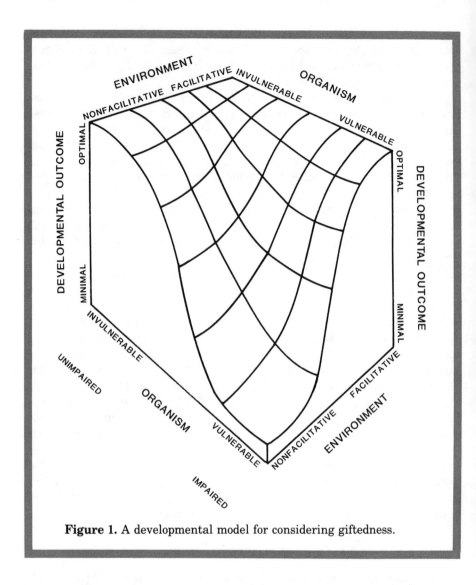

Figure 1. A developmental model for considering giftedness.

point in time. In this diagram, environment ranges across a crude continuum from facilitative to nonfacilitative of development. The organismic variables fall along two continua: invulnerable to vulnerable and unimpaired to impaired. The upper far corner of the surface represents superior to extraordinary developmental outcome—the portion of the surface where the gifted would fall. Conversely, the lower near corner of the model represents poor to nonfunctional developmental outcome—the portion of the surface where profound retardation or developmental failure would fall.

According to this model, a child's developmental status at any point in time and with respect to any behavioral domain is a joint function of three factors: the degree of the child's organic impairment and level of vulnerability and the degree of facilitation provided by the child's environment. In different domains, the child may be at different points on the surface. Thus, for example, an otherwise normal cerebral palsied child with high levels of motor compromise would fall into the lower near quadrant of the surface with respect to motor development, but in cognitive development might be more central or even in the upper far quadrant of the outcome surface. Were technology to make possible an environmental intervention to alleviate the child's motor impairments, the child's status with regard to motor development would change.

The history of the hereditary disorder, phenylketonuria (PKU) provides an example of how environment influences organic impairment. PKU is a condition whereby the failure to metabolize phenylalanine results, ultimately, in profound retardation. On our diagram, a child with organismic impairment and the absence of a known environment that could be facilitative of development would fall in the lower right portion, indicating retardation. When the metabolic impairment became fully understood, however, it was possible to engineer a facilitative environment for normal to near-normal development by prescribing a phenylalanine-free diet in the early years of life (Berman, Waisman, & Graham, 1966). Thus, although the child's place on the organismic continuum would not change, the degree of facilitation of the environment would be profoundly changed and the child's developmental status would be seen quite differently. In fact, it now appears that after five to six years on the phenylalanine-free diet, children can tolerate some phenylalanine. This change would be reflected in the model by moving the individual on the continuum from completely impaired to less impaired.

The organismic continuum of invulnerable to vulnerable can also be thought of with reference to relative conditionability or resilience. This continuum is proposed to account for individual differences in responsiveness to environmental variables: Some children appear to exhibit good development even in environments that appear to be nonfacilitative of development, whereas other children seem to be much more dependent upon environmental facilitation to reach similar levels of developmental outcome. Garmezy's work on vulnerability (1974); Murphy's work on coping (Murphy & Moriarty, 1976); Tyler's analysis of individual differences in responsiveness to environmental experience (1978); Chess and Thomas's and Escalona's discussions of individuality and the operation of temperament (Chess & Thomas, 1977; Escalona, 1968, 1973); and Werner and Smith's more recent report of children who were particularly resilient under poor environmental conditions (1982) are all compatible with a model that permits good to superior developmental outcome under conditions that are judged to be generally not facilitative of good developmental outcome.

The highly gifted child who comes out of an environment that is lacking in many of the basic elements thought to be important to good developmental outcome is an exemplar of the invulnerable child. The development of such extraordinary talent and creativity under seemingly adverse circumstances is sometimes posed as a challenge to the considerable evidence that contingently responsive and highly enriching experience with many opportunities for broad-based learning is required for good to excellent developmental outcome. According to the model proposed here, however, the degree of dependency upon a highly facilitative environment is an organismic variable. The model would predict that a small number of highly gifted individuals would emerge from totally impoverished and abusive environments. Of much larger consequence, demographically, are those children who are organically unimpaired and who, experiencing highly facilitative environments, function at the level of giftedness or are able to express and develop special talents. Many of the students in gifted programs around the nation are described by these circumstances. In less facilitative environments, these children's degree of vulnerability would influence whether they realized their potential for giftedness. The difference between the level of achievement attained and the level of achievement that might have been attained by these individuals is a measure of the loss of human resources to society.

From the viewpoint of the model proposed here, developmental continuity is not a matter of organismic characteristics but of the degree of consistency in the combinatorial processes of interaction between the organism and the environment. For some children, neither their placement along the organismic dimension nor the degree of facilitation of their environment changes across the course of development. In these cases, we would predict continuity over time in the child's relative level of functioning and developmental status. For other children, the degree of vulnerability or dependence on environmental facilitation may change as a function of differential constitutional expressions of these characteristics or as a function of learning history. If the nature of the facilitating environment does not also change, then we would expect discontinuity in development.

For example, for some children, development in the first two years of life may be relatively independent of environmental facilitation; a facilitative environment may become much more important and significant in later periods of development. If the environment is highly facilitative in the first two years of life and continues to be so in the next period, we would expect continuity in development; if the environment is not highly facilitative in the first two years but shifts to a level of excellent facilitation, we would also predict continuity although the functional equation accounting for the continuity would have changed. The reader can easily work out the combinations that would and would not produce continuity. Giftedness, according to this model, could be, in different individuals, either an inherent collection of characteristics of the child that is expressed with relative independence from environmental facilitation, or a set of characteristics that is fostered by, indeed is dependent upon, environmental facilitation. The task then becomes one of identifying the processes and terms of the developmental equations that produce repertoires that are defined as being gifted or talented.

Because there is such a large common-sense aspect to this model and its implications, it is tempting to consider it as a general heuristic rather than as a potential blueprint for a research agenda. Yet the model provides a structural framework for deriving a set of developmental research questions that encompass not only the general laws of behavior but also the individual difference variance around those laws. It permits the individual difference focus on the gifted and the talented to shift from one dominated by the tradition of psychometrics to one in which psychometrics is only one part of a larger picture. Having provided this conceptual background, we turn to an assessment of the major themes that have emerged from the chapters in this volume.

Major Themes and Issues in the Study of Giftedness

The Nature of Giftedness

Is giftedness a general characteristic or is it domain specific? Is there a central core of general intelligence that can be measured on a scale such that giftedness can be defined as performance above a certain arbitrary point on the scale? These and other questions have long been debated in the literature on the gifted, as Grinder (chapter 1) so aptly notes. The modern focus, he concludes, is converging on a search for the Spearman "g," exemplified by the information-processing characteristics proposed by Sternberg and his colleagues (chapter 2), the elements of which, according to Rabinowitz and Glazer (chapter 3), involve not only rapid retrieval of information but the organization of knowledge that provides for higher order analysis and synthesis.

Although giftedness might involve the use of novelty and some element of new thought or products, according to Wallach (chapter 4), as a general measurable ability, creativity does not take us very far. Perhaps creative acts occur at the point where quantitative analysis no longer applies and where a qualitative system reorganization occurs either within a domain or across domains. Thus, creativity might be thought of as an aspect of giftedness that comes into play only at certain points in highly competent performance, that is not always present, and that for some gifted individuals, may occur only rarely or not at all. Is creativity more necessary for gifted performance in those domains associated with music and art as opposed to science or politics, for example? Some interesting developmental aspects in the realization of creativity in art and music and perhaps in writing are suggested by the few retrospective studies of prodigies; are similar developmental processes operating in the cognitive and intellectual realms upon which investigators of giftedness traditionally focus? What are the relationships among talent in the artistic domains, general intelligence, and high levels of cognitive performance?

In a recent proposal Gardner (1983) parcels out intelligence into seven domains: linguistic, musical, logic and mathematical, visual and spatial conceptualization, bodily-kinesthetic skills, interpersonal skills, and intrapersonal knowledge. Gardner does not link the domains, so that highly competent performance in one does not necessarily imply gifted performance in another. Gardner focuses upon both the cultural and developmental determinants that affect which of the intelligences is emphasized, and he sees creativity in each realm as representing the highest level of functioning within the domain. In his view, however, there is also a biological component that determines natural inclinations and susceptibility to environmental shaping. Thus, Gardner's developmental analysis is compatible with the model proposed earlier in this epilogue.

An empirically intriguing aspect of Gardner's theory is his claim that each domain of intelligence has its own form of memory, learning, and perception. If this is the case, then the research on giftedness and creativity should be largely domain specific, and the quest for general processes across domains would be unsuccessful. The basic notion that there is some degree of domain specificity in gifted performance is one of the strongest points of convergence across the chapters in this volume, and the idea represents a major shift from much of the historic literature. From the evidence of some of the larger historic longitudinal data bases, however, one concludes that intellectually gifted individuals appear to excel in other areas as well (see Janos & Robinson, chapter 6). Whether there are some common higher order processes that operate across domains remains to be determined and is a concept that does not necessarily contradict domain specificity of giftedness. It may be necessary to distinguish between high general intelligence, in the sense of competent and efficient processes of information storage and retrieval, and truly gifted performance, which may involve qualitative reorganization of information. There is no reason to believe that human behavior will be best understood by an all-or-none approach.

The Gifted and Education

Much research on giftedness has been focused on intelligence and cognition. Educational programs for the gifted, with the exception of special schools and programs for the artistically talented, have been largely devoted to intellectual and cognitive development. The major issue in education has been whether enrichment and the broadening and deepening of knowledge ought to be the focus of educational programs for the gifted or whether gifted students should be given opportunities to accelerate their progress through the curriculum (see Fox & Washington, chapter 7). The case for enrichment, it would seem, is largely one against acceleration and derives from the belief that education should not get ahead of the psychosocial development of gifted students. According to many practitioners, acceleration threatens to do that.

Yet, Janos and Robinson (chapter 6) convincingly argue in support of Terman's original data on the overall high level of personal and social functioning among intellectually gifted individuals. This ought to have implications for educational practice in the direction of acceleration. If the intellectually gifted are, in general, relatively problem-free in the social and personal development areas, then it ought to be possible to fashion acceleration programs without necessarily creating psychosocial difficulties. Indeed, the evidence about psychosocial problems among the gifted suggest that the absence of challenge and the sense of marking time also produces difficulties. Fox and Washington (chapter 7) make clear that evaluations of educational models for gifted students are sorely needed, not only to ensure that gifted students receive the kind of training that will be most beneficial to them, but also to prove to educational administrators and policymakers that special programs for gifted students should have a high priority.

One of the key concerns with respect to educational programs for the gifted has been the criteria used to select participants. The most widely used criterion is performance on standard tests of intelligence. Humphreys (chapter 11) argues that this is the most sensible criterion, whereas Wallach (chapter 4) points out the low correlation between IQ scores and gifted out-of-school or occupational attainments. The use of IQ scores as the major criterion for giftedness is challenged by Baldwin (chapter 8) and Mistry and Rogoff (chapter 5), who contend that the difficulty of making cross-cultural comparisons using a single scale ultimately discriminates against minority or different populations.

Humphreys would not disagree entirely, although within a culture such as that of the United States, he does advocate a single criterion approach. This has been a central point in the national argument that has raged over the use and interpretation of standard tests of general intelligence for the retarded, the normal, and the gifted. The question that emerges in comparing the points of view about criteria and culture is one of values: To what extent should the pluralistic cultural basis of the United States figure into the definition of giftedness? The question can, however, be posed in such a way as to make it open to empirical study. If, for example, different subcultures in the United States foster different styles of thinking or different strategies of information processing, then different forms of Sternberg's metacomponents might be found in different population subgroups. If that were the case, then the nature of those metacomponents could be identified for each subculture. If, on the other hand, cognitive metacomponents are found to be the same in different cultural groups, then metacomponential function might be used as the criterion for selection of the gifted across ethnic groups in our society.

In this era of rapid technological advances, forms of thinking, communication, problem solving, and even interpersonal functioning are becoming increasingly ruled by logic strategies compatible with computers. The logic components and analytic strategies they exemplify are highly related to the basic elements thought to underlie the processes being tapped in standard intelligence tests. Indeed, the computer is considered to be a form of artificial intelligence, and advances in computer technologies are aimed increasingly at mirroring the base elements and capabilities of some of the more obvious aspects of human intelligence. What will be gained from group-specific criteria for identifying the gifted in a world increasingly dominated by computerized technology? One answer to this, extrapolated from the observations made by Baldwin, is that such identification might serve to give gifted members of such subgroups special access to intellectual and cognitive approaches that are commensurate with their potential. These approaches may offer ways to maximize the motivational and positive self-concept factors that can help keep those gifted individuals on a trajectory of realizing their full potential. The empirical challenge, then, is to describe the cognitive metacomponents and the knowledge acquisition and retrieval processes and to demonstrate that there is good transfer across culturally different realms by using early identification strategies that involve group-specific criteria.

Social Aspects of Giftedness

The discussion of the differential outcomes for gifted men and women (Eccles, chapter 9) occasions a group comparison analysis that is somewhat different from those related to different cultures and cultural subgroups. The early identification questions are not so central to the topic of gifted women; however, how giftedness is played out across the life span and the form and kinds of achievement it produces are, according to Eccles, highly related to psychological self-image factors and socially valued behaviors that are associated with either sex. The outcomes are seen as resulting from socialization processes rather than from either overt discriminatory practices or biological factors. It is, of course, difficult to sort out biological, discriminatory, and socialization factors, because of complex interrelationships among propensities, values, and socialization practices designed to represent values. It is important to recognize that mean differentials between the standard intelligence test scores of males and females, as is true of the scores of Blacks and Whites, are possibly much less informative than the fact that there is considerable overlap in the distribution of test scores for the two populations. The overlapping distributions and the early mean equation between the distributions point to the importance of the socialization process in producing differential outcomes in gifted men and women. Eccles also raises important questions about the selection of outcome criteria to evaluate the contributions of gifted men and women in our society. Intellectual and professional accomplishments cannot be the sole criteria for achievement as long as society's expectations for men and women differ widely.

The alternate forms that giftedness may take can also be considered to include morality (Gruber, chapter 10). Little attention has been paid to giftedness in such domains, except in biographical accounts of the lives of individuals. As with cultural issues related to intelligence and cognition, the area of morality immediately raises questions of social values, including the cultural definitions of good and evil. What does it mean to be morally gifted within a society? How does a person express moral giftedness? Are moral giftedness and moral leadership related? Are there cross-society standards for such morality, or must moral giftedness use different criteria for different societies? Is the development of moral giftedness subject to the same basic laws independent of moral content?

The major themes and issues that have emerged from the chapters in this volume serve to highlight the nature of the forms that public policy should take with respect to research on and provision of programs for the gifted and talented in this nation. Public policy has been most evident with respect to the mandating of educational programs (see DeLeon & VandenBos, chapter 14). But, as should be obvious, given the amount that we do not understand about the nature and development of giftedness, the effectiveness of educational programs is likely to be severely limited. Public policy about retardation has resulted not only in the development of programs for the retarded, but also in the major commitment of funds to systematic research on retardation. This has led to a better understanding of the biological, psychological, and sociological factors that affect retarded individuals and also to a technology of educational intervention that has improved significantly their level of functioning. A similar commitment to research on the gifted and talented might produce comparable results, with potential societal benefits that are difficult to quantify. The questions that might profitably form a research agenda have been repeatedly indicated throughout this book and in this discussion. It is useful to summarize them and to describe the dimensions of a useful program of research to which a public policy program might be committed.

A Research Agenda for the Gifted and the Talented

The Development Perspective

One of the most evident gaps in the research literature on giftedness has resulted from the failure of most investigators to assume a developmental perspective. Many of the answers to the issues and questions raised by the authors of the chapters in this book ultimately rest upon an understanding of the developmental course of highly competent and creative behavior and the nature of the forces that shape and maintain giftedness and talent. It goes without saying that a talented violinist will never express that gift nor share the talent with society if he or she is raised in an environment that has no musical instruments, that places little value on music, and that does not afford the opportunity to learn to play the violin. But one need not use such an extreme example to call attention to the fact that, without supportive environments and opportunities to learn, to be instructed, and to practice, even biologically based abilities are unlikely to develop and mature. Current knowledge, however, stops here. Psychologists know very little about the developmental course of giftedness or talent, about the nature of environmental opportunities that nurture their realization, and about the nature of the conditions that must change over time to ensure continued development of giftedness.

From a population point of view, giftedness and talent are individual difference phenomena. Are these individual differences largely inclinations and propensities that will have a particular developmental course depending upon the nature of the environment in which the child grows? Are they based in biological differences in neural physiology? The available evidence suggests that giftedness and talent, however defined, are not unchanging characteristics, even if detected. Thus, explication of the role of the environment is crucial in any case. To what extent are there natural developmental courses of abilities in particular domains that provide the base against which environmental factors operate? Is the developmental course similar in normal and in gifted children across such domains as music and microbiology, politics and photography? Are differences in the expression of intelligence mainly quantitative or qualitative? Clearly, the developmental context is an important dimension of the research agenda.

Similarly, though perhaps less immediately compelling, some of the research questions are likely to be answered only by longitudinal investigations. It is not always clear whether and when longitudinal research efforts will be profitable. The time and resources required are obvious concerns. Also, when a longitudinal study is formulated, the questions to be asked are based upon the state of knowledge at that moment. Subsequent discoveries are not easily incorporated into an ongoing study, leaving open the possibility that as time passes the research could become increasingly obsolete. Thus, it is with great caution that one embarks upon a major longitudinal effort. However, without a modicum of resources committed to longitudinal research, even the more simple questions about outcome cannot be addressed.

For example, the question of how gifted performance is maintained and nurtured is an important one. Using a variety of different criteria, based upon already existing measurement strategies, it would be useful to identify groups of young gifted children and to track them over the course of a 10- to 15-year period. The record of the children's environmental experiences and educational opportunities over this time, along with an assessment of which children continue to be classified as gifted, would provide a picture of factors that appear to be contributing most heavily to outcome. The sample would need to be sufficiently large and leveled for sex, minority/majority membership, geographical location, and socioeconomic status in order to permit analysis on these major dimensions.

It is clear that measures of intellectual and cognitive functioning, performance on standard assessments, creativity tests, and evaluations of personal and social functioning over time ought to form a major portion of the data collected. Additionally, periodic experimental analyses that take advantage of newly developed strategies for looking at components of information processing and for evaluating functioning in different domains of behavior ought to be planned. Although it may be a bit premature for a major national study of this type, it would certainly be useful to have a period of several years of planning, testing of measures, and pilot work in preparation for the design of such an effort.

Emphases for Future Research

From the wide-ranging reviews and reflections included in this volume, we have distilled three major emphases for future research: understanding intellectual processes and functioning in the gifted and the talented, determining social and personality characteristics that differentiate gifted and creative individuals from intellectually competent individuals, and assessing educational strategies. All of these, we believe, should be approached developmentally.

The first of these research areas encompasses investigations of knowledge acquisition, storage, and retrieval, as well as problem identification and solution. Efforts to describe these information-processing mechanisms should range across the life span. During infancy and early childhood it is possible to look at component aspects of intellectual and cognitive behavior, sensitivity to different modalities of stimulation (auditory, visual, etc.), and extraordinary responsiveness to social stimuli or self-produced stimuli. There is a well-developed set of methodologies for studying infant behavior that could now be profitably focused upon studies of individual differences and the stability of those differences in order to form hypotheses about characteristics of children who have unusual information-processing capabilities. A similar set of efforts aimed at the preschool and early school years and including short-term longitudinal components would give us some idea about stabilities from infancy to the early school years.

Returning to the model of development suggested earlier in this epilogue, however, looking only at the individual over time without a concomitant assessment of the individual's environmental experience during the intervening period will be only partially informative. The fallacy of most early-to-late assessments, be it with respect to performance on intelligence measures or with respect to characteristics of temperament such as timidity, is that they ignore the contributions made by environmental factors to the stability or instability of the behavior. Stability over time may have many causes. An individual attribute independent of environmental factors is only one of the possible causes. Only an investigation of the processes of change will provide the kinds of answers that can be said to increase our scientific understanding of behavioral development in a significant manner. This is no less true for the study of the gifted and the talented than it is for understanding the developmental course of any behavior in any population. The research agenda with respect to giftedness and talent requires (a) emphasizing early identification of highly competent performance in different behavioral domains, (b) tracking the course of the functions and processes involved in the behavior over time, and (c) describing the environmental conditions that are relevant and irrelevant to its developmental course. Including groups of normal children for comparison is recommended in these research efforts in order to increase the probability of discriminating those factors that are particularly distinctive in the gifted and talented.

A second, high priority, not unrelated to the first, is to expand the focus away from the intellectual and cognitive into social and personality factors that contribute to the expression of giftedness. It is clear from both research and personal observation that some highly intelligent individuals lead concomitantly creative and productive lives, whereas others do not. Socialization factors and availability of opportunity account for some of this difference, but motivation, energy, and individual choices also appear to influence the degree to which intellectual gifts are realized. Similarly, the factors that contribute to the uses of intelligence—for personal gain, intellectual pleasure, or the benefit of society at large—have not been described and their developmental course has not been delineated. Again, the kind of longitudinal research described earlier would be useful in investigating the role of personality or temperament variables, the potential differential influences of socialization practices on gifted versus typical children, and the career-related and personal decision-making processes engaged in by particularly gifted and talented individuals.

Finally, given children who are identified as gifted and talented, a significant increase in research on effective educational programs is needed. Children cannot wait to grow up until we investigators know all that we need to know in order to help them. In the here and now there are gifted and talented children for whose education we bear responsibility. Determining what kinds of programs most benefit what kinds of gifted and talented children will enable us to better target our educational resources. The gifted and the talented among our children represent one of the richest of our human resource potentials. We lose every time the educational experiences of these children do not maximize their functional capabilities. There is implicit recognition of this in the widely mandated programs for the gifted and the talented in the states across this nation, but it is worthwhile to develop and maintain these programs only if we ultimately have some evidence that they make a real difference in outcomes.

It is not possible to evaluate where we might be had we witnessed a systematic investment of research effort on the gifted and talented to the same extent that we have invested in the study of the retarded and even the normal child. It is, however, possible to speculate that the research called for in this discussion and by the authors throughout this volume would, if undertaken in even a less than all-out fashion, result in an eventual application of knowledge that could not help but be beneficial, not only to the children directly involved, but also to the society in which these children, their children, and all of their descendents will live. It is our hope that the compilation of knowledge about the gifted and the talented represented by this volume and the identification of a research agenda to expand our knowledge base will stimulate the commitment of resources and of the best minds in behavioral science to the task that has been described.

References

Berman, P. W., Waisman, H. A., & Graham, F. K. (1966). Intelligence in treated phenylketonuric children: A developmental study. *Child Development, 37,* 731–747.

Chess, S., & Thomas, A. (1977). *Temperament and development.* New York: Bruner/Mazel.

Escalona, S. (1968). *The roots of individuality.* Chicago, IL: Aldine.

Escalona, S. (1973). The differential impact of environmental conditions as a function of different reaction patterns in infancy. In J. C. Westmann (Ed.), *Individual differences in children* (pp. 145–157). New York: Wiley.

Gardner, H. (1983). *Frames of mind: The theory of multiple intelligences.* New York: Basic Books.

Garmezy, N. (1974). The study of competence in children at risk for severe psychopathology. In E. J. Anthony & C. Koupernik (Eds.), *The child in his family: Children at psychiatric risk* (Vol. 3, pp. 77–98). New York: Wiley.

Gesell, A., Amatruda, C., Castner, B. M., & Thompson, H. (1939). *Biographies of child development.* New York: Hoeber.

Horowitz, F. D. (1978). *Toward a functional analysis of individual differences.* Presidential address to the Division of Developmental Psychology at the meeting of the American Psychological Association, Toronto, Ontario, Canada.

Horowitz, F. D. (1982). Child development for the pediatrician. *Pediatric Clinics of North America, 29,* 359–375.

Horowitz, F. D. (1984). The psychobiology of parent–offspring relations in high-risk situations. In L. P. Lipsitt & C. Rovee-Collier (Eds.), *Advances in infancy research,* (Vol. 3). Norwood, NJ: Able.

Horowitz, F. D. (1985). *Making models of human behavioral development.* Manuscript in preparation.

Murphy, L. B., & Moriarty, A. E. (1976). *Vulnerability, coping and growth.* New Haven, CT: Yale University Press.

Tyler, L. E. (1978). *Individuality.* San Francisco: Jossey-Bass.

Werner, E., & Smith, R. (1982). *Vulnerable but invincible: A study of resilient children.* New York: McGraw-Hill.

Author Index

Page numbers in italic refer to authors listed in the reference lists.

Subject Index

TEIKYO WESTMAR UNIV. LIBRARY

BF 412 .G56 1985

The Gifted and talented
              (91-1933)

DEMCO